# POLITICAL THEORY AND THOUGHT

# POLITICAL THEORY AND THOUGHT

[For UGC-NET, M.A., UPSC and State Public Service Commission Examinations]

*By*
**MANOJ SHARMA**

**ANMOL PUBLICATIONS PVT. LTD.**
**NEW DELHI - 110 002 (INDIA)**

**ANMOL PUBLICATIONS PVT. LTD.**
4374/4B, Ansari Road, Daryaganj
New Delhi - 110 002
Ph.: 23261597, 23278000
Visit us at: www.anmolpublications.com

*Political Theory and Thought*



First Published, 2004

ISBN 81-261-1815-6



PRINTED IN INDIA

---

Published by J.L. Kumar for Anmol Publications Pvt. Ltd., New Delhi - 110 002 and Printed at Mehra Offset Press, Delhi.

# Contents


| | | |
|---|---|---|
| | *Preface* | *vii* |
| 1. | Ancient Indian Political Thought | 1 |
| 2. | Greek Political Thought | 52 |
| 3. | European Thought—I | 133 |
| 4. | European Thought—II | 246 |
| 5. | Contemporary Political Thought | 370 |
| 6. | Modern Indian Thought | 394 |
| 7. | Medieval Political Thought | 504 |
| 8. | Behaviouralism and Post-Behaviouralism | 522 |

# Preface

Political Theory and Thought as a paper is being taught at the graduate and post graduate level in Political Science syllabus in almost all the Indian Universities. The various courses conducted by various institutions at the Central and State level too have been considered in respect of their syllabus, course contents and requirements. Thus the material presented here would be of interest as well as great use to the students of Political Science. This book has been especially designed for UGC-NET Examination, M.A. (Political Science) Students and other competitive examinations by UPSC and Public Service Commission of various States.

The major topics dealt in this book are—Ancient Indian Thought; Greek Political Thought; European Thought; Contemporary Political Thought; Modern Indian Thought; Medieval Political Thought; Behaviouralism and Post Behaviouralism etc.

**Manoj Sharma**

# 1 Ancient Indian Political Thought

## KAUTILYA

Kautilya was a great political philosopher whose childhood days is yet to be discovered. So far no authentic biography of Kautilya is available. Taking recourse to legends and references, it is believed, Kautilya was born at Chanaka and therefore, came to be known as Chanakya. Dr. Ganapati Shastri holds the view that the venerable Acharya had been born in the Kutala gotra and hence, came to be known as Kautilya and since his parents were devotees of Lord Vishnu they called him Vishnugupta.

Though the exact period of Kautilya is unknown, it is believed, he lived during the period of Nanda dynasty and Alexander's invasion. Due to the humilation meted out to him by the Nanda king, he became revengeful and promised to destroy the Nanda dynasty. A nationalist in Kautilya also could not tolerate the invasion of India by the foreign invaders. Hence, in order to destroy the Nanda dynasty and to build-up a strong state, he trained his able disciple Chandragupta Maurya to dethrone the Nanda king and establish his own rule. This he did very successfully as Chandragupta replaced the Nanda king and occupied the throne of Magadha. The writings in the *Vishnupurana*, Dandin's *Dashakumarchrita* and *Somadeva's Nitivakyamitra* bear testimony to this.

The period during which Kautilya lived was marked by the emergence of studies by Manu, Brahaspati, Ushanas on one hand, Buddhism and Jainism on the other. All these scriptures gave contradictory and extreme views on social and religious life. But

Kautilya brought a synthesis of the extreme ideas given earlier, appealed to the individuality of man and tried to build up a new Indian polity.

Kautilya's period was also marked by the political disorder, maladministration and misrule of the Nanda kings and external attack by the Greek invaders. Kautilya through his king Chandragupta tried to create a strong and stable state with a benevolent king. He generated a sense of patriotism through his discourses and deliberations to fight against the foreign invaders. He also reorganised the administration of the entire kingdom to ensure an honest, efficient and compassionate administration. In accordance with his advice, Chandragupta built up a strong state, defeated the invaders, established a clean administration and subsequently became the imperial king of India. That is why, out of the three aims *i.e.*, Dharma, Artha and Kama, Kautilya highlighted Artha which in broader sense means the inhabited land or the state.

**Kautilya's 'Arthasastra'**

Kautilya's Arthasastra is a work of exceptional interest in the field of Political Theory and Public Administration. Because even if it signifies a study of wealth, in fact it is more a treatise on the statecraft. Its scientific and systematic expositions has surpassed all other contemporary works. Though some scholars view that this work may not be the creation of a single individual and contest the view that Kautilya was the author of the *Arthasastra*. But some distinguished scholars still regard the text as the genuine work of Kautilya, the Prime Minister of Chandragupta Maurya. But unfortunately this comprehensive work on politics and administration was completely lost and it was not until 1904 when an anonymous pandit (Priest) of Tanjore district handed over the manuscript of the book alongwith a commentary on a small part of it by a writer named Bhattasvamin to Dr. Shama Sastri who realised the importance of the manuscript and published it in 1909. But with regard to the year of its origin, scholars are divided, some believe that the Arthasastra was written around 4th century B.C. while other scholars maintain that it was written in the 3rd or 4th century A.D. But this controversy according to J.W. Mabbett is need less. According to him, there can not be any doubt that the Mauryan Kautilya wrote the Arthasastra.

The Arthasastra is divided into 15 Adhikaranas with 180 Prakaranas. This work is a combination of Sutra and Bhasya. Sutra probably applied to the headings of Prakaranas and Bhasya is a commentary on it with a certain mixture of verses. The purpose of the sastra is to lay down the means for the acquisition and maintenance of dominion over earth. The style of Arthasastra is simple but it is enigmatic in places. Its 15 Adhikaranas deal with different aspects of state and administration. The first part deals with the education, discipline of prince, the qualification of ministers, different kinds of spies, the duties of a king etc. The second part deals with the land and village administration, conduct of government servants, the officers and superintendents of the treasury etc. The third part determines forms of agreement, legal disputs, regarding marriage, agreement, sales and purchases etc. The fourth part deals with the removal of dangerous elements and criminal law, the fifth part deals with the methods to remove state enemies and fill the treasury of the king, the sixth and seventh part deals with the seven elements of kingship and six lines of policy, the eighth part deals with the vices of the king and calamities such as flood, fire etc., the nineth and tenth part deals with the military campaigns, the eleventh part deals with the corporation and guild, the twelfth and thirteenth part deals with the methds to win wars and how to be popular in conquered country, the fourteenth part deals with preparing powders and mixtures to produce illusive appearance, spread disease etc., the fifteenth part deals with the description of the plan of work.

Kautilya's Arthasastra carries significance because for the first time it liberated the science of politics from all sorts of limitations and developed a systematic tool of administration of the state. Its discovery, writes Parmar, radically changed the outlook of the western scholars in India.

## ORIGIN AND ELEMENTS OF THE STATE

Since the dawn of political philosophy, many philosophers of both East and West have involved themselves in answering the questions with regard to origin, nature, elements and functions of the state. In India many ancient works like *Satapatha Brahman*, *Manusmriti* and *Mahabharat* have dealt with the problem of origin of the state. But

Kautilya's *Arthasastra* essentially a book on the art of administration gave only passing reference to the origin of the state. According to Kautilya, the state originated to fulfil the desire of the people to have a peaceful society. It is said when the weak began to be oppressed by the srong, the people made Vaivasvata Manu their king and fixed one sixth of the produce of soil and one-tenth of merchandise as his share. Maintained by this payment, kings took upon themselves the responsibility of maintaining the safety and security of their subjects. Those who did not pay the fines and taxes took on themselves the sin of the kings and kings who did not bring about the well-being and security took on themselves the sins of the subjects. Thus, Kautilya speculated, Manu Vaivasvata was made the king through contract. Kautilya, hence, was the first contractualist in India like Thomas Hobbes, John Locke and Rousseau were the modern contratualists of the west. But Kautilya's social contract was more governmental and less social. Because he was not interested in creating a theory on the origin of the state. His intention was to replace the misrule of Nanda dynasty by Chandragupta who could make the state strong and powerful. Hence like Hobbes, he said, the system of Matsyanyaya (large fish swallowing the small ones) was prevailing in the society which marked the state of nature and to get rid of that a contract was made. But like the *Mahabharat*, Kautilya also believed in the Divine origin theory.

## THE SAPTANGA THEORY (ELEMENTS OF STATE)

Kautilya used the word 'Rajya' which according to Spellman, corresponds to the English word, 'State'. The state is defined for the first time in the *Arthasastra* of Kautilya as consisting of seven elements, a definition which becomes an axiom in the later sources.

The states as seven-limbed is contemplated by the ancient Hindu thinkers. In *Manusmriti*, Manu deals with seven Prakritis of the state like king, the ministers, the capital, the realm, the treasury, the army and the ally. This order of preference remained as a model for *Yajnavalkyasmriti*, *Vishnusmriti*, *Mahabharata* and *Kamandaka*. But Kautilya in his *Arthasastra* put the same in a different order like the king, the minister; the country, the fort, the treasury, the army, the friend and the enemy. Thus, he changed the previous order of priority and added a new element *viz,* the enemy. However, he agrees with Manu when he states, "Excepting the enemy, these seven elements, possessed of their excellent characteristics, are said to be the limb like elements of the state". Kautilya also reduces the elements of the state when he writes, "the king and his kingdom are the primary elements of the state". Because all other elements revolve round these two elements. However, it is necessary to highlight Kautilya's views on different elements of the state to know the nature and characteristics of the state.

**The King**

The King or the Swamin is the head of the state and occupies an exalted position in his polity. But in order to be the Swamin or the king, one should be bestowed with different qualities like high descendency, godly nature, virtues, truthfulness, gratefulness, resolute, courage and discipline. He should be free from vices and should be exemplary for his subjects. The king as the sovereign head of the state has different types of duties like the appointment of ministers, protection, of the people, ability to give justice and inflict punishment on the wicked. Happiness of the king lies in happiness of the people. Thus, Kautilya's head of the state resembles modern head of the state who is all powerful provided he does his duty.

**Amatya**

Amatya constitutes the second element of the state. But Kautilya refers to Amatya in a different sense. Amatya generally means the council of ministers. In the Arthasastra the Amatyas constitute a regular cadre of service from which all high offices such as Chief priest, ministers, collectors; officers, envoys and the Superintendents of various departments are to be recruited. Hence, Sharma writes, for Kautilya, Amatya does not mean only the ministers. The king can not rule the kingdom alone. According to Kautilya, a single wheel cannot move. There should be ministers to help him. But ministers should be men of wisdom, integrity, bravery and loyalty. The integrity of the ministers can be tested in four ways *viz.*, loyalty to the king, not falling a prey to monetary allurement, facing a crisis calmly and complete self-control under sexual provocations.

**Janapada (The Country)**

The implication of Janapada defined in the Arthasastra implies both territory and population. Because without either the population or the territory, a state can not exist. The territory should contain fertile lands, mines, timber, pasture grounds, forests and waterways etc. The people should include men with good character and loyalty, intelligent, wise masters and slaves. Thus, the country possessing the above type of territory and people, can be said to be a god country which is the third element of the state.

**Durga (Fort)**

Durga or Fort constitutes the fourth element of the state. Here Durga means the Fortress and resembles pura, the third element of Manu's state. As a synonym of Pura, it should be understood in the sense of fortified capital. Kautilya talks of Durgavidhana and Durganivesa in his Arthasastra. In Durgavidhana, he refers to construction of fortress and in Durganivesa, he refers to planning and layout of capital. The capital is to be built at a central place; areas are to be set apart for members of different varnas and for artisans as well as gods. Many functions like secret war, the readiness of the army and fighting the enemy are to be carried out from the fort.

**Kosha (The Treasury)**

Kosha or the treasury is necessary for the protection and maintenance of the state in general and army in particular. If army suffers from shortages it may desert the king or even kill him. The treasury should be filled with gems, gold, jewels etc., and should have the capacity to sustain the calamities for a long time. But according to Kautilya, treasury should accumulate wealth through righteous and legitimate means.

**Army**

The army constitutes the sixth element of Kautilya's state. Its main duy is to defend the country from external aggression and protect its independence. This element, according to Kautilya consists of hereditary and hired soldiers comprising infantry, chariots, elephants and cavalry. It is also described in the Santi Parva as the 'astanga bala'. Kshatriyas constitute the main part of the army. But unlike

Manu, Kautilya allows even the lower castes to to join the army if emergency arises. But according to Kautilya, the best army should be strong, obedient and happy. It should be invincible, trained in fighting various kinds of battle, skilful in handling various forms forms of weapons and should share the weal and woe of the king. They must also keep teir sons and wives well contented.

**Mitra (Ally)**

Kautilya's concept of Mitra (ally) is based more on ethical considerations. The real ally should be hereditary and not artificial. It should be one with whom there is no possibility of rupture and one who is ready to come to help when occasion demands it. But on the other hand, one is to be treated as an enemy who is gready, possessed with disloyed subjects loose character, addicted to mean pleasure, powerless and impotent etc.

Kautilya syas, it all depends on the king how he deals with the elements of the state. He can make even the poor and miserable elements of his sovereignty happy and prosperous but a wicked king will surely destroy the most prosperous element of the state. In fact Kautilya through his Septanga theory of state proposed to analyse and explain the nature of his policy different from tribal counterpart. As Parmer rightly observes that the theory of state in the Arthasasatra is little more than an analysis of the elements essential for an efficient operation of the political organisation.

## FUNCTIONS OF THE STATE

Modern political theory very often concerns itself with the problems of state activity. Some philosophers like John Locke, J.S. Mill and others envisage limited role for the state; but the political philosophers like Robertowen, St. Simon, Sydney Webb one one hand, Hegal and Green on the other argue for the greater role of the state. But such a dichotomy did not exist in ancient India as the state represented by an absolute monarch behaved like a Hobbesian Leviathan. It embraced all walks of human life. Accordingly Altekar writes in his book, 'State and Government in Ancient India'. The activity of the state as envisaged by the Mahabharata and the Arthasastra, relates to all aspects of human life—social, economic and religious...was and is to embrace the whole of human life, both here and hereafter". Kautilya assigns his state to discharge the role of a modern welfare state. Approapriately the state has different functions which are discussed here briefly.

**Protection of the People and Property**

Since the inception of vedic period, protection of the people has been the major function of the state. Kautilya also argues that the protection of people and their property is the foremost function of the state. The state has to protect the people from both internal insecurities and external attack. Kautilya deals in detail in his the Arthasastra (Part-IV) entitled "Removal of Thorns" the procedure of preventing anti-social activities like theft, robbery, murder, killing, cheating etc. and also provides remedies against the natural calamities like fire, floods, famine etc. Kautilya like a true nationalist suggests for the unethical measures like expediency, diplomacy, dishonesty, hypocrisy and even murder killing to be undertaken by the king to defend the state and make the state strong. Another function of the state is to protect the varna (caste) and the Dharma (duties) of the people.

**Developmental Functions**

To ensure prosperity and happiness to the people is the second important function of the state. The welfare of the people is the only objective of the state. Kautilya hence says, "in the happiness of his subjects lies king's happiness; in their welfare his welfare; whatever pleases himself he shall not consider as good, but whatever pleases his subjects he shall consider as good". Hence for the welfare of the people, the state has to carry out developmental activities like construction of dams, settlement of virgin lands, providing pastures for the cattle, opening trade centres, providing irrigation facilities etc.

**Economic Functions**

In the economic sphere, Kautilya suggests for the state ownership and regulation to some extent. "The King shall carry on mining operations and manufactures, exploit timber and elephant forests, offer facilities for cattle breeding and commerce, construct roads for traffic both by land and water and set-up market towns". Besides, the state should own industries like transport and cotton. But this should not lead to view Kautilya as a socialist because he allows private property and private ownership of industries. Even mines one to be leased out to private persons. Kautilya's economic system can be included under 'Mixed Economy System'. But the state retains the right to interfere in case of loss of production or over-production or workers problem. The state also regulates the trade to ensure good of the consumers. The state accordingly has to regulate the prices of the commodities, import and export, weights and measures etc. If any trader cheats people, he has to be inflicted with severe punishment. The state has to make provisions for market centres and market hours.

**Social Functions**

As mentioned earlier, the state has to protect the social order in accordance with the system of varnas (caste) and their Dharma (duties). The state has to promote education, learning and art. Kautilya makes special provision for the educated and learned in his state. Kautilya says, those who perform sacrifices, spiritual guides, priests and those learned in the vedas shall be granted Brahmadeya lands yielding sufficient produce and exempted from fine and taxes. The state has to take care of the health of the citizens. The physicians in the city and the villages are to control the diseases and check the spreading of epidemics. The state has also to help the poor pregnant women, orphans, the aged and the disabled.

Thus, according to Kautilya, the state activities have different dimensions. It has to protect the dharma, justice and the interest of the people. The state has to be Dharmadhikari, Nayayadhikari and Managalkari in ancient philosophical sense. The state has been provided with so vast powers and functions that one will conclude that the position of the King is very powerful. But it is not so. Kautilya puts and number of restraints over the activities of the king and makes him a saint and servant of the people rather than a monopolistic power wielder. Kautilya's views on state activities and its economic system resemble modern welfare state system.

## NATURE AND CHARACTERISTICS OF GOVERNMENT (STATE-CRAFT)

Kautilya's Arthasastra is a treatise mainly dealing with the state-craft or the art of government. Kautilya creates a stable government with welfare orientation. His government is based on an administrative hierarchy. The king is the head of the government and administration. He is the chief executive head of the state. He is assisted by many tirthas who help the king to administer the state. Those are Mantri (the minister), Purohit (the priest), Senapati (the commander of the army), Yuvraj (the heir-apparent), Dawarika (the door-keeper), Antarvanshika (the officer-in-charge of harem), Prashastra (the magistrate), Samahartr (the collector-general), Sannidhir (the chamberlain or the director), the commissioner, the city-constable, the officer-incharge of the city and superintendent of transactions, the superintendent of manufactories, the assembly of councillors and and heads of departments, the commissary-general, the officer-incharge of fortification, the officer-incharge of boundaries, the officer-incharge of wild tracts. In book II of the Arthasastra Kautilya talks about Adhykashaprachara and describes the duties of nearly thirty Adhyakshas. An Adhyaksha had under him a lekhaka (clerk), a rupadarshaka (inspector of coins), Samkhlyaka (accountant) Nivigrahaka (keeper of the balance), and an Uttradhyaksha (who watches the activity of the subordinate staff). There are also Yukta, Upayukta and Tatpurusha in every department. Yukta is the head of the department, the Upayukta is a subordinate officer and Tatpurushas are servants of the lowest categeory.

Like Manu, Kautilya also decentralised the units of administration. The entire state was divided into a number of provinces consisting of about 800 villages put under the princes. Each province was divided into different district administration to be administered by a group of officers under the general supervision of the pradeshtrs (the commissioner). Lastly comes village administration to be kept under the control of the village headman. The village headman was incharge of security, collection of revenue, president of the village council and custodian of the village records.

The main objective of the government having the administrative structure mentioned above is to guarantee security and welfare of the people through an honest, loyal and efficient adminstration. Besides the admnistrative structures, a study of Kautilya's theory of government also includes powers and position of the king, the council of Ministers, Public servants, law and justice, system of Espionage, was and foreign policy.

## POWERS AND POSITION OF THE KING

The king is the head of the entire governmental system. Nothing moves without his knowledge. He has enormous powers and occupies a unique powerful position. But the king has to be noble and benevolent. He has to lead the people by virtue of his own action. Hence Kautilya says, "if a king is energetic, his subjects will be equally energetic. If he is is reckless, they will not only be reckless likewise, but also eat into his works. Besides, a reckless king will easily fall into the hand of his enemies. Hence the king shall ever be wakeful". In other words, Kautilya created "a people's king" who should possess some qualities. Those qualities include sincerity, gratitude, firmness, strong determination, wit and humour courage and strength, quickness in action, freedom from passion, quality to study the situation etc. He should be qualified in the art of ruling and should lead a isciplined life. The king has various powers and functions. As mentioned earlier, the king has been vested with such power by the sacred laws and traditions not to exhibit his power over the people but to ensure the security and happiness of the people through his able administration.

### Executive and Administrative Powers

The king has the power of appointing ministers (Mantris), amatyas (Officer), spies, ambassadors etc. and build-up a system of administration. He has to maintain law and order in the state with the assistance of his ministers and officers. He has to defend his country with the help of his army, spies and ambassadors. In other words, he has to ensure security to the people both internally and externally. He has to prevent theft, robbery, murder and killing in his kingdom. He has to exercise his coercive authority (Danda) against the wicked. He has to take necessary steps to prevent the natural calamities like fire, flood, famine etc. He should be the protector of the poor and downtrodden especially poor pregnant women and orphans. He has also the power of punishing any official who turns to be currupt and terrorise the people.

### Legislative Power

The king is the symbol of law, authority and justice. But the king is not the law maker. He has simply to protect the law as prescribed by the sacred literature, divine revelation, customs and usages. At best, he enjoys the power of subordinate legislation whereby he can formulate rules and principles for the day-to-day administration but he is not empowered to legislate in the sphere of social norms. The king's legislative power is more in the form of delivering justice.

**Judicial Power**

The king is the fountain of justice. The king appoints the judges and also sees that justice is administered impartially. In meting out justice, a king is not supposed to distinguish between his son and the enemy. The king has the right to punish the judges when the latter does not inquire into the necessary circumstances, makes unnecessary delay in discharging his duty, helps the witness giving them clues etc. When a judge imposes an unjust corporal punishment, the king will punish the judge with the same type of punishment.

**Financial Power**

The king has the financial power of imposing tax and collection of revenues. He always makes his treasury filled with gold, jewels and jems etc. He has the right to ask for the statement of receipts and expenditure. Besides, he has the power to regulate trade, commerce and industry. He asks his officers to take care of mines and industries, regulate the mode of production. He should ask his officers to regulate the market price of the commodities and punish the traders who cheat the people.

**Military Power**

The king is the sovereign and has the power to declare war and conclude peace. He is the commander in chief. He inspects the elephants, horses, chariots and the infantry. The king has the right to adopt any method he likes to win the war.

**Power of Protecting Social Order**

Since the vedic period, the king has been empowered to protect the special order ordained by the divinity and prescribed by the Vedas. The king should see that every individual sticks to his Svadharma and carry out the duties assigned to their castes. Its basic objectives is to ensure the general welfare of the citizens and prevention of social disorder. It is to replace a competitive society by a society where strong and weak will dwell in cooperation.

Thus, the king has very vast powers and authorities. But as mentioned earlier, the king is to be a responsible and benevolent king. For the evil, the king can be absolute and ruthless but for good he has to be the most responsible king. Hence, Kautilya says when in the court, he shall never cause his petitioner to wait at the door, for when a king makes himself inaccessible to his people, he may cause confusion to his business. Kautilya also suggests his king to attend to the business of gods, of Brahman learned in the Vedas, of sacred places, of minors, the aged, the afflicted and the helpless women. The king is supposed to be the saviour of the poor and destitutes.

## RELATIONSHIP BETWEEN ETHICS AND POLITICS

Since the beginning of Political Tradition, political philosophers have differed on the relationship between ethics and politics. Those who view 'Politics' as a means to ensure the welfare of the people, establish a close relationship between the two but those who treat 'politics' as a 'pursuit of power' make a separation between ethics and politics. Kautilya belongs to the first generation of political philosophers who established a close relationship between ethics and politics in the internal administration of the state. M.V. Krishna Rao writes in his book, "Studies in Kautilya", "there is complete agreement between Aristotle, Plato and Kautilya regarding ethics and politics as identical and assigning a normal and spiritual significance to associate living and in believing that the happy life is virtuous life for the fulfilment of which the whole creation moves". Plato gives a picture of unattainable ideals; Aristotle of the descent of ideal to the real and Kautilya of the ascent of real through spiritual effort to the ideal. Some scholars view Kautilya as the Machiavelli of India. Because both of them have deep concern for the preservation, acquisition and expansion of the state. Both of them suggest for the use of force and fraud to consolidate the interest of the state. But such comparison are superficial and an in-depth study of their respective political approaches reveal their differences. The differences in the political outlook of Kautilya and Machiavelli are essentially rooted in the long Indian tradition of culture and politics on which Kautilya laid the foundation of his political philosophy. Because of this tradition, Kautilya did not divorce like Machiavelli political issues from the ethical ones. Kautilya no doubt emphasised the consolidation of political power but never viewed political power as an end in itself. In Kautilya, the separation between politics and morality is unthinkable and political power acquires legitimacy only when it promotes human happiness. But in external relationship with other states and during the time of war, Kautilya emphasised expediency and subordinated ethics to politics. But this is a temporary measure to be pursued by the king to establish supremacy of his state and bring back normally. Therefore, any analysis of Kautilya's view on the relationship between Ethics and Politics should be divided into two parts *i.e.*, part one deals with politics and ethics in identical terms, part two make a compromise with ethics for a greater cause.

**Identical Relationship Between Ethics and Politics**

As mentioned earlier, Kautilya's political ideas are grounded on the long Indian tradition of culture and politics. India's culture and politics have always been linked to religion and ethics or morality. So in Kautilya's political philosophy, there is no chance that his king will be indifferent to morality to pursue the political power. An immoral king will be most hated by the Indian psyche. Hence, "Kautilya's concern for moral values is obvious and his major pre-occupation is to restore and foster the ethical values of Hindu religion". According to Kautilya, the techniques and prescriptions of the *Arthasastra* are understood in the concept of Rajdharma which is supposed to lead to heaven.

Kautilya had deep faith in the vedic social order and wanted to pursue the social order through his statecraft. Like Manu, he also traced the origin of the state to divinity and made the king 'benevolent' instead of making him an 'absolute king'. He talked of four sciences like Anvishaki, the triple Vedas (Trayi), Varta (agriculture, cattle breeding and trade) and Dandaniti (Science of government). Anvikshaki comprises the philosophy of Sankhya, Yoga and Lokayata. Righteous and unrighteous acts can be determined from the triple vedas; wealth and non-wealth, potency and impotency can be decided through the science of government. Kautilya's faith in ethics and morality propelled him to talk of four sciences which could be adopted as guidelines by all sections of the society. Since the triple Vedas determine the respective duties of the four castes and of the four order of religious life, they are the most useful. Besides the duties assigned by the vedas, Kautilya says, harmlessness, truthfulness, purity, freedom from spite, abstinence from cruelty and forgiveness are the duties common to all. The observance of one's own duty leads to heaven and infinite bliss. When it is violated, the world will come to an end owing to confusion of castes and duties. Kautilya also instructs his king not to allow people to deviate from their duties; for whoever upholds his own duty ever adhering to the customs of the Aryas and following the rules of castes and divisions of religious life, will surely be happy both here and hereafter. Thus, Kautilya has completely identified his politics with the preservation of a moral and religious social order. He rightly advises his king to be well educated and well versed in all the four sciences. Kautilya's moral prescription for political rule becomes vivid in his statement when he says, "the king who is well educated and disciplined in sciences, devoted to good government of his subjects and bent on doing good to all people will enjoy the earth unopposed". But the king in order to be ethical should keep his six senses under control. Such six senses are lust, anger, greed, vanity, haughtiness and overjoy. By doing this, the king will refrain from doing harm to anybody and keep himself away from falsehood and unrighteousness.

Kautilya's politics was never power oriented. Like Machiavelli neither he defined politics as the art of capturing power and the craft of preserving it nor made his king the absolute wielder of power. Rather Kautilya made political power a means to achieve the ethical goal. Hence, Kautilya says, "in the happiness of his subject lies his happiness; in their welfare his welfare; whatever pleases himself he shall not consider as-good, but whatever pleases his subjects he shall consider as good". Thus, happiness and welfare of the people should be the only concern of the king. Kautilya warns the king that just as the king is powerful, his subjects are equally powerful. If the king becomes dishonest and reckless, his people will be more dishonest and reckless. The king should be the symbol of virtues and ethics.

Kautilya also talks of Danda (Punishment) to be based on law and justice. Even the king or judges are not free from such punishments. Laws are not the dictates of the king and justice is not what the king says it to be. It is rather based on religious scriptures and local usages. Secondly, Kautilya says when the law of punishment is kept in abeyance, it gives rise to such disorder as is implied in the proverb 'Matsyanyaya Mudbhavayati' (bigger fish swallowing the smaller ones) for in the absence of a magistrate the strong will swallow the weak but under his (magistrate) protection, the weak resist the strong. Thus, Kautilya establishes the rule of law and justice in his polity and does not leave it to the monopoly of anybody. His laws of punishment are more the reflection of a religious and ethical social order. He also creates a system of administration in which he suggests his king to keep close watch on corrupt officers and punish them. He always prescribes for an honest and efficient administration.

## CONCEPT OF SOCIAL ORDER

Kautilya's concept of society was founded on religious prescription. On the surface, Kautilya had no original idea of the social structure. He owed it to the vedas and the smritis. But an in-depth study of Kautilya's social order reveals that Kautilya went one step ahead and made his social order more progressive. In other words, Arthasastra society was more liberal and progressive than the society under Manusmriti. Kautilya's social order is based on the following foundations :

### Varna or Caste System

Kautilya believed in the vedic conception of society based on four varnas such as Brahman, Kshatriya, Vaisya and Sudra. These four varnas were assigned with different duties. The duty of the Brahman was study, teaching, performance of sacrifice, officiating in other's sacrificial performance, giving and receiving gifts. The duty of a Kshatriya was study, performance of sacrifice, giving gifts, military occupation and protection of life. The duty of a Vaisya was study, performance of sacrifice, agriculture, cattle breeding and trade. The duty of a Sudra was the serving of the twice born, agriculture, cattle breeding and trade.

### Four Stages of Life

Kautilya also gave importance to four orders of religious life to keep the individual and the society in the right order. Such four orders are House-holder (Grahastha), Student (Brahmacharya), Vanaprasta (Forest recluse), Ascetic (Paribrajaka). The duty of a house-holder is earning livelihood by his own profession, marriage among his equals intercourse with his wedded wife, gifts to God, ancestors, guests and servants etc., The duty of a student which is known as the stage of Brahmacharya is to learn the vedas; fire worship, living by begging, devotion to his teacher even at the cost of his own life etc. During the stage of Vanaprastha (Forest recluse) there should be observance of chastity, sleeping on the bare ground, wearing deer skin, fire worship etc. During the last stage a man has to lead an ascetic retired life from the worldly affairs. He has to lead the life of a Parivrajaka and should have the complete control of the sense organs abstaining from all kinds of works, disowning money, keeping aloof from the society etc. One should also have internal and external purity.

Kautilya had tremendous faith in such vedic prescription and believed if the world is maintained in accordance with such prescription it will move from progress to prosperity. He appropriately suggests his king to see that every individual and caste perform their duties in their own station of life.

**Position of Women in the Society**

Kautilya gave the women their due place in the society. The state should make law for the protection of women in the society. He was quite sympathetic to the cause of poor women and said, poor pregnant women should be provided with financial assistance. He also expected the state to protect the honour of women. Any forcible relationship with immature girls, rape of widows and orphans should be dealt with severe punishment. Even the daughters of prostitutes should be protected.

Another bright feature in the Arthasastra was the increased respect that was shown to women in the matter of marriage, contract and divorce. The system of marriage was sacramental; but it emphasised the importance of contractual obligations. "The women enjoyed a large measure of freedom and the relations between men and women were reciprocal in character. Neither of them could practice cruelty on the other. The obligation of a wife to serve her husband for a short or long period depended on the amount of maintenance and the caste of the husband. But Kautilya prohibited women of the higher castes who were married according to religious rites (Dharma Vivahat) from enjoying the privileges that were allowed for others". Kautilya gave the women the right to remarry under special circumstances like when the husband is outside for a long time or the husband suffers from incurable diseases or he is sterile. Widows can marry the brothers of their husband. Divorce is allowed only on the ground of mutual enemity.

## THE COUNCIL OF MINISTERS

The Council of Ministers constitute the second rank in the governmental hierarchy. No doubt there is centralisation of authority since the King alone has to take the final decision. But Kautilya as a realist could visualise the limitations of the king. The king alone cannot rule. However, powerful or competent a King may be he alone can not administer the state. He has to take the help of the ministers in the decision making and implementation of different plans and programmes. But Kautilya did not conceive of a personal government and hence, suggested for a council of ministers. Because all kinds of administrative measures are to be preceded by deliberations in a well formed council.

### Composition

Kautilya suggests that the king should appoint neither more nor less than three or four ministers. Because he argues "a single minister may be beyond control; two may quarrel and ruin the state or conspire against the king and a large number of ministers may affect the secrecy of the council". Thus, the council of ministers should consist of three or four ministers which will be an ideal consultative body. Who can be a minister? Only man of honesty and ability should be appointed as ministers. Secondly, the king shall employ as ministers such persons who are born or high family and possessed of wisdom, purity of purpose, bravery and loyal feelings. But a man with high character, well educated in the Vedas and the six Angas, well versed in the science of government and has the capacity to prevent calamities shall be appointed as priests. Over and above all these qualifications, Kshtriya says, four tests are to be administered to test their integrity. Such tests include the test of loyalty to the king, test of not falling a prey to monetary allurements, test of facing a crisis calmly and complete sex-control under sexual provocations. Of these tried ministers, those whose characters have been tested under monetary allurements shall be in charge of revenue; those who have been tried under love allurements shall be in-charge pleasure ground (vihara) both external and internal, those whose loyalties have been tested by allurements shall be appointed to immediate service and those whose characters have been tested under all kinds of allurements shall be employed as Prime Ministers.

**Functions**

Council of Minister's constitute the real wheel of the government because the king's decisions are to be based on the suggestions of the council of ministers and once a decision or a policy is finalised, it implementation is also the responsibility of the ministers. In other words, council of ministers have advisory functions and individual minister has executive function. For the security and welfare of the people, the king solely depends upon the performance and excellence of the individual minister. The council will be a small body of three to four ministers (not all). The king will have secret consultations with the council whenever he feels the necessity. The king may take their opinion individually or jointly. But when urgent matters are to be discussed, the meeting of the council of ministers should be summoned for consultations. The king should follow the course recommended by the majority if it is capable of leading to the achievement of the object. But if the king thinks that the majority view is not likely to help him to achieve his object, he is free to reject it and follow a course of action that will help him achieve the target. Thus, Mantri Parishad (Council of Ministers) is only an advisory body, it is neither like a modern cabinet nor a sovereign parliament.

The success of the king depends on the successful working of the individual ministers. Hence, ministers should have major responsibilities to guarantee security of persons and property, finding out remedies against calamities, recruiting a good army, collection of revenue and improvement of treasury etc. According to Kautilya, the king should ask the ministers to take care of the poor and destitute and should give emphasis on agriculture, industry, trade, food supply, labour, transport, morality and health. Since Kautilyas reference was to a welfare state, the ministers should work for all round development of the state.

## CONCEPT OF LAW JUSTICE AND DANDA

Kautilya deals with the subject of law in book-III of his Arthasastra. The basic objective of Kautilya's law has been to provide intellectual and spiritual freedom to man. In ancient India, law was the creation of divine revelations. During Dharmsutra period, the king had no law-making power. He had simply to protect and preserve dharma. But according to Kautilya, there are four sources of law like Dharma (Sacred law), Vyabahara (evidence), Charitra (History) and Rajashasana (edicts of the king). Kautilya gives importance to rational law or king's law. He says, in case of a conflict between Rajashasana and the three other sources, former should prevail.

Kautilya talked of seventeen types of laws such as marriage and allied topics, division of inheritance, disputes regarding property and building, non-performance of agreements, recovery of debts, rules concerning deposits, rules regarding slaves and labourers, co-operative undertakings, law regarding purchase and sales, resumption of gifts, sale without ownership, law concerning ownership, robbery (or forcible seizure of an object), defamation, assault, gambling and betting, etc.

Kautilya gives a detailed account of law. He makes a distinction between civil law and criminal law. Some of the civil laws and penal laws are presented below :

**Civil Law.** Kautilya in his Arthasastra describes in detail, civil laws concerning marriage, the duty of marriage, the properly of a woman and compensation for remarriage. Kautilya was quite liberal in his concept of marriage. According to him, any kind of marriage is approvable provided it pleases all those who are concerned in it. Property of women includes means of subsistence (virti) or jewellery (Abadhaya). Both husband and wife can make use of it during the time of necessity. Kautilya also gives the women the right to re-marry if a husband is of bad character or has long gone abroad or has become a traitor to his king or is likely to endanger the life of his wife or has fallen from his caste or has lost virility.

Laws of inheritance says division of inheritance shall be made when all the inheritors have become majors. A father distributing his property shall make no distinction in dividing it among his sons. If daughters are unmarried, they will be given adequate property payable to them on the occasion of their marriages.

Disputes concerning immovable property such as a house, a field, a garden, water-work, a tank and reservoir of water; are generally settled on the testimony of neighbours. The disputes-concerning property include disputes on the construction of houses and their adjecents, tenancy, sale of property, encroachment on another property.

Regarding the recovery of debts, Kautilya says, a debt the payment of which is not limited by time or place or both, shall be paid by the sons, grand sons or any other heirs of the dead debtor. But a wife who has not heard of the debt shall not be caught hold for the debt contracted by her husband. But husband may be caught for the debt contracted by his wife.

Regarding the slaves and labourers, Kautilya suggested laws prohibiting the selling or mortgaging the life of Sudra who is not a born slave and Arya in birth. In case it is done by his Kinsmen the latter will be fined. If persons other than kinsmen do the same, they shall be liable to capital punishment. Purchaser as well as the abettors shall be punished. However, it is no crime for the Mlechhas to sell or mortgage the life of their own offspring. But an Arya shall never be subjected to slavery. Wherever there will be slavery there shall be an agreement between a master and his servant and the nature of agreement shall be known to the neighbours. The servant shall get the promised wages. If the wages of the slave has been settled previously, the amount shall be fixed in proportion to the work done and the time spent in doing it. A servant neglecting or unreasonably putting off work for which he has received wages shall be fined 12 panas and be caught hold of till the work is done.

**Criminal Law.** Criminal law deals with matters of serious crimes and capital punishment. It includes robbery, theft, defamation, assault etc. On robbery, he says, sudden and direct seizure of articles lead to the act of robbery, fraudulent or indirect seizure is theft. Fine for direct seizure of articles shall be proportional to the gravity of the crime.

On defamation he says, character assassination, contemptuous talk or intimidation constitutes defamation. If persons of superior rank are abused, the amount of the fines shall be doubled; if of lower rank, it shall be halved. For defaming the wives of others, the amount of the fines shall be doubled. If any of a lower caste abuses the habits of one of the higher castes, the fines imposed shall increase from 3 panas upwards. If any of the higher caste abuses one of the lower castes, fines imposed shall decrease from 2 panas. Defamation of one's own nation and villages shall be punished with first amercement, that of one's own caste with middle-most and that of gods or temples, with highest amercement.

About assault, he says, touching striking or hurting constitutes assault. When a person touches with hand mud, ashes or dust the body of another person below the navel, he shall be punished with a fine of 3 panas. If the offence is committed above the navel, the fines shall be doubled. If anyone strikes any body with an instrument which causes swelling, he shall be inflicted with first amercement; if a man strikes leading to the chance of killing some body, he shall be punished with the middle-most amercement.

If one beats a person to death without causing blood or breaks some body's hand, legs or teeth, he shall be punished with first amercement. Kautilya does not condemn gambling out-rightly nor does he prescribe punishment for gamblers. He suggests a state control on gambling. He wants it to be centralised in places provided by the state and officers in-charge of such places are to collect revenues from the gamblers on behalf of the state.

Different types of laws as prescribed by Kautilya are presented above to provide a model for the modern legislators to follow in law making. Kautilya's codification of law is quite exhaustive, systematic and progressive.

**Justice.** Law becomes meaningless if it is not enforced by Judiciary. Law in the hands of ignorant people gets tempered and become partial. Hence, in the same Book-III of Arthasastra, Kautilya deals with law and the process of giving justice to the people.

**Organisation of Judiciary.** Kautilya prescribes for three members acquainted with sacred law and three ministers of the king to carry on the administration of justice. Since judges are to be guided by Dharma, they are known as Dharmasthas. However, the judges are to be appointed at different headquarters like frontier post, the headquarter of ten villages, headquarter of 400 villages and at the chief city with 800 villages around it. The purpose of arranging the judiciary in his way is to make the doors of the judiciary very much nearer to the people. So that irrespective of social and economic justice, people can knock at the door of judiciary.

Kautilya prescribes for two types of courts Dharmasthiya and Kantakasodhana. Of course Kautilya does not explain the nature and composition of these courts. Dharmasthiyas can deal with both civil and criminal cases. Kantakasodhanas deal with political and official cases. Kantakasodhana courts are chaired by (Magistrates) of amatya rank. In order to keep watch on the work of the officers and subordinates, Kantakasodhana courts are to be set-up in different provincial headquarters. On the other hand, Dharmasthiya courts are presided by the three learned judges of the rank of amatya. They primarily deal with the disputes between judges. Besides these courts, each village will have its local court consisting of the headman and the elders of the village.

**Judicial Procedure.** Kautilya says before the trial starts, the year, month, season, the date, the nature and place of the deed, the residence, the caste, the gotra, the name and occupation of both the plaintiff and the defendant both of whom must be registered first. Then the statement of the parties shall be taken down in such order as is required by the case. Such statements are to be thoroughly scrutinised. Both the plaintiff and the defendant are required to deposit the money so that the case can start. The defendant is supposed to reply to the plaintiff within a period of three to seven days. In case a defendant fails to reply within the prescribed period, he is to be fined. The complainant is required to submit his counter reply on the same day on which the defendant's reply is filed, otherwise, he will lose the suit and is fined suitably. The judges will interrogate the parties as well as the witnesses who are called in if the defendant contests the claim. Only those persons who are present at the time of transactions (happening of the incident) can be placed as witnesses. Such witnesses are called srotrs (hearers). Secondly the witness must be trustworthy and honest and should be acceptable to both the parties. But persons who are physically and socially disabled like blind, deaf or dumb and have vested interest in one or other party to the suit cannot be the witness. There may be two to three witnesses in a case.

Kautilya finally suggests five conditions to be followed by the judge to arrive at a decision. Such conditions are: a distincally seen offence, a voluntary admission, straight-forwardness in question (and answers) put in the court, reasoning and oath.

But Kautilya warns and cautions the judges to be careful and impartial while delivering the judgment. When a judge does not inquire into the necessary circumstances, makes unnecessary delay in discharging his duty, evades or causes to evade statements, helps witness, he shall be punished with the highest amercement. If he repeats the offence, he shall both be punished with double the above fine and dismissed. He was the-first ancient law giver who gave every men and women the right to move to court. He suggested for a system of immediate justice, equity and natural justice.

Kautilya's prescription of 'judicial organisation and procedure with high sense of honesty and impartiality has much relevance for the modern school of jurisprudence. If followed, it will help in the creation of a sound judicial system.

## THEORY OF DANDA (PUNISHMENT)

The theory of Danda has been reflected in the writings of many ancient philosophers like Manu, Yajnavalkya and others. But Kautilya has presented a comprehensive theory of punishment covering different types of crimes. According to Kautilya, Danda is the law of punishment or science of government. It has two primary objectives of establishing peace and order as well as giving justice to the weak. Kautilya says in the absence of Danda (law of punishment), Matsyanyaya (bigger fish swallowing the smaller ones or might is right) will prevail. Danda will give protection to the weak against the strong. Where Danda (law of punishment) will be applied, people belonging to different castes and order will do their respective duties. According to him, Danda or punishment may be broadly of four major types such as fine, mutilation of limbs, imprisonment and death.

**Fine.** It is the most common type of punishment suggested by Kautilya in his Arthasastra. It is meant for all types of crimes. Artisans like weaver, washerman, scavenger etc., shall, in accordance with their agreement as to time, place and form of work fulfil their engagements. Those who postpone their engagements under the excuse that no agreement as to time, place and form of work has been entered into, shall not only forfeit 1/4 if their wages but also be punished with a fine equal to twice the amount of their wages. Those who carry on their work contrary to the order shall not only forfeit their wages but also pay a fine equal to twice the amount of their wages. Secondly when a trader sells or mortgages inferior commodities telling it to be of superior type, sells articles of some other locality as the produce of a particular locality or gives adulterated things or deceitful mixtures to the customer, he shall not only be punished with a fine of 54 panas but also be compelled to compensate the loss. Regarding stealing he says, when any person steals articles of 1/4th to 1/2 a pana in value, he shall be fined 6 panas or his head may be shaved or he may be exiled. When a person steals articles of 1/2 to ¾ of pana in value, he shall be fined 9 panas.

**Mutilation of Limbs.** Mutilations of Limbs is another type of punishment suggested by Kautilya for different types of crimes like theft, kidnapping, murder etc. It includes both the government and the ordinary citizens. Kautilya starts with severe punishment for the government servants. When the government servants commit for the first time such offences as violation of sacred institutions on pick-pocketing, their thumb and the little fingers shall be cut off. Secondly, when any person enters into a fort without permission or takes away any valuable thing or wealth through a hole or passage in the wall of the fort, he shall be beheaded. When any person steals a big animal, abducts a male or female slave or sells the articles belonging to a dead body, both of his legs shall be cut off.

**Imprisonment.** Though Kautilya does not mention the terms of imprisonment for the quality, his reference to bandhangara and bandhanasthana (place of confinement) suggests jail for convicts of both the sexes. But imprisonment is not a common form of punishment. He suggests forced labour in state mines, payment of fines of huge amount as alternatives to the system of imprisonment.

**Death.** Kautilya suggests death as punishment for some types of crimes. It may be with or without torture. In other words, some will be inflicted with death sentence with torture and some others with death sentence without torture. When a man murders another in quarrel, he shall be tortured to death. But when a person wounded in a fight die within seven night, he who causes the wounds shall be put to death instantly. Any person who sets fire to pasture lands, fields, yards prepared for threshing out grains, houses, forests of timber or elephant, shall be thrown into fire. Any person who murders his father, mother, son, brother, teacher or an ascetic, shall be put to death by burning both his skin and head.

But the law of punishment should be applied with much care. Kautilya says, "whoever imposes severe punishment becomes repulsive to the people, while he who awards wild punishments becomes contemptible. But whoever imposes punishments as deserved becomes respectable." For punishment when awarded with due consideration makes the people devoted to righteousness and to productive works; while punishment when ill-awarded under the influence of greed and anger owing to ignorance, excites fury even among hermits and ascetics dwelling in forests. This implies that Danda when awarded in the right manner becomes positive and helps the people as well as the state. But if it is inflicted whimsically, it creates negative repercussions.

Kautilya's theory of punishment is relevant in the sense that it is uniformly applied. Whether one is an ordinary citizen or government officer or judge, law of punishment is applied to all. Judges when neglect their duty are to be fined if still neglects are to be dismissed.

## THE SPYING SYSTEM

Kautilya's emphasis on spying in different areas of the state constitutes an important aspect of his governmental system. Spying system is another important pillar of his system of administration. It has both internal and external objectives. Its internal objectives consist of giving secret information to the king regarding ministers, officers, army generals, robbery; theft, killing, murder, conspiracy against the king etc., its external objectives consist of giving information regarding the neighbouring states and their plans of war, to create dissension and trouble in foreign states, to envisage the plan to murder the enemy and to inform the king regarding the foreign spies. Thus, spying system helps the king in making his position secured, ensuring an efficient and honest administration to the people and establishing an independent and powerful state. The spying system is a unique contribution of Kautilya in the field of internal administration and foreign relation.

To pursue the objectives described above, the king shall give appointment to spies on the advice of ministers. In his Arthasastra Kautilya mentions about nine types of spies such as Kapatikachhatra (fraudulent disciple), Udasthita (recluse);

A Grihapatika (house-holder), a Vaidehaka (a merchant), tapasa (an ascetic practising austerities), a Satri (a class-mate or a colleague), a tikshna (a fire-brand) a rasada (poisoner) and a mendicant women.

**Kaptika-Chhatra (Fraudulent Disciple)**

Kapatika-chhatra is the most capable and skilful person who can easily study the mind of others. They are appointed either with honour or on the basis of salary. Their main function is to inform the king and the ministers regarding the crucade and wicked nature of people.

**Udasthitha (Recluse)**

Udasthitha is one who is an ascetic with strong character and foresight. They will be provided with money and disciples to start agriculture, cattle-rearing and trade. Out of the disciples he will send some for spying. Their main duty will be to detect crime committed in connection with the King's wealth.

**Grihapatika (A House-holder)**

Grihapatika is an intelligent, honest cultivator who has left his traditional occupation. He would spend his time and energy for encouraging the farmer for cultivation in the lands allotted to him. After gaining their confidence, he will engage them for spying.

**Vaidehaka (Merchant)**

Like Grihapatika, Vaidehaka is a trader with foresight and character. But he has left his profession. He will be appointed as a spy to carry on the manufacture of merchandise goods on the lands allotted to him for the purpose.

**Tapasa (An Ascetic Practising Auterities)**

Tapasa is a man with shaved head or bearded face who pretends to be an ascetic. He pretends to be a vegetarian, but he takes non-vegetarian food. His disciples may carry the message to the people that he is a man with supernatural power. His blessings will remove their miseries and bring their prosperity. He may through palmistry foretell such future events concerning the work of his born people in the country like small profits, destruction by fire; fear from robbers and execution of seditions etc. He will ascertain the validity of his forecast through nods and signs of the people. He shall also foretell not only the rewards which persons possessed of foresight, eloquence and bravery are likely to receive at the hands of the king but also probable changes in the appointment of ministers. According to such reports of the spy, the ministers will honour or give relief to those who have been unnecessarily victimised and give punishments indirectly to those who have escaped it.

**Satri (Class-mate or a Colleague)**

A satri is a class-mate or known man of the king who is appointed as the spy. Satri will be deployed to test the religious allurement of the ministers.

**Tikshna**

Those who are brave and fearless and can fight even with tigers or elephant are appointed as fiery spies (Tikshna). They espy the public character of those officers attached to the king.

**Rasada (Poisoner)**

Those who are very cruel and indolent are to be appointed as Rasada (Poisoner). Poisoners include sauce-maker (suda) a cook, a barber, the spreader of bed etc., and their duty will be to espy the private character of the officers.

**Bhikshyuki (A Mendicant Woman)**

A poor widow of Brahman caste who is very clever but an ascetic is appointed as a spy. Such spies have access to king's harem and residence of King's Prime Minister. She will be deployed to test the love allurement of the ministers and the officials.

Those spies who are skilful, loyal, reliable and well trained in putting on disguises shall be sent by the king to give secret information regarding the ministers, priests, magistrates, collector-general, the chamberlain, the commissioner, the city constables, superintendent of transactions, heads of departments, Officer in charge of fortifications etc. The institute of espionage will set the spies in motion in different departments. If any spy will be detected giving wrong information, he will be punished by the king. The modem system of administration has to borrow many ideas from the exhaustive system of espionage created by Kautilya.

## MANU

Manu was the first Hindu political philosopher who laid the foundation of India's political tradition in ancient India. Because if tradition begins with myth, Hindu mythology believes, all the dynasties that ruled India owed their origin to the primeval king Manu. Manu was not only the first king of ancient India, he was also the first philosopher who codified the law and created a new Hindu social and political order. His original brilliant masterpiece, the Manusmriti is the most influential Hindu law book which still determines the social and political orientation of many Indians. The study of Maim has become more relevant with the emergence of Hindu revivalism in modem India.

Who was Manu? Manu in its literal implication stands for wisdom and compassion. He was also considered to be the symbol of an institution or office of kingship. But it is said, Manu was the first progeny of the creator Brahma. Brahma in his plan of creation implanted the human race which started from Manu. Because the Agnipurana mentioned about Svayambhuba Manu. According to it,

Manu created himself and exhibited his power of kingship in different periods. He led the creation in different phases of history and became the source of knowledge, power and authority. Some scholars appropriately view. Manu as the symbol of office of the kingship. Some others view him to be the real king who existed in different periods and guided human generation through his ruling.

**The 'Manusmriti'**

The Manusmriti is the most unique and scholarly work of Manu. The Manusmriti has an extraordinary significance as a socio-religious work for the Hindus in all times. It is the most important treatise on society, religion and state-craft. The Manusmriti is like the ganges which has its origin in the Vedas. Hence, it is treated as the most authoritative work. It is the first work which codified the law in ancient India and for the first time created the political theory of a social order, government, Danda, law and justice. Manusmriti inaugurated a new era in the field of administration. But the Manusmriti was the work of first Manu who had the opportunity to listen to Brahma, the God and transmitted it to different Rishis and Maharishis like Bhrugu and Marichi. It is the essence of Manu's philosophical perception and political orientation.

Manusmriti consists of twelve chapters and 2684 hymns. The first chapter consisting of 119 hymns deals with the origin of the universe; second chapter consisting of 249 hymns deals with the different parts and duties of life such as hereditary occupation, process of purification, Brahmacharya (celibacy) and devotion to the Guru (the teacher); third chapter consisting of 286 hymns deals with house-holder's life, the system of marriage, rules regarding happy married life, evils of inter-caste marriage; fourth chapter consisting of 260 hymns deals with the rules of Grahastha life and Varna order; fifth chapter consisting of 169 hymns deals with pure and impure food, ceremonial purification and duties of wife; sixth chapter mentions about Vanaprastha and Sanyasa in 97 hymns; seventh chapter consists of 226 hymns explaining about the king's duties, the court and the payment of tax; Eighth chapter includes 420 hymns laying down the procedure of civil and criminal law, including the system of witness; Nineth chapter consisting of 336 hymns deals with the system of divorce and distribution of property. In this chapter also the civil law has been mentioned. The tenth chapter dealing with the creation, occupation and duties of different castes covers 131 hymns; the eleventh chapter covering 265 verses speaks about the system of penance through performances of sacrifice and rules of keeping away from the vices. The last chapter deals with the rules of social life, Moksha, self-knowledge, self-examination, duties towards the society and the state.

## CONCEPT OF SOCIAL ORGANISATION/SOCIAL ORDER

Manu was the creator of a social order based on division of the society into different castes. Such a social order was naturally having reference to a Hindu society. But such a social order was not new as it was prevalent in the form of functional divisions. Some scholars view that even in the Vedas reference is made to classification of the society into four categories. R.C. Majumdar in his book' Ancient India' observes a late hymn (x.90) of the Rigveda, known as Purushasukta, says that when the gods divided Purusha (the primaeval giant or creator) "the Brahman was his mouth; the Rajanya was made his arms; the being (called) the Vaisya was the thigh; the Sudra sprang from his feet. This is the only hymn in that vast collection known as the Rigveda in which occurs the names Rajanya, Vaisya and Sudra and the term Brahman also occur but very rarely. It would thus, appear that towards the very end of the Rigvedic period the distinction between four classes had just begun to take shape". Manu's work was like the Ganges which had its source elsewhere. Manu codified the caste system which he claimed to have done for the betterment of the society.

Manu said that the Brahmanas, Kshatriyas, Vaisyas arid Sudras sprang respectively from the mouth, arms, thigh and feet of the creator. But Manu introduced a system of rigidity and made it a part of the laws of the society. Secondly, he made that Brahmanas most privileged sections and superior even to the kings. But Sudras were to be the most deprived group of his social order. An attempt is made to give a brief account of the relative positions of different castes in his social order.

**Brahmana.** Brahmanas are the greatest among men. A Brahman is born for the fulfilment of the sacred law. He becomes one with Brahman. He is an eternal incarnation of the law. The main functions of Brahmanas are teaching, reading, sacrifice and sacrificing (as priests) for others. He exists for the sake of dharma and is for the existence of the Vedas. Because when a Brahman is born, he is born above the world. He is the chief of all creatures to guard the treasure of dharma. Thus, whatever exists in the universe is the property of the Brahman; for the Brahman is entitled to it all by his superiority and eminence of birth. He segregates Brahmins and elevates them to higher position by telling that the Brahman eats but his own food, wears but his own apparel, bestows but his own alms. According to Manu, a Brahman is an interpreter of law and hence, must read the sacred law carefully: A Brahmin is a twice-born who undergoes the process of sanctifying the body and purifying his life. He prohibits Brahmins to marry in other castes (Varna). A Brahmin's son can be a Brahmin only when he marries a lady of his own caste. A Brahmin has to undergo austerity and should stick to the vedic way of life, otherwise he loses the fruit of a successful Brahmin. These are the code of conducts for a Brahmin. Only a successful Brahmin can be a guide to the King. The king should respect the Brahmins.

Manu says, just like fire never gets polluted even if used in the graveyard, whether ignorant or learned, following noble or mean occupations, a Brahmin is a great divinity. Thus, Manu's social order has predominance of Brahmins which still pervades the modern society. He allows occupational mobility for Brahmins. Brahmin can join defence or agriculture.

**Kshatriya.** The Kshatriya sprang from the arms of the creator. A Kshatriya has to protect the people, to bestow gifts, to offer sacrifices, to study (the Veda) and to abstain from attaching himself to sexual pleasures. Like the Brahmins, Kshatriyas are also twice born and are to undergo the same type of purification. The son of a Kshatriya becomes a Kshatriya only when Kshatriya gets married to a lady of his own caste.

**Vaisya.** The Vaisya coming from the thigh of the creator constitutes the third rank in the social hierarchy. The main functions of the Vaisya are to tend the cattle, bestow gifts, offer sacrifices, study the Veda, trading, lending money and to cultivate land. That means Vaisyas are to carry out both agricultural and commercial functions. But Vaisya, according to Manu, are categorised under the group of twice born. Hence, Manu gives them the right to study the Veda but cannot teach the Veda. Like Brahmins he undergoes the process of purification. But the thread ceremony of Vaisya will be different from Brahmins and Kshatriyas. For example, Manu said, the sacred thread of a Brahman must be of cotton put on over the left shoulder; the thread of a Kshatriya must be of three fold and, hempthread, the Vaisya must have woollen thread.

**Sudra.** Sudra occupies the lowest position in Manu's codified law. The Sudras are to serve the other three castes. Naturally while the other three castes (Varna) are privileged, Sudras are deprived. Sudras are excluded from the twice-born. They do not have any right for sacred learning. He who explains the sacred law to a Sudra or dictates a per.ance to him sinks along with his pupil into hell. Like Plato and Aristotle undermining the importance of the manual labourers, Manu undermined the importance of Sudras and said, Sudras can never form a stable society. A kingdom which is destitute of twice-born people but contains many Sudras and which is infested by atheists is soon afflicted with disease and famine and utterly perishes. Brahmins should not reside in such a state. He also gives an insignificant position to Sudra women when he says if a son is born from a Brahmin male and Sudra female, he will not have the right of a Brahmin.

### Status of Women

In Manu's social order woman is given a peculiar status. She is bestowed with a major responsibility to be the real mistress of the house and made the wife, the uncrowned queen of the house. But a woman does not have the freedom in the society (na stri svatantryam arhati). Here is it worth mentioning that though women occupied a similar position with that of men during the Vedic period and some women like Gargi, Vachaknavi land Maitreyi participated in the philosophical deliberations with great philosophers like Yajnavalkya, Manu's ordinance prohibited women to study the Vedic literature. But

Manu suggested that women should be properly taken care of. Husbands should respect their wives so that the offsprings and the sanctity of the family will be properly protected. Wives should be given thc authority to manage the material and financial affairs of the house. Here Manu gives an elevated position to women in comparison to man. Again in some other verses he says if a wife tries to surpass her husband, she will suffer from many diseases.

Manu's social order was based on a social organisation marked by the gross inequality. It created an in-human tradition of social hierarchy in which Sudras, varnasankaras and women had no privilege, only deprivations. But such conclusions on Manu's social order will lead us to extremism. Because though Manu says, Sudras are born slaves and have no right to study the Vedas, in some other verse, he says, a man of faith may receive pure learning even from one of a lower caste, as he may receive the highest law from the lowest and an excellent wife from a base family. So also he allows in case of a second marriage, one may marry a woman of lower caste.

## THEORY OF GOVERNMENT (ORGANISATION AND FUNCTION)

Manu construct his idea of Government as an essential element of preserving the social order, the state and its governance. Manu says, for easy and better governance of the Kingdom, the king should have the assistance of ministers, officials and the army. Besides, Manu suggests for decentralisation of power in his theory of Government. He gives power to the village headman and creates a structure of local Government. Accordingly there is devolution of powers and functions in his governmental system but the final power of supervision, control and appeal remains with the king. His theory of government has organisational and functional aspects which are discussed below :

### Organisation of the Government

In the entire structure of the government, the king is the linchpin. Hence, Manu suggests the king to be honest, modest and learned. He must give up his vices and should exercise utmost control over his body and mind. He must get-up early in the morning, read the Veda and worship Brahmanas. He must be committed, sincere and untiring in his duty. The king is the holder of all the powers vested on him by different Gods and goddesses. He is the protector and father of the kingdom. All must obey him.

Ministers constitute the second ladder of his government. Manu realises that even an easy undertaking is difficult to be accomplished. Hence, to govern a kingdom which yields great revenues will not be easy to be governed without assistance. In the fitness of things, the king should appoint seven or eight ministers. Such ministers should be well versed in the sciences, skilled in the use of weapons and men of noble families, The king should have regular consultations with the ministers with regard to peace and war, the revenue, the manner of protecting and the sanctification of his gains. He must first ascertain the opinion of each minister separately and then he must do what is most beneficial for him in his affairs. But he must select the most distinguished Brahman and consult him on six important matters of royal policy.

Officials constitute another segment of governmental system. The king should appoint as many officers as he likes to meet the demands of administration. But he should appoint skilful and clever people as Officers. From among the officers, he should select the brave, the skilful, the high-born and the honest in offices for the collection of revenue, in mines, manufactures and store-houses but timid officers should be kept in the interior of his place. Besides such Officers, the king should appoint an ambassador who is expert in all sciences, understands hints, expressions of the face and gestures, honest, skilful and belongs to a noble family. The ambassador should possess a good memory, know proper time and place for action and should be handsome, fearless and eloquent. The ambassador will be in charge of war and peace. He should keep watch on the gestures and actions of the foreign kings through his confidential advisers.

**Local Government**

For the protection and governance of his kingdom the king should deploy a company of soldiers commanded by a trust worthy officer in the midst of two, three, five or hundreds of villages. Every village should be the unit of the government. It should have a headman. Then next higher administrative units should consist of ten twenty, hundred and a thousand villages. In every such unit there would be a Head or Lord. It will be based on hierarchical principles of administration. The Lord of one village shall inform the lord of ten villages of the crimes committed in his village and the ruler of ten to the ruler of twenty. But the ruler of twenty shall report all such matters to the lord of a hundred and the lord of a hundred shall himself give information to the lord of thousand. The lord of one village shall obtain those articles which the villagers ought to furnish daily to the king such as food, drink and fuel. This will be a type of salary for the village headman. Besides, the rulers of ten villages shall get one Kula (which means as much land as is sufficient for one family) and the lord of twenty villages shall get five Kulas, the lord of a hundred villages shall get the revenues of one village and the lord of a thousand shall get the revenues of a town. Manu suggests the king to appoint one minister exclusively for the village administration. One officer should also be appointed in each town as the superintendent of all affairs who is most formidable and work like a planet among the stars. The superintendent should personally supervise the work of all the officers and keep a watch on their activities through spies available to him. Because the officers who are appointed by the king to protect the interest of the people generally become dishonest and exploit the people. Manu says, the king should protect his subjects from such people and confiscate the property of those officers who are corrupt. Such dishonest evil-minded officers should also be banished.

**Principles, Policies, and Functions of the Government**

Manu traces the principles and policies of his government to three human ends like virtue, wealth and pleasure and assigns accordingly different functions to be carried out by the government. The basic objective of the Government headed by the king, Manu says, should be to acquire by his army what he has not gained, to preserve what he has not gained by careful attention, to increase what has been preserved in various ways and to bestow the increase upon the deserving. Ghosal writes, according to Manu, the general aims of a king's policies are four fold. These are, firstly, acquisition by force, secondly, preservation, thirdly, increase in various ways and fourthly, bestowal of the increase upon the deserving. Manu does not prescribe uniform policies of administration. It is rather composite and contradictory line of behaviour dictated by the exigencies of administration. The king, should act with justice in his own kingdom and chastise his foes with rigour; he should preserve his kingdom and destroy its opponents just as a weeder pluck the weeds and preserve the corn. The king should be both severe and gentle according to circumstances so that he will be highly respected. Manu also lays down the complex principles of the king's government especially in relation to the foreign enemy. Hence, regarding the principles and functions of the government, Manu draws a parallel with the animal behaviour. Like a tortoise we are told, the king shall protect the limbs of the state against treachery, like a heron he shall plan (his understandings), like a lion he shall exhibit his strength, like a wolf he shall snatch at his prey and like a hare he shall double in retreat.

**Guaranteeing Security for the Subjects**

The primary function of the government is to ensure security for its people. Because the king is the father figure and also the source of authority. The Ministers and Officers must assist him in the maintenance of law and order and prevention of crime. The king with the help of ministers, officers, lords of villages and the spies shall detect two types of thieves *i.e.*, the secret thieves and the open thieves. The secret thieves consists of Burglars, robbers in forests and so forth. The king, with the help of the officers and the spies has to find out the culprit and punish them. He has also to guard various public places with the troops and spies so as to keep out the thieves. The thieves who are caught with the stolen goods and the tools of theft in their possessions are put to death. The persons who provide the thieves with food and shelter are also put to death. On the other hand the open thieves are those who live by the fraudulent sale of various commodities and who take bribes. It also includes cheats, rogues, gamblers, fortune-tellers, high-officers and physicians guilty of improper conduct and so forth. The king should confiscate the property and banish the officers who misuse their office and accumulate wealth.

## Formation of Foreign Policy

The king with the assistance of his ambassadors will decide the foreign policy of his government. Manu speaks of six principles to be followed in the foreign policy making. Such six principles (Gunas) are alliance, War, Marching, halting, dividing the army and seeking protection. The king shall make an alliance for peace when he is sure of his own superiority in future and of his slight loss at present. An alliance may be of two types *i.e.*, when one marches together with an ally on the contrary when the allies act separately. He shall wage war when he finds that all his principal subjects (Prakritis) are very much contended and he is very strong. War may be of two kinds. One is undertaken in season by one self to meet his purposes and another is launched to avenge an injury done to a friend. He shall march against the enemy when he finds that his own army is strong and well disposed towards him while that of the enemy is weak. Marching is of two fold. It is undertaken by one alone when an urgent matter suddenly arises and the second one is undertaken by one, allied with a friend. The kind shall declare halt when he is very weak in chariots and troops or he may declare halt in favour of a friend. He shall divide his forces when the army stops in one place and its master in another in order to achieve some purpose. He shall take refuge in rich and powerful king when harassed by the enemies and to be known as the protege of a powerful king.

## Military Functions (War and Aggrandisement)

Manu suggests his king the techniques of war and aggrandisement. For the protection of the people if war is necessary, the king should not hesitate to take recourse to it. But the king should be cautious in his decision. Political wisdom requires that the war should be so organised that no ally, no neutral or foe may injure him. He should envisage his plan of attacking a hostile kingdom properly. He suggests his king to undertake the expedition in the month of Margasirsha (November-December) or towards month of Phalguna (February-March). Because in such months fodder and grain are abundant and the roads are dry. He can declare war at other times but only when he has a certain prospect of victory or when his enemy is in danger. Secondly, he must arrange all affairs in his kingdom perfectly, secure a base (military) for his operation and make his six fold army efficient. Thirdly, he should keep watch on friends who secretly serve the enemy and the deserters who return from the enemy camp. Because such people are the worst foes. Fourthly, the king should extend his troops in that direction from where he apprehends danger and he himself should encamp many array. Fifthly, he should deploy the commander in chief, the subordinate general and the superior officers in different directions. He should place troops of soldiers whom he can rely and keep such soldiers who are expert both in defending and offending fearlessly. When the king has been able to enter into enemy's town, let him destroy the tanks, ramparts and diches and instigate a rebellion in foe's kingdom and when the real opportunity comes let him conquer. Thus, Manu gives a theory of defence which can be compared with Machavelli's doctrine of aggrandisement.

**Administration of Justice**

Justice constitutes an important part of Manu's state. Hence, administration of justice in an honest impartial manner is highly essential. Manu says, "justice being violated destroys; justice being preserved, preserves; therefore justice must not be violated, lest violated justice should destroy us". The king himself must preside over the court but must be assisted by Brahmanas and learned councillors. In the absence of the king, a learned Brahman should act as judge assisted by three councillors. The judges must try to find out the truth by inferences as a hunter traces the hair of a wounded deer by drops of blood. "When engaged in judicial proceedings he must pay full attention to the truth, to the object, to himself, next to the witness, to the place, to the time and to the aspect."

Manu's theory of government is marked by its concern for the protection of the subjects, (internally and externally) formulation of a foreign policy based on expendiency, war and aggrandisement, a balanced policy of taxation and honest impartial truthful way of administering justice.

## MANU'S THEORY OF DANDA (PUNISHMENT)

Manu's theory of Danda (Punishment) or coercive authority constitutes the most important foundation of his polity. It reflects the different dimensions of political theory like sovereignty, law, justice, political obligation and the king's responsibility towards the law abiders. Manu was not the only advocate of the theory of Danda as it was also highlighted by Yajnavalkya and Kautilya. But thc originality of Manu lies in restricting the hands of the king in applying the canons of punishment and to make him cautious about his duty to be just and impartial. Manu's theory of Danda (coercive authority) is the centre of his socio-political system and has much relevance even for modem polity. Appropriately Manu says, Danda is the protector of all creatures, law and the Dharma; it is the king, the male, the director and the ruler. It pursues the rule of law and justice in the society. That is because neither the father, nor the mother, nor the friend, nor wife, nor son, nor the domestic priest is exempted from the king's Danda if they fail to discharge their duties in the right perspective.

**Objectives and Principles of Danda**

The king has to rule on the basis of Danda or coercieve authority for the purpose of protecting all creatures and the Dharma (Laws). Manu says, Danda which generates fear becomes the basis of the state. The state should have the allegiance of its subjects and their devotion towards duty. Force makes the subjects not only law-abiding but also duty bound. It will make the state strong and prosperous.

Manu uses Danda as the symbol of law, authority and justice. Hence, he says, punishment (Danda) is the king, the male, the manager of affairs and the ruler. It is also the source of people's security and prosperity. It makes the people happy when applied in the right perspective. Danda is awake when others are asleep. If Danda is not applied untiringly against the unjust, might will be right and the strong will roast the weak like the fish on a spit. The whole world is kept in order by punishment, for a guiltless man is hard to find. Danda also keeps the social order intact by asking every varna or caste to do his duty in his own station of life without meddling in the affairs of others. The king's name and fame will go on increasing if he applies the principles of Danda universally.

Some principles of Danda may be presented here for better understanding. The king should prevent the anti-socials by three methods—like imprisonment, putting them in chains and various corporal punishments. The king will be guilty if he does not punish the thieves and wicked. He who steals the rope or the water-pot from a well or damages a hut where water is distributed, shall pay one Masha (of copper) as a fine and restore the article damaged in its proper place. But if one steals ten kumbhas of grain or more than a hundred (palas) of articles like gold, silver etc. or he steals woman and the most precious gems, corporal punishment should be inflicted. If one steals more than fifty palas it is enacted that the hands shall be cut off. For stealing cows belonging to Brahmans, for piercing a barren cow and for stealing cattle of Brahmans, the offender shall forthwith lose half of his feet. An offence which is committed in the presence of the owner with violence, will be robbery; if it is committed in his absence, it will be theft. In case of a theft the guilt of a Sudra shall be eight fold, that of a Vaisya sixteen fold, that of a Kshatriya thirty two fold, that of a Brahman sixty four fold or quite a hundred fold knowing the nature of offence. Here Manu's objective has been to prevent the twice born from being a criminal which would disrupt the social order. A king who desires to gain the throne of Indra and imperishable eternal fame, shall not neglect to punish a man who commits violence. He who commits violence must be considered as the worst offender than a defamer or a thief. But Manu warns the king that if he neglects his duty to check or pardons the perpetrator of violence, he will perish and incur hatred. Manu suggests the king to deal with adultery committed with the wives of others by giving such an exemplary punishment that it would not be repeated in future. Because adultery would lead to mixture of castes (Varna) and destroy the entires social order. In the field of trade, Manu says, the king should confiscate the whole property of traders who out of greed export goods over which the king has a monopoly of the export which is forbidden. He should also regulate the prices of the marketable goods, mark the weights and measures. He should punish the traders who cheat the people.

Thus, Manu says, Danda or coerceive authority serves different objectives like protection of the creation, social order and the socio-economic interest of the people. Above all, its paramount objective is to establish a polity based on honesty, discipline and efficiency.

**Who can Apply Danda?**

Manu says, any one can not apply Danda. He warns the king to be cautions in applying Danda. That king can be a just inflicter of punishment who is truthful, who acts after due consideration, who is wise and knows the respective value of virtue, pleasure and wealth. Punishment is difficult to be administered by men with immatured minds. Manu therefore says, punishment can not be inflicted justly by one who is a fool, a covetous man or one addicted to sensual pleasures. On the other hand a man who is wise, pure, faithful to his promise and acts according to the institutes of the sacred law can inflict punishment. The king who is just in inflicting punishment will prosper but if he is voluptous, partial and deceitful, will be destroyed. Manu says, the fame of a king spreads like a drop of oil on the water if he applies Danda in the right manner. But the fame of a king who acts in a contrary manner and does not subdue himself, diminishes in extent among men like drop of clarified butter in water.

Manu's theory of Danda laid the foundation of a just legal order where like the modem democrates, Manu never left the coerceive authority to the monopoly of the king.

## VIEWS ON STATE

Manu as one of the law codifier of ancient India deals with the theory of the structure of the state (Kingdom), nature and functions of the government (king) and presents a system of law to deal with both the civil and the criminal cases and regulates the external human conduct. Manu's views on the origin and structure of the state are the reflection of both the divine origin theory and the organic theory of state. In his views on Government, Manu has followed the old Vedic doctrine of the two powers such as temporal and spiritual by bestowing ruling authority upon the Brahman and the King. This power is to be exercised by them over the people by divine ordination.

## 'SAPTANGA' THEORY OF STATE (ELEMENTS OF STATE)

Manu constructed such a theory of state in which the kingdom (state) will be politically stable, administratively efficient, financially sound, militarily and diplomatically strong. Manu's theory of state because of its unique contribution in the field of state-craft has remained a permanent treasure in the literature of political science. It is because of this fact we find the similarities of views on the 'saptanga' theory of state (seven limbs of the state) among Manu, Yajnavalkya and Kautilya.

Before going to discuss the theory of the elements of the state, Manu deals with the problem of origin of the king, the sovereign ruler. Manu gives a theory of the divine right of kingship. According to him, when the world was without a king and trembling with fear, God created a king for the protection of the world. The king is all powerful because of his excellence in every field. He is fire and wind, the Sun and the Moon, the king of justice, the Kuvera, the Varuna and the great Indra. Though a child, a king is not to be despised as a human being for he is a powerful divinity in man's form.

According to Manu, a state has seven limbs such as Swamin, Mantris and Amatyas, Janapada (the territory), Durga (Fort) Kosha (the treasury); Bala (the defence) and Mitra (ally). A brief account of each of the elements is presented here.

**Swamin (The Sovereign Ruler).** The king is the sovereign ruler of a kingdom. He is created by God with all the blessings from different gods like Indra, wind, yama and the Sun, fire and Varuna, the Moon and Kuvera. He cannot be challenged. Because Manu says, the king excels every one in the society. He is the right person to protect the social order. He is the representative of the divinity in human form. He is the symbol of justice. If any one ever dares to challenge the king ends in destroying himself. Manu said, "Fire burns only the individual but the fire of the king burns the race". Thus, Manu created an all powerful sovereign ruler like Thomas Hobbes, Machiavaelli and John Austin in Modern times.

**Amatyas (Ministers).** Manu advised his king to be carefully in the formation of council of ministers. Because such ministers constitute the government and appropriately form an important element of the state. The king should appoint seven or eight carefully examined ministers who are learned, brave, skilled in the use of weapons and have an outstanding heredity. The king should discuss with his ministers in matters of peace and war, conditions of the kingdom, wealth, protection of the territory etc.

**Pura (Capital-city).** For the safety of the king Manu suggests for a town fortified by a desert or water or even trees, by armed man or by mountains. The king should live in such a town. Manu argues, the desert occupied by the beasts and the deer, the water by crocodile, the trees by monkeys, the (Outposts) of men by men, constitute the best defence for the king.

**Janapada (The Territory).** Like the modern state system, Manu's kingdom also had a permanent territory. But Janapada should have both cultivable land and waste land. It is better if the territory is fit to be the source of good living and surrounded by weak neighbours. But it should not be marshy and unhygenic. It would be a better kingdom if it is inhabited by the Aryas. More specifically he advocated a kingdom having predominance of Brahmins. The kingdom should go by the Vedic doctrines. If it is dominated by the Sudras there is every chance that the kingdom would suffer from the famine and diseases.

**Kosha (The Treasury).** Manu emphaizes Kosha or the treasury for the proper maintenance of the kingdom. But he should appoint pure men (not greedy) to take charge of kosha which involves both the income and expenditure of the kingdom. Collection of revenues, location of mines, especially gold mines, production of grains by the labourers should be taken care of to develop a sound and stable finance.

**Bala (The Army).** Bala or the army is another important element of the state. Its objective is to protect the kingdom from the external attack. But the army depends on the offensive weapon it possesses and the type of discipline it has. It should be controlled by a minister who is skilled in war.

**Mitra (The Foreign Ally).** Manu gives preference to acquiring of ally as an important element of the state. The king should create friends for his own safety rather than going for acquiring land or money. Such allys who are weak today may be strong tomorrow.

Thus, Manu mentions about seven limbs of the state and pays equal importance to each one. No limbs is superior to any one. Here lies the difference between Manu and others like Kautilya or Yajnavalkya.

## THE KING (POWERS AND OBLIGATIONS)

Manu created a benevolent king for the protection of life of the people and maintenance of a social order prescribed by him. Manu was an advocate of divine right of kingship; As already mentioned in earlier discussions; there was at first no king. As a result, the people found themselves in trouble and fled in all directions. For their protection, the Lord created a king. Thus, the kingship was a divine creation but must serve the purpose of the people. In other words the king muṣt be both divine and benevolent. Besides, "Day and night he must strenuously exert himself to conquer his senses; for he (alone) who has conquered his own senses, can keep his subjects in obediences". One can be the best king if he sacrifices his sensuality, greed and wrath. Thus the king belonging to the caste of Kashatriyas is supposed to lead a pious life himself and worship Brahmanas. In other words, in Manu's Hindu policy, there will be supremacy of spiritual. power over temporal power as Manu favours a Brahminical social order.

### Powers and Authority of the King

Manu's conception of the powers and authority of the king is derived from the conjoint principle of the King's divine creation and endowment with a superhuman personality. So the king is extraordinary and excells others in the society through his action and activities and hence, claims obligations from the subjects.

The king is the culmination of all the powers possessed by different gods and deities. Since he has been created with eternal parties of Indra, the wind, yama, the sun, fire, varuna, the Moon and of the Lord of wealth (Kubera), he surpasses all other created beings. He is the source of law and justice. Manu argues, even an infant king must not be neglected because he is a great deity in human form. No one should challenge or disobey the authority of the king. Because the king is so powerful that his anger can destroy the whole family who hates him or resist his authority. The king has the power to make law for the happiness of his subjects and at the same time inflict pain on those who are defaulters. The king has the power to punish and create fear in every body so that no one deviates from his duty. Danda (punishment) should be inflicted on men who act unjustly.

Punishment alone governs all created beings; it alone protects them; it watches over them while they sleep, Besides, the king has the following powers.

**Executive Powers.** The king has also been bestowed with the powers to constitute his kingdom with seven elements such as Swami, Amatya, the territory, the Pura (the fortified town), Kosha (the treasury), the Bala (the army) and the ally (friends). The king is the chief soverign legislative and executive authority in the state. Besides his power to inflict punishment he has the executive power of appointments. He has the power to appoint ministers (eight) who are skilled in different fields like war, finance, and governance. The king has the power to ask for suggestions from his ministers and takes the decision finally on important matters. He has also the power to appoint officers of different departments. But such officers must be wise, firm and capable to implement the laws and collect the tax. The officers with skill and courage, high descendency and honesty should be given higher responsibilities like collection of revenue, mines, production and store houses. But the king should keep with himself the power of supervision and control. Besides, the king has the power to appoint ambassadors to take care of the relationship with other states. He has to find out the allies and give information to the king regarding the secret activities of other kings.

**Law-Making Power.** The king has also the law making power. But the king makes those laws with the help of the principles drawn from the local usages and from the sacred law (smriti). Such laws can be classified into eight categories like debts, deposit and pledge, theft, robbery, adultery, duties of man and wife, gambling and betting etc. The laws of the king can not be challenged in any court or by any person.

**Judicial Power.** The king has also the judicial powers. He can enquire into different cases and with the help of Brahmans and experienced councillors delivers justice on the matters mentioned above. The ring if fails to decide cases should entrust the job to a learned Brahman.

**Military Power.** The king has also the military power of declaring war against other kingdoms. He can also conclude peace, make treatise and enter into friendship. He has to decide the foreign policy of his kingdom with the help of ambassadors.

## CONCEPT OF LAW AND JUSTICE

In India's political tradition, Manu is regarded as the first law codifier. Manu creates a social order and a political system giving absolute temporal power to the king. But as mentioned earlier, Manu does not leave the subject to be ruled by the whims of the King. Manu therefore, talks of 'Law' as prescribed by the Vedas which means 'sruti' (revelation) and by smritis (tradition). Accordingly to some scholars, it will be wrong to describe Manu as the first law-giver of Hindu polity. Because his prescriptions of law are based on different sources of law. G. Buhler writes, "Whether law has been ordained for any person by Manu, that has been fully declared in the Veda; for the sage was omniscient". Besides, there are also other sources of law. The whole Veda is the first source of the sacred law, next the tradition and the virtuous conduct of those who know the Veda, the customs of holy Man and finally self-satisfaction. Here the self-satisfaction means the satisfaction of the virtuous. Manu gives a list of "eighteen titles of law" which includes non-payment of debt; pledges, sale without ownership, partnership and non-delivery of what has been given, non-payment of wages, breach of contract, revocation of sale and 'purchase, disputes between master and servant, the law of disputes about boundaries, assault and slander, theft, violence, adultery, law between men and women, partitions, dicing and games with animals. These eighteen laws drawn from the local usages and treatises guide the king to decide the litigation and give justice to the people. Besides, Manu talks of transcendental laws which give a code of conduct for the twice born and keep the social order intact. Such laws are exclusively based on the prescriptions of the Veda. Thus, Manu talks about two types of laws *i.e.*, the transcendental laws and the state laws. The objective of state law is to give protection to the people from theft, robbery, etc., to give justice to the people by punishing the wrong doers and save the foundations of a polity from corruption and exploitation. The state laws based on local usages and treatises may be of two types such as civil and criminal laws which are discussed below :

**Civil Laws**

Manu talks about some laws concerning ownership and inheritance of property, money lending, contractor agreement, partnership, sales without ownership, non-payment of wages, boundary disputes etc. Which can be grouped under civil laws meant for resolving civil cases. Since all the laws cannot be covered under this study, some portions of civil laws are discussed here for a clear understanding of Manu's concept of law and justice.

The king, Manu says, shall protect the inherited property of a minor until he returns from his teacher's house or until he becomes a major. The king should also guarantee ownership right to barren women, widow and women afflicted with diseases. Manu says, the just and righteous king must punish the relatives of such women who appropriate their property like thieves. In case of disappearance of ownership of property, the owner of the property does not know the time and place where it was lost, he is worthy of aline equal to the object claimed. The property stolen by the thieves must be restored by the king to the men of all castes (Varnas) but if the king uses such property himself, he lowers his position to the rank of a thief. When a creditor sues before the king for the recovery of money from a debtor, he must make the debtor pay the sum against which the creditor proves to be his due. The king shall order the debtor to repay the debt alongwith a small fine when a debtor denies the repayment of debt. Regarding the deposits, he says, a sensible man should make a deposit only with a person of good family, of good conduct and well acquainted with law. Manu says, he who restores not his deposit to the depositor at his request may be tried by the judge in the depositor's absence. An open or a sealed deposit must never be returned to a near relative (of the depositor during latter's time); for if the recipient dies without delivering them, they are lost. Regarding the sale without ownership, he says, a gift or sale made by any body else but the owner must be considered as null and void according to rule in judicial proceedings. But any one who' acquires a chattel (movable property) before a number of witness, posssses that chattel with a clear legal title by purchase. Regarding the non-payment of wages Manu says, a hired servant or workman who without being ill, out of pride fails to perform his work according to the agreement, shall be fined Krishnala and no wages shall be paid to him. But if he is really ill and after recovery performs his works according to the original agreement, he shall receive his wages even after a lapse of long time. In case of boundary disputes between villages, the king shall settle the limits in the month of Gyaistha (May-June) when the grass dries up and when the landmarks are most distinctly visible. The boundary lines of the villages should be marked by trees, tanks, temples etc.

**Criminal Laws**

Manu speaks about the laws regarding defamation, assault, hurt, theft, adultery, *etc.,* which can be clubbed under the criminal law. Manu says, different laws prevail for different castes in case they try to defame the other. A Kshatriya if defames a Brahman, shall be fined one hundred (Panas); a Vaisya one hundred and fifty or two hundred but a Sudra shall suffer corporal punishment. A Brahman shall be fined fifty (Panas) for defaming a Kshatriya; in case of a Vaisya the fine shall be twenty-five (Panas); in case of a Sudra only twelve. A once born man (Sudra's) tongue shall be cut off when he humiliates a twice-born with gross invective. Because he is of low origin. If he arrogantly teaches Brahmans their duty, the king shall cause hot oil to be poured into his mouth and into his ears. In case of assault and hurt, Manu says, if a man of low-caste does hurt a man of the three highest castes, his limbs shall be cut-off. A low-caste man who tries to place himself on the same seat with a man of high-caste shall be branded on his hip and be banished. But one who breaks the skin of an equal or fetches blood from him shall be fined one hundred (Panas); he who breaks bone shall be banished. If a limb is injured; wounded or blood flows, the assailant shall be made to pay the expenses of the cure or the whole as a fine to the king. Regarding theft, the king should be very careful, to prevent it. Because the king is worthy of honour who ensures safety. One has to suffer corporal punishment for stealing men of noble family especially women and the most precious gems. In case of theft, the guilt of the Sudra shall be eight fold, that of a Vaisya sixteen fold, that of a Kshatriya thirty two fold but that of a Brahman sixty-four fold. But the king should deal more severely with those who commit violence because such people are worse than defamer or a thief. Manu bans adultery strictly. He says, the king shall give punishment with terror to those who commit adultery. Because adultery shall destroy the Varna order. Manu defines adultery as "meeting the wife of another man secretly, offering her gifts, touching her dress, sitting with her on a bed, touching a woman in a place not to be touched." Manu prescribes separate punishments for separate castes.

**How to Render Justice?**

Manu gives a unique and permanent place to justice in his political philosophy, Justice is the only friend of man who follows him even after his death. Manu establishes the importance of justice by pointing out, "that justice being violated, destroys justice, being preserved, preserves; therefore, justice must not be violated, lest violated justice destroys us". If the king and the judges remain indifferent to injustice or falsehood, they themselves will be responsible for it and destroy themselves. Besides the man who commits crime and gives false witness will also be responsible. Manu thus, entrusts the king with the major responsibility of administering justice on the basis of, law described above.

The king must act as the highest court of justice and should be assisted by the Brahmanas and experienced councillors. He should daily decide one case after another which fall under the eighteen titles of law drawn from the local usages and institutes of sacred law. Detailed elaborations have been made above regarding such laws. The king should personally investigate the case. If he can not, he should appoint a learned Brahman to do the same. Besides, three other Brahamanas well versed in the Vedas should assist the judge. The court shall consist of four-faced Brahman. The king should cover his body and occupy the seat of justice. He should worship the guardian deities of the world with a concentrated mind before he begins the trial. But Manu says, the king should examine the causes of the suitors according to the order of the cases. He should also try to study the internal disposition of men by their voice, colour, motions, aspects, eyes and gestures while deciding the cases.

Manu gives importance to evidence and the honesty of witness in law suits. Trustworthy men of all the four, castes (Varna) may be-made witness in lawsuits. Secondly, the witness must have sense of duty and freedom from covetousness. But those who have an interest in the suit or those who are friends or enemies of the parties or persons suffering under severe illness or tainted by mortal sins can not be the witness. Manu also prohibits some sections of the society from being witness in any case. Such section of people include the king, the actors, a srotriya (Brahmin learned in the Vedas), an ascetic, a wholly dependent man a man, of bad fame, an aged man, an infant, man of lowest caste, man having deficiency in his organs, intoxicated man, a mad man, a man tormented by hunger and thirst, a wrathful man, or a thief. By preventing such people from being witness, Manu has tried his best to make justice lawful, impartial and honest. However, the king should try to know the honesty and ability of the witness. In case of disagreement among the witnesses the king shall accept as true the evidence of the majority. In case they are equal in number, the king must give importance to the witness of those who are distinguished by their good qualities. The statement of the witness must be received on trials. The judge should examine the witness personally. If no witness is available in a case and the judge is unable to really ascertain the truth, he may discover the truth by an oath. Manu says, the judge should punish those who give false evidence. If the witness is given through covetousness, one thousand Panas will be fined, if a man gives witness through fear, two middling amercements shall be paid as a fine, if one gives witness through friendship, four times of the lowest amercement shall be charged as fine. Manu says, such fine have been prescribed for perjury to prevent failure of justice and restrain injustice. After ascertaining the time and place of offence and considering the ability of the criminal to suffer and the nature of crime, the King (judge) shall give judgment and cause punishment to those who deserve it.

Manu's views on law and justice, as the two inseparable pillars of the state contribute highly to the literature of jurisprudence and the political theory for creating a system of rule of law.

❐

# 2

# Greek Political Thought

## PLATO

Plato was born in 427 B.C. in a noble family in Athens and claimed to have royal blood in his veins. He traced his origin to Greek God Pooeidon and that of his mother with the family of Great Athenian, lawgiver Solon. The period of his birth and that of death was historically important because hardly a year or so before his birth great Athenian statesman Pericles passed away and Athenians then got entangled in Peloponnesian wars in which his own native city had to suffer immense humiliations. It was during his life period that he saw that Macedonian militarism was sweeping away almost everything. From his life to his death he saw Greek legal system in trouble. He also saw the defeat of Athens in wars against Spartas and the establishment of tyrannical rule of reactionaries. He also saw the execution of his master at the hands of these reactionaries. The result of all these events was that he greatly felt perturbed and wanted to establish that the rule of a philosopher king was the only remedy to remove all these troubles. He also wanted to establish that law-abiding and noble citizens had no place in the tyrannical state. He felt that remedy to Athenian state problems was not in producing ordinary citizens but noble and brilliant sons, like Socrates.

Plato, like many of his relatives, had an ambition to start a political career. As a matter of fact he had the opportunity of joining the terror of 404 but he abstained there from till he was sure of their line of action. But soon he found that it was not possible for him to reconcile with their line of action. He developed great hatred for them when he found that they failed to condemn the death of Socrates. It was rather a turning point of his life career when he decided to leave politics to become political philosopher. His political philosophy contained politics, ethics, mathe matics and sociology combined together.

He was so much shocked and terrified by the death of Socrates and others who were forerunners of his philosophy that he left his native land and spent much of his time in travelling over Greece, Egypt and Italy. It is also believed by some writers that he also visited India and learnt philosophy of Indian Vedantas. He is also believed to have visited Persia.

It was during his travels abroad that he studied the causes of human discontentment, and political instability. On return, he established an institution for systematic and scientific study of all these problems and named that 'Academy', which is even today regarded by some as the first University of the ancient world.

It was in 387 B.C. that he wrote earlier dialogues of 'Republic' and also the 'Apology', 'Crito', 'the Gorgias' and 'the Protagoras'. From Egyptian philosophy he borrowed the idea of division of labour which he felt was definitely advantageous for running sound state administration. It was during his this visit that he met Dion at Syracuse who was converted to his view point. It was through the efforts of Dion that Plato got the opportunity of visiting Sicily again with the idea of converting its ruler Dionysu II to his views and putting his own idea of "Philosopher King" into practice. His mission, however, had little success.

Till the time of his death he made constant efforts for promoting just life and installing philosopher kings. It has been said about him that, "yet he never abandoned the belief that he had found a way of life, and he never ceased to train men to follow it..." In the words of Barker, "He thought to impart knowledge which should issue into action, and to teach a philosophy which should be a way and an inspiration to life".

He died in 347 B.C. at the mature age of 81.

Though luckily we have most of his dialogues' available to us in one form or the other yet unfortunately we have no recorded account of his lectures which he delivered at the 'Academy' established by him. There is considerable evidence to show that his lectures were more valuable expressions of his ideas and in their absence it is not possible to have fullest exposition and appreciation of his philosophy. In the words of Barker, "We have none of Plato's lectures, yet we have none of Aristotle's set writings. We have lost one side of Plato's work, just as we have lost the other side of the work of Aristotle. Our loss is more serious, as the real doctrines of Plato must have been communicated in lectures."

Plato's philosophy is now available to us in his about 3 dozen dialogues which could be preserved and have been passed on to the succeeding generations. It is only through these dialogues and lectures that Plato gave expression to his ideas. These dialogues, to a great extent, also reflect development of his ideas and philosophy. His main works which could be preserved are as under:

**The Apology and The Crito.** These deal with the relation of individual with the state–a problem arising out of the death of Socrates. He was specially interested in the study of this subject because he had been much pained by the death of his teacher.

**Meno and Protagorus.** These deal with political knowledge and instructions in Politis.

**Charmides and Laches.** In these dialogues problems like 'self-control', 'courage', 'virtue' and the relation of the individual with society have been discussed. The definition of these terms was of great significance for him because it was through them alone that a person could be judged.

**The Republic.** It is the masterpiece of Plato. The publication consists of 10 books out of which Books V-VII are very important. Book I deals with 'justice and humanity'. Books II, III and IV have been devoted to 'system of education' and subjects like 'reason', 'spirit' and 'appetite'. Books V,VI and VII are concerned with such subjects as 'ideal state' and the definition of good and bad. In Books VIII and IX Plato reviews the working of the state and the individuals. It is in Book X that Plato deals with the relation of philosophy with art and human soul.

**Gorgias.** It deals with value of knowledge and launches a serious attack on falsehood. It was the method of his study to expose others through their own philosophy. This he had learnt from his teacher, Socrates.

**Philosophy of Republic.** Republic was written by Plato when he was about 40 and as such it is safe to presume that the book represents his mature ideas and ripeness of his philosophical thoughts. Plato wanted to establish here that the state was a magnified individual and that both the individual and the state have identical virtues. According to him, both the individual and the state have common elements like reason, spirit and appetite. It can be termed as 'treatise on ethics'.

Plato's Republic is also considered by some as a 'treatise on justice' and by some others on 'Political Science and Jurisprudence'. It also deals with metaphysical and educational problems. Broadly speaking main problems discussed in Republic are:—

1. As to which is 'right' and 'wrong'?
2. What is the best educational system?
3. What are the qualities of an ideal citizen?
4. What are the qualities of a good government?

**The Statesman.** It was written in 360 B.C. when he was about 67 years. It deals with politics. Here plato has come one as a practical idealist while dealing with the subjects like the role of individual in politics and Political Science. He has also tried to discuss as to how the people should be governed. According to him, a true politician should try to educate the citizens and aim at promoting virtue and justice. He strongly felt that it was in the fullest development of these faculties alone that the state could best promote their interests and also achieve collective welfare of the citizens in a state. The treatise also depicts a remarkable departure from 'Republic' in the sense that here the author has lost much of his idealism and has also become considerably practical.

**The Laws (346 B.C.).** The book came out at the mature age of 80. He has tried to be more practical in this book. Now he had begun to realise that the laws are necessary even for the guidance of the kings. Here he has confessed that since it is difficult to find out a philosopher king it is essential that the ruler should not be kept above laws. He too has correctly assessed human nature and even given up the idea of communism of wives and property. On the contrary he has felt that human nature requires institutions like private property and family without which he even might not have perfect life. He has also now not favoured perfect state control system of education. He, however, still favours a sort of state control, and censorship over marriages. He pleads that the marriages should be of such a type that only good children were produced. The women should perform certain domestic duties because it was in proper performance of these duties alone that the family could lead a happy life. He however, did not favour the idea of giving a different type of education for men and women. According to him both should be imparted in equal manner.

It shall thus be seen that Plato started as an idealist and as he gained more and more experience he became practical in his thoughts. His Republic depicts him as 'Ideal' and his Statesman' and 'Laws' as practical idealist. His writings have left a lasting influence on the posterity and provide a guideline for political thinkers who have followed him. In the words of Maxey, "The writings of Plato touch every phase of the thought of his time, and constitute an imposing compendium of Greek learning and culture."

## PLATO'S IDEAL STATE

The father of the Idealist School as he is, Plato portrays an Ideal State in his Republic. His Ideal State is a utopia whose pattern was laid perhaps in heavens. What he depicts is the "model" of the best state— "the state as a type". He wanted to realise the idea of the Good in his Ideal State. He wanted to set a pattern as to what a State "should" be Plato's Ideal State was meant to be the state as such, a type or model for all places and all times. Sabine rightly points out "The general nature of the State as a kind or type is the subject of the book, and it is a secondary question whether actual states live up to the model or not." He was trying to show what in principle a state must be, if the facts are not like the principle, so much the worse for the facts. That is why Plato did not worry about the practicability of the institutions he proposed for his Ideal State. He was trying to show what in principle and in theory the state ought to be. He admits many times that is Ideal State, based on communism and Rule of Philosophy, is difficult to realise, Plato followed logic wherever it lead him.

Plato is a perfect artist in the depiction of his Ideal State. Just as an artist, bent upon sketching an ideal picture, would not bother whether or not the characteristic features of his picture are to be found anywhere in Nature, similarly Plato did not rack his brains to make his institutions possible of realisation. But we must not conclude that Plato made a complete break-away from the existing Greek institution. Plato's Ideal State is also pragmatic in the sense that it is also an improvement upon the then Greek City States. But it must be admitted that Plato did not bother much about the practicability of his institutions. Hence, Plato was as much a political realist as a political idealist.

Plato's Ideal State is the literary manifestation of the Socratic doctrine that reality inheres in the idea of a thing, According to Socrates, Beauty could exist without a beautiful thing. An ideal can exist without an outward concrete manifestation. What is more important is the Idea of the "Table", not the table itself. Plato's Ideal State is an Idea which according to Plato can exist without being realised in the concrete actual states.

## SALIENT FEATURES OF PLATO'S IDEAL STATE

Plato's ideal state has following salient features:

**1. Rule of Philosopher Kings.** According to Plato an ideal state must be governed by a philosopher king who should be a passionless person and seeker of truth and wisdom. He was above all types of prejudices and symbol of human wisdom. By his actions he commanded respect from all. He possessed high qualities of head and heart and could not be corrupted by concentration of Power in his hands. He combined in himself virtue and knowledge. He was bound by no laws. Such a king alone was in a position to look after the welfare of all.

**2. Equal Treatment of Men and Women.** According to Plato's ideal state, the philosopher king should make all efforts for building character of both men and women. Both should be brought up as useful citizens, as both were an integral part of the state and as such there should be no distinction between the two.

**3. Restriction of Art and Literature.** According to Plato in the ideal state there should be restrictions on the production of art and literature. According to him no cheap, unpopular or immoral literature should come before the people. The people should have only literature of a type which promoted high moral character.

**4. Functional Specialisation.** Plato believed in a system of complete functional specialisation. He did not like that each and every body should go on performing functions of the type which were not suited to his temperament and taste. He was of the firm view that every one should perform functions assigned to him and should not try to go beyond them. Thus, the king should rule and let soldiers fight alone on the battle field. But he wished that everybody should be completely devoted to the task assigned to him and should try to attain perfection in that field.

**5. Proper Administration of Justice.** According to Plato justice was an essential and integral part of a state and it kept various organs and individuals in close harmony with each other. Therefore, he pleaded that justice should be properly administered. His conception of justice was something different from that of modern one. It was not something to be measured in terms of courts of law. It was not a legal conception but something quite different from it. It was something in which there was functional specialisation and everybody was required to remain within his limits. Under it there was perfect hermony among various sections of society and none was to encroach upon the rights of others.

**6. Division of Classes.** Plato's ideal state has three classes, rulers at the head to govern the state, soldiers to defend, and peasants and artisans to fight for the betterment of the economic conditions of the people living in it. Each section of the society was required to attain perfection in the particular job attached to it. According to him, it was only in class division that each class could give security, prosperity and proper administration to the people.

**7. Specialised Soldiers.** Plato fully well realised that defence of the state was most essential for all the states. He therefore, gave this responsibility to the soldiers. He believed that these people should not be ordinary soldiers but persons specially trained for the purpose. Maxey says that Plato believed that these soldiers should be "specially trained for their task and of the very highest physical and mental fitness."

**8. State Controlled Education.** According to Plato state should have full and final control over education. According to him it was the only agency which could produce philosopher kings and train the minds and thoughts of the people in right and proper direction. Education had both social and individual aspects in his philosophy. In society, education should promote social welfare while individually it should bring soul closer to reality.

**9. Qualified Absolutism.** Ordinarily Plato did not wish to impose any limitations on the authority of the philosopher king. According to him it was virtue in action and could not be corrupted. In fact, a close study of the power and position of his philosopher king would reveal that he was hobbesian Leviathan. But still he put certain checks on his authority. According to him philosopher king should see that the fundamentals of the constitution were not violated and were always kept intact. It was required of him to preserve social order and honour natural laws to the extent possible.

**10. Bringing Up of Children.** According to Plato children were national possession and as such it was obligatory on the part of the state to bring them up according to their aptitude. He also believed that ultimately the children should be under state control and the state should not only provide them proper education, nourishment and development but proper work as well.

**11. Communism of Wives and Property.** He believed that if the ruling class was to progress and master it was essential that there should be communism of wives and property. As long as rulers were not free from the bondage of family life and rose above narrow interests of possessing maximum of private property they shall never be in a position to solely devote themselves to the state. Without such a communism there was every possibility of their becoming corrupt and selfish.

**12. Totalitarian Outlook.** Plato's ideal state has totalitarian outlook. According to him the people can only develop in the state and that was the only agency through which his personality could find fullest expression. The people should think in terms other than merging themselves in the state. The people can neither be above nor aside the state but an integral part of the state. Since the philosopher ruled the state and he was above individual or party considerations, there was no need to fear or think in terms of protecting one's interests. It should be left entirely to the state to look after the welfare of the individual.

**Criticism of Ideal State.** Platonic conception of an ideal state is to a great extent unconvincing. Some of the arguments advanced against this concept are:

1. ***Non-development of Human Personality.*** If, at all Platonic ideal state materialises, it is very much doubtful whether proper development of human personality shall be possible in such a state. Plato has preached functional specialisation which implies devotion to one's duty and perfection in a particular direction. Such perfection can only be achieved when other aspects are either absolutely ignored or are not properly developed. In other words, one aspect of life finds development at the cost of other. Then, another cause for this non-development can be traced in the ideas of Plato that state is ultimately responsible for human development. State is the custodian of development of personality of the people living in it. But who can deny that an individual can better look after his own interests than the state, no matter if state was governed by the philosopher king or not. Individual was always the best judge of his personal interests. It is feared that under Platonic arrangements individual could develop only 1/3 of his personality leaving the rest to chance or fate.
2. ***It is Totalitarian.*** The ideal state created by Plato is totalitarian in the sense that it completely merges the individual in the state and thus, pays no regards to the individual. It is also totalitarian in another way namely it

has very strongly tried to maintain privileged classes and has given not only due but also greatest regard to them.

3. ***Ignoring of Producing Classes.*** Like a true aristocrat Plato has ignored the role of working and producing classes. Not only this, that these producing classes form a bulk of population but also that they form the backbone of every state. The very idea of ignoring a particular class is undesirable and unwanted and does not fall in line with the philosophy of perfect or an ideal state. In fact in modern set-up no advanced state can afford to ignore the welfare of a particular class at the cost of other classes. Under his arrangements working classes are ignored so that they should provide leisure for other classes.

4. ***Wrong Analogy between Individual and State.*** Plato has drawn far-fetched analogies between the individual and the state. His analogy between three organs of state, namely Appetite, Reason and Spirit with those of individual, namely, Rulers, Soldiers and Producers is rather too much far-fetched and is likely to lead to confusion. In many cases, even otherwise, his analogies are confusing.

5. ***Anti-human State.*** Plato has tried to portray a state which is against human nature. Though it may be true in theory only to discuss the advantages of communism of wives and property yet in actual practice who can deny that communism of wives and property is against human sentiments and feelings. It is something which is rather anti-human and cannot appeal to normal human beings. Any attempt at the introduction of this communism is bound to lead to revolution and is most likely not to suit human thinking. 'But if communism of wives and property is eliminated the whole edifice of his ideal state is bound to collapse. Thus, in other words his whole state is anti-human, anti-sentimental and thus, unwanted.

6. ***Utopian State.*** An ideal state portrayed by him is more or less utopian. In accordance with his arrangements it is neither possible nor practicable to have 'philosopher king'

or state controlled system of education. Such institutions as the 'communism of wives and property' are anti-human and thus, cannot be put into actual practice. The whole arrangement is more or less ideal rather than real.

7. ***It can Result in Anarchy.*** Another criticism advanced against Plato's concept of ideal state is that it can degenerate into bureaucracy of the worst order. There is every danger that this class might try to identify its interests with the masses and thus, ultimately create confusion and disorder.
8. ***No Recognition to Law.*** It is strange that in the ideal state Plato has given no recognition to laws. He has tried to create a state in which rulers were above laws and usually the laws had less importance than what these should have in a well developed and civilised state.
9. ***Denial of Education to Lower Classes.*** Plato has practically denied the right of higher education to lower classes and has thus, tried to create class distinction. In his philosophy he has maintained a clear distinction between ruling and working class. Such a distinction is vitally injurious to the health of state and can result in the division of society into hostile camps.
10. ***Perpetuating Slavery.*** Plato has not only failed to condemn the institution of slavery but on the other hand in the framework of his ideal state he has tried to perpetuate it. He has done his utmost to justify the existence of this institution. Whatever might be the merits of this institution in his own philosophy it cannot be denied that it is a condemned institution. It sysmbolises the tyranny of man against man. It is an institution which creates a class of persons who learn to live at the cost of others. Under this system many toil and few enjoy. As a realist and far-sighted thinker he should have condemned the institution in very strong words but he acted just contrary to that.
11. ***The Rule of Philosopher King.*** His ideal state is to be ruled by a philosopher king. But philosopher king of Plato has his own problems. He is the person who is not trained in the art of governing the people. He is not the best diplomat and

little training is given to him about maintaining contacts with the people. He has no knowledge about finance and military tactics. To have such a ruler as the head of an ideal state is bound to have its own problems.

12. ***Fullest State Development not Possible.*** For the fullest development of state it is most essential that all should contribute whole-heartedly. But under Plato's arrangement bulk of the society is eliminated and disheartened in contributing to national development and growth. This is rather a serious problem.

We might thus, conclude that there is sufficient weight in the criticism advanced against his theory; but at the same time the most valuable contribution of his theory is that he set forth certain targets for the succeeding generations to strive for and to achieve those targets. The core of his philosophy still remains unchallenged. State controlled system of education is even today being introduced in many states. No civilised state can disown its responsibility of imparting education to its citizens. We also try to find the best disciplined mind and brain to head our state which is comparable to the idea of philosopher king and in one form or the other the state is assuming more and more responsibilities. A modern state is more a welfare than a police state. His stress on virtuous people is even today appreciated. He rather very correctly said and that is true as well even today that, "The states do not come out of an oak or a rock but from the characters of men that dwell therein and this being so he who wishes to study the characters of men will do well to study their states." It is not the number of people who live in the state which matters, but number of virtuous people count. If there are still certain defects in basic theory, due consideration must be given to the times in which he was working. His theory, in his own times and circumstances, was well suited and practicable as well as attainable.

## PLATO'S VIEWS ON JUSTICE

Plato's political writings were the outcome of his dissatisfaction with the prevailing degenerate conditions in Athens, his native city state. The Athenian democracy was on the verge of ruin. It was only a democracy in name. Actually there was the tyranny of, "The

Thirty." Plato found in the contemporary politics, two great and serious flaws which were, according to him, the cause of this ruin. One was the ubiquity of ignorance masquerading in the guise of knowledge. The other was the political selfishness of the rulers and the ruled (Barker). The first defect was manifested by the fact that the amateurs instead of the professionals were predominant in Athens. The Athenian democracy seemed only to mean the right divine of the ignorant to govern wrong. The system of lottery for appointment to public offices was mainly responsible for this. Any man, whatever his capacity might be appointed to the executive office only by the sheer chance of lot. The second defect which was even more formidable was the result of the Sophists's, teachings of the ethics of self-satisfaction. The Sophist taught that the individual was everything and that the state was a mere means for the fulfilment of his desires. The violent, excessive and gross spirit of individualism induced the citizens to capture the offices of the state or the better fulfilment of their own selfish purposes, and divided "Athens into two hostile camps of the rich and the poor, the oppressors and the oppressed." (Plato).

Evidently, these two factors—amateur meddlesomeness and excessive individualism became Plato's main targets of attack in the Republic. The attack came in the form of the construction of an ideal state in which "Justice" reigned supreme. The second title of the Republic *i.e.* "Concerning Justice" shows the important place which Plato gave to it. Actually the fundamental issue of the Republic is the discovery of the nature and habitation of Justice.

Before we proceed along with Plato in the search of Justice we must note the following five points:

1. That Plato is a deductive thinker who deduces all his political philosophy from certain fundamental assumptions. Incidently the most consistent thinker as he is always true to his plan, one cannot accept his premises and reject his conclusions.
2. One of his fundamental assumptions is the tripartite devision of man's mind into Reason, Spirit and Appetite—and the corresponding division of society into three classes *i.e.* the

Rulers, the Soldiers and the Farmers. We know that in this respect he is indebted to Pythagoras.

3. The father of the Idealist School in Politics and Philosophy as he is, he could conceive of "beauty" without there being a "beautiful thing". "Universal" carried a greater meaning for him than the "Particular". His indebtedness to Socrates, is evident in this respect.

4. In another aspect in which Plato was indebted to Socrates was his master's master-idea, that "Virtue is Knowledge". The latter epigram simply meant that there could be no virtue without knowledge.

5. In his attempt to discover justice, Plato adopts the negative approach. That is, he tells us what justice is not. It is only after exhausting this approach that he gives us his own theory of Justice.

Though it is very difficult to resist the temptation of following Plato's dialectical logic with which he refutes the "Prima Facie" theories of Justice, yet we shall console ourselves by giving very briefly the essence of his arguments against these theories.

The first theory is that of Traditional morality which considers Justice to be "giving to ever man his due." The latter phrase results in the view that it consists in "doing good to one's friends and evil to enemies". Plato refutes this on three grounds that :

1. One's supposed friends may be friends only in appearance.
2. To do evil to any body, including our enemies is in consistent with the most elementary conception of morality.
3. This view takes into consideration only the relations between two individuals on the individualistic grounds and ignores the social whole which is the raison d'etre of any theory of Justice.

The second theory is that of Radical morality held by the Sophists. The latter held two propositions:

1. That Justice is the interest of the stronger. That is, it identifies justice with potentia. The strongest and surest is

to get what he wants. And as a state the government is the strongest, it will get what it wants. Because if Justice is the interest of the stronger, the justice for the people will be "to seek the interest of the ruler." It will be unjust on the part of the subjects to pursue their own interests.

2. The second proposition of the Sophists is that injustice is better than justice. Thus, Justice consists in obeying authority where one must, and following one's own interests where one can. Injustice is following one's own interests and Justice conformity to the rulers interests. The Sophists, individualists as they were, went to the extreme of gross individualism.

It is this gross individualism that Plato wants the Republic to refute. He wants to show that the self is no isolated unit but part of an order with a station in that order.

But here Plato is satisfied with logically refuting the two propositions of the Sophists. To the first he opposes the Socratic conception of government as an art. All art is for the sake of the material it touches and handles and not for the sake of artist. The ruler practises the art of government not in his own interest but to bring about an improvement in the governed.

To the second proposition Plato replies that justice is always better than injustice and that a just man is wiser, stronger and happier than an unjust man for he knows his limitations too.

Third theory is that of Pragmatism which tells in part that Justice is an artificial thing, the product of social convention. Thus, theory is the precursor of the Social Contract Theory. In the state of nature there was no justice, or state. Many weaklings combined together and created the state. Thus, Justice is the child of fear and is based on the necessity of the weaker and not the interest of the stronger.

The common line of error in all the three Prima Facie theories of Justice, as it seems to Plato, is that they have all treated Justice as if it were something external, an importation, a convention. Justice, on the other hand, according to Plato is rooted in the human mind. It is intrinsically, a virtue. It is something internal. Justice does not depend for its origin upon a chance-convention.

Now a perfect artist as Plato is, he does not out-right give his theory of Justice. Instead of attempting at once an analysis of the human mind. Plato adopts the method of Large Letters *i.e.* the method of solving deeper mysteries with the help of more easily understandable mysteries of similar kind and thus, discovers and defines Justice with the help of his Ideal State. Justice exists both in the state and individual. But in the state it is a bigger and easily visible form. Accordingly, Plato proposes to consider Justice first as it exists in the state in its broadest form.

In this construction Plato proceeds by a psychological method in the Republic. He takes up each of the three elements of the human mind beginning with the lowest *i.e.* Appetite and proceeding to the highest that is Reason and shows how each of these in its turn contributes its quota towards the creation of the state.

The origin of the state, according to Plato, is to be found in the needs of man which can be satisfied only if they supplement each other. Men have many wants and no man is self-sufficient. Accordingly they take helpers and exchange with one another. Wherever there is society there is some sort of satisfaction of needs and some exchange of services for this purpose.

Sabine says, “This analysis introduced as simply by Plato into his construction of the ideal state was one of the profoundest discoveries which his social philosophy contains. Briefly stated this amounts to this : “Society is to be concerned as a system of services in which every member both gives and receives.”

But exchange of services implies another principle of almost equal importance, the Division of Labour and the specialising of tasks. For if needs are satisfied by exchange, each must have more than he needs of the commodity which he offers, just as he must have less than he needs of that which he receives. The farmer produces more food than he needs while the shoemaker produces more shoes than he can wear. Hence, it is advantageous to both that each should produce for the other, since both will be better fed and better clothed by working together than by each dividing his work to make all the various things he needs. This rests, acording to Plato, upon two fundamental facts of human psychology, first different men have different aptitudes and so do some kinds of work better than others and second, that skill is gained only where men apply themselves steadily to the work for which they are naturally fitted.

Upon this brief but exceedingly penetrating analysis of society and of Human Psychology, Plato's further construction of the state depends.

There can be no better description of Plato's justice than what is given by Sabine :—

"The analysis of the state shows that there are three necessary functions to be performed. The underlying physical needs must be supplied and the state must be protected and governed. The principle of specialization demands that essential services should be distinguished and it follows that there are three classes : the workers who produce and the guardians who in turn are divided, though not so sharply into the soldiers and the rulers, or the Philosopher-King if he be a single ruler. But since division of functions rests on difference of aptitude, the three classes depend upon the fact that there are three kinds of men, those who are fitted by nature to work but not to rule, but only under the control and direction of others, and finally those who are fit for the highest duties of statesmanship such as the final choice of means and ends. These three aptitudes imply on the psychological state three vital powers of soul—that which includes the appetitive or nutritive faculties, that which is executive or spirited and that which knows or thinks—the rational soul. It would seem natural that each should have its own special excellence or virtue. Wisdom is the excellence of the Rational Soul and courage of the active, but he hesitates to say that temperance can be confined to the nutritive soul. Justice is the proper inter-relation of the three functions, whether of the classes in the state or of the faculties in an individual.

"Thus, the construction of the ideal state culminates as it was planned, in the conception of Justice. "Justice is the bond which holds a society together, a harmonious union of individuals, each of whom has found his life-work in accordance with his natural fitness and his training."

In the words of Prof. Barker : "Social Justice may be defined as the principle of a society, consisting of different types of men—who have combined under the impulse of their needs for one another, and by their combination in one society, and their concentration of their separate functions, have made a whole which is perfect because it is the product and the image of the whole of the human mind."

This is Plato's elaboration of the Prima Facie definition of justice given by Cephalus *i.e.* "giving to every man his due." But Plato's interpretation is diametrically opposed to that of Cephalus because the latter was talking in terms of rights while the former in terms of duties. For what is due to him is that he should be treated as what he is, in the light of his capacity and his training, while what is due from him is the honest performance of those task which the place accorded him requires.

Plato's Justice is based on three principles of society:

1. The first is the principles of non-interference. No class should interfere with the task of other classes."It shall concentrate on its own sphere of duty and shall not meddle with the sphere of others." Only then and then only there can be unity in the state and the society as a whole can benefit by the work of the individuals.
2. The second is the principle of functional specialisation. Quite a detailed reference has been made to this principle earlier. A repetition is not called for.
3. The third is the principle of harmony. Human virtue according to Plato is divided into wisdom, courage, temperance and Justice. The first three he asigns one to each class. There remains Justice. The task of Justice is to harmonise the three virtues. The nature of Justice is "architectonic" in relation to other excellences, *i.e.* is related to them as the work of the architect or a master-builder in the construction of a house, is related to that of masons, joiners, wood carvers, and sculptors who work under his direction.

The conception of Social Justice (or righteousness) as the fitting by each man of his appointed sphere is the cardinal conception of the Republic (Barker). The conclusion of the whole matter would seem then to be this that each person should do his own appointed work in contentment. This in Plato's eyes is Justice, or in other words the true principle of social life. The Justice of the state is the citizen's sense of duty of his station issuing before the world in public action.

Such a conception of justice is the final and ultimate answer to the individualism in life and in theory which Plato combated. The conception postulates a view of the individual as not an isolated self but part of an order, intended not to pursue the pleasures of isolated self but to fill an appointed place in that order. The individual is not a whole but the state is a whole. The individual is a factor or fraction of it.

Before we attempt any criticism of Plato's conception of Social Justice, we have still to consider his defintion of Justice, in the individual. If the Justice of the state is the due performance of the function by each class, he argues, then "the justice of the individual (the discovery of which was the purpose of the whole argument, and the reason for the construction of and consideration of the state), will be equally the due performance of function of each part of the individual mind. The parts of the individual mind represent the same principles as the class of the state. So the justice of the individual means that Reason. Spirit and Appetite should keep within their proper bounds. To Plato justice of the individual is identifiable with virtue of excellence.

Thus, Justice is for Plato, at once a part of human virtue and the bond which joins men together in states. It is identical quality which makes man good and which makes him social. This identification is the first and fundamental principle of Plato's political philosophy. The Platonic conception of Justice as applied to the state may be subjected to the following criticism:

1. To a modern reader Plato's conception of Justice, sounds novel and striking for what it omits and for what it

includes. It is in no sense a juristic definition of Justice. It is not enforceable. Self-control and devotional self-abnegation in the interests of society lie at the base of Plato's Justice. These are moral principles having no legal sanctions behind them. Plato's Justice does not visualise and provide for clash of individual wills and conflicts between one interest and another.

2. It is not applicable in a modern nation-state whose population runs into crores. It is not physically possible to divide such a large population in three stereo-typed classes and to assign to them fixed functions.
3. It tries to leave 2/3 of the personality of the individual undeveloped. When the individual possesses all the three elements—Reason, Spirit and Appetite, he should develop all these faculties. But Plato would confine one class of individuals to the development of one faculty only. If he belongs to rulers' class he will develop reason only. Similarly if he belongs to the soldiers' class, he will develop spirit or courage alone. And again, if he belongs to the peasant class, he will develop the instinct of appetite. This attitude amounts to reducing the individual to 1/3 of his personality.
4. Plato's justice assigns asloute ruling power to one class *i.e.* philosophers only. Such a monopoly of political power in the hands of one class, however, well-trained morally and spiritually is bound to demoralise that class sooner or later and thus, corrupt the state. Lord Acton's statement that Absolute power corrupts absolutely is a truism which cannot be denied.
5. It might be said that Plato's justice with the Communism of Property and Wives (which is its logical and essential corollary) ignores the essentials of human psychology and denies satisfaction to the fundamental craving of the human soul. As such it makes too much of demand on the devotion of the individual towards his state and is therefore unrealisable.

6. Such a concept of Justice leads to totalitarianism pure and simple. Prof. Popper in his famous book, "The Open Society and Its Enemies" has criticised Plato's concept of Justice most vehemently on the ground that it leads to totalitarianism in contrast to humanitarianism. The humanitarian theory of Justice, according to him, makes three main demands or proposals namely:

   (a) The equalitarian principle proper, that is, the proposal to eliminate "natural" privileges.

   (b) The general principle of individualism.

   (c) The principle that it should be the task and the purpose of the state to protect the freedom of its citizens. To each of these political demands or proposals there corresponds a directly opposite principle of Platonism namely:

   (i) Principle of natural privileges.

   (ii) The general principle of collectivism; and

   (iii) The principle that it should be the task and the purpose of individuals to maintain and to strengthen the stability of the state.

   Similarly Crossman has very correctly criticised Plato in this way, "Plato's philosophy is the most savage and most profound attack upon liberal ideas which history can show."

7. As Prof. Popper again points out that Plato's Justice leads to a class-state in which ruling becomes the previlege of a particular class. Similarly carrying arms and fighting becomes the prerogative of a particular class. Naturally the same principle applies to the peasants class which has the monopoly of the production of articles of consumption. In Popper's words "Plato calls class-privilege just while we usually mean by Justice rather the absence of such privilege."

   We mean by Justice, "some kind of equality in the treatment of individuals."

8. The individual is reduced to means, the state becomes an end in itself. The individual, according to Plato exists for the state not *vice versa*.

Some of the criticism againt Plato's Justice can be ruled out if we know actually what the Greeks meant by Justice. Plato used the Greek world "dikaisune" for Justice which comes very near to the world "morality" or "righteousness."

The following are the elements of truth in Plato's Justice:

1. It is a true principle of social life.
2. It is an ultimate answer to an extreme individualism.
3. The proper working of three elements–reason, spirit and appetite–in the individual's mind is the sign of a sound and sane mind.

## THEORY OF COMMUNISM

Plato believed that in order to achieve an ideal state it was essential that the kings should be philosophers. A philosopher king could deliver goods to the society. The society would be healthy if philosopher king ruled the nation. His ideal philosopher king could be possible by getting proper training through an elaborate system of education. It was a positive method. Alternately he suggested communism of wives and property which was a negative method of his philosophy. The idea of communism of property was neither new nor unknown to the Greeks. In fact it had already been put into actual practice and the Greeks had known the systems of tilling the land on community basis. Similarly in the past in Athens the state controlled private property and in Sparta though the institution of private property existed yet the produce were put to common use by the community for the bulk of the society. We also find that in Crete public lands were tilled by slaves and so on.

**Platonic Conception.** Plato built up his theory of communism of property on political and psychological basis. According to him psychologically it was essential that the guardians, which included the rulers and the warriors should be relieved of the worry of mine and thine. According to his philosophy as long as the warriors and rulers are not relieved from this psychological burden they shall not become ideal kings.

From political and economic points of view Plato believed that it was essential that political and economic powers should be divorced from each other. Since philosopher kings had been vested with extreme political power, it was essential that he should not be vested with very many economic powers. Communism of property would end this concentration of economic power in the hands of a few or in the hands of philosopher king. Combination of economic and political powers might deviate philosopher king from the path of wisdom. He also believed that concentration of such powers might lead to discontentment and revolution. According to Barker, "It is from this practical consideration that Plato starts and in this sense his communism idealistic as it seems, is the most practical feature of his ideal state." He was so much particular about this that as Sabine has put it. "So firmly was Plato convinced of the pernicious effects of wealth upon Government that he saw no way to abolish the evil except by abolishing wealth itself, so far as the soldiers and the rulers are concerned."

**Communism of Property.** Plato was of the firm view that there should be communism of private property in the case of at least two classes, namely philosopher kings and also the soldiers. In the case of former he was of the view that combination of economic and political powers would lead to tyranny. Property might also make them greedy. In the case of soldiers he felt that the private property will deviate their attention from the noble object of defending their motherland from external aggression. The attraction might also make them weak both morally and culturally. He therefore stressed the necessity of communism of property in the case of at least these two classes. He himself says that the institution of private property is bound to mislead these two classes and they should be banished from that. "To cure the greed of rulers there is no way short of denying them the right to call anything their own." (Sabine)

He also did not favour the idea of retention of private property by those two classes, collectively called guardians because he felt that private property will underestimate the value of virtue. The criteria for selection for guardianship was virtue and if the guardians amass wealth then the people will most naturally be influenced by it. He thus, felt that ideal state with a philosopher king will never be achieved if guardians were allowed to retain private property. Abolition of private property will promote virtue and fair means for selection of candidates for ruling and defending the nation.

Plato also feels that the retention of private property might generate an idea in the minds of subjects that their rulers and defenders were also a party in the race of amassing wealth and thus, lose faith in them. Their activities might be seen with suspicion and thus, ultimately masses might revolt.

**Plato's Communism and Modern Communism.** Platonic communism is something different from modern communism as expounded by Karl Marx. *e.g.*, we find that basis of Platonic communism are evils of love for private property and thus, making an attempt at complete functional specialisation and devotion to duty. On the other hand Marxian communism stands for ending exploitation and relieving millions from untold miseries which the poor are undergoing. Then another difference is that Marxian communism believes that with the advancement of communism the state will gradually wither away, whereas according to Plato, if communism was practised the state would become ideal and get more and more powers. Yet another difference between the two is that Platonic communism does not touch the masses but only the classes. The masses which constitute majority of population and work on land are left untouched. In other words under his arrangements whole social set-up for practical purposes remains unchanged. On the other hand in Marxian communism whole social set-up is changed. The masses are touched and he vigorously preaches that change be brought both by evolutionary as well as revolutionary means.

It has also been pointed out that Platonic communism is national in character whereas modern communism is international in nature. Plato never wanted that his communism should be spread by evolutionary as well as revolutionary means, whereas Marx made his communism as science and said 'Workers of World Unite'. Proceeding further it can also be pointed out that Plato's communism was of a political character and aimed primarily at the unity of the state whereas modern communism is economic in nature. It intends to bring about economic prosperity. In addition to this, modern communism believes that religion is opium for mankind but in Platonic communism no attempt has been made to separate religion from politics. On the other hand attemt has been made to combine both.

**A Critical Estimate.** Plato's conception of the communism of property has been put under severe criticism. In spite of all what may be said against his theory it cannot be denied that his basic idea in advancing his theory was to promote national unity and to end diversity which was the main problem of his age. It has been said that Plato was not so much concerned with the abolition of private property as with the basic idea of the unity of the state. He firmly believed that property created disunity and he wanted to end that. It has been said about him by Sabine that, "He was not in the least concerned to do away with inequalities of wealth because they are unjust to individual concerned. His purpose was to produce the greatest degree of unity in the state, and private property is compatible with this."

**Aristotle's Criticism.** Though his theory has been criticised by others as well yet one of his staunchest critics was his own most sincere follower, Aristotle. He has criticised him on the following grounds:

1. Owning private property is human nature and to deprive him of it is anti to traditional human psychology. This instinct has developed since times immemorial. To make an effort to kill or suppress this instinct is something unnatural, uncommon and unpracticable. It is just fighting with a well established human psychology which in the long run may prove destructive.
2. All healthy social struggle is going on in each society only to acquire more and more private property. It is because of this zest for property that the people to compete with others and express what is best in them. They take initiative in the hope that each initiative will help them in acquiring

more private property. If the very institution of private property is abolished, then all this initiative and healthy social struggle will come to an end.

3. Plato's scheme is only for the rich and the kings as well as soldiers but he has failed to bring into his fold the workers, peasants or those who form a majority in the society. A scheme which excludes majority is bound to fail.
4. It is only through private property that such healthy social instincts as 'charity' or 'benevolence' develop which ultimately help in the formation of healthy society. If there is no private property such healthy instincts will not develop and the nation might be the loser in the long run.
5. If Plato's theory is put into actual practice it is bound to result in under production and over losses because there will be none to look after common and joint property. There will be no personal interest but impersonal compulsion which will definitely be unhealthy and not in the national interest.
6. And lastly Aristotle is of the view that communism of property whensoever adopted has not delivered social goods. It has neither worked satisfactorily anywhere nor are there very many chances of its working properly if and when put into practice.
7. Though Plato has tried to retain the institution of slavery on the plea that it will help in the development of philosopher king, yet it has not covered this class in his present arrangements.
8. Beyond all doubts growth of institution of private property is symbol of growth of our civilisation. If this institution is dispensed with then practically we shall be playing with our own civilisation and putting it in the reverse gears. It is feared that the march of civilisation will come to a standstill if private property is abolished.
9. If Platonic concept of private property is adhered to, that is bound to create groupism. In the name of equality it will

crush human freedom. It will result in over centralisation and excessive state control over citizens which can never help the development of state.

10. Plato's concept of communism of private property is a method for curing spiritual diseases. It is rather difficult to understand that material remedies will cure spiritual diseases. Accordingly it is difficult to understand the logic of his philosophy.

We may sum-up the criticism of communism of private property with Barker, when he says that, "Platonic socialism, it is obvious, is a way of asceticism."

There is no doubt that some of the points of criticism advanced by Aristotle against him are just and reasonable but to think that Plato's idea of communism of property is absolutely futile, unsound and impracticable is undesirable and it will be just under-estimating the value and importance of theory. It is practicable in the sense that as a shrewd politician he realised all consequences of the combination of economic and political powers. Moreover his conception was a logical conclusion of the theory which he built about justice and the philosopher king. His whole concept of justice and philosopher king would have collapsed in case he would not have advocated the idea of communism of private property.

## RULE OF PHILOSOPHY

Few thinkers have been so logically consistent as Plato. He is one of the greatest system-builders in the history of Political. Though, whose conclusions are the logical deductions from his basic assumptions. It is not possible to accept his premises and to reject his conclusions. As Sabine puts it, "Few books that claim to be treatises on Politics are so closely reasoned or so well co-ordinated as the Republic." Plato's conception of Philosopher-Rulers or Perfect Guardians with their unlimited and unchecked powers of rulership is the direct and logical result of his basic assumptions with which he starts.

Plato starts in his Republic with the following two assumptions:

1. Triplicity of human mind into Reason, Spirit and Appetite and the corresponding division of the state into three

classes—Rulers, Auxliaries and Peasants. The Rulers represent Reason, the Auxiliaries represent Spirit, and Peasants represent Appetite in the state. Just as Reason is the complete master of the human mind, the other two elements being sub-servient to it, naturally the Perfect Guardians who represent Reason are the complete masters in Plato's Ideal State which according to him is, "the embodiment of the human mind".

2. The Socratic dictum which is the second basic assumption of Plato's Republic is that, "Virtue is Knowledge". This preposition as Sabine says, "implies that there is an objective good to be known, and that it can in fact, be known by rational or logical investigation rather than by intention, guess-work or luck'. In other words "Virtue" and "Knowledge" are identical. The latter amounts to an identification of "goodness" and "wisdom". Now Wisdom according to Plato is a quality of greatest importance to the state. The basis of an ideal State according to Plato is scientific Knowledge. Without it the ignorant people would govern and the whole citizen-lot is bound to suffer. Plato during his own time finds ignorance of rulers as the main cause of the turmoil in city-states. Hence, Plato emphasises that the philosophers who know should have the ruling power. Only then there will be peace and happiness in the state. His dictum is, "The wise shall rule and the ignorant shall follow". Hence, of Virtue is Knowledge and the latter must be made the basis of the Ideal State, it naturally follows that the man who possesses Wisdom or who knows--the Philosopher or Scholar of Scientist--ought to have deceive power in government and that it is his knowledge or wisdom which entitles him to such a big role in the state.

Not only that Plato's conception of "Rule of Philosophy" is a logical deduction from his first principle but also induction from the current corruption in the various city-states. Hence, Plato's thinking in this respect is also pragmatic as he tries to remedy the then practices in all city states and particularly in Athens. In Athens Plato found as if "the ignorant had the right-divine to govern wrong." No special qualification was essential in order to become a ruler in Athens. Plato's utterances like this that, "in order to become a carpenter one needs some training but in order to become a ruler, a simple lottery will do", is clearly satirical on Athenian practice. Any fool could become a ruler by the simple chance of lot. This is intolerable for Plato who believed that only competent, wise and efficient people should have the right to govern.

## SALIENT FEATURES OF RULE OF PHILOSOPHY

**1. Seeker of Truth.** A philosopher king is always seeker of truth. He knows everything by virtue of his knowledge. Because of that intellectual brilliance he has better capacity to judge the things than any other ordinary person. He can look after the interests of community better than those who are ignorant.

**2. Outcome of Proper Training.** Rule of philosopher king was a noble idea. By this he meant that only those who had knowledge and proper training should rule and all others should be excluded from this category as they were incompetent to govern.

**3. Identical Interest with the State.** Since philosopher king is a perfect guardian and has rational character, he is selfless. He has no interests apart from the interests of the state. In other words, his interests and the interests of the state are always identical and cannot be separated from each other.

**4. Necessity of Cultivated Mind.** All do not have a cultivated mind to understand and follow the supreme and noble idea that 'virtue is knowledge'. Therefore, those few who have this cultivated mind should only be trained as philosopher kings. In the words of Edward Zellor, "The Platonic State can only be an aristocracy of virtue and intellect exercised by one or few."

**5. Flexibility in Rules.** Rule of philosopher king is better than the 'rule of the law' because the latter is not very much flexible and cannot give the people what is due to them whereas rule of philosopher king is flexible and gives the people their due.

**6. Product of Education.** Plato's philosopher king is product of a regular system of education. This education lasts upto the age of

35. In fact the system is so extensive and exhaustive that it continues for the whole life of the philospher king.

**7. An Absolute Rule.** The rule of philosopher king is absolute. A philosopher king is not responsive to public opinion. He is more or less devoid of customary laws and conventions though it is expected of him that he should honour and respect them.

**8. He has Many Responsibilities.** Philosopher king is supposed to check flow of property and wealth and maintain unity and self-sufficiency of state. He should also ensure that every citizen properly performs duties assigned to him and that they are responsible for maintaining and continuing the system of education.

**Criticism.** Plato's philosophy about philosopher king and role of philosophy has been put to severe criticism. Main points of criticism advanced against his philosophy are as under:

1. ***Failure in Practical Life.*** Plato has created a philosopher king to rule over the subjects, but in actual practice such kings have met with utter failure. In India one finds that Muhammad Tughlaq was a near philosopher king. By his policies and actions he brought untold miseries to his subjects and earned the title of 'wisest fool' of his times. Such could be the fate of any other philosopher king.
2. ***Chances of Democracy.*** By creating the institution of philosopher king as the embodiment of 'knowledge in action' Plato has practically closed all chances of direct and indirect democracies and elections.
3. ***Essential Subjects.*** Plato, in his system of education meant for the philosopher king, has provided for the study of music and astronomy but he does not provide for the study of essential subjects like finance, law, and so on which are of practical use to a ruler than the study of music.
4. ***Despotic Rule.*** Plato's philosopher king is more or less despotic. Despotism was neither welcomed at that age nor is it welcomed even today.
5. ***Ignores Masses.*** Plato feels that only those few who are trained for the specific purpose of ruling should govern. He

thus, ignored bulk of the citizens, their worth and capacity. It is undesirable and unhealthy.

6. ***Educational Facilities to Majority.*** It is deplorable that he proceeds on the assumption that majority of the people are not worth getting the education which a philosopher king can get. He thus, discriminately closes the doors of education on the masses.

7. ***Under-estimation Collective Wisdom.*** In his philosophy Plato has laid maximum stress on the wisdom of single individual namely the philosopher king. He makes us believe that this single individual is the embodiment of all wisdom and knowledge. But in the process he forgets the value of collective wisdom and underestimates that. Who can deny today that collective wisdom is always much superior than individual wisdom.

8. ***Anti-Democratic.*** Today his concept of philosopher king has also been criticised because of its anti-democratic nature. The people are supposed to simply obey the philosopher king and obey his commands. It believes that one single individual is above all others and thus, all are not equal in the state. A vast majority of citizens have been reduced to the status of dumb driven cattle and so on. All combined together make his philosophy anti-democratic.

9. ***Selfishness.*** A philosopher king can at any stage also think of combining his own interests with public interests and thus, might try to have unlimited powers and make the lives of citizens miserable. Power corrupts man and absolute power absolutely and this can be true of philosopher king as well.

10. ***Corruption.*** Kant has criticised the rule of philosopher king when he says, "That the king should become philosopher king is not likely to happen : nor would it be desirable since the possession of power invariably debases the free judgement of Reason."

**Training in India.** As already discussed, Plato has tried to impart a regular system of training through education to his philosopher kings. This education starts with the birth when he is to be separated from the family and left to the entire responsibility of the state and lasts up to the age of 35.

First phase of his education is over when he attains the age of 35 years but in fact education continues throughout his life. He gets education till the age of 60 years.

Such a type of training might have been possible in those days but it is not possible in modern times where theory does not matter but practical experience does count. To think of a man getting education upto the advanced age is not possible. Moreover, even if this education is given it will be worthless because we are living in an age of democracy rather than intellectual aristocracy. The ruler is required to understand the sentiments of the electorates and to act accordingly. In India and for that matter in every democracy a leader may not be a good student of Political Science, but he should essentially be a good politician capable of boldly facing hard realities of life and giving desired lead to his subjects.

## THE REPUBLIC AND THE LAWS

Plato's Republic was written at the age of forty only when he was quite young and full of inspirations. At that age he loved idealism and in many cases was rather devoid of hard realities of life. He then felt that much of what was ideal was practicable as well. This was also supplemented with his hate for Athenian democracy which had put his teacher Socrates to death and about which he had developed the idea that it consisted of people who were not competent to govern.

On the other hand 'Laws' was written at the fag end of his life when he was about 80. During this long intervening period of 40 years he had gained many valuable experience which made him wise. He had realised that all ideal was not always practicable. This work was brought out by his pupil. While giving his ideas Plato had realised by now that it was impossible to get an ideal king of his imagination. He was quite confident that the people were quite prepared to obey an enlightened ruler, provided such a ruler could be found out. Having thus, failed in his attempt Plato has given his second best state in his

'Laws' which Plato felt could be achieved. According to Sabine, "The Laws was definitely a work of his old age and all critics agree in finding in it evidence of declining power though this has very often been exaggerated."

As regards literary value of Laws it is beyond all doubts that Republic is his masterpiece. Its literary value still remains unsurpassed. In the words of Sabine, "In respect to literary quality there is no comparison between the 'Republic' and the "Laws'. This earlier work is conceded to be the greatest masterpiece in the whole range of philosophical writings. The Laws on the other hand, is distinctly hard reading."

## DIFFERENCE BETWEEN 'REPUBLIC' AND 'LAWS'

**1. Place for Law.** In 'Republic', Plato had given no place to laws. It was felt that a philosopher king, by virtue of his vast knowledge, was above laws and rather laws flowed from him. The laws had then no place in his arrangements. But in the 'Laws' he has assigned important place to laws. He now feels that laws must be given their due place in administrative set-up. As a realist he has now realised that unfettered authority could prove dangerous any time. Laws, to him, are now essential for a healthy society. In the words of Sabine, "The fundamental difference between the theory of the Republic and the Laws is that the ideal state of the former is a government by specially chosen and specially trained men, quite untrampled by any general regulation, while the state sketched in the latter is a government in which law is supreme, ruler and subject alike being sub-servient to it."

**2. Sobriety and Maturity.** The main difference between the two treatises is that of sobriety and maturity. 'Republic was written at a young age of 40 whereas 'Laws' was written at the mature age of 70. Thus, whereas the former represents vigour, zeal, energy and idealism, the latter represents his sober, mature and practical character. Both represent two different aspects of his life.

**3. Private Property and Family.** Republic pleaded communism of wives and property, for at least the guardian classes. In 'The Laws' he has however, changed his ideas to a considerable extent.

He now feels that both the private property and family should be retained to a limited extent by the individuals. In other words, he is not as hostile to these institutions as he was in the past. He now feels that both these institutions are essential for the development of the people.

**4. Change in Outlook.** In Republic Plato had attempted to present a poetical outlook. He had tried to make it a poem and piece of literary work. On the other hand, in his 'Laws' he has tried to represent a different outlook. He has now become religious minded and has started giving sermons.

**5. Difference in Scope.** In his Republic Plato has tried to cover a vast field. He has made it a treatise covering social, economic and political life of the city state. On the other hand scope of his 'Laws' is very limited. He has now touched only political life in this treatise and virtually touched no other aspects.

**6. A Touch of Reality.** In his 'Republic', Plato was idealist. He took everything in terms of his idealism *i.e.* as these ought to be and believed that with hard labour everything ideal was possible to be achieved. But in his 'Laws' he has stressed practicability and has sacrificed his idealism. We thus, find that in 'Republic', Plato was ideal whereas in 'Laws' he is realistic.

**7. Ideas about Self-control.** In his 'Republic', Plato had subordinated self-control to justice. Justice was virtue in action. It was real knowledge which could be combined with justice. Self-control had no place before justice, but on the other hand in his 'Laws' Plato has pleaded that justice should be subordinated to self-control. Now he feels that it is the duty of the legislators of the state to see that they inculcate spirit of self-control. He has thus, now subordinated justice to self-control.

**8. Changed System of Education.** In his 'Republic' Plato had pleaded for a state controlled system of education from the very birth. He then believed that education alone promoted knowledge and wisdom. On the other hand in his 'Laws' Plato has pleaded for a system of education where paid teachers were to impart education upto at least elementary and secondary education stage. Thus, in the

'Laws' the theory of complete state controlled system of education has been abandoned.

**9. Changed Views about Communism.** Plato has now altogether changed views about communism. In his Republic he has pleaded for communism of wives and property. He has even pleaded that children should be produced and brought-up under state supervision, care and control. Philosophers and rulers should not at all possess private property and family. Now, however, he has changed his views about communism. He feels that institutions of family and property are essential and must be maintained. Instead of communism he has put only certain restrictions on family life and use of private property. He has tried to regulate them so that their evil effects are reduced to the minimum.

**10. Harmony of Classes.** In his 'Republic' Plato did not discuss about the need and utility of various classes in the state. He felt that all classes should bow before the wishes of the philosopher king. In other words reason was to dominate courage and appetite. It was question of subordination of one class by other classes. In his 'Laws' he has, however, realised that it is not the subordination but only close harmony with each other which will serve the prupose. He has thus, replaced subordination by harmony.

**11. Ideas about Democracy.** In the Republic Plato glorified Spartan philosophy. In other words it meant that the state should get by force what they can. He gave every support to the idea of military actions for realising what state though was legitimate and proper. In his 'Laws' he has however, not glorified and supported this. On the other hand he has preached that states should try to live in peace with others. It is better to realise aims and objects through harmony rather than war.

**12. Place of Individualism.** In his Republic, Plato has tried to establish that there is no anti-thesis between the individual and the state. According he has established that individual cannot go beyond the state. Thus, for him question of individual freedom does not arise. But in his 'Laws' he has realised that there can be chances when interests of the individual might clash with the state. He has thus, pleaded for grant of limited freedom of expression to the individuals.

**13. Mixed Constitution.** In his Republic, Plato had practically assigned no place to constitution but in 'Laws' he has taken a different attitude. He has now begun to realise that main reasons for the fall of Greek city states were the tendency to take their ideals to the extremes. He quoted the example of Athens which had given maximum freedom to her citizens and Sparta which had become highly militarised. He, therefore, come to the conclusion that it was most desirable that there should be a constitution for each state which should rationalise its actions and also save it from becoming extremist. According to him, a constitution which combined monarchy with democracy was the best one. In the words of Barker, "Just as in adopting the rule of the law he already pays homage to the principle of consent in the form of persuasive preambles, so too in adopting the mixed constitution, he accepts that principle has the basis of administration."

## SOCIAL AND POLITICAL PHILOSOPHY IN 'THE LAWS'

The 'Laws' was written at the mature age of eighty and thus, represents Plato's mature ideas and his agelong experience. The greatest significance of his this last treatise lies in the fact that here he has come down from his idealism and become both a realist and practical thinker. His philosophy is now practical and reached near hard realities of life. He has become so practical that practically he has given up the idea of an autocrat, philosopher king ruling uncontrolled and not under the laws of the lands. He now contemplates a state in which there is a combination of elements like the monarch, rich, poor and the masses and in which there is impersonal philosophic code. In addition to this, he has now recognised the need and necessity of fundamental laws which should govern both the ruler and the ruled. He now believed that guardians must be the slaves and servants of rules. By now Plato is satisfied that it is impossible to achieve the ideal state and as such he has tried to depict the second best ideal state in his 'The Laws' in which he has portrayed a different social, economic and political life.

In his 'Laws' Plato has laid great stress on self-control which is the pivot of his discussion here. The need and necessity for self-control has increased because here the legislators have a hand in the election of their ruler. He even subordinates justice to self-control and feels that wisdom can work only where there is self-control. According to him, "No virtue is virtuous unless the complete virtue and self-control is first present, self-control is the prior condition or rather it is the necessary completion, alike of wisdom, courage and of justice." He has now abandoned the scheme of communism of wives and property because when there is self-control these institutions are unwanted.

**Nature of Law in 'The Laws'.** Plato has fully well understood and realised by now that rule of philosopher king may be ideal but is not practicable. He has conceived the notion of the second best state with some place and importance for the laws which both the ruler and the ruled should obey. He has felt the necessity of laws to the extent that a chapter has been devoted in his treatise to the subject. For him this has now become symbol of civilisation. According to him, laws are necessary because all have not sufficient self-control to lead to social life and laws shall pave way for self-control. Laws should control us from our birth to our death. He has also felt the necessity of laws because according to him all citizens do not work with the idea of following what is best in the national interest. On the other hand he has now realised that the individual preferred to follow selfish rather than national interests. Necessity of laws was also felt because it was felt that one should be clear to democrate between the good and the bad. In other words law is to crystalise good and eliminate.

According to him the laws should be the outcome of common customs adopted in a particular territory. The customs are essence of ages and thus, the laws based on these customs will be essence of experience of generations and most acceptable to the masses. The law should have universal application and should also influence all walks of life and death including social, economic and political aspects of our life.

The law must be considered and treated as sovereign. It should be thought that Government is product of law and that law is not a tool in the hands of persons in authority. The laws should however, be enacted in such a fashion that it gives maximum benefit to maximum number of people. It should not benefit either one community or a particular section of society. The law should be rigid and should not require change for quite considerable time. The laws should also regulate our moral life as well.

He, however, does not believe that fear of physical force should be sanctioned behind the laws but that the citizens should be educated in the spirit of laws. It should appeal to mind and conscience and should touch our heads and hearts. Obedience to laws should follow not from without but from within. It is in such circumstances that near perfect citizenship can be achieved and the state can feel proud of its citizens.

**Plato on Crime and Punishment.** Plato has also discussed about crimes and punishment in his laws. According to him it is wrong to believe that crime is an isolated action of the criminal. It is outcome of individual's social environments and frustrations. The state should neither treat the criminal in an isolated manner nor punish him inhumanly. The true state will try to find out real causes of the crime rather than finding out superfluous causes. The laws of the state should aim at reforming the criminal and educating him properly in the spirit of the laws.

His feeling shows that even the criminal does not feel pleasure in receiving punishment because justice is happiness and punishment unhppiness. Justice is spontaneous and punishment a compulsion. Since punishment or crime is unhappiness and compulsion, it is not the outcome of a person's natural instinct but the product of his injured feelings for which society is the main culprit.

Since the individual is not directly responsible for the crimes and is merely a tool in the hands of society, the punishment should only aim at reforming criminals and it should not be harsh or inhuman. According to Barker, "In this sense the state which inflicts punishment is the agent of the criminal who is punished : it does not merely stand for the rights of the injured person or for a violated scheme of order, but also for the better side of the criminal himself." Man's mind is good but only crime is wicked. Society gives birth to all corruptions though many a time due to lack of proper training of mind and thoughts man becomes an instrument for such corruption.

Though he aimed at reformatory punishment, yet he has not ruled out the chances of capital punishment and persecution in cases like religious disbelief or those who practise private religion. According to him honest religious disbelievers should be first put behind the bars and tried to be reformed rather than being out to death all at once. He believed that severe punishment in such cases will promote national unity and harmony.

**Geographical Location of the State.** Plato still believes that geographically the state must be far away from the sea shore. According to him a state near the sea shore was bound to be flooded with traders and moneyed people providing many allurements to the citizens, detracting them from the path of attaining perfection. He also suggested that the state should always be short of timber so that it did not indulge itself in ship-building activities. He was of the view that in the state there should be nothing in abundance because this will lead to trading activities, rivalries and corruption. He therefore, believed that in the state commercial activities should be kept to the lowest and efforts should be made to make the citizens as perfect as possible.

**Education in the Laws.** He had laid great importance on Education which, he felt, was training of a healthy mind. He felt that in the cabinet subject of education should be dealt with only by Prime Minister who will supervise problems dealing with educational administration, including controlling of attendance and also supervisors and inspectors in the schools. He will also be responsible for proper maintenance of school buildings and among other things encourage gymnasia. According to him education always provides proper training of a healthy mind and guides him to receive both pleasure and pain. He also went to the extent of saying that punishment was also an educative system which was necessary for unhealthy mind. According to him education should aim at promoting qualities of an excellent citizenship with the quality to rule and be ruled in the interest of justice and also training young mind for his higher ideals. They should be so trained through proper education that both by habit and as a matter of common instinct, they should obey these laws.

The educational system should be in the hands of only those who were mature and had been chosen from among the guardians.

He has, however, permitted to allow such a person to hold private property and family. Such a person in the governmental set-up was to be accorded highest position and prime place, not being occupied by any other person.

He believed in the system of universal compulsory education on the pattern of single school system. He also pleaded that both sexes should be trained on the same pattern. He did not favour the idea of co-education system after the age of 6 when both the boys and the girls ought to be separated and given training in different institutions.

The education was to be imparted at two stages, *i.e.* primary stage and secondary stage. The former started with the cradle and lasted upto the age of ten. Upto the age of three the babies are to be allowed to jump and play on certain tunes ; between three and six they are to be taken to village temples and play grounds where they are to work under the supervision of official matrons. Actual physical education is to be imparted after the age of six where the boys and girls are to be separated from each other. It is in the latter stage, *i.e.*, at ten that actual education starts. Here the boy is required to start with the study of literature, music, calculation and astronomy in addition to Geometry and Arithmetic. Each subject is to be taught almost for three years and it is supposed that by the age of 16 the pupil will have sufficient knowledge of reading, writing and music. Plato has also provided for military education which he felt was absolutely essential for safeguarding the interests of the state. According to Sabine, "The theory of education in the 'Laws', unlike that of Republic, is theory of system of educational institution." It has also been said that the salient feature of educational system in Law is, that it pleads education for the girls and also an organised system of school education.

**Economic Structure of State in 'The Laws'.** With the maturity of age, Plato has now realised that communism of wives and property is not practicable. Accordingly he has reconciled himself to the idea that these institutions should be retained. His sole idea now is that the state should be a self-contained agricultural community of a moderate size in which there will be no exploitation. The people shall neither exploit each other nor shall do any ignoble deeds. There will be no business based on vulgarity. The currency will have only local circulation and the citizens will not hoard either gold or silver. Lander shall lend money to assist the borrower in coming over his difficulty rather than with the idea of charging interest which was illegal and immoral. Import and export was to be done under very restricted conditions. The institution of slavery was still retained. A slave was paid for tilling the land. Each citizen had fixed piece of land which could be tilled with the aid of the slaves.

He has advocated the system of free marketing and trade. The aliens should devote themselves to trade and industry, the slaves to agriculture and the citizens to politics and development of their mind and personality. The prices of commodities should be fixed by the magistrates who will allow only a nominal profit. There shall be uniform price for a particular commodity in a particular market on a particular day. Retail trade was also permitted. The citizens were obliged to purchase pieces of art from the aliens who in turn were required to purchase foodgrains from the citizens. He discouraged the idea of citizens practising handicrafts or possessing gold or silver. He allowed them possess only few coins. He did not favour the idea of having any Hellenic currency. There should be no lending or borrowing of money on interest. He also argued that no borrower was under any obligation to repay the money once taken on loan. He suggested that by and large the people should be agriculturists.

**Social Structure in 'The Laws'.** Plato still adheres to the idea of city state with a population of 5040, in which each will have his own family and private property. The land shall be owned by each and will neither be sold nor mortgaged. The product shall be used for common good and thus, property will have to some extent public control. The farming will not be common and land will have individual or private character to be used for collective welfare. The right of holding private property is thus, basically recognised though it is suggested that it should be used for social welfare. According to him, it was essential that each family should have a child and those who have none should adopt one.

He still holds the view that in the society the women should take their place along with the men. He also believes in uniform system of education for both the sexes and that the marriage should be controlled in the public interest. The women should also be drawn in the public life and that they should contest elections along with men. He also supports the idea of giving military training to the women so that they also should be ready to fight for national integrity, if need be.

Plato favours monogamy where the pairs will have opportunity of meeting each other at religious assemblies which will be held every month with the idea of promoting friendship. He also pleads that before marriage both the boy and the girl should exchange certificates of health and should see each other stripped. The marriages should not be performed for the sake of individual pleasure but for welfare of the state and thus, should be mixture of opposites. The couples are to remain under family supervision for first ten years of their marriage. It is the duty of each couple to give maximum training to each child according to laws of the land. Each family should live a separate and independent life apart from its own family and thus, the impression of one generation will not be passed on to the other. According to him marriage is physical, moral and religious institution in which women shall have liberal place.

**Religious Structure in 'The Laws'.** It is for the first time that Plato has given any serious thought to religion and has taken some pains in explaining the subject. This might be due to his growing age in which everyone is likely to become religious minded. According to him now, religion and morals must go side by side and hand in hand and thus, cannot be separated from each other. He, however, believes that the religion should be state controlled. He does not favour the idea of individual religious exercises but collective worship in public temples. There should be authorised priests for performing rites and rituals. He forbids atheism and even goes to the extent of providing death penalty for it.

**Structure of Government in 'The Laws'.** In his Laws Plato has also discussed in some detail the Governmental organisation which he proposes to have in his sub-ideal or second best state. He provides for a popular assembly to be held exclusively responsible for conducting the election of deliberative body, known as council. The

Assembly should consist of all citizens but in order to be a voter it was essential that the citizens should have military training and wear arms while coming to Assembly. The citizens were divided into four classes. The Assembly also elected 37 guardians of law and Generals of army. The guardians of law were to be elected in triple ballots. The election of 360 members of Councils was to be held on the basis of classes. The members enjoyed only one-year tenure.

The Assembly was required to conduct election including that of members to the Council, local officers, market officers and generals of the army. It was also held responsible for punishing those who performed anti-social and anti-state activities. It also permitted the stay of the aliens in the state. But above all it gave approval of all laws, whether original or in the amended form. It thus, combined in one both legislative as well as judicial powers. There is however, nothing in 'The Laws' to show that it had any executive powers as well.

**Judicial System in 'The Laws'.** Plato has distinguished between private and public suits. The public suits were to be tried by the Magistrates who were to be elected by the Assembly. As regards private suits these were decided by the voluntary courts which consisted of neighbours or friends. It was supposed that these persons had best information about the dispute. Then there were tribal courts whose judges, were elected by lots. The idea of having these courts was that all should have a share injurisdiction. Then there were courts of selected judges which were elected from among the magistrates for a period of one year. The proceedings of courts and the decisions arrived at were announced in the public.

**System of Local Self-Government in 'The Laws'.** In the rural areas there were 5 inspectors to be elected by their inspecting tribes. These inspectors were elected only for two years and each one was required to choose 12 young persons. They all collectively toured the whole state and finished their job in two years. During their tour, in addition to sanitation and water supply arrangements, they also reported about roadways and defence measures.

In the cities there were 3 city inspectors who were from among the first class citizens. These inspectors were responsible for managing property and looking after city's roadways and waterworks etc. In addition to this, there were 5 market inspectors who were primarily concerned with properly regulating city's marketing system.

**Mixed Constitution in 'The Laws'.** Plato has provided for a mixed constitution in his second best state which, according to him, could be achieved. Such a Constitution was meant to promote harmony among divergent views. It was this principle which could be said as the fore-runner of the theory of separation of Powers as subsequently expounded by Montesque. He has tried to combine wisdom of monarchy with freedom of democracy. In other words, he attempted to save the state from extremes of either democracy or of aristocracy which would have degenerated in due course of time. An ideal state should contain the principles of both democracy and monarchy in one. He traced the fall of Persia and Sparta in nothing else but in their extremes in the Constitutions. Mixed Constitution meant wise government with consent. It was justified because the wise have a right to rule over the fool, strong over the weak and rich over the poor. When, however, he talks of monarchy or democracy, he means that the principles of only these two forms of government should be adopted. Though, he laid the basic principles of Mixed Constitution, these were subsequently developed by Aristotle and others who followed him.

## ARISTOTLE

Aristotle was born in 384 B.C., his birth place was on the Macedonian coast, and thus, he was not Athenian by birth. His father was a physician to the king of Macedon. Stagira, was not considered as true Hellenes because Macedon was governed by a monarch and had no faith in the 'city state' set-up. He had the opportunity of having first-hand information at the royal court, where his father was a physician, about working of state affairs. He also carried in blood, love for biology and thus, had disposition to view things from that view-point.

**Starting of Actual Life.** The family expected that Aristotle will also take to his father's profession and thus, shall become an eminent physician. But soon its conviction became an illusion but it became very clear that he would join Plato's Academy. He selected this place firstly because there was no other place for advanced studies in the whole of Greece and secondly he was much influenced by the writings and thoughts of his teacher. In fact, he proudly said that his teacher was the greatest son of his land. He joined Academy at the early age of 17 where he came in close and direct contact with Plato. He sat under his feet as a serious and earnest student for twenty long years. He left so great an impression of his philosophy that it was abundantly clear that he would head Academy, after the death of Plato. But in 347 B.C., after the death of his teacher, he decided to leave Athens. He remained out of Athens for 13 long years when he visited the courts of Hermeas and Mitylene in Asia Minor. He also availed this period in long travelling and studying different political institutions in different parts of the world. In the court of Hermeas he studied decadent despotism of Persia whereas in Mitylene he studied maritime fauna. It was in 342 B.C. that he was called to Macedonia to become the tutor of young Alexandra where he influenced monarchy and deeply studied this institution. He had however, to leave the place in 322 B.C. after the death of Alexander.

**Establishing a New School.** It was in 335 B.C. that Aristotle decided to set-up a new school to preach his own ideas, thoughts and philosophies. An institution known as 'Lyceum', sprang-up with the patronage and backing of his pupil Alexandra. For 12 years he personally headed this institution and produced many research scholars and pupils who politically carried his image. Since he himself was embodiment of human knowledge in all walks of human life, he made efforts to systematise the whole body of human knowledge. He even stressed on the study of comparatively less known subjects as logic and astronomy.

**Methods of His Writings.** Plato was ideal but his disciple Aristotle was a realist as well as a practical man. This is quite well reflected in his great treatise 'the Politics'. He has tried to portray the concept of an independent state. He has even not tried to make state independent of laws but has also substituted that to the authority of the laws. Such an approach to the problem is absolutely different and as such the methods of study of Plato and Aristotle are different as well. Plato was speculative and did not care much for historical facts as they stood. On the other hand Aristotle had scientific and biological background and thus, he had a systematic approach to the problems before him. As against deductive methods of Plato he followed inductive method for his study. According to Dunnings, "In Ethics and Politics, accordingly, while Plato working deductively from his Philosophical conception of the virtue and the good blended inextricably the two bodies of doctrines. Aristotle, proceeding by extensive observation and minute analysis of objective facts, marked out for each science an independent field." In addition to this, he employed comparative methods in his writings which Plato had considerably ignored. He is thus, analytical and dialectical and not metaphysical. Then, another method, which he employed was that of teleology which made him think that politics and ethics were branches of study of the same science and thus, could not be separated from each other.

Aristotle, both in his ideas and methods of writings, was conservative and had respect for traditions as against Plato who was radical and less traditional. He has further said that "Plato is more impressed by the unity of pervading phenomena ; Aristotle by the diversity. He had respect for accumulated knowledge of the past and was more a reformist rather than an exponent. He was moderate in view and believed in adjustment."

In his writings one finds extreme contentiousness about small points. He suffers from repetitions and at places it is doubted that he had failed to rightly and correctly convey his feelings and ideas. He is not very clear in his writings and it is difficult to even follow him closely. Many a time he is also irrelevant and indulges in unnecessary cross-references.

**Works of Aristotle.** Aristotle has written much. Some of his writings include. 'The Categories' : 'On Interpretation' and The 'Prior Analytics'. Then comes The Topics' which deals with dialectical reasoning; On Sophistical Refutations which deals with fallacious arguments and 'On the Soul' which explains that soul is the formal efficient and final cause of living. His 'History of Animal' deals with the classification of animals, whereas 'On the Part of Animals' deals with biological Sciences. His other works which deal with animals are 'On the Progression of Animals' and "On the Generation of Animals". In his 'Physics' he has dealt with the principle of natural bodies and natural motions. In 'Nicomachean Ethics' he has dealt with a comparatively complicated question as to whether goodness and happiness are identical. His other works include 'On Monarchy', 'Constitutions', On Colonies' and 'On Philosophy'.

But 'Politics' is the only important work available to us which can be associated with the name of Aristotle. Unfortunately this is also incomplete and it is very much doubted whether it was edited by this great philosopher or by his students at his school. According to some thinkers the treatise is the collection of lectures delivered by him at his school, others believe that it is a collection of notes taken by his students, while still others are of the view that it is a compilation of Aristotle's lectures. Some even go to the extent that 'Politics was not at all written by Aristotle but by his successors at his school at Lyceum. But the general view is that the treatise represents the collection of his notes prepared by him for delivering lectures at various places in different years. Thus, it can safely be said that the treatise represents his original views.

**Arrangement of Politics.** The treatise consists of 8 Books which can conveniently be divided into three groups. The first three books from the basis and provide material for superstructure. Books IV, V and VI, which form another part deal with nature of constitutions and their distinctions with each other. Books VII and VIII deal with the constitution of an ideal state most suited to a city state which is Platonic in nature. Thus, briefly speaking each book deals as under:

**Book I.** It was perhaps written last of all. It deals with slavery and introduces the treatise.

**Book II.** It deals with Plato's ideal state.

**Book III.** It deals with citizenship, normal and perverted forms of constitution and also with monarchy.

**Book IV.** It deals with various forms of Government.

**Book V and VI.** These deal with oligarchy and democracy.

**Book VII.** It discusses the constitution of an ideal state.

**Book VIII.** It develops the point discussed in book VII.

**Jaegar Views.** Professor W. Jaegar is of the opinion that the treatise was written at two different stages--first stage bears an influence of his teacher on him. Here he has discussed about ideal state and tried to condemn various theories prevailing at that time. This is available to us in Books II. III, VI and VII. This stage continued till the death of Plato and Aristotle finally decided to leave Athens. Second stage can be one in which Aristotle himself studied different world constitutions and saw the things as there were. He saw the advantages and disadvantages of oligarchy and democracy. This stage is expressed in other books of the treatise. In other words we can say that during his first stage he was an idealist and at the second stage he was a realist and discussed about the things as these ought to be. According to Sabine, "According to Jaegar's conception, therefore, the Politics was intended to form a treatise on a single science, but was never subjected to the rewriting that would have been necessary to bring the parts, written as they were over a period of perhaps fifteen years, into a well unified form."

**Politics–An Incomplete Work.** Though *Politics* is the only available treatise of Aristotle but unfortunately that too is incomplete. It is observed that it is not an artistically finished work devoted to public welfare but only a heap of arguments collected from here and there either by the author himself or by his successors. Had it been a finished work the posterity would have been much benefited and the world rich by many times.

We may however, conclude the importance of *Politics* in the words of Sabine when he says that, "The new general science of Politics, therefore, was not only empirical and descriptive, but even in some respects independent of any ethical purpose, since a statesman might need to be expert in governing even a bad state. The whole science of Politics, according to the new idea, included the knowledge both of the political good, relative, as well as absolute, and also of political mechanics employed perhaps for an inferior or even a bad end. This enlargement of the difinition of political philosophy is Aristotle's most characteristic conception."

## THEORY OF STATE

The starting point of Aristotle is the same as that of Plato. He, like Plato, begins by attempting to refute the Sophist doctrine that the institutions of Political Society are the product of "convention", not of "nature". This meant that the individual's allegiance to the state was not natural; and was something cramping to the individual's moral development. The best judge of his moral development was the individual himself and he could disobey the laws of the state whenever his Reason told him that obedience was inimical to his moral development. The effect of the Sophist doctrine was to strip the law of the state of all moral authority. In opposition to such a doctrine Aristotle, like Plato seeks to re-establish the moral authority of political laws. He wishes to show that the state is ordained by nature and its authority is moral. The individual without any hope for reward and fear for punishment should obey the state as the latter is natural. Hence the "Politics" opens with a consideration of the origin of the state. He wants to establish the natural character of the state by proving that it originates in the two natural instincts of the individuals. However, this is not the only argument which Aristotle puts forward in order to prove that state is a natural institution. He has another argument. This is his characteristic teleological argument. "The nature of a thing is its end" this in nut-shell is the Aristotelian teleological argument.Third argument is that the state is organism.

Let us discuss these three arguments in detail:

The first argument put forward by Aristotle is one of the most valuable analysis of the state in the whole realm of political speculation. In order to find the natural origin of the state he analyses it into its parts and studies it in its beginning. There are two primary natural instincts which compel human beings to associate themselves together– the reproductive instinct which brings man and woman together and the instinct of self-preservation which brings together master and slave. Thus, we get the first natural society of three persons–the family which is the association established by nature for the supply of everyday wants." The next stage is the village, which is a union of several families for the supply of something more than everyday wants. Aristotle does not specify these further wants, but we may conjecture that he had in mind that the village made possible a greater division of labour and therefore, the satisfaction of more varied needs, as well as more complete protection against man and beast.

The village, he adds, is formed almost naturally by the union of families by common consent.

Such is Aristotle's first argument to prove that State is a natural institution. One must appreciate Aristotle's wisdom in putting forward an argument which no body can refute. His argument is that the state is natural if family is natural. In other words, is family is natural, the state must be natural. The former propositions was almost a truism. No one would maintain that the family is anything but natural. Even the most ingenious Sophist could not prove that the family was an artificial institution of deliberate creation of the individuals or an imposition from outside. It is unanimously regarded as natural because it is clearly the natural expression of man's native instincts of sex and self-preservation. Now the natural character of the family is bound to be followed by the natural character of the state. The state is the logical development of the family since the state alone achieves completely what the family aims at and achieves partly–namely self-sufficiency. The fact that an individual is not self-sufficient is the very reason which makes the family necessary to him. But the family though it achieves a degree of self-sufficiency which the individual cannot, is still dependent upon support from without. The same natural necessity which makes individual combine in a family makes families combine to form a village and villages. In their turn to form a state. The state has, therefore, the same title to be called "natural" that the family has.

The second argument and the most typical of Aristotle is that "the nature of a thing is its end." This is the argument based on his teleology. His view of the world is teleological ; everywhere things are regarded as determined towards their end. Everything realises its true nature when it reaches its end. The apple fruit shows the true nature of the apple seed. The state shows the real nature of man. Man can get perfect develoment of his nature in the state only. Beyond the state he is no longer a human being. Man is not all animal his true nature in rational. The possession of the faculty of Reason is what distinguishes him from an animal. We can term the animal and rational nature is man as lower and higher nature respectively. As Foster says, "But according to Aristotle the state is nature not only in the sense that it supplies the nature and the environment for the development of his higher nature." And it is only in the State that an individual gets the opportunity for the development of his rational nature. The family and the village prove inadequate not only because they do not adequately supply the needs of man's animal nature but also because they do not supply the needs of man's rational nature. Since the end of all human development is to realise its rational nature, the latter is realised in the state only. Since "the nature of a thing is its end; where thing is when fully developed, we call its nature; hence the man by nature is a political animal." This is how Aristotle proves through his teleology that the state is a natural institution and that man is by nature a political animal.

To put it differently, since membership of a state is the end of all human development and since its end is the real nature or meaning of anything it follows that man has his real meaning as member of a state. "In the state, and as a member of the State, he lives and has his being : without the state and apart from the state he has no meaning. This is the meaning of the famous phrase : man is by nature a political beings". His real nature or meaning consists in the citizenship of a state, which is the end of his development. Until he has achieved his citizenship he has not attained his nature, and he is not man in the full meaning of the term. This is the meaning of the phrase. "The state is man's narural destination." This also explains the meaning of the sentence. "He who is unable to live in the state must be either a beast or a god."

The third argument which Aristotle gives in order to prove that the state is a natural institution is that the state is an organism which has developed and grown. The state is a whole of which the individuals are the parts. He is the father of all organismic theories of State. "According to him, the state is a natural community; and organism with all the attributes of a living being." It is clear from the preceding account of the state, the end or fulfilment of earlier forms of human associations like the family and village that Aristotle views it as a growing or developing thing.

These are the three arguments which Aristotle puts forward in order to prove that the state is a natural institution. But it is necessary to understand the sense in which the state is natural. Obviously, the state is not natural in the sense in which we describe mountains, rivers, earthquakes and other phenomena as natural, it is not a part of Nature and is not determined by physical causes. Again it is not natural in the sense in which a reflex act like the blinking of the eyes or the secretion of saliva when the eyes or the salivary glands are properly simulated is called natural. The state is natural in the sense in which the use of language or the building of houses is natural to man. The capacity to speak or to build houses is implanted in man by nature. So the State is natural in so far as the impulse to associate with other fellow men is implanted by nature in every individual.

The two propositions–Man is a political animal, and the state is natural–involve each other. The state is man's natural destination because he is a political animal, because he who can live beyond the state is either a beast or a god (and it is only for courtesy's sake that Aristotle uses "god"). The faculty which makes him a political animal is his "Reason". Other animals are gregarious, but man alone is political; he is the only animal endowed by nature with the gift of "Reason". Although the state is natural to man in precisely the same sense in which the bee-hive is natural to bee, the state differs from the bee-hive because man's nature differs from the bee's in being rational. The bee-hive is governed by laws, as the state is, but the bees do not live a political life because they do not understand the laws which govern them.

## THEORY OF REVOLUTION

Revolution conveys two-fold meaning to Aristotle:

(a) A major or minor change in the constitution means a revolution to Aristotle. If the constitution has changed from Monarchy to Aristocracy, revolution has taken place. Any small or big change in the constitution meant revolution to him. Even if oligarchy has become less oligarchic or democracy less democratic a revolution is deemed to have taken place. The example of big change can be : if oligarchic rule is overthrown by democrats or if, otherwise, the democratic rule is overthrown by oligarchs.

(b) Even if the constitution remains the same and the ruling power has been transferred from one man to another, revolution is supposed to have taken place *e.g.*, if one tyrant is replaced by another or one monarch is substituted by the other.

We know already any change in the constitution had far reaching importance. It meant a change in the social and moral rules of the state. The ruling power had great part to play in the cultivation of virtue. Hence, he does not restrict the meaning of revolution of political conception.

**Causes.** While discussing causes of revolutions, he distinguishes general causes of revolution from particular causes of revolutions and causes of revolution in particular kinds of states. Thus, we can discuss causes of revolutions under three kinds:

(i) General causes of revolution.

(ii) Particular causes of revolution.

(iii) Causes of revolution in particular kinds of state.

(1) We shall discuss them one by one. The most general cause of revolution Aristotle finds in the natural desire of every man to become equal to every other man. The masses aim at absolute equality of privileges and powers and opportunities. They envy the few who have better privileges and powers due to their superiority in wealth, ability or birth. That state will be prone to revolution more frequently in which there is greater inequality. The more the equality the more stable the state is. That is the main reason. Why Aristotle regards that state as the best-practicable one in which middle class is in majority. If the middle-class predominates there will be lesser inequality, and if there is lesser inequality, there are fewer chances of revolutions.

(2) After discussing the general cause of revolution Aristotle gives a long list of particular causes of revolutions. In this respect Aristotle's analysis is really praise-worthy. As Dunning says, "His remarks under the latter head exhibit his insight at its best, tracing as he does, political transformation to obscure social and economic sources." In more or less the same tune Maxe says, "There can be no

doubt, however, of the acuteness of Aristotle's insight into the basic causes of revolutions. One or more of the factors enumerated by him will be found to have been among the provoking forces of virtually every political revolution of which history has any record.

But before we come to the particular causes of revolution we must distinguish them: *(a)* Occasions of revolution; *(b)* temper of those who make revolution; and *(c)* the motives of those who make revolution. Occasions according to Aristotle are to be regarded as quite distinct from the causes. The former may be and often are incidents of trifling character; the latter are always profound. Aristotle gives a number of examples in order to support his position but they of course need not be quoted. Again causes are to be distinguished from the temper or the frame of the mind of men who make revolution. The revolutionary temper is created when the conception of justice of the persons does not get full satisfaction in actuality. "Men turn to revolution when they think that they have not their dues in proportion to their estimate of themselves." There can be no fellow-feeling when one section of the community is convinced that its rights are being denied to it and that justice is not being done. The democrats will resent the oligarchic monopoly of power. They will think that in spite of the fact that all are equal few rich persons control the government and hence deny justice to many. Similarly, oligarchs in democracy are apt to move towards sedition when they feel that they do not get the share in political power which they deserve on grounds of superiority in wealth, birth and education. Thus, the factor which produces the revolutionary temper or frame of mind is the feeling in one class that justice is not being done, that it gets less than what it deserves and another class more than what it should have. Then again, causes are to be distinguished from motives. The latter in Aristotle's words are, "the desire of gain and honour, or the fear of dishonour and loss; the authors of them want to divert punishment or dishonour from themselves or their friends."

The particular causes of revolution according to Aristotle are:

(i) The possession of the absolute powers by one or a few individuals so as to excite fear in the minds of the public.

(ii) The disproportionate increase of any part (territorial, social, economic or otherwise) of the state.

(iii) Contempt.

(iv) Electiontrigues.

(v) The universal passion for privilege and prerogative.

(vi) The over-reaching insolence or avarice of rulers or ruling classes which causes men to react against them.

(vii) Undue importance of certain individuals.

(viii) The endeavours of men guilty of wrong-doing to foment a revolution as a smoke-screen to conceal their own misdeeds.

(ix) Carelessness shown in granting public offices to disloyal citizens.

(x) The dissentions and rivalries of people of different races.

(xi) Dynasties and family–Feuds and quarrels.

(xii) Struggles for office and political power between rival classes and political factors or parties.

(xiii) The neglect of small changes which might assume large proportions later on.

(xiv) Dissimilarity of elements in the state.

(xv) Free immigration of foreign races with different notions of justice and law.

After narrating the particular causes of revolution Aristotle proceeds to causes of revolutions in particular types of states, most particularly democracies, oligarchies, aristocracies and politics. Democracies are overthrown by the excessive use of powers and unwarranted condemnation of the rich by the demagogues. They either turn into tyrannies or oligarchies. There are revolutions in oligarchies due to two causes :—

(a) Rivalry and dissentions among the ruling oligarchs themselves.

(b) Oppressive dictatorial rule. But where the rulers are harmonious and they are not oppressive, oligarchy is not easily overturned in aristocracies, revolutions break out due to the restriction of conferment of honours of the state on very few persons. There is revolution in polity due to the defective balance of the different elements combined in the constitution. It is due to maladmixture of oligarchic and democratic elements that there are revolutions in politics. Tyrannies and monarchies are liable to be overthrown due to three reasons :

(i) Hatred and contempt produced in the minds of the people due to the insolent and oppressive behaviour of the monarchy and the tyrants.

(ii) Personal insult inflicted on some notable persons.

(iii) Influence of foreign states of opposite character.

**Preventions of Revolutions.** Aristotle's account of the preventions of revolutions is again indicative of his penetrating knowledge of the then constitutions. In addition to laying down some general means of preventing revolutions or making the state stable, he touches upon particular remedies for particular diseases to be found in particular constitutions.

**General Preventions.** First, as the major cause of revolution is the feeling of the minds of certain section of the community that injustice is being done to them, the most general means of preventing revolution is to remove this feeling. And this can be achieved by treating the various classes with consideration. All offices of the state should be open to all who are virtuous. No class should have monopoly of offices. All persons and classes should feel that they are getting their due. Such arrangement should be made that proper allocation of rewards and offices is made to each person according to his worth or deserts. This Aristotle terms as Distributive Justice.

Secondly, the rulers should see that the spirit of obedience to law is cultivated and maintained in the people. The inculcation of this habit of law-abidingness is the most powerful instrument by which the stability of the state can be maintained. Lawlessness should not be allowed to creep in small and trifling matters.

Thirdly, small and petty changes in the status quo must not be overlooked. They should be carefully watched and attended to. Aristotle's penetrating analysis is really worth-appreciating in this respect. He rightly indicates that occasions of petty strifes though apparently is significant, yet lead to complete revolutions.

Fourthly, the citizens should be properly educated in the spirit of the constitution. Such equation is the best of all preventives of revolution. If the citizens are in the full knowledge of the manner in which their constitution works, they will adjust themselves accordingly and there will be lesser possibility of revolution. In Aristotle's words—"the greatest, however, of all the means we have mentioned for ensuring the stability of Constitutions but one which is now-a-days generally neglected—is the education of the citizens in the spirit of their constitution."

Fifthly, too much of political power should not be allowed to lie in the hands of one individual or a particular class of individuals. It is the exercise of extreme powers by one which is the cause of all troubles. If one person is too powerful, the others present and thus, the seeds of sedition are sown.

Sixthly, the government offices should be so organized that they are not allowed to become sources of gain. All precautions should be taken that the public offices do not become sinecures. The rulers should not be allowed to make money out of their offices. The economic motives should be totally separated from political ones. (The reader should note at this stage the similarity of approach between Plato and Aristotle). Bribes and other illegal methods of acquiring money on the part of the holders of offices should be rendered impossible. All offices should be made honorary i.e., without salary.

Seventhly, inequalities of offices and honours more than those of wealth drive men to rebellion. Therefore, honours, rewards and offices should be distributed as widely as possible. No person should feel that certain political honours and offices are impossible of attainment due to some reason or the other. But this distribution of offices is to be allowed with one qualification and that is the smaller offices should be given on a long tenure and the higher ones on a short one as the holding of the highest offices for a long time has an inherent corrupting influence.

Eighthly, no single person should be permitted to capture suddenly an office of great political importance. Access to position of power should be made gradual and slow. Moreover, no outsider or stranger should be ordinarily given political offices.

Ninthly, the internal details of the administration, particularly the administration of public finances should be made open to public scrutiny. The governing body can gain popularity only when the public is made confident that the treasury is not being exploited by the officials.

Tenthly and lastly, since every form of government calls danger to itself by its own excesses, it follows that every government should be moderate in the exercise of its powers. It should remain within limits. In oligarchies, the oligarches should adopt a very cordial behaviour for the democrats. Similarly, in other forms of government, the ruling class should be fair to the ruled.

**Particular Preventions.** After describing the general preventions of revolutions which can be applied in all constitutions, Aristotle passes on the particular means for preserving particular forms of government. The nature of means recommended for each is determined by the nature of the causes which tend to change it. The main cause of revolution in polity is improper blending of democratic and oligarchic elements. Hence, Aristotle suggests that, "especial care must be taken to detect the obscure beginnings of new conditions making for political change." In other words, proper care should be taken in order to maintain the proper balance between the democratic and oligarchic elements. Similarly, in aristocracies the government cah be made stable by treating the masses with fairness and by not allowing a single man to become too powerful, in oligarchies, by allowing the poor to participate in administrative functions, and in democracies by allowing the rich to participate in the administrative functions and sparing their estates etc. He says that a tyrant can maintain himself in power by following methods:

(a) By having under him an efficient system of espionage especially of female spies.

(b) By pursuing a policy of military aggression abroad.

(c) By alarming the people with fear of foreign attack.

(d) By keeping the people occupied and poor.

(e) By promoting distrust and a spirit of hostility between the various classes of the state.

(f) By chopping of the inconvenient tall poppies.

(g) By participating in public worship and religion and by respecting the people's religious sentiments.

(h) By enlisting in his favour as large a measure of social support as possible.

(i) By honouring the good.

(j) By winning the reputation for military virtues.

(k) By showing favours personally but punishing through others.

(l) By living a life of undisguished luxury and glamour which creates awe in the minds of the public.

(m) By destroying the intellectual life of the citizens.

(n) By increasing the material well-being of the people.

Such is Aristotle's most penetrating analysis of the causes of revolutions and their preventions unsurpassed by any ever since the beginning of political speculation. His objective description of means by which the rulers whether tyrants or oligarchs, can maintain themselves in power, anticipates Machiaveli. It is in his theory of revolutions that Aristotle completely separates ethics from politics. His theory of revolution is one of the greatest contributions which Aristotle had to make to Political Thought.

## VIEWS ON PROPERTY AND FAMILY

Aristotle vindicates for every citizen both private property and the family life and regards them both as institutions belonging to all by the order of nature, because he believes that the moral life of every citizen requires the equipment of private property and the discipline of family life. But these two institutions are only instruments. They are not ends in themselves.

We shall discuss Aristotle's views on family and property separately. First, something about family:

**Family.** In his zeal for the state Aristotle does not iike Plato, depreciate the family. The state is for him a "Community of Communities". But the family has its own function in the scheme of life. It constitutes the historical origin of the state. It is the first natural association arising out of the union of male and female on the one hand and the master and slave on the other. According to Aristotle, family is a natural association like the state.

But if the family is a natural association like the state, it is unlike the state not only in degree but also in kind. The similarity between the state and the family is only apparent. In reality they are very different from each other. It is one of his numerous criticisms against Plato that the latter had represented the state to be merely a large house-hold and the ruler of the state to be essentially the head of that family. Plato had set forth the view that a small state and a great house-hold will be essentially the same and the government of both but one science whether its name happens to be royal, political or economic. Such a conception, Aristotle holds to be false. State and family according to Aristotle differ not only in degree but in kind also.

Aristotle has mainly two arguments through which he tries to draw a line of demarcation between the state and the family.

First, in a state there is only one kind of relationship that of the ruler and the ruled. In the family on the other hand there are three different relations as the family consists of an individual holding dominion over wife, children and property including slaves. Hence, the head of the family has a particular type of relation with his wife quite a different relations with his children and again a totally different relation with the slaves. He rules the wife, not as an absolute despot, but a constitutional advisor, he rules the children not as an absolute despot but as the king, who looks to their good rather than his own, while property, both slaves and other, he rules in full despotism, for the exclusive advantage of himself. "In this manifold relation of the head of the house-hold to the subordinate elements lies the essential distinction between the house-hold and the state; for in the latter according to Aristotle, the relation of the ruler to each of the citizen is precisely the same."

Secondly, another point of distinction between the state and the family is that the latter exists for the sake of the physical needs of life, and the former for the moral and intellectual needs. The state which includes the house-hold is self-sufficient while the family is not.

In order to prove these two points of distinction between the state and the family, he enters upon an exhaustive analysis of the family in the course of which he sets forth his views on many fundamental economic questions.

**Property.** Aristotle's views on property are developed in direct reference to Plato. While criticising Plato's views on communism of property, Aristotle puts forward his own views on property which are of more general bearing and constitute to this day the ablest defence of private property. We have already discussed in detail Aristotle's criticism of Plato's communism and the repetition of the same here is not called for. But one fact must be known as in other respects Aristotle's comments on Plato's views on property are full of "inaccuracies and inconsistencies. In his polemic against Plato, Aristotle attributtes to him the advocacy of a communist scheme of property. In fact, Plato proposed nothing of the sort. The workers, the peasants and artisans live under a system of individual ownership and management of property. Only a small fraction of population which constitutes the ruling class has nothing to do with property as such. It has to consume in common the articles of food and clothing provided by the peasants class. Plato actually leaves the individualistic system of production intact. Nevertheless, Plato outlaws private property for the rulers as a possible menace to their sense of unity and devotion to the state.

Summing up Plato's views on property we can say that he regarded private property as:

(a) Non-essential for the moral perfection of the individual; and

(b) dangerous for the unity of the state. Hence, he abolishes the right of the rulers to hold any private property at all either in the form of estates or houses or silver or gold.

But Aristotle's views on Property are very different from Plato's. He less denies that private property is, in itself, a threat to moral perfection and he defends his view on the following six grounds:

1. There is his famous "incentive and progress" argument. The individual works harder if his self-interest is involved. If the individual works harder the society as a whole will gain and there will be greater social progress. He, "links the idea of self-interest with that of social progress through the greater individual effort and competence." In ever-green words which will not be forgotten for all times to come, Aristotle says, "When every one has a distinct interest, men will make more progress because everyone will be attending to his own business."
2. Private property is also a source of not a little pleasure, it is a form of self-love. The ownership of property gives great pleasure to man. "For all or almost all, men love money and other such objects in a measure." Aristotle sharply distinguishes such love of property from selfishness and considers it rather from the view-point of self-respect.
3. Aristotle advocates private property as an essential instrument of good life. It is a means to the development of human personality. Under a system of communism, the cultivation of virtues like generosity, liberality and hospitality is next to impossible Righteousness presupposes a certain amount of property.
4. A conservative as Aristotle is, he points out that here must be something deeply and enduringly human in the idea of private property, if it has existed for such a long time. The institution of private property must have been useful, otherwise it would not have survived the great upheavals in human history. And according to Aristotle "we should not disregard the experience of ages." As to communist

practices, "in the multitude of years these things, if they were good would certainly not have been unknown." Aristotle's views in this regard are essentially conservative.

5. The ownership of private property imparts a sense of civic responsibility to the individuals. An individual who owns property will look to the state for its protection. An individual who pays taxes will take interest in the state-affairs in order to see that his money is spent well. A person who on the other hand, does not own property and pay taxes will have no such interest in state. This is why, Aristotle makes the ownership of property as the condition precedent of citizenship.
6. The holding of private property requires property management. The experience of management of property is also useful in the management of state affairs. Hence Aristotle allows the right of citizenship only to those person who hold private property.

In a nut-shell, his argument is at bottom that property like the family is a natural and moral institutional extension of personality, a source of pleasure and an opportunity of good activity.

Such is the defence of private property put forward by Aristotle. But he is quite aware of the evils that befall men in a system of private property, but he says that, "they are due to a very different cause—"the wickedness of human nature." The cure for social imperfection is not equality of property but moral improvement of man through an elaborate educational system. As a matter of public policy, the legislator ought to aim at equitable rather than equal distribution of property. What seems most important to Aristotle is not who owns property but how property is used.

**Manner of Holding and Using Property.** There are three distinct modes holding and using property, according to Aristotle:

(a) Private ownership of property but common use of the produce.

(b) Common ownership and common use of the property.

(c) Commn ownership of property but private use.

Out of these three alternatives Aristotle prefers the first *i.e.* private ownership of property, but common use. "It is clearly better that property should be private, but the use of it common." Again Aristotle holds that though every man has his own property, he would use them in common use with his friends.

"And the special business of the legislator is to create in men this benevolent disposition".

In his views on the use of property, Aristotle is striking a very subtle balance between individualism and socialism. He combines the advantages drawn from the individual ownership with those from public use of property. Private ownership of property bring economic and moral advantages. The common use brings unanimity and unity. In defending private property he is an individualist; indeed no one has expressed the common-sense of individualism better than Aristotle. He is also a socialist in as much as he propounds the common use of property for the good life of the community. As a socialist he would also like to have property regulated through proper legislation. "He actually adopts a middle of the road course between the two extremes of individualism and socialism."

**Property as an Instrument.** Aristotle defines property as, "a store of instruments to be used in a house hold or in a state." Slave is also an instrument but he is an animate instrument. Property on the other hand is an inanimate instrument. The end to which property and slaves are instruments is the good life whether within the house hold or in the state.

From his definition of property as a stock of instruments to good life Aristotle draws many substantive conclusions:

1. Property is essential for the existence and proper functioning of the house hold. Man needs food to satisfy hunger, a house to live in, and garments to protect himself against the rigours of climate. The house-hold which is a condition of good moral life cannot function well without a certain amount of necessaries of life.
2. As wealth is an instrument to good life, "its dimensions are limited by the function for which it is intended." The

amount of property required for good life is limited. It is not necessary that endless amount of property should be amassed because it is as bad to have more than what is required as to have less than what is necessary for good life. The aim before people should be, therefore, the acquisition of wealth sufficient to make good life possible, and not the accumulation of an unlimited amount of it. Excessive wealth thwarts good life instead of facilitating it. Property is compared to a hammer by Aristotle. The latter must be heavy inorder to serve its purpose, but the object of the hammer maker will not therefore, be to make it as heavy as possible. The same function of the hammer which demands weight also sets a limit to the weight required.

3. For Aristotle the production of wealth has no philosophical significance. He regards it as a more or less disagreeable necessity incidental to the maintenance of good life and hence as a function of the hosue-hold, rather the lowest of its functions (as house-hold management has for its purpose rather to make the members of the family virtuous than to make them rich).

**Methods of Acquiring Wealth.** Aristotle distinguishes natural methods of acquisition of wealth from unnatural ones. The natural methods are those through which mere necessary subsistence is procured. Among these he enumerates cattle-raising, agriculture, and hunting the last including as subordinate species, fishing, rather chase of land animals and oddly enough brigandage. The unnatural methods of acquisition are those which aim not at the mere maintenance of life but at the endless accumulation of wealth. Trade, barter and commerce are the examples of unnatural methods if they aim not at the maintenance of life but at making huge profits.

## IDEAS ON SLAVERY

Aristotle believed that it was essential that house-hold should be properly maintained and for that the institutions of slavery and property were most essential. The slaves are animate instruments whereas property is the in-animate weapon for running a house-hold.

He did not agree with the Sophists that it was not a natural institution but had come to stay by convention alone. He also did not agree with the idea that since slavery was unnatural, therefore, rule of master over the slaves was also unnatural. According to him for making a complete house-hold it was essential to have both the slaves as well as freemen. Slave is a living possession of family whereas property is a lifeless possession. A slave differs from his master because of difference in power of reasoning and understanding, the master having far superior reasoning power than the slave. In the words of Maxey, "Wanting in their make-up is the ineluctable capacity for self-determination which a ruling class must have, and therefore, it is clear that nature has intended them to be used as instruments in the hands of others. Consequently it is just that they should be held as property and used as other property is used, as a means of maintaining life."

**Definition of Slavery.** According to Aristotle, a slave is living possession and property of his master. He possesses no reasoning power but has the power of understanding and following reason. He postulates that those who are not virtuous are slaves and it is possible to determine as to who is virtuous and who is not. He also starts with the presumption that men have different capacities and are unequal. Those who have lower capacities should be slave of those possessing higher capacities and capabilities. The slave belongs to master but master does not belong to slave. C.H. Mcilwain has properly expressed the views of Aristotle when he says that, "If by nature man is a political animal so is the slave nothing more than a domestic animal, a mere cattle, rabit of animate property, an instrument of action separable from the possessor."

**Justification for Slavery.** Aristotle has justified slavery on many grounds namely:

(i) It is a natural phenomenon that the inferior must be subordinated to the superior. As soul rules over the body or reason over appetite, similarly those who have more reasoning capacity should rule over those who have no superior reasoning capacity or less power of understanding. The former are naturally masters and latter slaves. The masters have superiority in wisdom and the slaves in physical strength. As a musician cannot live without musical instrument so a family cannot live without a slave.

(ii) Slavery is necessary because it will provide leisure for the virtuous which is most essential for the welfare of the state.

(iii) Since a slave does not possess rational faculty and cannot regulate appetite by reason, it is good for him and is in his own interest to be a slave because then alone he will be in a position to share in the virtues of his master and will thus be elevated.

(iv) Slavery is essential for the master because that will enable him so lead a good and happy life which is essential for productive and creative work.

(v) He justified slavery on the ground that in case the system was denounced whole Greek social system would collapse resulting in social disorder and chaos in the Greek life.

(vi) Slavery is manifestation of will of nature which is clearly indicated from birth and wisdom of people which is always of varying degrees. He said that, "for a being who is endowed by nature with a mind capable of reflection and fore-thought is by nature the superior and governor whereas he whose excellence is merely corporeal is formed a slave."

(vii) According to him since family is social unit it has two natural instincts namely sex and appetite. The relationship on the one hand is between the master and slave and on the other between husband and wife.

(viii) Accordng to him it is with slavery that perfection can be attained. Slaves and the masters are just complementary and not contradictory to each other. The institution of slavery is thus, a social necessity.

(ix) Nature has given every organ of body some function to perform. Accordingly that of the eye is to see and of the ear to hear. In society everybody has some duty to discharge. Similarly function of the slave is just to obey the command of the superior and intelligent. He has gone to the extent of saying that as man is natural for a woman for marriage, similarly slave is natural for a master for the proper discharge of his duties.

**Conditions Essential for Slavery.** Aristotle however, did not give unqualified support to the institution of slavery. He justified it only under certain specific conditions namely:

(i) Only those who are mentally deficient and virtuously not so superior as others, should be treated as slaves. He did not support the idea that all prisoners of war were slaves. He felt that it was not always essential that a nation capable of fighting a war was always and essentially superior in intelligence and wisdom. He therefore, condemned the idea that all prisoners of war were slaves. He thus, disapproved the idea of slavery by force.

(ii) Slaves should not be harshly treated but be given human treatment. Those who violate this established principle should be legally punished.

(iii) There should be provision for emancipation for those slaves who show good conduct and develop capacity for reasoning and virtue. According to Barker, "The slave can be treated as man in any respect, he ought to be treated as man in all and the admission that he can be regarded as a man destroys that conception of his wholly slavish and non-rational character without justification of his being treated as slave."

(iv) Slavery is essential for alround development, thus, an integral point of growth. Master has no right to misuse his power and authority. Slave is not his subordinate but only assistant.

(v) He was opposed to the idea of using force for slavery. Only those should be enslaved who were inferior in understanding and virtue.

**Criticism of Defence of Slavery.** Although Aristotle has tried to defend the institution of slavery on many grounds and has tried to portray it as a natural institution, yet his ideas have been put under searching criticism on account of certain inherent defects in his theory namely:

(i) There is self-contradiction in his theory. On the one hand he believed that the slave should be given some share in law and also be provided chances of emancipation but on the other hand he declares him merely as a piece of property of an animate kind. There is no reconciliation between these two contradictory statements.

(ii) Aristotle starts with the presumption that some are born intelligent while others have less potentialities. Thus, according to him the former are masters and the latter slaves. But practical experience has shown that all are born with equal potentialities and it is development which makes real difference. Thus, the bases of his theory are not correct.

(iii) Aristotle has not fixed-up any criteria to determine as to who is natural slave and who is not. By saying that some people are by nature slave, he has made it a hereditary institution which is most undesirable.

(iv) His idea that only few are capable of issuing orders and are virtuous, is again a fallacy and reducing a vast majority of people to slavery which is neither practicable nor desirable.

(v) He has started with the presumption that it is possible to divide humanity into two broad categories namely superior and inferior, which is not possible. Even if his ideas are accepted in this regard, it virtually means that the latter are not human beings in reality, which is something ridiculous and barbarous.

(vi) His basic ideas are founded on the philosophy of racial superiority in which pride of place has been given to the Greeks. The conception of racial superiority is a farce and most unacceptable to the modern world. Thus, the bases of his philosophy are not well founded.

(vii) If it is accepted that it is the will and wish of the nature that the superior should rule over the inferior then there would be many such classes in a society because in each society there are persons who are superior in one way or the other, over others.

(viii) In modern days retention of this institution is most unwanted and anti to the idea of equality.

(ix) Division of society into two groups namely the 'masters' and the 'slaves' is bound to do much harm to the unity of the state and thus, can result in the clash of interests. Those who are depressed may even sacrifice their national loyalties to some extent and at certain stages finding an appropriate opportunity might even deceive.

(x) His defence of slavery goes against his basic philosophy that men are by nature good and social beings. He also believed that men had potentiality of being moral which aspect should always be developed. On the other hand he has subjected a numerically predominating class to everlasting subjection which cannot be reconciled with his philosophy.

(xi) His theory and ideas about slavery are opposed to the concept of social justice. Under his arrangements the slaves are required to work for the good and accomplishment of the intelligent. In other words they are very essential for the wise to become perfect and in the process they are required to contribute and work hard. But when the wise and the intelligent have contributed they appear nowhere. Thus, their labour is not properly rewarded and recognised. It is against all concepts of social justice.

Though Aristotle's criticism today may not sound well because it is not suited to modern conditions, yet if it is seen in the light of circumstances in which he defended this institution, there seems to be some justification. If he would have refuted and repudiated the institution of slavery whole Greek social fabric would have collapsed. Therefore, there does not seem to be much justification in condemning his ideas to the extent to which it is being done at present.

His criticism may be justified from the point of view of expediency but there is practically no justification in saying that some are born to rule and others to be ruled. There is no class distinction on the lines demarcated by Aristotle. Undoubtedly all have equal faculties for development and the only question is as to how those are to be developed. Given equal and opportunate circumstances many talented persons may come to the front and those who are considered and meant for subjugation might prove as the best rulers. Since his plea for the retention of slavery is unwanted except for expediency, all advanced countries of the world have legally abolished slavery. The Constitution of India has adopted the principle of equality without any distinction and does not agree with the idea that some are to rule and others are to be ruled. Slavery is a legal offence in India today.

All the same it will be appreciated that he made lasting contribution to political philosophy by his theory of slavery. Maxey says about his contribution that, "There is but one answer to such reasoning, and that is to be found in the logic of force, a truth which Aristotle did not fail to perceive, as is shown by his repeated insistence that only persons truly slaves by nature can be justly held in bondage."

Some of the thinkers have gone to the extent of suggesting that even our modern world is not free from Aristotle's influence. In the words of Prof. A.R.M. Murray, "The modern world is not without examples of racial discrimination which are defended by essentially the same arguments as those employed by Aristotle. "Similarly Prof. Maxey says, "The learned apologists for negro slavery in the old south draw their best arguments from Aristotle." Such criticism levied against Aristotle in this regard will considerably come down, if we agree with the views of A.E. Taylor when he says, "The slaves of whom he speaks were house hold servant in small business. He had not before his eyes the system of enormous industries carried by the gangs of slaves under conditions of revolting degradation which disgraced the later Roman Republic and early Roman empire or the Southern States of North America."

## THEORY OF JUSTICE

Greek political thinkers attached great importance to the conception of justice. They felt that it was one of the most outstanding and important features of the state. It was virtue in action and worked on the basis of mutual cooperation in which each and every member of the society should try to discharge his duties towards the community as a whole. It was of general excellence and depicted moral development. It was moral virtue in social relationship.

Though Greek Political thinkers might differ in details about the conception of justice, yet its fundamental importance remained unshaken throughout the Greek period. According to Plato, justice was in proper performance of duties. He felt that the philosophers, soldiers and the peasants, who had been allotted a particular job, should perform that properly and honestly. The philosophers should rule, soldiers fight and the peasants serve the community as a whole with emotion and honesty.

**Types of Justice.** As regards Aristotle, justice for him was of two types namely 'complete justice' as well as 'particular justice'. Since the former was identifiable with moral virtue it was responsible for regulating all public and social relations. For him complete justice laid in law-abidingness and was possible only in an ideal society. According to him, particular justice was concerned with the distribution of offices and observance of rules of proportionate equality. It also consisted in proper and desirable distribution of wealth, honour and good things.

**Distributive and Corrective Justice.** Distributive justice lay in proportionate allocation of offices according to one's own worth. It was primarily concerned with political privileges. Each type of political organisation had its corresponding distributive justice, *e.g.*, in democracy it was birth; in oligarchy it was riches while in aristocracy it was in virtue. It counters confusion and distributes offices according to one's social contribution. In it mutual strifes are minimised. In other words in it rights are measured in terms of duties performed by one in the society or social services rendered by one. On the other hand corrective justice is mainly concerned with commercial transactions. It is negative in character. It aims at restoring back what one had lost due to social injustice. It prevents the encroachment of one on the rights of others. As part of the whole it restores what was forbidden to one due to one reason or the other.

**Corrective Justice.** Aristotle also mentions about corrective justice. According to him, it is a type of justice which prevents people from encroaching upon the rights of his fellowmen. He believed that, "It relates to voluntary and commercial transactions like hire, sale and furnishing of security etc. and with involuntary actions involving aggression on life, property, honour and freedom."

**Criticism.** But there appears to be no universality in the conception of justice. At many places it is self-contradictory *e.g.*, the definition of the term 'contribution to society' is something which cannot have any universal application. In democracies, birth and freedom are measuring rods and it is presumed that everybody is contributing to the society and hence all rewards and honours should be equally distributed. In oligarchies, it is presumed that only the wealthy contribute to the society and honours should be their monopoly. He has no doubt laid stress that the virtuous should rule and that they contribute most in the welfare of state but again virtue is something which is discrete and not concrete and hence cannot be accepted as a standard or measuring rod.

Then again, on the one hand he has pleaded that the cultivation of virtue should be criteria for distributing offices, but on the other hand, he has agrued that the masses should not be ignored and offices and honours should not be made the monopoly of few. He pleaded sharing of honour by all because according to him collective wisdom was better than the wisdom of the few virtuous and that the masses could bring about a revolution at any time.

Aristotle has given preference to duties over rights because people can claim a share in honours in proportion to their contribution to the society, but on the other hand in modern times rights are given at predominant place and the citizens on the whole are quick in demanding rights than discharging their duties. Not only this, but his conception of justice is a sort of workable democracy in which all have a share in the offices of honour but the virtuous have a preference over the common masses.

## ARISTOTLE'S IDEAL STATE

In that context we learnt that the subject matter of the "politics" is easily divisible into portions—Political Ideals and Political

Actualities. Broadly speaking Books No. II, III, VII and VIII deal with Political Ideals. In dealing with the latter Aristotle is greatly indebted to Plato and tries to depict his Ideal State. But the depiction on the Ideal State, in accordance with Plato does not suit Aristotle's taste and he shifts to the description of the actual states as soon as he finds the opportunity. Moreover, his potrayal of the Ideal State always remain incomplete. Hence, as Sabine says, "In truth his avowed purpose to construct an Ideal State eventuated, and the reader feels that the task was really little to his taste. What he does is to write a book not on an Ideal State but upon the ideals of the State." Again, in Books VII and VIII, he tries to describe the physical, mental and geographical conditions which are essential for the existence of the Ideal State. All these conditions are derived from Plato's "Law", not the "Republic". And as we know, in the laws, Plato depicts his second best State. Hence, it is very correct to say that "what Aristotle calls the Ideal State is always Plato's second best State."

Before we come to the depiction of conditions essential for Aristotle's Ideal State two facts of great importance are to be noted:—

First, Aristotle is not an absolutist like Plato. He is a relativist by nature. Plato prescribes that his Ideal State in the Republic is good for all communities for all times to come. But according to Aristotle we cannot pronounce which is the best government for a particular people without taking into account the special nature of that people. If in a particular community only one single person or family of extraordinary and proeminent excellence and political skill is available, Monarchy will be the ideal government for that. Again if there are a few instead of one, men of predominant virtue; Aristocracy will be the best government. Then again, if there naturally exists a war-like multitude able to rule and to obey in turn by a law which gives office to the well-to-do according to their desert the best government for them is Polity. Hence Aristotle, a realist and relativist as he is, takes into account the special nature of the people for prescribing his Ideal State.

Secondly, Aristotle's normal preference goes in for Monarchy as the Ideal State, since transcendent virtue is more likely to be found in one man than in any large number. "But this he recognizes to be an almost impossible ideal and accordingly the Ideal State which he later on (in Book VII) depicts is a government of high and enlightened virtue in which no one is admitted to citizenship who is not so qualified, and in which all citizens rule and are ruled in turn." Under Monarchy law could not be made supreme, as "good among men" could not be subjected to law. And according to Aristotle, in any good state the law must be the ultimate sovereign and not any person whatsoever. And if this be taken seriously, Monarchy is ruled out as the Ideal State.

**Features of Aristotle's Ideal State.** Aristotle's views regarding his ideal State are scattered here and there. Some in book III, others in Book VII and VIII. As noted earlier, Aristotle's Ideal State is a government by men of high and enlightened virtue, in which no one is admitted to citizenship who is not qualified, and in which all citizens rule and are ruled in turn. Now this Ideal State as depicted by Aristotle is an ideal according to him, which is pitched too high for human nature and is unrealisable. Hence, Aristotle puts forward his Best Practicable state—the Polity in which the qualification for rule is not high and enlightened virtue but the sturdy military virtue of a middle class. But at present we are concerned with the features of Aristotle's Ideal State whether realisable or not.

The following are the features of Aristotle's Ideal State:

1. Aristotle's Ideal State is always a small city-state. "Like Plato also Aristotle confined his Ideal to the city-state, the small and intimate group in which the life of the state is the social life of its citizens, overlapping the interests of family, of religion and of friendly personal inter-course." Aristotle could not visualise any state which was bigger than the city-state of the then Greek-world. Macedonian Conquest of the East and West had no effect on Aristotle.
2. In Aristotle's Ideal state law is supreme. There should not be personal and despotic rule of even the most virtuous person. There should be the impersonal rule of law which is the embodiment of the wisdom of the community since the ages. Here there is a fundamental difference of approach

between Plato and Aristotle. Plato in the Republic rules out the necessity of law altogether in his Ideal State as there is the rule of a Philosopher-king who is Reason personified. In the "Law", also in which he depicts his sub-ideal state, Plato recognises the law only as a concession to the frailty of human nature, not as a part of the Ideal. But Aristote accepts the sovereignty of law in his Ideal State not "as a concession to human frailty but as an intrins part of good government and therefore, as a characteristic of an ideal state." The role of law was well understood by? Aristotle even from the contemporary situation.

Aristotle learns that even the wisest ruler cannot dispense with law because the law has an impersonal quality which no man however good can attain. The law is 'reason unaffected by desire". Aristotle's Ideal State could be brought into existence. It was not impracticable. But Plato's Ideal State was impossible of realisation it depended upon the location of one person of extra-ordinary brilliance and virtue—the Philosopher-king. Hence, Maxey's statement, which is really full of meaning. Plato seeks a superman who will create a state as good as ought to be; Aristotle seeks a super science which will create state as good as can be."

3. The main function of the Ideal State of Aristotle is ethical. It aims at making man moral. The real purpose of the Ideal State is to try to bring about moral improvement among citizens as it is an, "association of men living together to achieve the best possible life." Aristotle's concept of self-sufficingness merely means that the state alone can provide all the conditions within which the individual can achieve the highest type of moral development. The state is the best state which enables every man, whosoever he is to lead a good and happy life. And good and happy life according to Aristotle is moral life.
4. As a corollary of the third feature, the fourth one is that a great emphasis is laid on Education in the Ideal State. Like

Plato. Aristotle also regards the State mainly as an educational institution. He also propounds the compulsory system of education. In order to make man virtuous, the State through education should aim at the formation of good habits among citizens. They must be taught how to practise virtue and moderation, to follow reason and to obey law and to rule also. Purely military training, as was imparted to the Spartans, is not sufficient for it does not develop all of a man power and conspicuously neglects the intellectual training. The whole man—the body, the appetite, the reason is to be trained. If perfect state is to be created its constituent members must be made perfect. Such perfection can be achieved only through the cultivation of moral and intellectual excellence by the citizens. And this can be accomplished through a system of uniform, compulsory; public education which, "is the first essential of the best state and the administration of such of system is the most important function of government." Hence, like Plato's Ideal State the ultimate function of Aristotle's Ideal State is pedagogic. In essence, Aristotle accepts Plato's scheme of Education yet in non-essentials he disagrees with the latter. For instance, the system of Higher Education is not obtainable in Aristotle's Ideal State. It must be realised that Aristotle's education was for citizens only and not for those classes which were conditions but not part of the state.

5. In Aristotle's Ideal State property is to be owned privately but is to be used in common. According to Aristotle, the land is to be distributed among the citizens on the basis of equality. In addition to the land, they can own personal property of the value of not more than four times of the original land. But the produce of the land as well as of the personal properties is to be consumed at common tables.
6. A particular principle of division of labour is to prevail in the Ideal State, according to which the agriculture is assigned to the slaves, commerce and trade to resident-aliens and political functions to citizens. Aristotle's Ideal State warrants slavery which he justifies on more than one

ground. The slaves, and the resident-aliens are to be excluded from the participation in state-activities. It is only those who have leisure that can actively participate in the exercise of sovereignty.

7. The size of Aristotle's Ideal State should be neither too small nor too big. A certain minimum of population is required for the state, if it is to be self-sufficient. But if we go beyond a certain maximum, good government and order become impossible. But unfortunately, Aristotle does not prescribe any definite maximum on minimum size of population. But he says that the population should be manageable. And the criterion of manageability is personal knowledge. All the citizens should know one another personally. From the point of view of the moderners it looks absurd. But from Aristotle's point of view this limit of population is justified. It implies that he completely rules out the big population of the modern nation-states. The ideal conditions cannot prevail if the population is big.
8. The territory of the Ideal State should be such that it enables the people to live free and leisured life. It must have economic resources sufficient to supply the needs of the population. But it should not create abundance of wealth. It should be neither small nor big. The critérion of judging the correct measure of territory is that it should be small enough to be taken in a single view.
9. The situation of the Ideal State should be such that it should have ample access to sea in order to have necessary imports. But, it should not be too near to the sea lest its defence should suffer, or excessive foreign trade should usher in or the citizens should take to sea-faring.
10. The Ideal State is self-sufficient in all possible respects. It is never aggressive. It does not attack any foreign country as it is self-sufficient.
11. It should be located at such a place whose climate is temperate *i.e.,* neither too cold nor too hot, it is congenial to both mental and physical activity.

12. In natural endowments, the citizens should resemble the Greeks who combine the spirit and courage of the northern races with the intellectual keenness of the Asiatics. The subtle combination of intelligence with spirit is the best possible character for the citizens of a state.
13. The population of the Ideal State is divided into many classes-*e.g.*: *(i)* husband-men (agriculturists), *(ii)* artisans, *(iii)* a war-like class, *(iv)* a well-to-do leisured class, *(v)* priests; *(vi)* administrators. Of all these classes, only the last four form the constituent parts of the state *i.e.* only they are citizens. The first two classes are non-citizens. The agriculturists and the artisans are the necessary conditions of the State. The citizens must own property in private and must perform at successive periods of life the functions of warriors (when young), administrators (when older) and priests when very old.
14. In addition to these important features of the Ideal State. Aristotle discusses many minor features regarding the internal ordering of the city *i.e.* arrangement of water supply and of streets. He is also keen to make necessary arrangements for defence against foreign attack *i.e.* fortification, both of walls and citadel, training in the use of the latest war-like weapons.

It would not be out of place, if we were to reproduce Mcilwain's Summary of Aristotle's description of Ideal State. "It is neither too rich nor too poor, secure from attack and devoid of the desire for great wealth or wide expansion of trade or territory, homogeneous, virtuous and cultured, a defensible unambitious community, self-sufficient but not aggressive, "great" but not large, a tight little independent city over which the supreme power will rest in a true aristocracy whose members rule and obey each other in turn in maintaining for themselves a life of freedom from mercenary pursuits, devoted to the highest possible measure of culture and virtue, of well-being, and true happiness attainable by each and by all; while work necessary to the State's mere material existence will be performed by those whose natural lack of virtue disqualifies them for the higher life and for political functions but does not unfit them for manual toil under the direction of their moral, intellectual and therefore, political superiors. These lower classes are necessary elements of the Polis, but politically speaking scarcely "parts" of it in an organic sense, whether they be legally free or slave."

Such is the depiction of his Ideal State by Aristotle. His depiction is not systematic. We do not find in Aristotle that logical, organised and systematic description of Ideal State which is characteristic of Plato. But Aristotle's Ideal State is not like Plato's Ideal State, 'A City in Heaven'. It is a typically Greek state realisable on this earth. But the depiction of his Ideal State remains incomplete as it was "little congenial to his genius". Maxey beautifully sums up the similarities and dissimilarities between Plato's and Aristotle's Ideal States "How unlike and yet, in some respects how like, the Ideal State of Plato is the model commonwealth of Aristotle. Plato's State is a fabric of abstract ideas to be translated in reality by a philosopher king who will sweep away all existing institutions and employ genetics and education to create a new and better race of men a perfect social order; Aristotle's is a fabric of materials already existing thoroughly tried, well-understood and lying at hand ready for use by an intelligent statesman who dares to try his skill at weaving them into patterns approximating the ideal. Yet both thinkers display the same ethical fervour, the same passion for order, the same love for moderation, the same devotion to justice and reason, the same confidence in education, the same faith in humanity, and the same concern for realization of the good life."

❐

# 3

# European Thought—I

## NICCOLO MACHIAVELLI

Machiavelli was born in the Republic of Florence in Italy of well-to-do parents, in the year 1469. His father was a lawyer of some consequence and the boy apparently was educated from youth for a public career. In 1494 he entered public life in the capacity of a clerk in Chancery where nothing could check his progress and he advanced so rapidly that in 1498, he attained one of the highest post in the government that of second Chancellor and Secretary. He retained this post until 1512 and these years comprise the period of his active political life. He was engaged during this time principally in conducting official correspondence, in diplomatic missions, both to other Italian States and to powers elsewhere in Europe and in the organisation of a Florentine militia. He lost his employment and was exiled from Florence when Medici family came into power. In 1513 he found himself in prison on suspicion of conspiracy against the Medici government. However, he was released through the influence of important political friends. As a condition of his release, however, he was compelled to retire from public life and abstain from all political activities. He accordingly took up his residence on a small farm which he owned at Sasciano and lived the life of an exile. During the daytime, he tells us, he occupied himself with farm work, but when evening came he would shed his peasant garb and array himself in his court dress. Having thus become a gentleman again, he would spend the evening in reading the works of great authors of the past and in writing down the results of his reflections upon them. His most notable literary works were produced at this time, though the quantity and variety of his literary output indicates that his pen must have been busy all his life. Gradually the hostility of the Medici relaxed and he was allowed to return to public life. From 1521 onward we find him again employed in diplomatic work, and he was making, an active bid for the recovery of his old office when in June, 1527, he was suddenly seized with a fatal illness and died.

**His Time.** Machiavelli was unfortunately living in times when Italy was divided into small fragments. There was no national figure to command the confidence of the whole nation. He was personally of the view that Papacy was more an obstacle in secular integration rather an institution conducive to national integration. Due to economic advancement and technical developments the old feudalism was much weakening and degenerating itself. In his 'Prince' he made an appeal for the national unity of Italy but again the unfortunate philosopher could not see the successful outcome of his political philosophy in his own life time.

**Growth of Trade.** The period saw the advancement of means of communication and transportation. This resulted in the growth of trade and new trading class emerged which could only grow with strong royal protection. The development of international trade could only be at the cost of national trade controlled by feudals. The age was thus throwing off the yokes of feudalism. This change was bound to bring absolutism in monarchy.

**Power for Monarch.** Machiavelli was also living in those days when Europe was passing through intellectual and spiritual crisis popularly known as Renaissance. The outcome of this crisis was gradual transfer to power from church to the state. The institution of monarchy was gathering more power and confidence that it had hitherto enjoyed.

**Dawn of Secularism.** Another significant feature of his times was the dawn of secularism. The weakness of papacy was bound to result in theocracy and so long as church remained in power there was no room for secularism. The spirit of renaissance resulted in secularism and indepenence of state from church. The church with the passage of time, became a voluntary organisation. They victory of state over the church was complete.

**Intellectual Reniaissance.** As far as common man was concerned it was a period of intellectual renaissance. He was gradually coming out from ignorance to knowledge, from faith to reason and from humiliation and complete subordination to reasoning and self understanding. By this time it had been discovered that the 'earth is round'. This was against common belief which had been preached by the church fathers that the earth was flat. The new discovery shook the faith of many from the church. Thus supremacy of Church and blind faith in it was weakened and shaken.

**Invention of Printing Press.** The invention of the printing press brought about a social revolution and brought together the persons of common ideology in all the corners of world and thus quickened the process of social and political integration. The process also tended to free human mind from the old bondages.

**Materialism.** The period of renaissance also brought individual instead of God, and this world instead of that world, to the front. In other words, the renaissance replaced spiritualism and brought materialism along with individualism. The entity of the individual came to the front.

Before Machiavelli put forth his political philosophy, the ideas of the middle ages were still prevailing and dominating world politics. The church was still firmly holding ground and the individual had no say in church affairs. Credit goes to Machiavelli, who laid the foundation of the modern political philosophy. For the first time he stressed on the need and necessity of absolutism of monarchs and pleaded the idea of the separation of religion from politics. His political philosophy based on secularism, as it was, also stood for individualism. He denounced the authority of church and like most of the Italians of his day, held that church was responsible for the present Italian degenerated state of affairs.

**Influences on Machiavelli.** Machiavelli was very much influenced by Aristotle and Marsiglio. It was from Aristotle that he learnt the idea of separation of ethics and politics. It was again from him that he picked up historical method of study. He borrowed from Aristotle the idea that the state was highest organisation of human beings. Like him he also divided State into Monarchy, Aristocracy and Democracy. Machiavelli was also influenced by Marsiglio in his political philosophy. It was from him that he derived the idea of secularism and also political utility of religion.

**Method of His Approach.** He was modern in the sense that unlike other political philosophers, he did not draw his conclusions from the past. On the other hand he based his political philosophies on what was happening in his own times. He, of course, followed historical method, as a supporting factor but did not take history and historical method as a source for arriving at his conclusions. As a modern political thinker, he made individual or human nature as the basis of his political philosophy.

As a modern political philosopher, we find his political philosophy as a universal ground work in power for all political philosophies. His political philosophies are not confined and are not meant for one state alone. No doubt he stood for a united and powerful Italy but his philosophy has mostly a universal character. He kept the state over and above everything else. He did not fail to advise the rulers to encourage and exaggerate public in security even by raising the spectre of external danger to the community. A. Hecker has said about Machiavelli that, "Power used to maintain the state is neither moral nor immoral : states should be judged not by the power but by what they define as their business once the enterprise has been solidly established."

**Product of His Times.** Machiavelli, though commonly known as a modern political philosopher, was only the product of his times. It was during his times that the changes were coming in the state. The renaissance was bringing about social, political and intellectual changes. The hold of religion was already losing its grip and church was giving way to state authority. Development of international trade had already brought trading class close to the monarchs and as such national resources were bound to be exploited. Feudalism was coming to an end and all along there was race and tendency to exalt the monarchs. Renaissance had brought man to the front and the individualism was getting its due place. If religion was losing ground that was due to its own evils which Reformation, subsequently brought to the front. In such circumstances Machiavelli was bound to write what he wrote. He did not go against the times in which he was living but on the other hand he moulded his philosophy in the spirit of his times. It is therefore very much right to say that Machiavelli was simply the product of his times.

## FIRST MODERN POLITICAL THINKER

"Machiavelli," according to Prof. Allen, "makes the first decisive break with the political thought of middle ages. He represents many new tendencies in his political ideas which have come to be regarded as a characteristic feature of the modern age." It is now universally acclaimed that modern political through begins with Machiavelli. He introduces a sect of new ideas which have been current ever since. He breaks away from the established line of thought of that time.

Let us now examine how he deviated from the political thought of middle ages and how he earned the title of first modern political thinker.

**1. Historical Method.** What was most original in the works of Machiavelli was his method of approaching the problem of politics. The true method in the science of politics was, in Machiavelli's opinion, the historical method. He was the first writer after Aristotle who made use of historical method to tackle political problems. Men had been, he believed, in all ages and places they seem as at present, had been influenced by the same motive, and had been called upon to solve the same problems with the same means. In his view only a study of the past can throw light on the present and the future. His method is thus one of generalisation from particular. To one who, like Machiavelli, takes men as they are and does not base his view upon what ought to be, the study of the past alone can be a guide to the future. But the past which Machiavelli studied in his own works, and from which he supposed himself to be drawing his conclusion, was almost exclusively the past of classical antiquity. It was Greece and particularly Rome that furnished him with political truth. "His work was as completely dis-severed (separated) from the long accepted political theories," writes Dunning, "as the contemporary work of Coloumbus was from the accepted system of geography.

Prof. Dunning holds the view that the method of Machiavelli was historical more in appearance then in reality. The actual source of his speculations was the interest he felt in the men and conditions of his time. Machiavelli did not really draw its conclusions from the past; they were mostly based on the observations of what was taking place in his own time. Of the circumstances of his own time he was a most accurate observer and a most acute analyst. This determined the method which he really depended upon. His conclusions were reached in empirically, and were then reinforced by appeals to history. To quote Dunning, he used 'Livy in the Discourses', rather for the purpose of sustaining, than for the purpose of discovering, principles. In the same spirit Sabine also remarks that "it is misleading to say that Machiavelli followed the historical method. He used history to support or illustrate a conclusion he had reached without reference to history. His methods, in so far as he had won, was observation guided by shrewdness and common sense." There seems to be much truth in the assertion. The conclusions of Machiavelli were not suggested by, and were not based on any historical research; they were mostly the outcome of a shrewd analysis of the actual behaviour of men with whom he came into contact in his official capacity.

**2. His Theory about the State.** He rejected the view held in the middle ages that the State or the political authority was of divine origin. According to Machiavelli the State is a natural phenomena and arises out of the play of natural forces. The Machiavellian State is in the completest sense and entirely secular thing. Not only has it no vital relation to the Church but it has also got no relation to God or to another supernatural power. According to Machiavelli the State needs religion only as an instrument for furthering its object. "In Machiavelli's views", writes Allen, "The State can be understood only in terms of human lusts and appetites and that the successful ruler must learn to control these forms.

**3. Nationalism.** Machiavelli was the first conscience writer who advocated nationalism. Machiavelli was the creator of the idea of a national State. Machiavelli perceived the advantage to a government having subjects similar in language, customs and habits of life. He was able to see clearly the rise of national States in his own age. He saw France and Spain solidly founded on what we should call a racial basis and attributed their strength party to that. Whatever may be the case, Allen writes, it remains true that from what he said or implied the concept of nationalism could easily be derived.

Machiavelli also shared with the modern age, his belief that a strong national State must expend. He defends national expansion on the ground that firstly, it is a means to keep off the minds of the subjects from sedition and secondly, it is the natural result of State's healthy disposition.

**4. Machiavelli's Denial of Divine Law.** Machiavelli does not believe in the cardinal tenet of Christian doctrine, that man is destined to a supernatural end. This does not mean that he confines man's end to merely material well-being. But these values which the recognizes over and above material well-being are all earthly and not heavenly ones. They are the values of greatness, power, and fame. Fame which will outlast his life is the only immortality of which Machiavelli thinks the individual to be capable.

Machiavelli believes that man has no supernatural end and hence there is no function to be performed by a Divine Law. The Philosopher of the middle ages (Aquinas) believed that man needed two types of laws because he was destined to two ends. They believed that Human law was needed for the welfare of the individual in this world and Divine Law was needed for the welfare of the individual in the next world.

The medieval theory had based the separation of powers upon this distinction of the two kinds of laws. The temporal ruler was the custodian of Human Law, the custodian of Divine Law was the Church; and, as these laws were distinct from one another, each with its separate purpose, it followed that these two authorities had each its independent sphere of action. Indeed, it followed not merely that the Church should be independent of the temporal power, but (since man's supernatural end was of more importance than his natural one) that it must be in a manner superior to the latter. Since Machiavelli does not recognize the distinction of these two laws he is led to deny any claim by the Church not merely to superiority but to independence of the State.

This does not mean that Machiavelli despises religion. Those who expect him to do so will be surprised to read the title of a chapter in his Discourses: "The importance of giving religion a prominent influence in a State, and how Italy was ruined because she failed in this respect through the conduct of the Church of Rome." Similarly, he says at the opening of the same chapter : "Princes and Republics who wish to maintain themselves free from corruption must above all things preserve the purity of all religious observances and treat them with proper reverence; for there is no greater indication of the ruin of a country than to see religion condemned."

**5. Denial of Natural Law.** Machiavelli abandoned the generally accepted idea of natural law and conceived law as a positive rule created by sovereign in the state and maintained by physical force. "The law of Nature", writes Dunning, "in which both ancient and medieval philosophy had placed the source of political science, perceive from Machiavelli scarcely the recognition of a passing allusion." The doctrine of natural law implies that there are certain eternal standards of right conduct of which the good man must conform. A man is virtuous only if he conforms to those standards. But Machiavelli judges the rightness of conduct by another standard.

He measures a man's 'virtue' by his ability to attain power and fame, and just as other moralists prescribe rules for the exercise of virtue, as they conceive it, so Machiavelli lays down rules for the exercise of 'virtue' as he conceives it. As they tell men how they may conform their conduct to the laws of right and wrong he tells them how they may direct their action to the ends of greatness and power Machiavelli's most famous book, 'The Prince,' consists mainly of such rules and counsels, addressed particularly to one in a position of political power; and this is what is popularly known as 'Machiavellianism.'

**6. Separation of Ethics from Politics.** The most distinctive feature of Machiavelli's theory is his separation of ethics from politics. He was the first realist in politics. He believed that the State should exist for its own sake, should aim at its own preservation and advantage, and should not be bound by the obligation that determine the action of private individuals. The main difference between

Machiavelli and the writers who preceded him was the attitude towards religion and morality.

Machiavelli separated politics from ethics, even to the point of pardon and scandal. For centuries, political thought had been a product of theology, and political issues had been confused with issues primarily religious in nature. Machiavelli subordinated moral principles to the necessity of political existence and welfare. The safety and the success of the State were made paramount, all other considerations were subordinated. "Machiavelli is in the fullest sense a student of practical politics and he seeks to determine the working of a real, not of ideal political life." (Dunning). "The essence of Machiavelli's Philosophy," writes Hearbshaw, "is the doctrine that end justifies the means." It implies the deliberate disassociation of politics from ethics. "The foremost among the ideas which the Florentine made prominent in political science was that of distinction between the standards of public end of private morality. (Dunning). "When the safety of one's country is absolutely at stake" writes Machiavelli in "The Discourses," "there need be no question what is just or unjust, merciful or cruel, praiseworthy or disgraceful and that course alone is to be taken which may save the country and maintain its liberty." It is well, according to Machiavelli, to appear to be merciful and honourable, humanise a religion and sincere and even to be all these so long as your mind is so framed that you can, when need arises, change to the contrary."

Thus Machiavelli formulated his political philosophy independently of ethics and theological influences. It is accurate to say that Machiavelli ends the medieval era and begins the modern era. His unprecedent position in political theory is presented in several different aspects in Machiavelli's thought. His tool, calculated cynicism, his frank and indistinguishing naturalism, his extreme individualism, his pragmatism, his devotion to classical antiquity, his rejection of religious sanctions in favour of philosophy and a hedonistic morality, in all these he is to a great extent characteristic of the modern mind." His naturally acute intelligence attracted the problems of politics and propounded solutions which in both method and results" writes Dunning, "were as distinct from those of the preceding twelve centuries as if those centuries had never existed."

## THEORY OF HUMAN MOTIVATION

As Allen puts it, "No writer, probably, has been so persistently used and abused or so little understood, as Machiavelli. From the beginning to the end of the sixteenth century rolled over him a chorus of denunciations, which continued through the seventeenth and eighteenth centuries. The misunderstanding of him was due partly to sheer ignorance of his writings. Few or none of those who, in the sixteenth century, denounced him has read his works or had read any of them but the misleading "Prince." He discussed human nature in the beginning of "The Prince." Machiavelli has given a dark picture of the human nature to such an extent that a reader starts thinking that the nature of human beings as depicted by Machiavelli is not less than that of animals. But this is partially true so far as Machiavelli is concerned. Prof. Jones has pointed out in his book "Masters of Political Thought" Volume II, that in his other book the "Discourses". Machiavelli has gone to the extent of saying that men are neither utterly wicked nor perfectly good. However, Machiavelli does not take pains to examine the above dictum of his. So the general impression about Machiavelli's concept of human nature is that human beings are selfish, ungrateful, fickle, wicked, deceitful, cowardly and avaracious.

Machiavelli's views regarding human nature as put forward in his book "Prince" are as follows:

1. According to Machiavelli, man is completely self-centred and egoistic. He always thinks in his own interest and always tries to promote his own interest. Man, he thought, cares for nothing but himself; he is rascally, mean, greedy, sensual creature, more ready to forgive the murder of his father than the seizure of his property; gratitude for him is but the hope of benefits to come and what he calls his love is but love of himself.

2. Human beings are wicked by nature. He is always ready to act against the interest of the community if he sees any benefits to himself from doing so. "Good is that which, in my own interest, I wish my neighbour to do; but my neighbour and I in our own interest, are always ready to do evil." Thus Machiavelli declared that all men are wicked.

3. Human beings are not only selfish but they are also aggressive. In the words of Sabine, "Human nature is, moreover, profoundly aggressive and acquisitive, men aim to keep what they have and to acquire more. Neither in power nor in possession is there any normal limit to human desires, while both power and possessions are always in fact limited by natural scarcity. Accordingly, men are always in a condition of strife and competition which threatens an open anarchy unless checked by the ruthless force of the State."

4. Machiavelli frequently remarks that men are, in general, bad, and that the wise ruler must construct his forces on ths presumption. According to him, men love property even more than his kith and kin. Hence his cynical remark that a man more readily forgives the murder of his father than the confiscation of his patrimony. The prudent ruler may kill but he will not plunder.

5. Man wills government and the State for his own profit and protection. He is a timid creature and a creature of habit. He dislikes what he is not to end seeks the lines of least resistance. He tends to follow the well-beaten tracks. It is a fact of great importance, practically, that it is generally easier and safer to conform than to rebel.

6. Human beings are insatiable by nature. The appetite of man is for ever insatiable. By nature he desires all things, but fate allots him a little. Man is eternally desirous and eternally unsatisfied, raging at the present extolling the past, hoping in the future. No human community, no human government, nay more than any single human being, is ever content with its position. Hence arises a constant effort after aggradisement and dominate in which leads, sooner or later, to ruin. Most men are stupid and irrational. Men are often deceived by an illusive good desire, which ultimately ruins them.

7. Men's conduct is primarily determined by two motives-first there is a "Love of Novelty, which manifests itself equally in those who are well off and, in those who are not. For... and with truth, men get tired of prosperity, just as they are afflicted by the reverse. This love of change then so to speak, opens the way to every one who takes to lead any innovation in any country. If he is a stranger they run after him; if he is of the country they surround him, increase his

influence, and favour him in every way, so that, whatever his mode of proceeding and conduct may be, he will succeed in making rapid progress. In the second place namely, love and fear; so that he who makes himself beloved will have as much influence as he who makes himself feared, although generally he who makes himself feared will be more readily followed and obeyed than he who makes himself beloved."

8. Men also desire liberty. That is they desire to be independent of others. They want to be free to lead their own idependent life. The only sure and certain way to be independent is to make others dependent. In other words, it means that men want to dominate. And therefore strife between individuals is inevitable.

9. Men are also ambitious by nature. Machiavelli holds that so powerful is this instinct in the hearts of men that men desire everything but are unable to attain it ; desire being thus always greater than the faculty of acquiring, discontent with what they have and dissatisfaction with themselves result from it. This causes the changes in their fortune; for as some men desire to have more, whilst others fear to lose what they have ; enimities and war are the consequences.

According to Prof. Maxey, "The average man'a conception of Machiavellism would probably be summed up in such well-known abhorism as might make right, the end justifies the means, necessity knows no law.

Machiavelli's views regarding morality, religion and politics are essentially based on his views regarding human nature. His views regarding human nature account for his ideas regarding all political phenomena. His views regarding human nature is a striking resemblance to those of Hobbes. He looked upon man as a purely selfish being and as never actuated by social impulses. In fact his judgment on the nature of man is even more cynical than that of Hobbes.

Generally speaking, he says, "Men are ungrateful, fickle, deceitful, cowardly and avaricious." From this he draws the conclusion that a monarch should aim rather to be feared than to be loved, "Whether is it better to be loved than feared or feared than loved? It may be answered that one should wish to be both, but, because, it is difficult to unite them in one person, it is much safer to be feared than loved, of the two either must be dispensed with...Nevertheless a prince ought to inspire fear in such a way that, if he does not win love, he avoids hatred ; because he can endure very well being feared when he is not hated, which will always be as long as he abstains from property of his citizens." "Love" he argues "implies a bond of obligation which men, being essentially selfish, break on every occasion where their own interest demands it, while fear, for the same reason, holds them indefinitely. Moreover, since man is fickle and deceitful he who wishes to deceive will always find some one to be deceived. Men judge others by their appearance and this gives an opportunity to the rulers to deceive the people. Moreover, according to Machiavelli, man by nature is not good, he is vicious by nature. To quote Machiavelli himself, "whenever a choice is open to them and they are to do as they like, everything is immediately filled with confusion and disorder. Men are more prone to evil than to good. As is shown by all who discuss civil government, and by the abundance of examples in every history, whoever organised a State or lays down laws in it, must necessarily assume that all men are bad and they will follow the wickedness of their own hearts whenever they have free opportunity to do so."

What makes them bad and depraved is their innate selfishness and aggressiveness. Every one wants to have the best things for himself and to have as much of them as possible. And further, if human nature remains unchanged from age to age, it necessarily follows that it can not be depended upon to reform itself. It is not possible for the State to reform it by education as Plato and Aristotle hoped, or by improvement in the social and economic institutions as the communists think.

According to Machiavelli, the prince should try to combine in himself the qualities of a lion and a fox. Like a lion he should try to inspire fear in others and lie a fox he should be cunning. It is even more important for a prince to be cunning than to be merely strong. A cunning person can easily deceive a simple-minded strong person.

In his work "The Discourses", Machiavellis follows polybius in throwing to the back ground the Aristotelian view of the social nature of man. According to him society originated not because man is social but has origin in a calculating self-interest on the part of the individual. Men have by nature endless desires and the craving for additional satisfaction of them is the main spring of all human actions. One of the greatest desires on the part of the man is a desire for private property. In 'The Prince' Machiavelli declares that "Men more readily forget the death of their father, than the loss of a patrimony." He, therefore, came to the conclusion that the prince may better pass a sentence of death on a criminal rather than confiscate his property.

Thus his views on human nature were thoroughly materialistic and his materialistic individualism is made the explanation of love of independence and self-government. Few individuals are actuated by the desire for independence for the sake of mere power. The republican government is desirable because it gives a chance of material gain to the majority of the people. Under monarchy, the prince absorbs all the property himself and independence is desired because wealth multiplies most in those days which are not subject to others.

**Machiavelli on Human Nature (Universal Egoism).** We have already discussed in some detail Machiavelli's idea about human nature. Briefly speaking Machiavelli like Hobbes, believed that human beings were essentially selfish and the only uniting factor in these selfish human beings was his desire for security. That states could only develop and survive if they exploited this weakness of the human beings. The subjects join the state because they find themselves insecure without the effective protection of the state. In addition to this, man has a tendency to acquire and to protect what has already been acquired by him. The desire is bound to result in anarchy, if it is not checked by the authority of a strong government. He, however, frequently remarks that the people in general are bad, and that the wise ruler will formulate his policies on this assumption. While awarding punishments, the state must prefer patrimony to murder.

**Criticism.** But his conception or human nature is not very much realistic because:

(i) The very basic fact that man is so selfish is not an acceptable proposition.

(ii) While defining human nature he has not taken universal but only the Italian society into consideration and that too of his times which was not a representative society in any way.

(iii) The people are not liable to easily forget the loss of their patrimony. He has also pleaded that the struggle for acquiring more and more property was human weakness and that the state should take advantage of this human weakness but who does not know that the struggle is the very essence of life and indication of a healthy society without which a society was bound to be stagnant and without any progress and development.

(iv) In addition to this, he believed that the people could easily forget their patrimony but not the loss of property–a proposition which is something cynical. No doubt people love their property but they have equally deep regard, love and affection for the patrimony.

(v) Machiavelli has also been criticised for his taking for granted certain notions about government but has failed to develop them because he could not reconcile them with his philosophy that 'man is wicked by nature'. Had he developed them he would have himself realised hollowness of his philosophy and in fact would have miserably failed to build super-structure. "Machiavelli constantly takes his conception of government for granted, though he nowhere develops it into a general psychological theory of behaviour. Machiavelli has taken for granted that man by nature is bad and selfish but who can deny that man has no inherited qualities of goodness and/or badness but he has certain impluses alone which become good or bad according to circumstances.

(vi) Another great fault of Machiavelli is that he has tried to build, rather preserve has state in an environment of fear or prohibition which was bound to react unfavourably on moral progress of the state. Doubtlessly, without high moral standard it is neither easy nor desirable and mostly impossible to have either the preservation or the expansion of the state and thus his whole super-structure of state falls down.

(vii) Then again if fear is human nature and a factor responsible for bringing him to state then what will happen of a man and state if this fear goes away even temporarily. Machiavelli has not elucidated the point. In this sense one then must think Aristotle better than Machiavelli when he says that state exists for the sake of the life and continues for the sake of good life.

**Machiavelli on Ethics and Religion.** Before him medieval political philosophers believed that the religion was the basis of the state. They felt that development of state could only be judged by the religious progress which it made. Throughout middle ages it was felt that state was only a department of the church and as such church fathers and papists assumed definite supremacy over state affairs. In fact, they pleaded that as soul had supremacy over the body so the church enjoyed supreme position as compared with the state. They could not think that state could function without the sanction of the church authortity. Aristotle tried to differentiate between the state and church functions but his work was undone in middle ages by Conciliar Movement. It goes to the credit of Machiavelli that he completely divorced religion from politics and separated them completely from each other. In fact he tried to subordinate religion to the state but at the same time agreed that morality had its own limited place in society which must be preserved and exploited. He thus became not immoral but unmoral. Since he did not bother about the morality of means for achieving the ends, he can be called the founder of utilitarian ethics. He also differentiated between public and private morality and assigned the former a preferential place and position over the latter. Patriotism is the only end of a good citizen.

**Machiavelli on Forms of Government.** Machiavelli, like Aristotle, has classified the governments into normal and perverted forms. In its normal form the government was monarchy, aristocracy and limited democracy or constitutional democracy while correspondingly perverted forms being tyranny, oligarchy and democracy. He, however, agreed with Polybius and Cicero that only a mixed form of government was the best or ideal attainable one. As a realist he felt that in a state there should be close rèlationship between economic development and political stability. According to him, the stability of a government depended on the economic development of its subjects. He liked rule of many on elected basis rather than rule of one on hereditary basis. He had definite preference for elected elements over hereditary system. He argued that the people no doubt were unable to understand intricate and complicated policy matters but their sharing of government in ordinary affairs was bound to bring stability to the state. He believed in this suppression and extripation of nobility as their interests were against the monarchy and middle classes. He also believed that training and equipping of a citizen army was the primary need of a nation and as such for a successful ruler it was most essential to know the art of war. He pleaded for compulsory military training for all able bodied persons.

**Machiavelli on Aggrendisement.** Machiavelli very strongly believed in the dictum that the state should either 'expand or expire.' He however, held the view that the state must go on expanding itself both in absolute monarchy or republic. From expansion he understood not blending of organisation but annexation of states to be dominated and governed by one Prince. He preached the use of arms for the purpose of achieving successful expansionist policy. He also pleaded that a Prince should not depend on the policy of taxation because that was not a dependable source of income but he should believe in royal plundering. A successful 'Prince' ought to believe in outward shows for catching the imagination of his subjects as well as the subjects of other states. This outward show will certainly influence all other subjects and create praise for his state in the minds of others.

## THEORY FOR REVOLUTION

Machiavelli is one of the most misunderstood or abused thinkers in the history of Political Thought. He is denounced for certain views which are wrongly alleged to have originated from his brain. This misunderstanding of Machiavelli arises due to the little knowledge that his critics possess about him. Very few people have read complete works of Machiavelli. They know him only by his misleading book the "Prince." But in order to understand his thought in totality and to do justice of Machiavelli, one must not lose sight of ideas expressed in his other Book "Discourses." Wrong inferences are drawn by his critics because the "Prince" bereft of "Discourses" is considered to be the representative of his political thought. A keen and disinterested student of Political Thought will not do this. He will study his ideas expressed in the "Prince" in conjunction with those expressed in the "Discourses." If one were to know Machiavelli only by the "Prince" one would regard him as the protagonist of the Monarchical or Despotic or Arbitrary form of government. If, on the other hand, one were to judge him only by his ideas expressed in the "Discourses" one would regard him, as the champion of the Republican or Democratic form of government. Some critics would try to find a contradiction in the two views. But actually there is no such contradiction. Only what is required is to understand his ideas in the proper context and perspective. The "Prince" has to be interpreted in the light thrown by the "Discourses".

He wrote his more famous books the "Prince" and the "Discourses" more or less at the same time. The subject-matter of both the books, as Sabine points out is the same *i.e.* "the causes of the rise and decline of states and the means by which statesmen can make them permanent." Nevertheless there is a difference in the sense that the "Prince" deals mainly with monarchy or absolute government and the "Discourses" mainly with the expansion of the Roman Republic. The difference is on account of emphasis on the Monarchy in the "Prince" and on the Republic in the "Discourses". Though the qualities for which Machiavelli is especially known are common in both the books–such as indifference to the use of immoral means for political purposes and the belief that government depends largely on force and craft, yet the "Prince" lacks that genuine enthusiasm for popular government which is predominantly apparent from even a casual reading of the "Discourses."

In the "Discourses" he makes a distinction between the Free States and Unfree States. Free states are those in which people possess high degree of what Machiavelli calls "Virtue". By "virtue" in this context Machiavelli means a vigour in the People, public-spirit, law abidingness, trustworthiness in public duties. If the people possess the "virtue", as defined above, the state is healthy and free. The most glaring examples of a free or healthy or vigorous state which Machiavelli gives is that of ancient Roman Republic in which people possessed the "virtue" and in their share came the right to participate partly in the affairs of the state. To such type of state Machiavelli gives the name of "Republic". To the surprise of many of his bitter critics, he regards the Republic the "best form of government". He has sufficient reasons for giving preference of "Rupublic" to other forms of government including "Princedom" or Dictatorship or Despotism. Machiavelli argued elaborately and at length in the "Discourses" to show that Republic or popular government is normally in most respects superior and in a few inferior to a "Princedom". According to him "the Mass is wiser and more constant than a prince.....I affirm that a people is more prudent, more stable and of better judgment than a Prince. Not without reason is the voice of a people likened to the voice of God." The capacity of judging of things is evidenced by the fact that they decide definitely in favour of the better when they hear two orators of equal talents advocating different measures. In the matter of election of or judging the performance of a Magistrate their view is sounder than that of a Prince. Moreover, the self governing people make much more rapid progress than those ruled by a Prince. He said explicitly that government is more stable whether is shared by many. He preferred election of heredity so far as made of selection of rulers is conceived. "Despite the cynicism of Machiavelli's political judgment there is no mistaking his esteem for the liberal and lawful government." The study of "Discourses" leads us to conclude that Machiavelli conceived of "Popular" government as a character of the healthiest, most vigorous and stable type of state.

Machiavelli deals with "Princedom" both in the "Discourses" and the "Prince." In the "Discourses" he denounces it and in the "Prince" he eulogises it. But as we have discussed above, these two apparently self-contradictory views must be understood in their proper context. There should not be any doubt about this view of Machiavelli, that "Republic" was the best form of government. In the just contrast to this "Princedom" or arbitrary government was, according to him, the worst form of government. This form of government is found among the people who do not possess virtue at all and have become diseased. It is to be found among those people who lack law-abidingness. Probity trustworthiness, loyalty to the conutry and all other qualities go into make good citizens. The more people lack "Virtue", the more corrupt they are. So the difference between Despotic government and Democratic government is difference of the absence and presence respectively of probity, spontaneous obedience of law on the part of citizens, and civic virtue. In a Republic citizens conform to the laws of the state spontaneously and in Despotism by compulsion or force. Republic is a form of constitution which not every people is qualified to bear since a high degree of "Virtue" in the people is needed in acts to sustain it. This was theoretical part of the issue which was dealt within the "Discourses." But when he comes to the practical aspect, which he discusses in the "Prince" he finds that his contemporary Italian people were not fit for Republican form of constitution simply because at that time they lacked "Virtue". The Italian society at that time had become a prey to the worst possible moral degeneration and institutional decay. They had forfeited all the qualities of a good citizen and to that extent they had become corrupt. Machiavelli had to deal with an Italy in which the restraints of religion, of respect for law, even the belief in moral obligation seemed almost to have perished. He had to suggest the remedy for the ills of the diseased body politic of Italy. In his days according to him men had so far degenerated that Republics were impossible; if they were attempted they turned out to be miserable failures. The people had become so lawless that drastic measures were required to reduce them to order. Those drastic measures could only be taken by a dictator; a despot, a prince with absolute powers in his hands. According to Machiavelli, in his time, "the only really feasible government is the Princedom ruled by a single individual with an iron hand." In Machiavelli's own words, "The only way to establish any kind of order there is to be found a monarchical government; or where the body of the people is so thoroughly corrupt that the laws are powerless for restraint, it becomes necessary to establish some superior power which, with a royal hand, and with full and absolute powers, may put a curb upon the excessive ambition and corruption of the powerful."

"Again and again Machiavelli returns to the theme of modern degeneracy as opposed to ancient virtue and probity and to be thesis that times and the customs require desperate measures." For making a stop-gap arrangement, for crushing the anti-social elements, the Dictatorship was the only most appropriate type of government. Historically speaking manarchies are easier to establish than Republic and usually represent the first stage of political development. A Republican government is not possible until conditions have become settled, the people united and secure, and habits of adjustment fixed by education and experience. Hence Republican government must follow, not precede, monarchical government. Hence according to Machiavelli for two specific purposes of founding a new state and reforming a corrupt state, Despotic government is the most suitable. But this cannot be a permanent system of government, it should be only a temporary state of affairs. Once founded a state can be made permanent only by a Republican form in which people get some share in the conduct of business of government and their laws, rights and property are given due respect. Sabine has summed it up beautifully; "Despotic violence is powerful political medicine; needed in corrupt states and for special contingencies in all states, but still poison which must be used with the greatest caution."

But Machiavelli certainly cannot be described as a royalist or a monarchist if by these terms we mean to describe one who holds that the rule of a single individual is the best. On the contrary he is of the definite view as we have discussed above, that people as a whole rule better than a single individual. Theoretically speaking he was an ardent champion of the Republican form of government, particularly of the type of Ancient Roman Republic. But because the people had become so bad Republic could not be established and hence he recommended Despotism. Jones has beautifully simplified this issue : "Despite his ardent republicanism Machiavelli does not appear to find these conclusions particularly distressing. Here his cynical realism and prudent selfseeking come to the top.

## THOMAS HOBBES

In the history of political thought, Hobbes was the first English philosopher who produced a comprehensive work on political philosophy. He was born in the spring of 1588 at Malmesbury. "Hobbes tells us in his own autobiography that in the year of the Spanish Armada his mother gave birth to twins—himself and fear." We are told by John Aubrey, not observant English biographer of Hobbes, that the extraordinary timorousness which marked Hobbes' entire life, was due to the circumstances in which he was born but how far Hobbes's biographer is correct is a matter of doubt. Because, as Prof. Jones says that, "certainly Hobbes's conduct in life did not show him to be a fearsome as he would have us (because it corresponded with his theory of human nature) believe him to be.

Hobbes was also the prey what is commonly known as a broken home. He was the second son of an undistinguished vicar of westport, near Malmesbury, who deserted his wife and children when Hobbes was still a child. Hobbes' biographer, Aubrey says, "In his youth, unhealthy, of an ill—yellowish complexion—and trod both his shoes the same way. From 40 he grew healthier.... He was witty and humorous.... Besides his daily walking he did twice or thrice a year play at terms (at 75 he did it). Hobbes is interesting not only as a political theorist but as a person also.

Hobbes received his early education in Wiltshire, (a place in Malmesbury), where he was born. After completing his early education, he joined the Oxford. He was 15 at that time. He graduated at the age of 19. Hobbes was not at all satisfied with the university education and found it barren and profitless. In the Leviathan he condemned universities for their frequency of insignificant speech and he spent most of his time in the shops of book sellers and stationers.

On leaving Oxford, in 1608, Hobbes took up the position as a tutor to the heir of William Cavendish, who later on became the first Earl of Devonshire. This contact with such a powerful and distinguished family lasted for whole of his life and brought him into contact with most important personalities of the period like Ben Jonson, Lord Bacon, Clarendon, Galileo, etc. According to Prof. Jones "his life-long connection with this powerful and distinguished family was certainly one of the greatest influences on his subsequent career....without the stimulus and the opportunities which this connection gave him, Hobbes would have died another "mute, in glorious Milton." In 1610 he travelled in Europe where he was impressed by the revolt against scholasticism. Hobbes was addicted to mathematics but the was over 40 years old before he looked on Geometry.

At the time when the civil war broke out in England, Hobbes had to fly to France because he had seen the fate of Laud and Stafford, the two leading supporters of royal absolutism. In Paris he joined the royalist group. He remained there for eleven years. It was this period in which he wrote his greatest book, *The Leviathan*, published in (1651). But the contents of the book brought him the disfavour of the royalists. It also attacked the papacy. All this made it an impossible task for Hobbes to stay more in France. He secretly fled to England and reached there towards the close of 1651.

When, in 1660, monarchy was restored in England, Hobbes was once more received at the royal court by Charles, who would witically say, when saw Hobbes appearing. "Here comes the bear to be baited". Hobbes very quickly won the favour of king Charles and was awarded a very pension. But this state of affairs did not last long. His political activity was totally banned. He spent last twenty years of his life in writing books on history, physics, law and the classical literature. "When he died on December 4, 1679, at the age of ninety-one, he left for the world, a tremendous body of literary works. At an advanced age of eighty-five he translated Iliad and the Odyssey because as he observed "I had nothing else to do, why publish it? Because I thought it might take off my adversaries from showing their folly upon my more serious writing and set them upon my verses to show their wisdom."

He formed the link between the Renaissance and the Restoration; travelled on the continent, sojourned in France from (1640 to 1651), where he made the acquaintance of Father Marsene and set to Descartes his objections to the Meditations. His doctrines attracted the attention of the Roman Catholic Clergy and he returned to England where he succeeded, not without difficulty in being left alone. After 1660 he owned much to the favour of Charles II. The last period of his life was spent in controversy and in literary works such as the translation of two above mentioned works.

**His Writings.** Hobbes wrote several treatises on history, physics, law, etc. The following were his chief works concerning politics, of which the first three were of great importance:

1. De Corpore (1655);
2. De Cive (1642);
3. Leviathan (1651);
4. De Homine (1659);
5. Two essays: Human Nature and De Corpore Politico (1640);
6. Thucydides (1628);
7. Elements of Law (1650); "He has eloquence, the charm of wit, the decisiveness of confidence and the sentitiousness of a mind made up; he is capable of urbanity and of savage irony".

**Contemporary Political Life in Hobbesian Period.** Hobbes saw many ups and downs in the political history of England during his long but valuable life of ninety-one years. He saw the most exciting period of English history—the period of English Revolution. He was a young boy of fifteen when James I came to the throne of England and advocated the theory of Divine Right of Kings, ignoring Parliament altogether. James I was followed by his son and successor Charles I. He was less stupid than his father. England's financial condition was going from bad to worse due to costly wars in which the country was involved. The whole country had fallen into a wretched condition. In 1642, the conflict between Parliament and King started and lasted till 1688, the year in which William of Orange ascended the throne of England. A constitutional monarchy was established in the country. During the first phase of the conflict between King and Parliament nothing important happened and this state of affairs continued till the appearance of Oliver Cromwell. Charles I was murdered, and the Protectorate under Oliver was established. But England could not breathe long the fresh air of republican government; and in 1660 monarchy was restored under Charles II. Hobbes witnessed the whole dream which profoundly influenced his political thought. Charles I was followed by his son and Charles II, and who in turn, was succeed by James II. Finally in 1688, under Prince William of Orange and his wife Mary, England adopted constitutional monarchy.

**Influences.** In the words of Prof. Jones, Hobbes "must have had in mind the scholastic logic and the Aristotelian science, to which he was then subjected when, years later, in the Leviathan, he condemned universities for what they called their `frequency of insignificant speech".

## MODERN POLITICAL PHILOSOPHY

Conflicting opinions have been expressed by scholars about the rank of Hobbes among political doctrines. One extreme view is that of Vaughan who remarked, "So far as the vital development of political thought is concerned, Leviathan has remained and deserves to remain without influence and without fruit fantastic hybrid, incapable of propagating its kind."

A little milder than the above is the view of Murray that "Hobbes's biographer could only find a solitary supporter, while his assailants were countless." The other extreme view is that of Sabine who remarked, "Hobbes was probably the greatest writer on political philosophy that the English-speaking people have produced." Prof. Oakeshott says that "the Leviathan is the greatest, perhaps the sole, masterpiece of political philosophy in the English language." Dunning declares that, "His work placed him at once in the front rank of political thinkers and his theory became from the moment of its appearance the centre of animated controversy and enormous influence throughout western Europe."

It seems very difficult to reconcile the high esteem in which Leviathan is held by Sabine and Oakeshott with Vaughan's condemnation of it. One and the same book cannot be regarded as the greatest masterpiece of political philosophy in the English language and a fantastic hybrid which has remained and deserves to remain without influence and without fruit.

Hobbes' philosophy has been criticised on the following grounds:

1. Firstly, it is very much correct at Leviathan met with little favourable response on its obligation; its materialism, atheism and despotism were assailed on all sides. Murray has also remarked that Hobbes' biographer could only find a solitary supporter, while his assailaints were numerous. Henry More, Cudworth, Cumberland and philosophers like Filmer bitterly criticised the doctrine of Hobbes.
2. Secondly, critics from Spinoza onwards (Vaughan) have pointed out that it is impossible for the monster of Hobbes State of nature ever to become law abiding and docile citizen of the social contract.

   In a nut-shell, Vaughan has pointed out how could there be an over-night change in the human nature at the time of entering into the contract and the formation of the State.
3. Another point of criticism against Hobbes' philosophy, according to Vaughan is, Hobbes has tried to make us believe that the sole bond of union among the individuals is a common terror, the fear of relapsing into the State of nature. In other words there is no bond at all. The only cement is the sovereign's word. It is due to the latter's fear that the members remain in commonwealth.
4. Fourthly, according to Vaughan, Hobbes theory is pernicious in the sense that it leads to despotism pure and simple. It does not leave any scope for the individuals to offer any resistance against the tyrannical rule of almighty Leviathan. The whole population is reduced to slavery.
5. Vaughan is of the opinion that Hobbes' personal predilections and prejudice determine the shape, his political philosophy was to take. Being a tutor of the royal family, all his inclinations forced him to take the side of the king in the

Civil War. He was out to defend the royal absolutism, throw a very ingenious scheme.

6. Vaughan is of the opinion that Hobbes had no immediate following. The next political thinker of some importance was John Locke who criticised him on every point. Thus, Vaughan concludes that his ideas are not fruitful and have no progency.

**1. Idea of Sovereignty.** Among the most notable omissions of Greek philosophy is the absence of any clear attempt to define the nature of sovereignty, to determine its seat or settle the ultimate sanction on which it rests. Its existence was indeed implied in Plato's and Aristotle's conception of politics as the 'architectonic science' of the State as the ultimate authority for controlling and harmonizing all diverse energies of its members. But no effort was made either to fix the place where this power resides, or to define its limits, or to determine precisely what it is that relies the community to obey it. Hints and fragments of answers to most or all, of these questions—especially the last—are to be found scattered about their writings.

It is within the Roman jurists that the idea of sovereignty first takes definite shape, in the doctrine of majestas. But with these writers the idea was inevitably so closely inter-woven with that of personal allegiance to an individual they were, moreover, so completely free from any speculated impulse-that we owe to them little more than the coming of a name, the invention of an apt term, round which might be crystallised the conceptions already dimly recognised by the Greek philosophers and eventually to be defined whichever-increasing clearness, by the course of history and the efforts of subsequent thinkers to interpret it.

So the matter virtually rested until the coming of Hobbes. The idea of sovereignty which he propounded is, no doubt utterly inadmissible. When pressed to its logical conclusion it is, in fact, manifestly self-destructive. For, by reducing the whole herd to slavery, he has left no State or the sovereign to govern. By striking out one term of the relation, he has robbed the other of all intelligible meaning. Yet, in spite of his and other perversions, he must take the credit of being the first to see that the idea of sovereignty lie at the very root of the whole theory of the State; and the first to realise the necessity of fixing precisely where it lies and what are its functions and limits. His solution of the three later points may have been pernicious and impossible. But the first step towards a satisfactory solution of the problem was to perceive that it was there, and that an answer to it must be found.

**2. Separation of Politics from Moral.** Hobbes was the pioneer in attempting to divorce politics from moral. Against this claim two objections—the one historical and the other philosophical-might possibly be lodged. Historically it might be argued that the honour is such it is to be reckoned, belongs rather to Machiavelli. And philosophically that what Hobbes did was rather to bring moral down to the level of politics than to mark out the frontiers between them.

The former of these objections rest upon an evident confusion. The question is not, who was the first to divorce politics from moral in the field of practice? If that were all, no questions could be more futile. The innovation is as old as the world. It goes back, doubtless as far as Nimrod, or Cain, the first recorded builder of a city. It has been followed by every monarch and every republic upon record. And all that Machiavelli did was to reduce the time honoured practice to systematic and illustrate it by examples profusely furnished by the Pope and princes of his time. Of any speculation theory—and it is that alone which is here in question, he was entirely innocent. In Hobbes we have at least a stubborn attempt to break the whole political life of man from first to last, upon nothing but self-interest; to admit none but self-regarding motives into the speculative origin and subsequent maintenance of the State. The sole bond of union between the members of Leviathan is a common terror, the fear of relapsing into the State of nature. Or to speak more correctly between one member and another there is no bond at all. The only cement provided is that which binds each of them, singly and separately, by shere terror to the tyrant who stands above them all. On his theory, the moral, no less than the political, life of man is governed solely by utilitarians—which, on his interpretations means purely selfish motives.. and that no doubt is enough to distinguish him from the idealist who admit disinterested motive in matter of personal conduct but steadfastly denying their legitimacy and even their very existence, in matter of State, who are idealist in the region of ethics but purely materialistic in that of politics.

But there are certain other writer who do not agree with Vaughan that Hobbes has made only two important contributions to political thought. He has also made contribution to political thought in other spheres. According to Dunning, Hobbes is the first Englishman to present a system of political philosophy that can stand among the great systems of history. His work placed him at once in the front rank of political thinkers and his theory became from the moment of its appearance the centre of animated controversy and enormous influence throughout western Europe. So skilfully did he blend all the most conspicuous of concepts of current political thought in his system and adapt them to his ends, that philosophers of all schools were forced to a recognition and discussion of his doctrine, whether by way of approval or by way of condemnation.

**1. Views of Human Nature.** According to Dunning, "His dogma that man is by nature unsocial and the enemy of his kind was in flat contradiction of the Aristotelian dogma which had been the accepted foundation of social and political science for centuries."

**2. His View of State as Machine.** According to Wayper, even if Hobbes makes Leviathan all powerful, he never forgets that it is something artificial. The State, he teaches, is a machine, an artefact, a contrivance of man. His very use of the contract is important here. Once men viewed the State as something made by themselves, they may think that they can build something other and better than Leviathan.

**3. His Individualism.** Thirdly, according to WAYPER, the Leviathan is not merely a forceful enunciation of the doctrine of Sovereignty and of the machine view of the State, it is also a powerful statement of Individualism Hobbes does not let us forget that the State exists to serve man's needs and that its moral authority derives from the consent of the governed. Hobbes is no liberal or democrat, but he is an individualist, not because he believes in the sanctity of individual man, but because for him the world is and must always be made up of individuals. For him there is no such thing as the people, and no common will, no general will, no common good exists. Nor does Leviathan feed upon individuals.

**4.** Hobbes was the first thinker to conceive of a State in whose creation God did not have direct or indirect hand. Prior to him, except Machiavelli, all thinkers believed in the divine interference in the affairs of the State. He removed the doubt from the mind of human beings that there is some mystery in regard to the State. He was perhaps the first thinker who advocated that State is not the creation of God but it is the result of human actions.

**5. Utilitarian.** Fifthly, Hobbes is the first modern thinker to view the State as the conciliator of interests. In this he is the forerunner of the utilitarians. It is no accident that Jeremy Bentham borrowed heavily from him here just as he did from Hobbes's ideas on Felicity. Succeeding ages have usually disagreed with him, but it is no exaggeration to say that they have found in him a mine well worth their while to work for the richness of the ore that it yields.

**6.** The most important contribution of Hobbes is his scientific method. This method was based on the presumption that road to knowledge lies through reason. The scientific method was logical, rational, derivative, deductive and geometrical. He firmly believed that all human ideas and social phenomena were derived from the moving particles.

**7.** Hobbes is also regarded as the father of the concept of empiricism. According to him, all human faculties are derived from sensation. Maxey remarks that he is the father of modern behaviourism. Hume learnt his empiricism from Hobbes.

**8.** Another important contribution of Hobbes to political thought was his conception of positive law. The concept of positive law was the brain child of Hobbes. Maxey has rightly pointed out that "by repudiating the classical doctrine of the law of nature and making clear that only man made law can be effective in human affairs Hobbes did much to pay the way for Bentham and the great movement for scientific legislation of which he was the guiding genius."

**9.** One of the most important contribution of Hobbes is his theory of Fictitious corporation. According to Sabine, "Consequently, to say that a body of men acts collectively really means that some individual acts in the name of the whole group as its accredited agent or representative. Unless there is such an agent the body has no collective existence... it is union which makes a corporation and union means the submission of the will of all to the will of one.

**10.** According to Prof. Oakeshott, Hobbes was the creator of a tradition in the history of political thought the tradition of Will and Artifice.

## NATURAL RIGHTS NATURAL LAW

Many of Hobbes's 'contemporaries, especially those with a liberal tinge in their political speculation, were perpetually talking about natural rights and natural laws. Generally, these two concepts were held to be identical. Hobbes was careful to distinguish between two ideas, though he accepted the validity of both.

In a State of Nature man has indeed natural rights. Natural right, Hobbes declared, signifies simply the liberty possessed by every man of doing what seems best for the prereservation of his existence. "Liberty" here means the absence of external impediments. Natural right allows him to do anything he pleases as long as he can "get away with it." He has a perfect right to murder or steal if he can do so successfully, for he is as yet bound by no law prohibiting these actions. Men would, Hobbes is sure, do anything to get out of this desperate position in which they find themselves. They can, he believes, get out of it because they are creatures of passion and imagination, reason and will. Passion and imagination teach them 'the fear of death' and 'desire of such things as are necessary to commodious living; and a hope by their industry to obtain them" Reason teaches them to obey Natural Laws.

The Laws of Nature, according to Hobbes, are nothing but the dictates of reason. The Laws of Nature are a sort of restrictions on the individuals not to exercise their natural rights. In other words, Natural Law implies primarily restraint rather than liberty. It designates a rule, found out by reason, forbidding any act or omission that is unfavourable to preservation. By right of Nature, every man has a claim to whatever will satisfy any of his desires. By the law of Nature he is obliged to renounce some part of his claim for the mere certain realisation of the rest.

In. Hobbes's words, "A Law of Nature (Lex Naturalis) is a precept, or general Rule, found out by reason, by which a man is forbidden to do that, which is destructive of his life, or taken away the means of preserving the same; and to omit, that, by which he thinketh it may be best preserved. For though they that speak of this subject, use to confound Jus, and Lex, Right and Law; yet they ought to be distinguished; because Right, consisteth in liberty to do, or to forbear; whereas law, determineth, and bindeth to one of them; so that Law, and Right, differ as much, as obligation and liberty."

"To Hobbes the equal natural rights of men are responsible for making the State of Nature a State of war, against each other. On the other hand, the laws of Nature are the general principles dictated by reason. If a man follows these general principles he can escape from the anarchy of the State of Nature and can easily achieve the goal of self-preservation fully in a civil society.

Hobbes enunciates as many as 19 Laws of Nature that concern the doctrine of civil society. Of these nineteen laws, following are the most important:

1. The first and most fundamental of these laws, the one from which all the others follow, is, "Seek to obtain and preserve peace." The State of Nature is a State of war, but in this State of war everyone suffers. Even the strong and able man is never safe from the attack of his enemies. At any moment the is liable to be caught in a trap, or be slain by the artifice of a weaker man, just as Goliath, the strong, was slain by David, the weak.

2. The second law is, "In order to secure peace, each man must be willing, when all other men are equally willing, to lay down his right to all things, and must be content with so much liberty against other men as he would allow other men against himself." Peace is impossible as long as each man preserves his natural right to do and to take what he pleases. For a man to give up his natural rights, however, if

all other men were to retain theirs, would be ridiculous. It would be tantamount to committing suicide. But if all were willing to forgo the right to seize forcibly what they please, in the long run all would work out to the advantage of everyone.

3. The third of the natural laws is, "Every man should carry out his covenants and promises." The State of war can only give way to a State of peace when each man promises, and abides by this promise, to give up some of his own natural rights. 'I give up my rights only on the strict understanding that you promise to give up yours. If you carry out this promise, the peace between us continues. If you do not, I shall naturally resume my rights and the State of war between us is recommended.' The basis of all peaceful intercourse between men is faith that men will keep their convenants and that those who break their covenants will be punished.
4. The fourth Law of Nature is this, that upon caution of the future time a man ought to pardon the offences past of them that repenting desire it.
5. The fifth is, that in revenges, men look not at the greatness of the evil past, but the greatness of the good to follow.
6. The sixth Law of Nature is that no man by deed, word, countenance or gesture declare hatred or contempt for another.
7. The seventh Law of Nature is gratitude. A man who receives benefit from another of mere grace, endeavours that he who gives it, has no reasonable cause to repent of his goodwill.
8. The eighth Law of Nature, is complaisance that is to say, that every man strives to accommodate himself to the rest.
9. The ninth Law of Nature is that every man must acknowledge the other for his equal by Nature.
10. The tenth Law of Nature is against arrogance that is to say "that at the entrance into conditions of peace, no man

requires to reserve to himself any right, which he is not content should be reserved to every one of the rest.

11. The eleventh Law of Nature is 'Equity.'
12. The twelfth Law of Nature is equal use of common things that is to say "that such a thing as cannot be divided, be enjoyed in common, if it can be; and if the quantity of the thing permit, without stint otherwise proportionally to the number of them that have right."
13. The thirteenth Law of Nature is that no man is his own judge.
14. The fourteenth Law of Nature is that no man is to be a judge, that has in him a natural cause of partiality.
15. The fifteenth Law of Nature is that credit should be given to witnesses.
16. The sixteenth Law of Nature is Lot.
17. The seventeenth Law of Nature is Primogeniture or First Seizure.
18. The eighteenth Law of Nature is that all men that mediate peace, be allowed safe conduct.
19. The nineteenth Law of Nature is submission to Arbitrator.

Commenting on these Natural Laws, Sabine says, "they are at once the principles of perfect prudence and that of social morality and hence they make possible the slip from the psychological motives of individual action to the precepts and values of civilised law and morality."

Zagorin says, "To him the law of Nature is not a pervasive principle of the Universe, expressing the rational constitution of a divine mind. It is only a name for the means which the calculating human intelligence finds efficacious to achieve its ends of preservation and contentment."

## THEORY OF SOVEREIGNTY

No writer has taken a more extreme view than Hobbes of the absolute nature of sovereignty. He is certainly the first thinker to offer a clear and full statement of theory of absolute and unlimited sovereignty. Greek philosophers did not have any notion about sovereignty. Roman thinkers had some ideas about sovereignty which found expression in their Imperial Potestas and Majestas. But Machiavelli was the first writer to conceive of an independent national State and hence indirectly contributed to the growth of the concept of sovereignty. Bodin was the first thinker to give a clear theory of sovereignty. But Bodin's sovereign powers were limited by divine law, natural law and law of nations. Hobbes made sovereignty all powerful and unlimited. While Grotius taught that the Law of Nature and of Nations was binding upon all States; Hobbes taught that the Law of Nature and of Nations, and even of God, was binding upon men only through the will of their own sovereign.

Hobbes' sovereign was the product of social contract. No sovereign existed prior to the contract. He defines sovereign in these words: "By this authority, given to him by every particular man in the commonwealth, he has the use of so much power and strength conferred on him, that by terror thereof, he is enabled to form the wills of them all to peace at home and mutual aid against their enemies abroad. And in him consists the essence of common wealth which is one person, of whose acts a multitude, by mutual covenants one with another have made themselves, everyone the author, to the end he may use the strength and means of them all, as he shall think expedient, for their peace and common defence." It follows that the essence of sovereignty lies in the power to determine on behalf of the entire community what should be done to maintain peace and order. The will of the sovereign replaces the separate wills of the individuals. The sovereign is the sole law making authority in the commonwealth.

The subjects have no right to resist sovereign's authority or interfere with his orders. Right to resistance is condemned on either of three grounds:

1. Every act of disobedience by a subject is unjust, whatever the ground alleged for the act. An agreement to recognize a new, in place of the former, sovereign without the latter's permission, is unjust, because it is a violation of the pact by which his will was recognized as the will of each of the persons contracting.

2. No breach of the original pact by the sovereign can be set up as a ground for its violation by the subject. For the sovereign is no party to the contract. It is an agreement of each man of a multitude with every other to give up his natural rights in favour of common or third party, but this third party, the sovereign, gives up nothing, and retains all his natural rights and powers. Hence the sovereign cannot do injustice to his subjects; for injustice is merely the violation of covenant, and the sovereign is by hypothesis not bound by any covenant.

3. There is no justification for resistance by the minority of a community on the ground that it did not choose the sovereign selected by the majority. The dissenters either did or did not agree to abide by the decision of the majority: if they did so agree, it is unjust not to conform to their agreement; if they did not so agree, they are, in respect to the rest, still in a State of Nature, and all the rights of war against them are available without any question of justice.

Sovereignty, therefore, implies an absolute exemption from any just resistance or interference on the part of subjects. Unlimited power and unfettered discretion as to ways and means are possessed by the sovereign for the end with a view to which civil society is constituted, namely, peace and escape from the evils of the State of Nature.

**Functions of Sovereign.** Hobbes' sovereign has the following rights and duties:

1. First, the sovereign has the power to make and repeal all laws; of hearing and deciding all controversies which may arise concerning any law; and of either punishing or pardoning those who break these laws.

2. Second, the sovereign has the right to appoint and dismiss all officials and magistrates, both civil and military. No man can claim to have an inalienable or hereditary right to any office. In like manner, the sovereign must be the fountain of honour, with power to grant such ranks and titles as please him.

3. Third, in contrast with Bodin, Hobbes insists that the sovereign must have full power to levy taxation in order to provide for the army and the civil magistrates. It is useless to grant the sovereign the right to raise an army and appoint magistratcs unless he also has the right to levy money from his subjects so that these persons may be paid.
4. Fourth, the sovereign has the right to maintain peace or conduct war with neighbouring States. This in turn means that the sovereign must have control over the armed force of the State. This control is in contrast with the old feudal levies in which the bulk of the soldiers were led by their own lords and were only indirectly subject to the commands of the monarch.
5. Fifth, not only has the sovereign the right to tax the private property of his subject, but the very ownership of private property and the laws governing this ownership are derived from the will of the sovereign. Other advocates of the social contract theory claimed that private property was a natural right governed by natural law. But in Hobbes' scheme a man possess property in a civil State only as the result of a grant on the part of the sovereign.
6. Finally, the sovereign has a right to censor and prevent the spread of all opinions which appear dangerous. Hobbes was frightened of the results which might arise from liberty of speech and liberty of the press.

In short, the possession of sovereignty, according to Hobbes, carries with it the right of immunity from civil or criminal action, the right of public censorship, the right of making laws to regulate all personal and property relationship, the right of adjudicating\ all controversies involving questions of fact or of civil or natural law, the right of making war or peace, the right of commanding the military forces, the right of choosing ministers, counselors, and other public officials, the right of punishing offences and rewarding merit, and the right of bestowing honours and regulating social precedence. "These are the Rights, which make the Essence of Sovereignty; and which are the makers, whereby a man may discern in what Man or

Assembly of men, the sovereign power is placed, and resideth. For these are incommunicable, and inseparable."

Hobbes thus refuted all the restrictions which Bodin levied on the sovereign. Bodin had claimed that the monarch could not change the laws of succession Hobbes, on the other hand, accedes this right to one sovereign, though he was prepared to admit that normally the monarch would permit succession by rules of heredity. Secondly, Bodin's sovereign is limited by the laws of God and law of Nature. In Hobbes'system the conflict between civil and natural law is rendered impossible. The purpose of Natural Law is to secure peace through the erection of an omnipotent State and hence State using these omnipotent rights in any way is pleases is merely following the dictates of Natural Law.

As regards laws of God, Hobbes could not way under the strong theological passion of the age that he laws of sovereign might be contrary to the laws of God, but he tackles this problem in the same manner as he circumvented the Laws of Nature. He asks what is the command of God? These are many persons and groups of persons who claim to have received God's law by direct revelation, but these persons usually contradict one another even on fundamental points, "How can man be assured of the revelation of another without a revelation particularly to himself?" and again, "If men were at liberty to take for God's commandments their own dreams and fancies, or the dreams and fancies of private men, scarce two men would agree upon what is God's commandment.....I conclude ....Therefore that... all subjects are bound of obey that for divine law which is declared to be so by the laws of the commonwealth."

Thus Hobbes dismisses as absurd the claims of the Catholic and of all other Churches to act as infallible judges of divine revelation. To him, the only possible Church is a Church established and controlled by the State, whose supreme pastor is the sovereign. Hence any body of men meeting for worship without the sovereign's command is no Church, but merely an unlawful assembly.

In short, Hobbes propounded the doctrine of an absolute and unlimited sovereign. He concentrated all social and political authorities in the sovereign. Law and morals are merely his will, and his authority is unlimited, or is limited only by his, for the good reason that there is no other authority except by his permission.

Sovereignty is indivisible and inalienable, for either his authority is recognised and a State exists or it is not recognised and anarchy exists. Hobbes relieved sovereignty completely from the disabilities which Bodin had inconsistently left standing.

**Limitations.** For Hobbes, there is one limitation on sovereignty, Sovereign may order the death of a person (for treason or other causes) and not act unjustly. But he cannot order any person to kill himself. The reason for this is not a horror of suicide, but because man enters into the contract in order to preserve his own existence. Hence the command to commit suicide is a direct breach of this contract and in such a case only, man is free from the obligations of the contract. This idea brings up another phase of Hobbes' theory. Hobbes is insistent upon the absolute obligation of subjects to obey the commands of their sovereign, except under one condition. When the legitimate sovereign has lost all powers to protect his subjects or to preserve them from injury, the duty of obedience ceases. The subject under the terms of the social contracts must blindly obey the de-jure monarch as long as the latter can maintain peace and order; but in the event of successful civil war, the de-jure monarch loses his power, and the duty of obedience automatically cases; the subject is free to seek peace by serving under the new *de facto* ruler.

**Criticism.** Hobbes' theory of absolute and unlimited sovereignty has been subjected to hostile criticism. His theory of sovereignty has been criticised on the following grounds:

1. Some critics have rejects Hobbes' theory of sovereignty as unreal—as unreal to facts. they hold that no actual Leviathan wields such absolute and unlimited power as this theory ascribed to him. Hobbes himself admitted that sovereign do not, infact, exercise such vast powers. But this criticism does not seem to be valid. It can be maintained that the purpose of Hobbes was not to give a factual description of the powers actually exercised by his Leviathan.

2. Critics like Vaughan reject the theory as pernicious and impossible. According to him, "The Theory of Sovereignty is pernicious because it leads to despotism; it gives the subjects no defence against oppressive and tyrannical rule of despot and reduces the whole herd to slavery. The sole bond of union between the members of Leviathan is a common terror, the fear of relapsing into the State of Nature.

   If it is admitted that the only force which keeps the members of Commonwealth together is the terror of the sovereign's word—the objection is well-grounded. It is to be admitted that there is sufficient justification for believing that in the system of Hobbes, the ties which bind the members of the Commonwealth together is subjection to the sovereign authority which ultimately rests upon force. The sovereign authority of the ruler will melt away like ice in the summer sun, in the absence of his control over the people and the army in the Commonwealth.

3. Prof. Jones has pointed out that paradox exist in Hobbes' theory of sovereignty because on the one hand, he has supported absolutism on the other hand he has given the right to resist the sovereign in case of danger to individual's life. Logic demands that either the subject has a right against the sovereign or sovereign is not absolute. It sovereign is absolute and supreme the individuals don't have the right to resist the sovereign.

4. Hobbe's theory of sovereignty justifies any defacto government, whether just or unjust, right or wrong. Hence he advocated the principle of might is right. Some critics point out that he wrote his 'Leviathan' to humour Cromewell who had assumed sovereign powers after killing the lawful ruler.

5. Prof. Jones further points out that the right to protect one's life against one's sovereign applied, clearly enough not only in the case of a subject against whom Criminal

proceedings are threatened, but whenever any act of the sovereign endangers the life of one of his subjects. Thus a subject has a right to refuse to serve when he "is commanded as a soldier to fight against the enemy." Pushing the argument, he gives an example of a criminal. According to him, the criminal has a right to his life only if he can preserve it, while the sovereign, on the contrary, has a right to punish the criminal only if can catch him. Thus the position is actually not satisfactory. For, if the sovereign has sufficient actual power to govern the State as Hobbes thinks, it required to be governed, it is clear that the subject's right is non-existent.

6. Hobbes has failed to convince us that the rational human beings, as his individual are depicted at the time of the institution of sovereign, will choose to live in a state of slavery under the sovereign. It is not correct that they knew that the slavery of the sovereign is in their own interest. Locke criticises Hobbes' theory by saying that it leads us to think that "men are so foolish that they take care to avoid what mischiefs may be done to them by polecats and foxes, but are content, nay, think it safety, to be devoured by lions."

7. Moreover, if men were as completely unscrupulous as Hobbes believes them to be, then only the brutal and ruthless exercise of force could keep them in order. But as Prof. Jones points out that "The existence of the great democratic States, and their survival even in a world at war, is evidence that Hobbes is mistaken and that most men conform to law for reasons—whether these be a sense of duty, altruistic sentiments, social feelings, or only habit and inertia—other than because they are compelled to do so."

8. Hobbes, according to some critics, was a firm supporter of absolutism, because he had wholehearted sympathy with the Stuart Kings. According to Prof. Sabine, "Hobbes' principles were at least contrary to the pretension of

> Stuarts whom he meant to support as to those of revolutionist whom he meant to refute, and more contrary to both than either royalist or parliamentarian was to the other. The friends of the king might well feel that Hobbes' friendship was dangerous as Cromewell's enmity."

## THEORY OF SOCIAL CONTRACT

Hobbes has conceived of the State of Nature. It was a state of war, a war of all against all, a war in which each was as a revenging beast to his fellows. There was constant fear. With the passage of time man wanted to discard the life of constant fear. His social self began to assert himself. He wanted an atmosphere in which his life and property were secure. According to A. Hecker, "This state of nature eventually proved to be either impossible or undesirable to maintain."

**Prerequisites of Peace.** Hobbes opines that two rules are prerequisites of peace:

1. That every man ought to endeavour peace as far as he has hope for obtaining it.
2. That man must be contended with so much liberty against other men as he would allow other men against himself.

The power of reason is too weak to control the selfish tendencies of man's nature. Hence there must be some other power so strong as to enforce the dictates of reason and punish the defaulters. Hobbes says that such a power may be found in the state or commonwealth. "The only way to erect such a common power as may be able to defend them from the invasion of foreigners and the injuries of one another... is to confer all their power and strength upon one man, or upon one assembly of men that may reduce all their wills...into one will."

This 'one will' can come into existence in the following two ways:

***(a) Commonwealth by Acquisition.*** By natural force, as when a man makes his children to submit themselves and their children to his government, as being able to destroy them if they refuse; or by war submit his enemies to his will giving them their lives on that condition.

***(b) Commonwealth by Institution.*** When men agrée amongst themselves to submit to some man or assembly of man, voluntarily on confidence to be protected by him against all other.

**Two Stages in the Argument.** There are two stages in the argument of Hobbes as under:

1. Men could live in peace by following certain rules called the laws of nature. The most fundamental law of nature is "to seek peace and follow it". Although there are some passions which lead to conflict yet there are others which make for peace i.e., the desire to avoid death or the desire of things necessary for commodious living. Reason makes a man seek peace.
2. Men want a sovereign to enforce the laws of nature.

**Necessity of Some Coercive Power.** Men, in order to get out of the terrible state of nature, enter into covenants to forego such of their natural rights which, being retained, will hinder the progress of mankind. Man is selfish and egoistical and therefore Glory and Fear are the two instincts which make him keep covenant. There must, therefore, be some coercive power binding men to their covenants by the terror of some punishment greater than the benefit they expect by the breach of their Covenant.

The instinct of self-preservation, supported by the planks of natural law and laws of motivation, instructed its inhabitants to advance towards the civil state by retreating from the state of nature. One of the natural laws immediately came forward to do the yeoman's service. It placed the services of contract at the disposal of those weary, tired and fed up people, through the using of which they emerged into the civil state.

**Establishment of Commonwealth.** In the second part of his Leviathan, Hobbes creates his commonwealth as—"The only way to erect such a Common Power as may be able to defend them (*i.e.*, men) from the invasion of foreigners; and the injuries of one another...is to confer all their power and strength upon one Man, or upon one Assembly of men that may reduce all their Wills, by plurality of voices unto one Will; which is as much as to say, to appoint one Man or Assembly of men to bear their Person; and every one to own, and acknowledge himself to be the Author of whatsoever he that so beareth their Person, shall Act, or cause to be Acted; in those things which concerned the Common Peace and Safety; and therein to submit their Wills everyone to his Will, and their Judgments, to his Judgment. This is more than Consent or Concord; it is real Unite of them all, in one and the same Person, made by Covenant of every man with every man, in such manner, as if every man should say to every man, I authorise and give up my Right of Governing myself to this Man, or to this Assembly of men, on this condition, that thou give up thy Right to him, and Authorise all his Actions in like manner."

**The Sovereign.** This sovereign is the great Leviathan, the Mortal God to whom individuals owe their peace and preservation. This sovereign power may be created in either of the two ways—*(i)* By institution when men of their own impulse unite, *(ii)* By acquisition when impulse to union comes from without. In both cases the motive force is fear, in the former case the fear of one another, in the latter the fear of the sovereign.

The above social contract institutes an office which may be held by one man or by an assembly of men but which is distinct from the natural person of the holder. By the transfer of the natural rights of each man, the recipient becomes their representative and is invested with authority to deliberate will and act in place of the deliberation, will and action of each separate man.

## NATURE AND CONSEQUENCES OF HOBBESIAN CONTRACT

**1. Parties to the Contract.** Many of the earlier advocates of the social contract theory argued that the contract is between the governor and the governed. The governed or subjects agree to do so provided the governor or monarch fulfils his obligations and treats his subjects justly and fairly. It leads to the conclusion if the governor acts unjustly, his subjects can claim that the contract has been broken and are justified in rebelling. Hobbes has discarded this theory. According to him, the social contract is not between the governor and the governed but between each and every member of the state—the sovereign, in fact, is not a party to the contract. The parties to the contract are individual natural men—not groups of any sort, not the 'people' vaguely defined, and not any superior being or sovereign.

**2. Minority Divested of Any Power to Resist.** There is designation of the sovereign by the majority and its complete submission to it. Hence there is no ground on which a minority can base its just resistance. Hobbes claims that a minority has no right to object to the choice of a majority in the selection of the sovereign power. Again, since minority never agreed to become members of the social contract with its necessary obligations, the minority must still be considered to exist in the primeval state of war. As such, it may be destroyed without injustice by the newly constituted state unless this minority submit to the decree of the majority.

**3. Conditions for Continuance.** The end sought by the parties—internal peace and defence from external foes—is an integral element of the contract, and must therefore be regarded as a condition of its continued existence.

**4. Fear of Being Relapsed into State of Nature.** By the third law of nature men are forced to stand by their covenants, otherwise they may relapse into the horrible state of nature—a state of wretchedness and terror and promiscuous rapine and slaughter. As such any attempt to rebel against or resist the commands of the sovereign is a violation of the third natural law and leads straight back to primeval anarchy.

**5. Ever-Binding and Irrevocable.** The contract is ever binding and irrevocable. The members of the newly formed state have no right to withdraw their promise of obedience whatever the provocation.

**6. Absolute Control.** By the terms of the social pact the sovereign obtains absolute and complete control over all the citizens of the state. There has been absolute surrender on the part of the subjects and absolute despotism on the part of the sovereign. The one is the inevitable counterpart of the other.

**7. Fear.** However, the persons who obey and respect the authority of the state purely on rational grounds are very few. The effective agency which socialises the man is the fear of punishment and not reason. As Hobbes himself puts it, "Covenants without sword are but words."

**8. Sovereign above the Contract.** The parties to the contract are individuals. The Sovereign is not a party to the contract. He therefore not only stands outside it but is also above it. Thus, Hobbes tries to justify absolute or despotic rule and denies all rights of resisting the state to the individual. According to Dr. Vibasi, "Instead of becoming a charter of human freedom the contract becomes in the hands of Hobbes a bond of human slavery."

**9. Commonwealth Based on Reason.** The Commonwealth or State is based on reason and not on fear. People render obedience to the authority of the state because of the rational apprehension. This rational apprehension is that their end of self-preservation is better served within the state.

**10. Sovereign—Not Guilty of Violation.** Since, the Sovereign is not a party to the contract he cannot be guilty of violating the contract. Justice lies in adherence to the contract and the sovereign cannot be unjust.

**11. Right to Live.** The contract was concluded primarily for the protection of individual's life. It implies that the individual surrendered all his rights, except the right to live, to the sovereign. Thus the sovereign can encroach on all the rights of the individual, except the right to live.

**12. No Right Against Sovereign.** The people are bound to submit to the will of the state or the ruler and enjoy no right against the sovereign. Hence some critics have remarked that the Covenant, instead of being the charter of liberty, it is a bond of slavery for the people. However, Hobbes permits the individual to disobey the sovereign if the latter commands him "to kill, wound or maim himself," or not to resist those that assault him or to abstain from the use of food, air, medicine or any other thing without which he cannot live.

**Some Implications of Hobbes' Contract.** Some implications of Hobbes' contract are as under:

**1. Justification of All Forms of Government.** Hobbes' contract justifies all forms of government i.e., monarchy, aristocracy or democracy. This is because at the time of contract the individuals could surrender their rights to one man or one assembly of men as they liked.

**2. State—An Artifice.** The state is not a growth or an organism but an artifice or manufacture. It is a machine, an artificial creation calculated to serve the specific end of maintenance of peace and order and preservation of lives of the individuals.

**3. Simultaneous Creation of State Society and Government.** Dr. Vibasi opines that the Hobbesian contract creates simultaneously the state, society and government. In fact Hobbes does not distinguish between state and society and between state and government. He also does not distinguish between De Jure and De Facto sovereignty.

**4. Individualism.** State is a mean to an end, which leads to the concept of Individualism.

**5. Absolutism.** In so far as the people surrender all their rights, except that of life, to the sovereign and have no right of revolution, it leads to Absolutism.

**6. State—An Outcome of Anti-Social Nature.** The state of Hobbes is not the outcome of man's sociability, as held by Aristotle, but of his *anti-social* nature. It has been created to meet individual self-interests and, therefore, there is no place for social welfare in it.

**Criticism of Hobbes' Social Contract.** Critics have pointed out so many flaws shortcomings and defects in Hobbes' contract formula. Some are as under—

**1. Sudden Change in Man Incredible.** The critics opine that the natural man as conceived by hobbes, is essentially anti-social and no juggling with words and contracts can ever make him a fit subject for society. Hence it is incredible that the same beings, who one moment have been flying at each other's throats, should, the next moment, with equal eagerness, be flying into each other's arms?

Vaughan remarks that, 'no powers or magic device can bring such a radical change. The Ethiopian cannot change his skin. Nor could the crafty cut-throat, the Machiavelli Attila, of the opening chapters, even have become the peaceful labourer, still less the cringing Helot, of the close." It is never expected of such a warry man that he will give up his vicious habits and nasty living so soon and almost all of a sudden. How can this monster be expected to exchange peace for war whose only delight was to cut the throat of his fellow beings. "In all the annals of religion, in all the fairy tales of the Kingdom of Darkness, there is no conversion so sudden, or so radical, as this".

**2. Contract can not be Possible before Settled Order.** The critics opine that the contract is possible only under a settled order of the state. But to hold that the contract had taken place before the state came into existence is simply putting the cart before the horse.

**3. Change in Nature Incredible.** The critics remark that it is not understood as to how the ignorant, brutish, selfish and anti-social man became enlightened and politically conscious.

**4. Choosing More Dangerous Course.** The critics remark that the step taken by the natural men of Hobbes for the constitution of a civil state was perhaps more dangerous than the state of nature itself. they argue that the covenant generated a despotic monarch who has reduced the status of his subjects to the position of menial staff. It is not understood as to how the natural men of Hobbes took the step which was to invite simple destruction and disaster for them. As Locke pointed out. "This is to think that men are so foolish that they take care to avoid what mischief may be done to them by polecats and foxes, but are content, nay think it safety, to be devoured by lions." Vaughan remarks, "The society instituted by this contract offers a state of things still more intolerable than the anarchy which it replaces. It is, in fact, no society at all. It is a herd driven together by sheer panic and held in the pen by nothing but the terror of the sword."

**5. No Real State.** The critics opine that the Hobbesian state is founded on pure and simple despotism with no rights and powers of the people, it cannot be termed state in the real sense of the term.

Vaughan remarks that, "The state of Leviathan is a state avowedly founded upon slavery: founded therefore upon a principle which is the very negation of all justice."

## SOVEREIGN POWER, NATURE AND SOCIAL CONTRACT

Hobbes was essentially product of his times and to think of him and his philosophy without his times will be rather his incomplete study. This will eventually be doing injustice with him and his political thought. It was the influence of his times that he felt that man by nature was nasty, brutish and selfish and that he required a strong authority to check or control him. He therefore pleaded for a strong monarch on the throne who could check selfish habits of the people.

**Hobbes on Human Nature.** Hobbes' conception of sovereignty is based on his idea about human nature, which was also fountain head of all his philosophy. In fact, his conception of human nature is the pivot round which his whole philosophy revolves. Hobbes has made a fundamental departure from his contemporaries by saying that man was essentially nasty, brutish and an uncivilised creature. He made individual, as against society, the spring board of his thought.

Hobbes came to the conclusion that men by birth were equal in intelligence but it was desire for heaving one and the same thing which made them quarrel with each other. Men would never have quarrelled had they no liking to get one and the same thing. He believed that competition, glory and difference make people brute and quarrelsome. It was an uncontrolled society with desirous human beings which changed the whole concept of basic principles of the society. His conception of human nature was essentially based on two basic factors. Firstly that men are equal.

Secondly, unlike Machiavelli, he believed that man was not an idle spectator in political drama but always ready to struggle and achieve something noble, gentle and higher. He has himself written in the Leviathan that "It put forth a general inclination of all mankind a perpetual and restless desire of power after power, that ceaseth only in death. And the cause of this is not always that a man hopes for more incentive delighter than what he has already attained to, or that he cannot be content with a moderate power, but because he cannot assure the power and the means to live well which hath present without the acquisition of more."

This desire makes men fight with each other. It is the desire which made man nasty and brutish while in the state of nature; and made him stand against the valid desires of others to satisfy his own desires. "Out of this view of man and man's relation with each other Hobbes constructs his political philosophy."

**Hobbes on State of Nature.** He believed that essentially and basically men were un-social, selfish and brute. In the state of nature he was without any society, art and culture but insecurity was the only secure thing in that pre-state society. He was secure as long as strong spared him. The man-made laws were not justified in any code of conduct. His life and property were always at stake. Briefly his life was nasty, poor and brutish. T.H. Haxley has defined those laws as 'tiger laws'. There was no common law and no common lawgiver.

**Origin of the Social Contract.** With the passage of time man wanted to discard the life of constant fear and his social self began to assert himself. He wanted an atmosphere in which his life and property was secure. According to A. Hecker "This state of nature eventually proved to be either impossible or undesirable to maintain. Therefore at a specific time the inhabitants of a natural state came together and consequently agreed to set up social and political institutions. This agreement is called a social contract or a covenant of sometimes a social compact. It marks the beginning of a social and political authority."

It was to remove constant fear that men thought of surrendering their right to a Lord Protector to whom they wanted to be the custodian of their rights, duties and social justice. They declared "I authorise and declare and give up my right of governing myself to this man or to this assembly of men, on this condition that thou give thy right to him and authorise all his actions like manner. This done the multitude so united in one person is called commonwealth."

The assembly of persons and their social instinct which motivated them to come out of this brutish and nasty state of nature to the civilised society, with a social order, was the basis of social contract and also the origin of the state.

**Creation and Characteristics of Sovereign.** According to Hobbes the person to whom rights were surrendered was the sovereign: a great Leviathan before whom all were to bow. He was the preserver of peace, hope for prosperity, development and security. According to Hobbes, "By this authority, gives to him by every particular man in the commonwealth, he has the use of so much power and strength conferred on him, that by error thereof, he is enabled to form wills of them all, to peace at home and mutual aid against their enemies abroad. And in him consists the essence of commonwealth and he shall think expedient, for the peace and common defence." The sovereign of Hobbes has some salient characteristics namely that sovereign shall not be party to the contract and shall remain above all laws. He shall accordingly retain all the rights which he used to enjoy in the state of nature. Since all have surrendered their rights willingly to the sovereign, the sovereign was the custodian of their rights. None should challenge sovereign, on ground of infringing his rights. The sovereign, according to Hobbes, had no constitutional checks, whatsoever. "For before the constitution of sovereign power, all men have right to all things...this property being necessary to peace, depending on sovereign power, is the act of that power, in order to the public peace."

He was the sole interpreter of law and his actions could not be pre-judicial to social interests. He could not be charged with breach of contract because he was not a party to the contract. He was the symbol of national unity and as such any challenge to his authority was irrational.

No contract can be quoted against the sovereign because he is final authority to approve all contracts. There could be no contract against him. Hobbes continued to say that the obedience to authority was universal. The minority should not disobey the commands of a sovereign on the grounds that it was not party to the contract. He could not reconcile himself to the idea of limited sovereignty, Sovereignty must be indivisible and inalienable. He wanted to vest the right of choosing his own ministers and magistrates in the hands of his absolute and inalienable sovereign. He, however, made it quite clear that he was in no way bound by the advice of his ministers or magistrates. Hobbes again says that the sovereign was the ultimate authority for "making war and peace with other nations and commonwealths, that is to say of judging when it is for the public good and how great forces are to be assembled: armed and paid for that end: and to levy money upon the subjects, to defray the expenses thereof."

Hobbes has thus created his absolute indivisible and inalienable sovereign. His sovereign was the dictator and one of the most undemocratic persons after having been elected in a most democratic way he has tried to stress that his subjects, magistrates and ministers might shine in his absence but they cannot find a place in his presence.

## MAN AND STATE OF NATURE

Hobbes insisted that any study of political society must begin with a consideration of the nature of man and he started with human nature in 'Leviathan. He says, "Nature.... is by the Art of man, as in many other things, so in this also imitated, that it can make an artificial animal. For seeing life is but a motion of limbs the beginning whereof is in some principal part within; why may we not say that all Automata....have an artificial life? For what is the heart, but a spring; and the nerves, but so many strings; and the joints, but so many wheels giving motion to the whole body, such as was intended by the artificer? Art goes yet further, imitating that rational and most excellent work of Nature, man. For by art is created...a commonwealth or State,...which is but an artificial man; though of greater stature and strength than the natural, for whose protection and defence it was intended....there is a saying....that wisdom is acquired not by reading of books but of men...there is another saying....by which they might learn truly to read one another, if they would take the pains; and that is Nocse teipsum, read the self...which was...meant...to teach us, that for the similitude of thoughts, and passions of one man, to the thoughts and passions of another, whosoever looked into himself, and considereth what he doth, when he does think, opine, reason, hope, fear etc., and upon what grounds, he shall read thereby read and know, what are the thoughts and passions of all other men, upon the like occassions....He that is to govern a whole nation must read himself, not this or that particular man; but mankind:...

The Universe, for Hobbes, is a machine, a machine made up of particles moving according to a mechanical law. Man is a microcosm, an epitome of the great Universe. According to Hobbes, 'man is the matter as well as he is the artificer of that artificial man, the State. He states with mechanistic doctrine of sensation *i.e.*, sensation causes to particles.

According to Hobbes man is selfish by nature. He can be moved only by the desire to get what he wants and preserve himself, and by the fear that he will be unable to get what he wants or to preserve himself. He tries to avoid pain and secure pleasure. His liking or disliking makes a thing good or bad. What man desires he calls good and what he dislikes he calls fear. Man is compelled by the very principle of motion which is operative till the universe to will what he desires and only what he desires. It is impossible for him to will what another desires. When man is successful till achieving what he wills, is said to enjoy felicity.

According to Hobbes, every individual is striving for the gratification of his appetites and these appetites vary from individual to individual according to bodily constitution, education and experience. But whatever diversity there may be in appetites, inability to satisfy them, there is for all practical purposes equality of all men. Conceding the obvious difference among individuals in physical and mental faculties, Hobbes holds that in the long run these substantially offset one another. Lack of physical strength is compensated by intellectual ability and vice versa. The man who is weaker physically may prevail by craft and cunning; and as to wisdom, the fact that each thinks himself the wisest is itself a ground for the inference that all are substantially equal. Such is the somewhat cynical form in which Hobbes sustains the dogma that all men are equal by nature.

As a result of the foregoing doctrines the normal condition of mankind is held to be that of unceasing strife. This condition has three chief immediate sources: first, the competition between man and man for the means to gratify identical appetites; second, the fear in each lest another should surpass him in power and third, the craving for admiration and for recognition as superior. In other words, the natural relations of each individual to every other is determined by motives of competition, distrust and love of glory. But these are the characteristics of actual or potential war. Contrasting men with bees and ants Hobbes says, "Men are continually in competition or honour and dignity, which these creatures are not; among men there ariseth on that ground envy and hatred and finally war." This will be more certain because of an inherent defect in man's intellect, vain, glory or pride. Men are apt to think themselves stronger than they are to underestimate the necessity of fighting continually for what they want, the fearless than they ought to fear the frustration of their desire and even sudden death.

Hobbes further says that man is endowed with a faculty of reason by which he acquires 'the knowledge of consequences and dependence by experience of one fact upon another'. Such knowledge is generally acquired by experience; it enables man to calculate the most effective means for attaining the objects of his desire.

Such is the nature of typical man according to Hobbes. In short, according to Hobbes, man is essentially selfish, quarrelsome, mean, wicked, non-rational, impulsive and self-centred. Hobbes's concept of human nature is more or less similar to that of Machiavelli. The only difference between the two is that Machiavelli did not give any scientific reason for the selfish nature of man while Hobbes has supported his contention with scientific reasons.

**Hobbes's Views about State of Nature.** Hobbes holds that originally man lived in a State of Nature in which the benefits of government were not available. All actions of men were controlled by individual egoism and the instinct of self-preservation. Man was essentially motivated by self-interest and each man was perpetually at war with every other man. Man in a State of Nautre was like the beasts in the jungle. He takes what he can with impunity, robbing and murdering the weaker and fleeing in terror from the stronger. An examination of human nature shows that there were three instincts which caused mankind to engage in civil war when left to itself. One was the acquisitive instinct, as the result of which man used violence to make himself master of other men's persons, wives, children and cattle. The second was possessive instinct as the result of which man endeavoured to prevent his neighbourers from securing those things which he himself possessed. The third was the love of glory, as the result of which each man sought the praise and envy of his fellows. There was utter distrust of man. In the words of Hobbes, "when taking a journey man arms himself and seeks to go well accompanying. When going to sleep he locks his doors, even when in his house he locks the chests."

In a State of Nature the hand of each was against all; and so long as there was no common superior to hold him in awe every man was the enemy of every man, "In such condition" says Hobbes "there is no place for industry because the fruit thereof is uncertain; and consequently no culture of the earth, no use of the commodities that may be imported by sea, no commodious buildings, no instruments of moving and removing such things as require much force, no knowledge of the face of the earth, no account of time, no arts, no letters, no society, and which is the worst of all, continual fear and danger of violent death and the life of man, solitary, poor, nasty, brutish and short...."

Prof. E.L. Woodward has rightly said, "there is nothing of the pleasant golden age about it."

Such is in essence Hobbes's celebrated theory of State of Nature. It is founded on the notion that man is purely egoistic in his emotions. From the assumptions already described the natural State of man presents logically the following practice:

1. First, there exists no distinction of right and wrong. The impulses which move men are the passions which are born in them, and there is no standard by which any one of these passions may be judged morally different from any other. Only when some rule is established by which to compare acts can rightness or wrongness be predicated; but such rule, or law, can be set up only after a lawmaker is agreed upon, and such agreement ipso facto terminates the State of Nature.

2. Secondly, there is no distinction of just and unjust in the State of Nature. Here comes in Hobbes's idea of justice—the antipodes of Plato's, where there is no common power over men, Hobbes argues, there is no law, and where, there is no law there can be no injustice. Justice and injustice are not faculties of the individual, like sense and emotion; and therefore they have a place, not in a consideration of the natural or solitary man, but only where men are regarded as united to one another by social bonds.
3. And finally, on analaogous principles there is no such thing as private property. Where each individual stands in precisely the same relation as every other to all external objects, might alone determine right; "only that to be every man's that he can get, and for so long as he can keep it."

This, then, is the State of Nautre in which man lives. "Neither right nor wrong, nor justice have place in it. Force and fraud are its cardinal virtues. And the only rule that men acknowledge is the good old rule, the simple plan that he should take who has the power and he should keep who can."

## INDIVIDUALIST AND AN ABSOLUTIST

Absolutism and individualism are two important aspects of Hobbes' philosophy. There is on the one hand the theory of sovereignty which makes Hobbes' sovereign absolute in all matters. No writer has taken a more extreme view than Hobbes of the absolute nature of sovereignty. He is certainly the first thinker to offer a clear and full statement of theory of absolute and unlimited sovereignty. Hobbes made sovereignty all powerful and unlimited. While Grotius taught that the Law of Nature and of Nations was binding upon all States; Hobbes taught that the Law of Nature and of Nations, and even of God, was binding upon men only through the will of their own sovereign. But we must remember that his theory of absolutism was derived from his individualism, pure and simple. His critics failed to realise that Hobbes had started with individual and ended with individual. Individual's security is the first round which all his other political ideas revolve. His critics never penetrated deep into his philosophy and got the superficial impression that absolutism was the central part of his political philosophy. But in reality absolutism was only an ally, a subservient idea of another idea i.e. individualism. In fact, Hobbes' absolutism derived its doctrines from individualism. Moreover, Hobbes' individualism influenced subsequent political thought more than the absolutism. His individualism gave rise to the theory of laissez faire. Bentham was greatly influenced by Hobbes' individualism.

'Prof. Sabine has rightly pointed out that, "The absolute power of the sovereign a theory with which Hobbes' name is more generally associated was really the necessary compliment of his individualism." Similarly Prof. Dunning remarks, "But notwithstanding his exaltation of the power of the State his theory was, in its foundation, wholly individualistic and rested on as complete recognition of the natural equality of all men as was even asserted by Milton or any other of the revolutionary theorists. "Even a commentator like Vaughan, who is otherwise very critical of Hobbes says, "While Hobbes' theory of sovereignty resulted in absolutism it was nevertheless based on the doctrine that all men are equal naturally and upon the belief in the desirability of a large measure of individual freedom." Prof. Wayper has rightly pointed out that "The Leviathan is not merely a forceful enunciation of the doctrine of sovereignty...it is also a powerful State of individualism." At a different place Prof. Vaughan says, "By a strange irony, it was reserved for the deadliest enemy of individualism to give the first formal statement of the theory upon which in the hey-day of its power individualism was universally held to rest. The whole work of Hobbes breathes the bitterest hatred not only of individualism as a theory, but even of those elementary rights which none but the most backward nations now deny to the individual in practice.

According to Prof. Oakeshott, "individualism as a gospel has drawn its inspiration from many sources. But as a rational theory of society of a school of thought it has its roots in the so-called nominalism of the medieval scholasticism. The essence of this doctrine was that, "the reality of a thing is its individuality...that which makes it this thing, and that both in God and man 'will' is precedent to reason."

But it is important to note that Hobbes' individualism does not postulate the fundamental right of the individuals. His concept of individualism neither contained the doctrines of democracy nor liberalism. In the words of Dunning Hobbes is, avowedly, "no liberal or democrat bu the is an individualist, not because he believes in the sanctity of individual man, but because for him the world is and must always he made up of individuals." For Hobbes there did not exist any such thing as people, or common will, or general will or common good as they exist for Rousseau.

It is generally believed that Hobbes started as an individualists and ended as an absolutist. But it is not correct to say that upto the institution of the sovereign he was an individualist and after the creation of civil society became absolutist. Hobbes was a consistent thinker and is not possible for a consistent thinker to start with one view and end with another. If we accept his premises we have to accept his conclusion. He was an individualist through and through. His absolutism does not destroy individualism. In support of our contention we give the following arguments:

1. Firstly, the dark view of human nature with which Hobbes started necessitated the creation of the absolute power. Human beings were depicted as animals and animals understand only one language i.e., force. Thus absolute sovereign has been created for the control of anti-social tendencies of the individuals pre-supposes their individuality and does not destroy it.
2. Secondly, Hobbes' sovereign is a means to an end and not an end in itself. In the words of Wayper, "The State is not the end of the individual, but the individual is most certainly the end of the State." The sovereign exists in order to fulfil certain ends. The absolute sovereign was created to provide sufficient security to the individual's life.
3. Thirdly, absolute powers of the sovereign are derived from the express consent of the individuals. He acts as their representative and he will not destroy the individuality of his constituents.

4. Fourthly, even after the creation of the absolute sovereign, his individuals have the liberty of thought, belief, trade, education, art, literature etc. They are free to do anything within the four-walls of the law. Law will interfere only when the life and security of the individual is involved and this power is transformed by the individuals themselves.

5. Fifthly, Hobbes' individual enjoys right to resist the sovereign in case the latter sails to give adequate protection to the individual's life or if sovereign asks the individual to commit suicide. That clearly shows that the individual still retains his individuality. Individual is a judge in every case, whether the action of the sovereign is detrimental to his life and security or not.

6. Sixthly, even after the creation of the absolute sovereign, there does not come into existence any collective will or common will or general will. There still remains "the only individual human beings each actuated by his private interests."

7. Lastly, according to Prof. Oakeshott, the Leviathan has not been created with the purpose of the destruction of the individual. It is, in fact, the minimum condition of the civilised society. He argues further that the sovereign is absolute in two respects only and neither of them is destructive of individuality : firstly, the surrender of natural rights to him is absolute and his authorization is permanent and exclusive; secondly, there is no appeal from the legitimacy of his command.

We can conclude with the remarks of Wayper that, "Hobbes, so frequently portrayed as the great absolutist, is perhaps the greatest individualist in the history of political thought. His is an extreme doctrine of individualism embracing everything. He is a nominalist of the school of Occam, and his individualism is quite unqualified more so, indeed than that of any other writer." Sabine has pointed out that "Individualism is the thoroughly modern element in Hobbes and the respect in which he caught clearly the note of the coming age.

Hobbes was at once the complete utilitarian and the complete individualist.

## SOVEREIGNTY AND LAW

Hobbes has not only expounded his political philosophy about the social contracts but has also given his ideas about many other important political problems like the liberty of the individuals and their rights etc. In all walks of life he has tried to tighten the grip of sovereign over his subjects. He strongly pleaded that church was a department of state. He was, however, more individualist than Plato who absolutely subjected his citizens to the sovereign.

**(A) Natural Rights and Natural Laws.** Hobbes was of the view that in the state of nature and even prior to that there were certain rights which were very dear and precious to man. He struggled and fought for their preservance and had a strong desire to retain them. In fact these rights were at stake when he thought of joining the civil state and subjected himself to the authority of sovereign in order to retain his those very rights. For their sake he gave up all his rights except those of life and property. He could give up everything but not these rights. He also reserved with himself the right to disobey the sovereign if at any stage he felt that such of his rights were being snatched.

Hobbes, however, clearly distinguished between natural rights and natural laws. He was of the view that the natural rights of men were based on their selfish views and if strictly and closely followed, these were the basis of war. On the other hand natural laws would positively lead to peace and avoid war. With natural rights men could struggle to preserve what they had with them; whereas on the basis of natural laws men gave up some of their rights in order to have sure realisation of rights of all. The natural laws according to Hobbes are "immutable and eternal". To him the essential characteristics of natural laws were that:

1. Every body ought to struggle for peace, as far as he had the hope of attaining that.
2. That every man must adjust his requirements according to the needs of others.

3. That none, by his word and actions, should hate anybody else.
4. That every body should believe in the equality of others.
5. That as far as possible men should enjoy at least those in common, which cannot be divided.
6. That all men who mediate peace be allowed safe conduct.

In addition to these laws, other laws are based on the similar ideas of cultivating the spirit of freedom and avoiding of any and every spirit of revenge. He has based his laws not on the basis of morality but utility. Bu the did not believe that utility was the only consideration for arriving at conclusions. On the other hand he felt that if left alone that would give an opportunity to a clever person to use these laws for their personal ends.

He believed that the laws of nature, by their very character, were eternal and necessary for the fullest desire and satisfaction of mankind. He also distinguished between the 'law proper' and the 'natural law'. To him the former was the will expressed by a person or assembly of persons who had command over others and had a right to get them obeyed but the latter were those laws by which the individuals mutually agreed to act in a manner which was conducive to peace and goodwill of the society as a whole.

He has however again and again stressed that the men would not honour the covenants enjoined upon them on account of the dictates of right reasons embodied in the natural laws. He has therefore pleaded the use of force as an essential element for the preservation of these dictates, for the covenants without swords were mere words on papers. In the words of Sabine "The law of nature really meant for Hobbes a set of rules, according to which an ideally reasonable being would puruse his own advantage, if he were perfectly conscious of all the circumstances in which he was acting and was quite unswayed by momentary impulse and prejudices. Since he assumes that men do not act in this way, the laws of nature state hypothetical conditions upon which the fundamental traits of human beings allow a stable government to be joined. They do not state values but they determine casually and rationally what can be given value in legal and moral systems."

**(B) Liberty and Rights of Individuals.** Hobbes had quite different and opposing views about the liberty and rights of the subjects. Hitherto, common views were those of Milton and Levellers, which were rather based on the most democratic ideas and stood for the freedom of the individual as a member of the social community. Hobbes clearly tried to distinguish between the liberty of the individual as a member of the society and state and the freedom of the state as an agency to regulate the rights of members of the society. He was of the view that the liberty of the state *i.e.*, of commonwealth was unqualified and absolute and that there were no checks upon that. But the freedom of individual depended on the factor upto which the state could allow that. The freedom of individual was thus a relative and not an absolute term.

According to Hobbes there were no checks on the liberty of the commonwealth but individual freedom consisted in what state did not forbid and permitted to do e.g., the purchase and sale of goods, freedom of movement and so on. The rights of self defence and preservation were examples of such rights. In the state of nature the rights of men depended on his might but in the civilised states his rights depended upon mutual consent of the sovereign and having legal sanction behind them. He, however, believed that liberty of the individual was not at the cost of the sovereign and did not impose any limitations on his absolute character and nature. He believed that except the right of self-preservation the sovereign could disallow, check or refuse any freedom. No individual could prefer his rights against the state.

**Estimate of Theory.** Thus we can safely conclude that Hobbes' ideas about individual freedom depended on the will and desire of his sovereign but it must be remembered that his individual had far more liberties than the individual of Plato who had stooped too low to regulate the affairs of mankind. Here he has also shown a sense of more practicability than Plato who thought that the state could effectively and efficiently regulate all aspects, of human behaviour. Hobbes believed that the individual should be left to regulate some behaviours of his life but neither at the cost of state nor that of the sovereign but at his own cost. He agreed with Aristotle that the unity was desirable, and could be achieved by vesting extensive powers in the hands of sovereign, who was the symbol of unity. At the same time he believed that too much of unity and denial of basic liberties to the individuals would positively not strengthen but weaken the state.

Though Hobbes believed in absolutism yet in many ways he was individualist. Basically his political philosophy depended on the individual nature of man. He gave his individuals great freedom namely to disobey the sovereign when his life and property was at stake and could refuse to serve in army if he was sure that his life was in danger.

**(C) Hobbes on Secularism.** As far as his political philosophy was concerned Hobbes believed in absolute sovereignty. He did not believe in the spiritual authority of the church and its right to even equate itself with the sovereign. His conception of over-lordship of sovereign, over every activity of the subjects, both temporal and spiritual, left no ground for the church to exert its influence. He was of the opinion that the church had no power whatsoever and that it was simply an assembly of persons believing in some particular religious doctrines. To him, technically speaking, they were to assemble without the permission of the sovereign and not without that. If they assembled without the permission of the sovereign or if the sovereign did not refuse permission that was his goodwill. He thus made church as a department of the state and not at par or above the state and the sovereign. He condemned ideas of both world religion and spiritual state. He believed that the church always tried to superimpose itself and sought for establishing his own authority over temporal lords but he bluntly and boldly declared that there was no spiritual government as the state was political in nature and character. He also declared that there could not be a world church as each church was confined to its own state and was its department alone. He preached secularism still further when he said that the sovereign was both temporal and spiritual authority and his authority was derived from God. In other words he placed sovereign as the deputy of God on earth and being representative of God there was no need to separate spiritual authority of church from that of the state. His philosophy in fact had no place for church state.

**(D) Hobbes on Law.** In his political philosophy Thomas Hobbes resembled Bodin at least in one respect. Both of them believed in the exactness of their definitions and conception of their terms. It was due to his exactness in definitions that while defining law, he divided it into three categories, law of nature, civil law and divine law. We have already discussed briefly what Hobbes meant and understood by the term the 'law of nature' and how he distinguished it from the 'natural rights'. He took the 'law of nature' as an integral part of the system which was responsible for maintaining and promoting peace. He preached that the law of nature stood for individual sacrifice in order to achieve social peace. He, however, desired that the law of nature should be supported by swords because the covenants without swords were words and had no value. He had also described the 'civil laws', as those laws and regulations which had the sanction of the sovereign behind them and were also permitted by him. Their obedience was to be checked by the use of force where necessary and considered as unsocial and revolt against the authority of the sovereign.

He believed that the civil laws could be sanctioned and interpreted only by the sovereign. As the fountain of laws and their interpreter, he was above all laws. He, however, agreed that the only exception to this were the 'customs' which were to be obeyed even by the sovereign himself and he need not act or enact in a fashion which was contrary to the established customs of the land.

He has described 'divine law' as the commands of God and as such all rational laws were indirectly 'divine laws'. These laws superseded the civil laws commanded by the sovereign over his subjects but the interpretation of 'divine laws' was the sole business of the sovereign, for, otherwise people will regard every law as the divine law and regard for civil law will simply vanish. He believed that the interpretation of laws given by the sovereign should be final and binding on all his subjects.

Whatsoever, the form of the law might be, Hobbes believed the interpretation and execution of the laws was the sole responsibility of the sovereign. The subjects either need not interfere or stand in the way of sovereign by disputing the validity of interpretation or the scope of the law. Thus even in the case of laws Hobbes has not weakened the grip of his Leviathan sovereign over his subjects.

## JOHN LOCKE

John Locke was born of a middle class puritan family at Wrington in north Somersetshire, in 1632. His father was a country lawyer and land owner of modest means. In 1642 his father was enlisted in the parliamentary army in the civil war and served as a captain of a company of volunteers.

Locke received his early education at home and later on he was admitted to Westminster school in a puritan upbringing. In 1652, he was sent to Christ Church, Oxford for higher education. At that time he was 22 when he entered Christ Chruch College, (Oxford). Locke's university career was not very shining because the narrow discipline of the place dulled his enthusiasm for formal studies. In 1656, he took his Bachelor's degree and after two years, in 1658, he became the Master of Arts. After taking the M.A. degree, Locke was appointed as a tutor in Greek, rhetoric and philosophy at Oxford.

"Locke's reading included Hebrew and Arabic and was brought into contact with the professor of the languages, Edward Pococke, whom he greatly admired. Pococke was an outspoken royalist. His interest in philosophy was aroused by the writings of Descrates and through friendship with Robert Boyle.

But he did not like the teaching profession. He gave it up and started learning medicine. He became assistant to David Thomas, who was an eminent physician at Oxford; and after two years of apprenticeship, Locke established himself as a doctor. In 1666, Lord Ashley, who later on became the first Earl of Shaftesbury, came to Oxford for his treatment under Dr. David. The association of Locke with Ashley lasted hardly for a year but the latter was deeply impressed by Locke and invited him to London as his personal physician and confidential secretary. Locke lived for full fifteen years with Ashley at London. Lord Ashley was a great public man of his time. Although a supporter of the royal cause in the beginning, he went over to the Parliamentary side later on. He was made a field-marshall in the rebel forces. But this state of affairs did not last long.

He became an opponent of Cromwell and was responsible for his overthrow. When Charles II came to the throne, he appointed Lord Ashley as his Lord Chancellor. In 1672, he became Earl of Shaftesbury.

In 1673, Shaftesbury was dismissed from his office and this naturally effected Locke's position. Both Locke and Ashley had to leave England for reasons of ill-health. For few years both of them lived in France and in the year 1679, Charles II again restored Ashley to his former office. Locke also took over his previous position.

In 1681 Shaftesbury was charged with the offence of conspiracy. He was involved in a plot against Charles and finally arrested and tried for treason. He was, however, acquitted but was compelled to leave England. Locke facing his persecution, left his job and sought asylum In Holland in 1683. Here he came in contact with William of Orange. in 1688 the Bloodless Revolution took place in England. William of Orange was invited to occupy the throne which was vacant due to the unexpected fight of James, II. Again, Locke's career took a turn. He also returned to England and was appointed by William III as Commissioner of Appeals in excise and in 1696 became a Commissioner to the Board of Trade and Plantations. He thus acquired experience of practical politics. His health, however, became unequal to the work he involved and he retired to the home of Sir Francis at Oates near High Laver in Essex. But he could not hold this post for a long time due to ill-health. He resigned form the office in 1700 and after four years of his resignation, he died in 1704.

## INFLUENCES OVER LOCKE

The contemporary events greatly influenced Locke in shaping his political philosophy. According to Prof. Jones "During this youth, Locke had an ample opportunity to see the raw and vicious aspects of human nature and, in his age, to have this impression confirmed during the years of distress which followed Shaftesbury's fall from favour, as well as in the political career which both preceded and followed in the interval of exile. Again, his ill-health which pursued him throughout his life might have excused an embittered attitude towards life. Nevertheless, he managed through all this, to see enough native goodness and kindness in his fellowmen not to turn on them the jaundiced and cynical eyes of Hobbes. This is all—important, because his political theory—his conception of the kind of government which men need and require-was naturally inevitably based upon his notion of what men are like. In this year the people, in effect, dismissed one sovereign for incompetence and, with a minimum of disturbance, elected another who, as they believed, would perform his proper functions efficiently and whom they could trust to recognise the rights and privileges which they claimed for themselves. The accession of William and Mary was thus a triumph for democracy and for the thesis that sovereigns rule by the consent and for the benefit of their subjects. It seemed to Locke to vindicate his belief in the ability of the people to rule themselves. It completely disproved Hobbes' conception of man as blindly irrational and utterly and narrowly selfish. It showed men to be possessed of a social sense which naturally brings them together, so that the pressure of force is not required to keep them from each other's throats. It was concrete evidence of the fact that men are sufficiently reasonable to see that their best interest lies in mutual and peaceful co-operation and of the fact that they have a sufficiently rational will to act in accordance with what they see to be good.

Again, though the Restoration of 1660 did not result in the establishment of either political or religious liberty, and another revolution became necessary, yet there was to be seen greater social stability during the period between 1660-1688. Due to the presence of this social stability, Locke who observed it, was not willing to surrender all the natural rights in exchange for political security.

Locke's father also exercised a great influence on him. In the Second Treatise on Government, Locke's accounts of family life show better than almost anything else could, the essential humaneness of his view of human nature. We cannot deny that this conception is based on his own practical experience with his father. Lady Masham, one of his friends, wrote that Locke never mentioned (his father) but with great respect and affection.

## LOCKE'S CONCEPTION OF THE STATE OF NATURE

To understand political power right, and derive it from its original, we must consider what state all men are naturally in, and that is a state of perfect freedom to order their actions and dispose of their possessions and persons as they think fit, within the bounds of the law of nature, without asking leave or depending upon the will of another man.

A state also of equality, wherein all the power and jurisdiction is reciprocal, no one having more than another, there being nothing more evident than that creatures of the same species and rank, promiscously born to all the same advantages of nature, and the use of the same faculties, should also be equal one amongst another, without subordination or subjection, unless the lord and master of them all should, by any manifest declaration of his will, set one above another, and confer on him, by an evident and clear appointment, an undoubted right to dominion and sovereignty.

But though this be a state of liberty, yet it is not a state of licence; though man in that state have an uncontrollable liberty to dispose of his person or possessions, yet he has not liberty to destroy himself, or so much as any creature in his possession, but where some noble use than its bare preservation calls for it. The state of nature has a law of nature to govern it, which obliges everyone; and reason,which is that law, teaches all mankind who will but consult it, that being all equal an independent, no one ought to harm another in his life, health, liberty or possessions; for men being all the workmanship of one omnipotent and infinitely wise Maker, all the servants of one sovereign Master, sent into the world by His order and about His business, they are His property, whose workmanship they are, made to last during His, not one another's pleasure. And, being furnished with like faculties, sharing all in one community of nature, there cannot be supposed any such subordination among us that may authorize us to destroy one another, as if we were made for one another's uses, as the inferior ranks of creatures are for ours. Every one, as he is bound to preserve himself, and not to quit his station willfully, so by the like reason, when his own preservation comes not in competition, ought he as much as he can to preserve the rest of mankind, and may not, unless it be to do justice on an offender, take away, or impair the life, or what tends to the preservation of the life, the liberty, health, limb, or goods of another.

And that all men may be restrained form invading other's rights, and form doing hurt to one another, and the law of nature be observed, which wills the peace and preservation of all mankind, the execution of the law of nature is in that state put into every man's hands, whereby every one has a right to punish the transgressors of that law to such a degree as may kinder its violation. For the law of nature would, as all other laws that concern men in this world, be in vain if there were nobody that in the state of nature may punish another for any evil he has done, every one may do so.

And thus, in the state of nature, one man comes by a power over another, but yet no absolute or arbitrary power to use a criminal, when he has got him in his hands, according to the passionate heats or boundless extravagancy of his own will, but only to retribute to him so far as calm reason and conscience dictate, what is proportionate to his transgression, which is so much as may serve for reparation and restraint, For these two are the only reasons why one man may lawfully do harm to another, which is that we call punishment. In transgressing the law of nature, the offender declares himself to live by another rule than that of reason and common equity, which is that measure God has set to the actions of men for their mutual security; and so he becomes dangerous to mankind, the tie which is to secure them from injury and violence being sighted and broken by him; which being a trespass against the whole species, and peace and safety of it, provided for by the law of nature, every man upon this score, by the right he has to preserve mankind in general, may restrain, or where it is necessary, destroy things noxious to them, and so may bring such evil on any one who has transgressed that law, as may make him repent the doing of it, and thereby deter him, and by his example others, from doing the like mischief.

Besides the crime which consists in violating the law, and varying from the right rule of reason, whereby a man so far becomes degenerate, and declares himself to quit the principles of human nature and to be a noxious creature, there is commonly injury done to some person or other, and some other man receives damage by his transgression; in which case, he who has received damage has (besides the right of punishment common to him, with other men) a particular right to seek reparation from him that has done it.

From these two distinct rights (the one of punishing the crime, or restraint and preventing the like offence, which right of punishing is in everybody, the other of taking reparation, which belongs only to the injured party) comes it to pass that the magistrate, who by being magistrate bath the common right of punishing put into his hands, can often, where the public good demands not the execution of the law, remit the punishment of criminal offences by his own authority, but yet cannot remipt the satisfaction due to any private man for the damage he has received. That heat who hath suffered the damage has a right to demand in his own name, and he alone can remit. The dammified person has this power of appropriating to himself the goods or service of the offender by right of self-preservation, as every man has a power to punish the crime to prevent its being committed again, by the right he has of preserving all mankind, and doing all reasonable things he can in order to that end. And thus it is that every man in the state of nature has a power to kill a murderer, both deter others from doing the like injury (which no reparation can compensate) by the example of the punishment that attends it from everybody, and also to secure men from the attempts of a criminal who, having renounced reason, the common rule and measure God hath given to mankind, hath, by the unjust violence and slaughter he hath committed upon one, declared war against all mankind, and therefore may be destroyed as a lion or a tiger, and of those wild savage beasts with whom men can have no society nor security.

By the same reason may a man in the state of nature punish the lesser breaches of that law. It will perhaps be demanded, with death? I answer: Each transgression may be punished to that degree, and with so much severity, as will suffice to make it an ill bargain to the offender, give him cause to repent, and terrify others from doing the like. Every offence that can be committed in the state of nature may, in the state of nature, be also punished equally, and as far forth, as it may, in a commonwealth. For though it would be beside my present purpose to enter here into the particulars of the law of nature, or its measures of punishment, yet it is certain there is such a law, and that too as intelligible and plain to a rational creature and a studier of that law as the positive laws of commonwealths, may, possibly plainer; as much as reason is easier to be understood that the fancies and intricate contrivances on men, following contrary and hidden interests put into words; for so truly are a great part of the municipal laws of countries which are only so far right as they are founded on the law of nature, by which they are to be regulated and interpreted.

To this strange doctrine—*viz,* That in the state of nature, every one has the executive power of the law of nature, I doubt not but it will be objected that it is unreasonable for men to be judges in their own cases, that self-love will make men partial to themselves and their friends; and, on the other side, that ill-nature, passion, and revenge will carry them too far in punishing others, and hence nothing but confusion and disorder will follow, and that therefore God has certainly appointed government to restrain the partiality and violence of men. I easily grant that civil government is the proper remedy for the inconveniences of the state of nature, which must certainly be great where men may be judges in their own case, since it is easy to be imagined that he who was so unjust as to do his brother an injury will scarce be so just as to condemn himself for it. But I shall desire those who make this objection to remember that absolute monarchs are but men; and if government is to be the remedy of those evils which necessarily follow from men being judges in their own cases, and the state of nature is therefore not to be endured. I desire to know what kind of government that is, and how much better is than the state of nature, where one man commanding a multitude has the liberty to be judge in his own case, and may do to all his subjects whatever he pleases without the least liberty to any one to question or control those who execute his pleasure? And in whatsoever he does, whether led by reason, mistake, or passion, must be submitted to?

It is often asked as a mighty objection, where are, or ever were, there any men in such a state of nature? To which it may suffice as an answer at present, that since all princes and rulers of "independent" governments all though the world are in a state of nature, it is plain the world never was, nor ever will be, without numbers of men in that state. I have named all governors of "independent" communities, whether they are or are not, in league with others; for it is not every compact that puts an end to the state of nature between men, but only this one of agreeing together mutually to enter into one community, and make one body politic; other promises and compacts men may make with one another, and yet still be in the state of nature.

## LOCKE'S VIEWS ON THE SOCIAL CONTRACT

To get rid of some of the inconveniences of the state of nature men entered into a contract, by means of which they passed out of the state of nature into a political society. There are 4 conspicuous features of Locke's social contract:

(1) "Men surrender only the right of enforcing the law of nature, all others right they retain as fully as before.

(2) Rulers were excluded from the contract. The agreement was between free individuals and not between rulers and the ruled. The rulers were merely given *fiduciary power* or trust to be exercised solely for the good of the community.

(3) Locke was the first writer to recognise distinction between society and government. By one contract the society was instituted, by the other government."

(4) Locke's use of social contract was only a majority rule.

The following additional features of Locke's contract may be noted.

(5) According to C.E. Vaughan, Locke's contract is a double, though he does not say so explicitly. The first puts an end to the state of nature and substitutes it by a civil society. After the first contract has been concluded the people in their corporate capacity enter into another contract—the governmental contract. This contract was of each with all. Under this contract each individual agrees to cede to the community as a whole. A body politic is formed by means of the social contract. Each individual giving up his personal right to interpret and administer the law of nature in return for a guarantee that their natural rights to life, liberty and property will be preserved. Prof. Gettell says, "The contract was thus specific and limited, not general as Hobbes had said."

(6) According to Locke, in the act of making the contract no one will accept any restriction upon his freedom of action.

(7) The sovereign power, thus created by the contract, vests not in a single man or any organ, but in the community as a whole.

(8) Though, individuals surrender their personal rights to interpret and administer the law of nature, yet they do not forfeit their natural rights, *i.e.* right to life, liberty and property.

(9) The civil community which is to interpret and execute the law of nature "remains as much bound by it as the individuals in the state of nature."

(10) Another feature of Locke's contract was that it must be unanimous. Locke says—"Men being...by nature all free, equal and independent, no one can be put out of this estate, and subjected to the political power of another, without his own consent." Locke holds that government would be based firmly upon the consent of the masses.

(11) The contract is irrevocable because after having once made it the people cannot revert back to the freedom of the state of nature.

## THEORY OF NATURAL LAW AND RIGHTS

The Second Treatise on Government opens with a consideration of political power and origin of the State. According to Locke State is not result of growth as Aristotle pointed out but it had been deliberately created by man who once lived without any State, that is, who once lived in the State of Nature.

**State of Nature.** Locke follows Puffendorf's modification of Hobbes' State of Nature. The State of Nautre as conceived by Locke is a pre-political rather than a pre-social condition. Locke did not agree with Hobbes in regarding the State of Nature as a State in which men lived in brutish reciprocal hostility in which every man's hands were against his fellows, a state of perpetual war in which life was short, nasty and brutish, but one in which peace and reason prevailed. Locke regarded the State of Nature as normally peaceful because of man's social instinct. Thus, as Laski says, Locke's "State of Nature, is in contrast to the argument of Hobbes' pre-eminently social in character." According to Prof. Maxey "the State of Nature was thus explained as a condition of right and reason; non-political but not non-social. In Locke's State of Nature there was no jungle war of everyman, no sentimental human brotherhood, but a reign of law predicted upon reason and equality." The State of Nature was defined by Locke as "a state of peace, goodwill, mutual assistance and preservation". Moreover, the State of Nature, Locke says, is a State in which men are equal and free to act as they think, within the bounds of the Law of Nature. His State of nautre as Jones points out is neither historical nor natural.

**Law of Nature.** The State of Nature is not a state of licence because though in it man is "free from any superior power on earth." nevertheless in it, he has "the Law of Nautre for his rule." "The State of Nature has a law of Nature to govern it, which obliges every one, and reason, which is that law, teaches all mankind who will but consult it, that, being all equal and independent no one ought to harm another in his life, health, liberty, or possessions." According to Locke the Law of Nature is a body of rules which govern at all times and at all places the conduct of men. Its arbiter is reason. Reason interprets that equality is the fundamental fact in men's relation to one another. On this foundation, Locke conducted his doctrine of natural rights which belong to every man in pre-political state and explains why this state is unsatisfactory. These natural rights are summed up by Locke as (1) Right to Life; (2) Right to Liberty; and (3) Right to Property.

**(1) Right to Life.** The right to life, that is the right to the preservation of life, the most primary motive of human action and whatever is reasonably directed to this end is everyman's privilege. Thus Locke agrees with Hobbes that everybody has the right to preserve life.

**(2) Right to Liberty.** As to the right to liberty, Locke departs from Hobbes and defines it as exemption for every rule except Law of Nature. Thus right to liberty means freedom to do whatever one's like as long as it is not incompatible with the Law of Nature. The Law of Nautre thus is not limitation upon freedom but on essential concommitant to it.

**(3) Right to Property.** Locke's right to property is his right to anything with which he has mixed his labour, provided he makes good use of it, since nothing was made by God for men to spoil or destroy. For Hobbes there was no right in the State of Nature. For Hobbes people have no inherent rights as private property. Ultimately the right to property is possessed by the Leviathan. Locke's conception of the right to property gave birth to modern conception of the right to property.

Thus natural law not only accords man's rights, it also imposes duties upon him. It commands him "when his own preservation comes not in competition" to do what he can do to preserve others. Thus Locke's State of Nature is such in which men have rights and acknowledged duties and which is moral and social in character. To Hobbes man is anti-social and has the right even to kill and robs others to preserve his life and therefore, Hobbes naturally conceives of Nature as one where life is normally "solitary, poor, nasty; brutish and short." To Locke, man is not anti-social by nature and is not always moved by bodily comforts. The man who heeds the voice of duty and is moved by love, sympathy and tenderness. In short, if Hobbes' man is animal, Locke's man at least is human animal. He is endowed with the faculty of reason and all men are equal to one another morally, and not phycically as Hobbes had said.

**Inconveniences of State of Nature.** Locke was sufficiently optimistic to believe that in ordinary circumstances mankind will obey natural laws, even in the absence of force or sanction. But he admitted that from time to time offenders will arise who will break the law by injuring their fellow men or by seizing their possessions. In a State of Nature there are not and cannot be special officials charged with the punishment of breahces of natural law. Hence it is necessary for each man to take justice into his own hands This situation necessarily brings about some injustice and confusion. Thus the State of Nature is not the last or the perfect model of society, but there can be improvement on this state of nature.The State of Nature, however, has its inconveniences. It is surely not a state of war, but it is certainly not a state where peace is secure. It is constantly upset by the "corruption and viciousness of degenerate men," where they make attempt on one's life, liberty and property by force. It is, therefore a "condition which, however free, is full of fears and continual dangers." In the State of Nature each man has its own interpretation of his right and there is a variety of interpretation of natural law. The result is chaos and weakness. According to WAYPER the State of Nautre leaves three essential wants unsatisfied:

(1) "the want of an established, settled, and known law;

(2) the want of a known and indifferent judge;

(3) the want of an executive power to enforce these decisions."

Thus Locke comes now to those processes by which these wants are satisfied by the substitution of civil for natural society. It is here that social contract emerges. The purpose of the social contract is to establish organised law and order so that the uncertainties of the State of Nature will be replaced by the predictability of known laws and impartial institutions.

**Criticism.** Though Locke's concept of State of Nature and law of nature are somewhat convincing, yet it has been criticised on the following grounds:

(1) Firstly, Locke's state of nature, as Jones points out is neither historical nor natural. "By saying that in a State of Nature men are free and equal he does not merely mean that there was a time in the past when men were in fact free and equal, he means rather to assert that they ought to be free and equal if they were not controlled by the political authority." In fact his conception of man in the State of Nature is not noticeably different from man in organised society.

(2) Secondly, Locke has conceived rights in the State of Nature. But rights can exist in the State only. When there was no State, how can right exist? The State is the creator of rights. Right also involves duties on the part of other individuals to respect the rights of other individuals. Only

State can force the individual to respect the rights of others.

(3) Thirdly, there is a contradiction in Locke's philosophy. On the one hand Locke says that no ideas are innate and on the other hand he says that individuals are endowed with certain inherent rights.

Inspite of the fact that Locke's concept of natural law and natural rights have been criticised, yet it is not difficult to understand the importance of the Law of Nature in Locke's philosophy. It is the cyphen which joins the State of Nautre with the civil society. According to Vaughan, "The controlling link in the chain forged by Locke is manifestly the Law of Nature. It is that which determines the character both of the State of Nature and of the civil state which eventually follows." In Locke's philosophy law of nature occupies more central place than in that of Hobbes. It governs the conduct of individuals in the State of Nautre and continue in the civil State also. It is a powerful check on the civil law because the latter cannot infringe the fundamental rights of the individuals which have been granted to them by the Law of Nature. Prof. Vaughan has pointed out that "It is clear that Locke has the best of the argument and that, on the premises which both accepted, it is not Hobbes but he who drew the correct and indeed the only possible conclusion." Moreover, his concept of natural rights has greatly influenced the political thought of the eighteenth century. Liberalism of 18th and 19th centuries is the direct product of Locke's concept of natural rights. Most of the democratic constitutions of the world contain fundamental rights which is nothing but the modernized version of Locke's natural rights. In short, we can say that the origin of the modern concept of fundamental rights lies in Locke's natural rights.

## THEORY OF PROPERTY

Political philosophers of all ages have expressed their views on the question of property. To Plato, its proper regulation was indispensably necessary for the health of social organism. To Aristotle it was something very necessary for the development of moral personality. Private possession and common use was as a remedy against the evils of this institution.

In the middle ages the ownership of property was universally held to imply duties as well as rights. In case, the duties were not fulfilled, the rights were forfeited. It was obligatory upon the property—owner to provide for the support of the poor. The possession of property was considered to be a trusteeship rather than outright ownership, and the trusteeship would be forfeited if the owner neglected his social obligation.

**Locke's Ideas on Property.** With Locke Property ownership became ownership by inalienable right. It was claimed that a property owner had the right to do as he pleased with his own. Locke asserted that a man has a natural right to that with which he has mixed the labour of his body as he does by enclosing and tilling his land.

**A Few Characteristics of Locke's Concept of Property.** A few characteristics of Locke's concept of property are as under:

*(1)* ***Property Given Birth by Labour.*** Locke believed that God had given the world to men in common and, therefore, no body had any exclusive claim to anything. Though the land and all inferior creatures belonged to all, yet every person had the right of property in his own person. The labour of his body and the fruit of his labour was his *i.e.*, was his own property. If he mixed his labour with the earth, the fruit of his labour became his own. Thus, by mixing his labour with something, man removes that thing from the common right of other men. A man's labour fixed his right of property in the thing with which the labour was mixed because it represented an extension of his personality. A man acquires the right of ownership in a thing which he 'forms' by mixing his labour with it. By mixing his labour with any gift of nature, he does enclose it from the common' for his exclusive use and ownership. Thus, "It is labour indeed that puts the difference of value on everything", and that "whatever a man removes out of the sate that Nature hath provided and left it in, he hath mixed his labour with it, and joined it to something that is how own, and thereby makes it his property". Locke's theory was, thus, responsible for the later development of labour theories of value in classical and socialist economics.

(2) ***Property Not Creation of Society.*** The right to private property is a right which each individual brings to society from the state of nature as he brings the physical energy of his body. Society, therefore, does not create this right.

(3) ***Inalienable Right.*** It is the inalienable right of the individual. The duty of the state is to watch zealously over it, a sacred trust—committed to its care, inviolable, unalterable, the very arch of the covenant of the commonwealth. It would be a blunder to make any attempts to regulate it, to redistribute it, and to nationalise it would be the grossest of usurpation. It can be regulated only to the extent that it is necessary to give it effective protection.

(4) ***Inherent Right.*** According to Locke, the right to property is a right inherent in the individual because his labour is inherent in him. The society does not create the right to property. In fact, the society and state instead of being creators of property are creatures of it. Man created them to protect the prior right of property.

(5) ***Indefensible Claim.*** It is an indefensible claim both upon society and government. It is a claim that society cannot set aside because society itself exists to protect it. The inevitable effect of it all is to set up a tyranny of the individual in one of the most deep-reaching.

(6) ***A Sacred Right.*** Locke held property to be a very sacred right. His natural rights are to life, liberty and property. Of these, the right to property is so important that Locke uses the word 'property' to denote any right. The individual, at the time of contract, does not relinquish his right to property. The society, therefore, cannot regulate his property and even tax him without his consent.

(7) ***Anterior to Society.*** Locke makes out property to be something anterior to society. Property is the inalienable birthright of the individual and was so even in the state of nature.

**Use of Property in Two Senses.** Locke has used the word property in two senses, narrow and broad as under:

(1) In the narrow sense in the state of nature people possessed property in common and no body originally had private property. In Locke's words, "Property is without any express compact of all the commoners. The Earth, and all that is therein, is given to men for the support and comfort of their being. And...all the fruit it naturally produces, and beasts it feeds, belong to mankind in common, they are produced by the spontaneous hand of Nature and no body has originally a private dominion." The private property is the property which a person produces by his labour or sweat. Locke explains this point thus "every men has a property in his own person. Thus no body has any right to but himself. The labour of his body, and the work of his hands, we may say are properly his. Whatsoever then he removes out of the state that hath provided and left it in, he hath mixed his labour with, and joined to it something that is his own, and thereby makes it his property. For this labour being the unquestionable property of the labourers, no man bu the can have a right to what that is once joined to".

(2) In the broader sense Locke uses the term property to include three natural rights of life, liberty and property. Locke has stated at various places that the individuals enter into contract and institute the state to preserve property. Here he is clearly using the term in the broader sense of the three rights referred to above. Thus property existed in the pre-civil society and the institution of state was created to preserve this right.

## JUSTIFICATION OF PRIVATE PROPERTY

Locke has justified Private Property on the following grounds:

**1. Religious Ground.** Locke believes that ownership of private property is justified on religious ground. He argues that God did not commit himself on public or private ownership of earth resources. Locke says, "That appropriate means for making use of the resources which God has given to men is for individuals to develop them so that they can actually sustain life."

**2. Property a Result of Labour.** The private property is justified on the basis that men have mixed labour in that. Locke said, "Every man has a property in his own person; thus nobody has any right but to himself. The labour of his body and the work of his hands we may say are properly his. Whatsoever then he removes out of the state that nature hath provided and left it in, he hath mixed his labour with and joined it to something that is the own, and thereby makes it his property." Men put in their labour by way of tilling and sowing the land. As such their labour makes the lands in private property.

**3. Social Product.** Locke argues that private property emerged in the society and continues to exist even today whether we like that or not. He says, "You shall see that some man will begin presently to enlarge his possession." The fact that property has got social approval throughout these ages is sufficient to make it an unobjectionable institution. It is natural to bulk of society as everyone has a desire to increase one's possessions.

**4. Guarantee for Individual Liberty.** Locke considered the institution of private property as a guarantee for individual liberties. He asserted that only those people have suffered under tyrannies who did not possess private property.

**5. Socially Sanctioned.** Possession of private property has social approval and sanction in so far as it has existed for such a long time. He says, "Property is legitimate because men who must live in its midst have consented to its existence... Rousseau will insist that consent must be an active process, one renewed each day in men's lives; while Burke will claim that genuine consent is found in the established customs which men unconsciously develop over generations and centuries.

**6. Historical Grounds.** Locke argues that history is a witness that only those have suffered under tyrannies who did not own property. Liberty of those people was snatched who were without private property. Once the institution of private property is encouraged, that is sure guarantee for all kinds of liberties.

## LIBERALISM AND INDIVIDUALISM

The 19th century is called as the Age of Liberalism because during this period appeared so many thinkers who laid special emphasis on human personality and Natural Rights.

"Liberalism" opines Laski is hardly less a habit of mind than a body of doctrine. The basis concept of Liberalism is that every person should possess the right to take decisions about his fortune and career with out any undue interference. Hobbes opines that the heart of liberalism is the understanding that progress is not a matter of mechanical contrivance, but of the liberation of living spiritual energy.

Liberalism has laid emphasis on confining state's activities. It has presented the following kinds of liberty *e.g.* civil liberty, fiscal liberty, political liberty, personal liberty, social liberty, national liberty, and economic liberty. Liberalism calls state as a necessary evil.

**Locke—'As a Liberalist'.** Locke comes before us as a liberal political thinker. The following arguments can be given in favour of his being a liberal political thinker:

**(1) Doctrine of Human Nature.** Like other liberal thinkers, Locke starts the study of his philosophy with his views on human nature. However, unlike Hobbes, Locke does not express his views about human nature in a systematic manner. Hence one has to collect his views from the scattered ideas in the Essays Concerning Human Understanding and the Second Treatise. Locke holds that human beings are basically decent and have been endowed with a natural social instinct. They are essentially peace-loving and not quarrelsome. They are not always selfish. Sometimes they are altruistic also. All human beings are equal, in the moral sense. Every individual enjoys certain natural rights *viz.* the right to life, liberty and property. He enjoys these rights not because of any position strength, wealth etc., but because he is a human being and possesses reason. However, unlike him he fails to provide any scientific basis for his views about human nature. This is why Prof. Wayper says that his views are "nothing like so profound, and certainly nothing like as consistent, as that of Hobbes." He holds that desire is the spring of all human acts and that a feeling of pleasure ensues when desire is satisfied and that of pain of uneasiness when it is thwarted.

**(2) Doctrine of State of Nature.** Locke' does not consider the state of nature as the state of war of each against all. On the other hand he considers it as an era of "peace, good-will, mutual assistance and preservation." He conceives the state of nature as a pre-political rather than a pre-social condition.

With Hobbes Locke believed that before man came in the civil state, he was living in the state of nature where there was law and order, peace and prosperity. It was a state of goodwill. The law of nature governed in the state of nature. Locke believed with Grotius that the law of nature is not only legal in character. It represented moral and rational reasoning of the society. In the words of Locke, "Man being born as has been proved, with a little to perfect freedom and an uncontrolled enjoyment of all the rights and privileges of the law of Nature, equally with any other man, or a number of men in the world, hath by nature not only power to preserve his property that is his life, liberty and estate against the injuries and attempts of other men, but to judge of and punish the breaches of that law in others." It is personal liberty rather than physical liberty that mattered in the state of nature.

**(3) Formation of Government by Consent.** Locke opines that the government cannot take away from any one his property without his consent. This leads to the principle of no taxation without representation. In actual practice, government by consent does not mean government by personal consent but through a representative assembly. It means constitutional government. Locke holds that consent to the formation of government once given is binding till the government is dissolved. He makes the consent binding because he wants to build up his theory of political obligation on it.

**(4) Popular Sovereignty.** The Lockean conception of the social contract points to the theory of sovereignty of the people, limited by the prior rights of the individual. At the time of the social contract and the institution of civil society, the individuals surrendered certain of their rights not to a man or assembly of men as in the case of Hobbes but to the entire community which became the source and seat of all authority in the state. The people retain the right of removing a government which betrays its trust or is inefficient. The people have the power to remove or alter the legislature. But this is not legal sovereignty and legal power.

**(5) Limitations on Government.** Locke abolishes the legal sovereign in favour of popular sovereignty. He has no idea of absolute and indivisible sovereignty. He is for a government based on division of powers and subject to a number of limitations. His limited government is as under—*(i)* It cannot command anything against public interests. *(ii)* It cannot violate or abrogate the innate natural rights of the individual, *(iii)* It cannot govern arbitrarily but must do so according to laws, *(iv)* It cannot tax the subjects without their consent. *(v)* Its laws must conform to the laws of Nature and of God. *(vi)* It is not the government which is sovereign but law which is rooted in common consent. *(vii)* A government which violates its limitations is not worthy of obedience. *(viii)* The state is created for 'certain conveniences' and it must justify itself by creating those conveniences. *(ix)* Locke, like Hobbes, is a utilitarian. He thinks that utility demands that the state should conform to a moral order by acting within its limits and not functioning autocratically.

**(6) Individualism of Locke.** Locke was a thorough-going individualist. He did not agree that the individual has no standing whatsoever and that he is only an insignificant and subordinate organ of the society. He believed that the individual has definite standing. According to Vaughan, "Everything in Locke's system revolves around the individual, everything is disposed so as to ensure the sovereignty of individual." That state is the best where the interests of the individuals are best protected. The foremost duty of the state is to preserve, protect and honour the inborn and natural rights of the mankind. That Locke is an Individualist is supported by the following agreements:

***1. Government Limited by Individual's Rights.*** Locke's theory of government is limited by the prior rights of the individual. His limited government cannot command anything against the public interest. He was opposed to all governmental paternalism.

***2. Negative Functions of the State.*** Locke considered the functions of the state entirely negative. The function of the state was to punish crime and thereby preserve the natural rights of each of its citizens. The state to him is at the most no more than a limited liability company.

***3. Real Sovereignty in Individual.*** Locke opines that the real sovereignty resides in the individual. It can be explained as under—

*(a)* The individual occupies a supreme place in his scheme of politics. *(b)* Nothing is done without the consent of the individual. *(c)* Locke regards consent as the very foundation of the state. As he writes, "Nothing can make a man a member of any commonwealth but his actually entering into it by positive engagement and express promise and contract."

***4. Individual Property Impregnable.*** Locke advocates that neither the legislature nor the community was authorised to take any part of his property save by his own consent.

***5. State's Meddling Opposed.*** For the state to meddle with either of them is an unwarrantable impertinence. The positive functions were completely denied to the authority of the state.

***6. Government and Individual's Role.*** Locke opines that the creating, maintaining and dissolving of government is done through the consent of the individuals. The individual enters the civil state with his moral sense fully trained, his moral code perfectly articulated, the individual owes nothing to the state on that side of the account.

***7. Govt. Exists for Individuals.*** Locke has subordinated government to the community. According to Sabine, "Government is indispensable and its right therefore in a sense is indefeasible, but it is also derivative in the sense that it exists for the well being of the nation." Locke has emphasised that the government exists only for the welfare of the individuals. According to Dunning, "There is in this conception nothing of that absolute and uncontrollable sovereignty which was the soul of Hobbe's system" Maxey says, "It was not his concern to exalt its political authority but to describe its limitation."

***8. Right of People to Revolt.*** Locke's individualism transpires from his ideas about the rights of the people to revolt against their sovereign. The people have power, to remove a government whose policies seem to be curtailing their rights. The people have certain basic minimum rights. No authority in the state has any right to snatch these rights from him.

***9. Division of Powers for Individual Freedom.*** To uphold his individualism Locke attempts at the theory of division of powers. He believes that this device is essential for preserving individual and his freedom.

***10. State for the Protection of Individual's Rights.*** The state was created for the protection of the natural rights and the happiness of the individual. Locke sought rights and freedom for all men without distinction. Prof. Dunning says, "Locke's equal rights...are so in-wrought in his explanation of political institutions as to appear indispensable to the very existence of an actual political community."

***11. Legislature the Trust of the People.*** According to Locke, the legislature is the 'supreme organ' of the state and the executive is subordinate to it. But behind this supreme authority stands embodiment of power, the people. The legislature is the trust of the people and must act for their benefit and well being. if it acts contrary to this, the supreme power *i.e.*, the people can remove it or alter it. Locke says, "The community perpetually retains a sword. The power of saving themselves from the attempts and designs of any body, even of their legislators, whenever they shall be so foolish or so wicked as to lay and carry on designs against the liberties and properties of the subject."

***13. Innate and Natural Rights of Individuals.*** Locke accords a fundamental position to the innate and natural rights of life, liberty and property belong to the individual due to the fact of his very personality. In other words he says that the natural rights are prior to the state.

***14. Negative Functions Only.*** Locke assigns to the state purely negative functions. It interferes only when the rights of the individual are endangered. Otherwise the individual is left completely free to pursue his moral, material and intellectual persuits. Locke could not reconcile with the idea of assigning positive functions to the state which could lead to state intervention in the personal affairs of the individual.

***15. Pleasure Pain Theory.*** His faith in the pleasure and pain theory, which forms the starting point of his philosophy, is a further pointer to his individualism. To him all, the actions of an individual are motivated by the desire for pleasure and avoidance of pain.

***16. Emphasis on Private Property.*** Locke's views on property further confirm him as an out-and-out individualist. To him property which was initially owned in common becomes private property of an individual after the mixes his labour with it or imparts a bit of his individuality to the common object. This is the best way to emphasise the importance and worth of the individual.

***17. Law of Nature.*** Locke assigns a prominent position to the law of nature and insists that even the state law must conform to it under all circumstances. Thus he places the state at the mercy of the individual and authorises even the minority to challenge the moral justification of a law passed by the majority. Prof. Vaughan says, "Locke lays a perpetual ferment for rebellion against the state on the part of any and every individual."

***18. Preservation of Natural Rights.*** Locke holds that the individual is everything and that state is a means to achieve certain ends. It is the supreme duty of the state to preserve natural rights of men. Revolution is justified when such rights were flouted, disregarded or disrespected.

Thus Locke was a thorough-going individualist. In fact some of the scholars have criticised Locke for carrying individualism to such an extreme. For example Prof. Laski says Locke reduced the state to "a negative institution, a kind of gigantic limited liability company." By assigning purely negative functions to the state Locke in fact ensures the domination of the strong over the weak and the rich over the poor. He omits the idea of ensuring social justice nor does he pay any attention to the moral upliftment of the individual.

## THEORY OF CONTRACT

The Second Treatises on Government opens with a consideration of political power and origin of the State. According to Locke State is not the result of growth as Aristotle pointed out but it had been deliberately created by men who once lived without any State that is who once lived in the State of Nature. The State of Nature is not the last or the perfect model of society. There were certain inconveniences in the State of Nature. To get rid of these inconveniences men entered into a contract. Here it is essential to point out that just as Locke's Natural State implies a natural man utterly distinct from that of Hobbes, so does Locke's social contract represent triumph of reason on a hard necessity.

(1) To get out of the State of Nature, Locke points out, men make contract to enter into a civil society. This is a contract of all with all. This is a social, or more truly a political contract, since it establishes political society. It is not a contract made with the government which is to be set up later on. The end for which the contract is made is the protection and the preservation of life, liberty and property—the three natural rights which people enjoyed in the State of nature—against danger both from within and without the community. In return for the security of life, liberty and property, each individual gives up his natural rights of interpretating, judging and executing the Law of Nature and punishing offences against the law, and not to give up all the natural rights. The contract thus, as Locke puts it is not a general one as with Hobbes, but limited and specific in character. Contract is no more than a surrender of certain rights whereby man's remaining rights shall be protected and preserved.

(2) It is a contract to which all must consent. Locke says, "Men being...by nature all free, equal and independent, no one can be put out of this estate, and subjected to the political power of another, without his own consent." A society thus becomes by the acts of individuals who formed it, vested with it the functions of determining what is offence against the law of nature and punishing violations of that law—and these functions constitute in Locke's view, the whole scope of political authority. The community becomes the sole interpreter and executor of the laws it makes for the protection of these rights.

(3) Though the original contract itself is unanimous, all parties, to it agree, henceforth "to submit to the determination of the majority." Since unless men agree to majority rule, decisions cannot be taken and the State cannot survive.

(4) The social contract once made cannot be revoked. He who has signed it "can never again be in the liberty of the State of Nature."

(5) This contract does not, as with Hobbes, put an end to the Law of Nature as it does to the State of Nature. Man in the State continues to be under that law, as he was before.

(6) According to Wayper, this contract is the first step to the drawing up of a trust. People, having formed a society, must then

institute a government. They do not do this by making a contract with the government—that, as Rousseau was so clearly to point out, would be to invest government with too much dignity and authority.

(7) It is a contract to which each generation must consent. For "a child is born a subject of no country or government." "Every man's children being by nature as free as himself, or any of his ancestors ever were, may, whilst they are in that freedom, choose what society they will join themselves to, what Commonwealth they will put themselves under." This is in contrast to Hobbes who had conceived of a contract in which once the agreement was made it was binding on all future generations.

(8) In this contract, "the community is thus both the creator and beneficiary of the trust." As creator of the trust the community might be said to make a covenant with the trustee or the government. But as beneficiary of the trust, the community makes no contract with the trustee "who accepts a unilateral obligation towards it. The acceptance of the trust by the government is at the same time its undertaking not to exceed the limits laid down by the trust." (Wayper). Locke here lacks clarity. He neither talks of any contract between people and government, nor does he deny it. But the use of the word trust shows that there was no second contract. So powers of the government are always derivative and hence limited by the covenant of the trust and thus the community is both the creator and beneficiary of the trust. Here, thus, it may be noted as Sabine remarks that the grant of trust be community to government divests the community of power so long as the government faithfully carries out its duties.

(9) Lastly, Locke was the first thinker to make a clear distinction between society and government. "Whenever, therefore, any number of men are so united into one society, as to quit every one has executive power of the Law of Nature, and to resign it to the politic, there and there only is a political or civil society. And this is done wherever any number of men in the State of Nature enter into society to make one people, or a single body politic, under one supreme government. For hereby he authorises the society to make laws for him. And this puts men out of a State of Nature into that of Commonwealth, by setting up a judge eon earth, with authority to

determine all the controversies and redress the injuries that may happen to any member of the Commonwealth."

**Criticism.** Locke's theory of Contract has been criticised on the following grounds:

(1) Locke's theory of social Contract is firstly subject to the general criticism against all contractualist that political society is the result of some contract whether between people themselves or with the ruler. The Aristotlian dogma that State is natural is equally, rather more appealing. Not to talk of any contract, it cannot be taken for granted that there was a State of Nature before the emergence of political society. Modern thought pins more faith in evolutionary nature of the State rather than the emergence of the State as a result of any contract. Locke particularly more subject to this criticism than Hobbes, because to Hobbes, the contract was only a logical concept whereas to Locke it was both logical as well as historical.

(2) As to particular criticism of Locke's social contract, Sabine remarks that the difficulty with his theory is that Locke is no where clear as to what precisely does arise by the "original compact." Is it society itself or only the government which arises from this "original compact? Locke no where concedes the later view though he does not deny it either. The continental writers like Puffendorf and Althusius had clarified this problem by assuming that there were two contracts—one between individuals that gave rise to the community and the other between the community and the government. Locke tacitly assumes some such position, though he nowhere states it.

(3) According to Locke the rights of the individual which he enjoyed in the State of Nature and to protect which the political society came into existence are indefeasible. Yet according to Locke the community or the government are to take decision by majority. Locke forgets that the majority can also be very tyrannical. There is no good reason why an individual should leave his rights to the decision of a majority.

(4) Moreover, the terms of the contract also cannot escape from criticism. As Wayper remarks Locke attributes superior power to no less than three different bodies namely to the community, to the legislature, to a single person if the executive power is vested in him and if he had also share in the legislature. At one moment we get the idea that community has supreme power over legislature for the later's power arises from the former, and at another moment we get the idea that legislature is bestowed to the supreme power and the community is to abide by its laws so long as it remains in office.

## JEAN JACQUES ROUSSEAU

The writer whose work most truly reflected contemporary conditions in France and aimed at a solution of the social and political injustice of the period was Jean Jacques Rousseau. He was born on June 28, 1712 at Geneva (Switzerland). His father, Isaac, was an able watch maker, but volatile and thrifltess. His father abandoned the profession of watches to become a dancing master. Shortly after his marriage to Rousseau's mother he left her to go to Constantinople. "She urged him to return," Rousseau tells us in his confessions. "He abandoned every thing and came home. I was the sad fruit of this re-union. Ten months afterwards I was born, ill and weak; I cost my mother her life, and my birth was the first of my misfortunes."

Kinsfolk cared for the motherless boy up to his tenth year—lovingly, but most haphazardly. He was not unnaturally spoiled by his widowed father ("No one ever forced me; no one ever crossed my will."), who kept him awake all night reading aloud romances adventures and stories. Looking bank on this early period, Rousseau says, "In a short time, I had acquired, by this method, not only a tremendous case in reading and comprehending, but also an insight into the passions quit unique in one of my age—I understood nothing—I felt everything. All of the obscure emotions which I underwent, one after another.....formed in me intelligence of a peculiar character and gave me wonderful and romantic impressions of life of which experience and reflection have never quite been able to cure me."

When he was ten, his father wounded another citizen in a street-fight and fled from Geneva to escape punishment. Young Rousseau was then taken into his mother's family and put to school under a pastor at Boissy. After two years he was brought back to Geneva and apprenticed to a notary, only to be dismissed after a few weeks because his master despaired of his ever being able to learn that simple calling. Then he was apprenticed to an engraver, who succeeded by dint of many beatings, in forcing the young good-for-nothing boy to learn the rudiments of the engraving trade. At the age of sixteen he rebelled and ran away, from home thus beginning a wandering career that lasted to the end of his life.

A tramp and beggar, fleeing from Geneva to escape capture and return to the hatred master engraver, Rousseau chanced to call at the door of the Catholic priest at Confignon and ask for good. He was converted to the Roman faith. The priest sent him to a Madame de Warrens at Arnecy, a young widow whose good works included caring for homeless proselytes. She sent him to a monastery at Turin. In the monastery school indocile pupils were not kept; and Rousseau was soon turned out. He made his way back to Arnecy and appeared again at her door. Madame de Warens took him in again and decided to give him an education. In 1730, she sent him on a trip to Lyons, apparently hoping to be rid of him. When he returned, he found that she had gone to Paris without leaving an address. So he took to the road again and roamed the country far and wide in search of his beloved. In 1731 he found her comfortably established at Chambery. She took him in, not merely as a ward but as a lover. He lived with her and largely on her bounty until 1740. In 1737 he made a brief visit to Geneva to receive his small portion of his mother's dowry. Though not long away from Chambery, he was gone long enough for his goddess to take another lover. However, she was broad-minded. When Rousseau returned she welcomed him and bade him remain as second-place lover, which for a time he did.

By 1740 Rousseau had become convinced that he had no longer a place in the life of Madame de Warens. Through Madame de Warens it was arranged for him to go to Lyons as a tutor in the family of a certain Monsieur de Malby. He proved to be a poor teacher and hated the work. After a year he resigned and went to Paris. And shortly came under the eye of the influential Madame de Broglic. She got him appointed Secretary to the French ambassador at Venice. In August, 1744, he was dismissed and returned to Paris. He opened a small hotel in Paris. Therese Leavasseur, a maid-servant, who served in his hotel, became his real and lasting friend and whom in 1770 he would finally marry—after she had borne him five children, all of whom were disowned and sent to the foundling asylum.

In 1750 came the event which raised him from obscurity and transformed him into a world figure. In 1749 the Academy of Dijon announced a prize for the best essay on the subject, 'whether the advance of once lived without any State that is who once lived in the State of Nature. In the State of Nature the individual lived a simple life—sinless, happy and careless existence. He was essentially a solitary being content to exist without any sort of society. He wears no clothes and feels no need of them. He finds his scanty needs amply supplied by the lavish bounties of Nature. No consciousness of the approach of death, no restrictions on his perfect liberty, his equality with his fellows was complete.

According to Rousseau, "Primitive man was near an animal than man; he lived a free, healthy, honest and happy life, an isolated life having no ties and obligations. He was guided by two sentiments—self-interest and pity, and having no moral obligation with other men he could not be good or bad, virtuous or vicious. He was a creature of impulse and instinct in whom the quality of foresight was slow in developing. He led a solitary and non-moral life in the State of Nature. Even speech was undeveloped, for speech presupposed communication and same social interplay. So primitive man was devoid of language and wandered about the primeval forests begetting his offspring by the way, hunting for his food, and, concerned only with the satisfaction of physical needs. In a word, the natural man was neither happy nor unhappy." "Natural man was an animal whose behaviour was purely instinctive, any though whatever is depraved. He wholly lacked language unless in the form of instinctive cries, and without language any general idea is impossible. Consequently the natural man was neither moral nor vicious. He was not unhappy but neither was he happy. Obviously he had no property, for property, resulted from ideas, forseen wants, knowledge, industry, which were intrinsically natural but implied language, thought and society."

In the State of Nature man has no property and does not want any. "In this primitive State, men had neither houses nor huts nor any—kind of property whatever, everyone lived where he could, seldom for more than a single night, the sexes united without design as accident, opportunity or inclination brought them together—the produce on earth furnished them with all they needed. And instinct told them how to use it." All this changed with the growth of inequality; inequality was due to the abandonment of solitude for society and the institution of society was due to the establishment of private property. Rousseau says, 'The first man who, having enclosed a piece of ground, he thought himself of saying, 'this is mine' and found people simple enough to believe him, was the real founder of civil society. From now many crimes, wars, and murders; from now many misfortunes, might not any one have saved mankind by putting up the ditch and crying to his fellows 'how are you listening to this imposter? You are undone if you once forget that the fruits of the earth belong to us all, and the earth itself to none." The private property gave rise to inequality. Thus inequality led to jealousy and then to strife to law and that led to police and thus the State came into existence. Man lost his primitive the sciences and arts had purified or corrupted morals.' He decided to try for the award. He thought that a strong case could be made for the thesis that man is natrually good and that our social institutons alone have rendered him evil. Setting to work at once on this theme, he quickly composed his essay and sent it to the Academy of Dijan. In Angust, 1750, the award was announced. Rousseau won the prize of a gold medal and 300 francs.

In the year 1753 the same Academy again announced a prize for writing the best essay on the subject 'What is the origin of inequality among men and is it authorised by Natural Laws?" But this time Rousseau failed to win the prize. In 1754 he returned to his native city, was received with a great ovation. He married Therese in 1770. At least on July 2, 1778, a stroke of apoplexy took him off.

According to Dunning, "Rousseau was sensitive, and emotional. He had self-conscious temperament, impatient of control even of self control and resentful towards every institution or convention that suggested restriction or regularity....Only one human being seems to have possessed the power to induce more than a feeble flicker of rudimentary social instinct in Rousseau, and this was the coarse and unlonely woman with whom for a third of century he lived in squalid and irregular domestic relations."

Between the years (1755-1761) Rousseau wrote several important books. Rousseau was a great literary genius. He adorned and illuminated the field of political theory with a large number of writings.

**His Works.** The following were the main works of Rousseau.

1. Discourses on the Moral Effects of Arts and Sciences (1751).
2. Discourses on the Origin and Foundations of Inequality among Men" (1755).
3. La Nuvelle Heeoise (1761).
4. Du Contract Social or Social Contract (1762).
5. Emile (1762).
6. The Dialogues : The Reveries of a Solitary Worker (1778).
7. Confessions (1782).

G.D.H. Cole has remarked that 'Social Contract's to be still by far the best of all text-books of political philosophy.

## POLITICAL PHILOSOPHY

In the Social Contract, the very first sentence contained the famous phrases to the solution of the understanding of political thought of Rousseau. It ran as follows—

"Man is born free, and everywhere he is in chains. One who believes himself the master of the rest is only more of a slave than they. How does this change come about? I do not know, What can render it legitimate? I believe that that question I can answer".

Man is born free only in the sense that freedom is his inforn right: it is the necessary condition for the proper development of the various potentialities of man. "We can say that he is born for freedom, that he ought to be free. The second part of the first sentence that he is everywhere in chains implies that conventions and customs of society alongwith state regulations imposed upon him contain artificial and unnecessary restraints which hinder the development of his personality".

## ROUSSEAU'S CONCEPTION OF THE STATE OF NATURE

In fact, his political theory is based upon the conception of a pre-political state of nature. According to Rousseau, "primitive man was near an animal than man; he lived a free, healthy, honest and happy life, an isolated life having no ties and obligations. He was guide by two sentiments—self-interest and pity, and having no moral obligation with other men he could not be good or bad, virtuous or vicious. He was a creature of impulse and instinct in whom the quality of foresight was slow in developing. He led a solitary and non-moral life in the state of nature. Even speech was undeveloped, for speech presupposed communication and same social interplay. So primitive man was devoid of language and wandered about the primeval forests begetting his offspring by the way, hunting for his food, and, concerned only with the satisfaction of physical needs. In a word, the natural man was neither happy nor unhappy". "Natural man was an animal whose behaviour was purely instinctive; any thought whatever is depraved. He wholly lacke language, unless in the form of instinctive cries, and without language any general idea is impossible.

In the state of nature man had no property. There were no industries. Such a state of affairs could not last long and a stage arrived when man changed his previous way of living and began to live in settled groups. Social institutions gradually evolved. What a man had been contended to look upon as his mere possessions, now that he had in a given portion of land and prosperity to care for, he wished to be regarded as his very own inalienable good. He wished that his possessions should be recognised as his personal property. The offsprings of this desire were very great.

Rousseau has sketched a very peculiar picture of the state of nature. We are further told by him that in the original state men were equal, independent, self-sufficient and contended. Their conduct was based on emotions of self-interest and pity. It was not based on reason. In due course, with the progress of civilization, certain evils arose. The division of labour that followed the development of the arts and the rise of private property created distiction between rich and poor that broke down the happy natrual condition of mankind and made it necessary to establish a civil soceity. "The natural man was neither energetic nor aggressive monster of Hobbes, ceaselessly driven by his passions to war upon his fellows. Life was simple, regular and solitary."

Rousseau says "Such was or may well have been the origin of society and law, which bound new fetters on the poor, and gave new powers to the rich, which irretrievably destroyed natural liberty, eternally fixed the law of property and inequality, converted usurpation into unalterable right and for the advantage of a few ambitious individuals, and subjected all mankind to perpetual labour, slavery, and wretechedness." This is the picture of the state of nature and origin of the state portrayed by Rousseau. Rousseau was an admirer of the noble savage, he admires the average man: he wants to level out the actual inequalities of men by stressing moral intuition and character.

**The Social Contract Idea in Rousseau**. The process by which political society is formed is a social contract, since only by agreement and consent can authority be justified and liberty retained. The terms of contract has been described by Rousseau in the following words:

"Each of us puts into a single mass his person and all his power under the supreme direction of the general will, and, in our corporate capacity, we will receive each member as an indivisible part of the whole."

## THEORY SOCIAL CONTRACT

According to Rousseau State is not the result of growth as Artistotle pointed out but it had been deliberately created by men who freedom and the poor were oppressed by the rich. Few haves and many have nots. This led to misery, wretchedness, violence, crime and disease. According to Hearnshaw, he gave the discription of France of his own days.

One question arises why not to return to the State of Nature and to enjoy freedom again. Because it was impossible at that stage to go back in the State of Nature. Men now could not give up all the ideals and the habits which they got from their social heritage. Because people had developed a sense of decency. Moreover, it was not possible to return to the blissful State of nature because there were 'no longer forests where the noble savage could run wild: no longer was the population of the world so small that solitude for each and all was feasible; no longer could the clothes be dispensed with without embarrassment and inconveniences; never again the habits of civilization be discarded : the knowledge of good and evil be forgotten; the fear of death eliminated. Hearnshaw writes, "The gates of the Garden of Eden were closed and an angel with a flaming sword prevented all approach, the fall having taken place and its consequence being ineradicable the new Jerusealam must be something wholly different from the Garden of Eden."

Now Rousseau asks, "What should be done in this soceity? "How could primitive liberty be recovered without the abolition of law? How could equality be restored without the surrender of property? How in short could individualism be harmonised with socialism? How could anarchic man and organised society be reconciled? One of the other, how could liberty be reconciled with authority ? or how could personal freedom be recognised to collective security—the fundamental problem of political science?"

Rousseau's problems in his words: "The problem is to find a form of association that will defend and protect with the whole common force the person and goods of each associate and in which each, while uniting himself with all may still obey himself alone and remain as free as before."

Now people decided to enter into a contract. Each unites with all and thus gets the protection of all. He gives the social contract. The individuals who proposed to transform themselves into a community meet together and simultaneously make the great surrender in the following words:

"Each of us puts his person and all his power in common, under the supreme direction of the general will, and, in our corporate capacity, we receive each member as an indivisible part of the whole."

**Implications of the Contract.** "At once, in place of the individual personality of each contracting party, this act of association creates a moral and collective body, composed of as many members as the assembly contains votes, and receiving from this act its unity, its common identity, its life and its will. This public person, so framed by the union of all persons, formerly took the name of city, now takes that of repulic or body politic; it is called by its members State when passive, Sovereign when active, and power when compared with others like itself." The will of the sovereign he calls as the general will. This general will enjoys all the attributes of a sovereign.

It would be at first sight this despotic monster should be no less hated than the unmitigated tyrant and envisaged by Hobbes, but Rousseau sets to work to show that this is not the case. The State is an organism, it possesses a personality, it is characterised by a corporate mind, a command conscience, a general will, which is a will for the good of all, the sovereignty resides in this general will. Thus this general will of the community is the real will of the community. It is the real will of every one of its constituent members. (Each has surrendered his sovereignty by one hand and has taken the same by the other hand). The general will is animated by a moral purpose and is for the good of all. Thus one as a moral being should do, is to do what is in the good of all. A moral person is one who will, a will for the good of all.

In short, the following points must be remembered in mind to have a clear cut picture of social contract.

1. The first point to be noted is that each member gives his all to the society; and thus making the community absolute. The community that is born as a result of the pact cannot possibly be oppresive; it cannot possible be opposed to freedom.
2. Under this pact no one is a loser but everyone is a gainer. Rousseau himself says, "Since each gives himself up to all,

he does give himself up to anyone; and as there is acquired over every asssociate the same right that is given up by himself; there is gained the equivalent of what is lost, with greater power to preserve what is left."

3. Thirdly, it should be noted that the surrender is made, not to an irresponsible sovereign as it in Hobbes, but to an entity of which every individual is a constituent part and "over whose activities he had the same degree of control as any other member of the community." In other words, according to Rousseau, the contract is between two aspects of the individual. Men are at one and the same time, a passive body of subjects and an active body of sovereign. It can there be said that each, giving himself to all, gives himself to nobody.
4. Lastly, the ideal society which is to be ushered in by the social contract is organic in character. It is not individualistic like the body politic of Hobbes' or Locke's conception. It is a moral and collective being having its own life, will and entity, Rousseau describes it as a public person.

**Criticism.** Rousseau's theory of contract has been criticised on the following grounds:

1. Rousseau's theory of social contract is firstly subject to the general criticism against all contractualist that political society is the resul of some contract between people themselves. The Aristotelian dogma that State is natural is moral appealing than the idea of contract, dogma that State is natural is more appealing than the idea of contract. Not to talk of any contract, it cannot be taken for granted that there was a State of Nature before the emergence of political society.
2. According to Sabine, Rousseau in view of his criticism of the natural man, ought to have avoided the notion of contract altogether as both meaningless and misleading.

   (i) "His contract is nothing to do with the rights and power of government, since the latter is merely 'the people's agent and is so devoid of independent power that it cannot be the subject of a contract.

(ii) The imaginary act by which a society is produced is not even remotely like a contract, because the rights and liberties of individuals have no existence at all except as they are already members of groups.

(iii) Rousseau's whole argument depended upon the fact that a community of citizens is unique and coeval with its members; they, neither make it nor have rights against it. It is an 'association' not an 'aggregation' a moral and collective personality. The word contract was about as misleading as any that Rousseau could have chosen.

3. Lastly, Rousseau's Theory of social contract is not compatible with his theory of General Will. If General Will is supreme then social contract is unnecessary and meaningless and if social contract is necessary then General will is not supreme.

Thus Rousseau's social contract lacks logic.

## THEORY OF GENERAL WILL

"The notion of the "General Will", remarks Jones, "is not only the most central concept of Rousseau's theory, it is also the most original, the most interesting and historically the most important contribution which he made to political theory."

Rousseau was much disgusted with the society of his own days. He thought that all led the lives of slaves and no body was free in the true sense of the word. He said, "Man was born free, but he is everywhere in chains." He gives the analogy of a tree and points out that as mal-formed tree is less truly a tree than it would have been if left severally alone, so man in a corrupt society is less truly natural than if left in the State of Nature. For Rousseau, like Aristotle nature of a thing was, what it was capable of becoming under the best possible circumstances. In Emile, he deal with education that can be expected to produce a natural man. In the 'Social Contract' he writes of the State in which alone the natural man can reach his full stature.

He states his problem in the form of a paradox i.e., that "By what inconceivable art has means been found of making men free by making them subject." He wants to constitute a society which will substitute justice for mere instinct, which will give to man's action that moral character which they lacked before; which would change man from a stupid and limited animal into an intelligent being and a man. The government must function as an agent or servant of society and the society is to be created in such a way that each one when united to his fellows, renders obedience to his own will, and remains as free as he was before. It men lose their freedom; it would defeat the ends for which men come together, those ends being the fulfilment of their nature, which slavery would make impossible.

According to Rousseau, the will of each individual is merged into a General Will. The General Will corresponds to the common interest of all the members of the community as in contrast with the particular interest of the individual. It was normally arrived at by asking each member to vote for what he believed to be common good and accepting the view of the majority. The majority could, of course, be wrong, but Rousseau believed that the majority would err less often the identifying the general will than any other group, because their interest in community welfare would not be as easily corrupted. As for those who voted against measures accepted by the majority, Rousseau suggested that they, too, will be benefitted.

**Distinction between the Real Will and the Actual Will.** Rousseau distinguished between two types of Will of the individual namely *(1)* the 'Real Will' and *(2)* the 'Actual Will'. From 'Actual Will' Rousseau understood the will which is selfish, irrational and thought of the good of the individual alone. Thus this will is contradictory to the General Will which aims at the good of all. On the other hand, 'Real Will' of an individual aims at the common good and not at the particular or selfish good of the individual. Real Will is something higher, nobler and supreme. Thus Real Will of an individual always coincide with the General Will.

"The General Will is what is willed by a community as a whole. It is a common will for a common interest and as such, it is different from and may be opposed to the particular interests of the individuals.

It is the common will of the people. General Will is my own real will. Hence in obeying it, I realise my own real nature and I am truly free. The General Will is something over and above the sum of all the individual wills present in the society, but it is not something completely apart from individuals. Each individual has both a private will, in which he isolates his desires from the social group within which they function, and a General Will in which his individual desires ; are at the same time the desires proper to his status as a member of society and a citizen."

**Distinction between the General Will and the Will of all.** According to Rousseau General Will is not a sum total of the will of all. Because all may be willing for their own selfish good and not for the common good. He says, "the General Will is always just and always aims at the public good, but it does not follow that the deliberations of the people are always right. Man always aims at his good, but he does not always know what it is.....There is often a considerable difference between the General Will and the will of all, the former aims at the common interest and the later aims at private interest and is only a sum of particular wills.

But if we take away from these wills the various particular interests which conflict with each other, what remains as the sum of the difference is a General Will." According to Prof. DUNNING, "Rousseau distinguishes the General Will from the will of all. This latter is but the sum of all the particular volitions of the individuals about their private interest.

The General Will may be called the will of the majority, if it aims at the good of all. But the General Will is not always the will of the majority because majority will at its particular good. The will of the majoirty or even the will of the single individual is the General Will when it aims at the good of all. But Rousseau says that the General Will is usually the will of the majority because the majority can err less as it is difficult for the bulk of the people to become corrupted and ignore their real wills.

But Rousseau is not satisified with this. He gives another way of detecting General Will when he says that the General Will registers itself automatically by making differences of opinion cancel each other. Thus opinion cannot be refuted but neither it be proved. Prof. Sabine observes. "This concept of the General Will amounted to ray that communists have an inscrutable faculty for discertning their well-being and proper destiny." Thus Rousseau originated the romantic cult of the group, and this way the fundamental between his social philosophy and the individualism from which he revolted.

**Attributes of the General Will.** The following are some of the features of the General Will:

**1.** ***Unity.*** According to Lord, "It makes and preserves the unity of the national Character and issues in those common qualities, which ought to expect to find in the citizens of a given State."

**2.** ***Unlimited Sovereign.*** The General Will will be sovereign. Rousseau gives his sovereign just as absolute and supreme powers as Hobbes has assigned to his Leviathan. "Whosoever refuses to obey the General Will" writes Rousseau, "Shall be compelled to de so by the whole body...he will be forced to be free"."If the State is a moral person whose life is in the union of its members, and if the most important of its care is the care for its own preservation, it must have a Universal and compelling force in order to move and dispose each-part as may be most advantageous to the whole."

**3.** ***"The General Will".*** Says Rousseau", "cannot be deligated in any way whatever. Any attempt to delegate it would mean its end. Rousseau expressed, "It is the voice of the people, that is, the voice of God". Nothing less than all the people together can be trusted to Will the General Will.

**4.** ***Inalienable.*** "The 'General Will," Rousseau says, must always be inalienable and indivisible". "According to Rousseau as JONES remarks, "The Sovereignty, being merely the exercise of the General Will, can never be alienated; and the Sovereign, since it is only a collective being can be represented only by itself. Power, certainly, can be transferred; but not will.....For the same reason that Sovereignty is inalienable, it is indivisible. For Will is either general or it is no, either the Will of the whole body of the people or that of a part only. In the first case, the expressed Will is an act of Sovereignty and constitutes a law; in the second case, it is only a particular Will, or an act magistracy—a degree at the most."

**5.** "The General Will" says Prof. Wayper "As Rousseau insists cannot be an executive Will". The people ought not to be responsible for the details of Government. Those who make the law should not carry it out for it is the characteristic of the Sovereign General Will that it must be impersonal and the decrees of Government may frequently be particular and personal. Hence Rousseau makes a clear distinction between the Government and the Sovereign people.

**6.** "According to Rousseau" as Wayper points out, "the General Will must be a Will which is general in every sense and which is particular in none." It must take amount of the voice of every citizen, since it was agreed in the contract that each is received as an integral part of our group. It must bind all equally......it must deal only with the generalites of legislation, with the common cause and not with private interests—though it alone will decide what is the common cause and what are private interests. It is, in fact, only the fundamental laws that shape the Constitution of the State that Rousseau regards as law, and therefore as the product of the General Will.

**7.** "The General Will" rousseau adds, "is infallible". He says that General Will is always right because it tends to the good of all. The General Will", says Rousseau, "is always right, but it is not always known". "It does not follow", he adds, "that the deliberation of the people are always equally correct. Our will is always for our good, but we do not always see what this is; the people is never corrupted; but it is often deceived."

## ROUSSEAU AS INDIVIDUALIST SOCIALIST

It is hardly an exaggeration to say that Rousseau to be found at the entrance of all the main patterns of political thought leading to the present. There is little difficulty in finding excellent authorty in Rousseau to support individualism, anarchism, democracy, socialism and absolutism. He has been praised as an individualist and condemned as a socialist. He is at once a democrat and at the same time an absolute. In fact Rousseau's philosophy is the support upon which many succeeding thinkers with opposite views have equally drawn. "The writings of Rousseau's writes Neill. "appear to consist of a mass of contradiction." In his 'Discourse in Emile' and in the opening chapter of the 'Social Contract', he displays himeslf as an extreme individualist, a passionate devotee of anarchic freedom, on the other hand, in his 'Political Economy', and in the later sections of the 'Social Contract', he advocates a collectivism so complete as to establish the unqualified authority of State over the citizens.

**1. Rousseau as an Individualist.** Rousseau's earlier work "The Discourse on the origin of Inequality" is characterised by a defined individualism and as Neill puts it is his "The Maker of Modern Mind". There are many individualists who get their theories of an anarchically organised State with practically no social control over the individual from Rousseau. Some of his bitter attacks on man-made institutions are also to be found in his "Discourse on the Arts and Science" as well as in 'Emile'. In 'Emile' he makes clear beyond debt that the people is to be educated for his own sake and not for any other. 'Emile' is subject to no restraints whatsoever because Rousseau that all restraints are unnatural. 'Emile' is taught to reagrd himself as an end and never as means. "Man is too noble a being", writes Rousseau, "to serve as an instrument for others and he must not be used for what suits them without consulting also what suits him. It is never right to harm a human soul for benefit of others".

Rousseau's Individualism is romantic individualism (when man enjoys liberty and follows the dictates of his heart) Rousseau's magic key for the right action is instinctive feeling. Instinctive feeling is God's blessing and the heart has reason, which reason knows not. Rousseau believed that man is basically good and is free and independent. To him whatever is natrual is good, that is natral man or natural society. A natural man following his instinct is always good to his fellows and is naturally honest to himself. Rousseau was hostile to reason in his works excepting social contract where runs an intense anti-social restarint. As Sabine points out, against intelligence, the growth of knowledge, and the progress of science, which the enlightenment believed to be the only hope of civilisation, he set amiable and benevolent sentiments, good will and reverence. As Rousseau himself remarks "a thinking man is a depraved animal".

**2. Rousseau as an Absolutist.** Most of the Rousseau's critics for example, Vaughan, Duguit Popper and Maine, all regard Rousseau as an absolutist and totalitarian. He is considered by them as a most terrible ally of despotism in all its forms. Duguit wrote "Rousseau is the father of jacobin despotism, of Caesarian dictatorship, and the inspirer of the absolutist doctrine of Kant and of Hegal".

In Social Contract, Rousseau justifies State in all its pomp and show. Here he casts aside the pearl of liberty for the sake of security which he has condemned in his earlier writings. Whereas his earlier works were thoroughly anarchistic.

His Totalitarianism is most evident from his theory of General Will. In the 'Social Contract', Rousseau tells us in the beginning that "Man is born free but everywhere he is found in chains." The Social Contract is an attempt to justify the chains in which a man found himself. He invents contract, with terms to fit the problem of man's forgiving the chains by creating a society to which he surrenders everything. What in fact happens is this : Men agree with each other to surrender themselves and their possessions to the community and this act of their resulted in the creation of the famous General Will which is supreme, absolute and infallible. Man as an individual must bow before the dictates of the General Will. Against it he has no right. "Whoever refuses to obey the General Will shall be compelled to do so by the whole body." This means nothing else than that he shall be forced to be free. so a man who disagreed with the General Will—which for all the practical purposes is the will of the majority—is really disagreeing with his better self. By coercion he is forced to be free—a truly terrible device by which he tried to reconcile freedom with authority or individualism with thorough-going absolutism.

**3. Rousseau a Democrat.** The critics regard the philosophy of Rousseau the call to all democratic revolutions. It particularly inspired the French revolutions. As cobden points out, "He is by general agreement taken, a true prophet if not the very source of fountain of the modern democratic State. "The people" writes Rousseau "took the place of God. He became the source of all power of all morality, of all justice." Rousseau supplants the despotism of king by despostism of the people—a despotism which is uncontrollable irresistable. Rousseau is convinced that man is both infallible and God. Rousseau was particularly influenced by the democratic tradition of his native State Geneva. The General Will is the sovereign, is nothing but the will of the people. The sovereignty of the General Will in fact means the sovereignty of the people. The government is merely a representative body set up by the people to carry out the law enacted by the people, Rousseau makes the individual both the subject and the sovereign.

Rousseau believed in the moral virtues of man; he believed that man is essentially good and virtuous. Democracy also presupposes the moral character of man. (Democracy all before self and not self before all.) For, otherwise there would be no will to accommodate others. People according to Rousseau are incorruptible. From this logically follows that people's Will is infallible. Thus he arrived at a belief that the people are supreme. that a slogan of the French Revolution of liberty, equality and fratetnity were directly derived from Rousseau.

**4. Rousseau as a Socialist.** According to some critics Rousseau's 'Discourses on Inequality' should be regarded as one of the principal source of the socialist movement of the 19th century. Critics believe that socialism had been influencd by Rousseau's view in more than one way. Locke in his "Essay on Rousseau" declares, "Rousseau's influence on socialistic thought is greater than that is generally thought."

One of the basic underlying principles of all socialistic doctrines is that private property must be abolished or at any rate must be reduced to a minimum. And Rousseau it would appear from his early works was the greatest critic of private property. To him private property was the major factor which disturbed the life of the noble savage. The institution of private property created struggle, jealousy and inequality and all other evils associated with the civil society. In his plan for a constitution of Carsica, Rousseau even said that the State ought to be the sole owner. But certainly he was not a Communist. In the article on 'Political Economy' he refered to property as "the most sacred of all the rights of citizenship" and even in the 'Discourse' itself he treated it as a quite indispensable social right. In the 'Social Contract', where he justifies private property and creates a State for its protection and for the maintenance of the distinctions between the haves and the haves not.

## IMPACT ON WESTERN POLITICAL THOUGHT

Rousseau claims to be one of those political philosophers of 18th century whose influence has been immense in his own times and has been gradually increasing in our days. Since Rousseau belonged to philosophical school of thought he was able to give new ideas and thoughts. He was one of the most controversial figures of his age. Lord Morley once remarked, "would it not have been better for the world if Rousseau had not been born?" Sabine opined that, "Rousseau's political philosophy was so vague that it can hardly be said to point in any specific direction." But Hearnshah has high opinion about him. He says that, "From numerous and varied sources we get an impression of a man of high originality and undoubted genious, an intense individualist important at any sort of restraint...sensitive to noble impulse, full of fury against tyranny and injustice, capable of copious weeping on any convenient occasion. He loved the human race, although he quarrelled with every specimen of it with which he was brought into but the most transient contact." Dunning opinen that, Rousseau was suggestive. His theory of General Will became one of the springboards for subsequent political philosophers who were interested in asserting the rights of men and believed in individualism.

**1. Importance of State.** Rousseau emphasised the importance of the state in the life of the individual and asserted that the fullest development of individual's personality was possible only within the state. However, he refused to treat state as an end in itself. It was retained as an instrument of general welfare of the individual.

**2. Development of the Concept of Nation-State.** Rousseau developed the concept of Nation-State by laying emphasis on the principle of common good, common interest, general will as well as unity and solidarity of the people.

**3. Concept of Common Good.** Rousseau gave the concept of common good. This concept was later on developed by the utilitarian thinkers like Bentham and Mill into the concept of "the greatest good of the greatest number."

**4. The Theory of Popular Sovereignty.** Although some thinkers before Rousseau, gave theory of soverignty but none of them emphasised the doctrine of popular sovereignty. His influence was so deep that in the later years it became a fashion to talks of popular sovereignty. Prof. Maxey says, "It is beyond dispute that in the sphere of Political Thought, Rousseau performed one service of incalculable importance. That was his formulation of a plausible and largely realisable theoy of popular sovereignty."

**5. Fore-Runner of English and German Idealism.** After Aristotle Rousseau preached that man was a political animal. Thus, he opposed Machiavelli and Hobbes who believed that man was egoistic and aggressive and that his impulses should be ckecked. Rousseau bade a good bye to the traditional theories of the middle ages. It has been said by Cole that, "He is, in fact, the great fore-runner of English and German idealism."

**6. National State.** Rousseau's philosophy preached unity, solidarity and national integration. Like Bodin and Hobbes he was responsible for giving the conception of nationalism and nation state.

**7. Nationalism.** It was quite clear to Rousseau that free citizenship was rather impossible in those days. He, however, contributed to the philosophy of his age by saying that there must be national solidarity and unity. Although he was not nationalist yet he stood for nationalism.

**8. Sovereign v/s Government Law.** Rousseau made a clear distinction between state and government and also between the sovereign laws and governmental decrees. He held that sovereign law is based on fundamental rights and constitution and has thus value and standing. On the other hand, Government law is temporary in nature and reason and thus based on immediate needs of the people.

**9. Nourishment to Absolutism.** Rousseau's theory of the General Will, provides nourishment at once for absolutism, democracy and socialism. Rousseau's sovereign is as absolute as that of Hobbes. Rousseau's individual, at the time of the contract, surrendered his person and all his rights to the community. Although after the formation of the civil society, he enjoys some rights, yet, in fact, he enjoys them as a citizen and not as an individual. The sovereign state can regulate these rights and even abrogate them at its will and convenience. The sovereignty of the state is absolute and unlimited. Rousseau assigns this absolute and unlimited power to the state because he takes an organic view of it. As an organism, the state has every power over its limbs *i.e.*, associations and individuals. Its absolutism is based not on fear or compulsion but on consent.

**10. Political People as Ultimate Authority.** Rousseau made a rich contribution to political philosophy by saying that, "The political people were the ultimate authority and source for giving all political authorities and that government was simple an agency to execute the directives given by this sovereign authority."

**11. Nourishment to Democracy.** There is a good deal in Rousseau which supports *democracy*. The basic ideas of social contract, used by Rousseau, is consent. Rousseau's theory of the General Will suffers with no dangers inherent in the ideas of consent. General Will provides continual consent of the individual and removes the danger of majority-tyranny. The basic idea of democracy is government of the people, for the people and by the people. Rousseau's sovereign is the people and works in the interests of the people. His sovereign community is a direct democracy which works through its against, the government.

**12. Socialism.** The basic idea of socialism is that the society is all important and that the interests of the society must have priority over the interests of the individual. The individual must find his good in the good of the society. Socialism is for maximising the functions of the state in the interests of the entire community. Likewise, Rousseau's General Will is for the good of the society in preference to the good of the individual.

**13. Sovereign Law.** His sovereign law is the ancestor of the modern fundamental or institutional law. His influence is evident from the insistence made now-a-days that the positive enactments of the government must conform to the fundamental law of the land.

**14. General Welfare of the People.** Through Rousseau the general welfare of the people and general will of the community assumed great importance and became the starting-point of all later theories of state. Rousseau's theory promoted unity and solidarity in the state and, therefore, Rousseau, like Bodin and Hobbes, is one of the creators of the modern national state.

**15. Emphasis on People.** Rousseau more than any other thinker laid emphasis on the ideas that the people is the ultimate source of all political authority; that government is merely the agent and delegate of the sovereign people. He holds that the common goods is the criterion of good legislation and administration; and that the state is not a mere mechanism but that it has an organic life. He makes it clear that true basis of political obligation is continued and rational consent; and that in the last resort freedom and authority, law and liberty, man and state are not antithetic to each other.

**16. Personality Theory of Rights.** Rousseau adopts the Personality theory of rights. The individual is free in the state because he does not surrender his rights to an outside authority but to a corporate body of which he himself is a member. Any restrictions on the liberty of the individual are self-imposed. "Obedience to a law which we prescribe is ourselves is liberty." The rights of liberty, equality and property are rights of the citizen and not, as with Locke, the innate and inherent rights of the individual. Liberty is civil liberty and not natural liberty. Men are equal by law and not by nature.

**17. Emphasis on Freedom.** Rousseau's theory of the General Will leads to a notion of freedom in an organic life, a freedom consonant with the good of the general body of the community even though it involves a restraint.

**18. Reconciliation Between Romantic Individualism and Leviathan State.** Rousseau's concept represents a reconciliation between Romantic individualism and the Leviathan state. The state of Rousseau is as unlimited and absolute as the Leviathan of Hobbes. But whereas the Leviathan of Habbes swallows the individual after the contract, the Leviathan state of Rousseau needs the individual's consent not only for the creation of it but the *continued* consent of the individual for the working of it *i.e.*, of the state.

**Weakness and Inconsistencies of Rousseau.** Some of the weaknesses and inconsistencies in Rousseau's thought arise from the fact that he holds both an organic and mechanistic view of the state. Then again, Rousseau had no systematic education, therefore, was devoid of intellectual moorings which explains his intense individualism of the *Origin of Inequality* and the intense collectivism of his *Social Contract*. Some of the Inconsistencies in his thoughts are as under:

**1. Contradiction About Rights.** There is a certain wavering in Rousseau between the rights of the individual and rights of the society. There is a certain contradiction, about his views on rights of men in society. The contradiction is as under—(a) On the one side, the society has absolute power over the individuals because the individual surrenders his life and all his powers at the time of contract, (b) On the other hand, says Rousseau, each man alienates, by the social contract, only such part of his 'powers, goods and liberty as is important for the community.'

**2. Use of the Term Nature in Varying Senses.** Rousseau uses the term 'nature' in varying senses. His natural 'man has been taken to mean a primitive man, an unchanging man and an ideal man'. Rousseau wails that 'Man' is born free 'but is everywhere in chains' but he ends by creating a leviathan which swallows the man.

**3. Reconciliation of Liberty with Authority.** Rousseau wants to reconcile liberty with authority but his liberty include forcing a man to be free.

**4. Abstract Theory.** His theory of General Will, is very abstract and metaphysical. It is unrealisable. Rousseau's insistence that the will of all is not the same thing as the General Will denies his theory any practical value.

**5. Lack of Logical Development.** Rousseau's political thought lacks proper logical development and has been woven round certain axioms. As a result there are numerous contradictions. Quite often his earlier affirmations and subsequent statements do not go together.

**6. Idealistic Concept.** Rousseau conceives state in purely idealistic terms which do not go well with the instinct and desires of human beings. It is too much to expect that there would be no clash of individual interests and the various wills shall be able to operate in perfect harmony. Rousseau is rather utopian to assume that men will desire common good instead of self-good.

**7. Emergence of Separate Personality Incredible.** Rousseau holds that as a result of contract a state with a personality of its own emerged which possesses a separate Will. It is incredible that there might be a separte entity independent of the individuals constituting the state. The State is something impersonal and cannot possess an independent personality its own.

**8. Contradictory Theories.** Rousseau holds faith in two contradictory theories of state *viz.*, organic and mechanic. These two theories are incompatiable with each other. If the state is man made, it could never be an organism. On the other hand if it were organism, it could never be created by human ingenuity.

**9. Blend of Individualism and Collectivism.** Rousseau's theory contains elements of both individualism as well as collectivism it is very difficult to group Rousseau in either of the two categories. This aspect has already been discussed in details, and need not be repeated.

In his *Emile*, he has given clear indications that he was an individualist. He has clearly said that the people should be educated for their own sake. All restrains on the individuals were unnatural. He said, "when a man renounced his liberty he renounced his essential menhood, his rights and even his duty as a human being." Rousseau believed that man was basically good, free and independent. Morley has said about him, "He is the extreme individualist, the latest and greatest of the individualist political theorists." Whereas on the one hand, Rousseau was an absolutist Maine and Duguit regarded him a totalitarian and a terrible despot. His General Will is absolute and infallible. Man has not rights against General Will. He is forced to be free only by coercion.

❑

# 4

# European Thought—II

## J. BENTHAM

Jeremy Bentham was born in a well-to-do English family in England in 1748. From his very childhood he was studious, hardworking and painstaking. He was hardly three when to the surprise of many, instead of playing he started learning Greek and Latin and even read Rapin's History of England. He started his educational career at Westminster School and subsequently joined Queen's College, Oxford from where he graduated barely at the age of 15. He qualified in law and joined the bar in 1772. His father, who himself was a great lawyer, had pinned high hopes on his son and expected that soon he would be on the Woolsack. But he soon found his hopes dashing to the ground when he saw that his son was neglecting his profession. To the utter surprise of his father he bade good-bye to his profession and set himself to the task of reforming the then existing legal system which had earned a bad name. The law then was the handmaid of a few who completely controlled the legal institutions and he took upon himself to set them on rational footings. In his opinion law should aim at justice and he worked with that end in view.

Bentham mostly stayed at London and therefrom took to the task of writing and addressing the people all over the world. It has been said about him that he was a careless writer and never had the time of revising and rewriting his original scripts. The burden of editing and publishing his works therefore solely fell on his friends and admirers.

Bentham's life can easily be divided into two parts i.e., his ideas to which he adhered in 18th century and his 19th century views. In the former part of his life he developed notions and conceptions of utility and aimed at reforming and codifying English laws. At this stage, for all purposes, he tried to secure for himself a seat in Parliament. He also wanted to reform prisons but as bad luck would have it, he failed both in securing a Parliamentary seat and reforming the prisons.

In the latter part of his life he came in contact with J.S. Mill who inspired in him deep faith in democracy and democratic institutions. It was primarily under his influence that he became a true and real democrat. In 1824 came out his 'Westminster Review' to preach rights for the people. He strongly pleaded that the people should have a share in their administration. His attempts were a success when in 1832, only a day after his death, Bill of Rights was passed in England.

The passing of 'Bill of Rights' was a clear indication and ample testimony to the fact that nation had deep regard for his ideals and philosophies. He was listened to with attention and the nation reaped the fruit of a man who laboured till his death at the age of 84. He did not die unknown but left behind a great name and fame. In the words of Doyles, "He was venerated by a group of disciples, as a patriarch, a spiritual leader, almost a God with James Mill as his St. Paul."

**His Works.** Bentham was a voluminous writer and it is believed that he wrote as many as 11 volumes, in addition to many unaccounted for letters and unpublished works. As already said unfortunately he was not a careful writer. He wrote with the intention of never seeing his scripts again. Without the aid and active interest of his friend Dumont, his writings perhaps would not have come to us. It was due to his keen interest that wide publicity was given to his writings. His well known works are:

1. Fragments of Government (1776).
2. Introduction to the Principles of Morals and Legislation (1789).
3. Discourse on Civil and Penal Legislation (1802).
4. The Theory of Punishments and Rewards (1811).

**His Times and Influences.** Bentham was living at a time when the people of England did not enjoy political rights. The Bill of Rights had then not been thought of. Legal system was defective and required over-hauling. The plight of prisoners was pitiable and required immediate attention but none had the time to draw the attention of the authorities to these problems. As in the past cause of manufacturing classes was only being preached and the labouring masses were being criminally ignored.

It was during his life-time that England became one of the most important and leading world powers. With the expansion of trade and industry and acquisition of more and more markets English people developed a new outlook based on colonialism and imperialism. Their approach to every problem was quite different from traditional way of living and thinking. It therefore fell on Bentham to adjust old ideology with the new one. He knew English love for traditions and also felt the necessity of adopting new ways of life to make his nation progressive. The task of adhering to the old and yet giving up traditional way of living and thinking was quite difficult and it goes to the credit of this mastermind who solved it by finding a via media in the concept of utility.

Among others, Bentham was very much influenced by Hume and Priestley. Hume's 'Treatise of Human Nature' and Priestley's 'Essay on Government' were mainly responsible for giving him the concept of utility. Though Prof. Hallowell has tried to establish that for fundamental conception of 'utility' Bentham is indebted to French philosopher 'Helvetius, yet that does not appear to be very correct. Bentham has himself confessed that he borrowed the idea of utility from Priestley and as soon as "I discovered it I cried out as it were in an inward ecstasy". Mention may also be made about Mill's influence on Bentham. Mill's love for democracy and democratic institutions deeply influenced Bentham. His writings bear ample testimony to Mill's influence.

**His Method.** Bentham was a radical in his approach to the problems. He had no love for the past as such and did not wish to adhere to any particular institution simply because it had proved its utility in the past. An institution should respond to the present and not to the past was his philosophy. In his 'Fragments of Government' he boldly challenged the then existing legal system which he felt had become a formality and was not suited to the times. He was strongly of the opinion that each institution must be responsive to its times, more so the legal system.

He had also a universal outlook towards common problems though with an eye on England. His legal codes were intended for the whole of universe and not for England alone. In general, he did not follow the method of historical interpretation for the study of institutions.

## BENTHAM'S CONTRIBUTION TO POLITICAL THOUGHT

1. Bentham holds an important place in the history of political thought. He was a legal reformer and jurist rather than a political philosopher. He had nothing original in his political philosophy. He did not create new ideas. He did not work out any systematic political theory or Comprehensive Constitutional change. As Dr. Wayper observes—"he took his theory of knowledge from Locke and Hume, the pleasure and pain principle from Helvetius, the notion of sympathy and antipathy from Hume, the ideal of utility from any of half a score of writers. Lacking of originality and full of prejudice in his speculations, he is as confused and contradictory in his own theoretical adventures as he is complacent." Regardless of the shortcomings, his contribution appeared to be enormous.

2. And from the above statement we should not presume that Bentham did not make any contribution to the history of political theory. He was the first to establish the utilitarian school of thought. The service rendered by Bentham to political thought can well be expressed in the following words of Prof. Maxey—"Here was a doctrine to rock the foundations of all accredited political theory. With ruthless logic Bentham had brushed aside the ancient verities of both radical and conservative thought; had erased all distinction in principle between free and despotic polities; had put it down that divine right, feudal right, historical right, natural right, contractual right and constitutional right equally and alike were rubbish and nonsene.

3. Bentham founded the school of utilitarianism. This was his greatest contribution to the history or political theory. Sorely narrates

two qualities of Bentham's mind—the firm grasp of a single principle and truly astonishing mastery of details. He further observes that "Every concrete situation was analysed into its elements and these followed out into all its elements and these elements followed out into all their ramifications...whatever did not yield to this analysis was dismissed as vague "generality". Applying this method with infinite patience, he covered the whole field of ethics, jurisprudence and politics. Every thing in human nature and in society was reduced to its elements and then reconstructed out of these elements and in each elements only on feature counted, whether in respect of force or of value—its quantum of pleasure or pain.

4. Bentham was a true reformer. He was a practical man. He took active interest in the political life of his country. That is why he was venerated by a group of disciples as a patriarch, a spiritual leader, almost a good, with James Mill as his St. Paul." "Jeremy Bentham stood out as the dominating philosopher of the radical group. He did not seek, like Rousseau, to escape from grim acutalities into mysticism. He approached his problem in the spirit of a scientist, convinced with the wrongs of the people where commensurable, that their happiness could be assured when once its measurement was ascertained......His theories of state and law were composed with a view to their practical application." Bentham advocated a number of reforms for bettering the lot of the people, such as the reformation in the theory of punishment, elimination of the obstacles that lie out in the way of justice.

Prof. Sabine further observes, "that it was in his theory of legal procedure and judicial organisation, perhaps, that Bentham developed his most characteristic ideas, and it was certainly here that he departed farthest from the liberal tradition as it had been before him. In his desire to simplify procedure and improve the efficiency of the courts he proposed to abandon almost entirely the checks and safeguards which had been deemed necessary to protect the subject's rights......He correctly pointed out that legal formalism and artificial rules about the admissibility of evidence were largely predicated upon a belief that the absolutive law is bad and that government is dangerous and argued that, if this belief is indeed true, the reasonable remedy is to improve the law, not to weaken the courts."

His theory of law established the point of view of analytic jurisprudence "which was almost the only system of the subject generally known to English and American lawyers throughout the 19th century." According to Bentham, the legislator has had to keep in view the 4 ends as under : *(1)* Security, *(2)* Subsistence, *(3)* Abundance, *(4)* Equality. The legislator can rear the fabric of felicity by the hands of reason and of law.

5. The injustice and severity of punishments provided in the criminal law and the way in which the prisons were administered, Bentham considered them as intolerable. He bitterly attacked conditions in the English prison and always demanded a reform thereof. He had utmost sympathy with Howard who was making efforts at prison reform. He felt a great need of the system of education and of useful labour for criminals. In this respect his scheme was of great importance. His plans were also applied outside Great Britain and "the reform of prisons and the institution of reformatories and industrial schools derived its impulse largely from his principles."

6. Bentham had put before President Madison of America, a proposal to draw up scientific code of law for U.S.A. A similar proposal was made to Czar of Russia. In 1822, Bentham appealed to all nations professing liberal opinions. Gettle says—"His confidence in his ability to create a system of laws guaranteed to promote the greatest good of the greatest number was unbounded."

7. Bentham was primarily a reformer, Bentham's practical reforms included *(a)* universal manhood, suffrage, (the adult being able to read). He eschewed the question of women suffrage. *(b)* Annual parliaments. *(c)* Vote by Secret Ballot for maintaining electoral purity against intimidation and bribery. *(d)* Equalising of electoral districts. *(e)* He disliked the hereditary character of House of Lords, and was against beggary and wanted poor laws to be reformed. *(f)* He advocated a system of National Education. *(g)* The institution of Frugality Banks Which has developed into modern Savings Bank. *(h)* A scheme for good health.

## POLITICAL IMPLICATIONS OF BENTHAM'S UTILITARIANISM

**1. Criteria of Utility.** Bentham was the first to use the term 'utility' in a systematic way, with great minuteness and considerable details. His utilitarian philosophy had wide political implications. His staight-forward statement challenging the then existing social and political institutions had universal appeal.

**2. Blow to Social Contract.** His philosophy gave a severe blow to social contract theory. He said that the state was not the outcome of any contract but only because the people saw advancement in the state.

**3. Challenge to State Supremacy.** Bentham challenged the spremacy of state. This was of great political significance in those days. In most of the cases the state had no right to punish the subjects because people committed crimes due to defective laws passed by the legislators.

**4. Individual Freedom.** Another political implication of Bentham's philosophy was that he stood for individual freedom and demanded that the people must have a share in running their own administration. He thus stood for individual liberty in England when Spain and Turkey were establishing and strengthening their empire.

**5. Democracy.** Bentham's philosophy prescribed democracy and democratic institutions. It was a bold step in those days.

**6. Re-examination of Institutions.** Bentham's utilitarianism shook many of the age-old institutions from their very foundations. He very boldly said that the age of an institution was neither any guarantee nor proportionate to its utility. An institution should be judged from the purpose which it served and nothing else.

**7. Political Reforms.** Though it suffered from some drawbacks yet Bentham's philosophy was seriously studied. This in itself bears testimony to his influence. It was due to his efforts that Bill of Rights was passed in England. In the words of William Ebenstein "He is the greatest single reformer in English History, particularly in the field of law. His main contribution to political science was not that he invented a new principle of political philosophy but that he steadily applied an empirical and critical method of investigation to concrete problems of government and administration."

**8. Middle Class Social Philosophy.** Bentham was a middle class social philosopher. The people of England are not extremists by nature. They are usually opposed to revolutions and radical social and political changes. Bentham was no exception to that. Throughout his political philosophy he did not preach revolution. He suggested only reforms. He wanted to reform the whole legal system. But he did not wish to out-right replace it with a new order. Similarly, he wanted to reform the prisons. His love for democracy in itself proves that he always felt that there was room and scope for reforms. He did not condemn any of the legislative institutions. All that he suggested was that the legislators should behave nicely and realies their representative character.

## THE PRINCIPLE OF UTILITY AS PROPOUNDED BY BENTHAM

As Prof. Jones says, "Bentham's principle is shortly stated. It is that, of the various possibilities open to us in any given case, we ought to choose that which will produce the greatest happiness *i.e.*, pleasure to the greatest number. Bentham found a number of obscurities, fictions and formalities in English law and judicial procedure. Knowing fully well that the English Common Law was based upon customs and traditions and could not be changed, easily, he urged that 'the law of today must be shaped, by the legislator of today in accordance with the needs of today; and that the sole criterion of these needs must be the greatest good of the greatest number of men". That is to say the laws old or new, should be judged by the usefulness or utility which they render to the masses.

All human actions are guided by the notion of *utility*. We prefer to do only those actions which may bring for us happiness. In his most important work, Introduction to the Principles of Morals and Legislation, he holds that, "Nature has placed mankind under the governance of two sovereign masters, Pleasure and Pain". "They govern us in all we say, in all we think: every effort we make to throw off our subjection will serve but to demonstrate and confirm it". This maxim, unchangeable and irresistible, as it is, should become the chief study of the Moralist and of the Legislator. To these two motives the principle of utility subjects every thing". To Bentham, all human instintats are equally natural and that they are good or bad depending totally upon their results. In the words of Prof. Gettell, "The principle of utility approved or disapproved of actions in accordance with their tendency to promote or to oppose happiness.

In Bentham's principle of utility there are seven things which we should take into account when assessing the pain and pleasure in relation to everything individual and they are as follows : The value of pleasure or pain depends upon.

1. Intensity, 2. Duration, 3. Certainty or Uncertainty, 4. Propinquity or remoteness, 5. Fecundity, 6. Purity, 7. Extent.

A legislator and a moralist should take into account the above mentioned circumstances that influence the sensibilities.

Bentham held "that the end of legislator should be happiness of the people. He said, "In matters of legislation, general utility should be his guiding principle. The science of legislation consists therefore, in determining what makes for the good of the particular community whose interests are at stake, while its art consists in contriving some means of realisation.".

**Sources of Pleasure.** Regarding pains and plessures in the character of punishment and rewards attached to certain rules of conduct, Bentham distinguished between four sanctions as under:

1. The physical or natural sanction which "comprises the pains and pleasures which we may experience, or expect, in the ordinary course of nature, not purposely modified by any human interposition".
2. The political sanction compromises "such pains and pleasures as we experience, or expect, at the hands of the magistracy, acting under law. This might, with equal propriety, be termed as the legal sanction".
3. The moral sanction "compromises such pains and pleasure as we experience, or expect, at the hands of our fellows, prompted by feelings of harted or goodwill or contempt or

reagrd; in a word, according to the spontaneous disposition of each individual". Bentham has also styled this sanction as the sanction of public will or of honour or the sanction of the pains and pleasures of sympathy".

4. The religious sanction comparising "such pains and pleasures as well may experience, or expect, in virtue of the forebodings and promises of religion".

To make the above mentioned four sanctions more clear, Bentham says, "man's house is destroyed by fire. Is it by reason of his own imprudence? If so, it is a punishment of the nature sanction. Is it by direction of the magistrate? if so, it is a punishment of the political sanction. Is it owing to the ill-will of his neighbours who withhold assistance. If so, it is a punishment of the popular sanction. Is it supposed to have been occassioned by the immediate act of some offended divinity?

Bentham distinguished pleasures and pains into two kinds *i.e.*, Simple and Complex. According to him simple pleasures were of fourteen kinds:

(1) The Pleasure of sense. (2) The Pleasure of wealth. (3) The Pleasure of skill. (4) The Pleasure of amity. (5) The Pleasure of repute. (6) The Pleasure of power. (7) The Pleasure of pity. (8) The Pleasure of benevolence. (9) The Pleasure of malevolence. (10) The Pleasure of memory. (11) The Pleasure for imagination. (12) The Pleasure of expectation. (13) The Pleasure of association. (14) The Pleasure of relief.

Similarly, he held that simple pains were of ill-repute kinds, *viz.*:

(1) Pain of privation. (2) Pain of senses. (3) Pain of awkwardness. (4) Pain of enmity. (5) Pain of ill-repute. (6) Pain of piety. (7) Pain of benevolence. (8) Pain of malevolence. (9) Pain of memory. (10) Pain of imagination. (11) Pain of expectation and of association.

Bentnam's "*Hedonistic calculus*" depended upon his concept of pain and pleasure. To him man does only that work which gives him maximum of utility or that producers greatest pleasure. This utility or pleasure, according to Bentham, could be measured by Hedonistic calculus. In other words Bentham's notion of Hedonistic calculus was a apparatus designed to facilitate the calculation of pleasures and pains as motivating forces. There are several factors which determine individual pain or pleasure, Bentham enumerated them as under: *1.* Health, *2.* Strength, *3.* Hardiness, *4.* Bodily imperfection. *5.* Quantity and quality knowledge, *6.* Strength of intellectual power, *7.* Fairness of mind, *8.* Steadiness of mind, *9.* Bent of inclination, *10.* Moral Sensibility, *11.* Moral biases, *12.* Religious Sensibility, *13.* Religious Biases, *14.* Sympathetic Sensibility, *15.* Sympathetic biases, *16.* Anti-pathetic sensibility, *17.* Anti-pathetic biases, *18.* Infanity, *19.* Habitual occupation, *20.* Pecuniary circumstances. *21.* Connections in way of sympathy, antipathy, *22.* Radical frame of body, mind, sex, age, ranks, education, climate, lineage, government, and religious profession.

## BRIEF CRITICISM OF BENTHAMITE UTILITARIANISM

Utilitarianism received bitter criticism on the following grounds:

1. That it was a purely materialistic theory. Utilitarianism and materialism could be identified. Prof. Murray observes, "If we take away conscience, as Bentham does, there is no such thing as a moral or immoral action though there may remain acts that are generally usefully or the reverse. As there is no individual conscience, so there is no collective conscience. The culprit does not feel the consure of the community."
2. The theory of utility is impractical. It aimed at the maximum good of the maximum number, which is difficult in practice to realise.
3. Bentham ignored the value of society and simply thought in terms of each individual's happiness. The whole thing is beautifully criticised by J.S. Mill in the following words—"It is better to be a human being dissatisfied than a pig satisifed, better to be Socrates dissatisfied than a fool satisfied. And if the fool or the pig are of different opinion, it is because they look only to their own side of the question."

4. Prof. Sorley observes that Bentham's whole system would be completely upset if the qualitative distinction between pleasures were admitted.

5. Prof. Jones offers the following criticism of Bentham's theory of utility:

   (a) His principle is ambiguous. Jones says "When Bentham urges us to produce the greatest happiness for the greatest number, he implies that in any given case there is one alternative which (if we knew it) would be the correct course of action to pursue. But suppose two possible actions, X and Y. Suppose X to be capable of producing 25 units of happiness for each of 5 people (25 × 5 = 125); and Y, 4 units of happiness for each of 25 people (4 × 25 = 100). Which is the correct course to be followed? If we are ruled by the recommendation to produce the greatest happiness we shall do X; if by the recommendation to serve the greatest number, we shall do Y. In other words "what appears on the surface to be a single, self-evident exhortation is really two separate exhortation which (more often than not) contradict each other."

   (b) By saying that every body does always aim at pleasure, Bentham oversimplifies the human motives. Though even allowing that men ought to keep nothing but pleasure, yet they are often moved by other considerations. Men are not moved by one motive but by many diverse ones, that there is not one satisfaction, (pleasure) present in varying amounts, but many qualitatively different satisfactions.

   (c) Bentham's principle is, in fact, inapplicable. His Hedonistic calculus is not, indeed, very satisfactory. He does not give any scale for weighing his various factors against each other. "It is all very well, for instance, to say that we must consider both intensity and duration. If we has two pleasures of equal intensity, we would know enough to choose the more durable. But suppose they vary both in intensity and duration, what then? How much intensity weighs against how long duration? Since Bentham does not tell us, his calculus is not of much use.

## IMPORTANCE AND PRINCIPLES OF BENTHAM

Jeremy Bentham was an English thinker who coined the term utility and extensively used it in his philosophy. He gave utilitarian philosophy a systematic touch and put it on a scientific footing by making it a school of thought. Before him Hume and Priestley in England, Helvetius in France and Beccaria in Italy also used the term 'utility' but failed to put it on a scientific footing. Bentham used the term in a most scientific way. He himself confessed that he picked up the term from Priestley. He was so much impressed when he read the term 'greatest happiness of the greatest number of people'that be got an inner ecstasy. Wayper has quoted his to say that "I cried out as it were in an inward ecstasy, like Archimedes at the discovery of the fundamental principles of hydro-statics Eureka."

## GROSS UTILITARIANISM

**1. Hedonism.** Bentham started with the presumption that the cherished desire of every individual is to achieve pleasure and happiness. Man by nature is repulsive to miseries pains. Everything in the society should be considered in terms of utility. Utility means maximum social pleasures and happiness. It is always in direct proportion to the pleasure. To that extent it avoids sorrow and dismay. According to Bentham, "Nature has placed mankind under the governance of two sovereign masters, pain and pleasure. It is for them alone to point out what we ought to do, as well to determine what we shall do. On the one hand, the standard of right and wrong, and on the other hand the chain of causes and affects are fastened to their throne. The principle of utility recognises this subjection and assumes it for the foundation of that system, the object of which is to rear the fabric of felicity by the hands of reason and law-systems which attempt to question its deeds in sounds instead of senses, in caprice insteed of reason, in darkness instead of light."

**2. Utility as Primary Criteria.** Bentham was of the opinion that Utilitarianism is a philosophy in which everything ought to be tested in terms of utility and usefulness. Utility of all laws and actions of our legislators should be measured in terms of pains and pleasures which they give. Bentham said, "To seek pleasure and to shun pain is his sole aim, even at the moment when he is doing himself the greatest enjoyment or courting the most severe penalties. This maxim, unchangeable and irresistible, as it is, should become the chief study of the moralist and of the legislature.

**3. Utility.** Thus for Bentham everything was to be valued, adjudged and measured only in terms of pleasure and pain. He said, "The principle of utility consists in taking as our starting point, in every process of reasoning the calculus of comparative estimates of pains and pleasures and in not allowing any other idea to intervene. An adherent to the principle of utility holds virtue to be a good thing by reason only of the pleasures which result from the practice of it, he esteems vice to be a bad thing by reason only of the pains which follow in its train."

**4. Calculus of Utility.** Bentham was of the view that intensity, duration, certainty, proximity, fecundity and purity were some of the measuring rods for testing the extent of utility which an action ultimately gave. By frequency be meant the 'quality of it being followed by the pleasure of the some sort.' From purity he understood no fear to pleasure from any corner. For the purpose of utility, he felt that everybody was equal to the other irrespective of his status and position in the society.

**5. Four Sanctions.** According to Bentham there are four sanctions regarding pains and pleasures:

*(i)* ***Physical or Natural Sanction.*** This implies those pleasures and pains which are not the product of any human efforts, but have been given by nature in the course of time.

*(ii)* ***Moral Sanction.*** This implies the sanction which is prompted by good-will or contempt at the hands of our fellow beings.

*(iii)* ***Public Sanction.*** This means legal sanction which is given to the individuals by the magistrates in exercise of their legal powers.

*(iv)* ***Religious Sanctions.*** This follows from religious doctrines.

**6. Hedonistic Calculus.** Every action should be judged on the basis of pleasure and pain. There were physical, religious, moral and political sanctions for pleasure. Utility must be clear and precise. It must have a single and sufficient account for motivation. It must be adjustable by means of a moral calculus. Bentham wanted to apply this principle on legislation also. Utility means share of people in legislation. This democracy and not aristocracy is the ideal form of government.

**7. Simple and Complex Pleasures.** According to Bentham pleasures are simple or complex. Simple pleasures are in sense, wealth, skill, beauty, repute, power, piety, benevolence, malevolence, intellect, memory, imagination, hope, association and relief. Simple pains are in enmity, ill name, privation, memory, expectation and awkwardness. Man is governed under the yoke of these two masters namely pleasures and pains. Complex, pleasures and pains arise out of these simple pains and pleasures in one from or the other.

## CRITICAL EVALUATION OF BENTHAM'S UTILITARIANISM

Bentham's theory of utility has been criticised on the following grounds:

**1. Over-Simplification.** According to Bentham embracing pleasure and avoiding pain is the motivating and moving force behind all human activities. He has tried to classify pleasures and pains into simple and complex ones. He has put them all into a tabulated form. Here he is victim of over-simplification. The problem is not so simple as to appears to be or what he has made it look like. When put into actual practice and tested on hard and real complexities of life, the whole concept is bound to prove a broken reed.

**2. Materialistic Theory.** Bentham made his theory purely materialistic. His theory assigns no place to moral and immoral actions which a person is bound to perform in his day-to-day life. Murray has rightly observed, "If we take away conscience, as Bentham does, there is no such thing as a moral or immoral action though there may remain acts that are generally useful on the reverse."

**3. Misunderstanding of Human Nature.** According to Bentham human beings struggle for having maximum pleasure because according to him each pleasure must be followed by another successive pleasure. This is a very narrow outlook of human nature. This is rather sensual. Wise persons restrain desires rather than increasing them. They try to attain a stage of perfection where pleasure and pain have no meaning for them.

**4. Underestimation of Society.** Bentham has failed to understand the importance of society as a whole. He has laid stress only on individual pleasure. The basis of his theory is neither society nor state but the individual. He has forgotten that human beings are social animals and depend on society. He has also forgotten that individual without society is incomplete. As a realist he should have pleaded for collective rather than individual pleasure. Wayper has rightly said, "In his study of the individual he has left out both society and history. In refusing to consider the importance of history and society he ignored the strongest forces that have made what he is."

**5. Impracticable Theory.** Bentham has been criticised on the grounds that his theory sounds impracticable. It is well high impossible to give greatest happiness to greatest number of people. In actual practice happiness is always the monopoly of those who are at the helm of affairs rather than those who are governed. It is confined to a few rather than to the greatest number of people.

**6. Wrong System of Studying Political Institutions.** Bentham tried to assess justification and soundness of political institutions in terms of happiness. Soundness of political institution is directly and proportiontely related to the pleasure which it gives to the people. He wanted to measure politics on the standard yard of mathematics which is ridiculous. It cannot be denied that politics and mathematics are not related to each other and to measure one on the yard stick of the other is absolutely of no use.

**7. No Measuring Rod for Pleasure.** Bentham has failed to provide any standard to judge whether pleasure has been achieved or not and to what extent. Without such a measuring rod the whole super structure of this theory based on pleasure and pain is bound to collapse.

**8. Unanimity on Pleasure.** The concept of pleasure differs from person to person and place to place. It has no unanimity and to give it a universal outlook is someting which is not only impossible but impracticable as well.

**9. Inconsistent Theory.** Bentham maintains that human beings struggle for their own individual pleasures. If that is true then how could they fight and care for social happiness. It is rather useless to expect from selfish individuals to act for a social action. It is difficult to reconcile egoism with altruism in his theory.

**10. Ignored Habits.** Even though Bentham makes us believe that the people always act under the influence of pleasure and pain but that is not always true. Many a time people become slave of evil habits and act under their influence without caring for the pains which would come to them out of these actions. Sometimes knowing well that his habits might bring him miseries in the long run a person is still forced to act contrary to his inner desire as is the case with drunken persons and gamblers.

**11. Ambiguous Theory.** In actual life there are actions which produce greatest happiness but not for greatest number of people and there are still other actions which though they give less happiness but give it to greatest number of people. Bentham has not suggested as to what course should be followed in such cases and which should be preferred especially when one and the same course might not produce greatest happiness for greatest number of people.

**12. Wrong Psychology.** Bentham's theory makes people selfish and self-centred. According to him every one cares for himself alone and not for anything elese. This is neither the quality of good citizenship nor an indications of healthy society. His theory is based on wrong psychology.

**13. Stress on Quantity.** By saying that maximum happiness of maximum number of people should be the aim of state, Bentham has laid stress on quantity. In every good philosophy, alongwith quantity, proper stress should also be laid on quality.

**14. Outdated Theory.** According to Bentham immediate pleasure is always to be preferred over deferred pleasures. When put into actual practice this idea is bound to lead to many difficulties. State spends mostly on projects which might not result in immediate benefits to the society but are means for the succeeding generations. Such types of expenditures are most inevitable. These are indications of an advanced society. According to Bentham's theory, however, these are unwanted and not suited to modern time.

Thus Bentham's theory of utility as based on pleasure and pain theory is faulty and impracticable. Taken to its logical conclusion it is bound to indicate that Bentham had a narrow vision of the things. He tried to mould certain basic facts according to his own ideas and has not very much succeeded in that.

## BENTHAM'S POLITICAL THOUGHT

**1. Origin of Political Society.** Bentham did not believe that the state is the product of any social contract. He was of the opinion that obedience to state laws is not the result of any social contract. Due to utility the laws were both respected and obeyed. Utility is the only consideration for obeying the state authoriy. The only justification of state existence is the promotion of utility. It is the foremost duty of state to adjust and reconcile conflicting interests. It should see that those laws were not passed which promoted pain and not pleasure.

**2. Natural Laws and Rights.** Bentham was of the opinion that 'nature' is a very vague term. The concepts natural rights and natural laws are equally vague, uncertain and undependable. Accordingly, He did not believe in these theories. He however, agreed with Hobbes that law is the command of sovereign and that state is the only source of law. Laws could be given by God and not by Nature. As laws were given by the sovereign, therefore, in every state there must be a supreme, undisputed and unquestionable sovereign authority to issue commands. The worth of laws always depended on the general obedience given to it and the utility which if promotes. Security, substance, equality and abundance were aims of a model law. People are punished mostly because of the mistakes of legislators who do not pass proper and healthy laws, sometimes even such laws are passed which are more respected in violation rather than in obedience.

The concept of Natural Rights is simple nonsense. It has neither any existence nor value. The existence of 'Private Property' is justified.

As the state is sovereign and supreme authority it is exclusively responsible for giving laws. There is no justification in claiming natural rights. Natual rights ar against state soverignty and hence absolutely unjustified. The state is a contrivance. It is the foremost duty of legislators to see that the laws passed by them promote utility. The laws can be passed both by 'Natural method' as well as 'Technical methods.'

**3. Resistance of Government Authority.** Utility is the sole basis to decide whether the individual or society have to resist the soveign or not. If resistance has utility it was worth while and justified but not otherwise. Ordinarily, the people have no right to disobey the sovereign but have a legal duty to obey his commands. In normal circumstances supremacy of sovereign authority is most vital and it is the pious duty of citizens to obey.

**4. Sovereignty.** Like Hobbes, Bentham also taught to give unlimited rights and authorities to his sovereign. Existence of sovereign authority is justified if the laws passed by him are popular and promote utility. The only justification for punishment for break of laws is that it checked evil and promoted utility. Constitutions must be written ones but the sovereign had every right to amend the constitution as and when he finds that there is necessity for that. Bentham did not favour the presentation of Bill of Rights by the people. Such rights were checks on sovereign authoity. A sovereign is not at all bound to obey individual rights because he is the source of all laws. Bentham categoried rights as 'moral' and 'legal'.

**5. Punishment.** According to Bentham punishment should not aim at retaliation. It should be only reformatory in character and corrective in nature. In should aim at good and should remove the evil. It should be a such of nature that the criminals do not repeat the crime and the likely criminals think in terms of avoiding crime in future.

**6. Proper Form of Government.** Bentham believed that Representative Democracy is the only form of government which could give greatest happiness to greatest number of people. The government should work in such a way that it promotes good and happiness rather than evil and pains. Bentham stood for elected parliaments based on adult suffrage and ballot system.

**7. Publicity to Law.** In order to end punishment people should be made law conscious and law abiding. The laws should be given wide publicity. The people should be made to understand them. Press should be given reasonable freedom. He wanted to separate Judiciary from executive. Judiciary should be free from politics. Bentham was also in favour of spreading education. The legal procedure should be simplified. Legal system should be made very simple and cheap. Everybody should be allowed to plead for himself in the courts of law.

**8. Administration of Justice.** Bentham stood for the condification of law. He pleaded that law should be so enacted that it is understood by all. There should be neither any uncertainty nor unnecessary expenses in getting justice. Justice delayed was justice denied. The present system of justice is such that in it justice is not given but only sold at different price, which suited the pocket of the lawyers. This is most undesirable and as such corrective measures must be taken immediately.

**9. Reforms.** Bentham was a great social reformer. All existing social and political institutions must be reformed, if these were to exist. There should be annual elections for the Parliament through universal adult franchise. In order to check intimidation and bribery secret ballot system should be introduced. Poor laws should be reformed. Hereditary character of House of Lords should be dispensed with. There should be a national scheme for improving the health of the people. There should be a national system of education.

**10. Private Property.** Bentham favoured the institution of private property. The state should not take over any property without payment of proper compensation. It should however, pass such laws which could result in equal distribution of wealth. Bentham favoured the idea of free trade, as propagated by Adam Smith.

**11. Church.** Bentham was opposed to the Church of England. He could not reconcile himself to the situation as to how the Bishops could become rich. He failed to understand how the prists chould usefully and purposefully sit in the House of Lords and contribute to its proceedings. He felt that the church activities should be checked and priest and bishops should desist from owning huge amounts and private property.

**12. Education.** According to Bentham it is only with the help of education that mankind may be improved. To begin with the student should be faught what was useful or most likely useful for him. He should be taught to learn what was easiest from him to learn. Due regard should be paid to learner's capacity. Each student has some natural inclination and aptitude. He should be taught according to that and not forced to read anything which did not suit his natural liking.

## BENTHAM'S UTILITARIANISM

Jeremy Bentham was an English thinker who, it is normally considered, coined the term utility and is also held responsible for giving utilitarian philosophy a systematic touch and putting that on scientific footing by making it a school of thought. But that is not very true. Long before him Hume and Priestley in England. Helvetius in France and Beccaria in Italy also used the very term 'utility' in their writtings but unfortunately they failed to put it on a scientific footing. Bentham's only praiseworthy contribution is that he used the term in a most rational way. Prof. Hallowell has suggested that he borrowed this term from Helvetius but Bentham himself confessed that he picked up the term from Priestley's 'Essays on Government'. Dr. Wayper is of the view that, "The founder of utilitarianism was David Hume; Priestley, Hutcheson, Paley professed it; it was fed from foreign springs of Helvetius and Beccaria. But it was first arouse Jeremy Bentham." According to him he was so much impressed when he read the term greatest happiness of the greatest number of people' that he got an inner ecstasy.

**Bentham on Conception of Utility.** Bentham started with the presumption that the cherished desire of every individual is to embrace pleasure and happiness. Man by nature is repulsive to miseries and pains which he always struggles to keep away. He therefore believed that everything in the society should be considered in terms of utility which to him meant maximum social pleasure and happiness. Utility is always in direct proportion to the pleasure and to that extent avoids sorrow and dismay. According to him, "Nature has placed mankind under the governance of two sovereign masters, pain and pleasure. It is for them alone to point out what we ought to do as well as to determine what we shall do. On the one hand the standard of right and wrong, and on the other hand the chain of causes and effects are fastened to their throne. The principle of utility recognises this subjection and assumes it for the foundation of that system, the object of which is to rear the febric of falicity by the hands of reason and law. Systems which attempt to question it deal in sounds instead of senses, in caprice instead of reason, in darkness instead of light."

It is thus clear that for Bentham everything was to be valued, adjudged and measured only in terms of pleasure and happiness. He made his conception in this regard still more clear when he said that, "The principle of utility consists in taking as our starting point, in every process of reasoning the calculus of comparative estimates of pains and pleasures and in not allowing any other idea to intervene. An adherent to the principle of utility holds virtue to be a good thing by reason only of the pleasures which result from the practice of it, he esteems vice to be a bad thing by reason only of the pains which follow in its train.

Bentham was of the opinion that Utilitarianism was such a philosophy in which everything ought to be tested in terms of utility and usefulness. He even went to the extent of saying that utility of, all laws and actions of our legislators should be measued in terms of happiness and pleasures which they give.

Bentham was of the firm view that intensity, duration, certainty proximity, fecundity, purity were some of the measuring rods for testing the extent of utility which an action ultimately gave. From fecundity he meant the 'quality of its being followed by the pleasures of the same sort'. Whereas from purity he understood no fear to pleasure from any corner. For the puproses of utility, he felt that everybody was equal to the other irrespective of his status and position in the society. In this way he has established it beyond doubt that he was only an individualist. He did not contribute to the idea that traditionally existing institutions or ideas could not be challenged.

According to Bentham there are four sanctions regarding pains and pleasures. It is physical or natural sanction which implies those pleasures and pains which are not the product of any human efforts, but have been given by nature in the course of time. Then there is moral sanction which implies the sanction which is prompted by good will or contempt by the hands of the our fellow beings.

According to Bentham there are simple and complex pleasures as well. Whereas simple pleasures the sense, wealth, skill, beauty, repute, power, piety, benevolence, malevolence, intellect, memory, imagination, hope, association and relief; simple pains are in enmity, ill name, privation, memory, expectation, awkwardness, and sense. He believed that man is governed under the yoke of these two masters namely pleasures and pains; both simple and complex, arising out of these simple pains and pleasures in one from or the other.

**Criticism.** Bentham's theory of utility has been severely criticised on the ground that:

**1. He is Victim of Oversimplification.** According to Bentham embracing pleasure and avoiding pain is the motivating and moving force behind all human activities. He has also tried to classify pleasure and pains into simple and comlex ones. In addition to this he has also put them all into a tabulated form. But unfortunately he is victim of oversimplification. The problem is not so simple as it appears to be or what he has made it look like and when put into actual practice and tested on hard and real complexities of life, the whole concept will prove like a broken reed.

**2. It is Materialistic Theory.** Bentham has made his theory purely materialistic. Whole of his theory has assigned no place to moral and immoral actions which a man is bound to perform in his day-to-day life. Murray has rightly observed when he says: "If take away conscience, as Bentham does, there is no such thing as a moral or immoral action though there may remain acts that are generally useful on the reverse. As there is no individual conscience, so there is no collective conscience."

**3. He has Misunderstood Nature of Man.** According to Bentham man struggles for having maximum pleasure because according to him each pleasure must be followed by another successive pleasure. In this way he has taken a very narrow outlook of man's nature. He has made him rather sensual. But again he is wrong. Who can deny that wise men restrain desires rather than increasing them.

**4. No Measuring Rod for Pleasure.** Then Bentham has failed to provide us with any standard to judge whether pleasure has been achieved or not and if already achieved to what extent. Without such a measuring rod the whole superstructure of this theory which is based on pleasure and pain is bound to collapse.

**5. It is an Inconsistent Theory.** Bentham makes us believe that man struggles for his own individual pleasure alone. If that is true then how could he fight and care for social happiness. It is rather useless to expect from a selfish individual as he thinks a man is to act, for a social action. There is real difficulty in reconciling his theory of egoism with altruism.

**6. He has Underestimated Society.** Another weakness of his theory is that he has failed to understand the importance of society as a whole. He has laid stress only on individual pleasure. In fact the basis of his theory is neither society nor state but the individual. He has absolutely forgotten that man is a social animal and must depend on soceity. He has also forgotten that individual without society is incomplete. As a realist he should have pleaded for collective rather than individual pleasure.

**7. It is an Impracticable Theory.** Bentham has also been criticised on the grounds that his theory sounds impracticable. It is well nigh impossible to give greatest happiness to greatest number of people. Who does not know that in actual practice happiness is always the monopoly of those who are at the helm of affairs rather than those who are governed. It is the order of the day that happiness is confined to a few rather than to the greatest number of people.

**8. It is an Ambiguous Theory.** In our actual life we find that there are actions which produce greatest happiness but not for greatest number of people and there are still other actions which though they give less happiness but give it to greatest number of people. In such cases Bentham has not suggested as to what course should be followed and which should be preferred especially when one and the same course might not produce greatest happiness for greatest number of people.

**9. Wrong System of Studying Political Institutions.** He has tried to give justification and soundness of political institutions in terms of happiness. In his opinion soundness of a political institution is directly and proportionately related to the pleasure which it gives to the people. In other words he wanted to measure politics on the standard yard of mathematics which is quite ridiculous. It cannot be denied that politics and mathematics are not related to each other and to measure one on the yardstick of the other is absolutely of no use.

**10. He has Ignored Habits.** Even though Bentham makes us believe that man always acts under the influence of pleasure and pain but that is not always true. Many a time man becomes slave of evil habits and acts under their influence without caring for the pains which would come to him out of these actions. Sometimes knowing well that his habits might bring him miseries in the long run a man is still forced to act contrary to his inner desires as is the case with drunkers and gamblers.

**11. Pleasure has no Universal Character.** Then comes another difficulty. The concept of pleasure differs from man to man and place to place. It has no universality and to give it a universal outlook is something which is not only imposible but impracticable.

**12. He Makes Man Selfish.** His theory has also been criticised as it makes man selfish and self-centred. He cares for himself alone and not for anything else which is neither the quality of good citizenship nor an indication of healthy society. Thus his theory takes it for granted that every man is selfish which might be largely true but cannot be universally so.

**13. It is an Outdated Theory.** According to Bentham, immediate pleasure is always to be preferred over deferred pleasures, but this idea when put into actual practice is bound to lead to many difficulties. State expenditure is mostly on projects which might not result in immediate benefits to the society but are meant for the succeeding generations. Expenditure on research work is also of this nature. But such type of expenditures are most inevitable and are indications of an advanced society. But according to Bentham's theory these are unwanted and not suited to modern times.

We can thus find that his theory of utility expounded on pleasure and pain theory is not only faulty and impracticable but when taken to its logical conclusion is bound to indicate that the philosopher had a narrow vision of the things. He has tried to mould certain basic facts according to his own ideas and has not very much succeeded in that.

## J.S. MILL

John Stuart Mill was born on May 20, 1806, in London. He was the eldest son the James Mill who was the disciple and close friend of Jeremy Bentham a philosophical radical. Mill started learning Greek language at the age of 3. At the age of 8 he started reading Latin. At the age of 12 he had studied the philosophy of some of the great philosophers, such as Plato, Herodotus, Homer, Aristotle, Thucidides, etc., from May, 1820 to July, 1821, he was in France where he learnt the French with great fluency. In 1823, he got an appointment in East India Company and by sheer dint of his merit was appointed Assistant examiner and chief of the office, in 1856. He was of frail physique and nervous temperament and possessed considerable charming personality. Gladstone once said of him in private conversation "when John Mill was speaking, I always felt that I was listening to a saintly man."

After returning back from France, Mill started reading Bentham which greatly influenced his outlook. He became a perfect Benthamite as his father wanted of him, whom, as Shields observes. "In the course of the daily drill and recitation and lectures and conversations... shaped as best as he could his son's mind to suit the Benthamite image". He formed the Utilitarian Society in 1823 and Speculative Society in 1826.

Mill was a man of latters and a man of generosity. He was a regular contributor of many articles to Westminster Review. Later on he became the editor of London Review. In 1831, he began his long and sometimes difficult friendship with Carlyle. At the age of twenty-five Mill came in contact with a highly talented and attractive woman, Mrs. Harriet Taylor, (in 1830). This association to Mill was the most valuable friendship of his life. Mill married in 1851, that charming lady (after the death of her husband) and both led a happy life for about twenty years. Mrs. (Harriet Hardy) Taylor died at Avignon (France) in 1858. Mill dedicated his most important essay on The Subjection of Women to his wife, "Who was the inspirer, and in part the author, of all that is best in my writings,—the friend and wife whose exalted sense of truth and virtue was my strongest incitement, and whose approbation was my chief reward". The work was published one year after her death.

In 1858, he retired on a pension. From 1866 to 1868 he sat in Parliament as a radical member for Westminster. As a parliamentarian he achieved no success. On May 8, 1873, John Stuart Mill died at Avignon (France) and was buried by the side of his beloved wife.

**His Writings.** Mill was a prolific writer and wrote extensively on many subjects such as ethics, logic, metaphysics, economics and politics. Of his writings mention may be made of the following:

1. A System of Logic, (1843).
2. Some unsettled question in Political Economy, (1848).
3. Essay on Liberty, (1859).
4. Considerations on Representative Government, (1861).
5. Utilitarianism, (1863).
6. Thoughts on Parliamentary Reform, (1859).
7. The Subjection of Women, (1869).
8. The Autobiography and the Three Essays on Nature, The Utility of Religion and Theism, (1874).

9. Essay on some unsettled questions in Political Economy, (1844).
10. Principles of Political Economy, (1848).
11. An examination of Sir W. Hamilton's Philosophy, (1865).
12. Dissertations and Discussions, (1859-75).
13. Inaugural Address at St. Andrews, (1867).
14. The Enfranchisement of Women, (1853).
15. On the Improvements in the Administration of India during the Last Thirty Years, (1858).
16. Admission of Women to Electoral Franchise, (1867).
17. England and Ireland, (1868).
18. Chapters and Speeches on the Irish Land Question, (1870).
19. Women's Suffrage, (1873).
20. Autobiography, (1873).

## MILL ON LIBERTY

John Stuart Mill is universally regarded as the champion of liberty. In the middle of the 19th century, due to the utilitarian reform, the scope of administrative activities increased. Parliament became the supreme law making authority and from time to time passed such laws which obstructed individual liberty. But every British citizen was becoming politically conscious. They demanded universal Franchise. Doyle says, "So on one side the growth of the Central Government of the country and the increase of social legislation emphasised the Importance of communal action over the welfare of the masses; and on the other side the extension of the Franchise of education and the revival of local Government emphasised the importance of individual effort."

**Mill was against the Tyranny of Majority.** Mill wrote his famous Essay on Liberty which equals in eminence to Milton's Areopagitica. His essay was a strong plea for the liberty of thought, expression, action against legislative interference as well as against the pressure of public opinion. Mill believed that limits must be set forth upon the authority of a popular government, because the people who "exercised power in a self-governing state are not always the same people with these over whom it is exercised, and the self-government spoken of, is not the government of each by himself but of each by all the rest... The limitation, therefore, of the power of government over individuals loses none of its importance when the holders of power are regularly accountable to the community. In political speculations the tyranny of the majority is now generally included among the evils against which society requires to be on its guard."

Mill feared that the growth of democracy and the increasing legislative power of the state tended to reduce individuals to a common type and to swamp them in the 'tyranny of collectivism'. He believed that social progress depended upon giving to each individual the fullest opportunity for free development of his personality. Accordingly, "Mill favoured freedom of thought, speech and action. He believed in toleration of opinions and unhampered freedom of discussion. He had confidence that truth would survive in the struggle of ideas".

In fact, Mill's theory of liberty required was a thorough-going consideration of the dependence of personal liberty on social and legal rights and obligations. Individual liberty, to Mill, was necessary for the development of human personality. Barker aptly remarks— "From conception of liberty as external freedom of action necessary, for the discovery and pursuit of his material interest by each individual, "Mill rose to the conception of liberty as free play for the spiritual orginality with all its results in individual vigour and manifold diversity which alone can constitute a rich balanced and developed society".

## ARGUMENTS IN FAVOUR OF INDIVIDUAL LIBERTY

Mill advanced many arguments in the defence of individual liberty. The defence is made on utilitarian grounds emphasising the importance of individual's freedom of both body and mind. Here we find his uncompromising individualism.

1. The object of this essay is to assert one very simple principle, as entitled to go govern absolutely the dealings of society which the individual in the way of compulsion and control, whether

the means used be physical force in the form of legal panalties or the moral coercion of public opinion. That principle is that the sole end for which mankind are warranted, individually or collectively, in interfering with the liberty of action of any of their number in self-protection. That the only purpose for which power can be rightfully exercised over any member of a civilized community, against his will, is to prevent harm to others. His own good, either physical or moral, is not a sufficient warrant. He cannot rightfully be compelled to do or forbear because it will be better for him to do so: because it will make him happier; because, in the opinion of others, to do so would be wise or even right. These are good-reasons for remonstrating with him, or reasoning within, or persuading him, or entreating him, but not for compelling him, or visiting him with any evil in case he do otherwise. To justify that, the conduct from which it is desired to deter him must be calculated to produce evil to some one else. The only part of the conduct on any one, for which he is amenable to society, is that which concerns others. In the part which merely concerns himself, his independence is, of right, absolute. Over himself, over his own body, and mind, the individual is sovereign."

2. Mill assumed that the activities of every individual are either self-regarding or other-regarding. The self-regarding activities may include those matters which affect the doer only, having no concern with others, e.g., gambling, drinking, etc. But in 'other-regarding' activities society has every right to interfere.

3. Mill pleaded that individual is sovereign over his body and mind and therefore, he must be left free in all that concerns himself alone. According to Mill, in this sphere society has no right to impose any restraint over the individual because restraint as such is an evil thing.

## LIBERTY OF CONDUCT

Mill's doctrine of the individual's liberty of conduct may be summarized under three heads:

1. "the advocacy of the due recognition of the place and importance of impulse and desire in man, as distinguished from intellect, though in close connection with it the

supreme need of amply acknowledging the active and energetic side of the individual nature.

2. Revolt against conventionalities of society that hinder, or seen to hinder the development, and expression of individuality against the despotic social custom."
3. Insistence on the view that spontaneity or individuality is a necessary ingredient in happiness of human welfare.
4. Mill's argument was based upon a negative conception of liberty. He objected to social control over what he described as 'self-regarding activities' because he regarded restrained as an evil. He believed that individual personality could developed and expand only in an atmosphere of freedom.
5. Mill believed in the individualistic or atomic conception of society. To him, individual is not responsible to society for his actions in so far as they concern the interest of himself and do not affect others. Mill viewed society as a collection of self-seeking individuals, and of the social good as nothing more than the sum total of their separate satisfaction.

## BASIC PRINCIPLES

Mill was living in an age when the doctrines of Carlyle and Bentham about utility were gaining ground. Bentham had preached that pleasure should be the only measuring rod for each and every activity. In other words Bentham believed that sole aim of life was to get enjoyment. The life was to be enjoyed and pleasure to be derived out of it. In a few quarters this theory of Bentham was interpreted as immoral, debasing and degrading. The main task thus before Mill was to save Benthamite theory from this attack and to raise it above the charge of "debasing and degarding". Mill, however, without any hesitation and with all courage declared that fundamentally he agreed with Bentham's principles.

Mill, however, differed from Bentham and even from his father James Mill, in so far as details were concerned. Bentham had held that it was quality and not the quantity of pleasure which mattered. But according to Mill whole concept was wrong. Qualities of pleasure have their definite places. "It would be absured that while, in estimating all other things, equality is considered as well as quantity, the estimation of pleasures should be supposed to depend upon quantity alone." He differed from Bentham when he said that it was not the pleasure that mattered alone but along with that there was another factor also namely the 'fundametal prestige'.

Mill again, differed from Bentham when he said that pleasure was the only cause and motive for individual's actions. He believed that individual pleasure did not give him maximum pleasure but it was collective pleasure which gave him maximum happiness and joy. He thus believed that pleasure comes from outside and not from within. This was quite opposite of Bentham who belived that pleasure came from within.

Bentham had held that his conception of utility was political and not ethical. He thus desired that legislators and administrators should determine it by way of giving good and useful laws. He also believed that a wise legislator must proceed on the basis of satisfaction in quantity. But as against that Mill gave the theory a moral colouring. He put political ends at the background and brought moral ends to the front.

Then again we find that Bentham and mill differ from each other in another way. Bentham wanted to establish identity between public and prosonal interests, which task he wanted to accomplish by way of super added pleasures and pains. He termed them as sanctions of utility' and categorised them under the heading 'physical, religious, popular and moral pleasures. On the other hand, Mill felt that these were external sanctions which were easily dissoluble and therefore, he wanted to find this relation on the basis of some internal sanction and sentiment of conscience. He therefore, felt that pleasure and pain conceptions, when confined to oneself alone, were external but when they related to 'others' these were internal and as such have bearing on conscience.

Still another difference between the two was that whereas Bentham did not favour the idea of plurality of votes, Mill favoured such an idea. He was of the view that the intelligent and the experienced people must be given an extra vote. They also differed in so far as the question of pleasure was concerned. Mill favoured collective or social pleasure whereas Bentham preferred individual pleasure over collective pleasure. In so far as the right to vote was concerned, there also Mill modified Bentham. Bentham believed in manhood sufferage whereas Mill was of the view that women should also be given the right to vote along with men.

**Estimate and Contribution of Mill.** John Stuart Mill was the last great Utilitarian about whose place and contributed there is divided opinion. According to some, Mill contribution nothing new to Bentham's political philosophy but simply adjusted that to suit his times. They also charge Mill with inconsistencies in philosophy. It is said that he was only an analyser and not a synthesiser of his analysis.

But in spite of all this, Mill holds a very important and pride place in English political system. He moulded and improved utilitarianism in such a fashion that it could face the challenge of the time and could survive in the face of all odds. Had Mill not appeared at the scene it would have been a different story altogether.

Then the credit for raising a voice for female sufferage goes to Mill. He was the first Utilitarian who stood for universal adult suffrage and not for manhood suffrage as was preached and propagated by his teacher Bentham.

Then again credit goes to Mill for raising a voice for individualism. Before him Bentham had also stood of individualism but his individual was an isolated entity struggling for his own pleasures and pains. But individual of Mill was thinking in terms of not external pleasures but in terms of internal sanctions and conscience.

Another salient point of his philosophy is that he preached for liberty which was a bold step in those days. He went to the extent of saying that he did not like that the indivdiual should be put in any way even under the control of their legislators. Like a very great realist and champion of liberty he stood for the combination of administrator and legislator.

Then another contribution which he made to the philosophy is his support for minority representation. Though this is still a problem yet he made an attempt to solve it. He thus was a true and real supporter of democracy. One cannot deny that unless minorities are properly representated the whole system of domocracy is bound to fail.

Then one cannot forget his ideas about the functions which he wanted the upper Houses to perform. No doubt this is a vexed problem both for the academicians as well as the politicians even today, but perhaps he wanted to have proper use of upper Houses by allotting them the functions of drafting the bills.

But still more useful estimate of his character is that he stood for qualitative instead of quantitative pleasure. The conception of quantitative pleasure had debased and degraded utilitarianism. But by giving it qualitiative conception he raised the idea of utilitarianism and utility high above in the eyes of people and political thinkers.

John Bowle has also paid him high tributes when he says that, "And if the calibre of writers is to be judged by their effect on policy, Mill must rank high. As logician, economist and political philosopher he was regarded as a prophet in this own age."

## INDIVIDUAL LIBERTY

**1. Contemporary Circumstances.** J.S. Mill was the champion of individualism and liberty. His greatest contribution to Benthamite school of thought was the changed concept of liberty to suit his times. Bentham had pleaded for reforms and with the passage of time the state had to yield to his opinion. This however, gave rise to the increased scope of state activity. The individuals were conscious and politically active. The individuals were conscious and politically growing. The parliament was concentrating all powers in its own hands. In the words of Doyle "So on the one side the growth of the Central Government of the country and the increase of the social legislation emphasised the importance of communal action over the welfare of the inasses; and on the other side the extension of franchise of education and the revival of local Government emphasised importance of individual effort." In his approach to the problem J.S.Mill was close to Socrates. He felt that liberty is most valuable to society. Mill thought a fresh on the relation between the individual and the society. Doyle has compared Bentham and Mill when he says that "Liberty of action and thought, the corollary of egoism and a necessity for development into self-consciousness was at stake." Mill thought that the society and the legislatures were organs which tried to impose their opinion on the individuals and hence required checking.

**2. Differences between Bentham and Mill.** Bemtham and James Mill both believed that liberty was essential for utility and thus was simply means to an end and not an end in itself. On the other hand, J.S.Mill believed that liberty was an essential ingredient for moral development of mankind and thus an end in itself. To quote Mill himself: "The principle is that the sole end for which mankind are warranted, individually or collectively, in interfering with the liberty of action of any of their number is self-protection. That the only purpose for whicht the power can be rightfully exercised over any number of civilised community, against his will is to prevent harm to others... He cannot be rightfully compelled to do or forbear because it will be better for him to do so: because it will make him happier: because in the opinion of others, to do so would be wise or even right... The only part of the conduct of any one, for which he is amenable to society, is that which concerns others.

**3. Champion of Individual Liberty.** According to Mill democracy, public opinion and collectivism were dangerous to individual liberty and must be kept within their sphere of activity. It is a bad tendency on the part of society to impose its will on the individuals. According to him "The tendency of the society is ussually to impose, by other means than civil penalties, its own ideas, and practices as rules of conduct on those who dissent from them, to fetter the development and, if possible, prevent the formation of any individuality not in harmony with its ways and compel all characters of fashion themselves upon the model of its own.

**4. Limitations on Liberty.** According to Mill man is free in so far as individual actions concerning his own self were concerned, and which did not prejudice his actions about others. But when his actions influence others man is bound by certain limitations. As Mill puts it "He must not make himself a nuisance to other people. But it refrains from molesting others in what concerns them and merely acts according to his own inclination and judgement in things which concern himself, the same reasons which show that opinion should be free to prove also that he should be allowed without molestation to carry his opinion into practice at his own cost." Mill put certain restrictions on enjoyment of liberty. Only those who were mature could enjoy liberty. Mill did not care for social customs and conventions. He had nothing to say about age-old institutions.

**5. Right of Expression.** According to Mill it is wrong to think in any way that any authority on earth has a right to suppress the opinion of others. Even a single dissent opinion should not be suppress because it is disgracing to human race. Its denial could possibly result in exchanging error for truth. It is, therefore, very essential that every one should be given essential basic liberties for expression of self. According to Mill "The peculiar evil of silencing the expression of an opinion is that it is robbing the human race, posterity as well as the existing generation, those who dissent from the opinion, still more than those who hold it. If the opinion is right, they are deprived of the opportunity of exchanging error for truth; if wrong, they lose, what is almost as great a benefit, the clear perception and liberation, impression of truth, produced by its collusion with error." It is always a mistake of those in power to forbid expression. Those in authority should be exonerated for such slips. Mill stressed the need and necessity of variety of opinions.

**6. Need of Liberty.** Mill stressed the conception of individual liberty on the grounds that such liberty is essential for the development of human personality. Without it one could neither develop nor progress but become stagnant. It is also essential for spiritual originality. Barker explains, "From the conception of liberty he meant an external freedom of action necessary for the discovery and pursuit of his material by each individual. Mill rose to the conception of liberty as free play for the spiritual originality with all its results in individual vigour and manifold diversity which alone can constitute a rich, balanced and developed society." Intentionally Mill did not discuss the problem of social evil doers who had scant regard for democratic institutions and the method by which they should be treated. The individual should be left alone in so far as actions concerning himself were concerned. Individual's activities are divided into self-regarding and other regarding. Since the latter are concerned with the communtiy as a whole, the state had a right to interfere in them.

**7. Liberty of Representatives.** Mill also stood for the liberty of the representatives of the people in the elected bodies. They should not be mere echo of the people. They should also have independence of views and expression.

**8. Doctrine of Individual Liberty.** Davidson has beautifully summed up Mill's doctrine of indiviudal liberty when he says that "Mill's doctrine of individual liberty of conduct may be summed up under three heads *(1)* the advocacy of the recognition of the place and importance of impulse and desire in man, as distinguished from intellect, though in close connection with it the supreme need of amply acknowledging the active and energetic side of the individual's nature, *(2)* Insistence on the view that spontaneity or individuality is a necessary ingredient in happiness or human welfare, *(3)* Revolt against the conventionalists of society that hinder or seem to hinder, the development and expression of individuality-against the despotism of social customs."

## G.W.F. HEGEL

Georg Wilhelm Friedrich Hegel was a Professor at University of Berlin. He belonged to aristocracy and believed in the importance of bureaurcray because he was the son of a civil servant who was in the service of the ruler of Wurttemberg. He believes that civil service should be placed in a proper heirachy. He favoured the absolutism of monarchy and thought it as an essential Institution. He was a great philospher of Zermany placing before us the doctrine of absolute state, absolute *Spirit and Mind*. He glorified the monarchy. "In spite of his great reputation and the pressumbly exicting character of intellectual development, Hegel's outward life was no more unusual than that of most academic persons. He was born at Stuttgart on August 27, 1776. He was sent to a Grammer School at Stuttgart. He was awarded the degree of doctor of philosophy in 1790. After several years as a tutor in Bern and Frankfurt, five years as a professor at the University of Jena, a brief period, as a newspaper editor, and eight years as head of a Gymnasium in Nuremberg. Two years later, Hegel at the age of 47 was appointed professor of philosopher at Berlin, where he soon became a favourite of the government and in a sense its official philosophy". As a personality he was unprepossessing and of meagre appearance, his delivery was painful and voice weak. He was a good family man and addicated only to snuff, he spoke apparently with a broad swabian accent. Hegel died of cholera at the age of 61.

Following are His Writings are:

1. Science of Logic, (1812-1816) in (3 volumes).
2. The Philosophy of Right, (1821).
3. The Philosophy of History, (1837).

   (Edited by his son, and published after his death in (1837).
4. The Phenomenology of Spirit, (1807).

After his death his influence was very great not only in Germany but also in England and the United States. In England, he was one of the main inspirations of late nineteenth century idealism. His influence has been great philosophers who covertly rejected his distinctive views. The Marxists, for example, took him very seriously, while John Dewy, whose matured philosophy would certainly had scandalized Hegel, acknoweledged that he found the latter infinitely fruitful and suggestive.

## HEGELIAN DIALECTIC

George Wilhelm Friedrich Hegel is the most self confident philosopher who ever lived. He aimed at nothing less than a complete reconstruction of modern thought. The two main points round which the thought of Hegel centres are the dialectical methods and the idealisation of the nation state.

**1. Greek Dialectic.** The sophists were the first philosophers to employ the term dialectic. According to them the dialectic was not a method of demonstrating known truth or of discovering new truths. It was a method of disputation whose primary aim was to trip up a speaker by showing that what he was saying is self rufuting. It centred round ambiguities of terms and grammatical constructions. According to Plato the dialectic was the process of thinking by which the dramatic conflict of ideas was resolved by definition.

**2. Hegel's Meaning of Dialectic.** According to Hegel, dialectic was not merely a process by which logical ideas developed. It was a process by which all ideals in the world developed in this universe, which is an organic whole. Every thing is the creation of ideal or the spirit of reason. Reason is the sovereign of the world. The essence of reason is self consciousness. In its attempt to attain self realization, Reason has been unfolding itself in various froms.

**3. Law of Dialectic.** The law of dialectic was the law of contradictions. Hegel explained his law by three terms-being, nothing and becoming. He gave the example of genus changing into specie as a result of the sublimation of differentia. The process of change involves a substance first negating itself and then engaging that negation into a higher form. Dialectic may be seen in the evolution of the life germ in an egg. The egg contains a germ (thesis) which when fertilized gradually consumes (negatives) the contents of the egg.

**4. Dialectic a Rational Process.** According to Hegel the unfoldment or development of Reason has taken place not in a positive or straight manner, but in a spiritual or zig zag form. The formula of unfoldment is that of thesis, anti-thesis and synthesis. "The thesis shows one aspect of reality; the anti-thesis and synthesis. The thesis shows one aspect; and the synthesis reconciles the two. The synthesis again becomes a thesis and comes in higher synthesis, and the opposition between the two is overcome in a higher synthesis and so on the progress continues.

**5. Political Dialectic.** Hegel rejects the view of Fichte that only the ideal state is rational whereas existing states are irrational. One the contrary, Hegel maintains that actual, existing states are rational an are, therefore, to be treated with all reverence. He, thus idealises the actual. This is a logical consequence of his conviction that whatever happens is so because the spirit need it and that whatever the needs is right.

**6. Social Dialectics.** To elaborate the process on the social level, despotism (the thesis) calls into being democracy (its antithesis), and from the clash between the two results constitutional monarchy (the synthesis). Similarly, family (the thesis) provides its anti thesis (bourgeois society), and from the clash between the two the state (the synthesis) emerges which is a higher from of social evolution. It was the ambition of Hegel to deduce the entire universe, which he describes as the Absolute Idea from the most abstract of all conceptions, the idea of pure being in accordance with the dialectic method.

**7. Real is Rational and Rational is Real.** For Hegel, the course of world development is completely determined. There is nothing like chance or accident in it. But what determines the evolution is not a material factor like climate or matter but Reason in its creative and unconscious form. Since the universe is the embodiment or expression of reason, it must be completely knowable. For Hegel, the real is the rational and the rational is the real.

**8. Result of Dialectic.** In short, dialectic seeks to explain the story of the continuous development of the spirit or Reason. I emphasizes the essential continuity of the historical process. It explains history is the story of not only of the quite unfolding but of the bounding forward of the spirit. To quote Wayper, "Dialectic thus claims to be a new system of synthetic logic, replacing the old system of analytic logic, a principle of self-movement through contradiction towards the final goal of perfect realization of spirit-a conception of ordered rational progress which explains away periods of apparent anarchy accompanying the collapse of old orders as being themselves the misundesstood sign of progress to higher goods, a theory which is both essentially conservative and fundamentally revolutionary". Hegel in and through his dialectic propounded the belief that reality could only be apprehended by a method of contrasting one thing with its opposite.

## HEGEL'S VIEW ON STATE AND SOCIETY

In Hegel's thinking most controversial point is, his view on liberty. He gave prominence to state and not to individual. According to him main duy of an individual is to obey the state and such man becomes only a slave or tool for the welfare of the state. Before discussing Hegel's view it is necessary to discuss the criticism of Hegel about the Kant's view about freedom.

**Hegel's Criticism of Kantian Conception of Freedom.** In Kant's philosophy free will of the individuals was upper most in his thought. According to him every individual was an end in himself and none was to be considered as a means to an end. Kant had a passion for the liberty of the individuals and he was not prepared to sacrifice the same on the alter of the state. It is true that the liberty of the individual was to be subordinated to the higher needs of social existence, but this did not mean that Kant was willing to abandon the liberty of the individuals.

Critics point out that Kant could not make up his mind as to whether he stood for the conception of "being left alone" or in the higher sense of providing opportunity for the development of man's higher faculties. According to Vaughan, Kant failed "becaue he hovered between the two entirely different conceptions of the state i.e. between individualism and idealism.

Hegel criticised Kant's conception of freedom as negative, limited and subjective. Barker is of opinion that Hegal sketched positive and objective conception of freedom and as such his views about the state were different than Kant.

Hegel considered Kant's freedom as negative because it has no place for freedom of conduct because according to Kant freedom lies in inner moral will. He stated, "To define freedom of Press as freedom to say and write" is parallel to the assertion to do as we please. Thus he was against freedom of Press.

It is limited because it remains in the inner consciousness of man and does not come out of its while actually freedom can be realized only in society. As such Kant in individualistic.

In the same it is subjective because it remains only as a consciousness of individual's mind.

According to Hegel main element of man's freedom does not lie in the inner consciuosness of man but in the social institutions. Hegel's freedom lies in outer world and as such it becomes social and positive. Hegal has put emphasis that man can feel freedom only by taking part of social activities.

According to Prof. Snbine. "The vital point of Hegelian conception of freedom is that civilization is not repressive of individual self expression, that social forces are a medium in which the individual always moves and from which he derives the elements even of his individuality; that to be man at all requires participation in the life of communities; that education and culture are in general a medium of liberation."

**Liberty is Possible Only in Social Life.** Hegel's idea of freedom was leased on the old Greek motion of an individual finding his true personality and his freedom in the state. Man had no inalienable rights and his freedom was a gift of state. The state not only allows but enlarges the freedom of the society. The state is "the actualisation of freedom." The social institution and environments are the media through which an individual finds self realization and freedom. There is little freedom outside the state and the civil society. For modern man freedom can exist only in a national state.

**Is Hegelian Liberty a Mockery.** According to Hegel the only duty of a good citizen was to conform to the existing affaris in society. Individual choice was merely caprice, sentimentality and fanaticism. It was superficial. The primary duty of the individual was mere obedience. As such scholars are of opinion that he sacrificed the individual at the alter of the state.

**Hegel Regards State as Omnipotent.** According to Hegel state is absolute, omnipotent and infalliable. The state is the march of God on earth. The state is God itself. "If is the divine idea as it exists on earth. The state is actualization of freedom. It was embodiment of reason and as such none possesses right against the state. He did not believe in any rights against the state as such critics are of opinion that Hegel sacrifices the individual at the alter of the state. Moreover Hegel did not make any difference between an ideal and actaul state. In short "Hegelian state is levithian in new form".

According to Hegel, law is not a manifestation of people's will. Hegel is of opinion that public neither frames the law nor it possesses power to frame the law. Laws are product of experiences of previous history recognised by the state.

**State is above Natrual Law and Morality.** Hegel is of opinion that true freedom or individulaity lies in conformity with our real will is identical with the general will and general is embodied in the state. This theory conceives state as an end in itself, as the sole criterion of morality and rights and as supreme incarnation of human reason. Hegelism exempts the state from moral criticism and defies it. The Hegelian theory of the state leads to state absolutism and makes it above natural law and morality etc. He stated, "Nothing short of the state is actualisation of freedom."

**State is Unrestrained in International Field.** Hegel's conception of national state did not leave any scope for any inernational law or international order. The state was omnipotent and absolute. There was no such thing as international law which could bind the will of the state. International law merely represented certain usuages which are accepted so long as they did not conflict with the supreme performance of the state. To quote him "As state is not a private person, but is itself a complete independent totality." States in their relation to one another are indpendent and look upon the stipulations which they make one another as provisional but now with the emergence of W.H.O. regional organizations, his views are outdated.

**Hegal is not a Pacifist.** According to Hegel "War is to national life what winds are to the sea. Peace corrupts and everlasting peace would corrupt everlastingly."

The state of war shows the omnipotence of the state in its individuality. In war, it is the world spirit which decides which of the contesting states is its true embodiment and victorious state is the truer personification of he world spirit.

**Criticism of Hegel's Conception of Freedom.** Prof. Barker is of opinion that in comparison to Kant, Hegal sketched a more positive and objective concpetion of freedom. It is true to certain extent as he emphasized the outer aspect of freedom which can be realized only in society.

Hegel is of opinion that freedom of an individual lies in the obedience of state is the actualization of freedom, but it is difficult to agree with the Hegelian conception that all orders of the state increase the freedom of an individual. Freedom has meaning only in relation to the individual and the society and the raison desire of the state is the welfare of the individual. The individual is the end of the state and should not be lost in it.

Prof. Sabine points out that Hegel never tried to show as to how the modern state could be a centre for all interests of a modern man. His mind was full of a strong desire to bring about unification of Germany and he did not hesitate to merge the individual in the state. He even sacrificed the individual at the altar of the state.

**View's of Green.** Green criticized the Hegelian conception of state as a realization of freedom in following words "to an Athenion slave who might be used to gratify his master's lust, it would have been mockery to speak of the state as a realisation of freedom and perhaps it would not be much less to speak of it as such to an untaught and underfed citizen of a London Yard with gin shop on the right hand and on the left. Hegel's conception of freedom goes not seem to correspond to the facts of society as it is, or even as, unalterable condition of human nature, it ever could be." The real difficulty in Hegel lay in mistaking remedies for accomplished facts.

**Evaluation.** Thus to a great extent it is true that Hegel sacrifices the individual to the alter of the state but is valuable as it insists on the dependence of man in society. He is right in showing that man is influenced by society. He has made the idea of liberty richer by showing that man's conception of it. leargely depends upon the institutions which have trained him and given him education. Critics who point out that in Hegelian philosophy, individual is only slave of the state, have not realised the importance of distinction between real and unreal state. Greatest defect of Hegal is that he makes state as an end and individual as a tool to achieve aims of the state. Thus Hegelian views possess only historical value and cannot be accepted now.

**Summary**

1. Freedom is essential to man.
2. Hegel's conception of freedom has been criticised because it sacrifices individual at the altar of the state.

3. Hegel came to conclusion that freedom of man lies in obedience of state.
4. Kant's conception of freedom was negative and limited as it depended on inner consciousness but Hegel put emphasis on outer or social aspect so it is positive.
5. According to him state is omnipotent law and did not depend on public opinion State is unrestrained in International field and is above law and morality and gets glory by war.

## POLITICAL PHILOSOPHY OF HEGEL

Hegel's political Philosophy was a response to the scepticism of the British thinkers who did not accept reason as an ultimate source of truth and reality. In his political philosophy Hegel emphasized that reason comprehended all reality. He identfied all that is or has been with reason. Hegel tried to synthesize in his political political philosophy its different aspects and made it all embracing and synthetic. He tried to show that other thinkers had grasped only a part of truth. He did **not** refute what they wrote but only showed that they had written partial truth. He studied philosophy and history and derived princples from which he developed his political philosophy.

**1. History as Unfoldment of Reason.** Reason is the ultimate reality. History is the unfoldment of Reasons in its various shapes. Reason is God.

**2. Dialectical Evolution of History.** The process of historical evolution is dialectical. Dialectic means the interaction or the conflict of contrary forces or powers. By its action in the world each force of power gives rise to its opposite. Each thesis generates its anti-thesis and out of the conflict between the thesis and antithesis the synthesis is born. The synthesis becomes in its turn the thesis which again generates its anti-thesis a new idea is born.

**3. War as a Virtue.** According to Hegel the essential principle of the state is self-preservation and perfection. War is not to be regarded as an evil but a virtue. "The state of war", says Hegel, "shows the omnipotence of the state in its individuality". War is to national life what winds are to the sea, 'Preserving mankind from the corruption engendered by immobility'. War effectively displays the 'irony of the divine idea". War destroys the selfish egoism of the individual. For Hegel, "peace corrupts and everlastig peace corrupts everlastingly". "War is the state of affairs which deals in earnest with the vanity of temporal goods and concerns - a vanity at other highest significance that by its agancy, the ethical health of people is preserved in their indifference to the stablizing of finite institutions; just as the blowing of the wind preserves the sea from the foulness which would be the result of a prolonged calm, left alone 'perpetual peace'. "Successful wars have prevented civil boils and strengthened the internal power of the state". The various weapons of war were not invented only by chance; they fulfilled an essential purpose. To quote Hegel, "The gun is not a chance invention". The same can be said about gun-power. "Humanity needed it and it made its appearance forthwith". Guns and gunpowder bear the stamp of civilization. "The rights of uncivilized people are, a mere formality."

The world spirit decides for itself throug war which of the warring states is its true embodiment. Succees in war is a conclusive proof that the victorious state represnts more fully and truly the world spirit. However, no state can ruge in justification of a war it has begun that it is acting at the behest of the world spirit, though it can always make that claim in justification of war that it has won. Thus, Hegel assigns a great role to war. The world spirit according to him, fulfils its aim through war. Therefore, war is a virtuous necessity.

**4. International Law is not Binding to Nation State.** To Hegel, the nation-state was the most rational thing. It was the expession of a higher rationality than could be achieved by the individual, or by any private group or corporation. The state was omnipotent and absolute, supreme and sovereign. Naturally, therefore, the state is not bound by principles of International Law. International Law represents only certain usages which were accepted so long as they did conflict with the supreme performance of the state. The other nations have no right against a state. To quote Hegel, "A state is not a private person, but it itself a completely independent totality. Hence the relation of states to one another is not merely that of morality and private right. It is often desired that the state should be regarded from the standpoint of private right and morality. But the position of private persons is such that they have over them a law court, which realises what is intrinsically right. A relation between states ought also to be intrinsically right, but in mundane affairs that which is intrinsically right ought to have power. But as against the state, there is no power to decide what is instrinsically right and to realise that decision. Hence, we must here remain by absolute command. States in their relations to one another are indepenent and look upon the stipulations which they make with one another as provisional".

**5. World State.** But to Hegel, nation-state was only a necessary step in the evolution of humanity towards a world-state. It is only when the nations have developed to their full maturity that they can march towards the idea of world-state. But Hegel did not write much on the world-state. The idea of world state was too abstract for him to speculate about it.

**6. Private Property.** Hegel was in favour of the institution of private property. Without it, the individual could not exert himself and make his personality grow.

**7. Constitutional Monarchy.** According to Hegel, the state manifests itself in a constitution. The three important powers in the state are legislative, administrative and monarchic. Out of these powers, the monarchic power is the most important. Hegel made this division of powers according to the formula of his dialectic. The legislative branch, which stands for the unviersal aspect of the state, is the thesis. The administrative organ representing its particular aspect is the antithesis. The constitutional monarch who may be regarded as their unity in the individual state is the synthesis. Hegel includes the judicial organ in the administrative branch. The constitutional monarch is the medium through which the legislative and the executive are brought into a harmonious unity. Thus, according to Hegel, the monarch is the symbol and embodiment of the unity and supremacy of the state. The sovereignty of the state resides in him and no in the mass of the people. Being constituional, the monarch can be no autocrat. He is bound to the concrete content of the advice of his councillors, and when the constitution is established he has often nothing to do but sign his name. His function is simply to say 'I will' in the name of the state. But this name is weighty; it is the summit over which nothing can climb. In accordance with his dialectic Hegel has tried to show that the completely rational state must not only be a monarchy, but a constitutional monarchy.

## IMPLICATIONS OF HEGEL'S PHILOSOPHY

**1. Restroation of German National Unity.** An examination of Hegel's philosophy shows something both very old and very simple. He reaffirmed the Greek view that man rises to his full stature only in the state which completes the training in pulbic spirit supplied at the lower level by the family and civil society. Hegel's real aim was to restore national unity of Germany which had suffered humiliation at the hands of France. State's own preservation was the first end to be kept in view before the individuals could claim any freedom for themselves. Freedom to Hegel was something positive, and not merely a negative absense of restraints.

**2. Objections to Dialectic.** Hegel cast his arguments in the rigid mould of dialectic, he opened himself to serious pitfalls.

*(i)* ***Determinism.*** To Hegel, dialectic was a law of logic, and indeed an iron law, leaving little or nothing to chance or even to consciuos human volition.

*(ii)* ***Disappearance of Individual Values.*** As a matter of fact, Hegel has reduced individual wishes and perverseness to the level of mere caprice. The actors in human history for him are not men but impersonal forces. The deeds of actual men are what Hegel calls 'moments' in the process by which the idea realizes itself in the state. The wishes of man are merely 'subjective' made legitimate only in so far as the 'inner drive' of the dialectic makes them coincide with the 'universal' ends of the state. As Lancaster remarks, "While Hegel's emphasis on the 'Transcendence' of the individual was a useful corrective to the extreme atomism of the English treatment, he carries it to the point where individual values disappear entirely."

*(iii)* ***Vagueness.*** But the most serious objection against dialectic is that it is extremely vague. The 'contradictions' discovered

by Hegel consist of so many sorts of different and opposite things that the dialectic frequently losses its plausibility. Thus to Hegel, civil society is the antithesis of family.

**3. Exaltation of State.** The most significant aspect of Hegel's philosophy is his exaltation of the state. He makes the individual not only a member of society but makes him the subject of a state which being the final embodiment of world spirit is supreme and omnipotent. The moral superiority of the state consists not in the fact that it is a means to meet the needs of man but in the fact that it is an end in itself, representing the supeme achievement of reason in human affairs.

**4. Worship of State Power.** State is the 'absolutely rational', the 'actuality of the ethical idea' 'the march of God on earth'. Individual has signficance only as the material upon which spirit works its will. The individual conscience is not to be trusted. The commands of the state are the spokesmen of infalliable morallity. To raise of state above and moral criticism was to contribute decisively to a disastrous worship of power.

**5. Value of Hegel's Teaching**

(i) ***Emphasis on Social Aspect.*** Hegel's individualism ignores the social character of man. Hegel emphasized the social aspect of man's nature.

(ii) ***Basis of Communism.*** Hegel emphasized that the state is not a policy state, instead it must be regarded as part of man's moral end. His dialectic became in the hands of Marx the basis of revolutionary communism. Marx converted the evolution, an evolution ending not in the exaltation of the state but in its abolition.

(iii) ***Revision of Liberalism.*** Hegel's philosophy led the English idealists of the last 18th century to revise liberalism and rid it of its abstraction which had viewed the individual as a solitary and pleasure seeking animal.

(iv) ***Rich Idea of Liberty.*** Hegel made the idea of liberty richer by showing that man's conception of its largely depends upon the institutions which have trained him and given him his education.

(v) ***Sociological Theory of Politics.*** Hegel's theory gave rise to the sociological theory of politics, because he showed that political power was connected with the economic, social and cultural forces in the state. He gave a new emphasis and importance to the state and greatly enriched modern political philosophy.

(vi) ***Dialectical Method.*** He set forth a new intellectual method, the dialectic which should bridge the gulf between reason, fact and value.

(vii) ***Synthesis of Ethics and Politics.*** Hegel grasped the connection between morals and politics and handled the same with a far greater insight than any of his predecessors. According to Prof. Sabine, "The philosophy of Hegel aimed at nothing leass than a complete and systematic reconstruction of modern thought."

(viii) ***National State.*** In his political theory Hegel set a value on the national state and its place in history which formed no small part of his influence. The social philosophy of Hegel had a direct and intimate relation to the national history of Germany. According to Maxey, "It will be many years before the full influence of Hegel's political though can be measured. His conribution to the warring ideologies represented on the one side by Lenin and Stalin and on the other by Mussolini and Hitler, consitutes but one part of his signficance and is no mere paradoxical than his influence in other directions. Both his view and his methodology have deeply affected the social science. Divergent strems of thought have also flowed from Hegel's subordination of the whole of civil society to the state. Liberals, seeking an escape from the nobilistic individualism similar to that of laissez-faire, have found in the Hegelian conception of the state a plausible basis for programmes of reform carried on by state action.

## MAIN FEATURES OF HEGEL'S POLITICAL PHILOSOPHY

Sabine says "that the philosophy of Hegel aimed at nothing less than A complete reconstruction of the modern thought. Political issues and ideas were an important but still only a secondary factor in it as compared with religion and metaphysics. In a broad sense Hegel's problem was one that had been grown steadily more acute with the progress of modern science *viz.*, the opposition between the order of nature and the conception, of it implicit in the ethical and religious traditions of Christianity."

The course of Hegelian political thought was determined by certain factors. Kant and Fichte exercised a great influence in shaping his political philosophy. Plato and Aristotle too profoundly influenced his writings. Rouseau's and Montesquieu's writings also influenced Hegel's philosophy.

Againts the philosophies of Hume, Rousseau and Kant, Hegel "proposed to set a bold speculative principle of synthesis. Morals and religion, he believed could be given a logic justification, but only if a newer and more powerful logic of synthesis could be discovered, transcending the analytic logic of science. What Hegel's philosophy professed to offer........was an enlarged conception of reason that should overlap and include what had been separated by the analysis of Hume and Kant, and the centre of his system was a new logic purporting to systematise a new intellectual method. This he called "dialectic". He held that its virtue lay in its capacity to determine a necessary logical relationship between the realm of fact and the realm of value. Accordingly "it supplied a new and an indispensable tool for understanding the problems of society and of morals and religion. It was to provide a strictly rational standard of value...to replace the law of nature, the philosophical weakness of which had been proved by Hume and the practical weakness of which had been still more glaringly proved by the French Revolution."

The dialectic of Hegel was adopted as the basis of communistic doctrine by Marx. The dialectic method postulated that "progress or development does not take place in a straight or linear form, but proceeds in a spiral or zig-zag course.' Its formula is "thesis, antithesis and synthesis." Sabine remarks, "His dialectic was in fact a kind of symbol for revolution and recovery. It acknowledged the destruction of obsolete institutions by living social forces, but it celebrated the re-establishment of stability by the creative forces of the nation."

An outstanding charcteristic of Hegelian political philosophy was the high valuation of the national state. Here he followed Fichte that each nation has its peculiar spirit and culture and makes its unique contribution to world civilization.

In Hegel's political thought there were three elements of primary significance, *viz.*:

1. The dialectic, "which he put forward as a method capable of yielding new and otherwise indemonstrable conclusions in the social studies."
2. A theory of the national state as the embodiment of politcal power.
3. The historical method. He viewed the history of civilization as a succession of national cultures in which each nation makes its own peculiar contribution to human development. "His political and social philosophy centred in the study of history and in the relation of history to the other social studies. The history of religion, the history of philosophy and the history of law were created as special subejcts of investigation largely under the influence exerted by his philosophy. The historical method was a mode of driving from the order of historical evolution standards of valuation by means of which the significance of particular stages in the evolution could be determined.

Sabine held "that Hegel's philosophy first stated the principles upon which the belief in a historical method, rested. The method assumed that there is in nature a single pattern or law of development which can be exihibited by a proper arrangement of subject-matter. This holds true for the whole evolution of society as well as for any sub-division of history. Therefore, it should be possible to put an orderly evolution of law, of economic institutions, of philosophic thought or of government. The special work of historical insight consists in bringing to light this pattern, which is of course concealed in a welter facts, and it is for this reason that historical and theoretical studies are connected. Hegel's purpose was not so much to predict the future course of events as discriminate the main current from the eddies and backwashes in the stream, and thus to arrive at an historically objective standard of values."

## FEATURES AND INFLUENCE OF THOUGHTS

Hegel was very much influenced by the writings of his predecessors and contemporaries. He was influeced by Kant, Fitche, Plato, Aistotle and no less by Montesquieu and Rousseau. From Fitche he got the idea that ultimate reality was reason and not matter. He did not agree with Kant that things were self contradictory but agreed with Fitches that reason was dynamic and there was nothing which was beyond the reach of human knowledge. It was from this logic that Reason was the ultimate truth and that change was not an illusion but a reality that he further developed his theory and gave it a technical name called 'Dialectic' which was subsequently borrowed by Marx. It was on account of this philosophy of 'Dialectic' that Hegel has been called the 'Marxist'.

According to Wright "The dialectic begins with the most abstract conception of pure logic......and terminates with most concrete phase of thought, the philosophy of absolute mind in its full comprehensiveness and conceitness."

Hegel borrowed from Rousseau the philosophy of speculative synthesis. He believed that if new and reasonable principles were given the nations could get new outlook both in religion and moral. According to him, this could be done by the system of speculative synthesis.

From Fitche he borrowed the idea of national state which he considered as the sysmbol and embodiment of national power.

From Montesquieu, he also borrowed the theory of 'separation of powers' which he believed was absolutely necessary for the efficiency and freedom of individual but that it should not be taken away too far least it became a method for mutual misunderstanding between three departments of Government.

**Hegel's Contribution to Political Thought.** Hegel is today considered as one of the most difficult political writers whose writings are considered as most abstract. But in spite of all this Hegel is considered as one of the most original writers in political philosophy.

He conributed to the political philosophy *(i)* the dialectic method *(ii)* the theory of national state and *(iii)* the idea of progress. Acording to Gettel "The personality of the national state, superior in importance to its individual member, was exalted to a mystical hight." Sabine makes us believe that he made an attempt at 'complete reconstruction of modern thought."

It was Hegal's philosophy of dialectic which reached a realistic conclusion that the world culture was not the monopoly of one nation but it was the essence of cultures of all the state and that world culture represented the best of all the nation.

Stressing the importance of the theory of dialectic, Sabine has said that "Throught the dialectic as revised by Marx he became the source of new proletarian redicalism, culminating in communism, which has steadily tended to displace the older middle class liberalism. Through his idealisation of the nation state he became a source for conservative nationalism, culminating in fascism, which has swallowed up the liberal nationalism of middle 19th century."

Hegel's another contribution is that he has tried to prove that the whole universe is a coherent whole. He believed in reason and perfection and like a realist felt that all rational was real and that all real was rational.

Then his contribution is that he has properly assessed the value of history and place of personalities and events in the making of history. Still more credit goes to him becaues he has clarified his stand without any ambiguity.

He also gave the idea that man was an end in itself and not means to an end and that state was to promote the welfare of man. This is valued even today.

**Influene of Hegel.** Through his writings Hegel influenced many who mattered much in his age. His influence on Bismark and Marx was immense. Hegel's influence in the University of Berlin was not only tremendous but also effective. Bismark actually followed his ideas into practice. According to Merbach "At the portal of Bismark's Century stands the life, thought, activity of Hegel like the thought before the deed. Megovern has expressed Hegel's influence on the state activities of Bismark when he says that "Bismark's emphasis upon the nation state based upon force or power as the supreme goal of human activities; his belief that the state is not a collection of individuals, but a single organic whole; his advocacy of an all powerful monarchy and bureaucracy in opposition to democracy; his nations of international relations were all rooted in Hegelian principles."

He influenced Marx in many ways: for example, Marx borrowed from him ideas like class struggle and mystical ideas about the ends of the state. It was again from him that he borrowed the idea that state was absolute. Hegel also gave him the idea that economic life of the people influenced their social and moral life. According to Sabine "The importance that Max attached to economic forces in politics quite definitely had its roots there, though Marx doomed Hegel's state to extinction."

Hegel's influence was not within the four walls of Germany alone. We find that he had his followers in England, Italy and U.S.A. In England T.H. Green was the greatst exponent of his philosophy and what he did was simply to change Hegelian philosophy in such a fashion as that suited the English convenience. In U.S.A. most of universities preached his philosophy and in Italy Prof. Augusto Vera of Millan University and political thinkers like Benedetto Croce and Giovanni Gentile were the chief exponents of his philosophy and like true Hegelians they glorified state. In U.S.A.Moris Palmer and John Deway were Hegelians in true sense.

**Drawbacks of Hegel's Philosophy.** But it should not lead us to the conclusion that Hegel's philosophy was most perfect. It has also certain inherent defects and some of the important ones are:

1. According to Hegel state was an Idea of Reason or that the state represented the reason and being embodiment of reason, it was the march of God on earth. But who can deny that most of the states are not ideal states and do not represent reason and as such are not the march of God on earth. The governments consist of individuals who have their own selfish interests and therefore the conception of

state being the march of God on earth might be rule in theory but cannot be correct in practice.

2. According to Hegelian philosophy there was already a Divine plan for every action and that great men play no role in making or unmaking the national cultures and history. But again this dos not seem to be correct. Who can deny that great men, by their dynamic personalities, have changed the course of action of many nations though for a layman that appared to be divine will.

3. According to Hegel, constitutional monarchy was an ideal from of government but who would deny that was more a question of personal preference rather than a univseral suitability.

4. Hegel has pleaded that the national culture did not consist of individuals but that was the essence of best cultures of the various nations which gradually influenced the nation. But this again is not correct because national culture represents the best of their customs, conventions and traditions and are rooted in the mode of living of that nation.

5. Hegelian philosophy pleads that expediency was the only law which should be followed by every state. He did not believed that state was bound by any moral laws. But this again its not correct. State, if it dit not follow moral laws was bound to suffer in morality. State represented morality and moral achievements of subjects more particularly when he believed that state was the Idea of Reason.

6. Hegel believed in the philosophy of 'historical process in which everthing was left to history, which if followed to its logical end will make men fatalist, inactive and end the national cultures.

7. Hegel has also been criticsed because of his ambiguous language, which has been characterised as ugly and shapeless. Wayper has gone to the extent of saying that "A technical terminology more shapeless, ugly, impenetrable

than any other jargon, a truly awful style made him still more unseemly by a love of ponderous paradox, yet adequately matched by that wonderful construction that makes the philosophy of Right such a difficult book to follows, these are the landmarks of Hegelian writings.

8. According to Hegel state was the highest expression of individual morality and thus was the agency which regulated the lives of the subjects including their moral life and was above all controls. But this philosophy was true in the Greek city states of whose chief exponent was Plato and from whom he borrowed this philosophy. But in the modern states, this philosophy does not hold good. The influence of church had then increased and it had established authority as the custodian for regulating moral life of the individuals and that weakned the authority of the state in regulating the moral life of men. The appearance of international agencies these days has given a great set-back to the supremacy of the states.
9. Hegel has subordinated his individual to the state and has thus used it as an instrument for the glorification of state which theory resulted in Fascism and Nazism which were ultimately responsible for world wars.
10. Hegel has also been criticised for imperfect knowledge of history and religion, in addition to Art. Wayper has gone to the extent of saying that even his concept of dialectic is defective and not up to the mark. According to him it is wrong to believe that all defects are beginning of victory.

## HEGELIAN CONCEPT OF FREEDOM

Hegel had the reputation of being the most difficult of philosophers. This reputation rested upon the complexity of the language in which he expressed his thought. He concerned himself with the persistent issues of politics as consent, freedom and authority. His principal pre-occupation was with freedom. He regarded his political philosophy as supplying the only valid reconciliation of freedom and authority. Hegel asserted that men are free when they obey the commands of the state.

**1. Value of Freedom.** Hegel was one of those young Germans who had enthusiastically welcomed the French Revolution. But as things developed under Napeolean, these young Germans had to re-examine their beliefs. Hegel's political philosophy is the most significant fruit of this reaction. According to Hegel freedom is the distinctive quality of man. In his words, "To renounce one's freedom is to renounce one's humanity. Not to be free, therefore, is a renunciation of one's human rights and even of one's duties". This truth Hegel gathered from Rousseau and Kant.

**2. Freedom as Social Phenomena.** The chief defect of the Kantian concept of freedom is that he did not show it to be a social phenomnenon. He viewed it as the attribute of men as an independent unit. He nowehere stressed the point that freedom can be realised only in and through participation in the legal and ethical life of the community. Hegel sought to emphasize that freedom is a social phenomenon. It is made possible only by paticipation in the moral life of the community. He reunited the individual with a social system and urged that freedom can be possible only and within the state. The main point which Hegel emphasizes is that civilization is not repressive of individual freedom; that 'social forces are a medium in which the individual always moves and from which he dervies the elements even of his individuality; that to be man at all required participation in the life of some short of communities; that education and culture are in general a means of liberation. For men freedom can exist only in a national state.

**3. Differences from Kant.** Hegel believed that Kantian conception of freedom was negative, limited and subjective on account of which the attitude of Kant towards the state was gruadging and individualistic. In opposition to Kant, Hegel put forth his positive concept of freedom and less individualisitic conception of the state and it's freedom.

**4. Freedom only in the State.** Freedom is possible only within the state and not outside it. The state is a necessary condition on freedom. The state sustains freedom. Man is free only when he lives in a state. Without it, he is completely in subjection. That is what Hegel means by his phrase that "nothing short of the state is the actualisation of freedom". But the state which Hegel conceives of is nothing short of the perfection of Spirit or Reason. He called it the "divine idea on earth" and the final embodiment of spirit, the concrete universal.

**5. Freedom is Obedience to Law.** Since the state represents the social morality in its highest from, therefore, obedience to its laws guarantees freedom. According to Hegel, freedom does not consist in the absence of restraints or in satisfying the desires and passions as they rise but in obedience to the laws of the state which represent Reason. The absense of arbitrary restraints may be a condition of freedom but is not its essence. Hegel does not make the individual conscience the final court of appeal because it is incapable of telling us what is eternally right. Moreover, individual consciences change from place to place and from time to time. Therefore, for realisation of freedom we must look to the state, for its laws alone represent the eternal reason. Freedom consists in the willing obedience to the laws of the state. Men are free hence they are aware of the necessity. The state regularizes and rationalises human desires and makes and away of their identity with it. Men see that what they really want is what the state commands. The contradiction between freedom and obedience is seen to be merely apparent. The obedient citizen is the only free man, because, in the last analysis he is obeying himself. In duty, the indivdiual acquires his substantive freedom. Thus, the second point to be noted in the Hegelian concept of freedom is that freedom consists in obedience to the commands of the state. The only way to secure freedom is voluntary submission to the more perfect expression of reason in the state.

## THE STATE AS THE REALIZATION OF FREEDOM

Since Hegel's interpretation of human freedom was intimately connected with the problem of the realtionship between the state and the individual, we must now turn our attention towards the study of Hegelian conception of freedom.

To Hegel, the state was a means of enlarging freedom. In his Philosophy of History, Hegel writes that, "The history of the world is none other than the progress of the consciousness of freedom." He declared that the oriental people did not know that man as such was free; to them only despotic ruler was free. But Romans and Greeks went a step further and realised that some men were free. In fact, it was left for German nation to attain to the highest consciousness that man as man is free. The starting point of Hegel's philosophy was the consciousness "that the essence of man is freedom." The truth, Hegel gathered from Rousseau and Kant. The State must be regarded as the ethical whole and the actualization of freedom.

Hegel's conception of freedom was quite different from that of Kant. Hegel held that individual freedom consisted in conformity to laws and customs of society and participation in its moral life. He endeavoured to show that true freedom involved in the outward realisation of what was subjectively demanded by reason. He thought that this could be accomplished only through law, through the rule of morality, and through the system of institution that made for righteousness.

Hegal believed that the development of the 'spirit' meant the development of feedom. He conceived of freedom as the essence of man, and the history of mankind as the history of freedom. To him, the state was the highest expression of the word-spirit and hence, the highest embodiment of freedom. Hegel maintained that there could be no opposion between the interests of the individual and that of the state. The individual realised freedom to the extent to which he identified himself with the spirit as manifested in the state and its institutions. Wayper observes "His (individuals) real will impels him to identify himself with the spirit. The spirit is embodied in the state. Therefore, it is his real will to obey the dictates of the state. Indeed the dictates of the state are his real-will. Thus the command of the state give man his only opportuity to find freedom........But if he obeys because he wishes to, because he has consciously identified himself with the will of the state, because he has convicned himslf that what the state demands he would also desire if he knew all facts, then he is subject only to his own will and he is truly free. The state, says Hegel, is that from of reality in which the individual has and enjoyes his freedom provided he recognises, believes in and wills what is common to the whole"

Hegel defined freedom in the follwing words—"Freedom is the distinctive quality of man. To renounce one's freedom is to renounce one's humanity. Not to be free is, therefore, a renunciation of one's human rights and even of one's duties."

## HEGEL ON INTERNATIONAL RELATIONS

As far as external relations are concerned, Hegel decalred that each state was independent and subject to no law. He said, "A state is not a private person, but in itself a completely independent totality. Hence, the relation of states to one another is not merely that of morality and private right. It often desired that States should be regarded from the standpoint of private right and morality. But the position of private persons is such that they have over them of law court, which realizes what is intrinsically right. A relation between states ought to be intrinsically right, and in the mundane affairs that which is intrinsically right ought to have power. But as against the state there is no power to decide what is intrinsically right and to realise this decision." Hence, we must here remain by absolute command. States in their relations to one another are independent, and look upon the stipulations which they make with one another as provisional." He taught that each state was subject to its own will. He emphasised the complete individuality of each member of the family of nations and asserted that the ordinary rules of morality that obtained among individuals could not be applied in the relations among states. He held that agreements made among states were only provisional. To him the object of treaty was to secure the particular interests of the state, in consequene of changing circumstances, treaties might be ignored.

In fact, war was the curcible out of which a state's 'true personality' developed. Perpetual peace led to internal corruption, successful war prevented internal unrest and strengthened the power of the state. Let us quote his own words:

> War is the state of affairs which deals in earnest with the vanity of temporal goods and concerns—a vanity at other times a common theme of edifying sermonizing. This is what makes it the moment in which the ideality of the particular attains its right and is actualised. War has the highest significance that by its

agency, as I have remarked elsewhere 'the ethical health of peoples is preseved in their indifference to the stabilization of finite institution; just as the blowing of wind preserves the sea from the foulness which would be the result of a prolonged calm, so also corruption in nations would be the product of prolonged let alone, 'perpectual' peace".

Like Fichte, Hegel too, believed that each nation has its unique spirit and culture and makes its peculiar contribution to world civilization. "The progress of history thus portrayed the gradual unfolding of the universal spirit". He said, "Each particular national geneius is to be treated as only one individual in the process of universal history". Hegel Jutifies and glorifies wars while. I.H. Green held that war can never be absolutely justified.

## KARL MARX

Karl Marx, the father of Modern Socialism, was born in Trier (Treves), in the Rhineland province of Prussia (Germany), on May 5, 1818. His father, Herschel Marx, who was a Jew, had embraced Chirstinity in 1824. They embraced Christainity when Karl Marx was only a child, but there seems to be no valid reason to connect this fact with Karl Marx's mature view. When Karl Marx was only 17 years of age, he became a law student at Bonn University in 1835. In 1826, Karl Marx went to the University of Berlin. In 1843, he married Jenny, daughter of Freiherr Ludwig Von Westphalen, with whose family he had long been closely intimate.

In 1841, Karl Marx took his degree of Doctor of Philosophy at the University of Jena on the subject "the Difference Between the Natural Philosophy of Democritus and Epicurus." The radical view of Karl Marx made him a suspect with the authorities and this suspicion prevented his employment as a University teacher. Then Karl Marx entered into field of Joulism. Karl Marx studied Hegel very thoroughly.

In the month of January, 1845, Karl Marx left Paris for Brussels. But before Karl Marx left France an important event had taken place which was to have a lasting effect on Karl Marx's life. Karl Marx had struck up a firm and lasting friendship with Friedrich Engles. Friedrich

Engels was norn in Barman near Dusseldorf, in the Northern Rhineland (Germany) in 1820. Engles was only two years younger than Karl Marx and came from a wealthy family. Engles was the son of famous textile manufacturer of Barmen. As the representative of his father's interests in Manchester, Friedrich Engels became well aware of the social conditions in England. Friedrich Engels gained for himself a great reputation and fame and writing a book, "The Condition of Working Classes in England" published in (1844). Before Engel met Marx, Engels had already accepted the tenets of revolutionary socialism. Engels was a man of quick mind and ready understanding. Friedrich Engels quick mind and ready understanding led Karl Marx to write to him, "you know that I am slow to grasp things and that I will always follow in your footprints." Engels wrote to Karl Marx that he was glad to do what "was meant for, to play second fiddle" to Marx's exceptional genius.

Marx-Engels collaboration is one of literary history's most famous friendship. Friedrich Engels became the friend, disciple and collaborator. In the summer of 1845 Engels accompanied Marx to England. It was Karl Marx's first visit to England. In England Engels introduced Karl Marx to the 'German worker's education Union that had recently been started in London.

"England has often been called the mother of Exiles. But this saying did not come true in the case of Karl Marx. England was never very good to Karl Marx. In England Karl Marx experienced great poverty and distress. Karl Marx had quite a big family. Karl Marx lived with his large family in a two-room flat while he was in England. Karl Marx's wife was often ill and in his later life Karl Marx was himself unwell. Food was quite scarce. Karl Marx was able to continue only because of the generosity of his friend Friedrich Engels." "He lives in one of the worst and cheapest neighbourhood in London. He occupies two room. There is not one clean or decent pieces of furniture in either room, everthing is broken, tattered, and torn with thick dust over everything....Manuscripts, books newspapers lie beside the children's bit and pieces from his wife sewing basket, cups with broken rims, dirty spoons, knives, forks, lamps, an inkpot, tumblers, pipes, tobacco ash—all piled upon the same table, on entering the room smoke and tabacco fumes make your eyes water to such an extent that at first you seem to be grouping about in cavern—until you get used to it....But all there things do not in the last embarrass Marx or his wife. You are received in the most friendly way and are cordially offered pipes."

In 1851, Karl Marx was asked to contribute articles to the New York Tribune. Karl Marx again called on his faithful friend Engels, who wrote articles for him. Afterwards for some time Engels translated Karl Marx articels from the German until Karl Marx could take over the work himself.

**Physical Appearance.** "Marx was of a think-set build and dark complexion and known to him family circle as the 'Moor', A Bohemian Intellectual. He lived in the utmost confusion, over-worked desperately and ruined his health in sedentary labour. He was a deeply cultivated man with an immense admiration for Shakespeare....He was an amiable family man, but quite unpractical in the affairs of life....In spite of the venom and biterness of his public life, he enjoyed simple pleasures....There were picnics to hampstead Health on Sundays when the family was in funds when Frauds Marx would bring a hamper containing a mighty roast of real and the Moor would amuse the children by riding a donkey. Marx suffered from a liver complaint, and his later years were dogged by illhealth, following decades of sedentary study." He was so short sighted that he was always doubtful, when returning home he was standing in front of his own house.

On March 14, 1883, Karl Marx died in London. In a speech over his grave in High Gate cemetery, Frendrich Engles declared that, "his name and works will endure through the ages."

**His Works.** Karl Marx was a gaint writer. In 1847, Karl Marx, with the help and aid of Friedrich Engles, prepared the "Communist Manifesto" (1847). According to Betrand Russell, the "Communist Manifesto," written with the aid of Fredrich Engles, is the best contribution that Karl Marx made to the history of Political Thought. "The Communist Manifesto" contains his clearest and compact statement of conception of the past struggle between economic classes, the modern bourgeoisie proletarian conflict, the inevitable movement of present-day capitalism towards division, destruction and the programme of action, working classes must adopt in order to fit in their efforts with the actual march of events. The "Communists Manisfesto" (in Part IV) concludes with the words, "Communists scorn to hide their views and aims. They openly declare that their purpose can only be achieved by a forcible overthrow of the whole extent of social order. Let the ruling classes tremble at the prospects of a communist revolution. Proletarians have nothing to lose but their chains. They have a world to win. Proletarians of all countries unite!"

The other great contribution of Karl Marx is 'Das Capital' (1867). The 'Das Capital' was planned by Karl Marx as his life's work. the 'Das Capital' consists of three volumes. The first volume was published in (1867). The second and the third volumes of 'Capital' were edited by Karl Marx's close associate and friend Friedrich Engles after Karl Marx's death in (1883). The second and the third volume of the 'Das Capital' appeared in the year 1885 and 1894 respectively. It is said about 'Capital' that, "The appearance of this book was an epoch making event in the history of International Socialism...It was conceived as a comprehensive treatise on the laws of morphology of the economic organisation of modern society-seeking to describe the process of production, exchange and distribution as they actually occur, to explain their present State as a particular stage in the development constituted by the movement of the class struggle.'

The other works include the following:

1. The Poverty of Philosophy, (1847).
2. A Contribution to the Critique of Political Economy, (1859).
3. Eleven Thesis on Feuerbach, (1845).
4. The Eighteenth Brummaire of Louis Banaparte, (1894).
5. Civil War and Class Struggle in France, (1849).
6. The Critique of the Goetha Programme, (1891).
7. Revolution and Counter Revolution.

The Poverty of Philosophy, (1847) was published as an answer to Proudhon's Philosophy of Poverty. Karl Marx was not at all in the favour of views expressed by Proudhon in the 'Philosophy of Poverty". Karl Marx accused Prodhon of thinking like a peasant wihtout any understanding of economics or history. Karl Marx' "Poverty of Philosophy" is a thorough going indictment of Utopian Socialism.

Another important work is, "A Critique of Political Economy", (1859). In this book he had pointed out that the value of a commodity was measured by the amount of labour put in.

## THEORY OF CLASS STRUGGLE

**1. Theory of Class Struggle.** Marx believed that since time immemorial one class has dominated other classes in every society. This tendency gave birth to class war. It was the direct result and outcome of misuse of political power. Since the most powerful classes gained power in every society these were bound to misuse the power as a wheel of oppression against the majority. Sabine has said. "It was characteristic of Marx that he was less interested in perfecting dialectical materialism as a philosophy of history than in applying it to concrete situations, with a purpose of finding a programme of action for consciously revolutionary proletariat."

**2. Materialism.** Karl Marx's theory of class struggle is closely interlinked with his theory of historical and dialectical materialism. Eery society is divided into two classes namely those who exploited and those who were exploited. This class struggle has resulted in all great movements in the universe. It has created social, economic and political changes.

**3. Need of Revolution.** When society fails to keep pace with the economic, social and political changes, revolution is bound to come.

**4. History of Class Struggle.** Marx could not reconcile to the idea that the nations were only fighting units and history was record of these events. He named past history as history of class struggle. Whole history of mankind is available in this strggle. All social movements are class movements. A constant struggle is always going on between economic and political classes for capturing power. To quote Sabine: "The for class had Marx a collective unity as the nation had for Hegel. It acts in history as a unit and it produces its characteristics as a unit, acting under the compulsion of its place in the economic and social system. The individual counts mainly through his membership in the class, because his ideas, his moral convictions, his aesthetic preferences, even the kind of reasoning that seems to him convincing are in the main a reflection of the ideas generated by the class."

**5. Capitalism Encourages Proletariat Organisation.** In the class conflict there was always a tendency on the part of bourgeoisie to expand. Every capitalist will like to go out of home market and expand trade in the foreign countries. The bourgeoisie will also like to create big factories. This tendency of creating big factories results in the concentration of labourers in factory areas. He will also evolve new methods of producton. This large scale employment in centres of production brings closer unity among the workers or the proletariats and enables them to decide their programme of further action.

**6. Weakness of Labourers.** According to Marx classes come into being because of the system of production in which the capitalists employ labourers. The labourers are interested in selling their labour. Unles labour is purchased, the labourer is bound to starve. Since his labour cannot be strored, he wants to sell that at any cost. This weakness of labourer results in exploitation and oppression. This system of production creates two classes-one intrested in capital and the other in labour.

**7. Selfishness of Capitalists.** Class conflicts arise because a modern capitalist produces for promoting his personal interests. He controls legal and political system which makes laws against the interests of the proletariat, *i.e.* working classes. Sabine has said "From this standpoint (of Hegel's philosophy) the history of senseless deeds of violence, all equally condemnable before the judgement sent of the now matured philosophic reason....but as the process of development of humanity itself."

**8. Interdependence of Bourgeois and Proletariat.** In the present system both the bourgeois and the proletariat are interdependent. The capitalist has his capital which is not perishable whereas proletariat have labour which is highly perishable. In the present set-up proletariat are emerging as a new force. A new system can come into power only by a revolutionary struggle. In this revolutionary struggle proletariat have support from all the exploited classes.

**9. Destruction of Capitalism.** Marx believed that the modern system of capitalism has outlived in utility. It has resulteded over-production which requires destruction. This system of over-production and destruction in itself indicated the inner instability of the system of modern capitalism.

Marx logically came to the conclusion that modern system of capitalism sows the seeds of its own destruction. As Coker has said, "The instruments which the owners use to enlarge their profits and rents are the instruments which when perfected, fall inevitably into the hands of the workers, to be used by them to demolish the whole capitalist system."

**10. Cause of Destruction.** This destruction is due to following causes which are creation of capitalists themselves.

*(i)* ***Large-Scale Production and Monopoly.*** A capitlaist tries to monopolise everything. He pushes small capitalists out of market. These small capitalists can not complete with big capitalists. Gradually increasing their number they become proletariat.

*(ii)* ***Wider Markets.*** The capitalist is not satisfied with his home market. He wants to get wider markets. This results in international coperation among the workers.

*(iii)* ***Local Concentration.*** The capitalist employs thousands of workers who come into contact with each other. This contact creates class consciousness and facilitates their mutual co-operation.

*(iv)* ***Creation of Economic Crisis.*** According to Coker "...the capitalist produces recurring economic crises. The labourers who consitute the great body of consumers, are paid enough to purchase only a very limited portion of what they produce; the products accumulate and crisis of entreme

over production takes place. Each crisis is more severe than the other. This recurring crisis results in loss of faith in the capitalist system."

(v) ***Increase in Misery and Ignorance.*** The capitalist tries to keep the workers ignorant and miserable. This results is hostility between the two classes. To quote Coker again; "Thus the capitilist system enlarges the number of workers, brings them together into compact groups, makes them class conscious, supplies them with means of inter-communication and cooperation on a world wide scale, reduces their purchasing power, and by increasingly exploiting them arouses them to organised resistance."

## CRITICISM OF MARXIST THEORY

**1. Unsound Theory.** Marxian theory of class struggle has only propaganda value. Whereas Marx has all along discussed 'Class Struggle' he has nowhere defined the term 'Class'. He has nowhere define the term 'bourgeois' class. Thus this theory is unsound.

**2. Neglect of Social Conditions.** Marx has failed to distinguish between the social and economic classes. He was of the opinion that economics decided the whole social order. A scientific theory must take both social as well as economic factors into consideration and should give them their due place.

**3. Over Simplification.** Marx has over simplified the things. He has taken many things for granted and has failed to foretell the complexities of problem. His whole spposition in this regard does not appear to be very correct. In the words of Popper: "Indeed, the divergence within the ruling and ruled classes go so far that Marx's theory of classes must be considered as a dangerous over-simplification, even if we admit that the issue between the rich and the poor is always of fundamental importance."

**4. Class Struggle not Inevitable.** It has been said that it is not correct to believe that all struggle is always a class struggle. On the other hand, it is mostly a struggle between the classes on the one hand and individuals on the other. The individuals will always fight with society even if there are no classes. According to Carew Hunt,

"For the cause of conflict in life is the inevitable opposition between the claims of the individual and those of society, a conflict which is not reducible to clas struggle and cannot be dialectically resolved because it is a part of the unchanging situation."

**5. Prophesy not True.** Marx's prophesy that capitalism will gradually weaken itself has, miserably proved wrong. On the other hand, capitalism has strengthened itself. It has changed its character with changing times. It has become more enlightened. It is trying to adjust itself to suit the needs of time. It has started extending facılities to the working classes. It has also successfully gaind the co-operation of workers in certain fields. The capitalists have even willingly given worker some share out of their profits in the form of bonus.

## DIALECTICAL METERIALISM

What is Dialectical Materialism ? Dialectical Materialism is not the original idea of Marx. He borrowed this from Hegel. Hegel believed that it was a process under which all ideas in the world developed. He took historical process as something intrinsically comprehensible. He made distinction between the rational and real. Hegel used dialectic as the solution for apparent confusion in the world. Cole said "What was happening in human history was not what seemed to be happening, but gradual and progressive actualisation of the reality immanent in the absolute ideas. Everything was present in potentiality throughout the entire temporal process of development: but potential could concome actual only by means of the long struggle of the idea towards self-realisation through the conflict of imperfect ideas as manifested in history."

## DIALECTIC IN HEGEL

According to Hegel the whole world is moving towards a definite object. Reality could not be achieved in the universe by *prima facia* seeing the things but by contrasting things with each other. Goodness could be realised only when compared with bedness and so on. Hegel presumed the first assertion as thesis and its contradiction as anti-thesis. Thesis and anti-thesis produced a new idea or something new which combined the qualities of both and he called it 'synthesis'.

## MARX'S FORMULATION

Marx was very much influenced by dialectical idea of Hegel. He used it while formulating his theory of social revolution. In the words of Sabine "Marx first formulated the theory of dialectical materialism in a series of works published between 1844-48 in which he both developed his ideas of philosophy and jurisprudence, first formed during his years of study in the universities of Bonn and Berlin, and reformulated by French Socialism in the light of Hegelian principles."

## DIFFERENCE IN HEGEL AND MARX

**1. Conflict of Nations v/s Classes.** Sabine has thus stated the difference between Hegelian and Marxian dialectical materialism: "Whereas Hegel had conceived that European history culminates in the rise of the Germanic nations and had looked forward to the advance of Germany to a position of spiritual leadership in European leadership, marx conceived that history culminates in the rise of the proletariat, as the chief social consequence of a developing capitalism, and loked forward to the advance of that class to a dominant place in the modrern history—for Hegel mechanism of history was warfare between nations: for Marx it was revolutionary struggle between classes."

**2. Application to History.** Marx found dialectical materilism very useful. He applied it to historical and social conditions of his times. He gave the idea of materialistic interpretation of history. It had been said that Marx missnamed it as 'Materialistic: Appropriately he should have named it as 'Realistic' interpretation of history.

**3. Application in Economic Field.** Marx believed that things should not be studied as isolated events but in close relation with each other. On the basis of dialectic he arrived at the conclusion that capitalism was alive only on the labour of labourers and thus could not be the servant of working classes.

**4. Materialism.** Marx believed that 'Reason or Spirit' could not be the moving forces in history. Political and social changes are determined by 'material conditions'. By material conditions he meant the forces of production and distribution of wealth; the former being *(a)* natural resources, *(b)* machinery, *(c)* man and his qualities, and *(d)* time involved in producing goods.

**5. Revolution.** Marx confessed that forces of production were subject to change. In the best set-up force of changing production must come in line with the social institutions. Whenever, social and political institutions fail to adjust themselves with the changing economic system then there is always the possibility of a revolution. The old institutions will never yield to new ones unless force is used. Marx interlinked class struggle with materialistic interpretation of history.

**6. Secularism.** In the words of Sabine, "The dialectic was for Marx a critical method of deflating dogmatically asserted absolutes and a way of enforcing the Hegelican distinction between the real and the apparent. Its materialist interpretation meant first and foremost secularism-a release from the symbolic meaning of religious dogma and ecclesiastical authority, and more generally way of determining religion as one of the great conservative or reactionary forces in society.

**7. Economic Determinism.** Only economic factors changed the history. Cultural life of nation is dependent on its economic life. Even justice, love, charity and humanity were interlinked with the forces of production. Marx said, "it is not the consciousness of men that determines their social existence, but on the contrary, it is their social existence that determines their consciousness". Engles said "In every historical epoch the prevailing mode of economic production and exchange, and the social organisation necessarily following form it, form the basis upon which it is built up, and from which alone can be explained the political and economic life of that epoch".

## CRITICISM OF MARXIST VIEW

**1. Economic Factors are not Alone.** It is true that economics has basic and essential effects on the social and political conditions of society. But at the same time one cannot deny that in the present complex human life economics is not the only factors which contributes to it. Other factors like religion, customs and conventions have their own roles to play.

**2. Economically Powerfull do not Always Rule.** Marx laid stress on the fact that it is always those who are economically powerful that wield political power. To some extent this might be true but it is not always correct. Papacy had no economic power yet they had considerable political influence.

**3. Role of Ideology.** Marxian theorists forget the role of ideologies. If economic factors give birth to ideologies, the ideleogies also give birth to various political and social conditions which change the economic conditions. Russian revolutionary ideology brought about a change in social, economic and political conditions.

**4. Role of Feelings and Sentiments.** While laying strees on economic factors, Marx does not take into consideration feelings and sentiments which are deeply rooted in the minds of mankind and which are more important in some cases than the economic factors. In our present democracies these sentiments and feelings are touched by the clever people for getting votes.

**5. Causes of Change in Production.** Marx has failed to explain the causes which bring about changes in the nature of production. These causes influence social, economic and political set-up.

## MATERIALISTIC CONCEPTION OF HISTORY

According to Engels, "The materialistic conception of history starts from the principle that production, and with production the exchange of in products, is the basis of every social order; that in every society which has appeared in history the distribution of the products, and with it the division of society into classes estates, is determined by what is produced and how it is produced and how the product is exchanged. According to this conception, the ultimate causes of all social changes and political revolutions are to be sought, not in the minds of men in their increasing insight into eternal and truth justice, but in changes in the mode of production and exchange; they are to be sought not in the philosophy but in the economics of the period concerned".

Marx's interest in social sciences and in social philosophy was fundamentally practical. He only wanted to discover the law and method of historical and social change. Karl Marx knew that the discovery of the law and method of historical and social change would make it quite possible and easy for him to formulate the tactics suited to the revolutionary proletarian theory.

Marx has best explained his theory of economic interaction of history in his book Critique of Political Economy (1859) as under:

"In the social production which men carry on they enter into definite relations that are indispensable and independent of their will, these relations of production correspond to a definite stage of development of their material forces of production. The sum total of these relations of producton constitutes the economic structure of society—the real foundation, on which rises a legal and political superstructure and to which correspond definite forms of social consciousness. The mode of production in material life determines the social, political and intellectual life process in general. It is not the consciousness of men that determines that being, but on the contrary, their social being that determines their consciousness. At a certain stage of their development, the material forces of production in society come in conflict with the existing relations of production, or—what is but a legal expression for the something—with the property relations within which they have been at work before. From forms of development of the forces of production these relations turn into their fetters. Then begins an epoch of socail revolution. With the change of the economic foundation the entire immense superstructure is more or less rapidly transformed. In considering such transformations a distinction should always be made between the material transformation of the economic conditions of production, which can be determined with the precision of natural science, and legal, political, religious aesthetic or philosphical—in short, idelogical forms in which men become conscious of this conflict and fight it out. Just as our opinion of an individual is not based on what he thinks of himself, so can we not judge of such a period of transformation by its own consciousness; on the contrary, this consciousness must be explained rather from the contradictions of material life, from the existing conflict between the social forces of production and the relations of production. No social order ever disappears before all the productive forces for which there is room in it have developed: and new higher relations of production never appear before the material conditions of their existence have matured in the womb of the old society itself. Therefore, mankind always sets it say only such tasks as it can solve; since, looking at the matter more closely, we will always find that the task it say arises when the material condition necessary for its solution alone exist or at least in the process of formation."

## KARL MARX'S VIEWS ON CAPITALISM

Karl Marx devoted a great part of his life to the study of capitalism as a social institution.

The characteristic feature of the feudal production was production for local consumption. Profit became the main and the only aim of prodcution in the modern world. In this new system of production, there was a complete change. Now the labourers produced things not for their personal use. On the contrary the production was now meant for the capitalist to sell for money. Now in this new system of production, things were produced not for consumption but for sale in the market. Things produced in this way are called commodities. In the new system of production labourers received their wages from the capitalist employer for his work and the capitalist employer received 'profit'.

Now Karl Marx was faced with a very interesting problem. The problem was—on what does the exchange value of a thing or product depend? Why do the different products have different exchange values? The exchange value of product, according to Karl Marx depends upon the "labour-time" spent in its production. A product has a greater exchange value if more human labour has been put into its production. Karl Marx had anoher question in his mind which is very closely connected to the previous question. The question is—what is the common factor between things produced under capitalism and labour power under capitalism which we know also has an exchange power? What is the basis of determining the wages of the workers? Labour time spent in producing labour power means the time spent in producing the food, shelter, clothes and other such things which are necessary for the labourer to maintain his family's life. In the modern capitalist society, a labourer is able to produce in a day more than is necessary to his survival, but he is paid by his employer a wage commensurate, with a subsistence level of existence. The difference is called surplus value. In the modern capitalistic society this surplus value is appropriated by the capitalist employer.

2. Under capitalism there is periodic economic crisis of under-production and over-production. There is overwhelming production of commodities as well as capital.

3. There is theory of profit working under capitalism, the source of profit being the severe exploitation of the worker.

4. There is great accumulation and concentration of wealth into fewer hands, and thus there is keen competition.

5. There is severe calss struggle, and these crisis are inherent contradiction, in capitalism.

6. The living standard of workers generally falls down, there is unemployment, misery, agony of the toil, slavery, ignorance brutality, and moral degradation.

Marx believed in the invitable destruction of capitalism because it has its own inherent self-contradictions. He conceived of a future socialistic sociey in which each would be paid according to his capacity. State will wither away. "In place of old bourgeoise society with this class and class antagonism we shall have an association says Marx, in which free development of all is the condition for the free development of each." "Marx predicted that the collapse of capitalism would be followed by a socialized or collective economy."

## THE SALIENT FEATURES OF CAPITALISM

(1) In the capitalistic economy production is not meant only for local consumption but for profit. It is the profit motive which is the guiding principle of production in a capitalistic system of economy. The capitalist invests money in any enterprise only because he wants to get more and more profit. Thus lust for profit is an essential features of modern capitalistic economy.

(2) In the modern capitalitistic economy, the labourers produce things not for their own consumption, but for their employers. The employers sell the commodities produced by labourers for making

money and thus they make great profits. In the opinion of Karl Marx the capitalist are in a position to make profits only because of the reason that they appropriate surplus value. There is always a difference between the exchange value of the product, produced by labourer and the value of labour-power. In simple terms, this difference may be called surplus value. Karl Marx was of the view that in each and every industry "the wages paid to the workers are not the equivalent of the full value they produce, but only equal to about half of this value or even less. The rest of the value produced by the worker during his working day is taken outright by his employer".

(3) This exploitation of the labourer by the capitalist results in the inevitable class-struggle.

(4) The economic life of any society is controlled by those persons who own the means of production. Karl Marx was of the opinion that person who own the means of production in any society, control not only the economic life of society, but they also control the political and social institutions of that society. As Prof. Laski says, "They identify social good with their own preservation. Attacks upon them they will punish as sedition. Education, justice, religious teaching are tempered to serve their interest. This is not, it should be insisted, a conscious effort on their part to exclude members of the non-possessing class from a share in social benefit; it is simply the natural reaction to the material environment. But the class excluded from the privileges of possession natrually, also, desires a share in them. Hence, arises in every society a struggle between classes for its control".

## CRITICISM

The Communist Manifesto is described by Laski as "One of the outstanding political documents of all times" Karl Marx's theory of "class struggle has been severely criticized by many thinkers. According to Prof. Lancaster, "As a propaganda this theory is excellent, of no other reason than that it puts the the workers on the side that it informs him is sure to win. As a science, it is conserably less satisfactory, since there are grave difficulties about the term 'class' and therefore about the reality of class struggle. In view of the fundamental improtance of the conception of class it is curious to see how little attention the Marxists give to defining it". Engels defining the term proletariat says, "the proletariat is that class of society whose means of livelihood entirely depends on the sale of its labour and not on the profits derived from capital ; whose weal and woe, whose life and death, whose whole existence depends upon the demand for labour, depends upon the alternations of good times and bad, upon the fluctuations which are the outcome of unbridled competition. The proletariat or class of proletarians is in a word, the working class of the nineteenth century". So far as the 'bourgeoise' class is concerned, there is no definition in the whole of communist literature.

Karl Marx was the first thinker who interpreted the events of history on the basis of class interests. The existence of social classes cannot be denied by any one. Social classes do exist in every society. At the same time no one can deny the existence of struggle between different classes for political power. There has always been a struggle between different classes for the achievement of political power. In explaining the role of social classes in history Karl Marx committed two great mistakes. Firslty, Karl Marx identified social classes with economic classes. For Karl Marx, the struggle between the capitalist employer and exploiter and the exploited labour or wage earner was nothing but class struggle. This is the main reason as to why Karl Marx called the struggle between the capitalist exploiter and the exploited labourer—the "class-struggle." Class-struggle cannot come into existence unless the social classes possess the solidarity and unity of purpose. Popper is apt in his remarks that "Indeed, the divergence of interests within the ruling and the ruled classes goes so far that Marx's theory of class must be considered as a dangerous over simplification, even if we admit that the issue between the rich and the poor is always of fundamental impórtance. One of the great themes of medieval history, the fight between popes and emperors, is an example of dissension within the ruling class. It would be probably false to interpret this quarrel as one between exploiter and exploited."

In the opinion of Prof. Carew Hunt, Karl Marx's theory of class struggle, as an explanation of history is quite untenable expressing his views regarding Karl Marx's theory of 'classtruggle'. Prof. Carew Hunt says, "Finally, Marx's thesis that all conflict among men arises from the class struggle, albeit of undoubted tactical value as calculated to convince the masses that there misfortunes are attributed to the capitalist system and will disappear with the victory of the proletariat, is nonetheless fallacious. For the supreme source of conflict in life is the inevitable opposition between the claims of the individual and those of society, a conflict which is not reducible to class-struggle and cannot be dialectically resolved because it is a part of the unchanging human situation.

## INACCURACIES OF MARXIAN PROPHECY

Now we may turn to an examination of some of the prophecies of Karl Marx, as given in the "Communist Manifesto." Karl Marx was of the opinion that with the increase of wealth of the numerically declining capitalists and with the increase of miseries etc. of the numerically increasing labour class, our modern society would be divided into two classes:

(a) Bourgeoisie; (b) Proletariat.

With the division of society into two clear-cut classes of boureoies and proletariats all the other classes were to disapper in future. But unfortunately this prophecy of Karl Marx has not come out to be true. Karl Marx expected that the class of small trades people, shopkeepers etc. would gradually merge with the proletariat class. But Karl Marx was not correct in making this prophecy. Against Karl Marx's expectations; a new middle class is now emerging. This new middle class is taking the place of old middle class. Thus we may conclude that Karl Marx's prophecy, concerning the clear-cut division of society into two classes—bourgeoisie and proletariat seems to be incorrect. Contrary to Karl Marx's prophecy we find several classes in our own society. the "Communist Manifesto" was written primarily with French conditions in mind. Karl Marx and Friedrich Engels looked upon the contemporary France only. In France, the proletariat consisted largely of urban factory workers and the bourgeoisie of the owners of industrial property. This is the main reason as to why Karl Marx assumed that the proletariat class consisted mainly of urban factory or industry labourers and the bourgeoisie class consisted mainly of the owners of industrial property.

The proletarian revolt which was expected to come quite soon has not yet taken place in the highly industrialized countries. The proletarian revolt was expected to take place in the highly industrialized countries. Though it is true that a revolution has taken place, but it occurred in a place where it was least expected. And at the same time it is also true that the way, in which the revolution took place was quite different from the way, Karl Marx had expected.

Another criticism raised against Marxian theory is that the Marxian's prophecy of the ultimate victory of the proletariat is not at all based upon scientific grounds. Karl Marx was of the opinion that capitalism is doomed to perish and communism triumphant. As Laski says, "the breakdown of capitalism might result not in communism but in anarchy from which there might emerge some dictatorship unrelated in principle to communist ideals." In declaring the ultimate victory of the proletariat Karl Marx has overlooked a few possibilities. At the breakdown of the old order it is quite possible that the working class might be incapable of running the administration. there is another possibility as well. In the words of Carew Hunt, "Negation of capitalism may lead to the emergence of a new class which is strictly speaking neither capitalist nor proletarian.

## THE DICTATORSHIP OF THE PROLETARIAT

In Communist Manifesto, there is the discription as this, "The first step in the working class revolution is the raising of the proletariat to the position of the ruling class." The dictatorship of the proletariat is possible only through a revolution. This revolution is organized against the bourgeoisie class and is called proletarian revolution. The proletarian revolution is directed towards the achievement of two ends. Firstly it has to destroy the capitalistic structure of society: (2) Secondly, the proletarian revolution has to replace all the social, political, legal and other institutions with new ones.

The proletariat will use its political supremacy, to wrest by degrees, all capital from the bourgeoisie, to centralise all insttruments of production in the hands of the state, *i.e.* of the proletariat organised as the ruling class; and to increase the total of productive forces as rapidly as possible.

Of course, in the beginning, this cannot be effected except by means of despotic inroads on the rights of property, and on the conditions of bourgeois production by means of measures therefore, which appear economically insufficient and untenable but which, in the course of the movement, outstrip themselves, necessitate further inroads the old social order, and are unavoidable as a means of entirely revolutionising the mode of production.

These measures will of course be different in different countries. Nevertheless, in the most advanced countries, the following will be pretty generally applicable:

1. Abolition of property in land and application of all rents of land to public purposes.
2. A heavy progressive or graduated Income Tax.
3. Centralisation of the means of commuinication and transport in the hands of the state.
4. Confiscation of the property of all emigrants and rebels.
5. Abolition of all rights of inheritance.
6. Centralisation of credit in the hands of the state, by means of a national bank with state capital and an exclusive monopoly.
7. Extension of factories and instruments of production owned by the state; the bringing into cultivation of waste lands and the improvement of the sort generally in accordance with a common plan.
8. Equal obligation of all to work. Establishment of industrial armies, especially for agriculture.
9. Combination of agriculture with manufacturing industries; gradual abolition of the distinction between town and country, by a more equitable distribution of the population over the country.

10. Free education for all the childern in public schools. Abolition of children's factory labour in its present form combination of education with industrial production, etc.

**MARX'S THEORY OF STATE**

The views of Marx on state can be summarised as under:

**1. Criticism of Capitalism.** Karl Marx criticised capital. He regarded it as theft because Capitalim was based on injustice and exploitation of the poor by the rich. It created calss barriers and divided society into mainly two hostile groups. It divided the loyalties of state.

**2. Real Democracy.** He opined that Capitalism is its own enemy. Because modern captialist system is sowing the seeds of its own degeneration. Its in place a new state will emerge. It will have majority of proletariats or the working classes. The democrary of the capitalist order is not natural or real one but an artificial arrangement. In this system the capitalists being in minority mould democracy to suit their convienence. In this way the Capitalists defeat democracy in the real sense of the term. But in the new society there will be real democracy. The reason is that instead of Capitalists class which is in minority the majority consisting of working classes shall rule the society. It shall be true and real democracy and shall be used for collective interests. To quote Communist Maniesto "In place of old bourgeois society with its classes and class antagonism, we shall have an association in which free development of each is the condition or the free development of all." It further says, "The proletarian movement is the conscious movement of immense majority in the interests of the immense majority."

**3. State Full of Coercion.** According to Marx, the chief attribute of the modern state is not its promotion of the welfare of its people not its right to political obligation and obedience but its coercion and that a class—coercion. The state is an agency of class-coercion in the hands of the dominant economic class rather than an association of citizens in pursuit of a common purpose.

**4. The State not Natural and Universal.** The state has not always been there. It arose out of the necessity of holding class antagonisms in check but it became an instrument in the hands of the economically dominant class to establish its rule.

**5. State Always Favours Capitalists.** Marx did not accept the conventional idea that state existed for the sake of good life or that it was a natural organisation. The state is an agency for exploiting the poor. History tells us that the state always stood by the side of rich or capitalists. Those who are economically strong control the society as well as legal, social and political institutions. Though the state poses to be impartial and above all class conflicts and claims to be natural yet in actual practice it has never played such a role is class organisation which reflects ideas of dominant class in society.It is only semblance. The state is class organisation which reflects ideas of dominant class is society. It is the constant endeavour of the state to see that the proletariats do not rebel against the bourgeoisie. The agencies like schools, colleges and the church are used by the state for exploiting the workers. In these agencies workers are trained for subordination and submission. They are given such an education as renders them speechless.

**6. Proletarian Revolution.** The differences existing among the classes may be reconciled only by revolutionary means and method. This proletarian revolution aims at destroying capitalist order and changing old institutions into new ones. Marx, says that "Between Capitlaism and Communism lies the period of the revolutionary transformation of the one into the other. There corresponds to this also a political transition period of the proletariats." In the present system majority is exploited by the minority i.e., the capitalists class but in the changed set-up majority will expropriate the minority or the bourgeoisie.

**7. Democracy.** The modern capitalists are always at their safeguard against losing the power. They have devised such means and methods that power does not easily shoft from their hands. Democracy also may be called such a device. It helps the capitalist in retaining its power and authority. The working classes, therefore, should win the battle of democracy.

**8. Nature of State.** In the opinion of Karl Marx the state is an agency for expressing the will of the ruling classes. He gives arguments in support of his views. The state maintains armies, prisons and similar other institutions to protect and safeguard the rights, interests and privileges of ruling classes hence it is essential it bring a change in the pressened society and state. However, the state and society could be changed and dislodged only with the use of force and not by peaceful means.

**9. Classless Society.** When the proletariats capture power from the capitalists and the means of production come under their control, a new system of production will emerge. This system will hand over means of production to the community as a whole. The proletariats shall capture authority. A classless society will emerge and the present class distinction will disappear. At present, the main reason responsible for class distinctions is the concentration of the production. This dominant class exploits other classes. When the proletariats capture power, present the means of production and there shall be none to be exploited. No able-bodied person will be allowed to be a parasite. All shall work for the common welfare or in the interest of the community at large. After the emergence of classless society the need for the state will disappear and the state will 'wither away'. Marx is not clear about the withering away of the state. According to Engels, the state would wither away because public functions would be changed from political into administrative functions.

**Criticisms.** Karl Marx's theory of state has been criticised as under:

**1. Basically Wrong.** Marxian theory of state is against the established classical theory of state. It cannot be accepted that the state is a wheel of oppression and is authority is used against the weak classes. It is also wrong to say that the state represented the will of the economically strong classes. It is a baseless allegation that the state has always represented economically better classes. History tells us that the rulers in the past were never economically the most 'powerful' nor did they always represent the economically powerful classes. Instead of it, they represented all the clases. In modern times also, the state is a welfare state and is meant for the welfare of all irrespective of any class distinction. Modern Parliaments have representatives from all classes of society. They look after the welfare of all rather than the welfare of a few.

**2. Peaceful Settlement of Disputes.** Marx holds that it is impossible to reconcile differences between the working classes and capitalists. But the developments of the present times have disproved his views. There are peaceful methods of reconciling the disputes more paticularly industrial disputes. Labour Tribunals, Trade Unions etc. now represent the labourers and on their behalf settle disputes.

**3. Continuance of Exploitation.** Marx accuses the capitalists, who are now in power of exploiting the working classes. But Marx has failed to give a logical system to ensure that when proletariats comes to power they will not exploit the capitalists. It cannot be admitted that in case power comes in the hands of the working classes that will not be misused. They will use it in the spirit of revenge. Marx has no methods to check this exploitation by the ruling class.

**4. Under-Estimate of Peaceful Methods.** In the views of Marx the only way to bring about a change was through revolution. But he failed to think of the peaceful methods for bringing about changes. Ebenstein writes, "If Marx had accorded the political factor its due weight, if he had fully grasped the importance of the Reform Act in England and of the Jacksonian revolution in the United State, he might have realised that socialism too, might be accomplished without violence in countries that possessed democratic traditions strong enough to absorb far reaching social and economic changes without resorting to civil war. A recognition of the cultural and political factors in the equation of scoial change would have amounted, however, to a virtual abandonment of the central position of marx; that history is the history of class wars and that ruling classes defend their position to the bitter end."

Thus it can be concluded that Marxian theory of state is not so sound as it might appear *prima facie*. His suggestion for armed revolution is rather too much. His revolutionary ideas and resort to violence cannot be justified especially today when nations are thinking more in terms of peaceful cooperation rather than war. Force brings with it hatred and counter revolutionary forces which bring instability in the society. Settlement of disputes by force will certainly result in hampering political and social progress. An armed and violent revolution is less durable than the changes brought about by peaceful means and methods. Power acquired at the edge of sword is lost also in the same way.

## MARXIST THEORY OF SOCIALISM

Marx believes in the inevitablity of destruction of capitalism. In communist manifesto Marx states "the history of all hitherto existing society is the history of calss struggles" from the fight of slave and slave owner feudalism came into existance. And due to antagonism of agricultural class and feudal class and on account of change in means of production, capitalist class emerged. But Marx states no society is stable and professes that a similar change is taking place in bourgeoise society. He adds "the weapons with which the bourgeoies fell feudalism, to the ground are now turned against the bourgeoise itself. But not only has bourgeoise forged the weapons that bring death to itself, it has also called into existence the men who are to wield these weapons—the modern working class—the proletariat" Thus Marx believes that with the emergence of proletariat, downfall of capitalism is inevitable. It had in itself seeds of self destruction as given below:

1. In capitalism production is motivated by profit therefore it results either in overproduction or in underproduction but did not occur according to the needs of society. This flaw gives rise to dissatisfaction and discontentment. Perhaps Marx did not realize that supply and demand influences the production.
2. In capitalism surplus value goes to the capitalist and on account of this exploitation, labour class's interests clash with the capitalists, interests this results in class war.
3. Expansion of capitalism follows increase in number of workers. Marx is of opinion that petty manufacturers or cottage industries or petty shopkeepers unable to compete with large scale production have to enter as wage workers to earn their livelihood. On the other hands number of

capitalist decreases as the concentration of industry takes place, only a few capitaists dominate the bourgeoise society due to this procedure.

4. In capitalism individuality is lost as everything is mechanised, therefore individual self satisfaction of a worker is lost.
5. In Capitalist system workers become poorer and poorer because capitalist employs a labourer on a low wage as he can earn living by paying low salary. In competiton capitalist can wait but labourer cannot wait, because labour is a perishable commodity and so a worker had to accept low wages and becomes poor.
6. Capitalism creates crisis due to overproduction, due to competition and conflict takes place between captalists themselves.
7. Tendency of capitalism is local concentration. Thousands of workers are centered at the great industrial centres. It becomes for them very easy to organise. It creates class consciousness and organisation through which they can compete with the capitalists.
8. Lastly capitalism addds to the misery and dependency of the workers. Probably it is not true as workers in mills and in cities are better than farmers and self employed people.

In short capitalist system enlarges the number of workers, brings them together in compact groups, makes them class conscious, supplies them with means of inter communication and cooperation on world wide scale, reduces their purchasing power and by increasingly exploiting them arouses them to organized resistance.

After the struggle between the proletariat and the burgeoise a quasi state or dictatorship of proletariat will be established. The ultimate aim is stateless and classless communist society. In such a society every person would contribute voluntarily according to his ability and would receive according to his needs. The state withers away as it is essentially a repressive organ of a society based upon exploitation and would have no purpose in a classless society. In it also management and administration in industry will vanish. The government of person is replaced by the administration of things and the direction of process of production is of more importance in a classless society (Engles). The dictatorship of Proletariat as envisaged by Marx, is the immediate consequence of proletarian revolution. In this stage by a violent overthrow the proletariat is supposed to have seized to power, and thus to have created a state which uses coercion in its own behalf. The dictatorship of the proletariat, therefore is like the bourgeoise state which it supplants, is an instrument of class domination. Its function is "the necessary suppression of the minority...the exploiters (Lenin) to destroy the brueaucracy of the displaced capitalist state, to convert the means of production into public property. Only when, these purposes have been accomplished "whitering away" begins and the probable duration of the dictatorship is left entirely to conjecture. Neither Marx nor Engles developed the dictatorship philosophy. It was obvious that the classless society if it were to become reality, would not spring over night into existence. Some transitional stage must be supposed. Thus it is yet to be seen whether the withering away of the state capitalism is working in U.S.S.R. from 1917 or in China etc. since 1949. But there are nowhere signs of lossening of government control.

Moreover it was wrong conception of Marx that classes are a compact unit and society is always divided only in the two groups but generally it was divided in more than two groups and generally conflict takes place within the group Conception of Marx that workers will become poorer has not proved true on the other hand their condition has improved. Fourthly, a middle class of lawyers, doctors, professors and of clerks has emerged which sympathises more to capitalist class than with the labour class. Class feeling prove do not strong in workers sometimes they fight internally. Capitalism has also changed itself according to circumstances and due to concept of welfare state, they have survived and may survive. In the strong hold of capitalism U.K., U.S.A. France, Japan and W. Germany the most industrialised countries revolution has not occured. The victory of proletariat is not the proof of the establishment of a classless society. It is possible that any other system may emerge or conflict may take place between the Russia and China. However at present emergence of a classless society is an utopian dream and it has got set back with its failure in U.S.S.R. and in Europe.

## REVOLUTION AND EVOLUTION

**1. Rise of Capitalism.** Karl Marx based his political philosophy on economic struggle which was going on between the rich and the poor. It was a struggle in which the rich were exploiting the poor and getting richer because of the labour of the millions of workers. The rich had wealth by which they controlled the means of production. The poor had labour which was a perishable commodity and could be preserved. The labourer is always in urgent need of selling his labour whereas the capitalist wishes to utilise it for his own selfish ends. The capitalist pays far less to the labourer than what is due to him and terms this surplus value as his profit. He goes on accumulating his profits and becomes and monopolist.

**2. Communism will Gradually Destroy Itself.** Karl Marx also believed that communism was sowing the seeds of its own destruction and that it will die its own death. In the words of Coker: "Although capitalism proceeds natrually to its own destruction, it does not create socialism. In other capitalism words, inevitable prepares the way for, but does not inevitably lead into socialism.

**3. Socialist Programme.** Under the existing system the capitalists were controlling private rents, interests and profis and decided about the line of action. These should be used in such a fashion that means of exploitation did not go in the hands of any particular class. Coker has said "The function of a socialist programme, Marx held, is to show wage workers how to convert their potential into an actual superiority or how to prepare themselves for transforming an automatic struggle into a consciously designed politcial struggle."

**4. Communist Revolution:**

*(i)* ***Peaceful Means.*** Marx opines that in order to control the means of production it was essential that the working classes should first of all try to win the existing battle of democracy. He suggested that working classes in all countries should form a group and try to come to power.

Once they have come to power by peaceful means they should then try to settle themselves permanently and should make themselves secure in their seats.

*(ii)* ***Socializing Capital.*** Once the working classes have found themselves secure then they should embark upon the task of socializing capital. The process should be gradul but the working classes will have to face initial difficulties and in certain cases will have to use force also. It requires use of both intellect and force to use capitalistic owned means of production for the whole community. To quote Coker again, "The particular steps cannot be the same in all states. For the most advanced countries the immediate measures, according to the programme of communist manifesto, are the following: abolition of private ownership of land, centralisation of means of the state; establishment of state monopoly of credit and banking; abrogation of right of inheritance, heavily progressive income taxation; prohibition of child labour in factories; enforcement of an equal liability of all to work.

*(iii)* ***Violent Revolution.*** Marx believed that the capitalists will not be willing to hand over the power easily. They will try to stick to it firmly and strongly. They will put serious obstacles in the way of working classes. In such circumstances the working classes shall have but to use force for the overthrow of the capitalism. In his Communist Manifesto Marx has said "Communists openly declare that their ends can be attained only by the forcible overthrow of all existing conditions. Let the ruling classes tremble at the communist revolution."

*(iv)* ***No Definite Programme.*** Marx, subsequenlty believed that it was not essential to altogether over-throw the laws passed by the capitalists. He belived that all these laws which made workers politically and economically strong should be retained. He, however, strongly believed that no definite programme could be given because programme hampered action.

*(v)* ***Organisation of Workers.*** Marx was of the considered opinion that whether the methods adopted by the working classes were evolutionary or revolutionary, these should be used in an organised fashion. The working classes shold combine together en-bloc. They should make out their programme as and when circumstances permitted. It is entirely left to the working classes to decide about the methods suited to the time and ought to be adopted.

*(vi)* ***Use of Force.*** Force is a necessary instrument for bringing about a revolution. Coker has said, "He generally recognised that means of securing political power might differ at different times and in different countries the method might be direct economic action at one time and place, and a revolution and slow achievement of political predominance at another. His attitude was generally pragmatic...The method of forcible rebellion is permissble where the circumstances are such as to make that method necessary and probably successful."

**5. Both Evolution and Revolution.** Thus, Marx's method of overthrow of capitalist classes by working classes was both evolutionary as well as revolutionary. He was not concerned with the methods but with the ends of the struggle. For a lasting peace and permanent achievements, however, it is not the end that matters but what matters is the method by which these ends are actually achieved.

## THOMAS HILL GREEN

Green was born in Yorkshire in a clergy-man's family on April 17, 1836, and died of septicaemia in 1882, at the young age of forty-six. He received his education, first at his home-town where he remained till the age of fourteen, next at Rugby where he stayed for five years, and finally at the Balliol College, Oxford, where he spent his entire active life. It was at Oxford that he came under the influence of the great Benjamin Jowett. He became a Fellow of Balliol in 1860, and a Tutor in 1866, and was finally chosen as the Whyte Professor of Philosophy in 1878. Besides lecturing on Philosophy at Oxford, Green took an active interest in the civic affairs of the city.

He was elected to the Oxford Town Council from a constituency in the city, and did much useful work in that capacity for several years. He was also an active member of the Oxford School Board, and was the chief agent in founding the City of Oxford School for Boys. He participated in the political life of the country as a campaign speaker for the Liberal party, but never sought election to Parliament. He was also an enthusiastic worker in the cause of temperance. In 1875, he opened a coffee tavern in the city as a counter-attraction to the numerous public-houses then existing there, and became the President of the Oxford Band of Hope Temperance Union. In 1864-65, he undertook inspection work of schools in Birmingham. These many-sided activities exercised a great influence on his thought. He realised, as few thinkers could, that it requires a good deal of disinterested devotion to civic duty on the part of ordinary men and women, if a modern democracy is to work successfully.

His most important works are the Prolegomena to Ethics and the Lectures on the Principles of Political Obligation, both of which were published after his death, The Lectures were delivered in the winter of 1879-80, His thought forms a systematic whole and falls into three parts : metaphysics, ethics and political philosophy. Of the three the ethical part is the central one, His primary aim is the discovery of the true vocation of man and the best way of fulfilling it. But before we can know in what true human well-being consists, we must first discover the real nature of the individual, the real nature of the universe and man's place in it. Ethics thus, must be preceded by metaphysics. After having discovered the true goal of human life, Green proceeds to determine the conditions of social and political life in which it can be best realised. His moral philosophy thus, issues into political philosophy or a doctrine of the state. The purpose of his lectures on the principles of political obligation was 'to consider the moral function or object served by law, or by the system of rights and obligations which the state enforces, and in so doing to discover the true ground of justification for obedience to law', In what follows we shall be mainly concerned with Green's theory of the state and shall refer to his metaphysical and ethical views only to the extent necessary for understanding the former.

**The Sources of Green's Thought.** In its completed form the philosophy of Green seems to have been derived from three or four different sources. Professor Barker assigns the first place among the sources of his philosophy to the study of the Greek Classics. The Republic of Plato and the Ethics and Politics of Aristotle formed part of the curriculum of studies in Philosophy in the Oxford University where generations of students learnt the great truths emphasised by these great thinkers; namely, that man is by his nature a political animal, that the State is a partnership in virtue, that law is the expression of pure and passionless reason, and that righteousness consists in the performance by each man of his appointed function in the life and action of the community. The ultimate basis of the political idealism of Green may thus, be found in the writings of Plato and Aristotle,

The second and no less important source was German Idealism as represented in its three great representatives, Kant Fichte and Hegel. The main idea in Green's philosophy, namely, that the universe is a single eternal activity may be said to have been derived from Hegel. Green holds that the vital truth which Hegel taught is, 'that there is one spiritual self-conscious being, of which all that is real is the activity or expression; that we are related to this being not merely as parts of the world which is its expression, but as partakers in some inchoate measure of the self-consciousness through which it at once constitutes and distinguishes itself from the world; and that this participation is the source of morality and religion.'

But it is in the purely metaphysical field that Green adopted Hegelianism; and even in this sphere he discarded the Hegelian dialectic as the account of the process by which the ultimate self-conscious being unfolds or develops itself. In the ethical and political field Green chose to follow Kant rather than Hegel. His thinking starts from the Kantian point of view and bases itself on the Kantian doctrine of the free moral will in virtue of which man always wills himself as an end. For Green, as for Kant, the one thing of value is the good will. In this theory of the functions of state as the hindrance of hindrances to good life Green appears to by primarily Kantian. This, however, should not be taken to mean that he is not influenced by Hegel. Hegel was one of the determining factors of Green's thought.

In the third place, Green was greatly influenced by the view of Rousseau that the State or sovereign represents the general will, and as such is entitled to the obedience of the citizens. He was also attracted by the idea that every act of the general will must be characterised by disinterestedness. Green agreed that what makes orderly and human government possible is the public spirited care for 'common objects' on the part of each individual.

The fourth source from which Green drew his inspiration was the non-conformists' attitude towards the various problems of life. If Hegel provided him with the basis for his philosophical idealism and Kant for his ethical thought, the non-conformists exercised a profound influence on his political thinking. From them he may be said to have derived his love for the two words, 'freedom' and 'morality'. The non-conformists called their churches 'free churches' and laid great stress upon morality; they demanded that government should place a ban on liquor-drinking, horse-racing and gambling; they were fiercely opposed to private ownership of land but were not so averse to private capital. Green, as we shall see, defended the principle of private property so far as capital was concerned but was opposed to landed property. It is thus, evident that in his views on temperance, property, morality, etc. It may also be noted that in England itself there was a reaction against Benthamism. Burke deprecated the role assigned by Bentham to reason in politics and propounded the theory of 'expediency'. Coleridge opposed the view that the individual was the only reality and society a fiction, and held that society is an organic whole, a moral unit. Green must have been influenced by the theories of Burke and Coleridge, which were echoed by men like Carlyle and Ruskin.

## GREEN'S POLITICAL PHILOSOPHY

Social Institutions are indispensable for enabling us to freely realise our capacities of will and reason; this constitutes their moral justification. The State and its laws have a similar justification; but as they are distinguished from other institutions of social life, like the family, the school and the church in so far as they imply force; and as the relation of force to moral life is a peculiar one, Green thinks that they need a special justification. His main purpose in his Lectures on the Principles of Political Obligation is 'to consider 'the moral function or object served by law or by the system of rights and obligations which the state enforces, and in so doing to discover the true ground or justification for obedience to law.' In his effort to define the true function of law and determine the ground of our moral duty to obey the law he examines the various theories of political obligation and the chief rights and obligations enforced in civilised states. We shall begin our survey of his political philosophy with an examination of the meaning he assigns to rights and their recognition by society.

**Rights.** We may begin our study of Green's conception or Rights with a definition of the term. From Green's thesis that liberty involves rights it follows that a right is a certain liberty claimed by an individual as necessary for pursuing ideal objects and developing his capacities of reason and will. This brings into clear relief the personal aspect of rights. Rights inhere in individuals; they signify the material or external conditions of life necessary for the realisation of the moral ideal by individuals. But a claim for liberty of action becomes a right only when it is recognised as such by society; in the absence of such recognition it remains an empty claim. A man is entitled only to that degree of freedom which is socially approved as desirable. Similarly, each individual can legitimately claim elementary education as necessary for the growth of his personality; it becomes a right only when society recognises it as necessary for social good and enforces it. This may be described as the social aspect of rights. Though they inhere in individuals, rights involve a clear reference to a society in which the common good is recognised by its members as their own ideal good. The reason why society recognises certain liberties of action as necessary for its members is that it is through their exercise only that they can attain the ideal of moral development and contribute to the common good. Without the conception of the common good society would not exist at all. Since an individual can claim and enjoy rights only as a member of a social whole, rights are essentially a social product; they can never be conceived to exist as the possession of isolated individuals. From this it follows that the theory of Natural Rights as postulated by the advocates of the Social Contract Theory like Locke, namely, that men possessed certain rights in the pre-political state of nature, must be rejected as untenable. Green rejects the Social Contract Theory as well as fundamental tenet that rights existed independently of society in the state of nature. He would have wholeheartedly endorsed the dictum of Bentham that the doctrine of natural rights as maintained by seventeenth century thinkers was non-sense. He denies that there can be any such thing as rights existing independently of and prior to society. As against the contractualists Green believes with Plato and Aristotle that man is essentially a social or political being, and that rights accrue to him only in virtue of being a member of society.

Though Green rejects the seventeenth century doctrine of Natural Rights, he does not discard the concept altogether, He retains the phrase and re-interprets it. He describes those rights as natural which should be possessed by every man because they are necessary for the fulfilment of his vocation as a rational and moral being. Such rights may appropriately be designated as natural because they are the necessary and indispensable means to an end which is natural to man.

'Natural rights are rights which should be enjoyed by a normally rational and moral man living in a rationally constituted society They belong only to men capable of being influenced by the idea of a common good and are effective only in a society whose members recognize a common good as contributing to their own ideal good. They are the conditions under which the realization of the moral capacity of a man is made possible'.

This passage makes it clear that, according to Green, rights are given to individuals so that they may contribute to social good. In the last analysis what determines rights is the well-being of the community and not the humanity of the individual.

Rights are natural in the same sense in which Aristotle regarded the State as natural. They are natural in the sense that they 'arise' out of, and are necessary for the fulfilment of, a moral capacity without which a man would not be a man'. We may better call them ideal rights; they are the rights which a society properly organised on the basis of good will should and would grant to its members. Since such an ideal society did not exist in the past, and we can look forward to it only in the future, natural rights are rights that lie ahead of us; they are not the rights which we are supposed to have enjoyed in the past before entering upon politically organised life; they are rather the rights to which we look forward as we grow from a less perfect to a more perfect state.

The natural or ideal rights are both broader and deeper than the actual rights granted by any given society to its members at a given time. They are broader, because they go beyond the actual rights; in the words of Barker, 'the actual rights embodied in the actual law of a community never quite square with an ideal system. Just as the circles which we describe on paper or make in pieces of wood can never attain to the ideality of the perfect circle as conceived by Euclid, so actual societies always fall short of the ideal organisation demanded by good will; though some of them approximate more closely to the scheme of natural rights than others. They can be said to be deeper than the rights actually granted by a given society at a given time in so far as they provide the standard or norm by which we may judge the latter; they remain in ideal to which actual rights ought to conform. Natural rights thus, differ from legal rights in their extent and depth.

Natural rights differ from legal rights in yet another respect; they stand in close relation to morality. When Green talks of recognition of rights by society, he means recognition by the moral consciousness of society and not by law. He does not accept the theory of Bentham that 'rights properly so-called are the creatures of law properly so-called'. Some natural rights may not be legally recognised; few states at the present day recognise the natural right of the citizen to work; some do not recognise even the right of the citizen to elementary education. Sometimes rights actually recognised may be opposed to natural rights, e.g., in ancient and medieval times slavery was a legally recognised institution, and even men like Aristotle and St. Thomas Aquinas defended it. In our own country unteachability was admitted by the moral consciousness of the Hindus until it was attacked by men like Ram Mohan Roy, Swami Dayanand and Mahatma Gandhi. Legal abolition of untouchability followed the recognition of its immoral character by the moral consciousness of the Hindus. Secondly, natural rights are relative to morality than to law, because they have value and significance in relation to the moral ideal which we pursue; because they constitute the conditions necessary for the attainment of the moral end of human life.

It must not, however, be assumed that they have no relation to law. They have got to be embodied in law, if they are to be enforced by the community. It should always be the ambition of a community to bring its actual laws as near to the system of natural rights as possible. The progress of a society can best be judged by the extent to which its laws breathe the spirit of natural rights and the degree to which they are incorporated in its legal system.

Thus, interpreted the theory of Natural Rights becomes intelligible and can be retained. It cannot be dismissed as non-sense as Bentham dismissed the older seventeenth century version of it. But even when thus, interpreted, it is not wholly free from difficulties. We need not attach much importance to the objection that no agreed list of such natural rights has been drawn up. No final list can be drawn up; because the conception of what rights should be granted to the citizens is liable to change and grow deeper with the growth or civilization. The ideal is not an immutable ideal, the same for all times and places. It is dependent on the moral conditions of society at any given time. The right to work and the right to education were not included in the list of natural rights until some time ago; the former is not so widely recognised at the present time as the latter. As our conception of welfare state expands, fresh natural rights are likely to be discovered. The main difficulty of the theory springs from the fact that though natural rights are admitted to be necessary for the full moral development of the individual, he is allowed little say in determining them; the main responsibility for determining them is that of the community. What society may think to be necessary for the moral development of its members may not coincide with what the latter may think about it, or with what may be really necessary. Green does not give any clear and definite answer to the question: 'Who is to be the judge of what natural or ideal rights are really necessary at a given time in a given society'? The white population of South Africa still thinks that the coloured people should not be allowed to mix freely with them; similarly, the European majority of the population of some of the southern states of the U.S.A. are not yet convinced of the justice of the removal of the colour bar. There is another difficulty of an academic or theoretical nature of which mention may be made. Green says that rights are made by recognition, but his position in regard to natural rights amounts to the admission that rights can exist in the absence of recognition. What else can be the implication of the assertion that natural rights are those rights which should be recognised as necessary for the fulfilment of the moral vocation of man? We can use this type of language only if some rights are not recognised. If a right is recognised there is no meaning in saying that it should be recognised. The question of 'should be recognised' can arise only in regard to what is not actually recognised. Hence, the implication of Green's stand is that natural rights lack recognition, that they are rights in advance of recognition. Not much stress need, however, be laid on this confusion in the thought of Green; it does not blur the great contribution made by him towards a modification of the political philosophy of Hegel in the direction of Liberalism. The kernel of his doctrine of Natural Rights lies in the assertion that in the final analysis 'there exists within the community an ethical system which is independent of the state and which gives the individual a standard whereby to criticise the state itself.

**Views on Freedom.** Like Rousseau and Kant before him, Green also puts the problem of Freedom in the forefront of his political thinking. He regards freedom as the greatest of all blessings, and its attainment the true end of all our efforts as citizens. This is because human consciousness postulates freedom as a necessary condition of its growth and development. It demands freedom because the eternal consciousness in which human consciousness participates in itself characterised by freedom. The content of human freedom consists of the various rights which demand the State for their enjoyment. The vital position occupied by freedom in the thinking of Green is beautifully summed-up by Barker in the following words : 'Human consciousness postulates liberty; liberty involves rights; rights demand the State.'

But though all would probably agree that freedom is the greatest of all blessings, all are not in equal agreement in regard to its meaning. Some mean by it the absence of all restraints. This is the central point in the theory of Laissez Faire. Though Green does not equate freedom with absence. of restraints, he does believe that an individual cannot be called free if he is not allowed to make his own choice. There are others who identify freedom with obedience to the State. Green is in sympathy with this view in so far as he maintains that freedom can be enjoyed by an individual only in and through membership of a state. But he is not prepared to go the whole length with Hegel and regard the State as the realisation of freedom.

Green solves the dilemma by developing the concept of positive freedom which he defines as 'the capacity of doing or enjoying something worth doing or enjoying in common with others'. A society can be said to grow in freedom when its members are in a position to develop their powers of contributing to the social good, when they are able, in a body, 'to make the most and best of themselves'. Green does not regard that society as growing in freedom 'in which the apparent elevation of the few is founded on the degradation of the many.' Let us see, how he develops his idea of freedom.

In his discussion of the problem or freedom Green 'begins from, always clings to, and finally ends in the Kantian doctrine of the free moral will in virtue or which man always wills himself as an end.' For Green, as for Kant, the one thing in the world which has absolute value is the good will. We have already seen that, according to Green, the goal of human life is moral activity and not the pursuit of external ends like pleasure or happiness or power. The State must not do anything which many interfere with the individual's freedom to cultivate an ideal of character; all it can do and should do is to remove all, those obstacles which stand in the way of the individual developing his personality. The State should not interfere with this self-determination on the part of the individual by repressive interference or excess of paternal government. This is why Green describes the role of state-activity in a negative formula, as consisting in hindering hindrances to good life; in other words, in removing the obstructions that lie in the way of our doing things worth doing. But though Green is powerfully influenced by the Kantian conception of free moral will, his view of freedom bears close resemblance to that of Hegel who maintained that it is positive in nature and can be realised only in and through participation in the life of the State.

Green begins by saying that the ordinary and commonsense definition of freedom as consisting in the power to do what one wants is not adequate, because it does not take into account the nature of the object in which the will finds satisfaction. In what sense can we regard a man as free who drinks himself to death or who ruins himself and his family through gambling ? Freedom depends more upon the nature of the object which the individual makes his own than upon his ability to identify himself with it.

In the former case an individual is free in the ordinary sense of the term, he does what he wants to do. But in so far as his self-satisfaction is not adjusted to the law which determines where true self-satisfaction should be found, he is not really free. The drunkard and the gambler are not free because they seek self-satisfaction in objects in which it should not be sought; it can be urged that they are no better than the 'bondsman who is carrying out the will of another and not his own'. In the second case in which the individual seeks satisfaction in objects in which it should be sought, he is really free. Here the satisfaction which is sought is not the gratification of this particular desire or that; it is rather the satisfaction which 'ensues when the whole self has found its object'. Green calls this self-satisfaction peace or blessedness. It presupposes the distinction between the self as a whole and the particular impulses which sway men in different directions from time to time. An individual is free when he sets his whole self against those impulses which do not tend to his true good, and masters them. He becomes a slave when, for any reason, these particular impulses master him and determine conduct by their. isolated strength. For Green, as for Kant, man ceases to be autonomous and becomes heteronomous if his will submits to the impulse of pleasure-seeking. But whereas Kant holds that man is free or autonomous only when his will is determined by the categorical imperative of duty or the law of Reason. Green urges that he is free only when his will is determined by an object appropriate to it. The difference between the two thinkers can be stated in the following way. Whereas Kant makes the realisation of freedom by the individual almost independent of his social and political realisationships, Green holds that it is made possible by the State. It is the social and political institutions maintained by the state which help the individual to fine objects adequate to his moral will. While freedom as understood by Kant is limited and subjective, it becomes objective and positive in the hands of Green. This shows the influence of Hegel. Green would endorse the saying of Hegel that Reason, 'the self-determining principle operating in man as his will' has found a perfect expression for itself in the State. Green would also admit that the Divine Spirit finds its highest embodiment in the State. We may, therefore, conclude that for Green, as for Hegel, freedom consists in identifying oneself with Divine Spirit as manifested in the State. It is a necessary consequence of Green's theory that as a member of the State an individual enters into social relations with others and, therefore, his good must also be social good. The true good in willing which the individual finds the fulfilment of his nature must be social good because, as we shall show later on, such is the nature of man that whatever an individual deems worth doing and enjoying is always something which he can do and enjoy in common with others. All this leads us to the conclusion that according to Green freedom signifies the liberation of the powers of man for promoting the social good.

But though Green approximates to the Hegelian conception of freedom and maintains that an individual can realise true freedom only as a member of the State, he criticises the German philosopher on the ground that he ignores the difference between the ideal and the actual and speaks of tendencies as if they were facts. Though there is no doubt that society or state alone provides the conditions under which an individual can best secure the determination of his will by reason as manifested in its laws and institutions, Green urges that it would have been a mockery if some one were to tell an Athenian slave who could have been used to satisfy the master's lust that the Greek state was a realisation of freedom. Hegel's account of freedom might be true of perfect men living in a perfect state; it does not square with the facts prevailing in a state like South Africa with its policy of apaprtheid, or in a totalitarian state ruled by a dictator. There is another defect from which Hegel's theory suffers. Liberty is apt to be identified with passive obedience to the authority of the State. We have already noticed the objection that Hegel takes away the edge of the principle of liberty by identifying it with obedience to the State. Green's account is free from this shortcoming. He insists that the realisation of freedom in a state can have significance only if the individuals attain freedom through influences supplied by it, only if they come to realise by a process of reflection that what conventional morality and the laws of the State expect from them is something which is absolutely and universally desirable. The individual would be free only when he feels that the determination of his will by an object which the universal of national will of the State has brought into existence is determination of will be itself. This presupposes the hypothesis that the self-realising principle which finds expression in the reason of the state also finds expression in the self-consciousness of the individual—a hypothesis which Green makes. He regards the eternal self-consciousness in which the self-consciousness of the individual somehow participates as a self-realising principle. By a self-realising principle Green means a 'principle which is determined to action by the conception of its own perfection, or by the idea of giving reality to possibilities which are involved in it and of which it is conscious as so involved'. It is because the principle of self-realisation is as much operative in the individual as in the State that the individual can consciously conceive that the lines of conduct expected of him by the laws and customs of society or state are common to him with all men; and so in being determined by them he is determined by his own will.

Summing up, we may say that according to Green what is sought in all willing is self-satisfaction and that, as a self-conscious and self-realising subject, man can find true self-satisfaction in the attainment of his own perfection and not in the gratification of his natural impulses. The natural impulses have to be overcome, not in the sense of being extinguished, but in the sense of being fused with those higher interests which have for their object human perfection in some of its forms. For the attainment of this perfection man requires freedom. An individual can be said to be free only when he is in that 'state in which he shall have realised his ideal of himself, shall be at one with the law which he recognises as that which he ought to obey, shall have become all that he has in him to be, and so fulfil the law of his being. True freedom is found in achieving self-perfection.

It is thus, clear that the freedom Green has in view is not the negative freedom to do what one likes without let or hindrance, i.e., absence of restraints; it is a positive thing. It is the positive power of doing or enjoying something worth doing or enjoying and that too something which we do or enjoy in common with others. It is the positive power of pursuing those ideal objects which the good will presents to itself; it is 'the liberation of all the powers of men for the social good'. As Sabine puts it, freedom means 'an actual possibility, in view of existing circumstances, of developing human capacities, a genuinely increased power on the part of an individual to share in the goods which the society has produced and an enlarged ability to contribute to the common good.' It may be mentioned that, according to Green, this liberation of human power for the social good does not mean the annihilation of our natural impulses, but their union with higher interests. This is the only way to realise the ideal of perfection. It is a necessary consequence of this view that only the goodwill is free and not the bad will. Will is good when it is determined by the thought of self-realisation ; it becomes bad when it is swayed by the external stimuli of pleasure and pain. In the next place, freedom as conceived by Green is determinate in character; in the words of Barker it is the power of doing 'something of a definite character, something which possesses the quality of being worth doing and not any and everything.'

**Green's Metaphysical Theory.** In constructing his metaphysical theory Green starts with the Kantian thesis that the nature of the ultimate reality can be comprehended by the aid of a pure reason with occasional flashes of intuition, and not by the empirical or inductive method. He was thus opposed to the empirical or sensationalistic approach of Hume. He was equally opposed to the Spencerian evolutionary approach which will be examined in a subsequent chapter. He held that we cannot comprehend the true nature of man and of the universe of which he is a part, if we view him merely as a part of physical nature and his activities as so many natural phenomena. The basic and fundamental fact with which Green starts in his analysis of the nature of man is his self-consciousness. Man differs from the rest of animal creation in being self-conscious, in being conscious of the fact that he is conscious. Lower animals are merely conscious; they feel pleasures and pains, hunger and cold, and respond to external stimuli, but are not aware of the fact that they are pleased or suffer pain, and do not become reflectively aware of their hunger.

Now self-consciousness implies reference to a self in human experience which cannot be identified with the passing states of consciousness. It is the centre to which each successive state of consciousness is referred. The 'I' in phrases like 'I think', 'I feel', 'I remember,' 'I decide,' refers to this centre; it is that which has the various experiences of thinking, reeling, remembering and deciding; it persists through all of them and unites them in a unity. Without the synthesising activity of this 'I' or 'Self' there could be no knowledge of any object as a unified whole, standing in relation to the knowing self and other things in the known world. This Self unites the elements of our experience into a systematic unity in the same way in which a piece of string passing through the beads constitutes them into a whole. Green describes this combining or synthesising principle as spiritual, because its activity consists in establishing thought-relations between the diverse elements of our experience; no material or natural phenomenon can be a source of such thought relations.

But Green does not accept the Kantian doctrine of things-in-themselves as the source of the material of knowledge. He holds with Fichte and Hegel that the world around us which we know must be of the same stuff as the knowing self; it must be spiritual or intelligible in character. Had it been something different from or other than a system of thought-relations, it could never have been intelligible to the self. Hence, Green concludes that the cosmos or the real universe around us must be an intelligible or ideal reality; it must be spiritual in nature. The Universe, as an object of knowledge, must be an all-inclusive system of relations, intelligible to our reason. These relations are not created by the mind of any individual like myself or yourself; they must be ascribed to a supreme intelligence which must be regarded as similar to our own. Otherwise, we could never have known and understood these relations. The supreme intelligence which has created these thought-relations and sustains them may be called God. Green prefers to call it the Eternal Consciousness. As the condition of the existence and knowability of the universe, it is the universal and all-inclusive consciousness; 'it is the systematic principle which establishes unity and all order, the whole in which every part finds its logical place, the universal towards which every particular strives, and which it needs in order to complete itself and without which it is nothing, the divine unity in which everything lives and moves and has its being. It would be obvious to the intelligent reader that, if the Self which Green finds revealed in the fact of self-consciousness is much similar to the Kantian Transcendental Unity of Apperception, his God or Eternal Consciousness bears a close resemblance to Hegel's Absolute Reason or Idea. As has been stated earlier, the vital truth which Green found in Hegel was the belief in the reality of Divine Spirit or Reason. Green further agreed with Hegel in maintaining that the Eternal Spirit manifests itself in all our institutions, associations, and communities. This, again, shows that Green read Kant with Hegelian spectacles.

From the foregoing argument it would be evident that in the system of Green the three entities—the human self, the world, and God—constitute a whole; they do not form a mere aggregate. The relationship between man and God is far deeper than is indicated by saying that the former is created and sustained by the latter; it may best be described in the following words of Metz : 'The individual consciousness is said to be the medium or instrument of the universal consciousness, and to have some sort of participation in the latter, but of the manner of this participation we are told nothing more than that the eternal consciousness is communicated to us under the limitations imposed by our bodies.' The notion that somehow or other the eternal consciousness dwells within each human being occupies a vital place in the thought of Green : several important conclusions follow from it in his ethical and political theories, In the first place, it implies that man is something more than merely a part of nature; he cannot be explained in purely naturalistic terms. He is a free intelligence, a self-realising and self-distinguishing consciousness, His good cannot, therefore, lie in the satisfaction of the physical or sentient side of his being as Hedonism believes. Pursuit of pleasure cannot be the goal of life for a being who partakes in the eternal consciousness; his true good must be sought in the full realisation of the divine element which is somehow present in him. Our moral life, so Green holds, must be an unceasing struggle for the higher life, for the attainment of the perfection we associate with God; it cannot be a life dedicated to the pursuit of the greatest amount of pleasure. 'The true good of man is the perfection of human life.' Green thus, rejects Hedonism completely as a theory of the moral end of life, though he acknowledges that it has been of great social value. In the second place, since the eternal consciousness or God is characterised by freedom, freedom must be the chief feature of our moral life also. Human consciousness postulates freedom on the analogy of divine consciousness. Not only this, the eternal consciousness communicates to man the idea of the social good which lies behind Green's conception of the State. In the third place, the belief that somehow man participates in the eternal consciousness led Green to lay stress on the value and dignity of the individual; it made him a radical in politics. Passionately believing that every individual has intrinsic worth, he concluded that the essence of human life must be found in the pursuit of its own betterment which includes the betterment of the society apart from relationship to which an individual is inconceivable. He could not, therefore, view the State as an end itself as Hegel was led to do; the State can have no other purpose than the full development of the personalities of the individuals who compose it.

There are a few other aspects of the moral philosophy of Green which follow from his cardinal thesis that in some inexplicable manner the consciousness of each individual partakes of the nature of the eternal consciousness, and which affect his political philosophy : they also deserve a brief mention. The recognition of the intrinsic worth of the individual leads Green to the concepts of human equality and human brotherhood. Since every person has absolute worth, humanity in each man should always be treated as an end and never as a means. Everyone is under a moral obligation to recognise and respect the personality of every other man. This means that no one is entitled to make others a means to his own betterment. This in turn involves the notion that the end at which every individual should aim is the cultivation of an ideal character and not the pursuit of external ends. Moral goodness lies in virtuous activity, in the development, of character and not in doing good things. The motto is : Be good, and not merely do good. This had a profound influence on Green's theory of state functions; it led him to modify Hegel's theory in the direction of liberalism. It saved him from falling into the error of Hegel and making the State an end in itself. It also led him to describe the functions of the State in negative terms as the hindrance of hindrances to good life and not the promotion of moral good. The State cannot make its citizens morally better; one cannot make a man good by legislation. All that the State can do is to provide circumstances in which the individual can develop his moral personality. In this respect, again Green is more a Kantian than a Hegelian. But in his insistence that a man can develop his personality fully only in the State, that he can realise the ideal of moral perfection only through civic institutions which supply the necessary material and environment for it, he is a genuine Hegelian.

Another thing worth remembering about Green's moral ideal is that, though he describes it as self-realisation, he fully realises its social aspect, The things worth doing and enjoying are the things which are done and enjoyed in common with others. Green's moral ideal is an ideal of a good common to the agent and others, Personal life is social life, A good citizen is a good man.

## TRANSITION TO POLITICAL PHILOSOPHY

In the foregoing section we have argued that according to Green the true goal of human life is self-realisation, or the perfection of human life; we should always be moving from a less perfect to a more perfect human life. He also holds that freedom is a necessary means for the achievement of this end, and that this freedom can be had only in and through membership of a civil society. So far we have not adduced any proof to show that self-realisation or the perfection of human life is possible only in society. What Green says in this connection forms a bridge from his ethical theory to political philosophy. His argument can be summed up in the following words of Barker which have been quoted once before: 'Human consciousness postulates liberty : liberty involves rights: rights demand the State.' We have already elaborated the first part of the statement; we may now proceed to explain the last two.

Green's argument may be stated as follows. Like the eternal consciousness in which he somehow partakes, man is essentially a consciously self-realising principle. By describing man as a consciously self-realising principle Green means to say that a human being is self-conscious and is determined to action by the thought of his own perfection; he is endowed with the capacity of willing the ideal objects which the good will presents to itself. Furthermore, he is not only conscious of himself as willing ideal objects, but is also conscious of the existence of other selves of like nature with himself; *i.e.*, of beings who are determined to action by the conception of their own perfection. In short, man is not an isolated being but lives as a member of a society; he has to seek his own realization along with others who have the same end in view. It, therefore, follows that the things which he does and enjoys as worth doing are things which he does and enjoys in common with others; his good is not merely his own good but is a common good; it cannot but be a common good. He cannot imagine any ideal thing which he does not share in common with others. Green thus breaks, the isolation in which the individual is made to stand by the utilitarians.

The reader would understand the above-quoted chain of reasoning, if he remembers that for Green Reality is a system of relations, that society is nothing other than the relations which subsist between its members, and that an individual, is constituted of the relations in which he stands to other individuals as father son, brother, teacher, friend, etc. His good is nothing else than the goodness of the relations with others. In other words, it is a social or common good. It is because his good is a common good and not something private, that in pursuing his ideal objects he can be sure that his claims would be recognised by others as he himself would readily recognise the claims of others. The condition on which alone a society of consciously self-realising beings can be organised is that each recognises in his fellow, and each claims from his fellow that he shall recognise in him the power of pursuing ideal objects; and each makes his claim with a sure confidence of its recognition by all.' The claims to pursue ideal objects become rights when they are recognised by society. Social recognition is expressed in the laws maintained and enforced by the State. In the absense of such recognition the claim to pursue ideal objects does not acquire any reality; it remains an empty claim, Society not only converts our claims into rights by granting them recognition, it goes, further; through civic and political institutions maintained by it, it enables us to freely exercise our capacities of win and reason, Green holds that the institutions of social life, apart from particular aberrations, 'render it possible for a man to be freely determined by the idea of a possible satisfaction of himself being driven this way and that by external forces, and thus, they give reality to the capacity called will : and they enable them to realise his reason, *i.e.*, his idea of self-perfection, by acting as a member of social organisation in which each contributes to the better-being of all the rest'.

The foregoing discussion should make it clear to the reader how liberty which is postulated by human self-consciousness involves rights and how rights demand the State. Since no individual well-being is possible apart from social well-being; in other words, since man needs society for self-realisation, Green's ethical doctrine issues into political philosophy to which we may now turn.

## NATURAL LAW

Before passing on to Green's theory of the State a few words may be added about his attitude towards natural law which, from a very early period, has been regarded as a court of appeal before which human or positive law may be brought for condemnation or approval. He subjects it to the same sort of reinterpretation as he applied to the parallel concept of natural rights. He rejects the meaning given to it by seventeenth-century thinkers like Hobbes and

Locke as something existing independently of social consciousness, but retains the concept as containing great truth. Any rule or institution which can be shown to be inconsistent with it can be rejected as wrong and harmful. According to Green natural law is that law which man as a moral being should obey, whether it is a part of the actual law of the state or not. Its content is to be determined by reason or ethics; it cannot be discovered by appeal to experience. In other words, it is the business of natural jurisprudence to determine what laws should be considered natural; they would be valid and enforceable whether or not they form part of the statute law of the state. Thus, it is not necessary that natural law should be enforced by the society : it should however, be capable of being enforced. It is this capacity of being enforced which distinguishes it from morality. In order to be enforceable a natural law should be recognised as necessary or at least desirable by the moral consciousness of the society. It should also be remembered that natural law is a growing and developing thing; its content varies from generation to generation as the moral consciousness of the community grows. It is definitely connected with the moral nature of man, and may be viewed as the ideal towards which society is tending.

## SOVEREIGNTY

So far we have been speaking about Green's conception of rights, and have tried to show that they follow necessarily from the concept of human self-consciousness as a self-realising principle. We have laid stress on the point that, according to Green, society grants to its members certain freedoms of action and acquisition, called rights, on the condition that they allow like freedom to others. We have also seen that the rights granted by the society are enforceable; nay, they have to be enforced. A right that cannot be enforced is no right at all; it is simply a moral claim. Therefore, there must exist in every society a power that can enforce rights against all those who, for one reason or another, refuse to recognise the rights of others and place impediments in the way of their exercise. The good will of a good Hindu readily accepts the fight of the so-called untouchables to enter a temple and worship the diety there, but there may be some Hindus whose actual will refuses to recognise this right and who, therefore, try to put all sorts of obstacles in the way of the Harijans' admission to the temples. The State has, therefore, to use force against the obstructionists in order that the Harijans may enjoy their right. Rights thus, demand the State as the only authority which can enforce them. 'Here we reach the paradox, the unavoidable paradox, of state-action. It uses force to create freedom. In order to face this paradox we have to inquire, in the first place, what is the body that uses force, and in the second place, how far its action is endorsed by the living and active will of the members of the society.'

The answers Green gives to these questions form the heart of his political philosophy.

Political philosophers generally use the term sovereignty to describe the coercive authority by means of which the State maintains the system of rights and obligations in the community, and regard sovereignty as the trait which distinguishes the State from other forms of human association. Different answers have been returned to the question of its location in society. Green discusses two of them and seeks to reconcile them. Rousseau places it in the General Will, while John Austin locates it in a determinate human superior who receives habitual obedience from the bulk of the society and is not in the habit of obedience to a like superior. These two views seem to be incompatible. The General Will of Rousseau cannot be identified with the will of any determinate person to persons; it can be expressed only by the vote of the whole body of citizens. Moreover, the General Will of which Rousseau spoke is incapable of exercising any compulsive power; it is something abstract and intangible, and compulsive power belongs to concrete hum tin beings made of flesh and blood. Green holds that a little analysis would show that the two views are not mutually exclusive, but can be treated as complementary to each other.

Realising that if law is to be law in the strict sense of the term, it must be formulated and enforced by a duly constituted and generally recognised organ. of government, Green finds no difficulty in conceding the truth of the Austinian theory that 'in a thoroughly developed state there must be some determinate person or persons, with whom, in the last report, lies the recognised power of imposing and enforcing their observance, over whom no legal control can be exercised.' The King-in-Parliament is such a sovereign authority in Great Britain to whom the people render habitual obedience and who is not in the habit of similar obedience to any outside authority. In the terminology of today this authority would be described as the legal sovereign. But when the Austinians go further and suppose that the real reason why the bulk of the people render habitual obedience to such a sovereign is its possession of coercive authority, *i.e.*, its power of compelling the people to obey its laws through fear of punishment, they are. According to Green the real determinant of the habitual obedience of the people to the laws prescribed by it is their conviction that the laws are meant for their good, and that the sovereign embodies and expresses the general will of the community. If we use the term 'sovereign power' in a less abstract and fuller sensc, and mean by it 'the real determinant of the habitual obedience of the people', Green says, that we must 'look for its sources much more widely and deeply than the "analytic jurists" do.' It would be found to reside in 'that impalpable conjures of the hopes and fears of a people, bound together by common interest and sympathy, which we call the general will'. (Section 86), For clarity's sake the general will may be described as the political sovereign. It does not reside in any determinate person or group of persons and exercises no compulsive power. It does not formulate and enforce laws, but performs a much more vital function. It is the power which sustains and guarantees the social and political institutions of society which are the precondition of the existence of rights. In so far as 'the institutions of political society are an expression of and are maintained by the general will', it can be said that the general will is the ultimate sovereign.

A democratic society provides the best example of the presence and operation of the general will; to it applies most appropriately the famous dictum of Green that will and not force is the basis of the State. But it can be maintained that the authority of even a despotic ruler ultimately rests on the general will. One may go even further and hold that general will is not altogether absent in a society ruled by a foreign power as India was during the British rule; the great patriarchs like Dadabhai Naoroji, Surendra Nath Bannerjee, Gopal Krishna Gokhale and Pherozeshah Mehta who founded and nursed the Indian National Congress welcomed British rule as a blessing and never contemplated the idea of India going outside the British Empire. The intelligentsia generally believed that the Britishers ruled over India for the good of the people. Under those conditions it would not have been wrong to assert that the British authority rested on the will of the people. But when political consciousness awakened among the people and they began to demand swaraj or self-government, and the foreign government tried to suppress the national awakening by force, its authority came to rest more and more on brute force. The Indian National Congress came to express and embody the general will of the people more and more.

Summing up, we may say that according to Green the presence of a supreme coercive power is necessary for the existence of the State; the protection of a common system of rights and obligations requires it. But it is wrong to maintain that the State is sustained by this coercive power; the real sustaining power is the General Will. Force can only vindicate rights; it cannot create them, Rights are created and sustained by the General Will, by 'the common consciousness of a common end which constitutes. the society'. In other words, however, necessary force may be for the effective performance of its duties by the State, it can never be said to constitute its essence. As Green puts it, 'Will, not force, is the basis of the State.' Force may be necessary for restraining the minority of citizens in whom, for one reason or another, the civic sense is not properly developed; it may even be necessary for 'the occasional reinforcement of the law-abiding principle in others'; but it cannot be said to constitute the essence of the State. When once the coercive power, which is merely an incident of sovereignty, becomes its characteristic feature in its dealings with the citizens, the conclusion may be drawn that the state has lost hold on the affections of the people and its disintegration is near at hand. In short, according to Green, it is a fundamental error of thought to identity sovereignty with the possession of supreme coercive power; its essence lies in the General Will. He writes thus:

'The sovereign should be regarded, not in abstraction as the wielder of coercive force, but in connection with the whole complex of institutions or political society. It is as their sustainer, and thus, as the agent of the General Will, that the sovereign power must be presented to the minds of the people, if it is to command habitual loyal obedience; and obedience will scarcely be habitual unless it is loyal, and not forced'.

## GENERAL WILL

Green is led to his conception of General Will through an examination of the theories of political obligation expounded by Spinoza, Hobbes, Locke and Rousseau. He thinks that their theories suffer from one and the same fundamental defect; they conceive of the two main elements of the State, sovereign and subject, in too abstract a manner. They view the subjects as possessing certain natural rights prior to and independently of the State, and the State as the supreme coercive authority which is external to them, and separate from them, but which they have to obey somehow. Their chief problem was to discover some sort of justification for the right of the State to demand obedience to its laws, and of the duty of the subjects to render that obedience. They sought to solve the problem by the theory of social contract. Green says that their assumptions were wrong and their procedure erroneous. Rather than start with individuals endowed with natural rights on the one side, and a supreme coercive authority on the other, they should have injured into the origin and development of society. If they had cared to know how it is that individuals come to be clothed with entertain rights and duties, they would have found that rights and duties are neither natural in the sense of existing prior to the formation of the body politic, nor derived from a sovereign power. They would have discovered that not only rights and obligations but all the institutions of society and society itself, are the product of the common consciousness of a common end. Society begins in the consciousness of a common good or interest. Green designates this common consciousness of the common good as the General Will. It is as members of society, as recognising common interests and objects, that individuals come to possess their rights and duties. This common consciousness not only creates these rights and duties but also creates that system of laws and institutions by which the rights are maintained, as well as sovereign authority whose mission it is to enforce those rights and sustain in full vigour the institutions which are the concrete embodiments of rights and of laws.

In this way Green tries to show that the State does not arise out of a social contract, but is the result of the desire of men for a common good and is the indispensable condition of its realisation. This was the essential truth which Rousseau wanted to teach, though he clothed it in the garb of the social contract. Green rejects the concept and terminology of contract but retains the vital truth of Rousseau that the State rests on will and not on force. It does not rest on fear or physical compulsion.

By this principle Green means nothing more than the fact that every society is constituted and held together by a conscious and intelligent recognition of the common good. Given a number of rational men who have the capacity to represent to themselves the idea or conception of a common good and determining their action by it, the State comes into existence with its system of rights and obligations and law. In this way Green is able to resolve the antithesis between the society and the individual which figured so prominently in the writings of Hobbes and Locke, and to a degree in those of Rousseau, and which they could not easily resolve. This also enables Green to give a more adequate solution of the problem of political obligation than his predecessors did, Rousseau included. The question, however, naturally arises, whether the idea of a common good or the consciousness of a common end is generally and normally present in every member of the community and consciously determines his behaviour, or whether it rises to full consciousness in some minds and only on occasions. Before attempting an answer to these questions a few more words of clarification about Green's theory of General Will may be added.

It should be observed that Green's theory is not the doctrine of the General Will of the State in whose name the Fascists committed so many crimes and which became in their hands an excellent stick with which to beat the minorities and to bludgeon even whole communities into obedience. It is rather the doctrine of the will for the State, of the will to maintain the State. In the words of Barker the General Will is 'rather an assertion that the ultimate moving force which inspires and controls political action is a spiritual force—a common conviction that makes for righteousness, a common conscience that alone can arm the ministers and agents of the community with power....It creates the sovereign whose mission is to sustain in full vigour and in complete harmony all the living institutions which are the concrete embodiments of rights and of law'.

We may now deal with the question raised a little earlier, and determine the extent to which the 'common consciousness of a 'common end' is operative in the lives of the 'untaught and underfed denizens of a London yard with gin shops on the right hand and on the left'. Does it not seem absurd to speak of the conscious presence of this idea in the minds of the ordinary citizens ? Green answers that he does not expect the common man who is engrossed in his daily work and does not probably know what he owes to the state to have any clear consciousness of the idea of the common good. To say nothing of the 'untaught and underfed' citizen in the street, even educated persons like teachers and lawyers and medical practitioners, and even those who serve the state as its agents, can have only an imperfect and inadequate comprehension of it.

This 'however' should not be taken to mean that the ordinary citizen has no notion at all of the common good served by the State. It is present in the minds of all the citizens, though in a very rudimentary form. If it were completely absent, the State could not exist and endure. We may say that it is present and operates much in the same way in which the idea of moral obligation is present and operates. Though all of us are influenced by the conception of the moral ideal, it rises to clear consciousness only occasionally and in few cases. According to Green the two concepts—the idea of the common good and that of moral obligation—have the same source. Very likely, the man in the street does not think of the State when he receives his weekly wages or draws water from the municipal tap, but in so far as he has a clear understanding of 'certain rights and privileges common to himself with his neighbours', he has the needful elementary conception of a common good maintained by law. Green is emphatic on the point that without the instinctive recognition of this elementary conception, an individual becomes an outlaw and the very foundation of the State disappears. It should be the business of the State to develop and cultivate this rudimentary conception and make the individual into an intelligent patriot by giving him a share in the management of public affairs.

## THE INDIVIDUAL AND THE SOCIETY

The great truth emerging from Green's discussion of General Will and its relation to sovereignty is that an individual, owes allegiance to the State and its system of law and government, because he realises, perhaps unconsciously, that it is a product of, and embodies, the common good. He also brings out clearly the other side of truth that force and the fear inspired by it can command only a temporary obedience of the subjects. He holds that in the long run people render habitual obedience only to those institutions which they believe to be in conformity with the general will. This raises the vital question as to what an individual should do when he finds that a given law runs counter to his conception of the common good. Should he conform to it or resist it ? This is a vital issue, the age-old issue of the conflict between loyalty to the ideal and obedience to an actual bad law, bad law resulting from the domination of personal interests hostile to the common good. Green faces the problem cautiously and answers it soberly.

The fundamental point to be borne in mind while examining Green's answer to the problem is that he repudiates completely the old doctrine of natural rights according to which individuals claimed certain rights as against society. For Green the entire notion of rights against society is a contradiction in terms. Since rights are given to individuals so that they may develop their personalities and contribute to the common good, an individual can have no rights independently of society and 'therefore' none against it. All that he can claim is to be treated as a member of society. Therefore, when he comes across a law which he regards as bad because it contravenes his conception of the common good, he cannot claim to act as he wishes; he should not resist or disobey it, but conform to it, and do all he can by legal or constitutional methods to get it cancelled. But so long as it remains on the statute book, his duty at an intelligent patriot is to obey it. He should obey it because, even though it is inconsistent with the system of ideal rights which ought to be maintained, it is a part of the whole system of rights which society enforces as vitally necessary for the liberation of the human capacity for good. The whole must not be sacrificed for apart; the existing system of rights must not be disturbed for the sake of adding a new element to it because of the risk of social chaos. As Green says :

'The common good must suffer more from resistance to a law or to the ordinance of legal authority, than from the individual confrmity to a particular law or ordinance that is bad, until its repeal can be obtained. It is thus, the social duty of the individual to conform, and he can have no right that is against his social duty.'

Persons who hold out the threat of the so-called satyagraha in our country if what they fancy to be social wrongs are not righted at once should carefully ponder over the words of Green. The spirit of law-abidingtiess is very necessary for the smooth functioning of democracy; it is a crime against democracy to encourage the spirit of defiance of law and organise kisan marches and morchas when means or constitutional agitation are available. Indulgence in anti-social acts like looting and setting fire to public property is never justifiable.

When all constitutional means of getting an obnoxious law repealed have failed, or when constitutional means do not exist, as they did not exist in Czarist Russia and British India, what should the individual do? Green says that the individual should arouse public opinion against the unjust measure as Gandhiji did against the Rowlatt Bills or as Mazzini did in Italy, and lead a resistance movement. Under such conditions resistance to despotic authority does not become a right; it, however, does become a duty. Green speaks of the duty of resistance but not of the right of the individual to resist the authority of the State. But he insists that the resistance must be made in the name of the public good and on grounds which the mass of people can understand and appreciate. There must be a strong and intelligent popular sentiment against the Government and in favour or resistance, if the danger of social anarchy is to be eliminated. Gandhiji prepared the country by intense propaganda before actually launching the movement or non-violent non-cooperation, and at a later date, civil disobedience. No precise rules can be laid down as to the conditions under which resistance to a despotic government becomes a duty. It is sufficient for our purpose to note that Green recognises that at times resistance to government does become a social duty; nothing reveals his departure from Kant and Hegel so much as this admission of the duty of resistance to the State. It should, however, be remembered that according to Green resistance does not becomes obligatory; all that he says is that under certain conditions it is justifiable. It is justifiable only in the interest of the state and not for promoting personal or private interests.

## RIGHT MAINTAINED BY THE STATE

From the preceding discussion it would have become clear that the true feature of a state is not the exercise or coercive authority by a determinate human superior, but a habitual and voluntary submission on the part or the citizens to a system of rights and obligations based on the consciousness that the rights and obligations maintained and enforced by it are necessary for the promotion or the common good. In other words, the coercive power of the State must be exercised in a proper way and for the maintenance of the system of rights and related institutions. The question thus, naturally arises : What are the rights and obligations which the State protects and promotes ? Green.s views concerning the nature and scope of state activity can be gathered from his answer to this question.

The most fundamental and pre-eminent of these rights is the right to life and liberty, or as Green prefers to describe it, the right to free life. No distinction can be made between the right to life and the right to liberty, for the right to mere life without the right to use his life according to his own will has no meaning whatsoever. The right to free life must be granted to every member of the society in virtue of his humanity; *i.e.*, in virtue of his capacity of determining his action by reference to a good common to him and to others. No society which denies this right to any class of men can represent more than a temporary phase of development. Hence, the institution of slavery in all its forms is wrong; the practice of untouchability and of apartheid or colour-bar must also be wrong; these institutions constitute an infringement of this fundamental right. This right is over-ridden by the State during wartime and limited in peacetime in various ways by its right to punish, and its duty to enforce prohibition and compulsory education, etc. Since in his attitude towards war and views on punishment Green moves away from Hegel to a considerable extent, a few words on these topics may be added here.

In opposition to Hegel who regarded war as virtuous activity and as necessary for the preservation and promotion of the ethical health of the people Green held that war is always an evil thing in as much as it is destructive of human life. He admitted that war might evoke certain virtues like patriotism and courage among the combatants, that sometimes its result might even contribute towards the moral progress of mankind; *e.g.,* in the case of the war fought for the liberation and union of Italy against Austria, or the war of Japan against Russia; that in some cases it might even be a cruel necessity, *e.g.*, when it has to be resorted to for undoing a wrong previously done. But all these admissions do not alter its essential nature as involving the denial of the right of the people to free life and, therefore, morally wrong. It may be relatively right in some cases, but can never be absolutely right. As Green wrote : 'No state of war can make the destruction of man's life by man other than a wrong although the wrong is not always chargeable upon all the parties to a war.

Green differed from Hegel not only in regarding war as an evil, but also in maintaining that the need and impulse of war can be completely eradicated. Green held war to be an attribute of the imperfect state; according to him wars result from the incomplete fulfilment of their functions on the part of states. The more perfect the internal organisation of states becomes and the better they are able to maintain and reconcile the rights of their citizens, the fewer would be the opportunities of war. To quote Green : 'The more complete that organisation becomes, the more the motives and occasions of international conflict tend to disappear, while the bonds of unity become stronger.

Green differed from Hegel in yet another vital respect. We have seen that the German philosopher regarded the nation-state as the highest form of social organisation, and refused to visualise any international world-order of which independent nation-states may become members. He also exempted them from the operation or moral laws. Green postulates a common general will of humanity, or the common consciousness of mankind, on the basis of which he arrives at the conception of a universal brotherhood of man. This notion of 'universal brotherhood is one of Green's distinctive conceptions and constitutes the theoretical justification of his denunciation of war as wrong. On the basis of the common consciousness of mankind Green thinks it possible to erect an ethical code by which we can judge of the morality of state actions at the international plane. In other words, Green believes in an international ethical code which may be regarded as an extension of the ethical system operative within the boundaries of a national state. All these ideas are connected with the right to free life which Green regards as the essence of citizenship.

## PUNISHMENT

The right to free life is limited and restricted by the right of the State to punish. No one denies the right of the State to interfere with individual liberty by punishing an individual for violating the legitimate rights of his fellow-citizens; but political philosophers have differed among themselves in regard to its nature and aim. Some of them hold it to be retributive in nature, others preventive, and others still reformative. Green says that it is primarily preventive in nature, but not merely so, An element of retribution enters into it. And if the criminal understands and appreciates why he is being punished by the State, it becomes reformative also. In other words, according to Green, correctly understood, punishment must be at once retributive, preventive and reformatory, though primarily it is preventive or deterrent.

It is primarily preventive because it is directed towards the maintenance of the system of rights and obligations by associating with the thought of wrong action a certain amount of terror sufficient to divert a would-be wrong-doer from his purpose; it is adjusted to the preservation of the external conditions necessary for the action of the free will. Green lays stress on the point that the idea of punishment implies, on the side of the person punished, a capacity for determination by the conception of the common good, and on the part of the authority punishing the conception of right founded on relation to public good. Where either of these implications is absent, there can be no punishment in the true sense; we do not punish animals and children for any damage or harm they may do. Nor do we consider punishment to be just if it is inflicted on a person for doing something which is not a violation of a recognised right. If the punishment is just; *i.e.*, if the person punished realises that what he has got is what he deserved and was his due, that it was his own act returning on himself, punishment becomes retributive but not in the sense of being motivated by the idea of revenge; its motive is highly different. Its object is simply to protect rights from violation.

In so far as the criminal accepts the punishment inflicted on him as his own act returning upon him, *i.e.*, as his desert, and is thereby awakened to the consciousness of the anti-social character of his act, punishment becomes reformative in its effects. It becomes reformatory to the extent it is really preventive. The reformatory function of punishment is thus, an incident of its preventive function; it means nothing more than that the criminal recovers from his criminal habits. It is not reformative in the sense that its direct aim is the moral reformation of the criminal. Green is emphatic on the point that in its judicial action the State does not, and cannot, look to the moral guilt of the criminal, and makes no attempt to adjust the amount of punishment to the degree of moral guilt involved. Since the degree of moral depravity implied in a crime is connected with the motive and character of the agent which cannot be known to the magistrate, the latter cannot take cognisance of it. Moreover, the State should not take into account the moral guilt of the offender, because it is not its business to punish wickedness.

'The state looks not to virtue and vice but to rights and wrongs. It looks back to the wrong done in the crime it punishes; not, however, in order to avenge it but in order to the consideration of the sort of terror which needs to be associated with such wrong-doing in order to the future maintenance of rights.'

Though Green insists that punishment is not inflicted with any direct reference to the moral guilt of the offender in the past, or with a view to his moral reformation in the future, it is not devoid of moral purpose and moral quality. We can say that its ultimate purpose is moral, since it is directed towards the maintenance of the system of rights and obligations which is necessary for the realisation of the moral purpose of life. It has a moral quality because it ends to induce the criminal to realise the true nature of his act also and to regenerate his will. Above all, it tends to liberate the capacity of the criminal for self-determination towards a common good.

❑

# 5

# Contemporary Political Thought

## V.I. LENIN

About the contribution of V.I. Lenin to political thought Coker said, "In his brief theoretical writings he set forth a systematic political doctrine with considerable dialectical skill and a fair historical perspective; he was highly effective as a speaker before popular audiences and as the head of the Government of Russia he displayed rare qualities of practical statesmanship is exceedingly difficult domestic and international situations."

**1. Modification of Marxism.** Lenin was an orthodox communist. He believed that ideas of Marx were not static, fixed or inviolable but living and developing. He wanted to mould Marxian philosophy to make it applicable to the whole universe. He laid stress on revolutionary rather than evolutionsary side of Marxian philosophy. He felt that many of the prophecies of Marx about capitalism and its withering away had not come true. He felt that unless revolutionary means were adopted the capitalists might be successful in defeating working class movements. He also laid emphasis on the organisation and working of the party which he felt was an essential agency for preparing proletariate for revolution.

**2. Analysis or Imperialist Capitalism.** In the words of Sidney "Lenin gave a few orientation to the Marxist analysis of Imperialist capitalism." He had seen that doctrines of Marx had not come true. Capitalism and capitalist theory of the state were becoming deep rooted. Business and trade was on the increase. The workers of the world had clung to their own countries and showed national loyalties during the World War. This was against Marxian prophecy. It was an embarrassing position for orthodox Marxians. Lenin took upon himself the responsibility of explaining the reasons due to which Marxian doctrines had not come true. This he did through the theory of Imperialism which he defined as "final stage of capitalism beyond which it could go no further." For him, it is a monopoly stage with no chances of free competition. In this imperialism goes in the hands of a few bankers and is run, controlled and managed only by a few industrialists.

**3. Basic Principles of Imperialism.** To Lenin the basic principles of imperialism were:

*(i)* ***Monopoly.*** That monopolistic conditions play a predominant role in the economic life of the people;

*(ii)* ***Export.*** Export of capital became unusually important and maximum stress is said on that;

*(iii)* ***International Monopoly.*** There is a tendency towards international monopoly; and

*(iv)* ***Finance Oligarchy.*** Finance capital creates finance oligarchy.

**4. Definition or Imperialism.** Lenin defined imperialism in the following words, "Imperialism is capitalism in that stage of development in which the dominance of monopolies and finance capital has established itself, in which the export of capital has acquired pronounced importance, in which division of world among the international trusts has begun, in which division of all territories of the globe among the biggest capitalist powers has been completed."

**5. Why Marxian Prophesies did not Come True.** Lenin was of the opinion that Marxian prophecies would certainly have come true but for the reason that conditions which Marx foresaw have considerably changed *(i)* Industry became monopolistic. *(ii)* Instead of relying on national capital the monopolist began to depend on banks for financing their capital. *(iii)* Instead of localised market the markets became world wide and international. *(iv)* Competition assumed international character. *(v)* National competition within state boundaries has been practically eliminated. *(vi)* Lenin believed that the imperialist powers were bound to lead the world to war due to their lust for capturing more and more colonies. The imperialists have a natural tendency for expansion. *(vii)* Imperialism leads to class war. Each imperialistic step and action for advancement is bound to result in class division and suppression of labourers and working classes. In the words of K. Kautsky, "Imperialism is a product of highly developed industrialism and capitalism. It consists in the striving of every industrial capitalist nation to bring under its control or to annex larger and larger areas of 'agrarian's territory, irrespective of what nations inhabit those regions." *(viii)* According to Lenin imperialism is bound to result in a conflict between imperialist nation and its dependent colonies. Capitalism reinstates class struggle as a permanent force in capitalist society.

In the above changed circumstances the prophecy of Marx about the death of capitalism did not come true. But according to Lenin such a state was not bound to last long because imperialism was the last stage of capitalism.

**6. Dialectical Materialism.** According to Marx dialectic was not an incidental phenomena. It was something integral and well connected, in which everything was well knit and well interlinked with each other. In dialectic no event was inseparable and there was always action and reaction. For understanding each phenomenon it should be linked with other events. It is not a state of immobility or stagnation but that of continuous movement. It is a continuous process of development and growth, disintegration and integration. In it the process of development is put very simple. It brings about fundamental changes in the process of development and growth. The stages of growth and development are rapid and abrupt. In the words of Engels, "it, does not move in an ethereally uniform and constantly repeated circle, but passes through a real history."

Lenin applied Marxian dialectic to science, social studies, literature and even to art. But his ideas and methods have not been accepted and appreciated by many. In the words of Dr. Wayper, it was "dreadfully dull, repetitive, dogmatic and superficial survey, chiefly of notes for its crude notion of materialism, hardly different from the materialism of Feuerbach which Marx attacked." Sabine has also given more or less the same ideas when he says, "Thus, dialectical materialism can set the mathematicism right about Euclidean and non-Euclidean geometry and can instruct the physicist about the record relations between matter and electricity."

**7. Revolution.** In the words of Coker, "The Communists, following Marx, insist on the differentiation of their programme from all programmes that seek to unite or reconcile opposing economic classes by mitigating the differences between them or by peacefully and gradually modifying the social institutions which have developed under the influence of those differences."

**(i) Marxian Revolution.** Marx believed that hostile groups must exist in the world as long as there were persons who lived on the labour of others. He also believed that capitalist system was inefficient and resulted in anarchy in production and disintegration of productive sources. Laws were made in the state to safeguard the interests of the capitalists. State maintains status quo. A capitalist controls everything in a state, even the democracy. In a healthy society capitalism must be replaced by socialism. This will come partly through its own degeneration and partly by creating conditions of concentration, over-production, unemployment and poverty. These make the workers ready for a socialist revolution. By developing the instrumentalities of large scale production the proletarians can use them for socialist purposes.

**(ii) Prerequisites of Revolution.** Lenin was of the opinion that Revolution in Russia was strictly in accordance with Marxist ideas. He, however, believed that there were certain prerequisites for bringing a revolution namely:

***(a) Group.*** There should be a group of resolute revolutionaries who should work with clear determination, object and view.

***(b) Followers.*** Common masses must be in a mood to support the people who are determined to carry on revolution and finally;

***(c) Discontentment.*** There should be discontentment among the people, irrespective of the consideration whether that had been due to political, economic or social reasons.

***(d) Appropriate time.*** The revolutionaries should select appropriate time for forging revolution. This was one when rulers had won the displeasure of masses by their actions of omission and commission.

**(iii) Value of Revolution.** Lenin laid great stress on revolution. It was an essential step towards socialism. It was possible only in the countries which has no healthy democratic traditions.

**(iv) Conditions of Success of Revolution.** According to Lenin revolution will go unrewarded if immediately thereafter individual means of production were not replaced by collective methods and means. Means of production and distribution should be brought under collective control. Wasteful energies in competitions should be preserved for constructive production. To quote Coker again, "A Marxist, said Lenin in 1917, must take congnisance of living life of true facts of reality... he must not continue clinging to the theory of yesterday, which, like every other theory, at best only outlines the main and the general, only approximately embracing the complexity of life."

Thus, Lenin tried to defend Marx. He explained how Marxist prophecies had not come true. But at the same time he gave new interpretations to Marx's ideas and philosophies. He ensured that it was passed on to the working classes both as a live creed and an acceptable philosophy.

## VIEWS ABOUT PARLIAMENTARY FORM

**1. Lenin's Criticism of Parliamentary Form.** According to Lenin in Parliamentary form of government the houses were simply talking shops. Representatives hardly worked. Lenin wished to replace this system by the Soviets.

**2. Soviets.** In the words of Coker, "A Soviet represents working men only and represents them in natural working men's constituencies—grouped in factories, workshops or unions—rather than in residence districts, which correspond to no real unities in the economic and social interests of working men. Parliamentarianism—it was formally at forth by the Second Congress of the Third International—is a "democratic" form of rule only for a bourgeois class society. It cannot be the form of the organization for the future communist society, which recognized no classes; and it cannot be the form for the transitional society of the proletarian dictatorship, for it undertakes to represent a "national will," which is purely "fictitious" made up of the imaginary wills of the several territorial wills." Lenin believed that the present constitutional monarchies should be destroyed. According to him, there should be no Upper Houses to represent the classes. From top to bottom authority should be vested in the people who are elected by the electorates to represent their cause and to protect their interests. In a lengthy description in his *The Soviet at Work*, Lenin has thus, described the working of the Soviets: "The socialist character of the Soviet democracy—that is of proletarian democracy in its concrete particular application consists first in this: that the electorate comprises of the toiling and exploited masses—that the bourgeois is excluded. Secondly in this; that all bureaucratic formalities and limitations of elections are done away with, that the masses themselves determine the order and the time of elections and with complete freedom of recall of all elected officials. Thirdly, that the best possible organization of the vanguard of the toilers—of the industrial proletariat—is formed, enabling them to direct the toiling masses, to attract them to active participation in political life, to train them politically through their own experience, that in this way a beginning has been made for the first time actually to get the whole population to learn how to manage and begin managing."

**3. Difference from Marx.** Lenin's ideas in this regard are quite different from those of Marx. He did not plead for the despotism of proletariats, he rather said that the proletariats should be raised to high position and authority. It was never the intention of Marx to confine voting rights to a particular class, *i.e.*, the workers alone but he put forth the idea of universal adult franchise. Marx never suggested franchise on functional basis. He stood for territorial system for electing representatives. In the words of Coker, "Thus, the proletarian dictatorship, in Marx's system, would be only, a special application of the traditional creed of the unlimited prerogatives of popular sovereignty. The doctrine of the Russian Communists does not recognise any such prerogatives." Marx believed that working class government should be steady to suppress the counter-revolution, with full might and force so that the order set by proletariats was fully well maintained. Lenin maintained the same view rather to a greater extent. He gave more importance that Marx to the use of force in state organisation and its consolidation. In his 'Foundations' Stalin has said, "The fundamental problem of Leninism, its point of departure, is not the peasant problem, but the problem of dictatorship of Proletariats, of the conditions under which it can be consolidated. The present problem is a derivative problem."

## LENIN'S VIEWS ON PARTY SYSTEM

**1. Role of the Party.** Lenin did not believe that consciousness would automatically come among the workers and peasants. Constant and regular efforts shall have to be made to introduce revolutionary tendencies among workers and party organisation. On the whole the workers had faith in trade unionism and the trade unionists were determined to improve their economic conditions but as soon as their conditions improve they left trade unions. It is through organised and channelised party system that revolutionary tendencies could be infused among the workers. The party should play a predominant role in national life. In the words of Sabine, "The party thus, becomes the staff organisation in the struggle of the proletariats to gain power and to retain it after it has been gained. It is the 'vanguard' of the proletariat, the most self-conscious and at the same time the most devoted and self-sacrificing part of the working class."

**2. Party Organisation.** Lenin believed that party organisation should be retained and strengthened even after the revolution was over. It shall be needed to deal with the remnants of capitalism and to foil capitalist attempts to re-capture authority and regain lost power. A sound party was only one which had a revolutionary programme. Unless a party had a revolutionary programme it could neither forge nor think of piloting revolution. Party should make workers revolution conscious and also channelise their energies in a manner that the state on the whole was benefited. It should work as a clearing house of ideas and a machinery through which the ideas be coined and propagated.

**3. Training and Role of Party Member.** Party members should be taught and made to understand basic principles of Marxian theory and party programme as well as line of action. Party members should guide the masses and create in them a sense of discipline. They themselves should also lead a disciplined life and be ready to sacrifice everything for the sake of party and enhancing its prestige. Party members should always gladly lead every revolutionary movement and should rather wait for such an opportunity. According to Lenin the party should become the custodian of the welfare of the people and also aim at collective welfare. It should make programme for the welfare of the workers as well as the common masses. Party members should not distinguish between party and non-party men. They should not aim at the welfare of one at the cost of the other. They should create a healthy and harmonious atmosphere acceptable to all. They should create such confidence among non-party workers that they should realise that their interests are being properly safeguarded and looked after.

**4. Restricted Membership.** Lenin was not in favour of throwing party membership open to each and every person. Only those who were intellectually and morally developed should be enrolled as members.

**5. Iron Discipline.** Thus, Lenin expected the party to bring about conditions for revolution to smash capitalist order and also to give a lead to the proletariats. It should consolidate what had been achieved. With this end in view there should be iron party discipline. None should be allowed to become disloyal to party hierarchy. This iron discipline *ipso facto* implied that all the members must think in the same terms. They should teach the masses and non-party men in the same language and the same principles. As time passed this tendency further degenerated itself. The party members began to think that they were the best judges to decide about all issues at national as well as international level and that the lead given to them by the party was honest and most acceptable. This was just to think of the people as dumb driven cattle who were to obey and follow rather than to suggest and give their view point. Lenin, however, justified his stand by saying that such a step was inevitable to promote discipline among the people as an undisciplined nation could not be supposed to progress and develop particularly In a hostile atmosphere.

## LENIN'S CONTRIBUTION TO POLITICAL PHILOSOPHY

**1. Practical Outlook.** Lenin was a practical Marxist. He tried to put Marxist philosophy into actual practice. Without him, Marxian philosophy would have become outdated. As the time passed the wisdom of many of Marxian prophecies about future events proved false and began to be doubted and questioned. Searching enquiries were made into the validity of the ideas preached by Marx. The world began to gain an impression that Marx's theories were appealing to reason but not true to actual life. The need of the time was a philosopher, a genius and a devoted personality who should give justification for the failure of Marxian philosophies. This task was accomplished by Lenin who interpreted political philosophy of Marx in a fashion that it became most uptodate and yet the fundamentals remained unshaken. There was only a twist and not a break. In the words of Sabine, "The historical continuity between Marx and Lenin was far less one of scientific ideas than of moral attitudes between the two periods both of which are revolutionary in temper and method. Consequently the temper of communism the moral attitude and presumptions which Lenin bequeathed to it is at least as important as its intellectual content. It was this which made communism a creed and a faith, time beyond the per-adventure of a doubt, that afforded at once a sense of a unique insight and a moral imperative for every contingency."

**2. Materialism.** Lenin's approach to life wits materialistic. He viewed the things as these were and not as these ought to be in an ideal state. In August, 1917 he wrote that, 'The way out of Parliamentarianism is to be found" of course, not in the abolition of representative institutions but in the conversion of the representative institution from mere talking shops into working bodies." This, along with his idea that cultural rights of the minorities should adequately be protected, makes it clear that his approach was not utopian, what he wanted and stood for was not ideal but materialistic. In the words of C.E.M. Joad, "While Marx's approach to life is a bit philosophical,

Leninism has no such fragrance; it is a scientific truth; not a dogma, purely a materialist approach to life and its activities."

**3. Party Organisation.** Lenin stressed party organisation. In this respect his approach was realist. It is realised even today that unless political parties are fully organised these cannot face the challenge of the time and that was more correct for Communist Party which was face to face with capitalism. In the words of Sabine, "Nothing satisfied him (Lenin) and his associates short of unquestioning obedience, and he combined a perfect assurance of his policies with perfect devotion to the cause of revolution and a complete lack of personal self-seeking. In fact the basic difference between Mensheviks and Bolsheviks was not the questioning of the validity of Marxian doctrines but only that of the role of organisation for implementing, policies approved by the party." To quote Sabine again, Lenin believed that, "the nucleus of the party should be an inner group of professional revolutionists, absolutely and fanatically devoted to the revolution rigidly disciplined and acting as the 'vanguard' of all the potentially though not actually revolutionary elements in trade unions and among the workers." Even the most democratic people cannot deny that it is through a strong, well disciplined party organisation that the governments of the nations are run and the character of the people is built.

**4. Theory.** Lenin maintained that unless there is a proper theory, there could be no proper action. He could not agree that theory should follow the action. He believed that theory should precede action. Sound action can be taken on a sound theory. Without a solid, reasonable and intelligent theory action cannot be taken.

**5. Party Personnel.** Lenin said that party personnel should comprise of men of high integrity and character with unquestionable morality. This has universal importance. Even today persons with doubtful morality in the party can neither inspire the confidence of the people nor can get their whole-hearted co-operation. Nation can get guidance and go ahead with determination and faith through intelligent party members with undoubted integrity.

**6. Democratic Centralisation.** According to Lenin the party should consist of office-bearers elected by its members. The decisions of the party should be taken on democratic principles. The members should be given freedom of speech and expression within the party and but once the party took decisions all should simply obey and accept the verdict of the party. The party should be highly centralised. The ideas preached by Lenin are accepted even today. These are adhered to by most of the political parties.

**7. Change in Marxian Ideology.** The greatest contribution of Lenin according to Sabine was the change in Marxian theory as expounded and interpreted by a Marxist. To Quote him, "The social revolution simply cannot be made by force or exhortation to run ahead of the underlying industrial development upon which a proletarian mentality depends. Knowing all this Lenin was quite aware that his concept was logically untenable without a corresponding change in the Marxian theory or ideology. Accordingly he made perhaps the boldest and the most drastic change in Marxist theory ever made by a Marxist who was concerned to preserve his orthodoxy. The usual Marxian argument, he asserted, confused the mentality or ideology of trade unionism with that of socialism. Spontaneously the workers do not become socialists but trade unionists; socialism has to be brought to them from the outside by the middle class intellectuals.

**8. Role of Peasantry.** As a practical thinker Lenin realised that revolution could not succeed without a significant role by the peasants. He assigned proper place to peasantry, more so in Russia. One cannot deny that peasants have a great role to play in all political and social revolutions, more so, in predominantly agricultural country.

## LENIN'S VIEWS ABOUT STATE AND GOVERNMENT

Lenin also held the same views about the state. He also believed that the state was a capitalist organisation. It represented capitalist society and crushed the workers and peasants who rose in revolt against the capitalists. In the words of Laski, Lenin believed that the "state is product and the manifestation of the irreconcilability of class antagonisms." Directly or indirectly the capitalists are in vast majority in the legislatures. The minority cannot think of justice in their hands. State helped the capitalists to control means of production and distribution. It created monopoly conditions by which the controllers successfully exploited the workers. Lenin agreed with anarchists that the only solution to the problem was that the state should be dispensed with all at once without any hesitation. However, Lenin used to say that, "toilers need the state only to overcome the resistance of the exploiters." Since justice is managed by the capitalists, therefore, the present judicial institutions also should not be retained because it was through these institutions that the capitalists tried to retain and perpetuate control over existing institutions.

**State and Government**

Lenin distinguished between the state and government. According to him the government tries to crush working classes whereas the state protects them. State is just whereas the government is unjust. Normally a capitalist Government does not represent what the state wants. In the words of Stalin, Lenin used to say, "Our state must not be confused, *i.e.*, identified without government. Our state is the organisation of the class of the proletarians as a state power, the purpose of which is to crush the resistance of the exploiters, organise socialist economy, put an end to classes and so on. Our government on the other hand, is the peak of that state organisation, the ruling peak."

## BASIC PRINCIPLES OF LENINISM

**1. Political Theory.** Lenin was a staunch supporter of Karl Marx. He was not only a theoretician but a practical thinker and philosopher. He wanted to make his theory appealing and reasonable. At the same time he laid great stress on the principle that the theory should have a bearing on practical life. It should not be devoid of practicability of life. Theory should be moulded in such a way that it suited the time and circumstances.

**2. Political Party.** According to Lenin the role of a political party should be the moulding of minds and ideas of the people. It should be the vanguard of all movements and originator of all new ideas. Party members should give a lead to non-party men in all walks of life. Party membership should be restricted only to those who possessed high qualities of mind and character.

**3. Religion.** Lenin did not favour religion, which he felt, was bound to develop blind faith among the people and thus, was against the spirit of communism. It was therefore, his belief that religion should be discarded and condemned. The state officials should neither participate in nor encourage religion or religious activities.

**4. Revolution.** Lenin subscribed to the idea of revolution. It was essential for bringing about a change. Evolutionary methods could not be applied for smashing existing capitalist order. Revolution was both a need and necessity.

**5. New Society.** Lenin visualised a society in which there would be dictatorship of the proletariats or the working classes. In such a society the means of production and distribution would be utilised for collective welfare. Maximum pleasure and happiness would be achieved in such an ideal society.

**6. The State.** Lenin was of the opinion that the present state was a capitalist institution to protect rights and interests of the capitalists. All laws were made for protecting the capitalist order. State officials were either directly or indirectly responsible to the capitalists and protected their interests. Therefore, Lenin pleaded that the present state should be abolished.

**7. Parliamentary Form of Government.** Lenin was against Parliamentary form of government. It is wrong to believe that a person could represent the interests of all those living in the same territory. It is wrong to hold elections on territorial basis. This procedure has been adopted only to safeguard the interests of the capitalists as against those of the proletariats or the workers.

**8. Imperialism.** According to Lenin the basic principles of Imperialism were those in which, *(a)* monopolistic conditions played a predominant role: in the economic life of the people, and *(b)* export of capital became unusually important. It was wrong to believe that Marxian prophecies about capitalism had proved wrong. On the contrary, Lenin believed that differences had come only because Marx could not foresee certain things.

**9. Nature of Leninism.** An 'ism' implies exposition of new ideas and philosophies. The philosopher should create new ideas and should see that basic principles of his philosophy are accepted and patronised by maximum number of people. From this viewpoint it is safe to say that Lenin did not preach any 'ism.' He was an orthodox follower of Marx. He subscribed Marxian ideas and viewpoints. He supported Marxian line in his argument. What he did was only to mould Marxian philosophy in a manner suited to his times and needs. It is, therefore, wrong to talk of 'Leninism' as against 'Marxism.'

**10. Leninism and Marxism.** Sabine has said about Lenin that "Much of his genius as leader consisted in this curious combination of rigidity suppleness—his ability to take instantaneous advantage of an opportunity to make a change of front appears as the logical next step, to change direction without abandoning his course, and in general to combine opportunism with what no doubt he himself sincerely regarded as rigid adherence to principle." For Lenin, Marxism was a creed and he wanted to make it most practicable. His main points of difference with Marx were as follows:

*(i)* ***Dialectical Materialism.*** According to Marxian theory dialectical materialism was applicable to social science alone whereas for Lenin it was to cover physical sciences as well. For Lenin it had universal application, leaving no branch of knowledge untouched. But here too he has in many ways twisted Marxian interpretation so as to go far away from Marxian ideas. He has maintained its spirit though given a wide interpretation and scope. In fact Marx had left it to his followers to interpret dialectical materialism in a manner which suited the times best.

*(ii)* ***Role of Party.*** According to Marx a revolution overthrowing capitalism will be a spontaneous action of the masses and the party had a secondary role to play. On the contrary Lenin believed that the party had a predominant role to play in bringing about the revolution. Party is the agency which influences ideas and makes the masses active. It should act as the vanguard of the people's movements. The party consisted of intellectuals and people with high moral standard. It alone is in a position to lead the masses on the path of revolution. Whereas Marx believed that it was the

condition of the people which was responsible for bringing about revolution, for Lenin it was not the condition but the ideas which forged revolution. A close examination reveals that the difference is not of kind but of degree alone. Whereas Marx laid more stress on conditions Lenin stressed ideas but essentially both stand for a successful revolution against capitalist order.

*(iii)* ***Nature of Revolution.*** According to Marx both revolutionary as well as evolutionary methods should be adopted for bringing a change in the existing order. If the end could be achieved by evolutionary means, there was no point in resorting to violent means. As against this, according to Lenin, evolution had no meaning and a violent revolution was necessary for bringing about economic, social and political change. Here, whereas in both cases the basic spirit has been maintained, there is difference of degree only and that of laying stress. In the words of Sabine, "Thus, Lenin wrote the utopian capstone of Marxian system but a realist to the end he was grateful to point out that the end may never he realised and the unthinking populations being what it is cannot now be definitely imagined."

*(iv)* ***Nature of Capital.*** Lenin differed from Marx in so far as the question of nature and character of capital was concerned. Marx was of the opinion that capitalism was bound to die its own death and that it was gradually degenerating and decaying. But as the time passed Marxian prophecy proved false. Instead of decay, capitalism, through an organised banking system, got world-wide importance. Instead of decrease the importance of capital considerably increased and Lenin had to give quite a different interpretation of capitalism. According to Lenin imperialism was a form of capitalism and in fact its climax. It was imperialism which was bound to decay and bring about a civil war among the capitalists themselves so as to forge an internal revolution. But it should not be confused that Lenin, in any

way, repudiated the theory of decay of capitalist system. He rather strongly defended Marxian philosophy which was proving false and becoming outdated. The basic idea of class struggle was retained and strongly adhered to. It was agreed by both Marx and Lenin that capitalistic or monopolistic order was bound to sow the seeds of its own destruction.

*(v)* ***Nationalism.*** According to Marx workers have no 'fatherland.' They are the toiling masses and the whole universe is their home. He believed that patriotism was a bourgeoisie virtue. On the other hand, Lenin had a soft corner for cultural minorities, which he felt, should be properly protected. This was based on his practical experience. He had seen that even the workers had very honestly stood by their governments and rulers in the critical times of outbreak of hostilities. At the time when the workers could give a great blow to their rulers they stood with them. Similarly he saw that even the peasants and workers maintained their lines of communication after getting concessions from their governments and fully sided with them. Sabine has supported the idea of Lenin by saying that, "Essentially this policy was an experiment in cultural autonomy and quality with local political autonomy, but with a strong integrated central power."

*(vi)* ***Role of State.*** Marx believed that the capitalist order is practically in a degenerated state. It is based on the exploitation of the poor by the rich. It is a completely hollow institution and bound to collapse automatically. On the other hand, Lenin believed that the state will not collapse of its own but concerted efforts will have to be made for giving it a death blow. Political experience has shown that instead of withering away the state was taking upon itself more and more functions and responsibilities. It was becoming more and more popular with very many subjects under its fold. Lenin therefore, felt that party workers should make specific efforts to see that this

> degenerated institution was given a forceful revolutionary blow so that it completely went out of picture and was replaced by proletariat society. In his, 'The State and Revolution' Lenin says, "If we look more closely into the mechanism of capitalist democracy everywhere—in the so called 'party' details of the suffrage (the residential qualification, the exclusion of women etc.) in the technique of representative institutions, in the actual obstacles to the right of meeting (Public buildings are not for the poor), in the purely capitalist organisation of the daily press—on all sides, we shall see restrictions upon restrictions of democracy."

To conclude this discussion with Sabine, "The simple truth is that the Marxian dogmas which Lenin piously abandoned when then came into conflict with his profounder belief in organisation and his will as a revolutionist. Lenin's formulas remained the formulas of Marx, the meaning of Leninism departed very widely from the meaning of Marxism."

## MAO-TSE-TUNG

Mao-Tse-Tung came under the influence of Marxism at very early stages. He plunged himself in the struggle for China's freedom. He devoted himself to the cause of propagation of Communism in China. He gave serious thought to Asian version of Communism and got considerable success in that. He gave a new approach and outlook to principles of Leninism and Stalinism in so far as China was concerned. Maoism is considered as Chinese version of Marxism today.

### China's Communism

Chinese Communism is based on four main ideologies:

**1. Marxism.** These include the theory of 'Surplus Value'; 'Dictatorship of the Proletariats; 'Theory of Class Struggle' and 'Dialectical Materialism.' These principles were seriously studied in China. They found their due place in Mao's philosophy.

**2. Leninism.** Lenin modified Marxism to suit his own times. He was of the view that imperialism forms a stage of capitalism. In the struggle against Capitalism the position and importance of colonies and semi-colonies cannot be under-estimated. While thinking of world revolution, opposition to imperialism cannot be avoided and is inescapable. Lenin recognised the role of the agriculturists in bringing about revolution. He said that, Communism will pass through bourgeoise democracy before coming to developing nations.

**3. Stalinism.** Which stream of ideology to Chinese Communism came from the philosophy of Stalin. Stalin laid stress on respectable behaviour with the minorities.

**4. Maoism.** But the most important stream of ideas came from Mao-Tse-Tung. He moulded whole ideology and philosophy of Communism in China and it began to be known as Maoism. Some of the main political ideas of Mao-Tse-Tung may briefly be discussed as under.

## POLITICAL IDEAS OF MAO-TSE-TUNG

According to Mao Marxian philosophy was interpreted to suit Chinese conditions. Communism could not find roots in the country. He was, not a blind follower of either Leninism or Stalinism. He interpreted Communism in such a way that even Communism of Russian type was challenged. He made Communism a living philosophy. He exposed that in such a manner that the people began to consider him as god. He was considered as the most progressive leader of the world.

**1. Revolution.** Mao felt that armed revolution was as necessary today as it was when Marx or Lenin pleaded for it. According to Mao, the working classes were the backbone of all revolutionary activities. Therefore, they should be well trained in guerilla activities. The revolutionaries should create an atmosphere by which civil wars are encouraged. They should try to dominate after the civil war had broken out. No revolution could be a success unless agriculturists and cultivators were association with that. The leadership will however, always vest in the hands of worker. Untrained and ill-equipped agriculturists will always need leadership. Without leadership there could be no real revolution. Mao identified revolution with peasantry. He pronounced that every aggression on peasantry was an offence against revolution. He stressed the role of peasants in revolution. In the words of Franz Schurman, " As Mao Tse Tung said in 1927, in the Hills of Hunan, a revolution is not a dinner party, or writing an essay.... But let us remember that revolution grew out of China's soil, that a hundred years of rebellion and suppression, of revolution and counter-revolutions had so brutilized China that massive violence was inevitable."

**2. Stress on Peasantry.** Marx, Lenin and Stalin had laid stress on working classes. But Mao felt that the peasants should be accepted as the leaders of the revolution. "They alone are the real backbone for overthrow of feudal forces. Mao said, "The gigantic struggles of the peasants—the peasants uprisings and wars-alone formed the real motive force of historical development in China's feudal society." Assessing the importance of peasantry in China, Subine said, "Whether Mao's stress on peasantry was heresy or enlightened application of Marxist-Leninist thought, it certainly had its roots in Chinese situation."

**3. Opposition to Capitalism.** Mao is also opposed to capitalism like Marxism, Leninism and Stalinism. Capitalism is definitely denigrating. The two world wars have given a very serious blow to capitalism. It only needed one strong blow. It is the foremost duty of communist countries that they should hasten that. These countries should ensure that capitalist countries which were regularly engaged in war be so engaged that these could not find time to suppress anticapitalist activities at home. These countries should encourage civil wars and guerilla activities as well.

**4. Philosophy of Power.** Mao Tse Tung supported philosophy of power. Everybody's thinking and approach can be changed by political power through political power even all social institutions can be controlled and managed in the way one liked. Economic conditions alone do not mould human thinking and institution. Ideas make the society. After ideas only military strength is most important. Political and military powers are closely associated with each other. Military strength is created with the help of gun. With gun each and everything can be done conveniently. In Mao's own words, "The world can be moulded only with the gun. Whoever wants to seize the political power of the state and to maintain it must have strong army." In the words of Sabine, "Few political thinkers, and indeed few communist leaders, have attributed such great significance to war and to military power."

**5. Stress on Villages.** Mao laid stress on villages. The villages should be well organised so that the workers and the peasants who hail from the villages, are well organised to face the aggression, which usually comes from the cities. In the words of Sabine, Mao believed that, "Where the revolutionary forces were still weak, it was necessary to build the backward villages into advanced, consolidated base areas, into great military, political, economic and cultural revolutionary bastions so that they can fight the fierce enemy who utilises the cities to attack the rural districts." Due to advancement and concentration of wealth in cities for sometime it might be possible that rural areas do not achieve their object, but ultimately revolutionary forces operating from the villages are bound to be a success.

**6. Stress on War.** Mao had to love for peace. Peace is nothing else but continuation of present system of capitalism. It is war which can bring the end of capitalism and install communism in its place the outcome of First World War was Russian Revolution. Revolution in China was accomplished as a result of Second World War. Third World War is bound to end capitalism and in its place sow the seeds of communism. Therefore, Mao favoured war over peace.

**7. The State.** In the philosophy of Mao state is a means and method for crushing one group by the other. Those who manage to come to power in the state make every effort to crush the opponents. The state should ruthlessly crush those who are working against working classes. Once the communists manage to come to power in the state, they should use their power to end the capitalists. State should be used as a means for crushing the capitalists and anti-communist elements in the state.

**8. Personality Cult.** Mao believed in personality cult. He believed in the worship of one individual, who should be considered above everything else. His words should be accepted as law. In China, Mao had created this position for himself. His words were accepted fully well to China. He was worshipped as God. His ideas about the cultural revolution are on the lips of every Chinese. Every

Chinese considers it his foremost duty to propagate Mao's Idea and not to question them. Due to personality cult Mao's authority is nor being questioned in China.

**9. Neutral States.** According to Mao, there is nothing like neutral state. Every state in the world must follow either capitalist or socialist policies. There can be no third policy. Therefore, Mao did not recognise any neutral state or group of states.

**10. Politicisation of Army.** According to Mao, the army should be thoroughly politicised. It should be made to realise that they are defending a particular cause and they should serve the arm as long as they are capable of defending that.

**11. The Policy of Fight and Talk.** Mao had initiated the policy of fight and talk. The capitalists were at present in a dominant position in the world. They do not like any challenge to their authority. Any challenge is intolerable for them. Therefore, first of all the capitalists should be engaged in war. This can be an open war or guerilla warfare method of it can also be civil war. All that is wanted is that in the war the enemy should be kept fully engaged and exhausted. An effort should be made to bring him on the table for talks, after he has been exhausted. The communist states however, should be very careful that they are not serious in making the talks a success. They should, therefore, put such conditions which are absolutely unacceptable to the capitalists. The talks should be prolonged. In the meanwhile, if need be some minor concessions should also be given to the other party. In the end an atmosphere should be created by which the enemy is alleged to be non-serious in his talks and charged with the breach of peace. This charge should be widely propagated. The world should be convinced about the failure of the enemy to seriously discuss. the problem at the negotiation table. Meanwhile, the time gained in talks should be used for military preparations and suddenly the enemy should be attacked. His territories should be captured and he should be forced to sign on the terms and conditions acceptable to the communist countries.

**12. Development of Politics after Revolution.** Mao spent time on the development of politics after revolution. In the words of Sabine, "Mao, however, is quite explicit about an open ended, ever continuing dialectical. process...Mao's explicit advocacy of a more open ended and flexible understanding of the dialectic is elaborately interwined with his problem of adopting a western theory to the peculiarities of Chinese situation." As a practical solution to post-revolution politics, Mao also gave the concept of 'New Democracy.'

**13. People's War.** According to Mao, imperialism and feudalism go hand in hand. Unless the former was ended in the later it could not come to an end. People were more important than the weapons in winning a war. The people weapons were a decisive factor, people's war was based on the broadest of possible common front of the masses. For power structure in China Mao wanted to establish four power blocs namely those of workers, peasants, petty bourgeoisie and national bourgeoisie. He wanted to have a limited front of masses to fight imperialism. He said that the peasants were capable of bringing revolution independently. The revolution should start from the rural areas before it spreaded out to the cities. Success in revolution must depend on masses, their enthusiasm and creativity. A good leader must come from the masses and struggle for them alone. This leader should take his ideas from the masses. The people should be involved in the task of national regeneration an also in all revolutionary process. Revolution should not aim at merely capturing power but using that for the transformation of society.

**14. Value of Knowledge.** In his history of knowledge Mao laid stress on practice rather than knowledge. He felt that maximum knowledge could be obtained with the help of personal participation in activities rather than their mere knowledge. To quote his own words, "If a man wants to know certain things or certain kinds of things directly, it is only through personal participation in the practical struggle to change reality, to change those things or those kinds of things, that he can come in contract, with the phenomena of things."

**15. Permanent Revolution.** According to Mao, permanent revolution can come only that has roots in the masses. If revolution was to last long it was essential that distinction between the leaders and masses, the government and society and various sections of society should be brought to an end. Mao did not agree with Marx that permanent revolution could be brought only by working classes. Such a revolution could be brought only by working classes in Asian peasantry. A permanent revolution was possible only when all class struggle and class distinctions were removed.

**16. Hundred Flowers Policy.** It was wrong to think that in any society there should be only one ideology or only one state. Mao believed that each thinking was a flower and in China let such hundreds flowers blossom and grow. It is only then that the society will come to know which are rotten and out-dated ideas and that which are fresh and acceptable ideas. Terror should not be used in checking the ideas and not allowing the flowers to blossom and spread their smell.

## CULTURAL REVOLUTION EXPOUNDED BY MAO

Mao launched Grand Proletarian Cultural Revolution in 1966. Masses of Red Guards were organised to propagate this revolution and made to work against well established sectors of Chinese society. Cultural Revolution was planned because Mao was disturbed by growing deviation from his teachings. He, therefore, thought of extensive cultural transformation and political purge. The main targets of Cultural Revolution were handful of party persons in authority who were taking capitalist roads. These people stood against masses of workers, peasants and soldiers. According to Mao, Red Guards were required to completely overthrow them. In the words of Sabine, "The cultural revolution seems designed to preserve Mao's Chinese Marxist Society from being overwhelmed by industrialisation and consequent bureaucratization of life that has characterised the modern West and is increasingly characteristic of Soviet Union as well."

### Aims and Objectives

The main aim of Cultural Revolution was the anxiety of Mao, because the people were deviating from his political ideas. He wanted that the people should accept his philosophy more vigourously and closely. Accordingly there was no denial that the masses were the source of all power and authority in so far as political life was concerned. In the words of Stuart Z. Schram, "In essence Mao's Cultural Revolution aims to go beyond the humbling of the existing bureaucratic and technocratic elite, and to extirpate the very roots of any stratification which might emerge in the future, by destroying respect for special status or the party member or the special knowledge of the expert." The same authority, while discussing the causes of revolution has said, 'It makes clear and explicit Mao's growing anxiety lest the right wing deviations in the party which he had described as widespread in 1955, lead to emergence of full blown revisionist tendencies such as he perceived in the Soviet Union, thereby ultimately jeopardising the very survival of the revolutionary movement to which he had devoted himself for over forty years."

**Main Ideas of Cultural Revolution**

Mao had given the following ideas about Cultural Revolution :

**1. Suicide.** About suicide Mao said that it should be rejected. Man's goal is to seek life and he should not go against the grain of his natural tendency and seek death. One should die fighting only.

**2. Marriage.** About marriage Mao said that under feudal domination marriage is barbaric and inhuman institution. To quote his words, "The whole feudal system of marriage, including power of parent to arrange marriage for their children, to exercise compulsion, and all purchase and sale in marriage contracts shall henceforth be abolished."

**3. Children.** Children are the masters of new society.

**4. Women.** The women of China are vast reserve of labour power.

**5. Cooperatives.** There should be collective production, through cooperatives. Therefore, the Cooperative should be encouraged.

**6. Companion.** The best companion is one, who is politically most important and dependable as well as cooperative."

**7. Feudalism.** Feudalism is the ally of imperialism and bureaucrat capitalism and the foundation of their rule.

**8. Peasants.** Only the poor peasants can and must be the basic force to be relied upon in the land reform.

**9. Agrarian Reform.** The work of agrarian reform should be carried forward by state and in an orderly manner.

**10. Economic Planning.** Blindness and anarchy in the economic field should be gradually eliminated in line with principle of unified planning and of considering the interests of all sections of society.

# 6
# Modern Indian Thought

## M.K. GANDHI

Mohandas Karamchand Gandhi popularly known as Mahatma Gandhi had a very insignificant past but his determination and persistent endeavour made him an encyclopaedic personality. He was born during the period when India's first war of independence had already taken place in the year 1857, and the spirit of renaissance was gradually ushering into the Indian polity. He was born on 2nd October, 1869 at Porbandar in Kathiawar, district of Gujarat. The state of Gujarat had been tremendously influenced by the teachings of Jainism like Truth and Non-violence. His father, Karam Chand Gandhi alias Kaba Gandhi and mother Putlibai were the fortunate parents to give him birth as their youngest son. Having no education at all Kaba Gandhi could manage to be the Prime Minister of Rajkot State for some time. Against this background a brief sketch of Gandhiji's life and contribution is presented below.

**School and College Days**

Gandhiji had his early education at Porbandar. He went to school at the age of seven. He was an average student. After completing his high school education from Kathiawar High School, he joined Samaldas College at Bhavanagar in January, 1888. Being influenced by Kevalram, an eminent lawyer, Gandhiji went to England to read Bar-at-Law. Before going to England he promised before his mother not to take wine, women and beef in England. He went through the Bhagavat Gita amd Arnold's 'Light of Asia' in detail while at London. He completed his Bar-at-Law in 1891, and came back to India.

**Journey to South Africa**

After coming back to India he started his public life as a lawyer but in the initial stage he was having a low profile. But gradually he became prominent when an offer was given to him by Mr. Abdullah, a rich Gujarati merchant. Mr. Abdullah requested him to go to South Africa to fight his case. Accordingly in 1893, he left for South Africa as the legal representative of Mr. Abdullah. South Africa changed the course of Gandhiji's life. He stayed there for 20 years. During his stay at South Africa he made a deep study of the socio-economic conditions of the Indians there. He was deeply shocked to see the inhuman treatment meted out to the Indians in South Africa. Indians had become the victim of the practice of apartheid in South Africa. Gandhiji was no exception to it. He was not allowed to travel in the first class compartment though he had purchased the ticket for the same. Because he was an Indian, he was branded as 'Coolie lawyer' and was thrown out of the compartment at Maritzburg while travelling in the train. This unfortunate incident at Maritzburg gave birth to a new Gandhi. He revolted within and promised to fight injustice inflicted on the Indians. He called a meeting of the Indians who lived in Pretoria. Gandhi made his maiden public speech in this meeting. In his speech he made an appeal to the Indian merchants to be truthful and save the prestige of millions of Indians. He launched Satyagraha a number of times from 1904 to 1914, in South Africa to give equal social and political rights to the Indians and to fight against the practice of apartheid. On the other hand Indians at South Africa were overwhelmed with Gandhiji's pesonality and looked to him for leadership. Gandhiji initiated the formation of a political party in South Africa. Accordingly the Natal Indian Congress was formed to organise the Indians living there. He inculcated in them the mantra of Ahimsa and self-sacrifice to achieve their rights of being a human first.

**Entry into Indian Politics**

In 1915, Gandhiji came back to India as a liberating force to emancipate the millions of Indians from the British rule. When he entered into the Indian Politics, the Indian National Congress was in a state of anarchy. It was ridden with the crisis of conflict between moderates and the extremists. It was also lacking in popular base.

Gandhiji's moral principles and charismatic personality could ride out all the crises in the National Congress and a new era heralded in Indian politics. After coming to India he first established his Ashram at Sabarmati in Ahmedabad in 1915. Sabarmati Ashram became the center of religious, social and political activities at a later period. His mission became to fight for the cause of the downtroddens and liberation of the masses from oppression and exploitation. He launched Satyagraha at Champaran in Bihar in 1917, to fight against exploitation and to give justice to indigo farmers.

Being influenced by Gopal Krishna Gokhale, the leader of the moderate group in the Indian National Congress. Gandhiji started his career as a moderate political leader in India. He extended co-operation to the British Government in Britain's war effort because at that time he had great faith in the love of the English people. But the Rowlatt Act, the Punjab disorder and the Khilafat Agitation completely bruised his faith. Especially the inhuman tragedy of Jallianwala Bagh caused by Sir Michael O'Dwyer and the British support for the same made Gandhi distrustful of British words and deeds.

**Role in the Non-Cooperation Movement**

In 1920, Calcutta session, be gave the first clarion call to organise a Non-cooperation movement against the Britishers. With this movement, there started a new era in India's freedom struggle in general and Congress in particular. He offered a practical alternative to the futility of verbal violence and the sacrificial folly of political crime. With his voluntary poverty, simplicity, humility and saintliness, Gandhiji struck some of the inner chords of Indian Humanity. His appeal for courage and sacrifice evoked a ready response because he was himself the epitome of these qualities. It was because he was simple and truthful and his life was one of austerity and self-sacrifice that a great emotional bond grew between him and the Indian people. Gandhiji was arrested by the Government and became a crusader against the british rule in India. But due to violence in Chauri-Chaura near Gorakhpur of Uttar Pradesh, he suspended the movement. He was severely criticised by other leaders like C.R. Das, Motilal Nehru, Subhas Chandra Bose, Jawaharlal Nehru for suspending the movement. But Gandhiji justified his action. Because for Gandhiji, non-violence was the first article of his faith. After being released from jail, he started his work on social reform.

**Role in Civil Disobedience Movement**

In 1924, he was elected President of the Indian National Congress. The Indian National Congress decided to launch the Civil Disobedience Movement in 1930, under the leadership of Gandhiji. Gandhiji himself led a Satyagraha to the sea shore at Dandi of Gujarat and violated Salt-laws. Gandhi was again arrested on 5th May, 1930. Congress was declared illegel. No doubt the movement was postponed after Gandhi-Irwin Pact in February, 1931, but this movement scored historic success. For the first time, this movement became a 'mass movement'. Because of the fight against salt-laws, poor peasants could be benefited.

**Role in the Quit India Movement**

The last manifestation of Gandhiji's charismatic leadership came in 1942, 'Quit India Movement'. Gandhiji's clarion call, 'do or die' worked as a miracle during the movement. No doubt the British government could suppress the movement but ultimately surrendered to the people of India. 'The Cabinet Mission' came to India with a proposal to constitute the constituent assembly and the constitution was framed. Finally, Lord Mountbatten came with a dubious objective of transferring power to India with an aim to divide the people. On 15th August, 1947, India became Independent.

**Partition of India and Gandhiji's Assassination**

Though Gandhiji was reluctant to agree to the partition of India, he was helpless and could not prevent the partition. After 1946, Gandhiji was the most 'neglected leader' who was undermined by his so-called power hankering followers. No longer they were Gandhiji's men. But the tragic part of Gandhiji's life came when he was most misunderstood for his pressure on the Government of India to give Rs. 55/- crore to Pakistan on account of division of defence store. Because this came at a time when Pakistan had been confiscating the property of Hindu people and Hindus became destitute refugees. This created serious resentment among a section of Hindu fanatics. But the entire nation had to pay the price when Gandhiji was assassinated by a Hindu fanatic, Nathu Ram Godse, on 30th January, 1948. The symbol of India's truth, non-violence, unity and integrity perished into thin air for ever, never to return again.

## VIEWS ON END-MEANS RELATIONSHIP

Gandhiji introduced a new era in Indian politics. With an objective of spiritualising politices, he conceived of a strong link between religion and politics. Because he always emphasized his principle that means justifies the end. He completely rejected the doctrine that end justifies the means. If the end is achieved by unfair means, it will not yield a permanent result. It will be like "ill got ill spent". Gandhi compared "the means to a seed, the end to a tree and there is just the same inviolable connection between the means and the end as there is between the seed and the tree". He strongly believed that "if one takes care of the means, the end will take care of itself". Since Gandhiji believed in the moral pursuit and achievement of man, he always interlinked the means and the end.

### Application of 'Means and End' Principle

Gandhiji not only talked about the moral means but also was committed to it during his life time. During the freedom movement of India he never conceived of attaining 'Swaraj' by any means. He always emphasized that India should win its freedom by means of truth and non-violence. By means of violence and falsehood one man bring victory but that victory will never be permanent. Because violence begets violence and the process continues for ever. Hence, Gandhiji decided to suspend the non-cooperation movement due to violent methods adopted by the Satyagrahis at Chauri-Chaura. He said, "it is true we can not rise till our political condition is reformed. But it is not true that we shall be able to progress if our political condition undergoes a change by any means and in any manner. . .Only a change brought about by pure means, that is by peaceful and legitimate means, can lead us to real progress". As a firm believer in the path of just and moral means, he never tried to take advantage of the weakness of his opponents. When the Boer war broke out in 1899, he was convinced that the Indians who claimed rights of citizenship were morally bound to help the government. He therefore, offered his help and that of the Indian community to the Natal Government in spite of their just grievances against it.

**Spiritualisation of Politics**

Gandhiji's doctrine of means justifying the end was manifested not only during period of our freedom struggle but also in its application in India's internal politics. He was the first political leader of Modern India who made a serious attempt to spiritualise politics and establish an organic link between religion and politics. But by 'spiritualisation' or 'religion' he did not mean any religious dogmas or fundamentalism. What he implied was the 'synthesis' of the values in all the religions. It is the 'rock-bottom' of fundamental morality. For Gandhi religion did not consist in worshipping God or reading a religious book; it encompasses all human activities. Religious life means identification with mankind. He regarded religion as self-realisation, suffering and sacrifice. On the other hand, he challenged the traditional view of politics, power and the difference between public and private morality. He never believed in the Machiavellian sense of 'politics as an art of capturing power'. 'Politics and Power' must aim at social reform and service to mankind. In this sense politics becomes as essential as religion. Gandhiji believed 'politics today encircles us like the coils of a snake from which one cannot get out, no matter how one tries, the only way of wrestling with the snake is to introduce religion into politics'. If politics is divorced from religion, it is like a corpse, fit only for burning. Thus, religious value can guide the political actions in the right direction. But Gandhiji totally descarded the idea of 'state religion' or 'subordination of politics to religion'.

**Value of Politics for Religious Man**

Just as Gandhiji attempted to make politics religious, he also tried to make religion practically relevant for the society. He thought that the saint and the revolutionary are not incompatible. The saint must not become an escapist who refuses to act and renunciates the society; the revolutionary should not be an opportunist who is ready to sacrifice principles. The true saint must be effective in society while the true revolutionary must possess the deepest integrity. According to him, just as religious values could purify politics,

politics could play a positive role in spiritual perfection of an individual. Through politics, Gandhi agreed with Budha that one can serve the suffering humanity and purify himself. He brought into lime light the path of Karmayoga, or spiritual realisation through social action.

Thus, Gandhiji while emphasizing the importance of 'means' over 'ends' made on attempt to 'spiritualise politics' and establish a correlation between religion and politics. Every action of the individual is based on the single objective of achieving perfect result whether that is spiritual, economic, social or political.

## CONCEPT OF NON-VIOLENCE

In the history of mankind, Gandhiji has been the true champion of truth and non-violence. Brute force has been the ruling factor in the world for thousands of years and mankind has been reaping its bitter harvest all along. So Gandhiji called upon the people to eschew violence. According to Gandhiji, non-violence is the only universal character that distinguishes the man from the rest of God's creation. Non-violence as a concept did not belong to Gandhi originally. The only thing that he did was to expand the idea of non-violence and apply the same in his mission of life.

### Source of Influence

In spearheading the cause of non-violence, Gandhiji was influenced by his own parents who were followers of Jainism and Buddhism. In no other part of India was the hold of Jainism on the life of the people greater than in Gujarat where Gandhiji was born and brought up. Gandhiji was also influenced by a British scholar Sir Henry David Thoreau's book *'Essays on Civil Disobedience'*. He also read Tolstoy's *'The Kingdom of God is Within You'* at a time when he was passing through the crisis of scepticism and said 'its reading cured me of my scepticism and made me a firm believe in AMIMSA.'

### Meaning and Implications of Non-violence

Gandhiji considered Ahimsa (Non-violence) as the supreme religious duty of every man. Any body having kindness, within himself must believe in non-violence. Non-violence is the means of achieving the end *i.e.*, truth. It refers to both physical and mental non-violence. Physical non-violence, means one should not hurt or attack or kill any wrong doer. Nor should one mentally harbour something bad against others. This is however, a negative meaning of non-violence. Positively it means one must have love, sympathy, compassion even for his opponent. Secondly, Gandhiji believed that non-violence is a weapon of the strong and not of weak. Those who apply non-violence are men with indomitable courage and strenght. One must face danger without causing any injury come what may. "Non-violence is not cowardice, Gandhiji said, where there is a choice between cowardice and violence. I would advise violence. . . . I would rather have India resort to arms in order to defend her honour than that she should in a cowardly manner become or remain witness to her own dishonour".

**How to Practice Non-violence**

But how non-violence can be applied by men. Gandhiji suggested the following methods to apply non-violence:

**(a) Fearless Self-suffering.** Gandhiji strongly believed that a votary of non-violence must be utterly selfless, altruistic and completely fearless. Because non-violent man undergoes conscious suffering as he has to suffer physical and mental injury caused to him by the evil doer. The main objective of non-violence should be to convert the enemy into friends. Non-violence is undoubtedly superior to violence. Strength does not come from physical capacity. It comes from an indomitable courage. Self-sacrifice of the innocent man is a million times more potent than the sacrifice of a million men who die in the act of killing.

**(b) Truthfulness.** Non-violence claims the practitioner to become truthful. Truth means there should not be any dishonesty of purpose. Truth is eternal. Gandhiji wanted to prove his strong faith in truth and accordingly postponed non-cooperation movement against the Britishers when the movement became violent. Because he believed truth to be more valuable than victory. Victory without truth becomes violent and temporary.

(c) **Persuasion.** Persuasion is another way of approaching the enemy through non-violence. Gandhiji believed that an evil doer if persuaded properly can change his mind from violence to non-violence. But one must understand and appreciate the cause of his enemy.

(d) **Self-Control and Fasting.** Gandhiji suggested that non-violence is possible only when one has self-control, patience and tolerance. For self-control Gandhiji advised fasting. Fasting makes the body and mind cool and disciplined. By way of self-control one can have patience to tolerate and understand the cause of his enemy.

(e) **Love and Compassion.** Lastly, he suggested the votaries of non-violence to develop love and sympathy for others. One should be sympathetic towards the ignorance of his enemy. One should love his enemy but denounce his action. Gandhiji said, 'we never fought against the Britishers but we were fighting against British rule in India'.

Gandhiji advised the path of non-violence not only for the individuals but also for the nations and the people in general. It is high time that nations give up violence and mad race for arms, which is bound to result in a slaughter house as has never occurred in history. Gandhiji said 'there is no escape from the impending doom except a bold and unconditional acceptance of the non-violent method with all its glorious implications'. Gandhiji's prophecy of non-violence became a guiding principle for all generations to establish the kingdom of peace and love.

**Concept of Satyagraha**

Satyagraha as a doctrine and a weapon undoubtedly rose into prominence due to the untiring effort of Mahatma Gandhi. But it was in practice prior to Gandhi in both Asia and Europe. Satyagraha at that time was in the form of 'passive resistance'. Right to resist injustice even offered by the king was enunciated in the mythical characters of Bamadeva and Bhisma in the Mahabharata. In modern India the doctrine of passive resistance was expounded chiefly by Aurobindo Ghosh as a political technique rather than a spiritual therapy. However, the term 'satyagraha' was coined by Gandhi in 1906, in place of 'passive resistance' which he thought was a foreign expression. Secondly, the use of the word 'passive resistance' did not connote the whole idea which Gandhiji wished to connote. Accordingly he used the word 'Satyagraha' which means the combination of truth (*satya*) and firmness (*agraha*) and serves as a synonym for force. However, Gandhiji has been influenced by many sources like Tolstoy, Bhagvad Gita, and Henry David Thoreau.

**Techniques of Satyagraha**

Satyagraha as a technique of redressing social and political injustice was first experimented by Gandhi in South Africa with a commendable success. It was then applied successfully in India's freedom struggle quite unique in human history. Gandhiji suggested different methods of staging Satyagraha. The methods of Satyagraha may be divided into different categories like purifying or penitential devices, method of non-cooperation, methods of civil disobedience, and the constructive programme. All these techniques may be adopted by individual, group or mass movements in the political arena as well as in different spheres of social life. Such techniques are discussed below.

**Purification.** The purifying method in a specific context will be determined by the rightness of purpose, degree and genuineness of non-violence displayed by the Satyagrahi. While judging the purity of the action of a Satyagrahi his character must be taken into account. A Satyagrahi should always under go self-examination. Under purifying and penitential techniques we may include the following instruments:

*(a)* ***The Pledge.*** It is a public declaration of a Satyagrahi 'that he or they will abstain from or perform certain acts to fight untruth or injustice'. It implies their sense of determination to be a crusader for truth and justice.

*(b)* ***Prayer.*** It is on doubt a religious act of generating 'soul force' but it may be secularised so as to mean one's determination to discover the general will or common good. Satyagrahi through prayer develops his quality of other regardingness.

(c) ***Fasting.*** It may be adopted for self-purification and as a means of resisting injustice and making the evil doer to realise his mistake. In other words through fasting the Satyagrahi sends a message to the evil doer to admit his wrong and rectify himself. Gandhiji used it in the form of a science and warned that the technique should be used with extreme caution. It must be used only on rare occasion and by those who are skilled in the art of fasting. Fasting requires a high degree of purity, self-discipline, humility and faith. The man who launches fast should have spiritual fitness and a clean vision.

**Non-cooperation.** Non-cooperation is a non-violent technique of resisting the illegal authority or order or any person of exploiting nature. Gandhiji argued so long one cooperates he is oppressed and exploited; if people cease completely to cooperate with an unjust or tyrannical system, it will ultimately collapse. "Even the most despotic government" Gandhiji said, "...cannot stand except with the consent of the governed which is procured forcibly by the despot". This is true for the government as well as to those who exploit. Through non-cooperation with the evil the Satyagrahi purifies himself and withdraws his part of co-operation from the inhuman and unrighteous evil doers. Non-cooperation emphasises the purity of means, purity of ends, purity of motives and intentions. The methods of non-cooperation include hartal, boycott, strike fast unto death and hijrat which are discussed below:

***(a) Hartal.*** It is temporary strike with advance notice as to its duration, the closing down of shop and business and sometimes the halting of the work of administration. It is a traditional form of protest in India. Hartal according to Gandhiji strikes the imagination of the people and the government.

***(b) Boycott.*** It is a means to protest against or paralyse an unjust political system. It may be applied to an institution involved in corrupt or unfairly discriminatory practices. Boycott may be economically intended to keep out foreign goods where their presence create unemployment or destroy local industries.

***(c) Strike.*** It is a weapon of the labourers for the redress of their legitimate grievances. Gandhiji's concept of strike is different from western concept. Unlike west, he suggested, strike should be directed against corruption, injustice, inefficiency and not to eliminate the 'capitalist' or simply seize power. The Satyagrahi should adopt strike in a non-violent way. It should not be imposed and no one should be compelled to join the strike. It is voluntary purificatory suffering undertaken to convert the erring opponent. But the demands of the strike according to Gandhi, must be clear, feasible and justified. It should not be emotional or sporadic.

***(d) Hijrat.*** It means voluntary exile or temporary withdrawal from the place where one cannot live with self-respect. This method was advised by Gandhi to the Bardoli peasants in 1928.

***(e) Fast unto Death.*** It is the last weapon to be applied by a Satyagrahi for self-purification and changing the attitude of the evil doers.

**Civil Disobedience as a Technique of Satyagraha**

Gandhiji defines civil disobedience as "the breach of unmoral statutory enactment". It implies the people's protest in a civil manner. His emphasis is on 'civil'. So that disobedience will not be violent. It should not be launched in a atmosphere of evil and hatred. Like fasting it should be practised by a select few in the first instance. Hence, for civil disobedience, there should be leader of the Satyagrahis. The method of civil disobedience includes picketing which means to prevent the entry of persons into the picketed place; marches, non-payment of taxes and deliberate definance of law. Civil disobedience is a complete, effective and bloodless substitute for armed revolt. But civil disobedience should not lead to outbreak of violence or lawlessness.

**Constructive Programmes**

Gandhiji came to emphasize constructive programme in the mid-twenties. According to him, constructive programme is the most novel mode of Satyagraha and Satyagrahis should engage in silent, active, constructive work of reform and social service. He believed that simply taking over the political power would not carry any meaning. Every Satyagrahi must spend his energy for constructive programme to rebuild the society and promote common good.

**How to Meet External Aggression through Satyagraha**

In case of external attack or war, Gandhiji said, there are two ways like allowing the aggressor to take possession but not to co-operate with the aggressor. People will prefer death rather than submitting themselves to the aggressor. Secondly, non-violent resistance will start against the aggressor. During the invasion the technique could consist to non-violent resistance upto death.

## CONCEPT OF FUNDAMENTAL RIGHTS AND DUTIES

Gandhiji was a true democrat. He was not only concerned with transfer of power from Britishers but also to create a system in which every man and woman will have the opportunities to improve their conditions. There should not be domination of any group or institution and complete decentralisation of power should be adopted. Appropriately he emphasized fundamental rights for the people which will not only ensure true swaraj for all but also guarantee a living condition for the people. Gandhiji himself moved a resolution on fundamental rights in 1931, Karachi session of the Indian National Congress. The resolution read "this congress is of the opinion that to enable the masses to appreciate what Swarajya is, it is desirable to state the position of the Congress in a manner easily understood by them. In order to end the exploitation of the masses, political freedom must include real economic freedom of the starving millions. . . ." From this resolution it was explicit that like Marx, Gandhiji also emphasized 'economic rights' of the people. He always stressed on work for the workless, 'Freedom from want' which were the basic elements of his economic theory. His views on fundamental rights are also based on secular foundations. However, Gandhiji suggested a number of rights which can be categorised as civil, economic and political rights.

**Civil Rights.** Gandhiji suggested a number of fundamental rights highly essential for the life of a civilised men. These rights also ensure social justice in India. Such rights include the following:

(a) Equal rights for all citizens without any bar on the ground of sex.

(b) Equal rights to all in regard to public roads, walls, schools etc.

(c) Freedom of speech.

(d) Freedom of conscience and practice of religion.

(e) Free primary education.

**Economic.** Gandhiji, as mentioned earlier in this context emphasized economic freedom of the people. With regard to economic betterment of the people the suggested different economic rights such as a living wage for industrial workers, limited hours of labour, Protection against the economic consequence of unemployment, labour to be free from serfdom, protection of women workers, provision against employment of school going children in factories, and control by the state of key industries.

**Political.** Gandhiji had strong faith in democracy and fought for 'right to rule' to be enjoyed by all. So he highlighted political freedom of the people which includes: *(a)* right to self-rule, *(b)* freedom of press, *(c)* equal rights to all for any office of power, *(d)* right of labourers to form union.

From the above discussion it is clear that Gandhiji was a socialist of first order and a committed democrat. His emphasis on economic freedom depicts his strong faith in an egalitarian social order. He strongly advocated to bridge the gap between the rich and the poor.

## CONCEPT OF STATE

Like the 'christian fathers' (except for Aquinas) and the ancient Hindus, Gandhiji looked upon the state as originating in the sins of man. But there was a difference between them. The ancient Hindus and Christian fathers because of their assumption of the "natural wickedness of man", recognised the necessity and value of the state and gave the state a place of repectability by entrusting it with the maintenance of law and order. But Gandhiji had tremendous faith in the infinite capacity of human nature to improve upon itself. Individual need not depend upon the state. In this way Gandhiji was a philosophical anarchist who conceived a 'stateless idealist society based on truth and non-violence. No doubt Gandhiji and Marx toed the same line of thought *i.e.*, 'stateless society', but with a difference. Marx envisaged a 'stateless' society but advocated a 'transitional all powerful state' with dictatorship of the proletariat who will be instrumental in establishing a classless' and 'stateless' society. But Gandhiji admitted the existence of a transitional state with limited power and society would be 'state less' gradually with the moral and spiritual development of the people.

**Repudiation of the State Authority: A Philosophical Anarchist**

Gandhiji, like Tolstoy was opposed to the existence of state based on immorality and violence. He argued that the existing state commands and whatever is commanded cannot respect the moral value of the individual's action. Because an action is moral only when it is voluntary. He also rejected the existing state whose authority is based on force and violence. 'The state represents', he said "violence in a concentrated and organised form. The individual has a soul, but the state is a soulless machine, it can never be weaned from violence to which it owes its very existences." The coercive authority of the state is antidote to the growth of individual's freedom and personality. Accordingly Gandhiji drew the sketch of a new 'Ideal society' in which there will be freedom, spontaneity of action, truth and non-violence. It will be a society free from oppression and exploitation as people have an abiding faith in God. Every social activity will be based on love, service and co-operation. Gandhiji hance, stated "to me political power is not an end but one of the means of enabling the people to better their condition in every department of life. Political power means capacity to regulate national life through national representatives. If national life becomes so perfect as to become self-regulated, no representation is necessary. There is thus, a state of enlightened anarchy. In such a state, everyone is his own ruler. He rules himself in such a manner that he is never a hindrance to his neighbour. In the ideal state, therefore, there is no political power, because there is no state." Like any other anarchist, Gandhiji also highlighted, 'individual freedom' and 'total democracy'. Appropriately he suggested that his ideal democracy, both stateless and classlless, will consist of a number of self-contained and self-regulated village communites. 'Panchayat' constituting of villages will be organised and work as a 'republic' having full powers even to meet foreign attack in a non-violent way. The self-sufficient villages shall be bound together in a voluntary federation. But individual will be the 'units' of this federation and not the provinces. Life will be simple; the civilisation will be rural, a federation will be free from 'centralisation', which connotes force and is inconsistent with the non-violent structure of society. Voluntary cooperation of the individuals is the condition of dignified and peaceful co-existence.

**Idea of a Non-violent State**

But like other anarchists such as Michael Bakunin and Kropotkin, Gandhiji never believed that the state will be abolished overnight by revolution. Gandhiji admitted that the idea of a classless and stateless non-violent society was unrealizable as "a government cannot succeed in becoming entirely non-violent because it represents all the people. I do not today conceive of such a golden age. But I do believe in the possibility of a predominantly non-violent society and I am working for it". Gandhiji suggested to make the existing state non-violent as far as possible. The nature of non-violent state will depend upon how the political power has been achieved. If it is achieved by the non-violent Satyagraha of the weak, the emerging state will be democratic. But exploitation will still continue, "because it is only by non-violent Satyagraha of the brave the resulting state can be a 'total democracy' minimising exploitation and coercion. The real purpose of democracy, Gandhiji argued, 'is that under it the weakest should have the same opportunity as the strongest. This can never happen except through non-violence. Secondly, Gandhiji discarded the idea of an all-powerful state. Rather the state should be a means for the promotion of human welfare. "it is better", Gandhiji said, "the state should be limited to minimum functions". Like Thoreau, he also believed, "that government is best which governs the least". Thirdly, interference of the Government should be minimum so that people can enjoy their freedom to the maximum. Most of the functions should be transferred to the voluntary associations so that a real self-government could be established in the country. He was in the same line of thought as the guild socialists like G.D.H. Cole, Gandhiji laid emphasis on democracy in the villages where life was simpler, power diffused and the economy decentralised. Consuming only what they produced themselves, the villagers would be self-sufficient. Fourthly, he advocated for more "autonomy to the rural communities in the state and those rural areas having self-sufficiency in matter of basic needs, should be given power for the administration of peace and justice". Fifthly, Gandhiji said that the existing system of direct election should be replaced by indirect election because direct election led to many evils like, corruption, manipulation etc. So he suggested that the Panchayats should be organised to run the village administration. Each village will have one vote to elect district administration; each district administration will elect provincial administration and each provincial administration a parliament on president. But the candidates in such election should be man of dedication and should not be after office. Canvassing for votes should not be allowed. Voters should be left to themselves to judge. Sixthly, Gandhiji while advocating for a pre-dominantly non-violent state did not rule out the need for 'police force' because in such a state also there may be anti-socials to create violence and break the law. But the police should be 'reform oriented' and should behave like servants rather than masters. Finally, the non-violent state need not go for a 'armed force' to save the country. Rather it will have an army consisting of 'true Satyagrahis' who resist the aggressors even at the cost of their life.

No doubt, Gandhiji's views on state and government reflected his 'anarchist ideals' but unlike other anarchists, he was both a visionary and realist. Describing Gandhiji as a 'Philosophical anarchist' totally will be a mistake. Because he had admitted the existence of the state for a short period.

## GANDHISM AND COMMUNISM

**Gandhism and Communism.** A close study of Gandhian philosophy is bound to reveal that Gandhism and Communism agree on some basic principles. For Example, both Gandhiji and Karl Marx wanted to have a classless society in which there would be no distinction between the rich and the poor and everyone would be appreciated by the qualities which he possessed. For them both class consciousness had created a rift in the society and thus, resulted in exploitation of the poor by the rich. Similarly both believed that state was based on violence and in its present form it had no justification to exist. Both even went to the extent of saying that state was an evil institution though Karl Marx went a step further by saying that ultimately it would wither away. Not only this, but both had identical views about capital, For them both capital was a theft and a few in the society had no right whatever to hold money with them and thus, deny its use for collective national welfare. For them both capital should be used for social welfare and those who possessed wealth, should be obliged to part with that. They should deem themselves as the trustees of wealth.

Karl Marx and Gandhiji both had very soft corner for the downtrodden and the people belonging to weaker sections of the society. Karl Marx used to say that history is witness that hitherto existing struggle in which the labourers and the poor are being constantly exploited by the rich who control the means of production, is class struggle. He, therefore, gave the slogan that workers of the world should unite and it was in that unity alone that the depressed classes would come up and have their rightful place in society. Similarly Gandhiji also had a very soft corner for the down-trodden and low castes in the society. According to him the so called scheduled castes are a part of our society. He lived and worked among them and for them. Through his *Harijan* he tried to vigorously plead their cause and saw that in all walks of life they were given due representation. Similarly both believed in the concept of social equality meaning theredy that all should be given equal opportunities for getting justice and the doors of law courts should not be closed on any particular class simply because that could not afford to purchase justice. He thus, stood to preach with Marx that there should be political and economic equality.

**Differences between Gandhism and Communism.** No doubt there is some similarity between Gandhism and Communism but there is vast difference between the two. Gandhiji made it amply clear when he wrote in, 'Young India' on December 11, 1924, "I do not believe in short violent cuts to success....I am an uncompromising opponent of violent methods even to serve the noblest of causes. There is, therefore, really no meeting ground between the school of violence and myself." At another place he expressed more or less similar views when he said that, "Whilst I have the greatest admiration for the self-denial and spirit of sacrifice of our socialist friends. I have never concealed the sharp difference between their method and mine. They frankly believe in violence and all that is in its bosom. I believe in non-violence through and through."

Gandhiji had deep faith in religion and believed that politics wihout religion was barren and both should go side by side. It is religion which brings life to politics. On the other hand Marx believed that religion had no place in politics and both should be separated from each other. For him religion was opium for the people and a method for making the people fatalist. He felt that it was a method through which the capitalists tried to content the poor and as such he discarded religion altogether.

Similarly we find that Gandhiji had faith in the existence of God which for him was a mysterious force but all-powerful and guiding our affairs. On the other hand, Marx did not believe at all in the existence of God and for him man was the architect of his own fate and there was no heavenly or super-human power to guide the destiny of mankind.

Again we find that whereas Gandhian political philosophy is based on spiritualism, Marxism is based on materalism. For Marx man is only means to an end whereas for Gandhiji he is an end in itself. Gandhiji had very high consideration for man. Whereas Gandhiji attaches too much importance to man and has high regard's for him, Marx has no such opinion about man. As already said, for him man is only means to an end and not an end in itself. Both, therefore, have altogether different approaches to problems of individual liberty.

For Marx state was above everything else whereas for Gandhiji it stood for realization of man's personality only. We also find that Marx stood to take the fullest advantages of discoveries and inventions of science. He, therefore, pleaded that there should be dependence on large-scale industrialization. On the other hand Gandhiji pleaded for decentralization and believed that there should be the system of cottage industries and modern large scale industry system should exist only in a transitionary stage till man is ready to discard this. He said, "I am not opposed to the progress of science as such. On the contrary, scientific spirit of the West commands my admiration, and if that admiration is qualified, it is because scientists of the West takes no note of God and its lower creation.....I detest the unpardonable slaughter of innocent life in the name of science and humanity so called, and all the scientific discoveries stained with innocent blood I count as of no consequence." He considered that men were living machines and that the cottage industries would help people in easing their economic and social conditions. A factory which provided employment only to a few hundred people rendered thousands out of employment. In his Harijan he wrote on September 14, 1935, "Dead machinery must not be pitted against the millions of living machines represented by the villagers scattered in seven hundred thousand villages of India....The present use of machinery tends more and more to concentrate wealth in the hands of a few in total disregard of millions of men and women whose bread is snatched by it out of their mouths."

Gandhiji believed in rightful means for having lasting and durable ends. For him, proper means are necessary for achieving proper ends. If the means are not good, ends can not be good. He said, "for me, it is enough to know the means. Means and ends are convertible terms in my philosophy of life." He, therefore, stressed on means saying that if proper means are followed, ends will autmatically be achieved. Defining the significance of means and their importance in actual life, Gandhiji wrote in Harijan on February 28, 1937, "They say, means are after all means; I would say, means are after all everything. As the means so the ends, violent means will give violent Swaraj." On the other hand, Marx does not believe in this idea. For him, ends justify the means and therefore, our aim should be to achieve ends, no matter whether means for achieving those ends are right or wrong.

For Gandhiji one should hate the evil and not the evil-doer, because evil-doer is always product of evil and unhealthy social system. He, therefore, believes that it is capital and not the capitalist which should be hated. He very clearly said, "For me the fight is never with individuals, it is ever with their manners and their measures." On the other hand Marx believes that both the evil and evil-doer should be hated. He, therefore, hates both the capital and the capitalist.

Gandhiji was a very strong and ardent believer of non-violence. For him, one should be non-violent both in thought, speech and action. For him, even if the property earned by a particular individual was to be snatched that should be done by persuasion alone and not by force. In unmistakable and clear terms he said that, "Ahimsa is a weapon of matchless potency...It is an attribute of the brave, in fact it is their all. It does not come within the reach of the coward." On the other hand, Marx believed that there was no harm in using violence for achieving the ends. No doubt he suggested that violence should not be used as a primary methods for securing the ends but for all practical purposes he felt that unless force was used neither capitalist order nor evil institutions could come to an end. Marx, therefore, stressed on violence rather than non-violence.

Gandhian philosophy does not believe in embarrassing the opponent and what Gandhiji always intended was that the opponent should be made to realise his mistake. On the other hand, Marx believed that the enemy should be put in a most embarrassing position so that he was obliged to agree to the demands put to him.

Gandhism thus, is not Communism minus violence but something beyond that. Both prima facie agree on certain principles but as they proceed the differences also widen up. Vinoba Bhave has said that, "If Communism is a solid and imposing structure of granite. Gandhism is an ever changing amoeba." Significantly Gandhiji himself pointed out another difference which should sum-up the study of this topic. He said, "Moreover, they seem to take their instructions from Russia, whom they regard as their spiritual home rather than India. I cannot countenance this dependence on an outside power."

## CONCEPT OF SWARAJ (SELF-RULE)

The concept of swaraj is not a totally new doctrine originating from Gandhiji's idea. In the earlier Indian political thought, the concept of Swaraj or self-rule connected with the nation of 'Swarajya' referred to a particular mode of securing self-determination for all sections of the society. But in modern India, Dadabhai Naoroji and Tilak gave negative concept of swaraj implying 'national independence' only. Gandhiji restored the older meaning of 'Swaraj'. His concept of Swaraj offers guidance in transforming what he called the 'nominal' democracy of the modern western type into a truer or fuller democracy, which he referred as to Purna Swaraj (complete or integral democracy).

**Meaning and Implication of Swaraj**

Gandhiji gave a positive concept of 'swaraj'. Swaraj means self-rule. It means 'not to allow any outside power in the world to exercise control over oneself and not to exercise power over any other. These two things together make swaraj no submission and no exploitation. Thus, swaraj has 'nationalist' as well individualist implications but leads to international and social responsibilities. For a nations Swaraj means, as mentioned above, freedom from foreign rule and in that sense Gandhiji also finally demanded the exit of Britishers from India. A free nation, in Gandhiji's opinion, can not be selfish and need not be an isolationist. Gandhiji was both a nationalist and internationalist. So he said Indian nationalism must organise itself for the benefit and service of humanity.

Another implication of Swaraj as mentioned above, is 'self-rule' for the individual. It is equated with 'freedom to choose' and 'freedom to decide'. Without individual freedom, national freedom becomes meaningless. He declared that the 'Swaraj of people means the sum total of the Swaraj (self-rule) of each individual'. It means real participatory democracy should be established where every individual must be in a position to rule himself (politically and economically) and participate in the functioning of the political system. Appropriately he said, 'Swaraj for me means freedom for the meanest of my country men. I am not interested in freeing India merely from English yoke. I am bent upon freeing India from any yoke whatsoever". In real swaraj it is not acquisition of authority by a few, but the acquisition of the capacity by all to resist authority when it is abused. He rightly argued, true democracy can not be worked out by twenty men sitting at the centre. It has to be worked out from below by the people of every village. Thought there will be a central government, it should not be on western model of democracy. The state should be there to carry out the will of the people and not to dictate them or force them to do according to its will. Democracy should not be converted to mobocracy. Democracy is an impossible thing until the power is shared by all. Hence, he made it clear that democracy should not be identified with the rule of majority. Swaraj will be an absurdity if individuals have to surrender their judgement to majority. Therefore, Gandhiji said, Swaraj should provide equal opportunity to all to express themselves and in which none suffers under forced opinion. Under it, there is no recognition of any separate race, caste or religion. Hence, he said swaraj of my dream is the poor man's swaraj. The necessaries of life should be enjoyed by all in common with those enjoyed by the princes and moneyed people.

**Means of Achieving Swaraj**

But how to achieve swaraj and maintain it? Gandhiji very strongly believed that swaraj can be achieved by the application of truth, non-violence and satyagraha. Swaraj achieved by a non-violence satyagraha can bring 'permanent freedom' for a country. But after the attainment of swaraj a country should develop a 'true democratic polity' in which every individual is capable of resisting the absolute authority and ventilate his views freely. There should be decentralisation of power and authority. As mentioned earlier, Gandhiji, no doubt recognised the need for a central government but he said it should be structured not as a pyramid but as an oceanic circle. To quote him, "In this structure composed of innumerable villages, there will be ever-widening never ascending circles. Life will not be a pyramid with the apex sustained by the bottom. But it will be an oceanic circle whose centre will be individual always, ready to perish for the village, the later ready to perish fot the circle of village, till at last the whole becomes one life composed of individuals, never aggressive in their arrogance but ever humble, sharing the majority of the oceanic circle of which they are integral units." Besides this structural suggestion, Gandhiji also suggested that Swaraj can be achieved by 'moral autonomy' which demands 'self-purification'. Because it enables the individual to claim individual rights on moral ground. Such claims are more effective in politics and society. Swaraj also depends upon the 'self-discipline of the individuals, and self-control. There should be 'mass participation' of the people who can bring mass movement and can educate the people politically. Gandhiji, hence, rightly said, "Purna Swaraj denotes a condition of things when the dumb and lame millions will speak and walk. That swaraj cannot be achieved by force but by organisation and unity".

**Concept of Swadeshi**

Swadeshi implies self-reliance and liberation from poverty and hunger, it is the means to achieve the end of swaraj. It helps the people to become patriotic by depending on their own labour and indigenous products.

**Meaning of Swadeshi**

Swadeshi has both negative and positive implications. Negatively it means boycott of foreign goods (British goods) as a mark of our self-rule. In an address delivered to the Missionary Conference held at Madras on 14 February, 1916, Gandhi defined Swadeshi as "that spirit in us which restricts us to the use and service of our immediate surroundings to the exculsion of the more remote" and applied the principle in the field of religion, Politics and economics. In religion, it would mean that Hindus, Muslims Christians and others should refuse to change their religion not because there are no defects in them but because such defects can be rectified. In political matters Swadeshi can be materialised in the observance and revitalisation of the true spirit of indigenous institutions like the caste and the Panchayat. In economic and industrial life, the Swadeshi ideal should direct India to produce everything for her requirements within her border. If we follow Swadeshi he added, every village of India will almost be a self-supporting and self-contained unit, exchanging only such necessary commodities with other villages where they are not locally produced.

**Source of Influence**

Gandhiji's concept of Swadeshi was framed by his deep ethical-spiritual conviction, his close involvement with the economic condition of the people, especially rural people and reading of Ruskin's book *'Unto This Last'*. Gandhiji was not after material progress but moral progress. His ideals of true economics was to 'manufacture souls' and not material plenitude.

**Objective of Swadeshi**

'Khadi' and 'Charkha' are the centres of Gandhiji's Swadeshi. Because 'Khadi' can be a symbol of our patriotism and self-reliance. Khadi and Charkha (spinning wheel) were deployed during freedom movement for carrying out boycott of foreign cloth, promoting the spirit of Swadeshi and checking the draining of our wealth to foreign countries. Besides, Swadeshi and Khadi serve as a remedy for providing economic minimum to the starving millions of the country. It helps in the complete decentralisation of forces of production and provide employment for millions of unemployed in the country. It has also some humanitarian goal. Swadeshi and use of Khadi will also check exploitation, concentration of wealth in a few hands and unhealthy competition. Gandhiji opposed industrialisation as it would replace human labour and increase unemployment. Above all, Gandhiji advocated Swadeshi and Khadi because he thought that independent India could only discharge her duty towards a groaning world by adopting a simple but ennobled life.

## RELEVANCE OF GANDHISM TODAY

Always a question lurks in the mind of the modern man with regard to the relevance of Gandhian thought. Modern man with all his accentricity, lust for power, science, technology of modern warfare laugh at the basic postulates of Gandhism. But for this, the present generation is not to be blamed. Nathuram Godse no doubt killed Gandhi, but his successors killed Gandhism for ever. Any concept of ideology if not reinterpreted becomes invalid for the present. The something happened in case of Gandhism. The post-independence era marked a complete departure from Gandhian idea and was dominated by 'Nehruvian' model of political and economic development. Above all the intellectual arrogance of Marxists and western liberals contribute more to the decay of Gandhism.

But Gandhism can never die. As we approach towards twenty-first century, we face the problem of pollution, ecological decay, poverty due to industrialisation and high technology. There is also growing threat of arms race and terrorism pushing the entire mankind to a state of unrest. Gandhiji has unmistakably foreseen this predicament the incoming disaster as early as 1909, in his 'Hind Swaraj'. Throughout his life he continued to warn against it and showed the way to avert it through truth and non-violence. He had characterised modern civilization as a 'disease.' Two weeks before his death he had made a prophetic statement, that "this modern civilisation is such that one has only to be patient and it will be self-destroyed". Taking the present world scenario, beginning from the threat of nuclear warfare down to environmental pollution, one must find the validity of Gandhiji's statement. Gandhiji has talked about peaceful co-existence of nations and establishment of internationalism. Every one of us is striving today to reach that Gandhian goal.

The most important concept of Gandhiji namely 'Swadeshi' find its revival today in Indian polity. Especially after the incoming of multi-nationals and monopolisation of the entire industrial products, people in the country talk of Swadeshi. Of course the modern name of 'Swadeshi' would be 'self-reliance'. The new spirit of 'Swadeshi' is to fight against new-colonialism with increasing grip over Indian economy and creating cultural erosion. It is a reflection of Gandhian Swadeshi. Because Gandhiji has developed this concept first as a weapon of economic independence and then as political independence.

In the economic field, Gandhiji's emphasis on small scale industry as a source of employment generation , economic decentralisation leading to self-reliant village and limiting human wants still holds the key to the removel of poverty and economic hazards from the society. The present day states man also emphasize 'austerity measures', which are all reflection of Gandhian model. Gandhiji was not opposed to industrialisation. What he wanted was use of simple machniery in villages and decentralisation of industries. Otherwise machinery and industrialisation would be instruments of exploitation. He also suggested state ownership of industries so that industries would work for the benefit of mankind. This is also agreed by socialists and even the Marxists.

His emphasis on political freedom of minority, decentralisation of political power have been accepted in the form of protection of minority rights and Panchayati Raj. Gandhiji's concept of Satyagraha, non-cooperation, Civil disobedience even today have proved to be successful as a non-violent struggle against colonialism, racialism and exploitation. The success of struggle against apartheid in South Africa under the leadership of Nelson Mandela bears testimony to this. The struggle that Gandhi had started in South Africa in the beginning of twentieth century has been successfully completed by Mandela with the help of the same Gandhian doctrine and philosophy.

Thus, 'Gandhism' though cannot be taken as a model in a strict sense, can be taken as a beacon. As present we have the task of revalidating Gandhian ideas by new interpretation of his thought and action. The entire mankind will be immensely benefitted if Gandhian thought is followed in the right perspective. Gandhi is dead, long live Gandhism.

## M. N. ROY

M. N. Roy was born during a period when the first war of India's independence had already taken place in 1857. An era of change had ushered in due to new thinking and new thought in the form of reformation and regeneration. Renaissance had already established its foothold. Bengal was preparing for a militant revolt against the British rule. Terrorists were organising themselves to overthrow the British. A brief sketch of his life and contribution is given below:

### Childhood

M.N. Roy, whose childhood name was Narendranath Bhattacharya, was born on February 6, 1886 at Arbella, a village in the district of 24 Parganas. His father, Dinabandhu Bhattacharya was the head priest of the temple of Goddess Ksheputeshwari at the village Kshepe in the Midnapur district of West Bengal. So every body thought that Naren (as M.N. Roy was called) would inherit the profession of his father. But history proved otherwise. Coming out of the cocoon of an orthodox middle class Hindu family, M.N. Roy proved to be an iconoclast and revolutionary. Naren went to school in his own village and studied upto class-VI. Later on, his father shifted to the village Kodalia in 24-Pargana where he pursued his study in a Anglo Sanskrit school. This village has given birth to many revolutionaries like Rajnarain Bose and Sivanath Sastri who had made the first attempt of founding a secret revolutionary society in late 19th Century and had inspired Nabagopal Mitra's Jatiya Mela'. On the other hand it was the year 1905, the year of agitation against the partition of Bengal. This agitation not only gave birth to religious nationalism advocated by Swami Vivekananda but also triggered off the revolutionary activities initiated by Bankimchandra Chhaterji through his nationalist coinage 'Vande Mataram'. Naren was a product of his own time. The revolutionary personality of budding Naren, a boy of only fourteen years provoked him to join the agitation for the violation of the order of the school headmaster. He was rusticated from the School. He joined a revolutionary organisation called Annushilan Samity. However, later on rustication order was withdrawn and he completed his matriculation examination. He then joined in the Bengal National College.

**Roy as a Radical Nationalist**

As mentioned above, Roy being influenced by the climate of militant nationalism, joined the radical nationalist movement against British but before riding the cadre of a top ranking militant nationalist, left the country for a broader role. He started his career as a fighter for the cause of country's freedom in the Annushilan Samity, a revolutionary organisation for physical, mental and moral regeneration of Bengali youths. Later on, he met Barin Ghosh, the founder of Bengali daily, *'the Juganter'* and Jatindranath Mukherjee a fervent revolutionary nationalist. Both Mr. Ghosh and Jatindranath became his friend, philosopher and guide in the war of freedom. The village Kodalia bcame the centre of revolutionary activities. The revolutionaries were to be trained in shooting and marksmanship at the same time bombs to be made and arms to be acquired. But there was paucity of funds to meet the expenditure involved in such activities. So Naren committed political dacoity at the Chingripota Railway Station on 6th December, 1907. The Station Master was assaulted and money was confiscated to give for revolutionary activities. Naren was arrested. But he was released on bail. Another politcal dacoity was committed by him near Diamond Harbour in the district of 24 Paragana on 25th April, 1909. While leaving the place of dacoity, he told the owner of the house, "We are only borrowing money to drive the British away".

Naren was again arrested and released on bail. But after the declaration of Aurobindo Ghosh to retire from politics and long term imprisonment for Barin Ghosh, the revolutionary activities went through rough weather. Naren took the initiative to organise the different revolutionary groups into one banner known as Jugantar and planned guerilla type warfare. His view was to remove the British from India and establish a people's government instead of a government by few. In the Howrah-Sibpur Conspiracy case, he was again arrested along. with 46 accused including Jatin Mukherjee on 29th January, 1910. He was charged with the conspiracy of raging war against His Majesty the King-Emperor and deprive him of Sovereignty of British India. However, after nine months of solitary imprisonment, he was released due to lack of suffcient evidence against him.

In August, 1914, the war between England and Germany started. The revolutionaries decided to take advantage of this situation and looked towards Germany for necessary help. German Counsel General was convinced in Calcutta. An agreement was made that Germany would give arm delivery at Bataria (Java). Accordingly Naren was selected to go for receiving the arms but went in the guise of a name 'Charles A. Martin'. Making necessary arrangements at Bataria (Java) for arms delivery through ship to Calcutta, East Bengal and Balasore, he came back to India. But the ship did not arrive, so again he went to Bataria but was disappointed to see the non-cooperative attitude of Germans. So he went to China and Japan for arms. In Japan, again he talked to German officers who suggested him to go to Germany to get the sanction for money to supply arms. But then came the shocking news of the killing of his revolutionary mentor, Jatin Mukherjee in a police encounter at Balasore. Roy was crestfallen. After the death of Jatin Mukherjee (popularly known as Bagha Jatin), other colleagues of the revolutionary movement were also arrested. Naren decided to change the course of his life.

**Leader of Communist International**

Naren's journey for the next phase of life started. He reached San Fransisco (U.S.A.) in June, 1916. Though he arrived in the name of C.A. Martin, but as reported by the local news paper he was suspected to be a Hindu, high-caste Brahmin revolutionary leader or an emmissary of the British government. This created problem for his free movement in U.S.A. Hence, as per the suggestion of an Indian friend in the campus of Stanford University, he changed his name to Manavendranath Roy. A new era with a new name started in the life of Naren. Form Narendranath Bhattacharya be became Manavendranath Roy and came to be popularly known as M.N. Roy. Here he was attracted to Marxist ideas. In August, 1916, he went to New York where he met Lala Lajpat Rai. But with the American entry into war in June, 1917, a criminal case known as the Hindu-German conspiracy case was instituted. Roy was arrested and was prosecuted in a New York Court. But this time also, due to lack of evidence he was released. The constant fear of arrest haunted him. He, therefore went to Mexico alongwith his wife, Evelyn Trent whom he had met at Stanford.

His stay in Mexico was a period of stride for a bigger achievement. His activities in Mexico brought laurels for him as a communist. Roy through his organisational ability became the General Secretary of the Mexican Socialist Party in December, 1918. Here at Mexico, Roy came in contact with Michael Borodin a representative of communist international. Borodin was very much influenced by Roy's writings. Their initimacy developed. Roy became a 'Convinced Communist'. This was also the period of success of communist revolution in Soviet Russia. The word communism was whispering in the ears of every intellectual of the period. So Roy took interest in converting the name of Mexican Socialist Party as Communist Party of Mexico. Thus, he became the first Indian who founded the Communist Party in a foreign country like Mexico.

M.N. Roy was subsequently invited by Borodin and Lenin to the Second Congress of Communist International to the held in Moscow. He went to Moscow in May, 1920. He participated in the Second Congress of Communist International where he presented his paper on 'Supplementary Thesis on the National and colonial question' to complement Lenin's thesis on national and colonial questions. Both the papers were adopted with minor changes.

Roy being recognised by the Communist International got engaged in Communist activities. Soon he rode the cadre of Communist

International and became the head of Eastern Department of Communist International and of Moscow Oriental University. He also became a member of the official policy-making bodies namely the presidium, political secretariat, the executive committee and the World Congress—a rare honour bestowed upon any Indian ever.

The Communist revolution had also occurred in China. Roy was selected as a leader of the delegation to China sent by Communist International. Roy advised the Chinese leaders for an' agrarian revolution' which was not acceptable to Chinese. The Chinese Communists were also divided. So Roy's mission failed. He came back to Moscow. His failure led to the failure of commintern in China, for which Roy was held responsible. He decided to come back to India.

**Roy in the Indian National Congress**

M.N. Roy arrived at Bombay in the year 1930. Always he was under apprehension of arrest by the British police. To avoid the arrest, he moved as Dr. Mahmud. But he could not escape. He was arrested on 26th July, 1931. He was tried for treason and sentenced to twelve years' transportation. The sentence was later remitted by the High Court to six years rigorous imprisonment. He was released on 20th November, 1936 from jail in Dehradun. Some Congress leaders greeted him at the jail gate and Nehru sent him a message to attend the provincial political conference at Bareilly. In spite of his ill-health he plunged into the political activities and attended the conference. It was here at Bareilly conference he was enrolled as a member of the Indian National Congress. He was also elected as a member of the Executive Committee of Uttar Pradesh Congress Committee. He attended the Faizpur session of the Indian National Congress in December, 1936. Roy was welcomed by Nehru and was requested to take the dias. Roy was not a Congress man in Gandhian uniform but a radical determined to revolutionise the Congress programme. He also met Gandhiji, but they were meeting to depart in the thought and course of action. Roy thought of developing an alternative leadership who can start an effective struggle against imperialism and possess a revolutionary ideal. Roy's idea was opposed by right-wing leaders of the Congress.

The World War-II broke out in 1939. In this war Britain was a party against axis powers. Roy nurtured the idea of supporting the British government in their war against Hitler. Gandhiji and other leaders in the Congress opposed this idea because Gandhi had lost faith in the British Government. So when the league of Congress men organised anti-Fascist demonstration, the Congress prohibited them. But it was of no impact. So Uttar Pradesh Congress Committee expelled Roy from the Congress party. Thus, Roy was delinked from the Congress.

**A Radical Humanist**

The League of Radical Congressmen formed a new party under the leadership of M.N. Roy. The new party came to be known as Radical Democratic Party. The Radical Democratic Party was to give emphasis on individual and moral values. To create a new socio-economic and political order in a scientific and moral way became its avowed principle. But this party was dissolved in 1948, in consequence of a philosophical new orientation. He worked for a new world order based on human ethics and scientific attitude. He devoted his time in writing extensively on national and international problems in his own journal called, *Radical, Humanist*. He also wrote in foreign journals and got a lot of offer to talk of different issues abroad. But his deteriorating health diverted the journey of his life to eternity on 25th January, 1954. It was the last journey of a firebrand nationalist, a communist and a radical humanist.

M.N. Roy as mentioned earlier was a versatile genius and a philosopher. The entire human generation will record with gratitude his contribution to the political literature. Some of his writings are: *(1)* Reason, Romanticism and Revolution, *(2)* Materialism, *(3)* New Orientation, *(4)* New Humanism, *(5)* India in Transition, *(6)* Future of Indian Politics, Politics Power and Political Parties, *(8)* Science and Superstition.

**ROY ON MARXISM : A RELUCTANT MARXIST**

Roy's rebirth at Stanford University drew him closer to Marxist ideals. So quickly he could ride the ladders of Communist leadership that he became the first Indian to be a Communist Leader of

International repute. He was also the first Indian to organise a Communist Party in a foreign country like Mexico under the influence of Borodin and Lenin. He led a delegation of Communist International to China to guide the communism revolutionaries. Thus, his attitude towards communism may be divided into two parts—one part indicating his faith in Marxism—second part a critic of Marxism.

**Influence of Marxian Principles**

He accepted communism mainly because he was convinced that political freedom without the content of economic liberation and social justice has no meaning—a true foundation of Marxist ideals. Hence, he agreed with Marx that a social revolution must precede political revolution. He was convinced of the 'Materialist' stance of Marxism. According to Marx, this world is an objective reality. There is nothing transcendental in this world. Marxism as a doctrine of humanism and individual freedom appealed M.N. Roy most. He also appreciated Marx's concern for 'man' and faith in the ability of man. The anti-imperialist policy of the communist also influenced M.N. Roy. Hence, he said, "As a philosophy, Marxism is the outcome of the development of thought from the dawn of history. Therefore, it is the heritage of humanity, it is the ideological equipment belonging to everybody for a better world". Accordingly he made a Marxist approach to his analysis of the problems of society.

But Roy never belonged to the tradition of orthodox and dogmatic Marxism. His experience in the Communist International, urge for human freedom and an original genius within him made him to travel from Marxism towards radical humanism. This he did through his critical analysis of Marxism.

**Differences with Marxism**

While agreeing with the Marxist theory that existence determines consciousness, he repudiated the economic interpretation of history by Marx. Roy rejected Marx's argument that history is a dialectical process governed by the conflict between forces of production and the relations of production (owner-worker). Economic forces, Roy argued, can not be the only factor in history. Intelligence, creative ideas and ideology also play an equally important role in determining the course of history. Roy said, "Philosophically, the materialist conception of history must recognise the creative role of intelligence. Materialism can not deny the objective reality of ideas." The early history of man was more determined by the biological urge of man. Such biological urge can not be clubbed under economic factor. The study of economic conditions of the early middle ages reflects that there was no casual connection between the rise of business class and the renaissance. Renaissance as a phase of history was more determined by the cultural and the intellectual revolution in man's mind. It was based on rational, scientific and secular ideas of ancient Greek civilization than by the economic interest or political ambition of medieval traditional class. Roy believed that ideas of men create history and transform their socio-economic environment.

M.N. Roy argued that though Marx was concerned for man but in his economic analysis, individual was viewed only as a part of 'class' or 'group'. Individual loses identity under his system. Economic determinism, Roy argued, precluded the possibility of man ever becoming free as an individual. Man needs, not only economic freedom and security, but also freedom from cultural and intellectual restraints. He clearly pointed out that since man is the creator of the social world, any social organisation which denies the sovereignty of individual, cannot be libertarian. Under a totalitarian cult like communism, there is no hope for individual freedom.

He did not accept the theory of class-struggle as enunciated by Marx. Because according to Marx, society is divided into only two classes. But history speaks of more than two classes. The contermporary society has not been divided into two anti-thetical groups as envisaged by Marx. No doubt tension and struggle exist in society but a strong social cohesion also continues. For all these reasons, Roy was doubtful about the scientific basis of Marxian class struggle.

Marx made a prophetic announcement that through the dialectical process class struggle will bring the success of the proletariat finally leading to the establishment of class-less society. Roy viewed that dialictical methodology introduced an element of idealism in Marxism. At the same time Marx behaved like a prophet leaving many things to fatalism. That is because he simply glorified the class struggle without paying any attention to the worth and significance of empirical individual. Hence, Roy clamoured for a revolt against the fatalism implicit in the prophetical sociology of Karl Marx. Marx has also proved to be false prophet. He predicted the disappearance of the middle class. But it has become just the opposite. There has been an increase in the middle class. Roy says rather the cultural and the political leadership of middle class is a patent fact of post-1919, World History.

He rejected the Marxian theory of dictatorship of the proletariat. For him the individual freedom is more important than the dictatorship of any class. Under the dictatorship of the proletariat there is totalitarian rule enslaves the individual. According to him, the conflict of the present age was between totalitarianism and democracy, between all devouring collective ego-nation or class and the individual struggling for freedom.

Lastly, he also differed from Marxian concept of revolution. He said, Marxian revolution paves the way for totalitarian system. Because the violent revolution of Marx reveals the cult of collective irrationalism in which individual is lost. On the other hand he preferred a peaceful revolution through educating the people. Revolution should be based on voluntaristic romanticism.

Thus, Roy, though had faith in the Marxian doctrine of humanism discarded some of its fallacies. He was a reluctant Marxist.

## CONCEPT OF FREEDOM AND RADICAL DEMOCRACY

M.N. Roy was a great crusader for the individual freedom. Beginning from his role as a teen-age terrorist in the freedom struggle till his theorisation of radical humanism in the eleventh hour of his life, 'man' and 'Freedom' have always been his primary concern. No doubt freedom of the individual has also been the primary objective made by other social and political thinkers but M.N. Roy's search is not for freedom only but for the freedom individual actually enjoys. Freedom needs domocracy. But the present democratic set-up is not the real guarantor of individual freedom. Hence, M.N. Roy discards the present institution of democracy and suggests for radical democracy as an alternative. However, an insight into his views on freedom and democracy will include his definition and nature of the individual freedom, critique of the existing institutions of democracy like party system and parliamentary democracy and suggestion for radical democracy in the form of a direct locally organised domocracy.

**Definition of Freedom**

Man is the centre of his political philosophy. That's why he had rejected both the Congress nationalism and communism as the antedote to the individual freedom. As a social scientist he has discovered the real potentiality and the rationality of man. According to him man has intelligence and creative faculty to make and unmake. He creates his own destiny and also creates his own society and environment. But for all these, he needs freedom. Because he defines freedom as "progressive disappearance of all restrictions on the unfolding of the potentialities of individuals as human being and not as cogs in the wheels of mechanised social organisation." In other words, where there is freedom there should be absence of any restriction to throttle the growth of the individual personality. Hence, a conducive socio-political atmosphere is necessary for the realisation of individual freedom. But freedom for him should never be in the form of 'licence'. It should not also be considered as an accident nor a passing phase in individual's life. It is an end in itself, the supreme virtue. Hence, he said, "the purpose of a rational human endeavour, collective as well as individual, should be the attainment of freedom in ever large measure, and freedom is real only as individual freedom". M.N. Roy's primary quest has been to develop a new model of democracy in the place of the present democracy.

**Critic of Party System**

M.N. Roy was critical of the political systems existing in different countries. Everywhere there has been a trend of centralisation. But like Bakunin and Kropotkin (Anarchists), he was opposed to centralisation of power. Because such centralisation paralyses the free individual initiative and autonomous choice. From his own experience, he argued, political parties with their organizational set-up, monopolise all the powers and act as agents of centralisation.

Secondly, political parties stand in between the government and the people. In the electoral politics, political parties limit the choice of the people. The aim of each political party is to capture power even by corrupt means. Every political party however, purified it may be, waits for an opportunity to grab power and behave dictatorially. Hence, he dissolved his own Radical Democratic Party and suggested for a new political order in which there will be neither political parties nor any orgnisation but only "spiritually free men" as the agents of change.

## Critic of Parliamentary System

Freedom, according to him, can be realised most where democracy is more participatory in nature and there is less socio-political and economic control. But in the existing democratic institutions totalitarian techniques are adopted to negate the individual freedom. Even parliamentary domocracy suffers from serious defects. People are powerless between elections. In critical times even the rule of law affords little protection. In other words, people become powerless after the election. Their sovereignty remains a legal fiction excepting the period to vote the new set of masters. On the other hand the party having absolute majority assumes dictatorial power. This abuse of power cannot be prevented within the legal frame-work of democracy. Thus, he said, parliamentarianism as such cannot defend domocracy and guarantee civil liberties under all circumstances. The liberal polity is democratic formally and is really controlled by few politicians and bureaucrats at the top.

## Locally Organised Democracy

M.N. Roy rejected any idea of replacing democracy by dictatorship. On the other hand, he suggested for a locally organised democracy. This is also known as radical democracy as it envisages a radical change in the structure of the state. In the new democratic polity, individual will not both be isolated or scattered leading to powerlesshess. But in the new polity, individuals will be roganised in the form of people's committee. There will be complete decentralisation of power. The political parties will have absolutely no role to play. It is the 'people committee' at the root end a 'group of spiritual men' who will work as agents of change. In other words, in the new political system, the business of the state is not the business of an exclusive coterie but of all people and of every individual. The individual is not sovereign theoretically during election but Sovereign in practice, People' sovereignty becomes a vital reality and ceases to be mere consitutional or legal fiction, truely inalienable and indivisible.

**New Structure or Organised Democracy**

The new state of structure will stand on a firm base of peoples' committee. Unlike the earlier system, in the new state structure power, development, decision-making or planning will start from the grass-root level (people's committee) and will move to the top. There will be complete diffusion of power throughout the country and remain vested in the people.

Peoples' committee will be local republics and constitutionally the local units of the state. Each village and city will have a local peoples' committee elected for one year on the basis of universal adult franchise. Peoples committee will comprise one member for every fifty voters. There will be the structure of sub-divisional and district peoples' Committee. They will perform function of the local-self-Government. At the state level, the highest authority will be a provincial peoples' council including the Governor. The Governor will be elected for five years and deputies for four years by universal adult franchise. But at the centre, Supreme Peoples Council will be the highest orgnisation. It will consist of two houses namely federal Assembly and Council of States.

The Organization of Roy's radical democracy has a reflection of Rousseau's direct democracy. The Local Peoples' Committee will have controlling authority and will assume greater role than the apex bodies. For example local peoples' committee will continuously pass resolutions to guide its representatives in the federal assembly and the provincial council. It will give its opinion on proposed legislation. It will also have the power of initiatives, referendum and recall. It can propose new legislation. The governor will dissolve the provincial peoples' council before its expiry on a demand by the local peoples' committees. The local peoples' committee representing one-third of the total number of voters can demand referendum for any provincial legislation. It will also have the right to recall an elected member, if approved by a referendum of the entire electorate of that constituency. Thus, the radical democracy, paramedical in structure gives a hand to the people in the government. M.N. Roy's view is based on the argument that the individual is prior to all organisations including the family and the society.

But who will act as agents of change? No political party with its power craze can do it. It is only a group of "spiritually freeman" with their 'determination' who can bring changes and usher in a new world order. But again that will not be an easy task. The establishment of people's committee will not be possible over night. Hence, a council of states should be constituted during the transitional period. This Council would consist of the representatives of the best intellectual and professionals like engineers, economists, scientists, doctors, jurists etc. All of them would be nominated by the chief executive of the state. It will have the power to plan and supervise the implementation of different programmes for the people.

## IDEAS ON ECONOMIC ARRANGEMENTS

In Roy's opinion capitalist system of economy is most rotten and outdated. Gradually all industries should be controlled by the people and with this end in view he has given his own system of planned and co-operative economy.

In his opinion if individual freedom is to be preserved then there should be perfect economic democracy and purchasing power of the people should be increased. That could alone be possible in a planned economy by two ways. First, the goods should be produced at very cheap cost and secondly, government should subisdise the goods to be exported; but in both the cases the burden should be put on the tax-payer who could in turn expect to get back the profits after sometime. In-so-far as India was concerned Roy was of the opinion that purchasing power of Indian masses could only go up if there was an extensive programme of setting up new industries. In his opinion burden should shift from land to industry as land is already over-burdened. He, however, does not fail to realize that in India there is uneven distribution of land which is responsible for the mal-production and mal-distribution of agricultural produce. He, has therefore, suggested a proper scientific re-distribution and adjustment of land so that there is rational and reasonable distribution and production of agricultural commodities. He also felt that if large-scale construction programme including that of roads and bridges etc., was taken up that might help in the distribution of wealth and thereby living standard of the labourers might go up.

**His Ideas about Cooperative Economy.** Roy favoured radical change in the present economic set-up. In his opinion in the present system of economy means of production and distribution were in the hands of only a few capitalists who produced goods in the way they liked, without taking into consideration national requirements. Not only this, but excess which the capitalists got in the name of profit was used by them for their personal welfare and as such this wealth was denied to the society. The result of all this was exploitation which was ever-increasing and had no end in sight. Roy therefore, wanted to end present economic setup and desired to replace that by cooperative economy.

Roy essentially believed that working with cooperation and in close harmony with each other was nothing new. According to him, in our present complex society each one depends on the other and thus, there is a desire to work in close co-operation both in personal as well as collective interests. He, therefore, concluded that if this spirit of cooperation was introduced in the economic field it would guarantee for economic security. The outcome of such a co-operative economy would be even distribution of the goods produced and realization of social needs in the manufacture of goods.

In cooperative economy there would be proper understanding and both the producers as well as the consumers would work in close cooperation with each other. In his co-operative economy there was a scope for owning private property provided that did not, in any way, result in exploitation. In such a planning there would be proper utilization of means of production and distribution and certain basic industries would be used for national service. He, however, admitted that for quite sometime some industry shall not pass on to private sectors, more particularly higher basic industries, and these shall have to be kept under state control. He also realized that for sometime to came the state shall act as a co-ordinating agency both in the public and private sectors.

In his economic set-up there will be a network of consumers and producers co-operatives which will take the fullest advantage of scientific and technological advancement. There will also be a planning body which shall be responsible for allocating priorities in the use of national resources and improve our social utility services. In the arrangement the superstructure of the larger scale production of basic needs of the society will be on co-operative basis. Such an arrangement is bound to end exploitation.

**His Views about Indian Economy.** Roy was conscious of the fact that his economic arrangement should be such which suits Indian conditions and environments. He, in fact, differentiated between the economies of industrially advanced and under-developed countries. In his arrangement, India rightly fell under the category of a country with an under developed economy. According to him, India advancement can only be possible when there is large scale industrialization. He however, realizes that introduction agricultural machinery was bound to result in unemployment of thousands of peasants and workers working on our fields. He, therefore, hesitated to suggest introduction of agricultural machinery for our peasants. He, has suggested that instead of manure we should use cattle dung. Similarly, he has also suggested the use of tubewells as an alternative to wells for watering our fields.

In his constitution of India he has devoted a section to economic organization of our society. Under his arrangement economically India will be a cooperative commonwealth where goods shall be produced primarily for satisfying the requirements of the people. There will be proper planning and regulation for production and distribution which shall ultimately be the entire responsibility of the state.

He has also suggested a national planning authority consisting of experts with proper representation of State Bank. Such a body shall be subordinate to the Council of States. In his arrangement industrial and agricultural enterprizes financed by the state shall be the collective property of the people and State Bank will control the entire credit system of the state. The ownership of land, underground riches and railways will be transferred to the people. The freedom of enterprise, individual as well as corporate, will be guaranteed subject to the condition that the production will satisfy the requirements of the people.

## ROY ON GANDHISM AND THE INDIAN NATIONAL CONGRESS

While constructing the contours of M.N. Roy's political philosophy, it is necessary to highlight two important horizons of political literature existing at that time *i.e.*, Gandhism and Communism. Any disinterested observation of M.N. Roy's political theorisation will reveal his sympathy, appreciation well as contempt for both the philosophies. Sudipta Kaviraj rightly observes Roy's assessment of Gandhi shows a peculiar evolution from a more complex appreciation to one increasingly simplistic and critical.

Roy was a critic of Gandhiji's leadership, Philosophy and programme of the Congress. Roy's profile and methods as a teenage terrorist and subsequently as a leader of the Communist International took him away from Gandhiji and the Congress Nationalism.

### Appreciation of Gandhi

But as mentioned earlier, M.N. Roy as a sympathetic critic appreciated Gandhism in one of his first articles in IMPRECOR. Through the non-cooperation movement he said the agrarian movement, the proletarian movement and the nationalist movement are moving concertedly towards one object, *i.e.*, national independence. Congress was the 'acknowledged head' of the nationalist movement 'Gandhiji had tried' to make Congress truly representative of national aspirations of all classes of Indians. Sudipta Kaviraj writes, even the Charakha, a particular but of Roy's derision in later year, was seen to have a practical symbolic value. Roy even compared Gandhiji with St. Thomas Aquinas, Savonavola and Francis of Assisst in his book—One Year of Independence. He acknowleged four constructive contributions of Gandhi, *(1)* Use of mass action for political purpose *(2)* Consolidation of the Indian National Congress, *(3)* Liberation of the national forces from governmental repression by the slogan of non-violence, and *(4)* The adoption of the techniques of non-cooperation, non-payment of taxes and civil disobedience. But soon such appreciations made an exit giving birth to contemptuous criticism.

## CONCEPT OF RADICAL OR NEW HUMANISM

Having rejected the defective tenets of Gandhism, Marxism, and liberalism, Roy made his last journey to radical humanism or new humanism. His concern for the identity of man and a passionate urge for the individual freedom made him to construct a new political model based on humanitarian, rational, scientific and individualistic order, which will ensure the real sovereignty of man. Man is centre of society and hence, must be free from all sorts of chains—even if it is golden chain. He must have the opportunity to exhibit his ideas of radical or new humanism has been reflected in his writings like, New Humanism, Reason, Romanticism and Revolution. The Problem of Freedom, Scientific Politics etc. The new order is known as radical humanism or new humanism. However, a highlight on M.N. Roy's Radical Humanism will centre round the discussion about the origin and source of the ideas of humanism, his own interpretation of humanism and the basic features of his humanism.

### Genesis of the Idea of Humanism

The origin of the idea of 'Humanism" cannot be traced to the writings of M.N. Roy. It existed much prior to his theorisation of New Humanism'. In modern time, it was the product of the period of renaissance representing the ideas of ancient Greece. The elements of humanism were evident in the writings of Western political philosophers like protagoras, Erasmus, More, Buchann and Herdor. But M.N. Roy was inspired by the philosophical radicals like Hutcheson, Shaftesbury, Bentham and Marx. The individualist approach to the ethical problems made by the radical philosophers influenced M.N. Roy deeply. But Roy was never domgatic. He had his own rationality. So he differed not only from the artist but also from the French and he German schools of humanism of 19th century. Hence, in August,

1947, he published the manifesto of his own political philosophy, which came to be known as New Humanism or integral scientific humanism. His New Humanism came to be based upon the natural reason and secular conscience. Due to modern science, Humanism can now go to the root of human problems and that is why he called his rationalism as Radical Humanism. Humanism refers to a system dealing with the needs of men and not with religious ideas. Roy's humanism was due to the fact that rationalist humanist ethics serves as a panacea for all the problems of man in the material world.

M.N. Roy developed his concept of Radical Humanism because 18th and 19th century humanism could not scientifically ascertain the position of man. Also individual freedom faced crisis due to the encroachment of authoritarianism. The individual was completely chained and lost his freedom and identity. The political philosophy of Marx could not protect the individual. Because in spite of its element of humanism, it did not pay special attention to 'man'. Man was submerged into the class or group and finally under the dictatorship of the proletariat individual lost his complete freedom. Secondly, M.N. Roy said, in the period of crisis which the humanity is undergoing only, capital v/s the labour is not the issue. He also rejected the Congress nationalism under which nation becomes powerful at the cost of the individual. Gandhism lacked a social revolution. It gave enough scope for the capialists and the feudal landlords to exploit the poor. Liberalism in the form of parliamentary democracy can not guarantee individual freedom because politicians and bureaucrats monopolise the power. So M.N. Roy expounded 'New Humanism' which would restore the 'sovereignty of man'. M.N. Roy's radical humanism has different elements which are discussed below:

**Emphasis on Man**

'Man' is the centre of M.N. Roy's radical humanism. There is reason and rationality within man. He has intelligence and creative faculty. He is the creator of society. institutions and politics. Man is prior to society. So the society has no business to impose itself as a Leviathan on man. Appropriately, social progress should be measured only through the development of men and the extent of liberty that it allows to its individuals.

**Individualism and Rationalism**

Man has come through evolution. Man is sovereign not because of the grace of any unknown superphysical being. But there is rationality within him to understand nature and his environment. In other words, there is reason and rationality within man. Man's rationality is a product of biological evolution. The reason in man is a reflection of the harmony of the universe. Radical humanism believes that because man is rational, he is moral. Morality within man grows as rationality develops. Man tries to understand others. Rationality within man propells him to be humanistic and ethical. So unlike the traditional humanism, the new humanism never admits the hands of any transcendental authority in making the man rational, moral and humanist. Roy argues that a rational and moral society is possible as man by nature is rational. Therefore, man can be moral not under compulsion, but voluntarily.

**Materialism**

M.N. Roy's humanist philosophy never represents a transcendental society; it very much takes cognizance of the materialist cosmology. In spite of his difference with Marxism, he retained his faith in materialism. New Humanism, therefore, is based on a materialistic metaphysics and not on poetic or romantic grounds of sentimental effusion. But man's creative idea is not always determined by matter, it has in independent existence.

**Scientific and Secular Outlook**

Radical humanism in its new form is based on a scientific and secular foundation. Radical humanism had taken over, Roy said, "the tradition of the founders of modern civilization, the tradition of revolt of man against the tyanny of God and his agents on this earth". This has been possible due to the blessings of Modern Science. New Humanism established the supermacy of man on the authority of Modern Science, which has removed all mystery regarding the essence of man. Modern Science has also helped in establishing man's relationship with nature in the right perspective. It has made man secular. Radical humanisam therefore, calls for a social order free from superstitions, religious dogmas and social evils. It envisages a scientific man with secular outlook. It truely establishes the great tradition of renaissance. It's ultimate objective is to liberate man from all sorts shackles—Social, cultural, economic and political.

**Freedom**

Freedom, therefore, is the primary concern in radical humanism. Everything that man does *i.e.*, scientific achievement, cultural progress., artistic creations have been stimulated by his urge for freedom. Roy says, "the purpose of all rational human endeavour, individual as well as collective, is attainment of "freedom in ever increasing measures. Freedom is progressive disappearance of all restrictions on the unfolding of the potentialities of individuals as human beings and not as cogs in the wheels of mechanised social organisation." In other words, as a liberal humanist thinker Roy highlights the absence of interference in the life of the individual. The individual becomes really free when he gets opportunity to exhibit has potentialities. Hence, he says freedom of a society is to be measured only by the degree of freedom, individual actually enjoys. Freedom is the supreme value from which all human values are derived. Individual's struggle for freedom is eternal. Though individual is a part of the universe, he can never conquer it. But his urge for freedom is perpetual which enables man to acquire knowledge, to realise the truth. Freedom, knowledge and truth are interrelated. Roy says' freedom' therefore, can not be attained by immoral means, nor can an enlightened man be a liar'. Here Roy's radical humanism comes nearer to the Gandhian way of thinking.

**A New Political Order**

To ensure real freedom for the individual a real democratic government based on moral values is necessary. Being critical of the existing parliamentary system he suggested for radical democracy in which there would be complete decentralisation. People through Local Peoples' committee would be real upholders of powers. Secondly, Radical Humanism envisages a government based on moral sense of the people and therefore, every man's moral sense must be highly developed.

Alongwith it a sense of justice, fair play and social responsibility must also develop in their fulness. It must have the highest confidence in man and should not ask him to surrender even in serious crisis.

**New Economic Order**

M.N. Roy rejected capitalism, socialism and state capitalism. Because under these system, man is reduced to a non-entity though he is the creator of all the institutions. Secondly, there is no economic freedom for the people. Just as political decentralisation is necessary so also economic reconstruction is necessary where in the economic problems of a particular locality can be solved through the local initiative by the local resources. This system can be possible through a system of co-operative where there will be production with freedom for the Individual.

**Cosmopolitanism**

Roy's radical humanism is based on cosmopolitanism and not on internationalism. Internationalism admits the existence of nation-states. But cosmopolitanism is opposed to the system of nations. Nationalism creates racial acrimony. It is reactionary to the extent that it neglects the social questions. Individual is asked to surrender at the alter of the nation. Hence, New Humanism suggests for replacing nationalism by world brotherhood. There should be a world federation of the moral and spiritual people. The national boundaries should be abolished both physically and mentally. People should be educated in enhancing their horizon of freedom and progress. They should think in terms of entire mankind and not in the form of nation.

**Emphasis on Revolution by Masses**

To bring into existence a new social order new Humanism requires a revolution in the moral, intellectual, mental political and social spheres. He rejected Marxian doctrine of class-war and said it is based on violence and it is leader oriented. Revolution must involve the masses. Hence, revolution should be brought through educating the people, making them literate and creating political consciousness in them.

Roy's new humanism, thus, envisages a new social and political order in which man will be really free and enlightened.

## AUROBINDO GHOSH

Sri Aurobindo Ghosh was born during the period when India witnessed the wave of renaissance. It had shaken the traditional foundation of Indian polity and brought about an intellectual, social, cultural, religious and political revolution in India. But though a product of this period, Sri Aurobindo Ghosh travelled in a different way. Like M.N.Roy, Jayaprakash and others, he did not change his political platform, but made a journey from extreme nationalism to social spiritualism. He became the most revered leader of the spiritual world. A brief sketch of his life and contribution is given below:

### Early Life and Youth

Sri Aurobindo Ghosh was born on 15th August, 1872 in Calcutta. His father Dr. Krishnadhan Ghosh was an English trained medical practitioner. He was famous for his untraditional and progressive attitude of life. After coming from England he refused to surrender to the demands of orthodox Hindus that he should perform Prayaschitta (Purification) for having travelled beyond the sea. He preferred to leave his village Konnagar in the Hoogly. Being influenced by English way of life, he sent his three sons to England in 1879 for study. He left them with an English clergyman, who was instructed to keep the children away from Indian influence. Sri Aurobindo Ghosh grew up in entire ingnorance of India, her people, religion and culture. Thus, when Sri Aurobindo Ghosh was only seven years old, he had to leave for England. He stayed at Manchester with Drewett family, who were Chirstians. Mr. Drewett, an accomplished Latin Scholar, coached him privately. Sri Aurobindo Ghosh was perfectly trained in English and Latin. Mrs. Drewett taught him history, geography, arithmetic and French. It was only in September, 1884, Sri Aurobindo Ghosh was admitted into St. Paul's School in London. He was registered as Aravinda Ackroyd Ghosh (middle name was named after an English lady Miss. Annettee Ackroyd who visited his house during his naming ceremony). Later on Sri Aurobindo Ghosh dropped the name 'Ackroyd'.

During his school career, Sri Aurobindo Ghosh faced much financial difficulties due to irregular remittances made by his father. But Aurobindo's high academic performance fetched him Senior classical scholarship of £80 per annum. He joined King's College in Cambridge as a student in arts stream. He passed the first part of classics Tripos in first division after two years. He got many prizes for his excellence in English and other literary activities. Though he qualified in the the I.C.S. examination, but got himself disqualified for not passing in the riding test. I.C.S. did not create any interest in him, because the God had kept a different mission to be served by him.

On the other hand, young Aurobindo came under a number of political influences which determined his future. His father's own bitter experience with the British in India led him to change his opinion. So his father started sending newspaper cutting to his sons. In his letters, he condemned British Government in India as heartless government. This had tremendous impact in Aurobindo's mind. He also came in contact with an organisation known as the 'Indian Majlis' founded in 1891, which was a revolutionary organisation. Later on he joined another secret society romantically called, 'The Lotus and Dagger'. This orgnisation made it an avowed principle to fight for India's independence. He was also influenced by Mazzini's (hero of Italian unification) Risorgimento and Irish Patriotic movement. A new era in Sri Aurobindo's life started, an era of struggle and sacrifice to liberate the motherland.

Sri Aurobindo Ghosh was waiting for the opportunity to come over to India. So when Maharaja Sayaji Rao Gaekwad of Baroda during his visit to England made an offer to him to join in the Baroda State service, he immediately agreed. In February, 1893 he came back to India. First, he was appointed in revenue department. But subsequently at the request of the College Principal, Maharaja appointed him the professor of English. By his calibre and popularity he was promoted to the post of Vice-Principal. During this period at Baroda, he tried to acquaint himself with the history, culture, religion and philosophy of India. The teachings of Hindu philosophy,writings of Bankim Chandra and Michael Madhusudan Dutta attracted him a lot.

**Role in the Freedom Movement**

Sri Aurobindo Ghosh from his London days had a clear perception of British Government. British Government should be driven out; India must achieve independence not by the offering or compassion of the Britishers but by an armed rebellion. Hence, he was highly critical of both the British Government's anti-Indian policies and the Indian National Gongress mendicant attitude.

Though Sri Aurobindo Ghosh entrered into politics directly only after 1905, his political participation in the form of nationalist writings and helping the secret societies started since his year of arrival in India. His first political writings entitled 'New Lamps for Old' was published in they year 1893, in English section of an Anglo-Marathi paper known as the 'Indu Prakash'. In this first series of articles he wrote the critique of working of the Indian National Congress and gave a clarion call to the people of India to revolt against the British Government. This created reaction in the mind of many Congress leaders and pro-British intelligentsia. Though under pressure from moderat like Mahadev Govind Ranade, the proprietor of the paper asked Sri Aurobindo Ghosh to change his tone of writing but the latter continued to have the same attitude towards the Congress and the British Government.

When the Indian National Congress was formed, like many Indians aspiring for India's freedom, Sri Aurobindo Ghosh also praised it as a proud banner in the battle of liberty. But the euphoria vanished soon. The working of the Indian National Congress made him the worst critic in th congress history. Excepting achieving some administrative reforms the Congress had failed to adopt a clear-cut goal of national freedom. He wrote, 'I say of the Congress, then, that its aims are mistaken, that the spirit in which it proceeds towards their accomplishments is not a spirit of sincerity and whole heartedness, and that the methods it has choosen are not right methods and the leaders in whom it trusts not the right sort of men to be the leaders; in brief, that we are at present the blind led, if not by the blind, at any rate by the one-eyed'. He also criticised the Congress as a 'middle class organisation' which failed to evoke the support of the vast Indian proletariats. He condemned the 'mendicant policy of the moderates who compromised with injustice and servitude. He said isntead of resorting to flattery and sycophancy, the Congress should have relied on the strength of the nation. He was critical of the constitutionalist approach of the Congress and suggested that the Congress should adopt more radical policy in the direction of India's liberation through purification by 'blood and fire'. He pursued such a view because the then leaders of the Congress like Dababhai Naroji, Firozeshah Mehta, G.K. Gokhale (moderates) followed the method of 'Prayers and petitions' and believed in the 'Providential role' of the British.

He lambasted the British poltical organisations and the system which emphasises institutions and not on freedom and equality. He wrote, 'the British policies in India had led to the stifling of the Indian spirit, the cramping of her potentialities for development and her economic ruin.

Hence, Sri Aurobindo Ghosh developed a positive programme of political action against the British. His objective became the complete freedom from the British domination and not through the charity of foreign masters but through the inner strength of Indian nation. Besides his revolutionary writings, Sri Aurobindo Ghosh had bcome a member of the secret society in Western India. He brought about a sort of liasion among these socieities which was haded by a prominent Rajput noble of Udaipur and the revolutionary group in Bengal led by P. Mitter. The objective was to organise the youth and train them in the technique of revolutionary action. This bears testimony to the fact that even before coming to Bengal in 1905, during his stay at Baroda, Sri Aurobindo Ghosh had been accepted as the intellectual leader of the revolutionary movement in Bengal. This was knonwn to only few persons like sister Nivedita an Irish disciple of Swami Vivekananda.

However, after 1905, Sri Aurobindo Ghosh directly entered into active politics. So, after partition of Bengal he left Baroda and came to Calcutta. By his inspiring articles in the 'Bande Mataram' he became almost overnight a national hero and the whole of Bengali intelligentsia waited breathlessly for his stirring pronouncement on current events. He entered into the Congress as an extermist and joined the group of extremist leaders like Tilak, Lala Lajpat Rai and Bipin Chandra Pal. Aurobindo's revolutionary writings published in 'Bande Mataram', 'Karmayogin', 'Jugantar', 'Indu Prakash' and also his secret activities to organise the youth for an armed revolt made him the target of British Police. He was described by 'Lord Minto' as the 'most dangerous man in India'.

## MIRACLE IN ALIPORE JAIL AND WITHDRAWAL FROM ACTIVE POLITICS

In 1905, Lord Curzon was replaced as Viceroy by Lord Minto. Under his instruction, the government made all ruthless effort to suppress the radicals in Indian politics. One of the Presidency magistrates of Calcutta Mr. Kingsford ordered a 15 year old boy, Sushil Sen to be flogged in his presence. The boy because of several beatings became unconscious and was half-dead. The revolutionaries like Khudiram Bose and Prafulla Chaki could not tolerate and decided to retaliate. Kingsford could guess trouble and had himself transferred to Mauzaffarpur. The two youths followed him and on April 30th, 1908, Khudiram threw a bomb at a carriage as it was coming out of a club thinking mistakenly that Kingsford was in it. But that was not so. Rather two innocent ladies, Ms. Kennedy and her daughter killed. The government went on chasing the revolutionaries and raided on revolutionary centres. Though Sri Aurobindo Ghosh was not connected with the incident, police raided his house in Grey street and arrested him on May 3rd, 1908. He was taken to police station at Lal Bazar and from there to Alipore jail. It was in this jail Sri Aurobindo Ghosh experienced the spiritual power bestowed upon him. He said immediately after his release from jail, "When I was arrested and hurried to the Lal Bazar 'Hajat' I was shaken in faith for a while for I could not look into the heart of his intention. Therefore, I faltered for a moment and cried out in my heart to him, 'What is this that happened to me. I believe that I had a mission to work for people of my country and until that work was done I should have thy protection. Why then am I here and on such a charge'. A day passed and a second day and third day when a voice came to me from within 'wait and see'. He also wrote about his mystic experience in the jail, "I looked at the jail that secluded me from me and I was no longer by its high walls that I was imprisoned, no, it was Vasudev who surrounded me. I walked under the branches of the tree in front of my cell but it was not the tree. I knew, it was Vasudev, it was Sri Krishna, who I saw standing there and holding over me his shadows". After his release from the jail, he realised that everything is determined by divinity. So whether he was there in the scene or not, India would get independence. He changed his attitude of life. He wrote two weekly papers *i.e.*, 'Karmayogin' in English and 'Dharma' in Bengali.

Being blessed with spiritual power, Sri Aurobindo Ghosh decided to shun politics and work for spiritualism. Though British Government was again planning to arrest him, he got a message from above in a voice well known to him 'go to Chander Nagore'. Accordingly, he went to Chander Nagore and reached Pondicherry on April 4, 1910. From a dreadful extremist he became a great Maharshi. An independent national boundary was no more his vision. He worked for the unity of entire humanity. He made lasting contributions to spiritual world through his valuable writings like *(a)* The Life Divine, *(b)* Savitri, *(c)* The Synthesis of Yoga, *(d)* The Ideal of Karma Yogi, *(e)* Essay on Gita etc. He left his body on 5th December, 1950.

## HIS POLITICAL GOAL

Sri Aurobindo Ghosh was a revolutionary and a visionary. Though he underwent transformation from a radical nationalist to a convinced spiritualist, his philosophy of life continued to touch the social and political foundations of the society. He started his political career as a radical and an extremist. The freedom for the individual remained his major concern. He was never satisfied with anything less than the complete freedom for India from foreign domination. Accordingly an intense nationalism remained at the top of his political goal. After his mystic experience in Alipore jail, he no doubt left for Pondicherry. But his integral philosophy which he developed through yoga at Pondicherry was never devoid of political thought. As he said, the metaphysical and cosmic understanding cannot be divorced from the socio-political existence of humanity. Hence, a wide insight into his political goals covers a range of ideals set by him as a militant nationalist and a great yogi. His political goals like complete political independence, spiritual nationalism, world unity, ideal of human unity, a spiritualised society, inner spiritual feeedom and the goal of a perfect society are discussed below.

## Complete Political Independence

Sri Aurobindo Ghosh was the first Indian to demand complete independence. He demanded this at a time when the ideas appeared to be a utopia. In the words of great moderate leader G.K. Gokhale, only man outside lunastic asylums could think or talk of independence.... there is no alternative to British rule, not only now but for a long time to come. Sri Aurobindo Ghosh very scornfully condemned this attitude of the modrates twoards the British rule. He demanded complete independence for various reasons. He strongly believed that without political freedom, no real development is possible in India. Political freedom must precede socio-economic and administrative reforms. Writing in *Bande Matarant*, he said, "No national self-development is possible without the support of Rajashakti the organised political strength, commanding and wherever necessary compelling general allegiance and obedience . . .". Political freedom is the life-breath of a nation; to attempt social reform, education reform, industrial expansion, the moral imporvement of the rece, without attempting political freedom, is the very height of ignorance and futility. . .Reforms would never change the structure of subordination to British rule and culture. Secondly, he said every nation has a right to live its own life according to its own culture and ideals. In the name of reforms without freedom, the British would impose their own system of thought and make us a 'captive' for ever. Besides these secular arguments he also advanced some spiritual arguments about the problem of independence. He viewed the nation to be a divine mother. Her liberation must be the primary objective of her sons. Above all, India must get independence for the sake of entire humanity. He was totally convinced that India is destined to spearhead the next phase of human evolution. India, through her treasure of spiritualism would guide the world on spiritual path. But India cannot play its role of a spiritual Guru of the world so long it is chained by the British rule.

## Spiritual Nationalism as Political Goal

Nationalism was another political goal of Sri Aurobindo Ghosh. But the nationalism of Sri Aurobindo was different from western concept of nationalism. He was an advocate of spiritual nationalism. For him, India is not only a geographic entity but also a spiritual entity. He compared India with the divine mother, who always needs sacrifice of her sons. A nation is an organism. It has a personality of its own. The fulfilment of the individual person can be achieved by identifying himself with the national will. According to him, nationalism is not a mere political programme it is a religion that has come from God. The liberation of India was necessary to play her role as the spiritual guide of entire humanity. But for this political independence was a pre-requisite. Political liberty is the very life-breath of a nation. Without political liberty, social-economic and administrative reforms would be meaningless. But political liberty was only the immediate goal, not the final goal. The final goal is the resumption by India of her role as a spiritual guide to mankind. Nationalism for Aurobindo has a religious activity. The nationalist movment is a religious movement. Nationalism for him is a religious aspiration and a 'moral attitude'. Thus, unlike others, Sri Aurobindo Ghosh talked of a spiritual, democratic and cosmopolitan nationalism. It is not aggressive or chauvinistic. Because Sri Aurobindo Ghosh believed, nationalism is to be a temporary phase to get independence and strengthen nation; the main objective of each nation should be to work for the entire humanity without any differences on the basis of caste, colour, creed, culture or religion.

**World Unity**

Sri Aurobindo Ghosh was a visionary. His objective was not limited with narrow nationalism. He never differentiated on the basis of brith, caste, colour, creed, nationality, rank and class. On the other hand, he advocated internationalism and the formation of World-Union. In his internationalism World-Union would be formed consisting in free nationalities free from subjugation inequality and subordination of one by the other. It would be based on freedom and equality. But every nation would grow out of national idea and subordinate their interest to the interest of mankind. There will be human unity, which cannot be achieved unless man is sacred to man. He not only gave the idea of World-Union but also emphasised the necessity of spiritual unity and human perfection. Every man must try to attend the spiritual freedom and work for the society. There should be common human sympathy and fellow feeling. Sri Aurobindo strongly believed, only a spiritually perfect man can establish true brotherhood and work for the entire humanity.

**Human Unity as the Real Goal of Society**

Sri Aurobindo Ghosh after his mystic experience developed a conception of Swaraj broader than merely political or economic. In order to pursue a spiritual and political improvement of the Indian society, he fully integrated his socio-political thought into his life divine. His philsosphy is an integrated philosophy.

Sri Aurobindo aruged, the present society dominated by Science and Technology has only led to 'alienation' of the individual. The individual has not only been isolated but also has become helpless and politically powerless. In twentieth century men do not know where they are going; they have no goals. He is ignorant of his real, authentic existence. His true existence does not depend on Science or Technology but rather can come only by living a spiritual life. This can be possible only when an ideal society is formed and gives support to each individual to develop his spiritual capability without interference. When individuals are transformed into spirituality as self-aware spiritual unity of man would be established.

**Inner Spiritual Freedom**

Another goal of Sri Aurobindo's political philosophy is the ideal of inner spiritual freedom. In modern politics, liberty has been the main highlight. Anarchism, democracy and socialism have evolved to protect human freedom. But for Sri Aurobindo neither democracy nor socialism can protect liberty. On the other hand he suggested for spiritualised society for the sake of attaining integral freedom. Man does not need liberty alone, he also needs freedom from want and material insecurity. That can be possible through spiritual freedom. He must be allowed to develop his creative spiritualism. He pleaded for the spiritual synthesis of liberty, equality, unity, peace and fraternity. He preferred a 'simple rich nad beautiful life' for all. He advocated for the spiritual synthesis of individualism and communism which reconciles political liberty with social and economic equality.

**Perfect Society**

Another goal of Aurobindo's political philosophy has been to explore the formation of a prefect society based on spiritualism. He was critical of the dominant social structure in the modern world. While making an analysis of the social structure of earlier societies, he said that the society evolved through different dominant types of societies like symbolic, typical, conventional and rationalistic-individualistic societies.

The symbolic society marked by the human relationship determine entriely in terms of religious symbols. Nothing can deviate from the symbol; everything must be made sacred everything in society is sacrament religious and sacrosanct. From the symbolic society, the typical society evolved. In a typical society, society was organised according to different types like priests, warriors, producers etc. Each group had their own honour and role in the society. The conventional society emerged out of typical society. It created a rigid, formal system of grades and hierarchies. As a result conventions became lifeless. So the individuals revolved and gave birth to an individualistic and rationalistic society. The individualistic-rationalistic society rejected the formal traditions of the church and the state in the medieval age. Rationality, reason and science replaced the medieval thinking. Physical Science became the new standard of life. The rationalistic-idividualistic society also recognised the importance and equal rights of each individual. But Sri Aurobindo also discarded such a society. Because such a society failed to recognise the deeper truth. He criticised the liberal, individualistic society as a reflection of barbarian mentality. In such a society man only ran after superficial comfort giving rise to capitalist monopoly. Education was meant for making the man fit only for competitive, production oriented society.

So, he argued, the rationalistic trend in western civilisation must be challenged by subjectivism. The development of the individual and the community must be based on an eternal truth—a 'self-manifestation of the cosmic spirit'. In other words, a perfect society should be organised by the process of spiritualisation. It means every individual must feel his being a part of the divinity. But this spiritual growth can be possible with a community. Because spiritual growth of the individual cannot be based on 'self-ego' or 'isolation'. It would be on the principle of equality and not on conflict. The quest for divinity by the individual will be meant for the good of the world. Society need not stand on the way of the individual. The individual must contribute to the well-being of the community and the community must satisfy the needs and aspirations of different individuals. It should be organic in nature. The politics of the society must be based on two principles like 'treat others as self' and 'help the other person in need'. This would set aside the conflicting relationship between the individual and the community. In this ideal human society, (perfect society) the socio-political structure of man must be determined by the spiritual perfection. He made an integrated approach of the relationship between the individual, the community and the humanity. Every individual will perfect his individuality by an internal development (possible through the spirtual methods like yoga, meditation). But he has to harmonise his life with the life of a social aggregate and for the growth of humanity. The law of every community should be to perfect its corporate existence by its internal free development and work for the free development of other nations or communities. The law for humanity is to pursue its upward evolution towards the finding and expression of the divine in the mankind.

He also said, there is an inherent relationship between liberty, equality and fraternity. Without equality, liberty is left to competitive individualism. Equality without fraternity becomes mechanical. But fraternity is grounded in the spirit, which needs that man should move from mind to super mind. In other words individual is to seek his own self-development within the purview of a 'spiritualised polity' based on the soul power of brotherhood. In such an 'integral society' there is an intimate concern to discover the divine in a holistic appreciation for education, administration, protection and the productive economy.

Thus, Sri Aurobindo Ghosh rejected the existing soceity based on an artificial materialsitic and mechanised life. He preferred it to be substituted by a perfect society with perfect individuals, where individual will have free movemnent and development and work for the entire humanity. The entire humanity through perfect individuals would transform itself to one divine family.

## CONCEPT OF NATIONALISM AND PATRIOTISM

Sri Aurobindo Ghosh was the prophet of 'spiritual nationalism' quite new and unique in the history. For the first time he added a 'spiritual identity' to the already existing geogrpahical identity of India. For him Nation is the manifestation of God. Nationalism is a religion gifted by God. His flaming patriotism no doubt provoked him to eulogise the nation as the 'divine mother'. But it never made him parochial and chauvinstic nationalist. His nationalism is broader and comprehensive than mere patriotism. Moreover his advocacy of a unique type of spiritual nationalism was never without western influence. The nationalist movement in Ireland and the writings of Mazzini undoubtedly influenced him. Mazzini gave an ethical and cosmopolitan orientation to the purely political character of nationalism. But Aurobindo's conception of India as the divine mother and not merely a geographical unity was purely Indian in Origin.

Aurobindo's nationalism was religious and spiritual. However, an indepth analysis of Aurobindo's concept of nationalism reveals severals components which are discussed below:

### Nationalism as a Religion

Sri Aurobindo Ghosh deviated from the traditional western way of defining nationalism as merely a political concept. He gave a religious dimension to it. Nation is the divine mother. It has to be adored with real devotion and sacrifice. Hence, while addressing a public meeting in 1908, in the month of January at Bombay he said, "Nationalism is not a mere political programme; Nationalism is a religion that has come from God; Nationalism is a creed which you shall have to live... if you are going to be nationalist, if you are going to assent to this religion of nationalism, you must do it in the religious spirit. You must remember that you are the instrument of God". In other words, for Aurobindo, who believed in the Indian concept of God and religion, oriented his nationalism as a religious practice. But it is not a 'religion' in the way an ordinary man thinks. Religion here is not taken as an inactive thougthful life rather a vibrant activie life. It is a 'creed of the faith, love and knowledge'.

**Historical Spiritualism as the Foundation of Nationalism**

Sri Aurobindo Ghosh introduced spiritual approach to politics; like Hegel, he also believed that the events of history are determined by divine will. History is the manifestation and progressive self-revelation of Brahman, the absolute. The French Revolution was due to the will of God. So also there was the will of God behind the rise of India as a nation. Being influenced by sister Nivedita's 'Kali the Mother', Aurobindo believed life and death are but the parts of cosmic dance of Kali, the mother, who creates and also destroys. Referring to French Revolution he said, as long as the leaders of the revolution like Mirabeau, Danton, Robespierre and Napoleon exhibited in their role the will of Kali, she allowed them to work. When they wanted to assert their egoism and vital ambition, she removed them from the state of history. This type of theodicy in Sri Aurobindo Ghosh or what Hegel would call the justification and rationalisation of History in divine terms represents a fusion of the ideas of the *Bhagavadgita* and German Idealism.

**Nationalism is Permanent**

He was of strong conviction that spiritualism on dharma is the basis of nationalism and hence, nationalism is permanent. In May, 1909, at Uttarpara he said, in India Sanatan Dharma is nationalism. The nation is born with Sanatan Dharma and it shall move and grow only with it. For Sri Aurobindo Ghosh, since nationalism is based on Sanatan Dharma it is beyoned region or community. It is universal and permanent. Hence, he said, "Nationalism is not going to be crushed. Nationalism survives in the strength of God and it is not possible to crush it whatever weapons are brought against it. Nationalism is immortal. Nationalism cannot die; because it is no human being. It is God who is working in Bengal. God cannot be killed, God cannot be sent to jail." This revealed the invincible nature of his spiritual nationalism.

**Nationalism Demands Sacrifice**

In the perspective of the Indian nationalism, Sri Aurobindo Ghosh argued, since mother India is in chain, every Indian must be ready to fight tooth and nail against the British rule to unchain her. We must offer all that we have to our motherland, the goddess. He warned and wrote, "if any thought of self-pollutes the sanctity of our love, than the mother will not be satisfied and will continue to withhold her presence". In order to build-up a strong nation, the individual, the family and the class must make their sacrifice. He gave an organic concept of nationalism and argued that the fulfilment of the individual person can be achieved by means of identification with the national will.

**Political Independence is a Prerequisite of Nationalism**

Sri Aurobindo Ghosh was the first Indian to use the word 'independence' instead of Swaraj. Because he realised that politicial freedom preceeds other freedom. Political independence is highly essential for the rebirth and the rise of a nation. He argued liberty is the first indispensable condition of national development *i.e.*, intellectual, moral, industrial and poltical. Liberty is also necessary because that will enable India to lead the world towards the spiritual and moral advancement.

**Cosmopolitan Character of Nationalism**

Aurobindo's nationalism bears a cosmopolitan outlook. It is above sectarian, aggressive and narrow fanatic consideration. India by its spiritual treasure will help mankind towards a life of fullness, equality and unity. It will never behave like a master. The nationalism is only a necessary stage in social and political evolution of man. Ultimately there should be human unity through a World-Union.

Thus, Aurobindo made a moral and spiritual appraoch to the concept of nationalism. It differed from the western concept of nationalism and from the nationalism advocated by Tilak and the moderates. It is more comprehensive, progressive, humanitarian and cosmopolitan in nature. Truly he was the author of a neo-nationalism.

## CONCEPT OF HUMAN UNITY AND INTERNATIONALISM

Sri Aurobindo Ghosh was a spiritual visionary and an internationalist. His spiritual approach to internationalism made him the indisputed leader of a new world order. Man to man relationship will be the foundation of his new spiritual, humanitarian, international society of World-Union. He completely discarded the present internationalism grounded on political diplomacy, economic sanctions and threat of war. There will be no place for colonialism or imperialism. It will be a perfect society of equals and brotherhood to be its cardinal principle. Thus, Sri Aurobindo Ghosh, unlike other internationalists, never talked of a superficial world-federation.

He founded his internationalism on the edifice of a spiritual man with a perfect society. Though a nationalist, his nationalism was meant for a temporary phase. He said, 'after a nation is independent and strengthened, its duty will be to work for the entire humanity and not for narrow, parochial considerations'. Nationalism, for Aurobindo, is to be a blessing for internationalism. Because his nationalism is spiritual nationalism where individual action is determined by the will of providence and based on a common faith that the entire human generation is the creation of God, the absolute.

However, Sri Aurobindo's concept of internationalism has several foundations which are discussed below:

**World-Union**

Sri Aurobindo's internationalism do not envisage the formation of a world community through compulsion or force. It also does not imply a world state where nationalities will loose their identity. It envisions a "World-Union of free nationalities". In this new world order, there should no subjugation or inequality or subordination. It will be based on freedom and equality and guided by the ideals of human unity. Every one must have to believe that they are the parts of God, the absolute and hence, are related to each other. He argued, unity brought by world organisation like UNO may not be stable and real. Because it is based on temporary and superficial techniques like diplomacy and coercion. On the other hand 'World-Union' should be founded on the edifice of spiritual unification of mankind. He suggested that for the peace and progress of the real world, an enlightened method of education and moral training will be necessary. Secondly, society will have to evolve a more scientific method of observation.

**Opposed to Aggressive Nationalism and Colonialism**

Sri Aurobindo Ghosh was a staunch adocate of the concept of nationalism. He fought for the political independence of India and envisaged a strong India. But his nationalism was more spiritual and democratic. Though he defined the national but he never supported the idea of aggressive nationalism. Hence, during Second World War he condemned the fascist forces like Germany and Japan for their aggressive natioinalist pursuit. For him, nationalism is a temporary phase to liberate and strengthen a nation. Its real mission should be to work for the entire mankind. Hence, he defined internationalism as the attempt of the human mind and life to grow out of the national idea or form and even in a way to destory it in the the interest of the larger synthesis of mankind". To establish real internationalism, every nation must subordinate its national and racial interest to the common interests of mankind. Colonialism, imperialism, racialism and militarism must end.

**Unity in Diversity (Right of Self-Determination)**

According to Sri Aurobindo Ghosh, in his scheme of World-Union, every nation should work for world unity retaining their own identity. He never believed in the abolition of national boundaries and surrender of national independence. Every nation will have the right to self-determination. On the other hand the people of the world must be allowed to group themselves according to their free will and their natural affinities, "Unity would be the largest principle of life, but freedom would be its foundation stone". "In a world ridden with political, social and economic complexities, free assimilation may face some difficulties. But this difficulty should not be solved by means of force, but by argument and arbitration." He said 'some kind of confederation of the people for common human ends, for the removal of all causes of strife and differences, for inter-relation and the recognition of mutual aid and inter-change, yet leaving to each unit a full internal freedom and power of self-determination, would be the right principle of this unity." In other words, retaining their own culture, religion and nationality, nations would not discriminate against one another. The Worl-Union would be based on freedom and equality. It would place man face to face with man on the basis of their common human sympathy, aims and highest interest of the future.

**Universal Brotherhood**

Sri Aurobindo Ghosh argued, for the realisation of World-Union through human unity, society must be recognised on the basis of liberty, equality and fraternity. But unfortunately liberty and equality have been achieved in a mechanical and superficial way. There is neither real freedom nor real equality in the absence of fraternity. Fraternity is treated as impracticable so long as individual continues with his own ego. Only through real brotherhood, such problems can be removed . But real brotherthood exists in the soul and by the soul. An individual cannot be guided by his soul without spirituality. So to attend perfection through spirituality should be the primary objective. Only then brotherhood will be materialised and unification can be permanent. Such spiritual oneness will create psychological oneness discarding any intellectual or outward uniformity. Spiritual oneness will make individual interest subordinate to social interest and the interest of the mankind. At the same time society will give full opportunity to the individual for his spiritual growth, So both the individual and the society must work for perfection.

**Religion of Humanity**

Another pre-requisite of internationalism is the rise of a religion of humanity. The religion of humanity believe that we all are one; the divinity will reveal itself through humanity. It is a process of awakening of the soul in man. If creates a faith in man that mankind is the god to be worshipped and served by man. It helps man to realise the truth that man has a complete and peaceful life only when he lives as fellow being with others in the society. It believe in the transmigration of a materialist animal life of an individual to that of a spiritual life.

Thus, Sri Aurobindo's internationalism is untraditional and comprehensive. It is not only secular, democratic and progressive but also humanitarian, ethical and spiritual.

## HIS POLITICAL TECHNIQUES

Sri Aurobindo Ghosh was the first Indian to use the word "Independence for India" at a time when it was a mid-summer madness to talk about its. Even Tilak did not dare to use it. As mentioned in his political goal, Sri Aurobindo's objective was almost crystal clear. He never thought of anything less than freedom for India. To achieve that any method may be adopted because mother India was chained and her socio-cultural and polilitical identity had been strangulated by the British. Just as a man to escape from strangulation resorts to any means to save himself, people of India also may resort to any means to liberate the country. His intense patriotism made him an extreme nationalist. He never bothered for the 'means' and highlighted 'liberation' as the only end. Hence, he was very much critical of the Congress attitude towards British. His extremist view depreciated the 'mendicant' methods of the moderate Congress leadership and dismissed their policy of 'Prayer, petition and protest' as a bankrupt policy. However, 'Political liberty' being the primary goal of his political philosophy, he advocated different techniques such as the revival of national spirit and the regeneration of India's glorious past, direct revolutionary action (armed revolt and terrorism), passive resistance and boycott. Boycott included economic boycott, educational boycott, executive boycott and social boycott. Such techniques are discussed below:

### Regeneration of India's Old Pride

Sri Aurobindo was a great patriot and nationalist. He was convinced that in order to create an atmosphere of struggle against the British for freedom, the basic pre-requisite was to generate a sense of pride in every Indian about the glorious past of India. A reminiscence of India's great cultural heritage, her achievement in the realm of politics and social organisation, art and literature, her unique contribution in the realm of religion and philosophy would create a sense of confidence in the heart of the Indians. Hence, he worte, "to bring in the mass of the people, to find the greatness of the future or the greatness of the past, to infuse Indian politics with Indian religious fervour and spirituality are the indispensable conditions for a great and powerful political awakening in India". He himself made an untiring effort to create a national awakening through his writings in the 'Bande Mataram' and 'Karmayogin'. He wanted to instill faith in the mind of the Indians that in art, literature, culture, politics and civilisation, India has its own originality and edge over the British. Hence, he called upon the people of India not to imitate the British culture, commerce and politics blindly. He reiterated that being the inheritor of a great tradition, every Indian must feel proud of his own nation and brave the situation to make sacrifice for the motherland.

**Direct Revolutionary Action**

Sri Aurobindo Ghosh was an extremist and firebrand revolutionary. For him any revolutionary action can be justified to liberate the country. Even the force and violence may be used by the people to drive out the alien rulers. He said, "liberty is the life-breath of a nation; and when the life is attacked, when its is sought to suppress all chance of breathing by violent pressure, any and every means of self-preservation becomes right and justifiable—just as it is lawful for a man who is strangled to rid himself of the pressure on his throat by any means in his power. It is the nature of the pressure which determines the nature of resistance. Where, as in Russia the denial of liberty is enforced by legalised murder and outrage, or as in Ireland formerly by brutal coercion, the answer of violence to violence is justified and inevitable". From those words written by Sri Aurobindo Ghosh in his book on *"The Doctrine of Passive Resistance"*, it was beyond doubt that he favoured the use of violence in the freedom struggle against the oppressor. It would be a violent revolution against the alien ruler who had chained mother India. However, direct revolutionary action may be of two types : *(a)* Organised armed revolt *(b)* Terrorism.

(a) **Organised Armed Revolt.** Sri Aurobindo suggested for an armed revolt against the foreign rulers. As a realist he made an analysis of the British military power at the time and said it was not that powerful that it could not be fought out. No doubt India did not have arms. So he further suggested that an armed revolt could be organised by proper organisation and bringing arms from outside; a guerilla warfare may be organised, a general revolt in the Indian army of that period may be triggered. In 1905, in his Bhavani Mandir Scheme, he also presupposed the possibility of a mass armed revolt against the British.

(b) **Terrorism.** Terrorism was another revolutionary action supported by Sri Aurobindo though he realised that it would be absurd to expect random act of assassination to bring out the country's freedom. Terrorism is resorted in the absence of a mass armed revolt, peaceful poltical activities on the one hand, violent oppressive and suppressive policy followed by the the alien rulers on the other. He blamed the British Government for encouraging clandestine terrorist activities by their ruthless suppression and zeopardising all means of peaceful political activities. Sri Aurobindo himself during his Baroda period was associated with a number of secret revolutionary organisations functioning in Bengal and Maharashtra. He had a strong conviction that the terrorists were great patriots who were determined to make any sacrifice for their motherland.

Thus, Aurobindo believed in both peaceful political activities through press and platform. At the same time, he advocated the use of force and violence for the liberation of motherland.

**Passive Resistancc as a Political Technique**

Sri Aurobindo's idea underwent change after Bangal partition in 1905. After witnessing the mass awakening in Bengal, he realised that besides carrying out armed revolt and terrorist technique, mass movement can be organised as a method of achieving independence. Hence, he advocated the technique of passive resistance, which he thought to be the most natural and suitable weapon under the circumstances. In the *Bande Mataram*, he wrote a series of ariticles on passive resistance from April 9 to April 23, 1907, which were later on published under the title of "The Doctrine of Passive Resistance'.

He made a distinction between aggressive or active resistance and passive resistance. The method of aggressive resistance implies that the aggressive resister should do something by which he can do positive harm to the government. But the method of passive resister is to abstain from doing something by which he would be helping the government. The objective in both cases is the same—to force the hands of the government only; the line of attack is different. The passive method is especially suitable to the countries where the government depends mainly for the continuance of its administration on the voluntary help and acquiescence of the subiect people. Sri

Aurobindo made it clear that the passive resistance may turn to be violent in case of ruthless suppression by the ruler. Otherwise to submit to the illegal or violent methods of coercion, the country would be guilty of cowardice and dwarfing the national manhood. In this way it differed from Gandhiji's technique of non-violent resistance. Sri Aurobindo Ghosh said that the aim of passive resistance was to make the British administration ineffective by an organised refusal to do anything which would help the growth of British trade and commerce resulting in the exploitation of the country.

**Boycott as a Political Technique**

As a part of his technique of passive resistance, he suggested for 'boycotting' the British goods and commodities, schools, colleges, British offices and judiciary. He called upon the people to resort to economic boycott by refusing to purchase the British products. That would make them financially weak. People should disobey the unjust law and refuse to pay taxes. He suggested to boycott British education. Because the British education had done nothing excepting in producing a number of clerks in the country. It had also ruined the Indian culture and values. The British judiciary should also be boycotted as it would not give justice to the people. Lastly, social boycott may be applied to those who betrayed the cause of India's freedom.

**A Critical Appraisal**

Sri Aurobindo's political ideas have been assailed by the critics on different grounds. His concept of spiritual nationalism has been dubbed as 'reactionary' because it only talks about Hindu religious symbol as the form of divine mother. It also does not take into account the economic issues like poverty, exploitation and inequality in the society. It generates a sense of disunity among the different religious groups. His concept of human unity and internationalism based on the idea of divine family, led the critics to comment it as "too much idealistic" and "too much abstract". The critics also assailed him for not paying due importance to social and administrative reforms.

But such criticism never took note of the real implications of his political ideas and activities. He never interpreted religion in the formal sense of having a sectarian outlook. He gave primacy to political freedom because without this social and administrative reforms would be artificial and throttle the hope for freedom.

Moreover, posterity will recognise gratitude the astounding and permanent contribution made by Sri Aurobindo to political theory and to the entire mankind. His concept of spiritual nationalism, doctrince of passive resistance and boycott, ideal of human unity and internationalism constituting the bedrock of his political theory would be a guiding model for both empiricist and idealist, occidentalist and orientalist. Generations to come will hardly believe that a hardcore extremist of the freedom movement, later on became the great Yogi and the hero of a spiritual world, the world yet to be discovered by human endeavour.

## JAYA PRAKASH NARAYAN

J.P. Narayan, was born in 1902, and educated in the U.S.A. It was here that he came in contact with many socialists and practically went under the influence of Marxism. It was also during his stay over there that he studied M.N. Roy, another revolutionary of India, who had escaped to the U.S.A. to save himself from arrest and was influenced by his virtual Marxian philosophy. For quite sometime he remained under the influence of Marxism but as the time passed he began to lose faith in that mainly because it denied individual freedom and stood for party regimentation. In 1934, he founded Indian Socialist Party in which subsequently he also admitted the Communists. However, finding them not very sincere to socialist doctrines he truned them out and thus, saved his party from infiltration. In 1940, Jaya Prakash Narayan openly denounced Popular Front of the Communists and in 1942, he actively participated in the revolutionary movement. He got virtual name and fame in 1942, during Quit India Movement. He remained in jail for four years and once he even managed to escape from Hazari Bagh Central Jail. In 1946, along with other socialists he planned for a mass revolution.

**First Phase of J. P's Thoughts.** Jaya Prakash Narayan, commonly known as J.P. was a patriot who during first phase which spread between 1929-1953, thought in terms of socialism for solving

Indias socio-economic and political problems. He considered socialism as a way of reconstructing Indian economy. According to him present socio-economic inequality in India was primarily because of disproportionate ownership and control of means of production. He has said that for country's development it was essential that institutions which create hurdles on the way of development of man should be removed. In 1934, All India Congress Socialist Party came out with its 15-point programme which had J.P's ideology.

**15-Point Programme of All India Congress Socialist Party.** In the programme which had J.P's ideology it was proposed that all power should be transferred to producing masses and that economic life of the country should be developed, controlled and planned by the state. All key industries should be socialised and foreign trade should be monopolised by the state. It provided that public debt of India should be repudiated and state should not make any distinction on sex basis. In production and distribution stress should be laid on co-operative system and landlordism and similar other institutions of exploitations should be abolished without payment of any compensation. State should not make any distinction on the basis of caste, community, creed or religion. In the programme it was provided that the system of adult franchise on functional basis should be introduced and land should be distributed to the peasants; everyone should be given land according to his need and each one should work according to his capacity and lastly the right to work should be recognised.

He had proposed complete spearation of India from British imperialism and that debts of peasants and workers should be liquidated. He proposed that the producing masses should have all political and economic power and land should be given to the tillers.

Accroding to J.P. objectives of socialism can be achieved by socialisation of means of production. He also stood for reduction of land revenue.

**Resolution at Ram Garh Congress, 1940.** In 1940, J.P. submitted a draft resolution to the Ram Garh Congress, in which he advocated collective ownership and control of all large scale production and urged the Congress to stand for nationalisation of heavy transport, shipping, mining and heavy industries. In his draft resolution he proposed that in free India nation will work for peace between nations and there will be total rejection of armaments. Efforts will also be made to have excellent friendly relations with neighbouring states. The state will guarantee full individual and civil liberty and shall not discriminate in any manner between the citizens of the nation. The political and economic organisation of the state shall be based on the principle of social justice and economic freedom.

The village shall be made self-governing units, to the extent possible. The land laws of the country will be drastically reformed on the principle that land should belong to the actual cultivator. The interests of the poor and down-trodden shall be respected. In state controlled industries workers shall be represented on the management.

In Indian states there shall be complete democratic government.

**Stress on Village.** J.P. believed that village should be made self-governing unit. He stood for co-operative farming. He wanted to end the exploitation of the tillers and liquidation of all agrarian debts. He favoured agrarian reconstruction.

**His Programme of Gramraj.** In J.P's philosophy India's problems can be solved when village is reconstructed. He stood for Gramraj. In 1946, he gave his scheme of constructive work for Gramraj. In that he suggested that in the villages cultural centres should be opened and problems of health and sanitation should be solved keeping problems of each village in view. Attention should be paid quick redressal of grievances and removal of untouchability. Other items which needed attention included co-operative marketing, setting of grain banks and prohibition.

**J.P's Fourteen-Point Scheme.** In 1953, J.P. put forth fourteen-point scheme for increasing co-operation between Congress and PSP of Jaya Prakash Narayan. Though no compromise could be reached, yet his scheme indicated his thinking. In the scheme he suggested that Constitution should be so amended that guarantess given to princes and civil servants are ended; second chambers are abolished and all those articles of the Constitution which stand on the way of bringing social changes are removed. He wanted that administrative reforms at all levels should be introduced, corruption cases should be sunmarily dealt with and legal procedure should be suitably reformed.

J.P. wanted that administrative map of India should be redrawn taking language, economic and administrative factors into consideration. Administrative costs should be drastically reduced and in order to remove economic inequality and exploitation, land should be redistributed. State should not deal with individual peasants but with them through their groups in a group or panchayat. Rural economy should be transformed to co-operative economy and fragmentation of land should be checked. Suitable steps should be taken for consolidation of land holdings.

In his scheme J.P. proposed that waste lands should be reclamated and all banks and insurance companies should be nationalised. State trading should also be progressively developed and selected number of plants in different industries should be owned and run by the state or co-operatives. Unions should become socially responsible agencies, coals and other minings should be nationalised and in state enterprises workers should be associated with management. Areas of activities between large and small scale industries should be demarcated and salaries of highly paid officials should be brought down. Hen wanted that spirit of swadeshi should be promoted.

During this phase of life he thoroughly stood for developing India on socialist principles. He laid stress on increased agricultural production and inequality and exploitation, land shouldbe redistributed. State should international communism because it denied civil liberties. He did not contribute to both state controlloed system of education and its complete control over national economy.

## POLITICAL IDEAS FROM MARXISM TO DEMOCRATIC SOCIALISM

In 1954, J.P. resigned from the Socialist Party, then known as P.S.P., and became Jeewan Dani for Sarvodaya Movement and devoted himself to the cause of bringing about a new society in India in which there would be no exploitation and decentralization of authority would be the basic principle. He was very closely associated with Vinoba Bhave in his Bhoodan Movement. He wanted to have a new society which he termed as Sarvodaya. In 1974, he gave the concept of Total Revolution, which had mass apeal. In 1975 internal emergency was declared in the country and he was jailed. In 1977 elections were held in India and because of his efforts anti-Congress forces could form Janata Party which snatched power from the ruling Congress and formed Government at the Centre and also in many States. To his dismay these disintegrated in 1979. He fell ill and died in October of that year.

**Differences with Marxism.** J.P. loved Marxism his love for it did not last long. He developed differences with that for serveral reasons. He did not support atrocities of Russian Bolshevik Party on the one hand and authoritarian regimentation of Russian Communism on the other. He also did not like Communist approach towards national freedom being launched under Gandhiji. They denounced it as bourgeoisie and Gandhiji as Indian brourgeoisie. He felt that Communists in India were tools of Moscow. He condemend their loyalties towards Russia than to India. He was opposed to Lenin's colonial policy. Though he developed differences with Marxism yet he could not go very near Congress viewpoint. He believed that Congress could not provide real socialist programme to the country and conduct the fight for independence in a more revolutionary manner with the result that he formed Congress Socialist Party with the help of some disillusioned Congressmen.

**Towards Sarvodaya (Second Phase).** J.P., stood for bringing socialism in India but after some years he realised that it could not take mankind towards freedom, equality, brotherthood and peace. At Bodh Gaya Sarvodaya Sammelan held in 1953, he was convinced that unless Socialism war transferred into Sarvodaya, people could not go near the goals of freedom, equality and brotherhood. He then completely broke away from Communism and proceeded towards Sarvodaya.

**Basic Principles of Sarvodaya.** The idea of Sarvodaya was first adopted by Gandhiji from Ruskins 'Unto the Last'. According to Gandhiji he himself felt a sort of inner happiness when he got this idea. Sarvodaya meant collective welafare in which also was indvidual's own welfare and that there was always respect for work and that all types of jobs were respectable. In addition to this, it also meant that simple living and high thinking was true life and there should be universal development for all sections of society. According to Vinoba Bhave, "Self sacrifice is the very foundation of the Sarvodaya which preaches the emerging of oneself in the good of all." On the whole both Jaya Prakash Narayan as well as Vinoba Bhave believed that Sarvodaya is a moral programme and line of action and that it should be a useful instrument for collective welfare. In addition to that, Sarvodaya is an indication of a political revolution by peaceful means through free and frank expression of ideas. It has been said, "Ideally such a structure would replace completely the compulsion of the State of individual initiative and voluntary organisation, it is a sort of enlightened anarchy." In the economic field Sarvodaya stands for decentralization of authority and that the means of production as well as distribution shall be controlled and managed by the society. In Sarvodaya society there will be co-operative system of production both in the industry as well as agriculture.

**Qualities of a Sarvodaya Worker.** A Sarvodaya worker was required to spin daily and use the cloth spun by himself. As far as possible he should use goods produced by cottage and small scale industries. He should try to use cow milk and should clean latrines or do other work relating to cleanliness of the village at least once a month. Where there are possibilities of introducing basic system of education he should try to introduce that. He should also try to learn at least one of the reginoal languages of India. Not only that but he should be an ideal non-violent person with a sense of self-confidence and belief in power of the masses. He should also try to promote unity among various religions and sections of the society and should boycott caste system and discourage the use of intoxicating goods. He should also promote female education and try to spread the idea that both men and women are equal. He should also try to spread regional languages and provincial cultures so that none of them felt neglected. He should aim at bringing about economic equality, growth of agriculture, help in the unity of labourers and uplifting the poor.

**Sarvodaya Society.** The Society which shall thus be established under Sarvodaya Samaj will be free coercive centralized authority and shall be more or less a loose federation consisting of self-government autonomous villages. Every village or unit shall be self-sufficient and believe in the system of economic decentralization. In Sarvodaya society there was to be no parliament of the type which we at present have and those who came to power were not be the rulers but servants of the society. He believe that State shall be unnecessary in Sarvodaya society, and as far as possible the authority of the State will considerably be reduced.

In his opinion State does not help in the development of individual faculties but on the other hand is an unhealthy check even on individual's healthy activities. He, therefore, felt that there was no need to load government with so many punitive weapons and authorities in actual practice hampered individual progress.

He felt that in Sarvodaya society there shall be no party system and the people shall sit together to decide their own affairs. They will not require representatives to speak and talk on their behalf but on the other hand shall get opportunity to express their own ideas themselves. He wanted that in Sarvodaya society consciousness among the people should be created and there should be real Lok Neeti instead of Raj Neeti. In other words in Sarvodaya society there shall not be party or power politics but only authority shall flow from the people themselves who will work in a sense and spirit of serving the people rather than of governing over them. Jaya Prakash Narayan believed that conflicts always arise in a society due to various reasons but in his opinion solution to such problems did not lie in equipping the government with more punitive powers but in creating awakening and consciousness among the masses so that they could adjust themselves in a better and reasonable way.

**From Socialism to Sarvodaya.** In his early life Jaya Prakash Narayan was a serious student of Marxism. In 1929, when Indian National Congress declared complete independence as the goal of its national struggle, Jaya Prakash then bade farewell to his Marxist ideology and actively participated in the civil disobedience movement launched by Mahatma Gandhi. He, however, wanted to introduce socialism in the Congress with the result that he founded the Congress Socialist Party which was subsequently responsible for giving socio-economic programme both to the party and also the country, he seriously studied Gandhi an philosophy and was convinced that spiritual foundation was required for a lasting peace. In addition to that, he began to realise the value of individual freedom, equality and brotherhood which were in practice missing from Communism.

A turning point, however, came with Vinoba's coming in the field. His starting of the Bhoodan Movement and getting a donation of 100 acres of land from Shri Ram Chandra Reddy changed the very course of his philosophy. He began to appreciate the importance and significance of the methods which he felt could bring about an economic revolution in the country if seriously implemented. He found in Bhoodan Movement a fair, better and effective alternative to Communist revolution which provided for snatching of land by forceful methods. According to him Gandhism taught us the method of Satyagraha which brought freedom to India and that Bhoodan and Gramdan Movement was bound to bring economic revolution and make our political freedom a reality. He was also inspired by the idea of Lok Neeti instead of Raj Neeti as expounded by Vinobaji. Gradually he was also convinced about the disriability of cottage industries and the system of democratic decentralization. He also wanted to change the face of India by introducing village autonomy and raising the down-trodden and the poor who form a vast majority of Indian population. In his opinion Bhoodan and Gramdan movements are constructive techniques and easy as well as practicable solution to India's problems.

## POLITICAL IDEAS OF JAYA PRAKASH NARAYAN

Politically, he believed that dawn of a new society for all, irrespective of caste and status, would emerge under Sarvodaya. His significant political ideas are as under :

**1. His Reservations about Parliamentary Democracy.** Jaya Prakash Narayan was a very staunch supporter of democracy and favoured democratic institutions. For him, democracy was both a creed and a way of life and that nothing beyond democracy could satisfy him. He was believer of individual freedom which could best be achieved only in democracy. He was however, not satisfied with the present democratic system which he felt was highly defective. In his opinion present system was highly centralized with the result that the people could not take any active part in the proper functioning of democratic institutions. The control of party bosses is so rigid that individual is practically ignored. He also felt that parliamentary system, in its present form, has a very narrow base because in that the authority starts from above rather from down below. It has thus, an inverted structure which cannot last long. He also condemned decmocracy because legislative bodies which governed in the name of majority were in fact minority Governments. In actual practice minority rules over the majority. Not only this but the decisions arrived at by the majority party are not unanimous. Similarly even in the Cabinet decisions are not arrived at unanimously and only a few powerful persons carry others with them. All this clearly shows that the majority is ruled by the minority.

He also felt that in our present parliamentary democracy the institution of party system is very unhealthy. It had practically denied liberty to the individuals. Party bosses try to dominate their members. There is an on going and continuous struggles for supremacy which divides the rank and file and also promotes insincerity. He has condemned democracy also because he finds that in it there is much unnecessary waste of national money. Jaya Prakash Narayan was also pained to see that in our modern democracies those who could speak well irrespective of any other consideration managed to come to power. He was also pained to find that in order to win the elections all healthy and unhealthy practices were being used. Even casteism and communalism which is not to be legally used in elections, is used to win the election.

**Qualities of True Democrat.** In his opinion a democracy in its true sense must have spiritual basis and that can only be possible when the people practising it begin to believe in truth. They should also truly follow non-violence and should be ready to face all oppressions and high-handedness with courage and boldness. They should love liberty and believe in the spirit of not only toleration and co-operation. A true democrat should also be ready to willingly discharge his duties and responsibilities. He should be a believer in human equality. There should be belief in the decentralization of aouthority. The power should flow from down to above and not flow from above to down below.

**Faith in Parliamentary Democracy.** In spite of all his reservations for parliamentary decmocracy, he had still hopes that it could deliver the goods. In it, there is every possibility of maximum decentralisation of authority. Again it is the system which can establish links and co-ordinate between industry and agriculture on the one hand and rural and urban activities on the other. It can also help in establishing self-sufficising system of government.

**Ideas about a Partyless Democracy.** As already said, Jaya Prakash felt that the introduction of party system in our present political set-up had degenerated democracy. The present day system encourages party politics and divides the nation. He, therefore, felt that the whole system should be changed. There should be a partyless democracy. His suggestion was that in each village there should be a Gram Mandal or a Conference consisting of elected representatives of the village, one at least from each farmily. Such a Mandal should meet monthly to decide all pending issues of the village. There should be no need and necessity of electing representatives to speak on behalf of the people but the people themselves will express their feelings and view-point. Each Mandal then in turn will become an electoral college to send representatives to the legislatures. The whole arrangement shall be of the kind and nature that the authority will go down from villages to the legislatures and thus, real democracy will emerge.

**Reconstruction of Indian Polity.** During sceond phase of his political development he tried to reconstruct Indian polity. He suggested that the defects of modern democracies which need be removed include corruption, expensive elections, centralisation of authority and partisanship attitude of political parties. Masses should be mobilised for active participation in democratic processes. There should be work-oriented education and that legitimate demands of the masses should also be met. Other suggenstions made by him include differentiation in the names of political system, checking of authoritarian domination, involvement of all adults in the political system, promotion of social collaboration, Gramdan, administrative efficiency, formation of Shanti Sena, undertaking of rural reconstruction programme and more autonomy for states. He wanted that our present day democratic set-up should be based on ancient Indian values. He also wanted that our whole system should be above all castes, creeds and religions so that all Indians without any other consideration could participate in that. According to him in real democracy there should be rule of law.

He also laid stress on moral values. He considered democracy not only a form of government but also a creed and way of life. It should be made to operate in a way that all get social and economic justice, there is equality of opportunity and also balanced development of industry and agriculture. He believed that political and economic democracies could not be separated from each other.

**His Ideas about Panchayati Raj.** According to Jaya Prakash Narayan real solution to our political problems laid in the introduction of Panchayati Raj system is our body politic. As far as authority is not decentralized among the millions in our villages, nothing concrete can come out. The proposal given by him was that in each village there should be Gram Sabha which shall from the basis of the entire scheme. The Sabha shall consist of all adult men and women living in that village and shall have the power to discuss about life and problems of the village. Gram Pachayat shall be the executive organ of this Sabha. Subsequently there shall be Zila Parishads and Block Samitis at the higher level. Block Samitis shall cover the villages falling in one block and a few blocks combined together shall from Zilas. Jaya Parakas Narayan fully well realized the difficulties which could arise in the establishment of Gram Sabha or Gram Conference. In addition to this, he also realized that caste system could also be one of the reasons for its not very successful working. He felt that if proper and effective steps are taken, there can no reason to think that all difficulties and complications which can come in the way of proper and successful working of Pachayati Raj cannot be overcome. One of the methods suggested by him in this regard, was that the people should be given proper education. As far as possible family feuds and party system should not be allowed to interfere in the Gram Panchayats and Gram Sabhas. These Sabhas should be given some effective powers and real authority should be given to the Sabhas so that these could effectively exert themselves. He also suggested that the Sabhas should be given sufficient economic resources and authority to control civil servants working under their jurisdiction. As far as possible the Sabhas and Panchayats should have a non-political character and there should be no intervention from the high ups in the sphere of their jurisdiction. Jaya Prakash felt that if this system was introduced in the villages a new life was bound to come in the country.

**His Economic Ideas.** Jaya Prakash Narayan believed in the socialisation of means of production and distribution. He also believed in the nationalization of industries and suggested that economic resources should be placed at the disposal of the nation rather than any individual. He also suggested reduction of land revenue and also limitations on expenditure. He favoured collective ownership and control of all large scale industries. He suggested that such heavy industries, as transport, mining or shipping should forthwith be nationalized. He, however, believed that co-operative effort alone could bring about balance between agriculture and industry. He wanted to have economic rehabilitation of the poor and the down-trodden. He also believed in agrarian reconstruction. He was a strong supporter of co-operative farming. In his philosophy there was very close relationship between culture and economics because the culture of a nation was reflected by economic conditions of its people. He felt that economic conditions of the country should be such that every individual got equality of opportunity and was given some minimum economic standard.

Jaya Prakash Narayan was a socialist of the first order. He tried to awaken the youth of India by telling them to remember the role which they played during Quit India Movement and gave them a call to re-unite themselves to perform that constructive duty. His system of democratic decentralization and Panchayati Raj and that of adopting democracy in its new form, if properly adopted, can bring a new outlook in India.

## CONCEPT OF TOTAL REVOLUTION

During first phase of his life Jaya Prakash Narayan came out of the influence of Marxism and propagated his philosophy of socialism, which for him was only solution to the problems of India. During second phase he devoted himself to the cause of Sarvodaya and became Jeevandani. Between 1970-72, he tried to end the influence of Naxalwad in Bihar. Because of his efforts in 1972, as many as 400 dacoits of Chambal Valley decided to surrender before him. They promised to live as peaceful and good citizens of India. He was however, not satisfied with many policies of Congress government then headed by Prime Minister Smt. Indira Gandhi and in 1974, he gave the slogan of Total Revolution. In order to achieve his objective he organised demonstrations and set-up students committees and held public meetings. Because of his activities, which had good response from the masses, on 26th June, 1975, internal emergency was declared and he was put behind the bars, where he remained till emergency was lifted in 1977.

**J.P.'s Concept of Total Revolution.** On June 5, 1974, J.P. gave a call to Total Revolution at Patna. The whole idea was to bring about a complete change in the existing structures of Indian society. He was of the view that power could not be transferred to the people through military strenght or violence because after bringing changes military does not involve the people in the formation of policies and programmes. According to his total revolution, which covered seven areas, the number of which could increase or decrease, could bring real changes in several ways.

**His Seven Revolutions.** His Total Revolution was combination of seven revolutions namely social, economic, political, cultural, ideological or intellectual, educational and spiritual. This number could increase or decrease as well *e.g.*, economic revolution could be split into agricultural, industrial and technological revolutions. Similarly, intellectual revolution could be split into scientific and philosophical. Similary spiritual revolution also could be part of cultural revolution.

The concept of Total Revolution had wide implications. It aimed at total transformation of both man and society. It has been viewed differently by different people.

**Economic Revolution.** In the economic field Total Revolution aimed at reducing grossly disproportionate inequalities in socio-economic fields. It also aimed at saving the villages from urban exploiters and transfer of land owership to the villages for solving the problem of inequality centering round land ownership. It also wanted that public co-operation pattern in industries should be made more popular and everyone must be provided need-based wages with guarantee of full employment. Effective checks should be put on price rise.

Workers should be considered as the trustees of large industrial establishments and the basic principles should be social ownership. In the indusrty similarly the idea of self-government should be developed. Rural based industries should be developed and strengthened and for the purpose massive and integrated programme may be developed. There should be real linkage between the prices of agricultural and industrial products.

**Political Revolution.** In the political field it was provided that the candidates for the elected bodies should be slected by the peoples committees and the people should be consulted for the purpose. Both the army and the police need not obey those orders of the government which aimed at killing the innocent or were manifestly illegal or tried to subvert democratic culture of our society. Governmental processes should be based on discussions and there should be comprehensive law against defection. For selecting candidates there should be combination of majority vote and list system. The system of recall of elected legislators who have lost the confidence of the people should be introduced. Everyone who holds high posts whether elected or otherwise should periodically declare assets and none should hold any political office for more than two terms.

**Educational Revolution.** In intellectual, moral, educational and spiritual fields Total Revolution aimed at avoiding violence and desired that educational and economic planning should go hand in hand. In order to promote good life some moral and ideal standards acceptable to all should be developed. Universities should be freed from nepotism and should also become pure centres of teaching, training and research. Only those should be allowed to pursue higher education who have academic orientation. Co-operation in every field of life should be encouraged. Consistent efforts should be made to develop good habits in the minds of the people. Science should be humanised and spirit of tolerance to appreciate the view point of others should be developed.

**Social Revolution.** In the social field revolution aimed at ending irrational and illogical customs, conventions and practices. The system of inter-caste marriages should be encouraged. Existing caste system should be replaced by one caste *i.e.*, human caste.

**His Line of Action.** In his programme of action he did not favour the use of violence, which according to him brought changes in the elites and not in the lot of the masses. He favoured the policy of Gandhian Satyagraha. He however, said that once goals were fixed there could be no dogmatism about the means provided goals and values were kept in view. On the basis of experience the means could be changed as well. He favoured persuasion and where necessary the policy of non-cooperation could also be used. All bureaucratic pressures should be countered effectively and vigorously by the people. Youth and student power should be fully mobilised because that can go a long way in bringing Total Revolution. He favoured civil desobedience and civil resistance and also direct takeover of the management and running of the enterprises.

**Critical Assessment of Concept of Total Revolution.** J.P.'s concept of Total Revolution was a good synthesis of socialist dynamism and rural realism which J.P. developed during second phase of evolution of political development. It was a comprehensive concept and had several dimensions. It aimed at bringing radical changes not by violent means but with the help of persuasion. It hed lofty ideal of reducing both poverty and craze for power. It wanted social control over means of production and distribution. It also wanted to end social stagnation and use youth and student energies in constructive channels. It touched most impotant problem of rural reconstruction on the one hand and checking of urban exploiters rural masses on the other. It wanted to push to remote corners casteism and communalism which are chronic problems of Indian society and great impediments in the way of bringing social harmony. It also wanted that by distribution of land to the cultivators not only production would increase but land thirst of many would also be satisfied.

But unfortunately his concept of Total Revolution was viewed differently and before it could hold ground J.P. was arrested in 1975, and released in 1977, after remaining in jail for about 19 months due to declaration of internal emergency. During these 19 months no agitations were allowed and the concept did not draw much attention.

**Last Days of J.P.** After lifting of internal emergency J.P. organised some non-Congress (I) political parties which formed Janata Government at the Centre, after 1977, elections. It was crowning success of the his efforts, but soon he realised that his efforts were not to give fruit for long because of internal bickering of constituents of Janata Party. He would have tried to unite them again, but he hiself fell ill and died in 1979, as a frustrated man.

## B.R. AMBEDKAR

In the Post-Vedic period, 'caste' became the predominant feature of Hindu polity. It brought social inequality, rigid social divisions and disunity among different people. It gave supermacy to Brahmins but the Sudras and untouchables remained underprivileged. The system perpectuated till the advent of British rule in India. But it was only during British rule, caste rigidity came to be under challenge. The incoming of Renaissance in India also gave brith to a number of Social Reform moevements which challenged the validity of caste system and fought for the cause of untouchable; prominent among the leaders of social reform movements were Raja Rammohan Roy and his Brahm Samaj, Dayananada Saraswati and his Arya Samaj, Swami Vivekananda and his Sri Ramakrishna Mission, Justice Ranade of Maharashtra and Jyotiba Phuley, who founded Satyashodak Samaj in 1873, in Maharashtra to fight against Caste System and untouchability. It was during this period B.R. Amberkar was born on April, 14, 1891.

### Childhood

Bhimarao Ramji Ambedker was born at Ambedgaon village in Ratnagiri district of Maharashtra. He was born in an untouchable

Sakbal Mahar Community. His father Ramji Maloji Sankpal was a military man and was a disciple of Kabir, the preacher of Bhakti cult. His mother's name was Bheema Bai. But Bheema Bai died when Ambedkar was only six years old.

Ambedker underwent an inhuman treatment from his childhood because he was an untouchable. The bullock cartman refused to carry him, the barber declined to cut his hair and in the school, the teacher did not touch his note-books due to fear of being polluted. He continued his study in Government High School, Satara beginning from standard one itself. His school name was Bhiva Ramji Ambavadkar. But there was a teacher-cum-social reformer named Ambedkar in that school. The tracher loved him and inspired him so much that Bhimrao began to call himself Ambedkar and followed the footprints of his teacher-reforemer. Ambekar passed his Matriculation examination in 1970. This was a great event to be remembered as a boy from the untouchable Mahar family passed the Matriculation. A meeting was organised to congratualte him under the Presidentship of S.K. Bole, one of the leaders of Satyashodak movement. But during his school career Ambedkar had to marry Ramabai, a girl of only nine years as there was child marriage system.

**His College Days**

Because of the progressive attitude and helping hands of the Maharaja Sayaji Rao of Baroda Ambedkar could dare to pursue his higher education. He joined Elphinstone College. He was granted a scholarship of rupees twenty five per month, Professor Muller gave him clothes and books. But Ambedkar's humiliation did not change. The college hostal-keeper who was a Brahmin did not give him tea or water. But Ambedkar did not bother for such things because he was determined to pursue his education. With much hardship he completed his graduation in 1912. In the mean time his father died on February, 2, 1913. Ambedkar lost an inspiring friend and father.

But again the Maharaja of Baroda Gaekward sent him to USA for his higher study. Accordingly he joined Columbia University as a Gaekward Scholar. He became the first Mahar untouchable to read in a foreign university—a unique opportunity for an Indian indeed.

Professor Seligman, well-known economist, was his teacher at Columbia. In June, 1915, he obtained M.A. degree for his thesis "Ancient Indian Commerce". In may, 1916 he read a paper on "The castes in India, their mechanism, Genesis and development' at the Anthropology seminar sponsored by Dr. Goldonweiser. In June, 1916 he submitted his thesis for Ph.D. degree on the topic 'National Dividend for India: A Historic and Analytical Study'. This was later on published in the form of a book entitled 'The Evolution of Provincial Finance in British India'. From Columbia University he went to London School of Economics as a graduate student. But as his scholarship was terminated, he had to come back to India.

He was appointed as Secretary in the department of Defence to the Maharaja of Baroda. Had there been a boy from higher caste, he would have been extended a warm welcome. But Alas! Poor Ambedkar was an untouchable. He was deprived of such compliments in spite of his scholarly achievement in a foreign country. Rather he was ill treated even by the peons of higher castes. Peons flung office files on his table and drinking water was not available to him in the office. Ambedkar could realise the condition of millions of his untouchable brothers. He resigned his post, left Baroda and came to Bombay. He served as a Professor of Political Economy in Sydenham college, Bombay. But here also, social treatment did not change. He left Bombay and went to London to pursue his study in law and economics. He entered into Gray's Inn to qualify as Barrister. His wife Ramabai managed herself by selling her ornaments but declined to take any financial help from anybody. In June, 1921, he presented his thesis 'Provincial De-cerntralisation of Imperial Finance in British India' and got M.A. degree in Economics from London. He also completed his Bar at Law and came back to India to join the Bar in April, 1923.

**Social Revolutionary**

Ambedkar proved himself to be one of the great intellecutals of India. Eleandor Zelliot writes, "the influence of these years (education in foreign countries) seems to have been the development of pragmatism and self-confidence, faith in education and a deep belief in flexible Parliamentary democracy. Curiously enough, any sort of doctrinaire socialism left no mark on him and he had no alliance with

European political groups. He seems to have returned with the idea that India must evolve its own form of Parliamentary democracy and its own cure for its problem of inequality. Rather Ambedkar was deeply influenced by Buddha, Kabir and Jyotiba Phooley. Buddha and Kabir shaped his philosophical conviction of human equality, Jyotiba Phooley, a social reforms taught him to fight against higher caste supremacy and elevation of the masses through education and economic upliftment. Ambedkar's idea became to establish a society based on liberty, equality and fraternity. He was determined to fight against the caste system. He gave precedence to social change over political independence. His mission became to oppose the orthodoxical social arrangement and fight for political rights of the untouchables. Both society and politics became his area of operation.

Ambedkar appealed the people of lower castes to reform their way of life. He urged them to stop the carrying of dead cattle out of the village. He advised them to give up eating carrion, alcoholic drinks and begging. He wanted them to educate themselves and dress well.

On the other hand, he resorted to non-violent agitational method to arouse people's conscience and to protest against some of the Hindu laws. He called upon the people to burn the *Manusmriti* which according to Ambedkar perpetuated the social, economic and religious and political slavery of the untouchables. The *Manusmriti* was burnt on December 25, 1927.

He also started Satyagraha to enter into Kala Ram Mandir temple at Nasik in May, 1930. Because this temple was previously prohibited for the Harijans. About 15000 male volunteers and 500 females volunteers joined the satryagraha. A long procession proceeded towards the Kala Ram Mandir but the doors of the temple were closed. So they proceeded to the Ghats of the Godavari River. The higher caste Hindus threw chapals and pelted stones at the gathering.The tension between the caste Hindus and the Harijans continued. The temple was closed for on year. Ambedkar himself never believed in temple worship. So the programme of temple entry was more for social than for religious purpose. Such programmes continued till 1930. After 1930, he frought for the political rights of the untouchables.

The first Round Table Conference was convened in London in November, 1930 with Indian representatives. Dr. Ambedkar was invited to attend the conference as the leader of the untouchables. Ambedkar presented the entire picture of the inhuman condition in which untouchables in India were leading their life. He also lambasted the British government by saying, "150 years of British rule did not alter even a little the position of the untouchables. They were prevented from drawing water from the wells, from entering into temples etc. by the caste Hindu society. The Government itself prevented their recuritment in the police and the military service on the ground that they were untouchables." He demanded separate electorates for the depressed backward classes. In the second Round Table Conference when he reiterated his stand on separate electorate, Gandhiji opposed it by saying that this would perpetuate untouchability for ever. When both Ambedkar and Gandhi came into conflicting oppinion the British Prime Minister Ramsay MacDonald declared communal awared by which the depressed classes were granted separate seats in the provincial Assemblies and they were given the right of double vote. This was not accepted by Gandhiji; hence he declared fast unto death. Ambedkar was unperturbed and said, "Mahatmas have come and Mahatmas have gone but the untouchables have remained as untouchables". Finally the matter was resolved when 148 seats were accepted as the reserved seats by the Congrees and Ambedkar agreed to it. This came to be known as famous Poona Pact. Gandhiji broke the fast but asked everyone to work for the abolition of untouchability within a protracted period. Accordingly in 1938, the removal of Civil Disabilities Act was passed by the Madras Legislature. In July, 1939, at the instance of the Gongrees leaders, the temple at Madurai was opened to the Harijans. Thus, Ambedkar actified the Congress and Gandhiji to fight against untouchability. Ambedkar was also one among the few social reformers who made a political approach to the social problems of the oppressed classes.

**Ambedkar as the Labour Member, Law Minister and Chairman of Drafting Committee**

Dr. Ambedkar was appointed as the Labour member of Viceroy's Executive Council. He accepted it to prove that the untouchables also can administer. As the Labour member, he was always in favour of the labourers. He said that labour ought to work for the total control over the government. It was not enough that India should get Swaraj; it was more important in whose hands the swaraj would be. As labour member in April, 1944, he moved an amending Bill proposing holidays with pay for industrial workers employed in perennial factories. He also moved a Bill to amend the Indian Trade Unions Act, (1926). this Bill sought to compel an employer to recognise a Trade Union. The measure was unique as it safeguarded the interests of working class. He resigned from his post in the last week of May, 1946. It was during this period that he initiated the formation of All India Scheduled Castes Federation. It functioned as a political party which contested the General Election of 1946, but was completely routed. The motive behind the formation of this organisation was to keep the untouchables away from the organisation with higher caste dominance.

Ambedkar was elected to the Constituent Assembly of India by the members of the West Bengal Legislative Assembly, but lost from Bombay. He was also elected as the member of Drafting Committee in the Constituent Assembly. After partition of India, Ambedkar became very much realistic and decided to work alongwith the power that be. His attitude made the Congress support his candidature for the post of chairmanship of the Drafting Committee. He was elected the Chairman of Drafting Committee. Even Gandhiji said, an intellectual like Ambedkar was worthy of holding such a post. The other members of the Drafting Committee were N. Gopalswami Ayyanger, Sir Alladi Krishnaswami Ayyar, K.M. Munshi, Sir Muhammad Sadulla, N. Madhav Menon and D.P. Khaitan. B.N. Rau was the constitutional adivser. Dr. Ambedkar's original genius and his rich experience in different constitutional system of the world contributed highly in the constitution making process of India. He guided all the deliberations and decisions of the Constituent Assembly and shared the benefit of his wisdom in creating a constitution with the noble ideals of liberty, equality and fraternity.

The interim Government came into existence after the visit of Cabinet Mission Plan and assumed office on Spetember 2, 1946. This government continued even after Independence. Ambedkar was made the first Law Minister of independent India in Nehru's cabinet and he was the first untouchable to become the Cabinet Minister of Independent India. Ambedkar softened his attitude towards the Congress and Gandhiji to build-up a new India where the people of depressed classes will really be free. As the Law Minister of India, he wanted to bring uniform civil code for the Hindus. Hence, he introduced Hindu Code Bill in the Parliament which included abolition of the doctrine of rights by brith, aboslute right over property given to women, provision for inter-caste marriage and divorce. But the Bill could not be adpoted because of the conspiracy of some higher caste Hindu leaders and Ambedkar resigned from Nehru's Cabinet on September 27, 1951.

**Conversion to Buddhism**

Ambedkar realised that individual and group mobility were impossible with Hindu religion. The untouchables would not get justice under Hinduism. Hence, he renounced Hinduism and converted to Buddhism of 14 October, 1956. This was a part of his promise in 1936, that he would not die as a Hindu. Though many religious leaders of the world requested him to convert to Chirstianity and Islam, he converted to Buddhism. This he did because Buddhism, he said is a part of Indian culture and secondly Buddhism as a religion is based on three principles of knowledge, right path and compassion.

**End of an Era**

He went to Kathmandu to attend the World Buddhist Conference. He delivered lecture on 'Buddha and Marx'. He came back to New Delhi and attended a function organised at the honour of the Dalai Lama. On 4 December, 1956, he was present in the Council of States. But unfortunately on 6th December, 1956, he never got up from his bed and joined eternity while in deep slumber. With his death, the era of self-less crusade for the cause of the depressed class and the downtroddens came to an end.

## Views on Indian Political System

B.R. Ambedkar was a social revolutionary and true liberal who worked for a new polical order and envisioned a 'people's India' as well as a 'united India'. Indian polity since long has been undergoing a process of modernisation. Many greatmen have immensely contributed for modernising the polity. But a microscopic few like Ambedkar have played a multi-dimensional role in the modernisation process of the entire country. He is one among the few who realised that modernisation of the polity remains vague without social change. Accordingly he started his career as a social revolutionary. He awlays held the view that Hinduism was responsible for the disorganisation and demoralisation of Indian Society. With strong determination to fight social justice, Amebedkar started his social reform movement under the banner of Bahiskrita Hitakarini Sabha. Ambedkar was the first among the galaxy of social reformers in India who made a legal and political approach to the social problems in India. Indian National Congress also undertook the problem of untouchability under the leadership of Gandhiji but it was more based on religious and spiritual thinking. Dr. Ambedkar made a positive attempt to elevate the position of untouchables. He gave them a call to stop consuming carrion, alcoholic drinks and dragging of dead cattle out of the village. From 1930, onwards he devoted himself for the educational development of untouchables. Among a number of social reformer he was the first to fight for the political and legal rights of the untouchables because according to him, a revolution is merely transference of political power form one party to another party. Real social change will occur if the revolution is accompanied by a redistribution of power among the forces operating in the soceity. He prepared a declaration of fundamental rights safeguarding cultural, religious and economic rights of the depressed classes and submitted it to the minorities sub-committee. He was very much emphatic in his demand for abolishing untouchability and establishing equal citizenship. He also demanded separate electorate for the depressed classes as he knew that depressed classes would not have any identity within the Hindu fold. Not doubt, Ambedkar was misunderstood by the leaders of the Indian National Congress but whether it is giving evidence before the Simon Commission, or Round Table Conference or demand for separate electorate, Ambedkar's objective has always been to establish true social democracy in India. Ambedkar was not a

Marxist but he strongly realised that social and economic democracy must precede political democracy. He was not only concerned about the untouchables in India but he was equally worried about he degrading position of women in India. He fought for their liberation from male chauvinism. Women should have equal position with that of men in the soceity. An egalitarian social order demands equality not only between men and men only but also between men and women. Dr. Ambedkar as a member of Bombay Legislative Council fought for the Maternity Benefit Bill to recognise the dignity of women. As the Law Minister of India, Ambedkar introduced the Hindu Code Bill on February 5, 1951. The Hindu Code Bill introduced only four new things in their existing law. They were, abolition of the doctrine of the right by birth, right over property to women, share to daughters from the parental property and provision for divorce. Also it, insisted upon the consent of the wife to the adoption of a son by the husband. A daughter was permitted to be adopted. Thus, he was a feminist of the first order in India. The main objectives behind Ambedkar's movement for social change has been primarily to establish an egalitarian social order, which will be the real foundation of a modern Indian democratic polity. He always emphasized that, "the first condition which I think is a condition precedent for the successful working of democracy is that there must be no glaring inequalities in the Society." Another objective has been to establish true 'integration' of different sections in the mainstream of national life.

Ambedkar's another mission has been to make the Indian polity free from economic exploitation. Because he strongly believed that "casteless" and "classless" society should be the main foundation of Indian polity. During 1936-37, he organised the Labour Movement and also the independent Labour Party of India. His main plank was to abolish 'Landlordism' and 'Capitalism'. In 1937, after being elected to Bombay Legislative Assembly, he toók up the economic problems of the peasant, agriculture labourers and the workers coming from all sections of society. It may be mentioned here that in the first popular provincial assembly Ambedkar was the first legislator of India to introduce a Bill for the abolition of serfdom of agriculture tenants. He also dealt with the problems of landless labourers, small holding collective farming, land revenue, currency system, universalisation of education and abolition of landlordism. As a labour member in the Executive Council for two viceroys in India, he made significant contributions in the field of labour legislation and welfare in the country. It was during this period that the Factory Act was amended to ensure holidays with pay, the Indian Mines Act and Maternity Benefit Act were amended to provide larger benefits and better facilities to workers. He always emphasised the demands of the labourers for food, clothshelter, health, education and cultural amenities. He laid importance on equal treatment for labourers, whether industrial or agricultural. But it was the constitution of Statutory Welfare Funds, Joint Labour Management Committee, Esablishment of Employment Exchanges and the break through in the field of "Social Insurance" for which Dr. Ambedkar will be long remembered.

What Ambedkar aimed at was to bring a structural change in the economic life of the people so that there would be no scope for exploitation. Hence, he had strongly warned during the debates in the Constituent Assembly "...How long shall we continue to deny equality in our social and economic life? If we continue to deny it for long we will do so only by putting our political democracy in peril. We must remove this contradiction at the earliest possible moment or else those who suffer from inequality will blow up the structure of political democracy which this Assembly has so labouriously built up". In view of the present social and economic crisis in India, Ambedkar's warning is still relevant.

Dr. Ambedkar was a great visionary. His vision was to build up a "People's India", which would be strong and united. His pragmatic approach to achieve his goal made him different from others. He believed that a country may be independent but its people may not be independent. Only a privileged few may monopolise the entire gamut of power with in state. A polity having oppressors and the oppressed, was not acceptable to him. Appropriately Ambedkar as a pioneer of Indan Constitution fought for the safeguards of the interest of the suppressed and oppressed people in India. Without freedom of all sections of the society, real national unity cannot be established. He said, "without freedom nationalism would become a means of internal slavery forced labour and organised tyranny for the poor and servile classes". National unity and integrity would be dream without establishing People's India. By having mere political equality, he argued that we should not claim to have a democratic polity because political equality stands on the base of social and economic equality. Dr. Ambedkar could sense that the socio-economic inequality may create imbalance in society and this may result in hampering the process of national integration in India. As a part of his mission to make India modern and civilised free from disharmony and disunity, he also undertook other problems of the polity. After taking over as the chairman of constitution drafting committee, he tried his best to shape Indian Political System of his own thiking though he was not allowed to do so in all the cases. He was the man who suggested for the induction of the word "Fratenity" in the preamble of Indian Constitution. He wrote, "...the need for fraternal concord and goodwill in India was never greater than now..."

He viewed communalism as a 'group' based on narrow interest, claims and demands and create anti-national activities. But he suggested that communal question should not be solved by the policy of appeasement but by the adoption of same definite principles for all sections of the society. Spreading caste and communal disharmony are totally antagonistic to Ambedkar's ideals. Ambedkar was a great nationalist. He believed in a common Indian culture. His ideal was to establish one man, one value system. Hence, he preferred to adopt Buddhism though he was influenced by Christian and Muslim leaders to adopt their religion. Because he viewed that Buddhism which preached equality and fraternity, is a part of Indian culture. His acceptance of Buddhism was an unparallel example of is patriotism which ultimately became a blessing for millions in Indian society. Had he accepted any other religion, it might have created a political problem.

Another important contribution of Ambedkar was with regard to the federal structure of the policy. If our present states have not torn themselves from the rest of the country as the Republic of Soviet Union have done, we must be grateful to Ambedkar for what he did in spite of the resolutions of the Constituent Assembly and the two reports on central and provincial governments presented by the committees headed by Nehru and Patel. The Union Constitution Committee report submitted by Nehru contained proposals for Federal Parliament, citizenship of the Federation, Federal law and an elected Governor. But Dr. Ambedkar called for describing India as a 'union' although its constitution may be federal in structure and also changed the idea of an elected governor for the provinces. The committee headed by Ambedkar suggested for an "appointed governor". Thus, important povisions which made the Indian Government strong enough to resist the temptations of any state to be free were curbed by the Drafting Committee and subsequently Dr. Ambedkar in the process of his masterly propagation of the principles of constitution in the Constituent Assembly.

Dr. Ambedkar also undertook the problem of language keeping in view the unity and integrity of India. He had suggested for one language, many states formula. He was against the creation of linguistic provinces. He said, "A linguistic state with its regional language as its official language may easily develop into independent nationality. The road between an indepedent nationality and an independent state is very narrow. If this happens, India will cease to be the Modern India we have..." The patriotic mind of Ambedkar never thought of any threat to India's Unity in the name of language. He strongly warned that just like one language can unite people, two languages are sure to divide people. In the draft constitution, he made Hindi as the national language and Lion Capitl with Ashok Chakra as the national symbol of India. He wanted India to be a nation of peace and universal brotherhood.

Dr. Ambedkar was both a visionary and a revolutionary. He was a liebral with a strong sense of nationalism. His unfathomable contribution for individual freedom, social justice, equality, unity and integrity of the national will be long remembered by the people of India. His pragmatic approach to the socio-economic and political problems of the country is still relevant today. In view of the present atrocities on the women and depressed classes in India which has become a every day's affair, exploitation of the working class people and secessionist, linguistic problems Ambedkarism provide solution.

## VIEWS ON RELIGION AND SOCIETY

**Ambedkar's Views about Religion.** Ambedkar on the whole was not an atheist but at the same time he never spared time for going deep into the mysteries of religion. According to him religion was not pure spiritual consciousness. For him, Hinduism, which he left for embracing Buddhism, was another version of caste consciousness and name of Brahmanism. He did not believe in religious rituals. He said that Buddhist Dharma is different from Hindu Dharma. For him some of the important evils of Hinduism were:

1. It tends to disprove moral life of freedom and spontaneity.
2. Hindu laws are not uniformally applied to all.
3. It reduces life the externally imposed rules.
4. It has no loyalty to ideas.
5. Hinduism believes in fixity.
6. Hindu laws are made by those who do not know law.

He considered religion important because it is essential for human beings who are social animals and also because man is an intellectual being. In his own words, "Man cannot live by bread alone and he has a mind which needs food for thought". He further said that, "The religion which discriminates between two followers is partial and religion which treats crores of its adherents worse than dogs and criminals and inflicts upon them insufferable disabilities is no religion at all.". He did not agree with Gandhiji that Shashtras cannot be proved right or wrong by the learned people. He disagreed with Gandhian view that religion does not live by learning. It lives in the expreiences of saints and seers in their lives and sayings.

**His Preference for Buddhism.** Ambedkar very much preferred Buddhism over Hinduism and that is the reason as to why he left the latter and accepted the former. In his view Buddhism was better because it had certain principles which were close to real life. He further said that whereas Buddhism believes in the principles of liberty and social justice, Brahmanism is based on the principles of exploitation and injustice. He also said that Buddihism alone could check rising trend of Marxism, which was causing worry for the whole world.

**His Views about Hindu Society.** Ambedkar was very pained by caste system of Hindu society, which had completely degenerated and divided the whole nation. About Hindu soceity he said that it was in bad need of moral regeneration which was dangerous to postpone. He also said that Hindu leaders were quite unfit for the job. They appeal to the ideals of the past which have ceased to have any connection with the present.

He said that even practices of sati and forced widowhood arose because of the problem of surplus men and surplus women created by endogamy. He believed that the basis of caste was process of superimposition of endogamy on an exogamous population. For him endogamous caste system requires practices like forced widowhood and Sati. He was convinced that originally Hindu society was class society of Varnas. It was subsequently that it converted itself into caste society. First Varna or class to undergo this transformation was Brahmin class and subsequently spread to non-Brahmin classes. He said that non-Brahmins became a caste by following the preceedent set by Brahmins. Some groups became separate castes because of mechanism of ex-commuication followed by Brahminic caste. He clearly said that caste has nothing to do with religion.

Ambedkar very clearly said that whole ideas of division of society on caste basis was rooted in the oppressive ideology of the caste system. He was convinced that nothing could emancipate the outcastes except the destruction of caste system.

**His Views about Hindu Religious Books.** He had not much regard for religious books and in his opinion their teachings should be dispensed with, if a breach in caste system is desired. In his 'Annihilation of the Caste' he bluntly said, "If you wish to bring about a breach in the caste system then you have got to apply the dynamite to the Vedas and the Shashtras, which deny any part to reasons to morality."

**His Ideal Society.** While giving his views about ideal society he said that it was society which should be mobile. In it there should be many interests and free points of contacts with other associations. In this society there should be interactions among different components. But he said that Hindu society has ceased to be an ideal society of his imagination.

He wanted to uplift the depressed classes and even did not hesitate to criticise Gandhiji and Arya Samaj, which were also interested in opposing the lot of the depressed classes and stood for the abolition of caste system.

## CONCEPT OF AN IDEAL SOCEITY (NEW SOCIAL ORDER)

Ambedkar was the protagonist of a new social order. His views on Social problems like caste, untouchability and women constitute the foundation of this social-political ideas. His own experience in life and his intellectual faculty made him sceptial about the Hindu religion and its social order. His pragmatism and idealism prompted him to work for a new social order based on social justice so that the future of Indian democracy would be strong and stable.

Ambedkar once said, his ideal society or new social order would be a society based on liberty, equality and fraternity. An ideal society should be mobile, should be full of channels for conveying a change taking place in one part the other. In an ideal society there should be many interest consiously communicated and shared. There should be varied and free points of contacts with other modes of association. In other words there must be social endosmosis. Ambedkar argued, a society based on fraternity would only make the democracy possible. He said, democracy is not merely a form of government, it is primarily a mode of associated living of conjoint communicated experience. It is essentially an attitude or respect of reverence for fellowman. In democracy there should be freedom to choose one's profession. To talk of democracy and not to allow this freedom is to perpetuate slavery. Though equality in absolute sense is not possible but equal treatment of men is possible. Since caste and untouchability negate such Ideas, he damanded that the caste and untouchability in any form should be abolished. In fact he was one among the fiew social revolutionaries who demanded total abolition of caste and removal of Hindu rulers. His approach was not religious, but legal, political and scientific.

## CASTE SYSTEM

Ambedkar denounced the caste system as totally unscientific. Because caste has no scientific origin. Some justify caste system on eugenic ground. If caste is eugenic, origin of sub-caste must also be eugenic. If sub-caste is eugenic, why then there is bar against inter-marrying and inter-dining? Regarding prohibition on inter-dining he said, inter-dining cannot infect blood and can not be the cause of rise and fall of a race. Caste is a negative thing. It merely talks about prohibtion of inter-caste marriage, inter-dining etc. It does not give positive method of selecting life partner within a caste. Some justify caste on the ground of division of labour. But Ambedkar said, in no civilised society, there is unnatural division of labour into water-tight compartment. Caste is not only unnatural division of labour, it is also an undemocratic system in which division of labourers are graded one above the other, Social and individual efficiency requires us to develop the capacity of an individual to the point of competency to choose and to make his own carrer. This principle is violated in the caste system in so far as it involves an attempt to appoint tasks to individual in advance, selected not on the basis of tained original capacities but on that of the social status of parents. He said, unemployment among Hindus is due to the caste system because there is no readjustment of occupations. Caste, thus, does not result in economic efficiency; It cannot and has not improved race. It has completely disorganised and demoralized the Hindus. It prevents common activity and by doing so, it has prevented the Hindus from becoming a united society. But how to abolish caste? Ambedkar said, caste cannot simply be abolished by forced inter-caste marriage and iner-dinning. What is needed is national change. Hindus observe caste not because they are inhuman. But because their religion and religious shastras (Scripture) have taught them so. People being religious minded observe it blindly. Hence, he said, make every man and woman free form the thraldom of the shastras, cleanse their minds of the pernicious notions founded in the shastras and he or she will inter-dine and inter-marry, wihtout any body telling him or her to do so. He called upon the people to disobey the unscientific, inhuman and unsocial rules of the shastras.

**Untouchability.** Ambedkar himself belonging to the group of untouchables, deal with the problem from both historical and social perspective. He made a detailed analysis of the origin and the practice of untouchability in his book entitled 'The Untouchables': who were they and why they became untouchables published in 1948. He repudiated "The racial ethnic or occupational for the origin of untouchability using anthropometric and ethnographic evidence. His conclusion was that untouchables clung to the faith and practice of Buddhism in the early centuries of the christian era and were pushed aside in the struggle for supremacy between Buddhism and Brahmanism which has so completely moulded the history of India." Ambedkar's theory rejected the ideas of pollution attached to the untouchables. He argued that there was no racial difference between the Hindus and the untouchables. Thus, he condemned all the misconceptions and the practice of untouchability as baseless. Purification and defilement attached to untouchability can neither be applicable to a group nor it can be on hereditary basis. An individual can be impure or defilement is observed in case of birth, death etc. It can not be imposed over any group or race. Hence, Ambedkar demanded total abolition of untouchability. That can be possible by both social and legal ways. Socially the untouchables themselves should rise to the occasion. They should give up traditional occupations like carrying dead cow out of the village and should give up drinking. They should be educated. Secondaly, he fought for the cause of representation of all the untouchables at all levels of government. As a result, by Poona Pact, agreement was made for reservation of seats in general electorate. According to Ambedkar, untouchables must be seen as a minority as a separate people so long as they are treated as a separate people. And so long as they have special needs, those needs must be represented in the government by the untouchables themselves.

**Women.** Ambedkar was influenced by Buddha's views about women. Buddha described women as one of the seven Treasures and a thing of supreme-value. A family can be saved from debacle by placing a woman in authority over their affairs. He blamed Manu for giving women a degraded position in the society. He said, "according to Manu, Women have no right to study the Vedas". This view of woman was both an insult and injury to the women of India. It deprived women to acquire knowledge. She was also debarred from all religious activities by the Brahmins. But Patanjali's Maha Bhasya shows that women were teachers and taught Vedas to girl students. He said, Manu also deprived women from their social freedom. As a result in modern time also women are suffering from oppression, and humiliation in the society. Hence, he fought for giving justice to women. In his speech in D.C. Women's College in July, 1942, of Amraoti, he said that he measured the progress of a community by a degree of progress which women had achieved. He asked them to be clean, to educate their children and to remove inferiority complex. Through Hindu Code Bill, he gave them the right to inherit the property. He also gave them the right to be consulted by the husband in case of adoption of child.

Ambedkar was not a Marxist but he believed that a social revolution must precede political independence. Ambedkar ventilated this view during the freedom movement and was misunderstood. But now the entire national realises the relevance of his social ideas.

## AMBEDKAR AS A CONSTITUTIONALIST

Dr. B.R. Ambedkar was a great Constitutional expert and has been called as the architect of Indian Constitution. As a Chariman of the Drafting Committee he very ably defended every provision of the draft constitution and present constitution owes much to his genius. He has, therefore, very rightly been called as Manu of our times. He did not allow personal preferences to creep in while framing provisions of the constitution, but while doing so he kept national interests above every thing else.

**Dr. Ambedkar's Imprints on Constitution.** One cannot pin-point any part of the constitution which did not carry his imprint because he was Chariman of the Drafting Committee. There can be controversies and differences about his role as social reformer, his views about Hindiusm and Hindu society, but there can be no controversy about his role as constitutional expert. Because of his overwhelming contribution to the making of constitution that K.V. Rao has remarked that he is not only father but also mother of our constitution. It has been said that, "the achievement of independence would go to the credit of Mahatmaji and its consolidation to one of Mahatma's worst critic, viz., the great architect of our constitution, Dr. Ambedkar."

**His Role in the Constitutent Assembly.** From the beginning till the end of he work of the Assembly, Dr. Ambedkar dominated it. All looked towards him and listened to him with rapt attention. At the early stages he feared that the Assemby would be dominated by caste Hindus and that the interests of the depressd classes and castes would be ignored but gradually he relaxed his hard attitude and decided to co-operate with Congress leadership. He felt that this co-operation would enable him to safeguard the interests of the untouchables.

**Champion of Fundamental Rights.** Dr. Ambedkar was great champion of fundamental rights. In his opinion such rights are essentially needed for the development of the people, both mental and moral. Without such rights, those belonging to depressed classes shall never come up in the society. It was because of his efforts that a separate chapter on Fundamental Rights was included in the constitution. He, therefore, suggested and the Assembly agreed that these should be made justifiable so that neither executive nor legislature could deprive citizen of any Right given to the people. He provided safeguards, so that these Rights were not misused.

**Supporter of Strong Centre.** Dr. Ambedkar was supporter of strong centre and he made his views very clear in the Constituent Assembly. In the Assembly he supported even wider powers to be given to the centre for the unity of the country than what the centre had under the Government of India Act, 1935. He, however, favoured the idea of country's being a federation. It was because of his views that Indian was called as 'Union of States' rather than a 'federation.'

**His Support For Federal Set-up.** Dr. Ambedkar very strongly believed that in India a unitary system could not successfully and efficiently work. It was administratively difficult to rule over India from one single centre. He, therefore, supported federal type set-up for India. About the nature of this set-up he said in the Constituent Assembly, "Both the Union and the states are created by the constitution; both derive their respective authority from the constitution. The one is not subordinate to the other in its own field; and the authority of one is co-ordinate with that of the other." He was convinced that a strong centre in federal type set-up was absolute necessity for India both for the security of nation and checking fissiparous and devisive forces. It was also necessary for uniformity and stability in administration. That is the reason that in the constitution division of subjects was made in such a way that centre became very strong and made critics comment that India is an over centralised federation. He, however, asserted that it was wrong to believe that a strong centre would make India less federal.

**Justification for Emergency Provisions.** Constitution of India incorporates emergency provisions under which under certain circumstances head of the state can declare emergency conditions. Once emergency is declared federal structure gets converted into unitary system and Fundamental Rights given to the people under the constitution are abrogated. This provision of the constitution was badly criticised in the Constituent Assembly. Dr. Ambedkar, however, defeneded these provisions pointing out that all federal systems are placed in a tight mould of federation.

**Assessment of Work.** Credit goes to him for providing in the constitution abolition of untouchability and making India a secular polity. He, provided for a mix of rigid and flexible constitution, freedom of worship, expression and equality of opportunity.

He could convince the Assembly for providing reservation of seats for them in the elected bodies for SC and ST. Similarly he realised that future of India laid in secularism, but what he meant from secularism was something wider and broader than what it is now being followed. While explaining what he meant from secularism he said, "Secularism does not mean that we shall not take into consideration the religious sentiments of the people. All that a secular state means is that this Parliament shall not be competent to impose any particular religion upon the rest of the people. This is the only limitation that constitution recognises." He had power of conviction, courage and boldness.

## VINAYAK DAMODER SAVARKAR

**His Early Life.** V. D. Savarkar was born in 1883, in Ratnagiri district. He got his early education in India. During his school days he showed a visible tendency of his love for Hindu religion. He even organised student groups to check the excesses of Muslims, whenever he came to know of these. As a student he took active interest in politics and gave all possible support to Swadeshi Movement. He organised a compaign for burning foreign cloth with the result that he was expelled from his college.

In 1906, he got a recommendatory letter from Tilak which enabled him to get scholarship from Shyamji Verma, an Indian revolutionary in England, to study in England. The real aim was to organise and consolidate revolutionary movement for India in England. It was in England that many revolutionaries came in his contact and were inspired by him. As the time passed he became an eye-sore for the British Government and was arrested in 1910, for certain speeches to have been made by him in India in 1906, however, when he was being brought to India as a captive, he jumped from the ship into the sea but was re-arrested. The Government of India found him guilty of taeason and deported him to Andamans. In 1923, he was brought back to India and interned at Ratnagiri. His release was on the specific condition that he would not participate in active politics. He remained in this conditions till 1937. This period, however, he utilised in consolidating the Hindus, and pointing out the evils of Hindu society. After his release from Ratnagiri he activily associated himself with Hindu Mahasabha and became its life and soil. For many years he was its President. In 1948, when Mahatma Gandhi was shot dead. Savarkar was also tried but acquitted by the trying judge. Due to over exertion his health however, began to deteriorate and ultimately on February 26, 1966, he left this world for his heavenly abode.

**His Works.** Savarkar was an inspiring personality. He wrote and spoke to awaken the Hindus from their deep sleep and made them ready to face the hard realities of life. Some of his signifcant works are:

1. My Transportation for Life. 2. Hindu Pad Padshahi. 3. Hindutva. 4. The Indian War of Independence of 1857. (This was prescribed soon after its release in 1909, and made available to public only in 1947).

**Political Ideas of V.D. Savarkar.** Savarkar was a revolutionary and for him everything revolved round Hindutva.

**His Views about Hindutva.** He developed and defined the term Hindutva, which according to him was different and broader than the term Hinduism. In his own words. "Therefore those who love the land that stretches from Sindhu to Sindhu from Indian to sead, as their fatherland and consequently claim to inherit the blood of the race that has evolved, by incorporation and adaptation, from ancient Saptasindhus, can be said to possess two of the most essential requisits of Hindutva." For him Hindutva has three essential qualities namely *(i)* Rashtra, *(ii)* Jati, and *(iii)* Sanskriti. From Rashtra, he meant that the person concerned should respect the territorial integrity and geographical sanctity of our national borders. He should be most willing to sacrifice his everything for the sake of protecting these geographical boundaries. He should have no extra-territorial attachements. From Jati, he meant that a believer of Hindutva should belong to a family which has Hindu blood, in other words his ancestors should be Hindus. Third test is that the person concerned should have faith in the superiority of ancient Indian culture and civilisation and should take pride in Hindu Sanskriti. Thus, according to him such minorities as the Muslims and the Christians which do not feel proud of our cultural heritage or in whom the blood of Indian ancestors does not flow, do not come under Hindutva.

**His Views about Hinduism.** Savarkar was a true Hindu and a great moving force in Hindu Mahasabha, which was primarily responsible for the consolidation of enegries of Hindus of our times. For him, Hinduism was the most ancient religion in the world and that too with rich traditions. Hinduism has not decayed itself only because it is a dynamic religion which can absorb all other religions. It has a homogeneous and heterogenous outlook. It is the religion which is very rational and appealing to mind and soul. Many other world religions have drawn inspiration from Hinduism. In his philosophy modern degeneration and prevention is only due to our rulers who are deliberately disfiguring our religion and misinterpreting that so as to shake our faith in our religion and thus, to make us spiritually poor. It was this Hinduism which made India the spiritual leader of the world.

Differentiating between Hindutva and Hinduism he said that the former was broder and more comprehensive than the latter. For him Hindutva was a social, economic and political concept. It was clsoer to nationalism than religion. On the other hand Hindiusm was a religion and as such it had closer affinity to morality than politics. In other words Hindutva was political whereas Hinduism was a religious concept.

**His Faith in the Capacity of Hindus.** Like Madan Mohan Malaviya, he had great faith in the capacity of Hindus to run and manage their own affairs. He was of the view that the Hindus had great capacity to run and manage their own affairs and for centuries they had very well managed their own affairs. Referring to the capacity of Hindus he said that the very fact that Hindus were on the forefront of our national struggle bore an ample testimony to the logic that they had capacity and strong desire to achieve their independence. For him, that capacity shall further develop after the alien rule has come to an end.

**His Views about Non-Violence.** For Savarkar, it was not desirable to accept non-violence as a creed. For him, it was equally undesirable to adopt violence as a method for solving our social as well as political problems. It was partially desirable and as such it should be treated only as a relative and not as an absolute term. To adopt it as a method of life and mode of struggle was impracticable under Indian conditions and circumstances. It could be adopted only where the conditions were normal and opponent also believed in smiliar methods and understood the same language. In so far as India is concerned, the imperialists are not at all willing to listen to this language and not supposed to leave India with the use of this moral force. He, therefore, suggested that violent means should be adopted, if necessary, to achieve our objects. In so far as Indian National Congress was concerned for him that was a useful forum to express national opinion and view-point, but the way in which the leadership was handling the situation was not suited to our conditions. He was even opposed to Quit India Movement of Mahatma Gandhi, on the plea that India was as yet not ready for such a national struggle.

**His View about the Partition of India.** Savarkar believed in the idea of a United India. He felt that the partition of the country was suicidal and against national interests. He could not at all reconcile himself to the idea that our territorial integrity should be violated or the demand of Pakistan should be accepted. He was very bitter when C.R. Formula for the partition of the country was made public. He was also pained to see that the National Congress was drifting towards partition of the country by following policy of appeasement of the Muslims and giving them concessions one after the other which were prejudicial to our national and collective interests.

**His View about Participation in World War.** In 1939, when 2nd World War broke out and Congress Ministers resigned from offices in the provinces in which they were in power, a new problem came to the front. Indian National Congress was of the opinion that India should boycott war efforts till government came forward with an assurance tha India would be granted independence after the war was over. On the other hand Savarkar extended his hand of co-operation to the Government, as in his view such participation shall provide Hindus an opportunity to get military training. They shall be in a position to get acquainted with latest war equipments and methods of struggle. It was with this view-point that he could convince Hindu Mahasabha to pass a resolution to that effect.

**His Views about Minorities.** For him, India was a homogeneous country in which various communities and persons belonging to all religions were living together since ages. He was however, pained to see that some minority communities were not contributing in national progress and on the other hand were standing in the way of national progress. He made it amply clear to them that irrespective of the consideration whether they co-operated with the majority community or not, India shall go ahead with its ambitous programme of attaining independence. It was in the interest of minorities themselves that they should co-operate with the majority and thus, get its goodwill.

**His Views about Hindu Rashtra.** Veer Savarkar had unshakable and undisputed faith in the superiority of Hindu culture. He wanted to see India a Hindu Rashtra. He did not conceal his feelings in this regard and clearly said that the Hindus had a priority right to live in India. They have their gods and goddesses who are Indian. The Hindus consider India as their motherland. They love Indian cultural heritage and take pride in that. They respect everything that is Indian. They have no extra territorial attachments. They have sentimental attachments with everything that is Indian. On the other hand the Muslims, who form a vast minority in India, have extra-territorial affiliations. they go out for Haj. They have no sentimental attachment with our gods and goddesses. They have more respect and regard for Hazrat Muhammad Sahib and the land of his birth, than India. In his own words, "A Hindu patriot worth the name cannot but be an Indian Patriot as well. To the Hindus, Hindusthan being the fatherland and Holyland, the love they bear to Hindustan is boundless. That is why they predominate in the national struggle that is going on for the overthrow of the British yoke. Even buried bones in Andamans would assert this fact." In 1936, while delivering his Presidential address from Hindu Mahasabha platform, he expressed more or less similar views. He said, "While the Hindus love those affinities which bind a Hindu to a Hindu and to dwell on them with pride, the Muslims hate the very mention of them and are trying to eradicate the very memory of it all. Some of them fabricate histories and genealogies to contract their origin with the Arabians and Truks; they are trying to carve out a separate language for themselves and graft it as best as they can on the Arabian stock." Savarkar, therefore, said that very safely it could be taken for granted that India is a Hindu Rasthra. But this should not lead one to the conclusion that in this country religious minorities can not live or develop. In his arrangement all shall have the right of growth, prosperity and development but clearly understanding that they are a minority and that a numerical majority in every country has certain special rights. They will also have to realise that minority cannot be a hindrance to the growth and development of majority.

**His Views about Nationality.** Savarkar could not reconcile himself to the idea that residence of a person for a particular length of time within the geographical limits of a country should be the deciding factor for conferring nationality on a particular individual or community. In his philosophy, the measuring rod should be that the person or community should believe in cultural heritage of the land and should as well have sentimental and emotional attachement. For him Hindus in India are entitled to such a right.

**Savarkar's Interpretation of Indian Histroy.** According to him there have been six glorious epochs in Indian history. The first was Maurayan empire founded by Chandra Gupta Maurya under the guidance of great Chankya. Second was when Pshyamitra destroyed Greek power in India. Vikarmadiya's age was third such period. During his days there was revival of political and cultural heritage of India. Fourth epoch period in his view was one when Yasho Dharma of Malwa defeated the Hans at Mandasore in about 525 A.D. Foundation of Maratha power was another epoch making period, as it challenged Muslim forces in India and last and sixth epoch making period was the period of succesful repulsion of the British power in India. His whole interpretation of History is based on passionate glorification of Vedic Hinduism. He was opposed to the cult of forgiveness. In his view at time Buddhism in even gave set-back to the cause of Indian independence and Indian empire.

He was all praise for Shivaji for having set up a Hindu independent state. In his views Marathas had loftier ideas of nationalism than Harsha Vardhana. For him Sipoy mutiny of 1857, was really first war of Indian independence.

**His Social Ideas.** Savarkar raised his voice against untouchability and very strongly pleaded that it should be ended. For him it was a curse on the fair name of Hindusim and that in its present form it was very much unwanted. One of the methods which he suggested was establishment of mixed schools in which boys of all castes, both high and low, were required to study together in a spirit of oneness and brotherhood. Then another method was that the untouchables should be allowed to enter the temples. In his philosophy God had no religion. He even helped in the erection of a Patit Pavan temple in which the low castes and down-trodden were to be permitted entry without any hesitation. Still another effective method which he suggested was that dinners should be arranged in which people belonging to all communities should dine together. He even went to the extent of suggesting that there should be inter-caste marriages so that the myth of caste superiority was exploded. In other words his basic idea was that the Hindu society should be reformed in a way that it became ideal and got rid of all evils which were curse on its fair name.

Savarkar was a revolutionary by birth. He tried to consolidated Hindu nation and gave it a concrete programme and policy to follow. His concept of Hindu Rashtra was suitable reply to the cry of Pakistan. His association with Hindu Mahasabha made that an All India body. If the Sabha suffered a serious set-beck during the general elections and went in the background it was mainly because the moving and forceful personality of Savarkar was bedridden and thus, those personal contacts which inspired millions of Hindus in India could not be established. The very fact that glowing tributes were paid to him at the time of his death even by Congress leaders who differed from him in his approach to political problems is sufficient evidence of the respect which he commanded among the masses.

❑

# 7

# Medieval Political Thought

Middle Ages usually can be characterised as non-political which *Ipso facto* implies that these times on the whole were barren of all political activities. But it is not totally correct because political activity was there though that was not subordinated to theology. The Middle Ages are well remembered for giving ideas about monarchy, which was considered as the best form of government. Stress was laid on the office or institution of monarchy rather than the person of the monarch, who could be removed by the people. The concept of law was re-oriented and it was considered as belonging to the common folk. It was thought that law was supreme and the authority behind the king for governing the masses. Universalism was preached and on the whole it was believed that spiritual and temporal authorities were of mutual help to each other. The authority of church and Papacy considerably grew, which was also supported by the feudal lords who wanted to see weak monarchs on the throne. Pre-Christian civilisation was studied by Christian scholars. Theology was given more importance and a movement known as scholarsticism spread which continued to influence the Middle Ages. Theory of Corporation on the whole was accepted as the principle of governing the people. Ultimate authority was not vested in the individual but organisation assembly, or council. Composite character of the state was stressed. It was also believed that the state was result of a convention—an idea held ground for considerably long period. They did not believe in the idea that the sovereign was absolute. A sovereign was bound by the rules of community, law of nature and also their authority was challenged by the feudal lords and church fathers. The system of representation was quite common, though the representative was considered as a trustee and not an agent of the People The period was dominated by a struggle for supremacy between the church and the king in which both tried to establish their power and authority. There was institution of feudalism which meant a contract as well as personal loyalty. Both these things existed side by side though modern thinkers upto today have not been in a position to scientifically adjust the ideas. On the whole system was complex and complicated.

It is very much uncertain to authentically lay hand on a demarcating line between ancient and medieval period. Moreover, the expression Medievalism is not absolute but relative with reference to each country. Usually, however Mechiavelli (1469—1527) is considered as the first modern thinkers, with whom medievalism also ends. The period, however, on the whole lasted for over 1000 years which was usually without any political speculation and is called 'Dark Ages'. There was no origination of new ideas in political field. There was also usual lack of intelligence among the rulers and education was neglected. But Barker has however differed from this usual idea by saying that, "There was abundant political thought in the Middle Ages, just because they were ages of formation and formulation, in which the Christian Heaven the great new thing in the world was steadily permeating society and the fresh Germanic influx into the ancient world was finding its place and level." The idea of corporation and self-government was mooted. This was a step forward in support of monarchy.

The Germanic, who succeeded the Romans, were not very intelligent. They believed in the supremacy of law and gave birth to the idea of nationalism. The period is absolutely not dead but had life for, to some extent, in so far as political philosophy of breaking of new ideas was concerned. Prominent features of the age were:

**1. The Idea of Monarchy.** Medieval Political philosophy practically believed in the theory of Divine origin of kingship. It was believed that God was overlord of all kings and earthly lordship flowed from the Divine Lordship. Monarchy was considered as the best and normal form of government and political organisation. But as Barker has said, "The popular business and the popular right of critics of monarchy are cardinal tenets of medieval theory." They believed that though the king was representative of God yet the community had a right to control him. Reconciliation between the two might appear paradoxical yet it got reconciled throughout the Middle Ages because of amalgamation of Germatic and Christian ideas. Throughout the Middle Ages monarchy and not the monarch was exalted. The office and not the person was infallible and that the subjects should obey not the individual but the office. Unjust monarch could be disobeyed and resisted. Ruler was not absolute in the exercise of his authority but was bound by certain limitations namely those of the law of nature and of the community etc. Monarch was supposed to promote peace and justice. He had certain obligations towards community which he could not defy. He should have regard for customs which are the product of wisdom of men. He was not supposed to make laws but promulgate them. They believed that the laws made the king. In the words of Bracton, "The king himself ought to be under no man, but under God and under the law, because law makes the king". In the words of Sabine. "The king was not the head of the state, as he became in the era of absolute monarchy at the opening of modern period." The king should protect the subjects as the kingship was a service rendered to the people.

**2. The Idea of Law.** The law, throughout Middle Ages, was tribal and personal. It was never national or territorial. The law belonged to the folk and was common possession of the people. The source of law was unknown but usual belief was that the customs, Law of Nature and God's laws were the basis of folk laws. These were accordingly considered permanent and eternal. Since the customs were the basis of laws, there were usually un-written. Law was custom of community and its obedience a habit. Indirectly it was accepted that real authority behind the laws was the will of the people. According to Sabine, "Law seems regularly to have been issued in the name of the whole people definitely with the sense that their consent is an important factor in its validity."

The law was established as supreme authority in the state and even the king was required to obey that. None was competent to revoke laws. It was considered that law alone authorised king to rule. As against the modern practice, at that time government or the king was subordinate to law and not that the law was subordined to the government.

**3. Universalism.** The people of the Middle Ages believed in the idea of existence of a universal or cosmopolitan society. This was borrowed perhaps from Roman conception of world civilization. The church and the state were considered as two-different aspects of same indivisible society. These two organisations were headed by the Pope and the Emperor respectively but both were the members of the same society. Though both were different from each other in their jurisdiction yet were of mutual help to each other. There was universalism in another way also, namely that all believed that spiritual salvation was the sole aim of all human beings and that all human activities should be directed with this end in view. This goal was be-all and end-all of all human efforts. Even all political activities were directed to achieve this supreme end.

**4. Growth or Papacy.** Middle Ages are also known for the organisation of church into a mighty organisation. It was a general conviction that for Heaven's blessings church was essential. The Pope ruled as the deputy of God on earth and he demanded that all Christians should obey him. The monarchs began to invite Pope on their coronation ceremonies to seek his blessings. Gradually it also began to interfere in the temporal affairs as well. Its organisation was gradually strengthened and began to be considered as one of the soundest organisations in the world. As the time passed the state became only its department. The causes for this rapid growth were the destruction of Holy Roman Empire and also the rise of feudalism. The former weakened the temporal authority thereby giving the church an opportunity to exert itself whereas in the latter case it strengthened the hands of Pope against the Emperors, The feudal lords usually clashed with the Emperors. However, it was against the interests of the feudals to have a centralised authority. Their interest was to see a weak king on the throne which could only be influenced through a powerful church.

**5. Scholasticism.** Middle Ages are also known for medieval scholasticism. It included in its folds persons like Thomas Acquinas and Albortus Magnus. These intelligent Christians—realised the need and necessity of studying pre-Christian civilisation and thus, were not conservatives. According to Foster it was a representative civilisation and product of "Union of Christianity with the ancient culture of the Graeco-Roman world." These scholars believed that philosophy did not come into conflict, with theology. They assigned foremost importance to theology and as Dunnings says, Scholasticism was a system of thought in which philosophy in the purely rational sense was subordinated to the established theological doctrines." Hearnshaw says, "Scholasticism of the 13th century is a master key to the understanding of medievalism." Foster has said, "Scholasticism was the representative characteristic of the civilisation of Middle Ages who arose from the union of Christianity with the ancient culture of Graeco-Roman world."

**6. Theory of Corporations.** The theory of Corporations was quite common in the Middle Ages. It was believed that even the church and the state were Corporations. All human groups were considered as Corporates. The theory, which was due to Dr. Gierke and Dr. Figgis Maitland, was widely used during the Conciliar movement. The church was considered as the body corporate of the believers. Throughout Middle Ages, by virtue of this theory, attempt was made to decentralise authority rather then concentration of power in the hands of a person. The Pope was just like a presiding officer of the Councillors of his Church Council and the same principle was applied to the king in respect of his court councillors.

The theory also implied that collective wisdom was superior than the individual one and as such individual interests should be sacrificed over collective interests. In addition to this, it also promoted the idea that inspite of its non-composite character organically the state had composite character. It also gave the idea that ultimate sovereignty resided in the people and that the monarch simply was representative of the masses and thus, for all purposes the theory contributed towards pluralist theory of sovereignty. It was the influence of this theory that effort was made to distinguish between the state and the Government. Modern Fascists and the Syndicalists also draw their inspiration from this theory.

**7. Theory or Sovereignty.** There was no specific theory about sovereignty in the Middle Ages. It was quite unknown to the people of that age that sovereign was supreme over external and internal affairs, Carlyle has said, "There is nothing more characteristics of middle ages than the absence of any theory of sovereignty." Divine reason and moral order prevailed over political authority which was not considered absolute, Church authority was also a limitation on the king. The Law of Nature was equally considered a limitation or check on the authority of the king. The law on the whole was considered supreme which was usually unchangeable. It was also felt that the community had a control over the king and could dispose him of, if he was tyrant or despotic. The sovereign authority was also challenged by feudal lords who were always interested to see the kings weak. In other words the Middle Ages did not like the conception of absolute sovereignty but stood for limited or constitutional sovereignty.

**8. The Origin of the State.** Barring Acquinas all medieval thinkers usually believed that the state was the result of a convention though it was against the philosophy of Plato and Aristotle which preached that the state was the product of nature or that it was natural. They believed with Romans and church fathers, that it was artificial arrangement—the state being the result of an agreement between the king and the subjects or the result of sins of man. The theory held grounds for considerably long time and was appreciated by our modern thinkers till it was shaken by Montesquieu and Rousseau.

**9. Theory of Representation.** The Medieval Ages are known for the system of representation but the representative was considered as a trustee or agent of the people to whom he represented. The representative was elected with the object of promoting the welfare of the people. Leaving aside the question of nature of work which a representative was required to perform, in this arrangement, modern representative system is indebted to this age for this philosophy. The fundamentals of this system shall remain unchanged.

**10. Controversy Over Secular and Spiritual Supremacy.** Throughout Middle Ages it was believed that the state and church were two other different organisations. The church should have autonomy and be free from temporal control. It should have an independent character of its own. A conflict however, ensued because the temporal authority did not wish to part with its traditional power and refused to reconcile to the idea of absolute spiritual autonomy. This resulted in the theory of two worlds which implied that spiritual and temporal aspects of a man should never be combined. The kingly and priestly duties should be separated from each other and Pope should be obeyed in religious matters and the king in secular affairs. An attempt was made to establish that Pope was superior to the king because the former derived the authority from God. The Pope could check the king either by interdiction or ex-communication. The Secularists on the other hand pleaded that the king was equally representative of God on earth. He exercised both spiritual as well as secular powers before the establishment of the church. The church was thus, a usurper and nothing less than that. In other words religion and not politics dominated the Middle Ages which made Dunnings remark that Middle Ages were unpolitical. In additional to this, throughout the Middle Ages no political investigation was carried out which established the idea that age was berren of any new political philosophy.

**11. Feudalism.** It was another important institution of the Age which influenced economic, social and political life of the people. In the words of Sabine, "feudal institutions dominated the middle ages as completely as the city state dominated antiquity." Carlyle says, "It affected the life of every class in the medieval community from the king or the Emperor." It was mostly product of Roman and Teutonic institutions. It came to the front as the result of disruption in Empire and subsequent anarchy which followed. Barons got land from the monarchs and in turn gave that to the tenants who not only tilled the land but were also obliged to owe allegiance to the baron or feudal lord. According to Carlyle, "Feudalism is a system of relations, of judicial order, and of political order." The system effected accordingly, social, economic and political aspects of that age. It was almost obligatory on the part of a tenant to work on the terms and conditions of a bond executed with the baron which was expected to be honoured by the former but was usually dishonoured by the latter. It was virtually withdrawn when the tenant withdrew his personal loyalty from the lord. Though *prima facie* it might appear difficult to reconcile the ideas of contractual system with that of personal loyalty yet, it is a historical fact that the tenants worked on contact system and owed personal loyalty to the immediate superior, not knowing about the higher one to whom his superior owed allegiance.

## CHURCH—STATE CONTROVERSY

Before the establishment of church, the king was considered as the most powerful authority in the state. He was supreme overlord in the land whose authority was usually unquestionable and undisputed He combined in one both temporal and spiritual authorities. But controversy however, grew and gradually became hars has the church began to assume more and more powers. The popes began to assume the power of ex-communication and also directed the subjects to defy the orders of a defiant prince. The church made definite and pointed efforts to exert end assert its authority against the state. It is however, quite paradoxical that when the Roman empire was enjoying glory and was at the height of its power no attempt was made to settle an outstanding problem namely whether the Emperor derived its authority from God or the masses or that he had some temporal or spiritual character. There was also no settlement and division of powers between the church and the emperor and both could not reconcile themselves to the idea that they had co-equal powers. It was, however, usually believed that the church and the state were two departments of the same social organisation. This clash however, became acute in 11th century when Gregory VII declared that, "no ecclesiastic should be invested with the symbols of office by a secular ruler under penalty of ex-communication" Emperor Henry IV and Pope Gregory got each other ex-communicated which opened a sharp controversy which lasted with acute bitterness for more than two-centuries. The position of the church was sound till the 18th century. The most important and the potent cause being the decentralisation and disintegration of the Roman Empire. Situation however, changed in the 14th century when secular authority of the king began to establish supremacy over papal authority. The weakness of the feudal system and the establishment of nation states highly elevated the position of monarchy. The conflict was primarily over jurisdiction such ad might arise between the two officials of the same state on the proper jurisdictions about exercising of authorities.

According to Maxey "At first the church distinctly had the better of it. No temporal lord was strong enough to prevail against her. Her enormous wealth, her universal and smoothly functioning organisation, her highly centralised political system, her hold upon the superstitions of classes and masses enabled her to rout all opposition. Upto 13th century it was known the age of enthroned papcy and the church triumphant." The position however, changed for the better for the monarchs only In the 14th century. In the conflict and controversy which followed for centuries both the rival parties had their own claims.

**Argument for Papal Supremacy.** After 9th century, the church tried to claim its jurisdictions even over temporal affairs. It was to the good luck of the church that the Pope Gregory who had a dynamic personality and high character was successful in introducing many changes in the church organisation, He could also solve many problems and remove many difficulties which had weakened the church, This enhanced the prestige or the church. Even some of the thinkers went to the extent of saying that the church had jurisdictions even over the princes. The weak Roman empires had to face and fight the strong feudalism and practically had to accept unquestioned supremacy of the Pope and the church. Its weak organisation could not face the strong and militant organisation of the church. The arguments for this supremacy were:

**1. The Idea of Oneness.** According to the supporters of the church mankind was one and oneness only could be achieved when God governed the people and the state and this. He is doing through His representative, the Pope who, "is their priest and their king, their spiritual and temporal monarch, their law giver and judge in all causes supreme." The church, therefore, claimed that for the sake of oneness and unity the Pope alone should be supreme and not the king because he could not touch spiritual aspect of mankind. According to Grieke, "The Head of all this embracing state is Christ. But as the unity of mankind is to be realised already in this world. His Celestial Kingship must have a territorial presentment... The Pope is the wielder of what is in principle an emperor over the community of mortals. He is their priest and their king, their spiritual and temporal monarch, their law giver and judge in all causes Supreme."

**2. The Theory of Two Swords.** The theory propounded that the church and the state were two distinct and different organisations. According to Carlyle, it was believed by the exponents of this theory that, "Of these the greater weight is with the priests in so far as they will answer to the Lord even for the kings in the last judgment." This theory is known as also Gelasian argument.

**3. Idea of Supremacy of Soul.** According to church Fathers as soul was superior to the body similarly church was supreme over the state because state represents body and church its soul. In other words Pope was superior to the King. Accordingly it was felt that spiritual development which was the concern of the church should be given pride place over the development of body which was the concern of the state. It was, therefore, argued that emperor, was the highest vassal of the Pope. The Pope is guardian of kingship and it is his duty to protect and enhance the prestige of secular authority but not more than papal prestige, The pope is the competent authority to hear complaints from the king because he had definite and clear superiority over the king.

**4. Divine Sanction of the State.** The church Fathers believed that the state has only divine sanction through the authority of church. It had no Divine origin. The state originated only due to the sin of the man and his tailing and falling character. The state is governed by human laws whereas church is governed by Divine laws. Human laws are inferior to divine laws and as such secular officers are subordinate to spiritual officers.

**5. Church Obligation.** Church Fathers believed that it was their foremost duty to do spiritual doctoring for the state. According to them they only can discharge this duties and obligations only when they have a right to interfere in state affairs. In case this right is denied church shall not be in a position to discharge this obligation properly. Therefore, in order to discharge its obligation properly church must interfere in state affairs.

**6. Coordinating Power of the Church.** The supporters or church believed that it was the coordinator of all authority. It claimed that after the fall of the Roman empire it was the only agency which coordinated all activities. They also believed that while all other agencies were unstable it was the only stable agency and that it was through church alone that all social, political and economic ferments could be checked. They therefore, strongly pleaded that this coordinating agency must be strong, powerful and influential.

**7. Arguments from Bible.** The church Fathers tried to support their arguments from Bible as well. Old Testament, according to them, bore testimony by way of preaching that Jews were governed by the Priests from the time of Moses. The first king in the real sense of the term was coronated by the Priest. They also supported their argument from the New Testament by quoting famous argument "feed my sheep" which implied that Pope was the guardian of flock of Christ and thus, the protector of all including the king.

**8. Historical Argument.** The supporters of church said that it was a historical fact that monarchs sought the blessings of the Pope. They quoted historical example of coronation of Emperor Charlemagne by Pope Leo III where the Pope conferred authority on the monarch to rule. It was argued that if the Pope could bless a monarch he could also ex-communicate secular ruler as well.

**9. Moral Argument.** Morally the state is inferior to church, therefore, there is no justification for the officers of the church to obey the officers of the state who are inferior to them. On the other hand there is every justification for the officer of state to obey the officers of the church who are superior to them and from whom the officers of state can draw much inspiration.

**10. Will of God.** Church usually claimed that it was the will of God that church should govern the Christians. The church should ex-communicate and punish all those who did not obey it, because in disobedience of church was the disobedience of God. The church punished those who refused to carry out the will of God and thus, there was every justification in church's awarding punishment According to Dunnings, "with a wide basis in custom and public sentiment for the exercise of jurisdiction over many classes of legal controversies, with an exclusive control of such as could be shown to be spiritual in character with the facility of extending this control that inherited and the doctrine that it embraced whatever actions were, in any way, tained with sin : and with power to enforce its interpretation of its authority by the despotism of secular rulers from power the—medieval church was infact, if not in theory, a most potent political institution."

**Arguments for Secular Supremacy.** The monarachs or the kings had equally strong ground to hold and could advance equally weighty arguments to face strong arguments of Papacy. The powerful monarchs tried to dispense with the Pope and wanted to exercise uncontrolled sway over the secular affairs. But salient feature of this controversy was that usually the monarchs adopted defensive attitude and were not on the offensive. They only effectively repulsed the onslaught and did not take offensive attitude. They basically agreed that the church and the state were two distinct organisations and that the state should content itself by claiming rights and supremacy over the secular affairs and that the Pope should have right over spiritual and not over temporal affairs. Thus, the secularists were moderates and never extremists. According to Sabine, "The position taken by the imperialist parties to the investiture controversy was on the whole more defensive than that of the Paplists." The claim for church supremacy over secular affairs was challenged on the following grounds:

**1. Theory of Divine Origin.** It was claimed by secularists that the state was of Divine Origin and it was not mere delegation of authority by the church. The king was deputy of God on earth and thus, exclusively responsible to Him for all his actions. They pleaded that the state had as much Divine blessings and sanctions as the church and thus, they were at par with each other. Accordingly the question of subordination of one over the other does not at all arise. "Fear God and Honour the King" was quite commonly acceptable idea.

**2. Moral Basis of the State.** The secularists agreed with Plato and Greek that the state was based on morality and that it was one of its foremost duties to promote morality and justice. They therefore felt that it alone was not the duty of church to promote morality but that the state had a share in it. The state was as much responsible for enforcing morality as the church itself.

**3. The Theory of Harmony.** The monarchs believed that the church and the state were two essential social organisations and that social harmony could develop only when both worked in close cooperation with each other. Monarchs pleaded that harmony could only be achieved if Pope claimed supremacy over religious affairs and left the state with exclusive control in temporal affairs. In other words they did not interfere with each other in their working and honoured their mutual jurisdictions.

**4. Gelasian Argument.** According to this argument the theory of two swords was preached which gave a specific and clear theory that the state and the church were two separate departments. Accordingly the secularists claimed that since the two departments were quite separate from each other, therefore, equally independent and each having exclusive jurisdiction over the other. They pleaded that even according to this theory, the state was independent of the church.

**5. Biblical Arguments.** The secularists also quoted from Old as well as New Testament, which said that, "the powers that be of are ordained of God. Whosoever, therefore, resisteth the power resisteth the ordinance of God." They therefore, claimed that all were responsible to God alone and to hone else. Therefore, to claim supremacy over the state by the church was to resist the authority of God.

**6. Legal Argument.** During 11th century when Roman law was studied deeply, one of the important Roman Jurist Bortolus, clearly stated that legally sovereignty was inalienable and to dispute it was sacrilege. The other jurists similarly declared that power of the Emperor was unshaken. The will of monarch was command and thus, unquestionable. They also said, though not without much reality, that, "Holy Roman Emperors were rightful successors of the Emperors of Rome." Since the emperors enjoyed unquestioned authority, their successors should also enjoy that authority undisputed and unquestioned by the church. It was also legally pointed out that according to hereditary law of Roman Empire, property inherited was the private property of the monarch and thus, unquestionable. Since kingdom was passed on to him by hereditary methods it was unquestionable by the church, and as such it assumed the character of personal property of a ruling sovereign.

## ORGANISATION AND WORKING OF FEUDAL SYSTEM

**Growth of Feudalism.** Downfall of Roman Empire was one of the most important events of the Middle Ages which resulted in political and economic changes. Its influence also lasted throughout the Middle Ages. The Germanic people who unseated the Romans, found much incompatible and made new adjustments which in some cases came in conflict with the old order. It was anarchy after the disintegration of the Western Empire that contributed most in the growth of the feudalism and the defenceless owners of land were obliged to seek protection and shelter of the barons. These small land owners known as fiefs, were the vassals of the barons and had certain obligations like that of bearing arms and were obliged to assist their lords and barons by men, money and material. They, in turn, got protection. from outside attack and were responsible to maintain his property. Even one person could be vassal of so many barons. Political authority was confusingly segmented.

Then was the attack of the barbarian tribes known as Franks, Lombards and the Goths etc. These races had an imagination of new set-up both social as well as governmental which was nomadic in character and nature. These were based on the relationship or tribal chiefs, heads of tribal families and the conquered people. This set-up was essentially of a military character and thus, the product of continuous military pressures. The object was to provide peaceful life to the people and also to collect maximum of revenues. The organisation on the whole, subsequently developed as feudal system. According to Bhandari : "Feudalism was the natural out of growth of many institutions and customs of Romans and Teutonic origin and grew from both the bottom and the top simultaneously" According to Sabine: "The first result of the impact of the barbarians on Rome was the disruption of the Empire and the establishment in its place, of a number of loose-knit kingdoms whose organisation was more tribal than national.

**Organisation of Feudalism.** This was very complex setup about which, it has rightly been said, that even so far it has not been found possible to scientifically reconcile and adjust it. According to Sabine, "The first result of impact of barbarians on the Rome was the disruption of the Empire and the establishment in its place of a number of loose-knit-kingdoms whose organisation was more tribal than national. The system was the product of the idea that 'Might is right' and this idea had direct bearing on its organisation. Those who were weak sought the protection of those who were mighty and powerful.

The term feudalism derives its origin from the word 'fief' which means feudal and was the most common feature of the Middle Ages. It was based on the system of *(i)* holding of land by fiefs who were to seek protection from lords and barons and *(ii)* division as well as sub-division of lands. In the words of McIlwain, "Feudalism is the term descriptive of the later traditional form in the development of European institutions out of those of the tribal into those of the national state." It was essentially a military system which was created under an incessant system of warfare. It aimed at making the defence easy at the time of emergency and yet at the same time on the essential basis of land tenure provided a peaceful and settled life. Under this system there was no proper gradation of barons and lords and frequent distribution and redistribution of land made the whole system unscientific and its growth difficult. According to Bhandari, "It was a system in which public relation depended on private relations and political rights depended on land rights, resulting in some confusion between private and public right." It was a system which compromised patriarchal and imperial state type societies. It destroyed the idea of sovereign and nation type states. According to Maitland it was a system in which, "the whole government system—financial, military and judicial—is part of law of private property." The whole system was like a hierarchy in which serfs were at the bottom, kings at the top and in between were the barons and lords. Every free man owed allegiance to the king. Under the system there was complete decentralisation and localisation.

**Political Obligations of Barons.** Under this system each baron and fief was required to perform some political functions because at that time social and political functions were very closely knit and inter-linked with each other. Main functions required to be performed by Barons and fiefs were:

1. The king had no regular army and the army was provided by each baron and lord to the king as and when the need arose. Thus, each lord and baron was obliged to give military aid to the king.
2. Each baron or lord was required to give customary dues to the kings, which was his only source of revenue.
3. The kings were not required to interfere in the judicial system of a lord or a baron, For the purposes of justice in his own jurisdiction, lord was considered as final court of appeal.

**Difficulties in the Study of Feudalism.** Feudalism was a very important and significant institution but there are certain serious difficulties in the study of this institution. It was a system which was of very complex origin and nature, concerning and influencing every aspect or human life. The study of the system also became difficult because it was based on personal loyalities and had neither uniform growth nor did it originate at one and the same place.

**Political Significance of Feudalism**

(i) The theory gave the idea that each landowner must set to the community both in time of war as well as peace.

(ii) That the ruler and the ruled were both subject to law.

(iii) It promoted the idea that the land was not an ownership but leasehold of hereditary character and thus, promoted best interests of the king who looked after the land to the best of his capacity.

(iv) It prevented the idea of absolute authority because as soon as church entered the system there was conflict between the church and the state. It thus, gave the idea that none enjoyed absolute sovereignty.

(v) Instead of centralisation of authority, it promoted the idea of decentralisation which was in the national interest,

(vi) Law, to them, was based on custom and thus, it come manded more respect and was closely connected with social fabric. It also gave the idea that law based on customs was well governed.

(vii) The system interlinked social and territorial relationship with each other.

## MEDIEVAL SCHOLASTICISM

Throughout the middle ages a fierce controversy continued which influenced every individual and institution of the age, namely what was the relationship between the church and the stale and that out of the two who was superior and had a right to dominate the other. It was argued out by the church that the state could not claim and in fact should not claim exclusively right of control of the subjects. church Fathers put forth the doctrine of two swords by which they argued that each and every individual had two aspects of his life namely temporal and spiritual. It was most essential that both these aspects should be fully developed. The state could develop only his temporal and physical aspects and it was the responsibility of the church to develop spiritual aspect of the life of the people. They, therefore, suggested and argued out that the people were under only limited obligation to obey the state. They strongly put forth the argument that the people should, "Render unto Caesar the things which are Caesar's and unto God the things that are God's." Not only this but the church fathers also claimed a superior right of getting prior obedience of individuals because in their opinion soul had a superior role than the body and that the church represented the soul, whereas the body was represented by the state. The state, however, did not accept this claim of the church and challenged that. This resulted in the theory of two swords, which implied that each and every individual had temporal and spiritual aspects and both must not be combined together. This according to Dunnings was starting point in all medieval theories on politics. But the church Fathers always claimed that, "The Omnipotent God has willed that the teachers and priests of Christian religion shall be governed not by the civil. law or by secular authorities, but by Bishops and Priests." Their main arguments were that the king had no right to interfere in spiritual affairs namely:

(1) Soul was superior to body and that it befell on church to develop soul. The king was responsible for the development of body and also that the king had no right to interfere in the affairs of the soul. The two were altogether different from each other and must not be mixed together.

(2) It was argued that those who were engaged in spiritual pursuits had nothing to do with physical pleasure and that undoubtedly the former was much superior as compared with the latter.

(3) It is difficult to think that one and the same person will have tastes both for temporal as well as spiritual advancement and as such only such taste should be developed in which one had shown inclination. This taste should be developed by the agency which is most suited for the purpose.

(4) Since the church and the state have altogether different spheres of activities, therefore, it is most desirable and reasonable that both should not interfere in each other's affairs. The state has its own administrative laws and principles, which are quite different from those of the church.

Throughout the Middle Ages, therefore, a controversy continued which divided the society. The controversy known as 'Theory of Two Swords' believed that both the church and the state had different fields of activities and that the both, should not interfere in each other's affairs. In the words of Foster, "The greatest dispute of the Middle Ages centred round this principle (The Theory of Two Swords); but the principle itself was never disputed."

❒

# 8

# Behaviouralism and Post-Behaviouralism

The process of development of a new science of Politics, which has now come to be known as Modern Political Science, began with the coming of Behavioural Revolution. The deep dissatisfaction with the nature, scope, methods and conclusions of Traditional Political Science led to the emergence of a revolution—the Behavioural Revolution in Politics. This Revolution led to the emergence of Behavioural Approach in politics. Thus, development, however, could remain popular for only two decades. Under the weight of its own weaknesses as well as due to several new developments it got replaced by a revolution from within—The Post-Behaviouralism. As such a study of Modern Political Analysis must begin by a review of these two developments—Behaviouralism and Post-Behaviouralism.

## BEHAVIOURALISM : REASONS OF GROWTH

The deep dissatisfaction with the nature and method of investigation. of traditional political science turned into a revolution after the end of Second World War. This revolution came to be characterised as the Behavioural Revolution or Behavioural Approach or Behaviouralism, and within its broad ambit involved all such approaches, protests and reactions which were developed by many political scientists as alternative methods or investigation necessary for making political science a real science of political behaviour in place of its traditional nature as a philosophy of state and government. The legal and institutional approaches were rejected as parochial, formal, configurative, static and inadequate for the study of politics. The political scientists now came forward to advocate the need for building a behavioural science of politics capable of explaining all processes of politics and all aspects of human political behaviour.

**The Challenge of Behaviouralist Approach.** Since 1945, the behavioural approach has posed the most serious challenge to traditional approach. Political behaviouralism represents one of the most challenging developments in contemporary political science. Though the roots of political behaviouralism stretch back to the beginning of the century in the works of such European scholars as Max Weber and Graham Wallas, its phenomenal post-1945, development has been primarily the work of Americans. As Evron, M Kirkpatrick has observed, "The challenge to traditional political science of behavioural approach deserves to be ranked as the most important single recent development in political science." Similar views have been expressed by Somit and Tanenhaus : "Among the changes that have affected political science in this quarter of century, perhaps the most prominent has been the behavioural movement. In fact, few political scientists would deny that behaviouralism has been the single most important issue facing the discipline." Behaviouralism Vs. Institutionalism or Behaviouralism Vs. anti-behaviouralism has been, since early 1950s, a hot subject of debate in the discipline. Although the initial fireworks of the behaviouralism have passed away in favour of Post-Behaviouralism. Its impact on political science has been deep and big. Contemporary political theory owes a large debt to Behavioural Revolution.

## REASONS FOR THE COMING OF BEHAVIOURAL REVOLUTION

The centre of the origin, development and subsequent decline of Behaviouralism has been American Universities. It had its antecedents at the University of Chicago in the 1920s with Charles Marrians and his students. However, it has phenomenal growth and its vituality came only in early fifties after the Second World War and in other American Universities.

Several factors contributed to its origin and development. The late development of political science as an autonomous academic discipline in American Universities, the dissatisfaction with the nature of traditional political theory, the existence of several other factors and forces together made possible the emergence of Behavioural Revolution. In fact a number of forces contributed to the development of Behaviouralism. As S.L. Wasby has observed, "Stimuli which affected its development were : the arrival of sociologically-oriented European scholars during the 1930s; World War II, in which a number of American political scientists were involved in large scale government research projects; support from the Social Science Research Council (S.S.R.C.) and the Carnegic, Rockefeller, and Ford Foundations; and the growth of the survey method permitting study of voting behaviour and public opinion. In ways not previously possible." In fact as Bernard Crick has observed, "the rapid flowering of the behavioural approach in the United States depended on the existence of some key attitudes and pre-dispositions generated in American culture—pragmatism, fact mindedness, confidence in science and the like."

Robert Dahl, while analysing the factors which favoured the rapid development of Behaviouralism in the U.S.A. holds that there were at least "five specific inter-related, quite powerful stimuli." These were:

**1. Work or Social Scientists Particularly the Ideas and Efforts of Charles Merriam.** The first factor, according to Dahl, was the pioneering work of the social scientist Charles Merriam. Under the leadership of Merriam, the University of Chicago, the Department of Political Science was the centre of behavioural approach. According to Dahl, a number of political scientists who subsequently were regarded widely as leaders in introducing that approach into American political science were faculty members of graduate students there; for example: Harold Lasswell was a faculty member and V.O. Key, David Truman, Herbert Simon and Gabriel Almond all were graduate students in Merriam's department before the Second World War. However, Chicago was not the only place where the new behaviouralism, the new mood of scientific empiricism, was strong. Catlin at Conwell University was busy in expounding similar views which found expression in his book "Science and Method of Politics" published in 1927.

**2. Migration or Several European Sociologists and Psychologists to the U.S.A.** The second factor, according to Dahl was the arrival in the United States in the 1930's of a considerable number of European scholars, particularly German refugees who brought with them the sociological approach to politics which strongly reflected the specific influence of Max Weber and the general influence of European sociology. American political science had always been very strongly influenced by the Europeans. Dahl is right when he says, "Not only have Americans often interpreted their own political institutions most clearly with the aid of Sympathetic foreigners like Tocquivile, Bryce and Brogan, but also American scholars have owed specific debts to European scholarship. The first American University Chair in Political Science (actually in History and Political Science established in 1848, at Columbia) was occupied by the liberal German refugee Francis Lieber. In the second behalf of the 19th century many of the leading academic advocates of a "Science of Politics" sought to profit from the methods and teaching in some of the leading European Universities.

**3. The Work Done by Social Science Research Council (SSRC).** Fourthly, Dahl says, "Possibly an even bigger impetus—not unrelated to the effects of war—was provided by the Social Science Research Council (SSRC), which has had an enormous impact on American Social Science. A leading spirit in the Council for two decades has been a distinguished political scientist E. Pendleton Herring. His own work, before he assumed the Presidency of the Council in 1948, reflected a concern for realism, for breaking the bounds of research confined entirely to library and for individual and group influences on politics and administration."

**4. Impact of Second World War.** Thirdly, the "Second World War", according to Dahl "also stimulated the development of behavioural approach in the United States for a great many American political scientists temporarily vacated their ivory towers and came to grips with day-to-day political and administrative realities in Washington and elsewhere : a whole generation of American political scientists later drew on these experiences. The confrontation of theory and reality provoked in most of the men who performed their stint in

Washington or elsewhere, a strong sense of the inadequacies of the conventional approaches of political science for describing reality much less for predicting in any given situation what was likely to happen."

**5. American Philanthropic Foundations.** "Last but not the least important is, the influence of American institutions—the great philanthropic foundations, especially Carnegie, Rockfeller, and more recently Ford—which, because of their enormous financial contributions to scholarly research, and the inevitable selection among competing proposals that these exert considerable effect on the scholarly community." Without the financial support the behavioural approach could not have been popular, as Dahl has said, "If the foundations had been hostile to the behavioural approach, there can be doubt that it would have had very rough sledding, indeed for characteristically, behavioural research costs a good deal more than is needed by the single scholar in the library and sometimes as with studies of voting in presidential elections, behavioural research is enormously expensive."

All these factors, coupled with many others, of course, came to function in the decade of 1954's, Dahl writes that, "The behavioural approach grew from the unpopular views of minor sects into a major influence. Many of the radicals of 1930's, professionally speaking, had, within two decades become established leaders in American Political Science. Today many American departments of political science offer undergraduate or graduate courses in political behaviour. Indeed, in at least one institution (the University of Michigan) political behaviour is not only a course but a field of graduate study paralleled with such conventional fields as political theory, public administration and the like, and recently butteressed with some fat fellowships."

Besides these stimuli which provided the impetus to the development of behavioural approach, Waldo, as quoted by Dr. S.P. Verma, has listed several negative and positive reasons which made this approach so popular that it came to be characterised as a revolution in political science." Negatively, behaviouralism set itself against 'mere' description, raw (barefoot) empiricism; 'simple' factualism, against metaphysics, abstract speculation, and deduction from 'first principles', against 'ground' interpretations of history, the contemporary world, and future evolution, against legalistic methods of thought and 'institutional' modes of analysis; against entangling political science with moral or ethical matters... Positively, it favoured studying successful sciences to learn and know how to apply proper scientific modes of thought and methods of research, focussing attention on actual observable behaviour, *i.e.*, on what actors in fact do of political significance, seeking, carefully appraising, and testing empirical theory, *i.e.*, theory about behavioural world, fully and scrupulously gathering data, but doing so with theoretical guidance and for theoretical purposes, learning and applying as much mathematics and especially as much statistical quantitative methodology as the phenomena or data permit; working hard towards the attainment of 'higher level' generalisations, *i.e.*, those which explain more phenomena with greater clarity, simplicity and economy, in general, striving towards the goals of explanation, prediction and control."

## BEHAVIOURALISM VS. BEHAVIOURISM

The answer to the question, 'What is Behaviouralism?' must follow the understanding that Behaviouralism is not Behaviourism. In other words, we must understand the fact as to why Behaviouralism is called Behaviouralism and not Behaviourism.

**Behaviouralism is not Behaviourism.** Behaviouralism, as Easton points out, should not be confused with Behaviourism. Behaviourism is a concept in psychology which stands associated with the name of J.B. Watson. It was adopted to eliminate from scientific research all reference to such subjective data as purposes, intentions, desires, or ideas. Only those observations which were obtained through the use of sense organs or mechanical equipments were to be admitted as data. Observable behaviour generated by external stimuli rather than inferences about the subjective state of mind of the person being observed was to constitute the subject-matter of research. In other words, human behaviour was to be analysed In terms of Stimulus—Response (S—R) paradigm. In the intervening years, since behaviourism was enunciated, most psychologists recognised that between external stimulus and observable responses, subjective experiences occur that influence the interpretation and effect of the stimulus and thereby the nature of the response. David Easton writes, "The original behaviouristic paradigm S—R (Stimulus-Response) has yielded to the more intelligible one S—O—R (Stimulus-Organism-Response) in which feelings, motivations, and all the other aspects of the subjective awareness and reaction of the organism are taken into account as partially useful data. This has, of course, spelled the doom of behaviourism, as a term." The study of human behaviour through S—O—R paradigm came to be known as Behaviouralism. The type of the behaviourist paradigm (S—R) as suggested in psychology has nowhere been used or applied in political research. In the context of political science, the study of human political behaviour is based on S—O—R paradigm *i.e.,* subjective awareness and reactions alongwith stimulus and responses form part of the study of human political behaviour. Hence to describe this kind of research as 'political behaviourism' is to be guilty of a very loose usage of words. Easton says that, "Support for the clear distinction and difference between the terms is lent by its use in such institutions as the Centre for Advanced Study in the Behavioural Sciences at Stanford, the section of the Ford Foundation now liquidated, that was known as the Behavioural Science Division, and the Institution of Behavioural Science at the University as well as the Journal of Behavioural Science and the American Behavioural Scientist." The use of the term "Behaviouristic" for "Behavioural" would, as Easton says, be entirely confusing and misleading about the scope and direction of interest of the institution or publication involved.

**Definition of Behaviouralism.** It is indeed very difficult to precisely define Behaviouralism because it has been used as an umbrella by the behavioural political scientists to record their protests, for the rejection of traditional political theory/approach, and for advocating the building up of a science of human-political behaviour through empirical, mathematical and statistical analysis of data leading to scientific generalisations. Even during its hay days, it was differently defined by a very large number of political scientists, who, despite differences regarding its, nature and scope, took pride in describing themselves as behaviouralists.

Evron Kirkpatrick has objectively summarised the situation : "Between World War II and the mid-fifties. the term political behaviouralism represented both an approach and a challenge an orientation and a reform movement, a type of research and a rallying cry, a "hurrah" term and a "boo" term. Debate about behavioural techniques and methods was often accompanied by vituperations. Discussions were more often aimed at vanquishing adversaries than at clarifying issues."Sharp differences among the behaviouralists rendered it very difficult, almost impossible to record a precise, universally acceptable conceptualisation behaviouralism. As Waldo has pointed out "Behaviouralism was not and is not a clear and firm creed, an agreed upon set of postulates and rules". It is, infact, a loose collection of views and ideas with distinct broad similarities with several differences and dissimilarities. Behaviouralism has been defined by many as a protest movement and by several others as a mood.

## DIFFERENT WAYS IN WHICH BEHAVIOURALISM HAS BEEN CONCEPTUALISED

**1. Behaviouralism as a Protest Movement.** It has been held by several political scientists that behaviouralism came as a protest against the formalistic legal-institutionalism of the traditional political science. In the words of Dahl, "Historically speaking behavioural approach was a protest movement within Political Science.... It was associated with a number of political scientists, mainly Americans who shared "a strong sense of dissatisfaction with the achievements of conventional political science" and who believed that" additional methods and approaches either existed or could be developed that would help to provide political science with empirical propositions and theories of systematic sorts, tested by close, more direct and more rigorously controlled observations of political events."

**2. Behaviouralism as a Mood.** Sometime behaviouralism was described as a mood. Robert Dahl examined in details such a characterisation and observes: "At a minimum, then, those who were sometimes called "behaviouratists, shared a mood: a mood of skepticism about the current intellectual attainments of political science, a mood of sympathy toward "scientific" mode of investigation and analysis, a mood of optimism about the possibilities of improving the study of politics. " Was or is the behavioural approach ever anything more than this mood? Are there definite beliefs, assumptions, methods or topics that can be identified as constituting political behaviour or the behavioural approach? Dahl gives three different answers to this question:

(i) "The first answer is an unequivocal 'Yes'. Political behaviour is said to refer to study of the individual rather than larger political units. This emphasis is clear in the 1944-45, SSRC report that fore-shadowed the creation of the Political Behaviour Committee. This was also how David Easton defined the term in his searching analysis and criticism of American Political Science published in 1953. In this sense Tingsten. and Lasswall's studies of voting behaviour are prime examples of behavioural approach".

(ii) "The second answer is an unequivocal 'no'." Vernon Von Dyke remarks, "Though stipulative definitions of political behaviour are sometimes advanced, a when a, course or book is given the title, none of them has gained general currency." Alfred de Grazia speaks with authority for this Dahl says, "Grazia denied the term referred to a subject matter, an inter-disciplinary focus, quantification, any specific efforts at new methods, behaviourist psychology, "realism" as opposed to 'idealism', empiricism in contrast to deductive system or voting behaviour or, in fact, to anything more than political science as something that some people might like it to be. He proposed that the term be dropped".

(iii) The third view is no more than an elaboration of the mood mentioned above. Dahl says that in this view the behavioural approach is an attempt to improve our understanding of politics by seeking to explain the empirical aspect of political

> life by means of methods, theories and criteria of proof that are acceptable according to the canons, conventions, and assumptions of modern political science. In this sense, a behavioural approach is distinguished predominantly by the nature of the purpose it is designed to serve, the purpose is scientific.

Behaviouralism is more than a mood. It is also not merely a protest movement. It stands for the study of political behaviour instead of formal political institutions. It advocates empirical analysis instead of abstract and philosophical theorising. It stands for interdisciplinary forces and for making political science a correct science of political behaviour of human beings in society.

Explaining the main theme of behavioural approach, Almond and Powell have observed, "Whit it means, very simply, is the study of the actual behaviour of the incumbents or political roles, rather than of the content of legal rules or ideological patterns". Describing Behaviouralism as a movement for bringing political studies into closer affiliation with theories, methods, findings, and outlooks in modern psychology, sociology, anthropology and economics, Robert Dahl defines it as, "an attempt to make empirical component of political science more scientific. It aims at stating all the phenomena of government In terms of observed and observable behaviour of men......". Dahl then proceeds on to enumerate the basic assumption or features drawn from the views and writings of a large number of behaviouralists. Infact, the only and best possible way of comprehending the meaning of Behaviouralism is to know the characteristics and assumptions of Behavioural Revolution or Behavioural Movement or Behavioural Approach or Behavioural Mood or Behaviouralism or the Behavioural Challenge to traditional political theory.

## CHARACTERISTICS OF BEHAVIOURALISM

In order to know the characteristics of Behaviouralism we have again to study the views of several eminent scholars—David Truman, Heinz Eulau, Samuel J. Eldersveld and Morris Janowitz, and David Easton.

**A. David Truman's View.** David Truman defines Political Behaviouralism as the science of political behaviour. "Where political behaviour means all "those actions and interactions of men and groups which are involved in the process of governing.....At the maximum this conception brings under the rubric of political behaviour any human activity which can be said to be a part of governing." He specifies that Behaviouralism stands for two features: *(i)* Research must be systematic, and *(ii)* it must place primary emphasis upon empirical methods. By the first *i.e.,* systematic research, Truman means, "A precise statement of hypothesis, and a rigorous ordering of evidence" and by the second *i.e.,* empirical methods, he means research and theory building through data analysis and empirical testing. The ultimate goal of the student of political behaviour is "the development of the science of political process." He favoured a controlled use of inter-disciplinary focus. He even admitted the usefulness of historical knowledge. It can be "an essential supplement to contemporary observation of political behaviour."

Robert Dahl whole heartedly accepts the views of David Truman and believes that if these characteristics of behavioural political science had been properly understood and accepted by all the behaviouralists and their critics "much of the irrelevant, fruitless and ill-informed debates over the behavioural approach over the past decade need never have occurred, or at any rate might have been conducted on a rather higher level of intellectual sophistication".

**B. Views of Heinz Eulan, Elderseld and Janowitz.** In an introduction to their Book Political Behaviouralism : A Reader in Theory and Research, Heinz Eulan, Eldersveld and Janowitz specify the following four characteristics of the political behaviour approach:

1. It specifies as the unit or object of both theoretical and empirical analysis, the behaviour of persons and social groups rather than events, structures, institutions, or ideologies.
2. It seeks to place theory and research in frame of reference common to that of social psychology, sociology and cultural anthropology. In other words, it favours inter-disciplinary focus.

3. It stresses the mutual inter-dependence of theory and research. Theoretical questions need to be stated in operational terms for purpose of empirical research. And, in turn, empirical findings should have a bearing on the development of political theory. It is self-consciously theory oriented.
4. It tries to develop rigorous designs and to apply precise methods of analysis to the political behaviour problems. It stands for scientific procedure of research.

Thus, "political behaviour approach seeks to understand political action and, whenever and wherever possible, it employs quantitative and statistical methods."

**C. Views of David Easton.** David Easton has identified the following eight major assumptions or characteristics of Behaviouralism:

**1. Regularities.** There are discoverable uniformities in political behaviour. These can be expressed in generalizations or theories with explanatory and predictive values.

**2. Verification.** The validity of such generalizations must be testable, in principle by reference to relevant behaviour.

**3. Quantification.** Precision in the recording of data and the statement of findings requires measurement and quantification, not for their own sake, but only where possible, relevant and meaningful in the light of other objectives.

**4. Value.** "Ethical evaluation and empirical explanation involve two different kinds of proposition, that for the sake of clarity, should be kept analytically distinct. However, a student of political behaviour is not prohibited from asserting propositions of either kind separately or in combination as long as he does not mistake one for the other."

**5. Techniques.** "Means for acquiring and interpreting data cannot be taken for granted. They are problematic and need to be examined self-consciously, refined and validated so that rigorous means can be found for observing, recording and analyzing behaviour."

**6. Systematization.** Research ought to be systematic, that is to say, theory and research are to be seen as closely inter-twined part of a coherent and orderly body of knowledge.

**7. Pure Science.** The application of knowledge is as much a part of the scientific enterprise as theoretical understanding. But the understanding and explanation of political behaviour logically precede and provide the basis for efforts to utilize political knowledge in the solution of urgent practical problems of society.

**8. Intergration.** Because the social sciences deal with the whole human situation, the political research can ignore the findings of the other disciplines only at the peril. of weakening the validity and undermining the generality of its own results. Recognition of this inter-relationship will help to bring political science back to its status of earlier centuries and return into the main fold of the social sciences.

These eight assumptions definitely form the common core of the views of almost all the behaviouralist. However, at the same time it reflects the inherent weakness of behaviouralism. As Easton has himself observed that: It is "less a tightly structured dogma than a congeries of related values and objectives."

On the basis of the above description of the characteristics and assumptions of Behaviouralism, we conclude that : Behaviouralism seeks to study politics as an aspect of human behaviour in a framework of reference common to other social sciences and prescribes the use of empirical research, mathematical-statistical-quantification techniques of data collection and analysis with the purpose of building a scientific theory of political behaviour.

## LIMITATIONS OF BEHAVIOURALISM

Behaviouralism has been subjected to serve criticism particularly by the supporters of the traditional approach to politics. In fact the differences and divisions among the behaviouralists and the concerted opposition that they had from the traditionalists has made behaviouralism face a severe criticism. Even during its hay days there was lack of agreement among the behaviouralists regarding its meaning and definition. As Evron Kirkpatrick has observed : " It was general enough to comprehend a variety of peoples, propensities and activities, ambiguous enough that its proponents and representatives disagreed about its definition, specific enough to inspire articulate opposition from some proponents of traditional political science". Behaviouralism served as, "a sort of umbrella capacious enough to provide temporary shelter for a heterogeneous group united only by dissatisfaction with traditional political science and comprised of persons who would probably move out in quite different directions once the storm of protest against innovation was passed."

The criticism or Behaviouralism has been directed against its major assumptions as well as against its general approach towards politics. The main points of criticism have been:

(1) That human behaviour as the object of study is bound to be problematic and even fruitless.

(2) That all aspects or human behaviour cannot be observed and stated in empirical generalisations.

(3) That behaviouralism makes political science dependent upon other social sciences, particularly Psychology, Sociology and Anthropology.

(4) That behavioural advocacy or study of facts to the exclusion of values is neither possible nor desireable, nor even can it be useful.

(5) That the differences among the behaviouralists have tended to reduce it to a congeries of several views, both related and unrelated from one another.

(6) That scientific method, particularly as used in natural sciences cannot be applied to social sciences, particularly political science.

(7) That behaviouralists were obsessed with methods and techniques and that they failed to concentrate upon the substance of politics.

(8) That beviouralism reflected a bias in favour of liberal democratic systems since empirical research can be really possible only in such systems.

(9) That behaviouralists in their passion for 'Scientism' have created a riduculous complicated gargon.

(10) That the 'value-neutralism' preached and practised by the behaviouralists was destined to make it a less-relevant if not non-relevant theory of human political behaviour.

(11) That the behaviouralists failed to make real headway towards the professed objective of theory-building. They remained lost in trivial research and failed to come to grips with the brute realities of politics.

It has been along these lines that Behaviouralism stands subjected to severe criticism, particularly by the proponents of 'traditional' political science. Scholars like Leo Strauss Voegelin and many others have strongly criticised Behaviouralist's empiricism and value-neutralism. Several political scientists have analysed the major limitations of the behavioural approach. We quote here the view of Albert Somit, Tanenhaus, Christian Eay, Sibley and Wasby.

**(A) Albert Somit and Joseph Tanenhaus have Pointed out the Following Limitations of the Behavioural Approach:**

(1) Political Science is not, nor is it ever likely to become a science in any realistic sense of the term. It can't become a science for a number of reasons. The phenomena with which political scientists deal do not lend themselves to rigorous study. Human behaviour cannot be treated, whether individual or social, with the dispassion needed for scientific knowledge. Neither political science nor any other social science is commendable to experimental inquiry. We cannot employ the test tubes and laboratories, which are the only paraphernalia of physical sciences. 'Laws' of political behaviour cannot be stated for a sentient creature such as man, because he is free to modify his actions in keeping with or in violation of such laws once they are made known.

(2) Second, the overt behaviour tells only part of the story. Different individuals may perform the same act for quite different reasons. To understand what they do, one must go beyond, or behind observable behaviour. Moreover, individuals and groups act within an institutional or a social setting, and a knowledge of that setting is essential to any meaningful explanation of their behaviour. The anti. behaviouralists hold that the larger part of political life lies beneath the surface of human action and cannot be directly apprehended.

(3) Whatever the theoretical merits of quantification, for most practical purposes, it is now and will continue to be an unattainable goal. Quantification requires precise concepts and reliable metrics—and political science possesses neither. Significant questions normally cannot be quantified, questions which can, are usually trivial in nature.

(4) There are many areas where an inter-disciplinary approach may be useful but care must be taken to preserve the identity and integrity of political science. All too often, the anti-behaviouralists feel, there has been an indiscriminate borrowing of concept and techniques which are simply inappropriate for political inquiry.

(5) Significant political issues invariably involve moral and ethical issues. Political Science has historically been, and must continue to be, concerned with the questions of right and wrong, even if these cannot be scientifically resolved. Were the discipline to turn its back on such matters, it would have little justification for continued existence. Going considerably beyond this, one wing of anti-behaviouralism claimes that values cannot be demonstrated true or false and that political scientists are necessarily condemned to an eternal philosophical relativism.

(6) Self-consciousness about methodology can be and has been, carried too far. Overly critical and unrealistic standards impede rather than evidence the pursuit of knowledge. This same obsession has led many behaviouralists to exalt technique at the cost of its content. Technical rather than substantive considerations have been permitted to set the area of Inquiry. In any case many of these technical innovations are too sophisticated and refined for the raw-material with which political scientists must work. As for scientific-objectivity, there is almost universal skepticism among the anti-behaviouralists that it is attainable and considerable doubt that it is inherently desirable.

**(B) Christian Bay has Referred to the Following Limitations of Behaviouralism:**

(i) Behaviouralists avoid the "substance" of politics for the techniques. Bay claims that in the attempt to achieve a science the tendency of the behaviouralists is to avoid politics. He argues that most current political behavioural work fails to articulate its very real value biases. He says that behaviouralists think that American liberal democracy is the best form of government and their main task is to support democracy through the behavioural tools. He says that a basic dilemma confronts these behaviouralists : how simultaneously to achieve value neutrality and to support democracy.

(ii) He further argues that behaviouralists often assume that stability is the most important social goal. Pluralistic democracy in some countries, particularly in, America, is a "protective shield" for the interests of the middle and upper classes. Thus, current "preoccupations with pseudo behaviour carries conservative and anti-political implications." Bay suggests distinction between politics and pseudo-politics and designates behaviouralism as "pseudo-politics. " He says, "I would define as "political" all activity aimed at improving protecting conditions for the satisfaction of human needs and demands in a given society or community according to some universalistic scheme of priorities. Pseudo-political refers to activity that resembles political activity but is exclusively concerned with either the alleviation of personal neurosis or with promoting private or private interest group advantage, dettered by no articulate or dis-interested conception of what would be just or fair to other groups." The concern of the behaviouralists is with pseudo-politics.

(iii) Behaviouralists evade and avoid "substantiative political responsibility." Christian Bay comments, "The lack of political responsibility in most of political behaviour literature relates to the substantive level which involves articulate attention to questions of fundamental commitment in social and political research literature. Problems of human welfare (including justice, liberty, security and so on), the objects of political research and politics, can be adequately studied, and dealt with, only if their "ought-side" is investigated as carefully as their "is-side." Ought-side inquiry must pertain to wants as well as needs. Political communication must be analysed carefully so that we may learn what aspects of wants are most salient and could be frustrated only at the cost of resentment. alienations or upheaval." Since behaviouralists are not concerned with all this, Bay calls them traitors who have deliberately indulged in "intellectual treason".

**(C) Mulford Q. Sibley has Chosen to Specially Criticise the Value Neutralism of Behaviouralists. He Rejects it and Argues that:**

*(1)* The very selection of subjects for investigation is shaped by values which are not derivable from investigation; *(2)* in the end the concepts and values which do determine what and how one studies are related to one's judgement of the goals, which one identifies with political life and to one's general "life-experience"; *(3)* once the investigation is launched, there are definite limits to what one can expect from behavioural studies; *(4)* behaviourally oriented study will remove one from the stuff of everyday politics and cannot be related to that stuff except by means which would usually be regarded as non-behavioural; and *(5)* if clarification on thought policy-making is one objective of the politicist, behaviouralism, although destined to play a significant role, is restricted in which it can be expected to do".

Sibley says that, "Values are prior to any investigation, whether in politics or in any other area. The political investigator, no less than other must have same notion of his own order of priorities before he proceeds to use behavioural or any other approach. He presumably holds; that "political" sphere is more important for him to investigate than any other area. Whatever the reasons for his judgement, imputations of value are always present". Sibley, further comments "How", one account for our experiences? It would seem clear that value statements in the ultimate or primary sense cannot be validated or verified by what are ordinarily thought of as empirical and behavioural methods. Behaviouralism will inevitably be used within a framework of value judgements which cannot be supported through behavioural techniques alone. The behavioural investigator is confined by an unbehaviourally derived set of primary value judgements just as he is restricted by a whole frame-work of ultimate assumptions about the nature of the things he is investigating."

All this has been summed up nicely by Arnold Brecht in his book 'Political Theory'. He gives two propositions:

1. The question whether something is "valuable" can be answered scientifically only in relation to:
   (a) some goal or purpose for the pursuit of which it is or is not useful (valuable), or to
   (b) the ideas held by some person or group of persons regarding what is or is not valuable, and that consequently.
2. It is impossible to establish scientifically what goals or purposes are valuable, irrespective of:
   (a) the value they have in the pursuit of their goals or purposes, or
   (b) of someone's ideas about ulterior or ultimate goals or purposes.

To prove that the study of politics cannot be 'value-free, Sibley says that it is impossible to study the behaviour (value-biases) of the behaviouralist himself. 'It would seem that, although the observer can provide scientific accounts of those he observes, he cannot explain by behavioural methods as usually understood his own behaviour as an observer. He might, indeed, provide an interesting hypothesis to explain his conduct but this could hardly be verified by the statistical and other methods which he uses to study the behaviour of groups.

**(D) S.L. Wasby Points Out the Following three Limitations:**

1. "Because of the heavy emphasis by behaviouralists on methods, the criticism that they are more interested in techniques than the results they obtain, does strike home with a certain accuracy. Some, although clearly not all behaviouralists, appear to have chosen topics for the study solely or largely on the basis of the applicability of available techniques rather than for their theoretical importance. The drawback of habit is this that there is a delay in the development of new techniques needed to examine some theoretically important questions. Valid data will not be obtained without proper instruments, and instruments do not just happen but must be developed through testing." Wasby further adds that "the emphasis on techniques in

behavioural approach also means that behaviouralists need to be committed to constant retooling so that they may be equipped to use the most recently developed effective techniques, a commitment which involves much hard work because of the lag of even graduate curricula behind the current needs."

2. Also, as Wasby points out that, "It has been recognized that behaviouralists at times concentrated so heavily on aspects of political phenomena previously neglected that they went from the institutionalist's failure to consider behaviour to no consideration of institution. Studies of voting behaviour at times lacked examination of factors such as registration requirements and ballot forms; which might effect respectively the rate of turn out, or direction of the vote...the fact that almost all early studies of voting behaviour took place in the United States or within single communities or states made it easy for researches to forget the possible effects of institutional environment on electoral activity."

3. Thirdly, Wasby says that, "the behaviouralists have been criticized for concentrating on description of static situations. They undoubtedly felt justified in limiting their initial efforts to the study of "normal" and static situations to remedy the deficiencies they perceived in the picture of politics and government left by the institutionalists. But then they over-emphasised the study of the static situations and thus, neglected the study of political change and revolutionary situations involving the phenomena of conflict and violence."

Despite these limitations and points of criticism, it cannot be denied that Behaviouralism has played heuristic role in the development of the discipline. It successfully focussed attention upon the limitations of the traditional approach. The behaviouralists can legitimately claim credit for inducing, popularising and improving the scientific method of social science research and the use of statistical and mathematical techniques in the discipline. However, in the process, they became overwhelmed by concern for techniques, methodological sophistications and technical proficiency in research. As such what is needed is to be cautions of and refrain from the 'extremism' of the behaviouralism in favour of 'technique' and 'method' as well as for 'behavioural studies' to the near exclusion of the study of government and institutions. As Joseph la Palombara has observed, "The behavioural approach is objectionable per se but only when and in so far as it leads the political scientists too far away from the processes of government and their consequents. The best way to guard against this danger is to stress upon political and indeed governmental institutions and process in political analysis." In fact Post Behaviouralism has successfully secured several well-needed reforms in Behaviouralism and today, as Wasby points out, "The behavioural approach to the study of politics has now become fully established, and many of those initially hostile have come to use behavioural concepts and techniques, regularly." The traditionalists have come to recognise the merits of the behaviouralists and the behaviouralists turned post-behaviouralists have come forward to adopt a better and more objective view of some of the main ideas of the traditionalists.

## POST BEHAVIOURALISM

Behaviouralism came as a revolution and like every revolution could hold real ground only for a short-span of time. Within twenty years, right from mix sixties, there appeared several cracks among the behaviouralists and many of them started advocating the need for "reforms". While almost none of them advocated a rejection of Behaviouralism, all of them came forward to accept and advocate the need to get away from "Orthodoxism" and to be futuristic. For this, they accepted the need to take into account the experiences of the behavioural research as well as the limitations of Behaviouralism. Such political scientists, who accepted Behaviouralism but at the same time wanted to reform it, came to be known as Post-Behaviouralists and their views as Post-Behaviouralism.

**The Coming of Post-Behaviouralism.** In his presidential address at the sixty-fifth meeting of the American Political Science Association held at New York in September 1969, David Easton, himself one of the leading advocates of Behaviouralism, made a powerful attack on the behaviouralist position and advocated the need to restate, readjust and reform behaviouralism in the light of post-experience and the need of the society. Like many other Behaviouralists,

David Easton admitted that too much time had been lost on trivial and quite often irrelevant research under the banner of Behaviouralism. As Dr. S.P. Verma has opined, "that while the Behaviouralists were busy in sorting out controversies developing techniques and building-up of various paradigms, models and theories, society was facing more and more social, economic and cultural crises which were ignored by the Behaviouralists. In the American Society. there were signs of increasing stress. strain and conflict resulting from several factors *viz.* Civil Rights Movement and the Negro-White riots, internal cleavages in the United States in which civil war and authoritarian rule had become frightening possibilities; the American involvement in the undeclared war in Vietnam, the youth unrest in America, particularly on the issue of Vietnam war; the fear of nuclear war and several other factors. These were such conditions which political scientists, neither the traditionalists nor the behaviouralists had predicted. Behaviouralists in their near obsession with techniques and value-neutralism failed to take note of these problems and maladies. Some of the behaviouralists, like David Easton, realising this weakness came out to raise the questions : "Must we be committed eternally to an unchanging image of the discipline, behavioural or otherwise ? Is it not incumbent on us to take account of changing conditions and to be ready and willing to reconsider old images and modify them to the extent necessary ?"

While pondering over this question and similar other problems several behaviouralists accepted the need for making Behaviouralism fully relevant and action-oriented. The deep discontent with the direction of behavioural research in politics further impelled them to accept and advocate the need for reform within Behaviouralism. Many suggestions were made and accepted by most of the Behaviouralists who came to be designated and they accepted the designation, "Post Behaviouralists."

## WHAT IS POST BEHAVIOURALISM?

**(i) Post Bebaviouralism is not a Revival of Traditionalism.** In order to understand the meaning and nature of Post-Behaviouralism, we must, at the very outset, understand that it is not reversion back to traditionalism. Post Behaviouralists were Behaviouralists, they accepted the merits of the behavioural political approach over the traditional approach, nevertheless they accepted the need to reform behaviouralism with a view to eliminate some of its defects and to up-date it. "Post behaviouralism should not be confused with traditionalism", writes S.P. Verma, "though both are highly critical of behaviouralism. The difference between the two approaches lies in the fact that whereas traditionalism denied the validity of behavioural approach and reiterated its faith in the classical traditions of political science, the post-behaviourslists accepted the achievements of the behavioural era but sought to push political science further and towards new horizons."

**(ii) Post-Behaviouralism is a Reform Movement within Behaviouralism.** David Easton, in his presidential address to APSA 1969, identified Post-Behaviouralism as a New Revolution in political science and described it as a reform movement. He gave a call to the political scientists to push the development of the discipline towards relevant and action oriented research. To quote David Easton, "The political scientists should take the initiative by calling for the establishment of a federation of social scientists......The tasks of such a federation would be to identify the major issues of the day, clarify objectives, evalute action taken by others, study and propose alternative solutions, and press those rigorously in the political sphere". The post-behaviouralists want action-oriented research which could be relevant to social situation.

**(iii) Relevance and Action as the Two Hallmarks of Post-Behaviouralism.** Two main pillars of Post-behaviouralism have been **"Relevance"** and **"Action."** That the research and theory building must be relevant to actual social conditions and the brute realities of politics, and that political scientists have a practical role to play in society. Knowledge of politics has to be put to use for helping the society to preserve and protect human science—a sense of commitment and action must characterise entire research in political science.

We can say Post-Behaviouralism is not a reversion to traditionalism, on the other hand it is a reform movement, a future oriented intellectual tendency among the behaviouralists.

## FEATURES OR CHARACTERISTICS OF POST-BEHAVIOURALISM

David Easton, who had earlier drawn up a list of eight characteristic features of behaviouralism and called them the "intellectual foundation stones" of the movement, now came out with seven major characteristics of post-behavioursIism. He described them as the "Credo of Relevance" or "a distillation of the maximal image." These are given below :

**(1) Due and Primary Importance to Substance of Study Alongwith the Techniques.** "Substance must precede technique—if one must be sacrificed for the other—and this need not always be so; it is more Important to be relevant and meaningful for contemporary urgent problems than to be sophisticated in the tools of investigation. For the aphorism of science is that it is better to be wrong than vague. Post-behaviouralism would substitute a new dictum that it is better to be "vague than non-relevantly precise". In Political Science substance must come before techniques.

**(2) Emphasis upon Change.** Political Science should place its main emphasis upon social change and not on social conservatism as behaviouralists seem to be doing. "Behavioural science conceals an ideology of empirical conservatism. To confine oneself exclusively to the description and analysis of facts is to hamper the understanding of these facts in their broadest context. As a result, empirical political science must lend its support to the maintenance of very factual conditions it explores. It unwillingly purveys an ideology of social conservatism tempered by modest incremental change."

**(3) Study of all Facts/Realities of Politics.** Behavioural research has been guilty of ignoring the study of the brute realities of politics. The need, however, is that the political scientists should always concern themselves with the realities of political life, including the social stress, social strains, social conflict and crises. "Behavioural research must not lose touch with reality. The heart of behavioural inquiry is abstractions and analysis and this serves to conceal the brute realities of politics. The task of Post-behaviouralism is to break the barriers of silence that behavioural language has necessarily created and to help political, science reach out to the real needs of mankind in a time of crisis."

**(4) Protection of Human Value as the Major Role or Intellectuals.** "Members of a learned discipline bear the responsibilities of all intellectuals. The intellectual's historical role has been and must be to protect the human values of civilization. This is their unique task and obligation. Without this. they become mere technicians, mechanics for tinkering with society. They thereby abandon the special privileges they have come to claim for themselves in the academic sphere, such as freedom of inquiry and a quasi-extra-territorial protection from the onslaughts of society."

**(5) Values cannot be Totally Eliminated from Political Science.** Post-behaviouralists advocate a rejection of complete value neutralism, as advocated by the behaviouralists. The total emphasis on scientism and empiricism was an unhappy and unworkable stand. "Research about and constructive development of values are inextinguishable parts of the study of politics. Science cannot be, and never has been evaluatively neutral despite protestations to the contrary. Hence to understand the limits of our knowledge, we need to be aware of the value premises on which it stands and the alternatives for which this knowledge could be used."

**(6) Political Science is to be Developed as an Action Science and Contemplative Science.** "To know is to bear the responsibility for acting and to act is to engage in re-shaping society. The intellectual as scientist, bears the social obligation to put bis knowledge to work. Contemplative science was a product of the nineteenth century when a broader moral agreement was shared. Action Science of necessity reflects the contemporary conflict in society over ideals and this must permeate and colour the whole research enterprise."

**(7) An Active and Essential Role or the Professional Associations and Universities in Actual Process of Politics.** "If the individual has the obligation to implement his knowledge, those organisations composed or intellectuals—the professional associations and the universities themselves, cannot stand apart from the struggles of the day. Politicalisation of the profession is inescapable as well as desirable."

Summing up the characteristics of Post-behaviouralism. David Easton observed : "No one Post-behaviouralist could share all these views. I have presented only a distillation of the maximal image. It represents perhaps a Weberjan ideal type of the challenge of behaviouralism. As such the credo brings out most of the salient features of the Post-behavioural revolution as it appears to be taking shape today."

Post-behaviouralism as such advocates the need to make Political Science Research 'substance' oriented, relevant to social phenomena and action oriented. To quote David Easton again, "It (Post-behaviouralism) pleads for a more relevant research. It pleads for an orientation to the work that will encourage political scientists. even in their professional capacity to prescribe and to act as to improve political life according to human criteria." Post-behaviouralism rejects the thoroughgoing empiricism, value-neutralism and technique-obsession of the Behaviouralists. It attacks the craze or obsession for a scientific research and seeks to offer an integrated view, combining in a subtle way behavioural advocacy of empiricism with normativism of the traditionalists.

**Critical Evaluation.** Post-behaviouralism involves a bold attempt to reform some of the weaknesses of Behaviouralism. By advocating primacy of substance over technique. socially relevant research over pure science, political action over academic neutrality and social change over social conservatism. Post-behaviouralism definitely tries to come out of orthodox scientism of the Behaviouralists. It seeks to accommodate and reconcile the traditionalists support for value studies with behaviouralists advocacy of thoroughgoing empiricism. As Dr. Shriram Maheswari has observed, "As a result of Post-behavioural movement, a synthesis appears to be emerging in Political Science. The methods of science have come to stay in Politics, but they are tempered with an appreciation of their limitations, and what is more, they are to be combined with a sensitivity towards political values and an application of political knowledge."

Post-behaviouralism cannot be regarded as a reversion to traditionalism, though such a charge is preferred against it by strict behaviouralists. It accepts the behavioural approach, but alongwith some reforms. The Post-behaviouralists do not deny the importance of technical proficiency but they do not agree that scientists in the name of value-neutrality should completely remain cut-off from society. Values cannot and should not be kept out of scientific research. Since it was the responsibility of the social scientists to analyse social problems with a view to find solutions, it was an imperative necessity that they should keep in mind and help the society to preserve the human values of civilisation.

□